PHILOSOPHERS ON EDUCATION

"Philosophy is implicitly pedagogical . . . meant to correct the myopia of the past and the immediate . . . to transform the way we think, act and interact. Philosophers have always taken themselves to be the ultimate educators of mankind . . . They thought that interpreting the world aright would free us from illusion and direct us to those activities that best suit us . . . A vital and robust philosophy of education inevitably incorporates virtually the whole of philosophy; and the study of the history of philosophy mandates reflection on its implications for education."

from the Preface

Theories of knowledge (Descartes, Locke) imply educational reforms. Most ethical theories (Hume, Rousseau, and Kant) were meant to redirect moral education. The practical application of political theories (Hobbes, Mill and Marx) is directed to the education of citizens. Metaphysical systems (Leibniz, Spinoza and Hegel) provide models for inquiry, and hence set standards for the education of the enlightened. Some philosophers (Locke, Rousseau, Bentham and Mill) made their educational programs a central feature of their philosophy.

Philosophers on Education is intended to return education to philosophy, and philosophy to education. It presents a comprehensive history of philosophers' views on the aims and directions of education.

Amélie Oksenberg Rorty is the Director of the Program in History of Ideas at Brandeis University. She is the author of *Mind in Action*, and has edited many anthologies, including *The Identities of Persons*, *Essays on Aristotle's Ethics*, *Essays on Aristotle's Rhetoric*, *Essays on Descartes' Meditations*, and *Explaining Emotions*.

PHILOSOPHERS ON EDUCATION

Historical Perspectives

Edited by
Amélie Oksenberg Rorty

London and New York

First published 1998
by Routledge
11 New Fetter Lane, London EC4P 4EE

Simultaneously published in the USA and Canada
by Routledge
29 West 35th Street, New York, NY 10001

Typeset in Perpetua by Keystroke, Jacaranda Lodge, Wolverhampton
Printed and bound in Great Britain by TJ International Ltd, Padstow, Cornwall

British Library Cataloguing in Publication Data
A catalogue record for this book is available from the British Library

Library of Congress Cataloging in Publication Data
A catalogue record for this book has been requested

ISBN 0–415–19130–0 (hbk)
ISBN 0–415–19131–9 (pbk)

To the contributors
— past and present —

and to

Mrs Martina Hancy
Mrs Evelyn Saldick
Mrs Schwarz,
exemplary educators

CONTENTS

CONTENTS

CONTENTS

CONTRIBUTORS

Elizabeth Anderson is Associate Professor of Philosophy at the University of Michigan.

Annette C. Baier is Professor of Philosophy Emerita at the University of Pittsburgh.

Frederick C. Beiser is Professor of Philosophy at Indiana University.

Eva T. H. Brann is Dean and Tutor at St John's College, Annapolis.

M. F. Burnyeat is a Fellow of All Souls College, Oxford.

William Galston is Professor at the Center for Philosophy and Public Policy, University of Maryland.

Daniel Garber is Lawrence Kimpton Distinguished Service Professor in Philosophy and Associate Provost for Research and Education at the University of Chicago.

Peter Gay is Sterling Professor of History Emeritus at Yale University.

Alvin I. Goldman is Regents Professor of Philosophy at the University of Arizona.

Moshe Halbertal is Professor of Philosophy and Jewish Studies at the Hebrew University of Jerusalem.

Tova Hartman Halbertal is Lecturer in the School of Education at the Hebrew University of Jerusalem.

Simon Harrison is a Research Fellow at St John's College, Cambridge.

Barbara Herman is Griffin Professor of Philosophy at UCLA.

Genevieve Lloyd is Professor of Philosophy at the University of New South Wales.

Alasdair MacIntyre is Arts and Sciences Professor of Philosophy at Duke University.

Richard W. Miller is Professor of Philosophy at Cornell University.

Roy P. Mottahedeh is Professor of History at the Center for Middle Eastern Studies, Harvard University.

Adam Phillips is a clinical psychiatrist in London.

Philip L. Quinn is Professor of Philosophy at Notre Dame University.

C. D. C. Reeve is Professor of Philosophy and the Humanities at Reed College.

Patrick Riley is Professor of Political Science at the University of Wisconsin.

Amélie Oksenberg Rorty is Director of the Program in the History of Ideas at Brandeis University.

Emma Rothschild is Director of the Centre for History and Economics at King's College, Cambridge.

Alan Ryan is Warden of New College, Oxford.

Richard Schacht is Professor of Philosophy and Jubilee Professor of Liberal Arts and Sciences at the University of Illinois at Champaign-Urbana.

Josef Stern is Associate Professor of Philosophy at the University of Chicago.

Richard Tuck is Professor of Government at Harvard University.

Thomas E. Uebel is Lecturer in Philosophy at the London School of Economics.

Jeremy Waldron is Maurice Hilda Friedman Professor of Law and Director for the Center for Law and Philosophy at Columbia Law School.

Allen W. Wood is Professor of Philosophy at Yale University.

Paul Woodruff is Mary Helen Thompson Professor in the Humanities at the University of Texas at Austin.

John W. Yolton is John Locke Professor of the History of Philosophy Emeritus at Rutgers University.

Zhang LoShan (pseudonym) is a professor of ancient philosophy in the People's Republic of China.

ACKNOWLEDGMENTS

For permission to reprint previously published articles, I am grateful to:

- Oxford University Press for permission to reprint Jean and John Yolton, "Locke: Education for Virtue," pp. 1–2, 14–34 © Oxford University Press 1989. Reprinted from *Some Thoughts concerning Education* by John Locke, ed. John W. and Jean S. Yolton (1989).

Columbia University Press for permission to reprint Peter Gay, *Locke on Education* (1964), pp. 12–14.

The Aristotelian Society for permission to reprint Annette Baier, "Moral sentiments and the difference they make" (Supplementary Volume LXIX, 1995), pp. 15–30.

The Philosophy of Education Society for permission to reprint Alvin Goldman, "Education and social epistemology," *Philosophy of Education Society* (Urbana, Ill., 1995), pp. 68–79.

Harvard Middle Eastern and Islamic Review for permission to reprint Roy Mottahedeh, "Traditional Shi'ite education in Qom" (vol. 2/1, 1995), pp. 89–98.

Harvard University Press for permission to reprint William Galston, "Civic education in the Liberal State," reprinted by permission of the publisher from *Liberalism and the Moral Life*, ed. Nancy Rosenblum, Cambridge, Mass.: Harvard University Press, pp. 89–101. Copyright © 1989 by the President and Fellows of Harvard College.

Royal Institute of Philosophy for permission to reprint Amélie Oksenberg Rorty, "Rousseau's Therapeutic Experiments," *Philosophy* (1991), pp. 318–51.

Israel Scheffler was, for many years, the mainstay of the philosophy of education at the Harvard Graduate School of Education. His publications were models of calm and penetrating clarity; he was a generous teacher who attracted and influenced educators from Japan, Eastern Europe, the Middle East. While announcing a continued commitment to some courses in the philosophy of education, HGSE closed the doctoral program on Scheffler's retirement. "We need to concentrate on subjects that are at the core of education," Jerome Murphy, the Dean of the School, said by way of explanation. I am grateful to Dean Murphy and HGSE for demonstrating the need for this book.

Without the counsel, the scholarship and dedication of many people, this book would not have been possible. First and foremost: the contributors undertook a task that did not initially stand in the direct line of their researches. The contributors to this volume are historians of philosophy who have thought deeply about an important figure; their essays develop the implications of his work on education, broadly and largely construed. They were asked to project how (as it may be) the epistemology, the ethics and political theory, and the philosophy of science of these significant thinkers affected – and perhaps should continue to affect – the policies and practice of serious educators. They were invited to write essays – not journal articles, not entries for encyclopedias – and to speculate freely about the counsel their figure might give to reflective educators. Rather than stopping abruptly with the far-reaching implications of the Vienna Circle's Enlightenment revival, we have extended our historical perspectives by adding two papers on other philosophic traditions, that of the Shi'ite education of a mullah, and that of education in a traditional Yeshiva. Finally, to bring history to the present, we've included two papers on contemporary issues in the philosophy of education: the implications of recent social epistemology on education; and the problems that arise for civic education in a pluralistic liberal state.

A collection of this kind is inevitably somewhat arbitrary: why are Montaigne and Bacon absent? What, no Luther or Durkheim? No Thomas and Matthew Arnold? Why do many of the contributors say nothing about the relevance of their figures to current issues in educational theory? The answers are clear. Even a generous and public-minded publisher sets constraints on the size and scope of its publications. And even a wildly hopeful editor must match subjects/topics with qualified, willing and sympathetic contributors. Many of them generously responded to an intrusive editor, who asked them to address additional questions, or – in the interest of brevity – to omit a section of their papers. I am grateful to Jeffrey Michels and Stasia Sutermeister for their generous assistance in producing this book. I received counsel from an anonymous reviewer for the publishers, and from Eva Brann, Myles Burnyeat, Jane Cohen, Catherine Elgin, Steve Harris, Simon Harrison, Michel Oksenberg, Lawrence Sager, and Gisela Striker. I am grateful to Ronald de Sousa, Tracy Kosman, Genevieve Lloyd, Jay Hullett, Jay Rorty and William Ruddick for much needed encouragement and sustaining friendship.

A.O.R.

1

THE RULING HISTORY OF EDUCATION

Amélie Oksenberg Rorty

Philosophers have always intended to transform the way we see and think, act and interact; they have always taken themselves to be the ultimate educators of mankind. Even when they believed that philosophy leaves everything as it is, even when they did not present philosophy as the exemplary human activity, they thought that interpreting the world aright – understanding it and our place in it – would free us from illusion, direct us to those activities (civic life, contemplation of the divine order, scientific progress or artistic creativity) that best suit us. Even "pure" philosophy – metaphysics and logic – is implicitly pedagogical. It is meant to correct the myopia of the past and the immediate.

Philosophical reflection on education from Plato to Dewey has therefore naturally been directed to the education of rulers, to those who are presumed to preserve and transmit – or to redirect and transform – the culture of society, its knowledge and its values.[1] Every historical era is marked by a struggle for power, as it may be the authority of tradition or of manifest power, that of philosophic, spiritual, or scientific knowledge, that of artistic creativity, mercantile or technological productivity. It is only quite late in the history of liberal democracies that educational policy was formulated for, and directed to presumptively autonomous individuals, determining their own ends, structuring their own lives. Nowhere is the philosophy of education more important, nowhere is education itself more crucial – and nowhere is it more neglected – than in a liberal participatory democracy whose egalitarian commitments make every individual both legislator and subject.

The disputes at the heart of contemporary discussion of educational policy (What are the directions and limits of public education in a liberal pluralist society? How can we best assure an equitable distribution of educational opportunity? Should the quality of education be supervised by national standards and tests? Should public schools undertake moral and religious education?) reenact the controversies that mark the history of philosophy from Plato to social epistemology. Fruitful and responsible discussions of educational policy inevitably move to the larger philosophic questions that prompt and inform them: those issues are most acutely articulated and examined in moral and political theory, epistemology, and the philosophy of mind. What are the proper aims of education? (Preserving the harmony of civic life? Individual salvation? Artistic creativity? Scientific progress? Empowering individuals to choose wisely? Preparing citizens to enter a productive labor force?) Who should bear the primary responsibility for formulating educational policy? (Philosophers, religious authority, rulers, a scientific elite, psychologists, parents, or local councils?) Who should be educated? (Everyone equally? Everyone according to his potential? Each according to his need?) How does the structure of knowledge affect the structure and sequence of learning? (Should practical experience, or mathematics or history provide the model for learning?) What interests should guide the choice of a curriculum? (The achievement of a competitive advantage on the international economic market? Religious, political and ethnic representation? The formation of a cosmopolitan sensibility?) How should the intellectual, spiritual, civic and moral, artistic, physical and technical dimensions of education be related to one another?

Because we are the inheritors of the history of conceptions of the proper aims and directions of education, that history remains actively embedded and expressed in our beliefs and practices. It provides the clearest understanding of the issues that presently concern and divide us. Most theories of knowledge – certainly those of Descartes and Locke – were (among other things) intended to reform pedagogical practices. Most ethical theories – certainly those of Hume, Rousseau and Kant – were meant to redirect moral education. The practical import of political theories – those of Hobbes, Mill and Marx – is not only directed to the structure of institutions, but to the education of citizens. Comprehensive metaphysical systems – those of Leibniz, Spinoza and Hegel – provide models for inquiry; and thus implicitly set directions and standards for the education of the enlightened. Some philosophers – Locke, Rousseau, Bentham and Mill, for example – made their educational programs a central feature of their philosophical systems. Others – Descartes, Spinoza and Hume – had good reasons for not making the educational import of their systems explicit.

If educational policy is blind without the guidance of philosophy, philosophy rings hollow without critical attention to its educational import. A vital and robust philosophy of education inevitably incorporates virtually the whole of philosophy; and the study of the history of philosophy mandates reflection on its implications for education. The full force of the Cartesian and Leibnizian revolution emerges in its consequences on the role of mathematics in education of scientists; the point of Locke's and the Encyclopedists' views on epistemology is expressed in their insistence that successful learning begins in experience and practice; the full impact of Hume's and Rousseau's views on the imagination is revealed in the role they assign to the imagination in forming habits of mind and action. Hegel's transformation of philosophy marks the study of history, widely conceived, as an essential part of education. Since educational policy is formulated by those who counsel the rulers who apply and implement it, the philosophy of education is typically addressed to rulers and their counselors.

We can usefully reconstruct the features of the *dramatis personae* of this history: the continuing battle between the claims of (varieties of) civic legislators on the one hand (Plato and Aristotle) and (varieties of) spiritual directors on the other (Augustine and Loyola); the arts of Renaissance statecraft (Machiavelli and Castiglione); the assertion of spiritual self-determination (Luther and Erasmus); the early Enlightenment focus on (varieties of) scientific and technological knowledge (Descartes, Locke and Diderot); later Enlighten-ment reflections about the priority of developing social sentiments or strengthening an autonomous rational will (Hume and Kant); reflections on the civic and humane benefits of universal education (Adam Smith, Condorcet, Bentham, Mill); Romanticism's emphasis on the poet's aesthetic sensibility as the ultimate legislator of the world (Goethe and Schiller); the education of individuals as free citizens (Rousseau and Dewey). In other philosophic traditions, the Shi'ite focus on the education of a Mullah as an interpreter of the Koran and a traditional Yeshiva's education of interpreters of the Torah and the Talmud. Although they rarely mention historical figures, contemporary theories of education carry on the tradition: Goldman considers the effects of social epistemology on educational policy; and Galston addresses the principled issues that arise in a pluralist liberal state.

Both Plato (*c*.427–347 BC) and Aristotle (384–322 BC) take the education of citizen-rulers as a primary aim of the *polis*: it pervades every aspect of civic activity and it never ends. It assures the security, continuity and harmony of the city; and it expresses the distinctive character of its form of life. Plato argued that rulers (men and women alike) should be selected for their capacities to engage, and to be guided by philosophic inquiry as the culmination of a lengthy regimen in which intellectual and moral education are fused. Truth-bound myth, solemnly measured music, gymnastics and military training prepare citizens for political *philia*; mathematics and harmonics – the sciences of proper proportion – provide the theoretical foundation and the practical skills of justice; astronomy reveals the ordering principles of the cosmos that serve as a model for the *polis*. Beyond the obvious qualifications of a good memory, a passionate non-combative persistent love of inquiry, philosopher-rulers should be able to think critically and dialectically, ordering their beliefs into a unified system. Critically, because they must evaluate the assumptions that guide their questions; dialectically, because they must be able to adjudicate among, and eventually to reconcile apparently opposing claims; systematically, because they must engage in "all things considered" reasoning, bearing in mind the connections among the far-reaching consequences of their policies. They must learn to think of the city as a kind of precarious cosmos, whose parts are to maintain a stable harmony with one another, all united by the recognition of the ordering power of the Form of the Good.

Like Plato, Aristotle thinks that the institutions of the *polis* – its laws and political structures, its customs and observances – are its central educational instruments, forming the mentality, the typical motives and habits of citizens. (*Pol.* 3. 15 1286a23.ff; *NE* 10.9 1180a33ff.). Plato and Aristotle agree that "those who command . . . should first have learned to obey" (*Pol.* 1333a2); and that "three things make men good and virtuous: nature, habit and reason" (*Pol.* 1331a11). But while Plato thinks that rulers should be distinguished by their philosophical abilities, Aristotle strikes a different balance between the respective contributions of reason and habit to a life of practical virtue. There is no assurance that the highest and best life – the life of *theoria* directed to eternal truths – can provide guidance for practice-oriented virtue. The practical reasoning that serves virtue and political deliberation is not modeled on mathematics, but is embedded in disciplined well-formed habits of perception, emotion, thought and action. Acquired by sound experience and imitation, it involves the ability to discern and achieve what is best and most reasonable in radically different circumstances. Although the virtues are exercised for their own sakes, they are essentially directed to the good of *eudaimonia*. Despite the central role of reason in the good life, *theoria* and *praxis* have distinctive aims, and require the development of different sorts of abilities.

Although Augustine's (354–430) early education centered on Greek and Roman literary and rhetorical works, he moved from the study of rhetoric to philosophy, to the neo-Platonists and Stoics; and eventually, with his conversion to Christianity in 386, to the biblical scriptures. These shifts mark a radical revision in his views about the proper directions of a human life; they also redirect his views about the aims of education. Because every individual is essentially a citizen of the City of God, and only accidentally a citizen of his *polis*, his education should be directed to bringing his soul to harmony with the divine order. Augustine's early neo-Platonism and Stoicism initially projected the coincidence of philosophic and spiritual education: both involve a relatively direct progressive movement, deciphering the intentions of divinity as they are signified and embedded in the cosmic order. Like the scriptures, the world is a divinely encoded text that expresses and reveals the word of God. Semantic analysis – reading the world and the scriptures aright, interpreting their significant analogies – is a mode of spiritual illumination. But after his passage through Manicheanism, Augustine's account of moral and spiritual education becomes more complex, and darker. Original sin blocks the soul's direct access to God: not only our desires, but also our perceptions and interpretations of the world are awry, idolatrously centered on the self. Proper education requires not only the redirection, but the reconstitution of the soul: divine grace must intercede to provide a new Will. Scripture and spiritual directors, philosophy and astute interpretation can at best provide the occasions, the moments for the illumination of grace. But Augustine did not abandon his trust in a solid classical education: though the abilities to think and speak clearly and critically cannot bring salvation, they remain essential allies of the Good Will. He appears not to have faced the implicit tension between the educational directions of his Hellenistic cosmopolitanism and those of his post-Manichean emphasis on the individual's spiritual preparation for Grace.

The Renaissance *Città* reclaims the classical frame and the directions of education. Machiavelli (1469–1527) represents the political, Castiglione (1478–1529) the social ordering of the city-state. In *The Prince* (1513), Machiavelli describes the discipline of the successful ruler; in *The Discourses* (1517), he turns to the political institutions that form the civic virtues of the citizens and the glory of the state. Because his first duty lies in assuring the security and continuity of the *Città*, the Prince must have the *virtù* of knowing how to grasp and to hold power. Statecraft requires an astute sense of timing, a bold and ruthless ability to seize opportunities, the ability to inspire fearful obedience, to control appearances, to command his militia, to manipulate both allies and enemies, even to develop a laconic rhetorical style. But as his power is exercised for the glory as well as the security of the city, the Prince must also know how to gain the admiration as well as the obedience of citizens. Since it is unwise for him to delegate responsibility, he must be able to control the ordinary governance of the state, to plan its economy and agriculture. Becoming an exemplary Renaissance man is a practical necessity for the Machiavellian Prince: identifying himself with his *Città*, all his discipline, all his *virtù* is directed to achieve the glory as well as to assure the security of civic power.

4

Castiglione's *The Courtier* (1528) served as the model for generations of handbooks on the education of the well-formed gentleman. Leaving matters of direct rule to the Prince, the Courtier is to exemplify a transformed sense of grace: the human excellences exercised for the sake of the beauty of their perfection. He is, in a way, the precious jewel of his court; and the court is, in turn, the representation of cosmic order. The arts of war have become ornaments: riding, archery, fencing. The Courtier is to craft his gifts of mind and body into a work of art: he must dress elegantly, dance well, compose brilliant verses and engage in refined, witty conversation. Far from being a superficial and showy mask, all the charm of the Courtier's artifice manifests his honor, provides the world with a model of integrity.

In radically different ways, Loyola (1491–1556), Luther (1483–1546) and Erasmus (*c.*1469–1536) bring new measures of integrity, new criteria for the unity of the inner and outer man. Rather than providing a guidebook for acquiring virtuosity in the expression of *virtù*, they chart a regimen that is meant to rectify and redirect the soul/mind. But they differ dramatically in their conceptions of salvation and of the disciplinary education it requires. Equally subtle psychologically and astute politically, the educational writings of the Jesuit order fall in two categories. Loyola's *Spiritual Exercises* (1526/1556) is a handbook for spiritual directors who are charged with reconstituting the minds – the senses, imagination, desire and so, also, the will – of the faithful. The exercises take the form of traditional staged meditations, each preceded by prayer: the contemplator undergoes a period of rigorous sensory deprivation, during which he is to imagine – in as specific detail as possible – each of the stages in the passion of Christ. He is to suffer with Christ in carrying the cross, to share his moment of despair. Loyola's conception of spiritual education reverses that of Augustine: instead of the grace of a new will permeating and re-forming the senses, imagination and desire, Loyola works from the senses towards the mind and the will. Ironically, he prepared the way for later romanticism, introducing the education of the imagination to effect the kind of empathic identification essential to morality. *The Constitution* of the Order of the Society of Jesus (1556) prescribes the selection and character of both pupils and professors of the Order, as well as curriculum and the pedagogical methods of the Schools. The Order is in principle open to all; education is suitably graded to initiates' intellectual and spiritual abilities. But since the future soldiers and diplomats of the Church Militant are to succeed in influencing princes, the hierarchy of the Order must be gifted: well-born, intelligent, eloquent, and preferably of a commanding and handsome presence. Their education in philosophy, languages, rhetoric, scripture, theology and moral theory must be scrupulously controlled for its orthodoxy: Aquinas and Aristotle in philosophy, the Council of Trent and the Bible for theology, Cicero for rhetoric, expurgated versions of Thucydides, Homer and Hesiod and "others of this nature" for general learning. Authors hostile to Christianity are to be read sparingly, and only under careful supervision: the servants of Christ must be wholly obedient to the rule of the Order.

Luther, himself educated within an Augustinian order, launches yet another revolution in his "Letter to Mayors . . . on behalf of Christian schools" (1524) and "On the duty of sending children to school" (1530). Since scripture is the only authority on morality and religion, children must learn to read. To the extent their abilities and situations permit, they should be taught Hebrew, Greek and Latin. Despite the primacy he accords to spiritual preparation for the grace of faith, Luther places the responsibility for education with civil rather than with religious authorities. They are under the obligation to compel citizens to send children to school, and to provide a curriculum that encompasses sciences and the arts, jurisprudence and medicine, chronicles and histories. The proper expression of spiritual grace essentially extends to civic life: the man of good will is a good and constructive citizen. Lutheran intervention brought a dramatic extension of education: though its aims remained spiritual, it was mandatory, universal and regulated by civic authority.

Of a more skeptical turn, Erasmus' *Education of the Prince* (1516) provides a counterbalance to his predecessors. The virtues of the Prince are not vices exercised to noble ends: they are the simple virtues of early Christianity, to be exercised by all alike. Civic harmony and peace, rather than glory or canny force provide the best security of the State. The foibles and weakness of human nature – ignorance, mutual fear, the diversity and strife of passions – set severe limits on the hopes of dramatic revolutionary reforms. The controversy between Erasmus and Luther over the freedom and the power of the will was all the more heated because they were in close agreement about the corruption of the Roman church, its misuse of authority. That exchange – Erasmus' *De libero arbitrio* (1524), Luther's reply in *On the Bondage of the Will* (1525), countered by Erasmus in *Hyperaspistes* (1526) – had far-reaching implications for education. While they both assign the task of preparing for salvation to individual conscience, they disagree about the resources to which the individual can turn. Although Erasmus believes that conscience is the ultimate guardian of the individual's soul, he counsels Christians to remain within the tutelage of a suitably reformed Roman Church.

Cosmopolitan, at home in the Lowlands, Paris, England, Louvain, Rome, Basel, Freiburg im Breisgau, Erasmus established the model for scholarly clarity and precision in his translations and commentaries on the New Testament and early Patristic writing. Difficult as they might be to apply, the rules of scholarship were simple and straightforward: analyze and test manuscript variants, present both sides of controversies fairly, admit ignorance and claim no more than you can prove. In his hands, clarity and breadth of mind, rectitude of conduct and simplicity of faith were mutually supportive moral instruments. Ironically, Erasmus provided the directions and the textual support for the dramatic turns of the Reformation, which he himself regarded as both excessive and dangerous.

Although Descartes (1596–1650) did not explicitly discuss education, the *Regulae* (1628) and *Principia philosophiae* (1644) have powerful pedagogical consequences: the analytic method provides the basis and the model for inquiry; the mathematical scientist is the new authority. As the will cannot by itself correct malformed – that is, confused, misinformed – passions, moral education requires the development of *habitudes* of sound thought. (*Passions de l'âme*, I.45, III. 152–3 (1649)). *Estime de soi-même* and *generosité* – the dispositional passions that are the virtues of the mind – remind the will to suspend its judgment in the face of unclear and indistinct ideas. Scientific discovery – construed as the discovery of divine order – is the essential activity of the mind; happily it also provides the most reliable source of ideas that can, in principle, elicit countervailing corrective passions. Although he takes scientific truth to provide the new moral authority, Descartes nevertheless adheres to a provisional morality: he will obey the laws of his country and follow the guidance of the

6

Church, presumably in the unexpressed hope that scientific advances would eventually improve those institutions and their laws.

Locke's (1632–1704) *Some Thoughts Concerning Education* (1693) blends antiauthoritarian liberalism with economic conservativism. A handbook for the education of the sons of gentlemen, it is a marked contrast to his *Proposals for the Bringing Up of Children of Paupers*. Gentlemen's sons were to be educated by tutors who could mould the habits and direct the minds of their pupils towards practical pursuits. Learning by doing is the great pedagogical innovation: the languages were to be acquired by conversation and travel rather than by the study of the classics; scientific education was, as much as possible, to be grounded in observation and direct experience rather than expounded as a deductive system. Although Locke thought that Divinity endowed man with both mathematical and moral ideas, he believed that moral knowledge could best be conveyed by a study of history, biography and the scriptures rather than from theology or casuistry. Once set in the right path of common sense and social responsibility, the gentleman is meant to bring order to the rest of society. By contrast, the children of the poor are to learn a trade so that they can become independent and repay their benefactors. Gratitude is their great moral lesson.

Eloquent advocates for universal public instruction, Adam Smith (1723–90) and Condorcet (1743–94) argued that it is an intrinsic good; and that it conduces to a mild mannered, reflective, and "discursive" society, capable of judicious civic deliberation. Moderating the extremes – and the separation – of an elite classical education and one focused on occupational training, they justified public education as a liberal and humanizing activity, by no means merely an economic instrument to increase "human capital."

Hume (1711–76) reintroduces the imagination as a central protagonist in moral education. The passions of self-love and self-interest are our primary motives; fortunately, the mechanism of sympathy – a natural endowment of the human mind – makes the needs, passions and, to some extent, the thought of others as imaginatively vivid to us as if they were our own. Although we have some natural moral sentiments – benevolence, charity, kindness to children – these are, in themselves, insufficiently strong to promote the steady, reliable sentiments of a robust moral life. Like the other artificial virtues, justice arises when we have taken "a general point of view," having been enlarged by the imagination and informed by the understanding to consider whether an action or a character trait is typically useful or pleasing to our fellows. The conventions of justice are initially formed by considerations of self-interest, "but a sympathy with public interest is the source of the moral approbation which attends that virtue" (*Treatise of Human Nature*, III. 2. 2) (1739–40). It is, Hume argues, easier to be moved by a sympathetic understanding of the interests of one's fellows in a homogeneous society. But even in a diverse society, moral education can so enlarge the scope of the imagination to take the "general point of view," that sympathy can succeed in enlivening ideas of the common good with the force and vivacity of motivating passions.

D'Alembert's (1713–84) "Preliminary Discourse" for the *Encyclopédie ou Dictionnaire raisonné des sciences, des arts et des metiers* (1751–72) announces old motifs in radically new combinations. Knowledge is doubly progressive: it is cumulative and it simultaneously serves virtue and happiness; the understanding engages the interdependent faculties of sense, imagination, reason and memory. All knowledge, including moral and spiritual knowledge, arises from reflection on sense experience that is approximately the same for all men; it is, and ought to be, equally available to all and all are equally obliged to contribute to its advancement; it forms a logically coherent system that encompasses productive activity and scientific inquiry; the arts and crafts provide essential contributions to the moral as well as to the theoretical sciences. Resisting what he considers the empty pretensions of metaphysical deductions of science and morality, D'Alembert praises the (1560/1–1626) confident and patient incremental approach to knowledge. In contrast to the abstract metaphysical spirit of system that proceeds formally and deductively, the systematic spirit begins with established facts and proceeds practically and constructively towards the substantive organization of knowledge.

Kant (1724–1804) returns to the spirit of system, now formulated in egalitarian terms. While his rationalism does not deny the moral utility and propriety of sentiment – indeed he considers respect for the moral law to be a central pivot of the moral life – strict morality requires being able to will to do what is right, solely because it is right. In principle, anyone who grasps the law of non-contradiction can determine what is right: the maxim that directs a moral duty can, without contradiction, be willed as a universal law. The task of moral education is that of bringing children to understand and to follow what reason, properly understood, demands. The child must not be lured into morality by a desire to please, or from fear of punishment, or even because virtue is the best road to happiness. While the exercise of autonomous critical rationality cannot, as such, be trained, the moral educator can provide the conditions for its awakening: the child is to develop habits of self-reliance, while also recognizing that "he can only attain his own ends by allowing others to attain theirs" (Kant 1960, p. 28). Children are to be given models of respect and self-respect; the maxims that are embodied within those examples must be articulated, and applied fairly and equally to all, without exception.

Although Kant's views on morality were, by his own admission, profoundly influenced by those of Rousseau (1712–78), it is the latter who seems, superficially at least, our congenial contemporary: fully acknowledging the inevitability of moral ambivalence, he nevertheless describes the political and the educational regimen that promotes the morality of free men. The two agree that morality requires rational autonomy; they also agree that freedom consists in treating oneself both as subject to the moral law and as its universal legislator. But Rousseau projects our natural condition as far more benign and our social condition as far more troubled than does Kant. Because his writings are focused on the politics and the psychology, rather than the logic of morality, he appears to provide the moral educator with clear guidance.

Rousseau's writings on moral education fall in three categories: (1) *The First and Second Discourses* (1750, 1755) and the *Letter to d'Alembert* (1758) are cautionary tales, attacks on the debilitating and corrupting effects of society and its arts, as they inflame the imagination and develop erratic, disturbing passions. (2) *Émile* (1762) outlines the stages of the psychological formation of a free man and a loving mother. All education comes "from nature or from men or from things" (*Émile*, I); early education consists largely in allowing the young child the freedom of its natural activity. Instead of becoming passive by being taught, or resentful by

8

being punished, the child must learn from experience, from seeing the natural consequences of his actions. To be sure, the tutor often manipulates the child's world: Émile acquires an understanding of property and of injustice by seeing the results of his labor arbitrarily despoiled; he learns about promises by being placed in a situation where he himself proposes a mutually satisfactory agreement (Émile, II). Rather than answering Émile's questions about natural phenomena, the tutor is to engage his activity in discovering the patterns they exemplify. Émile is to be kept away from society as long as possible: by introducing habits of dependency, this transforms active and unselfconscious amour de soi into slavish amour propre. When adolescence awakens the power of sexual emotions, Émile – who is by this time a sensible and healthy young man – can be sent to learn the ways of the world. Sophie, who is to be his wife and the mother of his children, is to have quite a different sort of education, focused on familial sentiment and service rather than on rational autonomy. Although their education is meant to be morally equal and beneficially complementary, Sophie's sentimental education blocks her impartial rationality. Because she is not qualified to be an active citizen, it is only by ambiguous courtesy to the purity of her sentiments that she can be accounted a moral being.

(3) *The Social Contract* (1762) provides an account of the political conditions in which men can hope for morality from one another. Sharply distinguished from social dependency, active political life both forms and expresses men's moral capacities. It is by becoming a sovereign subject of the body politic, legislating the general principles of the laws to which he willingly subjects himself, that the individual achieves the promise of his nature. A new set of civic sentiments enables citizens to identify their interests with the General Will; the formation of those sentiments is to be fostered by the rituals of civic religion.

Schiller's (1759–1805) *Letters on the Education of Mankind* (1794–5) endorses Kant's view that aesthetic experience provides an intimation of freedom from both the receptivity of sensation and the preconceived categories of the understanding; he also agrees with Kant that freedom is a precondition for morality. Putting these two insights together, he emerges with a wholly un-Kantian conclusion. Morality is the expression of the spontaneous play of aesthetic expression; it transcends the necessities governed by reason. The progressive constructivism of the Encyclopedists is preserved but radically reinterpreted: the ultimate moral legislator is the inventive and playful poet or composer, rather than the craftsman or scientist. Morality is not served by technical skill or by objective knowledge; nor is it acquired by imitating exemplars. Schiller was as critical of Goethe's attempts to assimilate scientific, artistic and moral "genius" as he was of Kant's rationalism. A robust and vigorous sense of agency – the gift of spontaneous improvisation that is the mark of true morality – cannot be acquired by studying nature or by imitating exemplars. It can only be developed by allowing the spontaneous creative play of the mind to express itself objectively.

Bentham (1748–1832) and J. S. Mill (1806–73) agreed that the ultimate aim of education was the promotion of happiness, broadly construed as the satisfaction of critically and widely informed desire. It was precisely because their utilitarianism was complex and qualified, that they took the education of desires, as well as the calculation of consequences seriously. Logic, mathematics and the sciences were to be studied for their uncompromising attention to empirical detail, their liberal hospitality to counter-evidence: all three served as models of rigorous self-critical reasoning. Bentham notoriously declared pushpin as good as poetry; Mill enlarged education beyond facts and logic, to the education of social and civic sentiments, both as a human good and as an instrument for the formation of wise public policy. Education is to include history, classics and literature. History is the record of political experience; the classics provide models of rhetorical argument and of dialectical reasoning; literature develops social sentiments and strengthens the capacity for sympathetic imagination. All these avenues of education, taken together and properly ordered, are intrinsically as well as instrumentally valuable.

Strongly influenced by his study of Hegel (1770–1831) and of Rousseau, Dewey (1859–1952) thought that moral education coincides with democratic civic education, and that both involve the ability to mediate the never-ending tensions between the spontaneous expression of individual subjectivity and the objective cooperative work of citizenship. The work of morality begins with the practical problems that arise from social conflict; it involves the exercise of a set of second-order problem-solving skills that are acquired through experience; and it issues in the development of intelligent, continuously adaptable habits. The democratic citizen is the new ruler; intelligent activity has become both the aim and the expression of morality. Dewey's recommendations for moral education follow the pattern of his general educational proposals. They direct society to provide the material conditions – the physical, psychological, social and political conditions – that permit the individual to educate himself: he will himself naturally attempt to enlarge the scope, refine the skills and enrich the repertoire of his cooperative activity. Goldman's analysis of the ways that social processes structure knowledge develops one side of Dewey's legacy; another side is developed by Galston's discussion of civic education in a multicultural society.

Even if we wished, we cannot put this history behind us; it forms and informs our conceptions of our aims and our needs. But while European and Anglo-American countries share some highly general educational aims, their distinctive political and religious histories, and their different socio-economic conditions, set them quite distinctive moral and educational problems. Because the issues that are the substance of contemporary educational controversies are morally laden, we tend to suppose that their solution is philosophical and general. These controversies – disputes about the place of religious education in public schools, about the representation of ethnic, race, gender and cultural differences in the curriculum, about whether music and the arts should play a significant role in public education, about whether educational policy should be local or federal, about the separation of professional and technical training from a shared liberal and humanistic education – raise fundamental political, as well as moral issues. As the details of the problems of moral education naturally vary with national circumstances, so too the philosophic grounds for their solutions must vary. Aristotle's views on moral education have a radically different import in Great Britain from those they have in post-war unified Germany; the differences between Loyola, Luther and Erasmus have distinctive consequences on the educational systems of Ireland, Sweden and the Netherlands. As they are introduced in France or in Portugal, Cartesian principles of education bear little resemblance to their introduction

10

in the United States; a moral education focused on the primacy of social sentiment takes a different form in a nation whose citizens share a common culture than it has in one in which a dominant culture faces a growing multicultural population. Kantian education wears one face in Austria, quite another in Australia. And all this, without even beginning to think about how the history of moral education emerges in the second and third worlds, or how Islamic, Jewish or Chinese educational ideals support – and conflict with – the momentum of the global economy that awaits them. As is so often the case, philosophic theory moves to history and ends with geo-politics.

NOTE

1 Etymology is always revealing: "education" derives from *e-ducare*: to bring out, draw forth and from *e-ducere*: to lead out. Its double etymology suggests both drawing something out of the learner; and leading the learner out to a new place. *Erudire* typically suggests taking someone or something out of a rude or crude condition. Our "doctrine" and "indoctrinate" come from *docere*, to teach; and of course *disciplina* covers both senses of the English "discipline." "Instruction" comes from *in-struere*: "to build into." Hence the German *Bildung* to shape, form, cultivate. The German *erziehen* gives: to bring up or train. The verb "to school" derives from the Greek *schole*: discuss at leisure, and *scholion*: a commentary, interpretation. The French use "formation" as well as "education." Greek has the general term *trophe*: rearing, and *paideia* which refers to the bringing up of young children, both surprisingly limited.

SELECT BIBLIOGRAPHY

For more detailed and scholarly bibliographies, readers may wish to consult the notes appended to each essay.

Aristotle (1987) *Nicomachean Ethics*, trans. J. A. K. Thomson, New York: Penguin Books.

—— *The Politics*, ed. Stephen Everson, New York: Cambridge University Press, 1988.

Augustine (1995) *Against the Academicians* and *The Teacher*, trans. Peter King, Indianapolis, Ind.: Hackett.

—— (1993) *On the Free Choice of the Will*, ed. Thomas Williams, Indianapolis, Ind.: Hackett.

Bacon, Francis (1974) *The Advancement of Learning* and *New Atlantis*, London: Oxford University Press.

Bentham, Jeremy (1983) *Chrestomathia*, ed. M. J. Smith and W. H. Burston, London: Oxford University Press.

Brann, Eva (1989) *The Paradoxes of Education in a Republic*, Chicago: University of Chicago Press.

Castiglione, Baldassare (1978) *The Book of the Courtier*, Harmondsworth: Penguin Books.

Condorcet, Jean Antoine (1971) "Rapport sur l'éducation publique," in *French Liberals and Education in the 18th Century: La Chalotais, Tugot, Diderot and Condorcet on National Education*, ed. and trans. François La Fontainerie, New York: Burt Franklin.

D'Alembert, Jean Le Rond (1965) "Preliminary discourse," *Encyclopédie ou Dictionnaire raisonné des sciences, des arts et des metiers*, trans. Nelly S. Hoy and Thomas Cassirer, Indianapolis, Ind.: Bobbs-Merrill.

Descartes, René (1985) "Passions of the soul," *The Philosophical Writings of Descartes*, 2 vols, ed. John Cottingham, Robert Stoothoff and Dugald Murdoch, Cambridge: Cambridge University Press.

—— "Principles of philosophy," in Cottingham, Stoothoff and Murdoch (eds) *Philosophical Writings of Descartes*.

—— "Rules for the direction of the mind," in Cottingham, Stoothoff and Murdoch (eds) *Philosophical Writings of Descartes*.

Dewey, John (1916) *Democracy and Education*, New York: Macmillan.

—— *Experience and Education* (1938) New York: Houghton Mifflin.

Durkheim, Émile (1961) *Moral Education*, New York: Free Press.

Erasmus, Desiderius (1968) *Education of a Christian Prince*, trans. Lester Born, New York: Norton.

Galston, William (1991) *Liberal Purposes*, Cambridge: Cambridge University Press.

Gutmann, Amy (1987) *Democratic Education*, Princeton, NJ: Princeton University Press.

Hobbes, Thomas (1947) *Leviathan*, London: Oxford University Press.

Hume, David (1987) *Essays: Moral, Political and Literary*, ed. Eugene Miller, Indianapolis, Ind.: Liberty Press.

—— *Treatise of Human Nature* (1978) ed. P. H. Nidditch and L. A. Selby-Bigge, 2nd edn, London: Oxford University Press.

Jefferson, Thomas (1930) "Bill for the more general diffusion of knowledge," in *Thomas Jefferson and Education in the Republic*, ed. C. F. Arrowood, New York: McGraw Hill.

Kant, Immanuel (1960) *Lecture Notes on Pedagogy*, trans. Annette Churton and published as *Kant on Education*, Ann Arbor, Mich.: University of Michigan Press.

Locke, John (1989) *Some Thoughts Concerning Education*, ed. John Yolton and Jean Yolton, London: Oxford University Press.

—— (1964) "Proposals for the bringing up of children of paupers," *John Locke on Education*, ed. Peter Gay, New York: Columbia University Press.

Loyola, St Ignatius, *The Constitutions of the Society of Jesus*, St Louis, Mo.: Institute of Jesuit Sources, 1996.

—— *Spiritual Exercises*, trans. W. H. Longridge, London: A. R. Mowbray, 1955.

Luther, Martin (1890) "Sermon on the duty of sending children to school," in *Letter on Education*, ed. F. V. N. Painter, Philadelphia, Pa.: Concordia Publishing House.

—— "Letters to the mayors and aldermen of all the cities of Germany on behalf of Christian schools," in *Letter on Education*.

Machiavelli, Niccolò (1983) *The Discourses*, ed. Bernard Crick, trans. Leslie J. Walker, New York: Penguin Books.

—— *The Prince* (1995) trans. George Bull, New York: Penguin Books.

Mill, James (1969) *James Mill on Education*, ed. W. H. Burston, Cambridge: Cambridge University Press.

Mill, J. S. (1963) "An inaugural address at the University of St Andrews," in *Collected Works*, Toronto: University of Toronto Press.

—— *The Subjection of Women* (1988) ed. Susan Okin, Indianapolis, Ind.: Hackett.

Pestalozzi, J. H. (1951) *The Education of Man*, trans. Heinz Norden and Ruth Norden, New York: Philosophical Library.

—— *How Gertrude Teaches her Children* (1915) trans. Lucy Holland and Francis Turner, London: Allen and Unwin.

Plato, *Republic* (1992) trans. G. M. A. Grube and C. D. C. Reeve, Indianapolis, Ind.: Hackett.

Rousseau, Jean Jacques (1979) *Émile*, ed. Allen Bloom, New York: Basic Books.

—— *The Discourses and other Early Political Writings* (1997) ed. Victor Gourevitch, Cambridge: Cambridge University Press.

—— *The Social Contract and other Later Political Writings* (1997) ed. Victor Gourevitch, Cambridge: Cambridge University Press.

Russell, Bertrand (1926) *Education and the Good Life*, New York: Buni and Liveright.

Schiller, Freidrich (1965) *Letters on the Aesthetic Education of Man*, trans. Reginald Snell, New York: Ungar Publishing.

Smith, Adam (1982) *Theory of Moral Sentiments*, ed. D. D. Raphael and A. L. Macfie, Indianapolis, Ind.: Liberty Classics.

Smith, Wilson (ed.) (1979) *Theories of Education in Early America 1655–1819*, Indianapolis, Ind.:
    Bobbs-Merrill.
Tamir, Yael (ed.) (1995) *Democratic Education in a Multicultural State*, Oxford: Blackwell Publishers.
Whitehead, Alfred North (1967) *The Aims of Education*, New York: Free Press.

2

SOCRATIC EDUCATION

Paul Woodruff

Socrates denies that he is a teacher, and the people he questions often deny that they have anything to learn from him. These denials are tinged with irony, of course, but they contain a grain of truth: Socratic education puts the responsibility for learning on the learner. Nothing is more important to this kind of education than the resources that learners bring to it: their experience, their conceptual and logical abilities, and their desire to know the truth. Still, Socrates is more teacher than he admits; he has firm beliefs himself about the rough outlines of knowledge and human virtue (his main subjects of inquiry); and he often questions people to bring them to see that they too must accept such beliefs, on pain of inconsistency with their deepest commitments. Socrates speaks humbly enough, but his aim is not modest: it is to transform people's lives by coaxing them into thinking as a philosopher thinks. And Plato, in writing about this, faces hard questions about the value of the education for which Socrates stands.

Three salient features of Socratic education are illustrated in Plato's work:

1 an emphasis on critical and consistent thinking;
2 a unique concept of teacherless education, contrasted with teaching both as it occurs in Athens and as it would occur in ideal circumstances;
3 the hope that education in philosophy has the potential to transform people's lives for the better.

By "Socrates" I mean the character of that name in Plato's dialogues, which are largely historical fiction.[1] Socrates is famous for obscuring himself, his aims, and the state of his own knowledge by means of irony. On many points, readers are left to their own devices. Some think Socrates truly finds himself without answers to his own questions and sincerely continues to seek them. Others hold that Socrates knows the answers, but conceals them, leaving hints accessible only to the most philosophical audiences. And there are positions in between as well. In Socrates, Plato has drawn a personality that consists largely in shifting screens of irony, and we can do little but ask which is the predominate mask that Socrates wears. In this essay I will not try to peer beneath that mask. I will take it that Socrates is serious when he says that he lacks the knowledge he seeks, and that because he lacks such knowledge he cannot be a teacher. That is why his method places the primary responsibility on the learner.

14

1 CRITICAL AND CONSISTENT THINKING

What, then, does Socrates do by way of education, for whom does he do it, and what is his aim in doing so? A large part of his work is critical and issues in refutations of his companions: "With what group do I belong?" asks Socrates on one occasion. "I am with those who would be pleased to be refuted if I should say anything that is not true, and pleased to be the refuter of anyone who should say anything that is not true – more pleased, in fact, to be refuted than to refute. I think that's a greater good, you see, insofar as it's a greater good to be relieved of a great evil than to relieve another of the same" (*Gorgias* 458a). He is apparently willing to provide this service for anyone, regardless of age or level of education. His aim is to goad his companions into examining their beliefs and their lives, especially in relation to virtue or the good condition of the soul. During his trial, he tells how he would respond if ordered to change his way of life:

> as long as I breathe and am able to do so, I will not cease to practice philosophy, exhorting you and charging anyone of you whom I happen to meet, with my usual words: "My very good friend, you belong to Athens, the greatest city and the one most famous for its power and cleverness; aren't you ashamed that you are concerned to have as much money, fame, and honor as you can, while you are not concerned with true wisdom or the condition of your soul – that it be the best it can – and you do not give this a thought?" And if one of you disputes this and says he is concerned I will not immediately let him go or leave him, but I will question him and examine him and test him, and if I find that he does not possess virtue when he says he does, I shall reproach him for taking the most important subjects least seriously while giving more attention to trivia. These things I will do for anyone I meet, young or old, citizen or visitor . . .
>
> (*Apology* 29de)

We do not find Socrates doing exactly this in early dialogues other than the *Apology*, but we have a report of this kind of Socratic education from the most famous of Socrates' young companions – and one of the worst behaved. The effect was that the young man came to be ashamed of his life and to wish for improvement (Alcibiades, in *Symposium* 215a–216a).

What sort of improvement can come through Socratic education? We shall see that consistency as Socrates understands it requires high standards for knowledge claims, so that Socratic learners will be modest in what they claim to know. He also holds that a consistent and well-examined life will serve certain moral ideals, particularly the Socratic thesis that it is worse to do wrong than to suffer it (*Crito* 49ab).

Who is to be educated?

Socrates' practice of philosophy is an education for everyone, including himself. He demands no prerequisites of the boys and men he draws into his conversations, and he claims no special qualifications for his own project in self-education. Education as Socrates conceives it is a lifelong pursuit.

Socrates' opponents make this a point of ridicule, considering philosophy a subject fit only for the very young (so Callicles at *Gorgias* 484–5). Socrates, however, did not come at an early age to the sort of philosophy he practices (*Phaedo* 96a, ff), and in one later context argues that philosophy is not appropriate for the very young: people who are not yet fixed in their moral views can be thrown by the critical element of philosophy into disrespect for what is just and noble, and so the Socrates of Plato's *Republic* sets the starting age for philosophy at age 30 (537–8). The danger is real. Young students may learn from the critical element in Socratic education to question conventional morality, but they might not follow philosophy long enough to find in its positive element a solid basis for morality. Readers are probably supposed to think of characters who famously lost their moral bearings after spending considerable time with Socrates.[2] Plato leaves us to wonder whether this is really Socrates' fault, however, and shows him elsewhere, both before and after the *Republic* questioning people who are well below his official age for philosophy.

There is no one too young or too old for a challenging conversation with Socrates. With very young people Socrates takes a different line than he does with companions his own age; he is kinder, more encouraging, and less cutting in his use of irony.[3] With the brilliant teenager Theaetetus, he takes on the encouraging role of midwife, and he is respectful to the elderly Cephalus (*Republic* 1). But when men of mature years lay claim to knowledge, Socrates subjects them to the irony that he would be their pupil, if only they could say something that would stand against his questioning. Again, there is a grain of truth in this. Since he will not take the role of teacher, Socrates will not take his companions' education on his own shoulders. His aim in these conversations must therefore be self-education for his companions, as he says it is for himself. He is always bent on learning something, or at least on examining his own beliefs, and he tries to draw his companions into their own projects of self-examination.

In his own case, the project evidently continues throughout his life (*Hippias Major* 304c–e). It pre-empts all other studies, as we learn from the *Phaedrus* (230a, 235c). Its purpose is self-knowledge, according to the *Phaedrus* passage, but in most dialogues its result is mainly negative – a constantly revived sense of the philosopher's own ignorance on matters of the greatest importance. There is some irony in Socrates' repeated disclaimers of knowledge, but he seems genuinely committed to the view expressed in the *Apology*, that his human wisdom lies precisely in this gentle paradox: in his knowing that he is not worth much so far as wisdom is concerned (23b).[4] What Socrates knows best is how to maintain his own sense of ignorance by examining himself directly; and Plato also shows Socrates indirectly challenging his own views by questioning partners who have adopted Socratic positions but are unable to defend them. Such dialogues illustrate dramatically the failure of Socrates' best opinions to count, by themselves, as defensible knowledge.[5] All in all, Socrates spends much of his time examining himself, reflecting on his own views, and protecting himself against the conceit that his opinions should be taken for knowledge.

Such a sense of ignorance Socrates knows well how to convey to others, although they do not seem to be able to maintain it when they are away from his questioning. In the *Apology* he tells of working through the ranks of people who claim expertise – politicians, poets, craftsmen of all kinds – and proving that they did not have the knowledge that they claimed, or at least that their claims presupposed (22a–e). Elsewhere we see him engaged with

16

sophists (*Protagoras*, *Gorgias*, *Hippias*), students of sophists or orators (*Meno*, *Phaedrus*), and with army generals (*Laches*). Occasionally he engages the young in conversation (Cleinias in the *Euthydemus*, the boys in the *Lysis*, and Charmides and Theaetetus in the dialogues named after them). There is too the famous slave-boy of the *Meno* whose one qualification for the enterprise is that he knows Greek (82b). And of course Socrates is reported to have been involved with the handsome and irresponsible Alcibiades, who tries without success to make a teacher of him (*Symposium* 216b).

Socrates will talk with anyone; but not everyone is in a position to learn from talking with Socrates, because not everyone has the appropriate resources. We shall see that a learner should bring to Socratic education at least a respect for consistency and a serious desire to learn.

Example: an expert on piety

Plato's *Euthyphro* is an elegant short example of Socratic questioning. At the entrance to a court of law, Socrates falls in with a younger man who has just lodged an unusual charge against his father. Euthyphro is a self-proclaimed expert on matters of piety, which is the virtue that traditionally governs morality insofar as it concerns the gods. Euthyphro is confident he is right in his curious mix of traditional and radical notions about piety. In particular, he claims to know that prosecuting his father is pious, and he has no fear that this action may turn out to be impious, even though piety requires special respect for parents. Socrates says he wants to know what is and is not pious because he has just been charged with impiety. Claiming to be impressed by Euthyphro's knowledge, he presents himself ironically as a sort of pupil to Euthyphro (5c). In what follows, Socrates takes the unstated assumption that, if Euthyphro had the knowledge he claimed, he would be able to say what piety is – would be able, in other words, to offer a satisfactory definition.[6]

Socrates begins by asking a rather technical question, which sets forth part of what he requires in a definition (5d): "Isn't piety the same in every action, itself to itself, and isn't impiety the opposite of all piety and the same as itself, and doesn't anything that is going to be impious have one form in its impiety?" Euthyphro answers, "Entirely so, Socrates," thus setting the stage for Socrates' principal question: "What is piety?"

Euthyphro says that it is what he is doing now, prosecuting a wrongdoer. Socrates does not find this to be adequate teaching on the subject of piety, for piety occurs in contexts other than prosecutions. And so he asks again to be taught what is the one form that piety takes in all pious actions. This time Euthyphro gives the sort of answer Socrates wanted: Piety is what the gods love, and impiety is what they hate. Now Euthyphro has already declared that the gods are split on many issues, and so Socrates shows that Euthyphro is committed to holding that some gods can hate what other gods love. If so, then Euthyphro's definition implies that the same action could be both pious and impious. This conclusion would not have embarrassed Euthyphro's peers, for in ancient Greek mythology there are gods who hate what other gods love, and there are humans such as Orestes whose actions appear to be both pious and impious.[7] Euthyphro, however, cannot defend this result by appeal to traditional mythology; he has already shown that he has new and controversial ideas, and he has already agreed with Socrates that impiety is the opposite of all piety (5d). The result is that his definition of piety is inconsistent with his other beliefs about the matter, and he must give it up. He has not answered Socrates' question, not even to his own satisfaction. At this point it should be clear that Euthyphro is not the expert he claims to be, though he will not admit his difficulty until later (11b).

Socrates will try to save Euthyphro's general idea by helping him to reformulate it; he will later offer some ideas of his own, coax more answers from Euthyphro, and reformulate them as well. But all these proposals will fail. As Euthyphro's beliefs fall away, the discussion becomes more and more an illustration of Socrates' critical reflection on his own views. We might therefore see later parts of the dialogue as supporting Socrates' general claim that even his own best opinions on such subjects cannot pass the test of knowledge, but the text leaves open a number of possible interpretations. The dialogue becomes more technical soon after the refutation just described, and the opinions of scholars on the later sections are divided. Let this initial direct examination of Euthyphro, then, be our example of Socratic questioning.

Although Socrates has controlled the discussion and led it to this point by design, Euthyphro must take responsibility for the result because of his own commitments to the premises of the arguments. Because of those commitments, also, the discussion bears on the concrete issue of how Euthyphro should live his life – even though the argument seems to turn on abstract points of logic and metaphysics.

Euthyphro's career has prepared him for meeting Socrates. As we saw, Socrates set the stage for refuting Euthyphro by having him agree to certain ground rules at the outset: (a) an account of piety must be the same for all cases of piety; and (b) it must be such that no action can be both pious and impious. Euthyphro's way of living his life has already committed him, more deeply than anything he could say, to the sort of approach Socrates is taking: (a) in prosecuting his father, Euthyphro acts on his belief that piety is the same in every context;[8] (b) in affirming his confidence that there can be no impiety in this prosecution, he acts on his conviction that impiety is the opposite of all piety.[9] Euthyphro does not even have the luxury of saying that he does not care if he contradicts himself, for he is already committed to consistency (6a). A more nimble debater, who had no such commitments, might challenge Socrates' rules. Such an adversary might evade the question by declaring that piety is different in different cases, or he might stave off defeat by allowing that piety can coexist with impiety in the same action. But this conversation is not a debate; Socrates and Euthyphro do not treat each other as adversaries. An adversary would be merely playing a game, trying to win the argument as if it meant nothing to his life or to the beliefs that guide it. Euthyphro is a good candidate for Socratic education because he takes his subject seriously, as if his career depended on it, and does not play games with it. He follows Socrates' most important rule: to say only what you believe when you are questioned.

This conversation will end by circling back from one refutation to an earlier one, and Euthyphro will suddenly remember that he is in a hurry to be somewhere else. When all is over, what exactly will Euthyphro have learned? Plato does not tell us, and we readers are left to conclude on our own what Euthyphro ought to have learned. Perhaps Socrates has taught him something about piety.[10] At least Socrates has taught him something about himself: that he does not know what he thought he knew, and that he should therefore be more modest in his claims. Ideally he has learned that he should continue to reflect critically on his ideas about piety and, like Socrates, seek to improve them at every opportunity. Whether or not Euthyphro profits from the encounter will depend on how much he wants to learn in the future, and on how eager he will be to continue thinking along Socratic lines.

Method

We are now in a position to look at the general method schematically. Socratic education consists mainly of questions asked by a teacher (who may nevertheless deny he is a teacher) or a learner (who may nevertheless deny he has anything left to learn). To avoid the confusion that is threatened by these denials, I shall call these characters Philosopher and Companion respectively, keeping in mind that one person may play both roles, as Socrates does when he examines himself. Here are the main features of the practice:[11]

1 Philosopher denies he is a teacher and takes the attitude of a learner.
2 Lectures uttered by Philosopher are rare, and when given are framed in such a way that Philosopher is not responsible for their content.
3 Questions from Philosopher to Companion are the main form of interaction.
4 Companion is held responsible for any answers that emerge.

Philosopher's hope, often stated, is that Companions will furnish answers that are truly their own, on the basis of their prior education or inner resources; and Philosopher usually has grounds for this hope in the context in which his questions arise (as we have seen in the case of Euthyphro). Philosopher will hold Companion responsible for the answers that emerge, and Philosopher will not take responsibility for what he says himself, never putting himself in such a position that he must defend a claim or be questioned by Companion as to his personal meaning.[12]

The pedagogical justification for such teaching seems clear: learners are more likely to take a lesson to heart if they feel that it belongs to them and was theirs from the beginning. At the same time, because they are forced by Philosopher to take responsibility for their views, they are practicing the skill of thinking in ways that are both disciplined and independent. Here "independent" should not be taken to imply that Companions are to be sole judges of the quality of their answers. Philosopher will not let them get away with sloppy thinking, with inconsistencies, or with unsubstantiated knowledge claims. The method is not dangerously relativistic, for it will not approve just any internal consistency, and it produces only certain kinds of results. Generally, the method leads either to a negative conclusion (Companions find they do not have the knowledge they claimed) or a positive one (Companions find they hold a positive moral commitment they had initially denied).

The negative method requires that knowledge claims must be consistent with unwaveringly tough standards:

5 Questions may aim at an answer that would be evidence to support Companion's knowledge claim.
6 Philosopher introduces standards for knowledge, usually with Companion's consent.

Companions concur with Philosopher's negative finding just insofar as they agree with Philosopher's standards for knowledge, i.e., just insofar as they have a common goal in the discussion. This is the main point on which the method must be distinguished from that of later skeptics who took Socrates as their model: ancient skeptics did not subscribe to any standards of knowledge for their own part, but used only such standards as their opponents had explicitly stated in advance. Socrates plainly does subscribe to certain standards and introduces the same ones for most discussions in which knowledge is at stake. As we saw, he assumes that Euthyphro's knowledge of piety implies an ability to give a definition of piety satisfying certain conditions, and he makes similar assumptions in a variety of circumstances. Such assumptions are not neutral; they belong to a partial theory of knowledge that enters the history of philosophy with Socrates.

The positive method requires that answers be consistent with Companions' most deeply held beliefs, some of which may come to them as a surprise. In such a case, the questions aim to show that Companion cannot deny a certain moral proposition without coming into conflict with himself (as Socrates proposes at *Gorgias* 482b).

7 Questions may elicit positive statements of belief from Companion, to which Philosopher also subscribes.
8 Consistency requires that Companion therefore reject an earlier statement.

This leaves Companion in a new positive position. Socrates holds, for example, that it is worse to do wrong than to have wrong done to you; when someone attempts to deny this, he uses the method to show that his companion really holds the Socratic position – as would any human being, he says – and for this result he holds his companion witness (*Gorgias* 474c–475e). In this case the companion finds the new position very strange (480e), and his more assertive friend thinks what Socrates has done is childish (481b). Still, Socrates is convinced that no one can disagree with him on this point without being soundly refuted (509a), apparently because he believes that the method can be relied upon to elicit true beliefs and by this means to refute false ones.

Generally, and not surprisingly, the method is successful with companions to the extent that they are in agreement with Socrates on fundamental points at the outset. Much of the first half of the *Laches*, for example, shows that there is concord between Socrates and a pair of generals, on the topic at hand and on the standards for knowledge, with the result that they are more willing than most of Socrates' companions to accept the result of the method. Euthyphro is a very different case. Although he is responsible for the negative result of the conversation as far as we followed it, he is not willing to recognize this, and so he tries to put the blame on Socrates (11c). Socratic education works best for those who are already committed (as the generals are) to seeking knowledge that meets the highest standards, whether or not they are fully aware of the implications of this commitment at the outset.

Consider the contrast with a currently popular method of education, what I shall call open-question teaching. In modern classrooms, questioning often leaves students free to take a question as they will. In such a classroom, students learn to be accepting of each other's answers, and teachers are careful not to be critical in ways that would weaken a student's confidence. The aim of such questioning is to encourage discussion. Teachers of this kind try to seek positive value in each student contribution: not merely to tolerate, but to praise diversity of opinion. In this atmosphere students learn both to articulate their views and to listen with sympathy to the views of others.

Teachers trained in this method tend to be fascinated by Socrates, but many are shocked to the point of anger at his method, which strikes them as manipulative and over-directive. Open-question teaching does not control the evaluation of answers. It seeks to set students thinking for themselves in the strongest sense: it leaves students entirely free to be the judges of their own answers. This is a good way to draw out students to entrust their precious ideas to discussion. Most teachers who are inclined to philosophy in younger classrooms are not Socratic: far from refuting their students, or teaching them to set a high value on being refuted, they teach them to be accepting of each other's ideas, to follow each other's intellectual leads with respect, and to impose no rule but that of an open mind. The same is often true at the college level.

Criticism of the method

Plato shows Socrates facing a number of objections to his sort of education. One set of objections is related to age: students who are too young for it may lose their moral bearings, as we have seen. On the other hand, philosophers of mature years are accused of wasting their time with a childish pursuit that will not help them to get along in the world.[13] Plato seems to accept both points in the *Republic* and to have designed the ideal city as a response to them. He restricts philosophy there to older students (537–8), and he admits that philosophers in an ordinary city – if they exist at all – will be able at best to keep their own lives free from injustice and impiety, taking shelter as one does in a wind-driven storm behind a wall (496d). Socratic education is useful mainly in the moral sphere, and will therefore have the most public utility in a society that is organized along moral lines. That is one reason his method is not politically effective in democratic Athens (which, Plato and Thucydides would agree, is not organized along moral lines). Another is that Socrates neither wants nor is able to influence a large audience (as must be done in a democracy), and he condemns traditional rhetoric as merely the knack of pleasing a crowd.[14] The critics are right: Socrates has given up the ability to affect policy in democratic Athens. He is able to affect people by his method only one at a time at best.

The critics would add, however, that Socrates is not able to affect anyone for the better, because his method depends on arousing an irrational response: shame.[15] Socrates shames people in two ways, directly in his exhortations to virtue, as promised in the *Apology* and described in the *Symposium*, or indirectly through the sort of refutation illustrated frequently in Socratic dialogues. Shame is a powerful motivator for good or ill, but it is subject to two serious complaints because it normally depends on people's fear of public exposure: (a)

Such fear is irrational, because the public may have conventional views that are wrong. Shame, as many Greeks understood it, is a capitulation to public opinion at the expense of reason.[16] (b) Such fear often leads people to avoid exposure, rather than to change their behavior for the better.

Socrates would be able to respond positively on the first point, for unlike many of his peers he treats shame as rational. Although the values he supports are often traditional, and although shame plays a conventional motivating role for him, the shame he invokes is something new. The main point is that it is explicitly internalized: when Socrates shames his companions he exposes them to themselves alone in relation to values they recognize. No one else's opinion matters.[17] Again and again Socrates points out that he is performing for an audience of one, and that the court to which he speaks has only one witness and one judge, and that this judge-witness – his companion – must speak only his own mind and be consistent only with his own views. Socratic shame is a rational emotion because it comes from the recognition that one's life or beliefs harbor an inconsistency.

On the second point, Plato's dialogues support the criticism to a certain extent. By shaming people with his questions, Socrates seems to teach some of them only to stay away from his sort of questioning altogether. Even those who face it can miss the point and fail to improve.[18] Too often a dialogue ends with Socrates' partner slinking away in sullen apathy, or worse, in murderous anger against Socrates. Socrates' answer to this criticism is that his companions ought to rejoice in refutation, because the force of shame might make them better people (*Gorgias* 458a). Whether it succeeds or not must be up to them; Socrates will not be a teacher to them.

The critics might respond that for all his disclaimers Socrates acts like a teacher. Whether he is the hard questioner or gentle admonisher, Socrates seems to his companions to be in control of their conversations, so much so that they are often left with no sense of ownership in the conclusions to which he leads them. 'Draw your own conclusion," Protagoras will tell Socrates near the end of the dialogue that bears his name, plainly alienated from the entire proceeding (360d). Socrates is, indeed, so thoroughly in control of his method that his disclaimer of teaching is hard to credit.

2 TEACHERLESS EDUCATION

In what sense is Socratic education teacherless? On the positive side, Socrates believes that human beings generally have sufficient resources to take responsibility for learning. On the negative side, Socrates is convinced that he does not know enough to be a teacher as he understands what that is.

Resources of the learner

Socrates evidently believes that his companions already know a large part of what they appear to learn from his company. This learning includes both method: how to think clearly and consistently, and substance: the content of a companion's bedrock beliefs about good and evil.

On method, Socrates must be right in an important sense. No one can teach a student to think, because no one can teach anything to a student who does not already have basic thinking skills. Teachers remind their students to think clearly; they coax them and challenge them to think; they criticize them for thinking badly; but none of this will help a student who cannot recognize a contradiction or has no sense of what is relevant to what. Philosophers of today sometimes justify their subject in the general curriculum by claiming (among other things) that it teaches students to think – or at least to think better. The arrogance of this claim does not go unnoticed among their students, who have done a great deal of thinking before they come under their care. And if the students had not, if they did not already know how to think, and to think well, what hope could their teachers have of overcoming this deficiency with teaching? Sophisticated learning depends on resources already in the command of the student: resources including basic concepts and the abilities to draw inferences and reject contradictions when these become evident. But students come equipped for more than this sort of reasoning. They already know how to tell whether an image is appropriate or far-fetched (for example), and they are experts at picking out and labeling for oblivion all of the many things they find irrelevant to their concerns. This thinking ability is theirs from childhood, and has grown as they grew, so that they are no strangers to validity or relevance, even if they are unable to explain the terms.

Content is more difficult. Socrates' method presupposes that each of his companions has a set of true beliefs about such matters as good and evil, and that they cannot depart from those beliefs without coming into conflict with themselves.[19] The method also presupposes that his companions have a basic grasp of the concepts he asks them to define – piety, courage, or justice – sufficient to allow them to see the deficiencies of their answers. Socrates does not examine his own method critically in the contexts in which he uses it, and so he does not explain to his companions how it is that they know what he says they know. In other contexts, mainly in dialogues later than those in which Socrates engages in education, Socrates states a theory of recollection: all human beings are born with a kind of knowledge that is largely forgotten at birth, and which can be recovered through questioning. The role of a Socrates, on this theory, is to jog people into recalling knowledge which is already theirs. We moderns would say that this is a kind of teaching, but Socrates' disclaimer of teaching does not cover this.

Ideal teachers

Socrates knows what teachers are like in Athens, and he has a fairly clear idea of what a teacher would be like in ideal circumstances. His standards for teaching are high, based on his high standards for knowledge. He has as good a reason for thinking he is not a teacher as he does for thinking he does not have the knowledge he seeks.

Plato presents us with two models of education, one for ordinary Athens, where people must fend for themselves in the absence of real teachers, and the other for the various ideal cities he considers, where the knowledge of the rulers will make philosophy-based teaching both possible and valuable to the citizens.

The ideal cities educate all their citizens on plans designed by philosophers. Their aim is to develop in each child the character appropriate to that person's role in the web of society (*Statesman* 308e). Character, according to the *Laws*, is cultivated by training children to find pleasure and pain in what they ought, and is maintained in adults through the arts (653b–c). The system of education and the arts which Plato designs in the *Laws* to achieve this end is a rigid curriculum running from pre-natal care to the grave, including every element of culture, from games to music, articulated in different ways for the various ages of the citizenry (Books 7–8). Every element in the culture will be part of the educational system, and all of this will be in the control of experts who know what human virtue is and how best to teach it to different sorts of people. This knowledge they will have achieved through the successful practice of philosophy.

The knowledge Socrates seeks, in the contexts in which he denies he is a teacher, is just what ideal philosophers will have: knowledge of human virtue and how best to teach it. His refusal to teach, he says, is due to his recognition of ignorance. Philosophy as Socrates practices it in Athens is the loving search for knowledge he does not possess, whereas in ideal circumstances philosophy would actually yield this knowledge. In the ideal cities, philosophy makes its students into teachers and the rulers of teachers; in Plato's Athens, philosophy makes Socrates abstain from teaching. There, philosophy is for everyone; but in the ideal cities it is for a select few. The *Republic* reserves philosophy as the highest discipline for selected mature students, aged 30–5, of good mind and character, who will not lose their moral convictions when exposed to critical argumentation, and who will grow into philosopher-kings, able to secure through knowledge the virtuous order of the city (538d–539d). In ordinary Athens, however, we shall see that philosophy must play a different role, safeguarding not the state but at most the individual philosopher.

The *Republic* presumes an extraordinary context which allows philosophers to offer moral teaching with some guarantee of reliability. Outside the ideal cities, apparently, there is no reliable teaching of virtue. Socrates is the best of Athenians in Plato's Athens, but his career, as recounted in the *Apology* and illustrated elsewhere, proves that even he is unable to teach virtue successfully in the conditions of Athenian life. His companions do not all turn out well, and some turn out very badly. The texts leave open the question of how much this is due to Socrates' ignorance, how much to the temptations and corruptions of life in Athens, and how much to the individual failures of his companions. In any case, because Socrates places responsibility on the learner, he can give no guarantee of success. That is part of what Socrates means when he denies that he is a teacher.

Occupational, professional and craft training

Socrates would admit, however, that teaching of a sort goes on in Athens. When Socrates denies he is a teacher he is (among other things) distinguishing Socratic education from practical training, from the liberal education promised by sophists, and from the wisdom tradition of sages. That which can be taught in ancient Greece beyond the elementary level generally falls in the category of *technē*: professional or craft knowledge.[20] This concept underlies all talk of education in Plato, because before the advent of sophists most teaching of adults in Greece was modelled on the transmission of professional, practical or craft knowledge. Exactly how one ancient shoemaker trained another we will never know, but it is easy to imagine that master shoemakers simply showed their apprentices how to make shoes, letting them practice the craft, and correcting them as necessary. In ordinary cases such teachers need not be wise or articulate; they need only know how to do well what they teach others to do.

According to Socrates, however, a teacher of a craft or profession will be able to identify his own teachers, bring forward his own successful pupils, or at least succeed in answering questions about the goal of his profession (*Laches* 189d). Those who cannot satisfy at least one of these conditions, but are nevertheless able to do good work, are declared by Socrates to have had divine assistance. By this he means, for example, that there is no human explanation for how a performer can interpret Homer, or how a statesman can govern Athens at a professional level of competence, when the one cannot answer Socrates (*Ion*, *passim*), and the other cannot teach what he knows to his sons (*Meno* 99cd with 94b). For his part, Socrates tells us that he is aware of having no knowledge of his own; and apparently he fails to satisfy any of his three conditions: He has not found the teacher he seeks, he cannot point to successful pupils, and he cannot answer his own questions.

Socrates has good reason for putting special emphasis on the third condition. Each *technē* has a defining goal, and Socrates expects craftsmen and professionals to know what their goals are and to be able to explain them. The goal of medicine is health, for example, and a professional healer should be able to show verbally that he knows what that is. This is not only because such practitioners are called *sophoi* in Greek (like sages), or because some of them are masters of crafts that make use of words (such as orators or politicians). The crafts, occupations and professions are only as good as the uses to which they are put; a good professional must therefore aim at a good result, and to do that must either know what is good or be directed by someone else who does. That is why Socrates treats such professionals as if they should have the qualities he expects of a sage: a true professional, he seems to hold, should know what is good and be able to answer questions about it consistently.[21]

Liberal education and the sophists

The idea of a liberal education distinct from mere literacy on the one hand, and professional training on the other, was promulgated in the late fifth century BCE by sophists and other teachers for whom Plato's historical fictions are our main source. The best known of the sophists, Protagoras, rightly insisted that the education he offered was distinct from training in a *technē*. Protagorean education was supposed to take students who had no need to learn a trade and make them better citizens and better managers of their homes (*Protagoras* 312b–318a).

We can derive a sketch of Protagorean education from a number of sources. Protagoras trained students to think critically by examining apparent contradictions in literature; he taught the correctness of words and exercised students' verbal powers by teaching them to correct great poets, attuning the poets' language to their purposes; and he taught some elements of persuasive speaking. Most importantly, he also taught the sort of good judgment that is displayed in deliberative oratory, in speeches that look to the effects of various courses of action and attempt to lead an audience down the path that will be best for them.

The form of reasoning on which good judgment depends is known by current logicians as defeasible; in the ancient world it was called *eikos* in Greek, or *probabile* in Latin, words best translated not as "probability" but "reasonable expectation." Such reasoning is all we have to go on for shaping our thought either about the indeterminate future or about past events for which we have no witnesses. Its conclusions are uncertain and its method unreliable; training in this falls far short, therefore, of what Socrates would accept as professional knowledge. Good judgment is essential, however, to decisions in the world of our experience, to public assemblies, to business, and to the battlefield.[22] The best judgment considers the widest array of options and also the widest range of circumstances that might defeat a reasonable expectation; the worst judgment cleaves to one point of view, listens to no other voices but those that agree with it, and usually ends in disaster.[23] Good judgment is a democratic idea, and Protagoras was probably a democratic thinker who supported the idea of a government in which many voices were heard.

With part of this, Socrates plainly agrees; Socrates also seeks by education to help people think more clearly and thereby to become better citizens. But Socrates will not entirely dispense, as Protagoras does, with the ideal of professional training. This is because Socrates sets a high value on reliability in moral and political matters, whereas Protagorean education depends on forms of reasoning that can only be unreliable. *Technē* continues to furnish Socrates with his standard for evaluating teachers. He will allow that professional trainers are teachers of a sort, but by this standard, Protagoras and Socrates both fall short of being teachers. What distinguishes Socrates from Protagoras is that Socrates knows of himself that he is not a teacher.

Wisdom of sages and poets

A true teacher, in Socrates' expectation, should have both the authority of a practitioner and the articulate wisdom of a sage. Socrates capitalizes on an ambiguity in the Greek concept of *sophia*, which can mean either the wisdom of a sage (such as Solon) or the cleverness of a master at a craft or a profession (*technē*). By contrast with our Philosopher, a sage is one who gives answers to questions, but these answers may be enigmatic or at least challenging to the questioner. A sage may choose not to answer at all, to be a silent teacher.[24]

Sages are familiar models in both South Asian and East Asian traditions, and they are found among the Greeks as well. Solon is the best known Greek sage, and his conversation with Croesus the best known anecdote about this sort of wisdom (Herodotus 1.30ff. with 86ff.). Croesus is slow to see the truth of what he has been told, like most arrogant kings of Greek mythology. Solon's answer has been a surprise to him, and as such it should have been a provocation to further, deeper thought – an activity for which Croesus lacks patience.

Ancient Greek tradition generally accords to poets the honor of sages, and poetry can be as hard to understand as the utterances of sages. It can be ambiguous or appear inconsistent with itself, and in such cases there is no one a learner can ask to find out the poet's true meaning. Living poets cannot answer Socrates to his satisfaction, and dead ones leave us a legacy of unresolved debate.[25]

The teachings of sages and poets are difficult to understand, and therefore put a heavy burden of interpretation on the learner. We saw that Socrates, in asking questions, makes his Companions take responsibility for learning; we now see that sages can have a similar aim in giving answers that are difficult and frequently ambiguous, so that students must think for themselves to see what the answers might mean. And the silence of a wordless teacher is the plainest way to make students see there is no substitute for their own thought. Sages and poets, by speaking or writing as they do, generally leave learners free to go wrong by misinterpreting what they say; Socrates, with his relentless questions, will catch his companions if they go wrong and at least remind them to think more clearly about the matter.

Sages use ambiguity to liberate their pupils' minds, while Socrates tends to press his companions to avoid ambiguities at all costs. Here the contrast between Plato and his Socrates is especially striking. Plato is the most sage-like of western philosophers, in that he generally sets his readers free to pursue the truth in the matters he discusses, exploring the multiple ambiguities that lurk in the ironical stance of Socrates himself. To readers, the dialogues are a splendid opportunity for independent thinking, as they would be to those who look on as Socrates questions someone. But the experience of a direct conversation with Socrates is more limiting.

In any event, Socrates will not allow his companions to appeal to the authority of poets or sages, and he is reluctant even to discuss their utterances: "We should set aside the poets, you and I," he says to Protagoras after an inconclusive discussion of a poem, "and have a dialogue all by ourselves, just with each other, testing the truth and ourselves" (*Protagoras* 348a).

PHILOSOPHY

To learn from Socrates you must be guided, as he is, by the desire for knowledge and you must set the highest value, as he does, on learning. To live under the influence of this desire is to be a philosopher as Plato understands the term: a lover of wisdom. Socrates has been the model teacher in European thought since his own time, and he has been the model philosopher for the same reason. He is dangerous, exciting, a fountain of dissatisfaction, spreading a plague of yearning to know what is evidently beyond human powers to know.

His peculiar sort of teaching depends on turning his mind to philosophy in opposition to traditional forms of teaching and culture. In representing the life of Socrates in his dialogues, Plato develops and defines a concept of philosophy as a distinct practice, with its own aim, its own standards, and its own methods. If individuals turn to philosophy, their lives are changed; they set wisdom and virtue as their goals in place of power, wealth, or reputation; and their peers may fear that they have become useless. If a city-state were to be taken over by philosophy (as is imagined in the *Republic*) it too would be changed, as its culture and economy were given new aims by the philosopher-kings. The critical character of Socrates' philosophy seems to threaten traditional religion, morality, and perhaps also the foundations of democracy. We may see the quarrel between Socrates and his accusers, like the contest between Socrates and the sophists, as at bottom a disagreement about the value of Socratic education.

When successful, Socratic education is a kind of seduction into a way of thinking characterized by discontent with easy answers – discontent with any answer that falls short of knowledge. Socratic education aims to make people want to hold themselves to the painfully high standards to which Socrates holds himself, standards you can tolerate only if you value knowledge above success. A philosopher is someone who is entirely given to the love of knowledge understood in a certain way.[26] From the *Apology* to the *Phaedrus* and beyond, Socrates moves through Plato's pages defining his life in opposition to the practices of his contemporaries and to the traditions of ancient Greece – he stays out of politics, eschews discussions of poetry, attacks teachers of rhetoric, gives up speculation about cosmology, keeps clear of attempts at the rational understanding of religion, and reverses the usual polarity of love.

Philosophy, however, is not just another subject for education; it is not competing in the syllabus of Athens against more traditional genres for the time of its students. Philosophy threatens to transform the lives of its devotees altogether, and, as it does so, to transform the things people do. Love in the life of a philosopher is turned from personal erotic desire into a shared passion for knowledge. Rhetoric in Socrates' crucible is no longer the knack of pleasing a crowd with plausibilities; in the *Phaedrus* it will become the art of writing with knowledge in one person's soul (276a), a development of Socrates' method of questioning. Politics as Socrates practices it takes place not in the Council or Assembly, but wherever two people can meet to ask how best to live their lives. Even poetry may come to meet the standards of philosophy, though we are never told just how this could be (*Republic* 607). These transformations raise a serious question for Socratic education: what is the value of thinking like a philosopher in ordinary, untransformed Athens? Plato takes this question very seriously, chews on it in many of the dialogues, and responds to it, as we have seen, by devising ideal states where philosophy will be useful.

Athens, however, is not a safe place for philosophers. Socrates himself is the supreme product of Socratic education; but Socrates does not know enough at the end of his life to win his case in a people's court against the twin charges of fostering religious innovation and corrupting the youth. Plato drives home the point repeatedly: philosophy is no training for success in Athens. That may be why Socrates fails with many of his companions who, lacking Socrates' love for knowledge, are drawn more to success.

Socrates' life was devoted to unceasing education, for himself and for those about him, and it has been both a gift and a challenge to the concept of liberal education that was emerging then under the name of *paideia* – a gift because of Socrates' power to draw people into philosophy, and a challenge because of Socrates' refusal to turn philosophy to uses his society considered practical. Philosophy, as Socrates pursues it in Athens, seems to lead nowhere but to more philosophy. At most it serves to secure the conditions in which philosophy itself can best be practiced, either in an ideal city or in the mind of a philosopher. There, as in an ideal city, philosophy depends on watchfulness, on guarding against the passions, the desires, and even the perceptions that threaten the purity of the philosopher's mind in its quest for knowledge. But philosophy is more than mere watchfulness. In Socrates' life philosophy is primarily the cultivation of his passion for knowing the truth.

NOTES

1 Plato's portrayal of Socrates is not consistent on all points throughout his work. This essay treats Socrates as he is shown in the dialogues considered early, that is, in the *Apology* and other works that are consistent with it. In addition, the essay draws on passages from other dialogues that either reflect on, or further illustrate, Socratic education as we find it in the early dialogues. On the scholarly issues, which are hotly contested among scholars, see the works cited in the bibliographical note.

2 Alcibiades was accused of several crimes against religion and later aided the Spartans against Athens; Critias and Charmides were among the thirty tyrants.

3 With Cleinias in the *Euthydemus*, and with the boys in the *Lysis*.

4 Socrates' disclaimer of knowledge must be reconciled with many passages in which he says that he knows something or other. Evidently there is a kind of knowledge he thinks he does not have, and a kind that he does think he has. On the scholarly issues, see the works cited in the bibliographical note by Vlastos and Woodruff.

5 Several Socratic positions are undermined in the *Charmides*, and famously Socratic definitions of courage and beauty are refuted in the *Laches* and *Hippias Major* respectively. The interpretations of these dialogues are controversial; Vlastos, for example, holds that the dialogues of self-examination illustrate a different method from the one Socrates uses in the *Euthyphro*. See the works cited in the bibliographical note.

6 In what follows I give a simplified paraphrase of the argument, passing quickly over a number of difficulties in interpretation.

7 Orestes appeared to be pious in avenging his father, impious in doing violence to his mother.

8 He believes, for example, that no matter who the wrongdoer is, piety demands that he be prosecuted – an instance of rule (a) (5e).

9 He must hold that what he does cannot be impious if it passes his test for piety, an instance of rule (b) (4e, 8b).

10 Some scholars believe the dialogue also teaches positive views about piety, for example that it is service to the gods of the sort Socrates carries out in his project of educating his companions. See works cited in the bibliographical note, especially the article by McPherran.

11 Socrates' method of questioning is referred to by some scholars as *elenchus*, a Greek word meaning "test," "refutation," or "shaming." On the interpretation of the method, see especially the works of Vlastos cited in the bibliographical note, along with the summary discussion in Brickhouse and Smith.

12 Diotima, for example, is supposed to be responsible for Socrates' speech in the *Symposium*; and the speeches in the *Phaedrus* are attributed to a number of factors: Lysias' influence, Phaedrus' desires, inspiration from deities. Even the lengthy account of Simonides' poem in the *Protagoras* leaves Socrates exempt from further questioning. Simonides is the one who should be held to answer for his poem, but he is not present, and the discussion must be dropped, leaving Socrates with the last word. In the *Cratylus* Socrates attributes his account of language to nameless givers of words. In all these cases the responsible party is absent.

13 *Gorgias* 486, *Republic* 487d.

14 *Gorgias* 475e, 481. On this issue there is a poignant epilogue in Gregory Vlastos' *Socratic Studies*: "Socrates and Vietnam."

15 The charge is made explicitly by Polus and Callicles (*Gorgias* 461b, 482c–e), but could be made in other cases as well. Shame is related to the root-meaning of the Greek word *elenchos*, which is used for Socrates' method.

16 Homer had seen the pitfall in the *Iliad*: Hector's overactive sense of shame kept him outside the gates of Troy where he could do nothing but offer himself as a sacrifice to appease the anger of Achilles. Thucydides' new-fangled speakers avoid the language of shame, although it is still in use by conservatives such as Pericles and the Spartans.

17 Polus, for example, capitulates not, as Callicles has it (*Gorgias* 483), to the force of popular opinion, but to the surprising discovery that he himself – Polus – is deeply committed to certain views in spite of their being conventional.

18 Alcibiades claims to have been shamed repeatedly by Socrates (*Symposium* 216), but we know he has not profited at all from the experience. Shamelessly, he attempts to draw Socrates into a sexual liaison; and shamelessly, thereafter, he pursues a career unmarked by any clear moral commitment, giving many Athenians the fear that he might grow into a tyrant.

19 This way of understanding Socrates is due to a famous essay by Vlastos. The latest version is in *Socratic Studies*, from which see especially p. 25.

20 Socrates' use of the term *technē* covers crafts and professions ranging from statecraft to shoe-making and presupposes a number of striking parallels among them.

21 It is not clear how widely Socrates means to apply his requirement that a professional be guided by knowledge of the good: orators must meet the standard, but should shoemakers? Crafts-people who do not know the good may have to depend on experts at statecraft, and if so their own claims to knowledge must be modest. On the difficulty, see *Gorgias* 511–13, *Euthydemus* 290d, 291c, and my article in Benson 1992.

22 Such reasoning also had a use in forensic oratory, in defense of people accused of crimes; and it is on this usage that Plato brings his criticism in the *Phaedrus* (272–3).

23 Athenian tragedy illustrates cases of such bad judgment in kings such as Pentheus in Euripides' *Bacchae* or Creon in Sophocles' *Antigone*.

24 The Sung Dynasty poet Su Tung-p'o writes of the Buddhist teacher Vimalakirti, who "bowed his head wordless, though at heart of course he knew," when asked about the Dharma, and comments that his clay image is the same as the wordless teacher, "nothing added, nothing lost" (trans. by Burton Watson).

25 *Apology* 22bc and *Protagoras* 347e.

26 *Gorgias* 482, *Republic* 474–80.

BIBLIOGRAPHICAL NOTE

Dialogues that illustrate Socratic education or self-education include the *Charmides*, *Crito*, *Euthydemus*, *Euthyphro*, *Gorgias*, *Hippias Major*, *Ion*, *Laches*, *Lysis*, *Protagoras* and probably Book 1 of the *Republic*. Reflections on Socratic education are to be found in Alcibiades' speech in the *Symposium*; a somewhat similar method is illustrated by Socrates with a slave in the *Meno*; and there is an important discussion of education as midwifery in the *Theaetetus*.

On the cultural context of education in ancient Greece, Werner Jaeger's *Paideia* remains a masterpiece (2nd edn, Oxford, Blackwell, 1945, trans. Gilbert Highet). Sources for our knowledge of education by the sophists are translated by Michael Gagarin and Paul Woodruff in *Early Greek Political Theory* (Cambridge, Cambridge University Press, 1995).

On the Platonic Socrates, the greatest modern scholar has been Gregory Vlastos. Most of his relevant work is to be found in *Socrates: Ironist and Moral Philosopher* (Ithaca, NY, Cornell University Press, 1991) or *Socratic Studies*, ed. Myles Burnyeat (Cambridge, Cambridge University Press, 1994). For a fine corrective see now Charles H. Kahn, *Plato and the Socratic Dialogue: the Philosophical Use of a Literary Form* (Cambridge, Cambridge University Press, 1996). The best comprehensive book is *Plato's Socrates* by Thomas C. Brickhouse and Nicholas D. Smith (Oxford, Oxford University Press, 1994). A number of useful essays are collected in Hugh H. Benson (ed.) *Essays on the Philosophy of Socrates* (Oxford, Oxford University Press, 1992); the articles by Burnyeat, McPherran,

Nehamas, Vlastos, and Woodruff bear especially on Socratic education. For a general treatment see Henry Teloh, *Socratic Education in Plato's Early Dialogues* (Notre Dame, Ind., Notre Dame University Press, 1986). Richard Kraut's *Socrates and the State* has a fine chapter on teaching (Princeton, NJ, Princeton University Press, 1984) as does C. D. C. Reeve's *Socrates in the Apology* (Indianapolis, Ind., Hackett, 1989). On Plato, consult Samuel Scolnicov's *Plato's Metaphysics of Education* (London, Routledge, 1988).

3

PLATO'S COUNSEL ON EDUCATION

Zhang LoShan

Plato's dialogues can be read as a carefully staged exhibition and investigation of *paideia*, education in the broadest sense, including all that affects the formation of character and mind.[1] The twentieth-century textbook Plato – the Plato of the myth of the cave and the divided line, the ascent to the Good through Forms and Ideas – is but one of his elusive multiple authorial personae, each taking a different perspective on his investigations. As its focused problems differ, each Platonic dialogue exhibits a somewhat different model for learning; each adds a distinctive dimension to Plato's fully considered counsel for education. Setting aside the important difficult questions about the chronological sequence in which the dialogues were written and revised, we can trace the argumentative rationale of Plato's fully considered views on *paideia*, on who should be educated by whom for what, on the stages and presuppositions of different kinds of learning.[2] Those views are inextricably connected with his views about the structure of the soul, about the virtues and the *politeia* that can sustain a good life; and about cosmology and metaphysics.

PLATO'S PLOT

The early Socratic dialogues raise formidable problems about how we learn and about what constrains our ability to learn. Among other things, they exhibit the beginning – and the limitations – of inquiry, of learning and not-teaching. Aside from the kind of mimetic learning that forms the larger part of a person's habits of speech and action, most learning begins with received opinions and practice: a storehouse of a culturally solidified way of life, with commonplace distinctions and classifications, with an evaluatively charged vocabulary. By a process of encompassing critical reflection, inquiry attempts to move to a reasoned closure, one that ideally corrects as well as explains belief and practice.[3] But the early maieutic or elenchic dialogues, each apparently set to answer a specific definitional question ("what is [courage, piety]?") are manifestly incomplete. Taken in isolation, they do not issue in adequate definitions, both because the virtues are interdependent, and because all well-reasoned definitions are interdependent. As the epistemological triad of the *Theaetetus*, *Sophist*, and *Statesman* show, they ramify to form a complex structured system.

The middle transitional dialogues distinguish Socrates' quest for knowledge from the performances of the sophists and the "teachings" of the poets. They lead directly to the

Republic, an investigation of the educative role that the *nomoi* of a polis – its ethos and institutions – play in forming the pre-reflective opinions and habits upon which all inquiry rests. Because opinion is embedded and expressed in social practices and political institutions, the task of the wise educator has political ramifications. Since a sound *politeia* is the central condition for a sound education, Plato turns to the education of philosophic rulers who structure the life of the polis. Platonic rulers are to be guided by a concern for what is true as well as by what seems good and desirable: their education raises vexed practical and philosophic questions about the relation between civic and philosophic education. In what sense, if at all, does a sound civic life depend on philosophic inquiry? By whom is the inquiry to be conducted? To what effect? The late dialogues articulate the ontology that supports the possibility of well-formed knowledge and action-from-knowledge. Reasonably, then, the late dialogues exhibit and elaborate another technique of inquiry: the discovery/construction of a taxonomic schema that locates the genus and differentia of basic classifications within a structured schematic whole. Rather than addressing "What is a sophist/pleasure/statesman?" questions seriatim, apparently independently of one another, the later dialogues exemplify a systematically structured investigation into such questions.[4] All the maieutic practices and methods of analysis that are dramatically portrayed in the various phases of the Platonic corpus remain in place within Plato's fully considered counsel on *paideia*.

PLATO'S SOCRATES

Plato designed the early dialogues to show Socrates innocent of the charge of impiety and of corrupting the young. The manifest topics of those dialogues – the virtues that are central to Athenian civic life – circle about the issues that would best reveal whether Socrates deflected his companions from the values and gods of Athens. The drama of the dialogues – Socrates' conduct in discussing these virtues – shows that he did not overtly introduce new, unorthodox views, indeed that he didn't introduce views at all. Socrates' procedure in shared inquiry – and there is no other kind – is informal. Because it is closely fitted to the experience, temperament and opinions of his companions, it cannot be neatly formulated as a set of rules.[5] (Consider how the temperaments of Thrasymachus and Theaetetus, Laches and Nicias, Crito and Euthyphro, Protagoras and Glaucon affect the unfolding of their discussions with Socrates.[6])

While the manifest focus of the dialogues is ethical, their latent focus is logical and methodological: they are dramatic exhibitions, enactments of Socrates' attempts to develop – to formulate and analyze – the methods and techniques of sound reasoning. In a way, they present a dramatic performance of the origins of logic. Whether the content and method of these early dialogues reveal a Socrates whose tentative, provisional opinions, whose relentless cross-questioning and ironic unmasking presented a genuine threat to Athens' conception of itself is a dark question. A passionate friend of shared inquiry, ready to talk about anything and everything with all-comers may indeed have been an enemy to Athens' self-conception and self-presentation.[7]

But does the Plato of the *Republic* and the early maieutic dialogues think that (as Aristotle was later to put it) all men by nature desire to know, that they can tolerate an open-ended examination of received pieties? Plato seems of two minds about the matter. On the one hand, the Socrates of the early dialogues is ready for unbridled inquiry with any and all comers. He believes that every man strives for the good; and in truth, knowledge is among those goods. The ascent up the divided line – the movement from phantasia to opinion, from opinion to systematic reasoning and finally to insight – is internally impelled by erotically charged reflection. That movement represents inquiry as a natural unforced progression towards an encompassing teleologically-ordered explanatory system that reconciles the apparent contradictions of unexamined opinion. On the other hand, most of the participants in the early dialogues are like the prisoners in the Cave; they resist seeing things as they are. Their heads must be forcibly turned, they must be dragged towards the light of truth. At best – and this is an improvement – they become confused and dimly see that they did not know what they thought they knew. By the end of the *Republic*, fundamental philosophic inquiry is reserved for a few well-tested, well-educated few.

Plato seems equally evasive about the qualifications for wise rule. On the one hand, wise rulers must have unfettered minds, capable of seeing and internalizing the multiple perspectives that must be harmonized in the polity. On the other hand, they should not be weathervanes shifting with the prevailing winds of public opinion: they must be firmly and properly directed, prepared to form rather than to express opinion. They must be ideologically correct. A theory of mind stands behind these apparent dilemmas. Knowledge does not consist of isolated items of information or insight. Mind and character – beliefs and desires – are thoroughly fused; their proper developments are inseparable. In current western terminology, an opinion or belief is neither a psychological event nor a statement (to be put) in propositional form, to be evaluated as true or false, validly or invalidly inferred. Its meaning and evaluation rests in a person's – indeed in a society's – systematically ordered aims and commitments. As *Republic* 2 would have it, the significance and propriety of judgments about reliefs on the Parthenon (or a decision to build the Long Walls) are measured by their service to civic thriving. In a Chinese context, this would mean that the significance and correctness of a Unit Leader's judgment about production quotas is in part the function of the ideological origins of his judgment and its consequences in political action. In this mode, Socrates and Plato can be read as psychological/linguistic functionalists – with an added ideological dimension. Yet Plato nevertheless presents Socrates as holding that the mind's best insights carry it beyond its civic functions, indeed beyond the physical world, beyond its own embodiment. In this mode, Plato represents Socrates as a proto-neo-Platonist. Whether or not he deliberately intended to do so, Plato shows the Socrates of the early dialogues to be less in command of the movement of the elenchus – the critical investigation of the larger, systematic consistency of a belief – than recent commentators suggest. It is, of course, Plato rather than Socrates who is in command of the development of the dialogue, in command of the representation of Socrates at work.

After the introductory dramatic performances that exhibit some of the participants' pre-reflective assumptions and practices, Socrates engages his companions in a critical examination of the commonplaces they offer as definitions of central civic virtues: piety, courage, friendship. The participants typically begin with a set of core examples. Since these are merely examples, they manifestly do not qualify as definitions. But they remain as (corrigible and reinterpretable) test cases for further proposals. Other definitions are offered: some are, in the light of the rest of the interlocutor's opinions, shown to be too broad or too narrow. The evaluative implications of others do not accord with the views of the (presumptively) wise or with deeply entrenched practices of praise and blame. The critical examination of these opinions exhibits, and attempts to articulate, relatively formal criteria for sound definitions. So, for instance: a definition of justice, courage or friendship should characterize all, and only those, instances that exemplify it. The definition should not be so narrow as to exclude what seems a clear example, nor should it be so broad as to include instances that seem (by common opinion) to lie outside its scope. And above all, it should retain the evaluative connotations of the concept. For instance: courage and justice are, as virtues, *kalos k'agathos*, shiningly admirable and good. A proposed characterization that permits harmful or undesirable actions to qualify as genuinely courageous or just must therefore on that account be defective. The early dialogues do not issue in definitions; but the reader (though rarely the participants) may have learned – from examples – something about how to test candidates for an adequate definition.

The Socratic model of learning and inquiry rests on a set of guiding presuppositions:

1 Whether he realizes it or not, every reasonable person intends his beliefs and desires to form a consistent system. Because we all naturally and unselfconsciously strive for our good, truth is the obscure object of every belief, and what seems good – conducive to a well-lived, admirable life – is the obscure object of every desire.
2 An individual's entrenched habits of thought and action are at least as revealing expressions of his opinions and desires as what he sincerely reports himself to believe.
3 Opinions and desires are not idiosyncratic: even when they are mistaken or express constitutional and temperamental quirks, they reveal and express the practices and assumptions of a culture and society.
4 Although it is often difficult to diagnose the sources of intellectual disagreement, it is always a sign of confusion, bias or error. In principle, the fundamental beliefs of reasonable people should coincide.

As Plato represented them, Socrates' discussions exposed inconsistencies and ambiguities within his companions' budget of beliefs and desires. Since the participants in the discussions express the range of socially accepted commonplaces, those discussions also reveal implicit tensions within their culture. The success of such an inquiry depends on participants sincerely saying what they think, as concisely and clearly as they can; they are to avoid long-winded, evasive speeches; they must answer difficult questions honestly and be willing to follow the argument where it leads. (But an astute reader should see that it is the puppeteer Plato, working through Socrates, who leads the argument.) The inquiry is intended to issue in increasingly general, more encompassing, systematically unified and justified opinions. Socrates knows how to bring inconsistencies to light, often to the discomfiture of his partners in discussion. But while he can hint at the direction of a resolution, he cannot confidently proclaim it, without undertaking a similar systematic investigation of the

35

standing of each proposed solution, seriatim. As he rightly insists, he is too ignorant to teach anyone anything. There is no short-cut solution to the problems of the apparent circularity of Socratic inquiry: in a sense every inquirer knows, and yet does not know, the object of his inquiry. If he doesn't know what he's trying to discover, he won't be able to evaluate proposed answers; if he does know, it seems he does not need to inquire.[8] For all that, Plato's Socrates is not a philosophic skeptic: he is not so foolish as to announce a self-refuting general thesis. He means what he says: if he is too ignorant to teach anyone anything, he is certainly not about to expound a general doctrine, and certainly not one as blatantly self-defeating as dogmatic skepticism. Quite on the contrary, he resolutely commits himself to the continuity of inquiry. Having, in the *Meno* (84ff.), come perilously close to skepticism in formulating the paradox of inquiry, he brings the discussion to a proposed "solution": if the soul were immortal, then it might – even in its present embodied finite condition – be able to recover or recollect what it once knew. It would then in one sense know, and in another not know, what it seeks. But Socrates is careful not to offer this solution as something he himself knows or can demonstrate. There is no more eloquent credo for the continuity of inquiry than Socrates' response to his dilemma: "I am not altogether confident of all of this [i.e. that the soul can be ignorant of what it seeks, yet be critically able to recognize it]. But that we shall be better and braver and less helpless if we think we ought to inquire into what we don't know than if we give way to the idle notion that there is no knowledge, and no point in trying to discover what we do not yet know – for this, I am ready to fight as best I can in word and deed" (*Meno* 86BC). His resolve is his resolution to the (alleged) paradox of inquiry. That resolve leads Plato to attempt to articulate a theory of oppositions/contraries (between morality and immortality, ignorance and knowledge, ugly and beautiful, bad and good) that is prefigured in Diotima's lyrical *mythos* of *daimones* as messengers between the divine (or souls of the Golden Age) and an individual mind. The details of Plato's view of contraries is, I believe, one of the preoccupations of the post-*Parmenides* dialogues: the *Sophist* and the *Statesman*.

The consequences of this phase of Plato's account of education indicate inquiry to be an unending task, one that is more akin to Peirce's fallibilism than it is to Descartes's analytic method. Education prepares a person for the patient reflective work of bringing opinions and practices into a consistent, well-reasoned whole. Because the process engages character traits as well as habits of mind – because Plato links the two at their deepest level – the formation of character and of opinion are coordinate.[9] The early dialogues appear to counsel educators to engage every participant individually in the active work of inquiry: to test (what they think) they believe, to extend the scope of those beliefs by elucidating their interconnections, and to adjudicate conflicts between opinions and practice. This is an excruciatingly painful and risky enterprise. Because it involves the entire scope of an individual's habits and practices, because it can set him at odds with his culture and society, it can engender confusion and despair. Socrates' partners in discussion must really want to know the truth about something, or at least to sort out what seems confused or contradictory.[10] Since the Socratic figure challenges and disturbs their unwarranted confidence in unexamined opinion about matters of fundamental importance, he must be seen as trustworthy, having their real interests at heart. The relation between inquiring companions is dominantly erotic, subdominantly eristic. The constructive discovery/ recovery of truth and the destruction/unmasking of empty pieties go hand in hand.

PLATO'S REFLECTIONS ON SOCRATIC INQUIRY

With examples of Socratic inquiry at hand, Plato turns his attention to its philosophical implications and presuppositions. The *Meno*, *Symposium*, *Gorgias*, *Protagoras* respond to the charges that Socrates is a masked and evasive sophist, and a dangerous one at that. These dialogues begin to formulate the general philosophical views that are implicit in Socrates' attempt to discover truths by patient cross-questioning, his giving tradition and inspiration voice – without according them ultimate or automatic authority.

Socrates' discussions might seem to endorse Protagoras' view that man is the measure of all things. Indeed he might seem to be a Protagorean, but one who, unlike Protagoras himself, runs the further risk of leaving his companions shaken in their beliefs without finding sensible guidelines for practical life, and so worse off – in their own terms – than he found them. Plato must show that Socratic inquiry moves towards, and is guided by what is true, that Socratic irony is not merely a tendentious and destructive mask intended to expose the emptiness or confusion of common opinion. These transitional dialogues differentiate inquiry from sophistry, systematically well-grounded knowledge from traditional platitudes or ad hoc opinion. Sophists and orators attempt to bring their audience (what passes for) power, elegance and success. Socrates questions the measures of success: he distrusts fame, pleasure and political power, unless they are directed towards achieving the Real Good.

EDUCATION IN THE *REPUBLIC*

The beginning of inquiry is culturally specific, but its aim goes beyond the contingencies of time and place. The movement from the particular towards the universal and necessary is, at least for the guardians, rulers and philosophers presented in the *Republic*, a carefully staged affair. The starting-point of that education forms a common culture shared by all members of the polity: "children's pastimes," myths, music, gymnastics, and public art, the statues and sculptures in the city and on the temples. As it is projected in the *Republic*, the program of education is strict and strictly enforced against novelty (423–4). The point of earliest education is "to instill a spirit of order and reverence for law." Needless to say, myths and public art are to present admirable figures of gods and men for imitation. Waywardness and license are not to be represented at all. Even when they are shown to come to a bad end, they capture the imagination; and what captures the imagination, sets the beginnings of imitation. Music must be simple, calm, well-proportioned, designed to promote measure and harmony in the soul (*Republic* 3.398–403). Similarly, gymnastic training should be designed to strengthen a healthful well-balanced body, capable of ascetic endurance (*Republic* 3.409–11). Beyond the education common to all, that of the future ruler-guardians continues to arithmetic, plane and solid geometry, astronomy, harmonic theory (*Republic*

7.521–37). Finally, a few steadfast and trustworthy inquirers, men and women with philosophic ability and temperament begin the formal study of dialectic.

What do each of these studies, taken individually and cumulatively, contribute to individual and civic thriving? Arithmetic goes far beyond the kind of practical calculation used in the crafts, trade and farming (524d–526c). The habits of mind it develops set the stage for rational planning, for seeing beyond the confusions and contradictions of appearances to their true proportion and measure. In coming to understand of "the properties of units and number that can be grasped by pure thought," future guardians acquire the ability to distinguish a true unity from a conglomerate, a well-formed from an unbalanced proportion. Geometry further develops the ability to abstract from the physical properties of objects, to recognize that they exemplify and are explained by their formal properties. It should not be surprising that Plato thinks that both arithmetic and geometry help "to bring the soul to consider pure truth"; but it is surprising that, without any explanation, he also says that the guardians are to study arithmetic and geometry "with a view to war" (525–6).

Like the task of constructing Chinese puzzle boxes, solid geometry adjusts different "figures" to one another to form a well-ordered whole. Of what use are such studies to a ruler *as ruler*? These are the very abilities exercised in constructing a complex unity composed of distinctive parts. The parallels between constructing a well-formed polis and understanding the construction – the architecture – of a well-ordered cosmos should be obvious. Taken together, the synoptic study of mathematics evokes the synoptic vision of the *Timaeus* and the *Republic*: the Demiurge structures the cosmos from various geometrical forms, and rulers structure the complex unity of the polis from the various types of souls that constitute it. Both are guided by the Good, as a unifying principle. The generic rectifying ideas of mathematics – *unity*, *harmony*, *proportion* – are ingredients in morality and politics.

Astronomy moves the study of cosmic harmony to a yet more abstract level. When it is properly studied (mathematically rather than by observation) it carries the mind to the intelligibility and beauty of the motions and relations of abstract "objects": it strengthens the soul's participation in cosmic harmony. The abstract principles of harmony complete and perfect mathematical studies. Beyond legislating the music of childhood and civic festivals, they serve as guidelines for constructing a harmonious city and concordant soul. Of course in a sense children had been studying harmonics – music and music theory – from childhood; and it is an important feature of music that it is *both* sensuous and abstract. But in one sense, children hadn't, strictly speaking, been doing harmonics. Although they had been continuously moving towards such knowledge, awakening it in themselves, they had initially only been absorbing discrete and unconnected bits of partial proto-"knowledge." Similarly: the earliest introduction of primitive arithmetic and solid geometry typically use visual examples. But when properly taught, they dispose the mind to see the structure of interconnected Forms within physical phenomena, and then to contemplate them as pure Form.

Why should mathematics – largely conceived in all its forms – play such a crucial role in the education of rulers and philosophers? Why should its increasingly synoptic structure seem central to the construction of a just polity? Consider a speculative tale, a reconstruction of a Platonic train of thought. Suppose that the discovery of the incommensurability of the side and diagonal of a perfect square was initially perceived to threaten the Pythagorean hope that the cosmos exhibits – instantiates – a measured, rational order. Suppose that Theaetetus and Eudoxus discovered a formula – a *logos* – that provides a rational solution to the threat of irrational incommensurability. Suppose Plato thought that harmonically sensitive mathematics provides a rational solution to the generic threat of cosmological disorder expressed in mathematical incommensurability. Suppose that he thought that coordinating the different "parts" or classes of the polity, each with its distinctive temperament and aims, presents a problem directly analogous to that of (apparent) geometric incommensurability. If the distinctive aims and desires of the various classes – characterological temperaments – are fundamentally incommensurable, the dangers of conflict and irrationality may also seem to threaten the possibility of a stable political order. (More about this later.) Suppose that Plato became convinced that harmonically sensitive mathematics holds the key to knowledge of the Good as the principle (*archē*) of cosmic order, and so implicitly the key to the direct connection between mathematics and justice as "giving each his due." In this frame of mind, Plato might reasonably assign increasingly abstract, synoptic mathematical studies pride of place in the design of an educational program. An educational program organized around a mathematics synoptically focused on the study of harmonically sensitive proportional formulae might help assuage Plato's fears of political irrationality: it might offer the hope of rationalizing apparent incommensurabilities. Far from recommending mathematical education simply on the grounds that it is useful in implementing public policies (building bridges, constructing effective warships), Plato is making the more radical claim that it is at the core of deciding *whether* building bridges or warships is a Good Thing.

Of course none of these studies, ranging from "children's pastimes," myths and music to the highest and noblest reaches of astronomy, are school "subjects," information to be absorbed or rules to be applied; nor are they cordoned off from one another as separate "fields." As measures to be instantiated in the ordinary practices of the city, they are designed to form habits of thought-and-action, active dispositions and skills to be acquired as second nature. And they are to be integrated with one another (531c–d). These studies combine theory and practice; they are simultaneously abstract and applied; they are intended to form the character and habits of a rational soul. They are selected and structured to enable rulers to instantiate and construct a well-formed *polis* as a harmonious whole composed of properly proportioned interdependent parts, guided by the Good as a Unity-that-harmonizes-distinct-parts.

But there are some ideas (those of mathematics and of justice) and some abilities (those involved in recognizing inconsistencies) that cannot, without circularity, be derived from elenchic reflection. The education of wise rulers must therefore move towards a vision of the Good, to the ideas and ideals that govern any well-proportioned order. Men and women who have absorbed the mathematical-logical structure of cosmic harmony, and who have the passion and the aptitude for philosophic devotion, are introduced to dialectic (*Republic* 7.531–40).

But unless we take the whole of the *Republic* to exemplify it, Plato does not offer a description of dialectic, let alone an analysis. Recognizing the inadequacy of the "early" elenchic dialogues that address "What is [courage, piety, philia]?" questions in isolation, seriatim, philosophically minded citizens and philosophically minded readers are prompted by the *Parmenides* and the *Theaetatus* to turn to the triad of epistemological dialogues. Investigating the relations among the Intelligible Forms, they treat knowledge as an interconnected system of explanation. Future philosopher-rulers acquire the techniques of the method of division: they practice "cutting at the joints"; they map taxonomies, tracing the proper differentia of such generic classifications as "pleasure," "sophist" and "statesman." Eventually, after fifteen years of carefully guided practical experience in coordinating civic life, they move from assumptions and hypotheses to the contemplation of the Good as the unity and order of these systematically connected Forms. Although Plato doesn't actually say this, these studies of abstract Forms seem all the more perfect – all the more beautiful – because they show how the Good rules the world. The Good is (if we can put it this way) all the more perfectly Good because the abstract Ideas of forms and motion can be used as models for structuring the world – and the polis. And properly seen, abstract form and motion are all the more perfect because they can also serve as models for well-ordered systems.[11] To be sure, Plato prefers eternity and transcendence to change and contingency. But (what we might call) his proto-neo-Platonism allows him to take the immanence of the Good – the activity of instantiating harmony – as an additional mark of its beauty and perfection. I must confess that we Chinese have difficulty understanding Plato as a nearly-neo-Platonic-Platonist. We appreciate the admiration of abstract balance and form, but move our attention quickly to its instantiation in the cosmos and the polity.[12] Please do not mistake me here: in stressing the harmony between pure theory and its instantiation/ application, I am not swerving Plato to a western conception of pragmatic utility as the test of mathematics and values. Metaphysics, physics and ethics do not reduce to economics and political necessity. On the contrary, they are critically interdependent, bound together in mutual correction.

It takes all of this to answer the questions posed in Book I of the *Republic*: "Why be just? Is the just life more flourishing, happier (*eudaimon*) than the licentious or luxurious life?" The fully considered answers show that a sound *paideia* radically transforms common conceptions of "pleasure," "honor" and "power" as constituents of a *eudaimon* life. Under-standing the proportions of cosmic harmony, instantiating them in his own soul, moves a philosopher to attempt to bring it about in the mini-cosmos that is the polity. The conjoined development of mind and character enables philosophically-minded rulers to order themselves towards justice. Properly understood, a *eudaimon* life "gives each thing its due." The education of philosophic rulers should have equipped them to structure a harmonious polis; and that of the philosophers should have set them to investigate the harmony of the cosmos. Of course the claims of justice sometimes requires them, as it does other citizens, to make sacrifices, tethering the independent exercise of their distinctive skills and temperaments to serve the common good. Consenting to serve the common good, giving priority to the whole of justice rather than to their particular role, carries some residual reluctance. Temperamentally, philosophers prefer to contemplate the eternal Forms, the order of the cosmos without returning to the messy and sometimes despairing work of ruling. Nevertheless, since they are also temperamentally ruled by reason, they will, for a time, make those sacrifices willingly and wholeheartedly. (More about this later.)

EDUCATION FOR THE *REPUBLIC*

Taken as a whole, the Republic, with its background in the *Protagoras* and *Gorgias*, appears to have dramatic, revolutionary consequences for education. The education of the rulers is pivotal for all education: they structure social practices and institutions; they regulate and direct culture; they effectively form the opinions, desires and practices of all sectors of the polis. The mentality and character of ordinary folk like Euthyphro, Meno, Lysis, Nicias and Laches, the interlocutors of the early dialogues, express the *ethos* and *nomoi* of their polis. To be sure, they often disagree with one another. Their individual constitutions, experiences, temperaments and abilities, even their family genealogies, affect their habits and perspectives.[13] And significantly, their disagreements reveal the cracks and fissures, the conflicts that indicate – without diagnosing – the malformation of their culture.

While these differences can indicate individual idiosyncrasies in constitution and upbringing, the features that are significant in distinguishing responses to Socratic inquiry, and to types of education, can be characterized by reference to the general structure of the tripartite soul. All three parts of the soul – the appetitive, the spirited and the rational – are species of desire active in every soul, each make a distinctive contribution to the vitality of the whole. Differences in their strength and configuration differentiate types of individuals: it marks their primary desires and potentialities as producers, soldier-guardians, or as philosopher-rulers. Ideally, each type requires somewhat different educational discipline to achieve its best potentiality in a justly ordered soul. So, for instance, productive souls focused on pleasure and gain need to acquire a special weight of moderation and temperance; soldier-guardians set for courage must remember what is genuinely worth fearing and preserving when they might be most inclined to flee or to fight for honor; and of course wisdom, as the ability to think "all things considered," giving each thing its proper due and measure, is the virtue of philosopher-rulers (441c–445b).

Any viable, relatively enduring complex polity depends on the contributions of distinctive psychological types, each marked by its subsidiary aims and functions. Differences in the relative power and configuration of these classes distinguish types of political systems, as they are organized for production and wealth, or for military activity, or for philosophic rule (434d–441d). Each type of political system projects an educational regimen (they believe) best suited to maintain their priorities. In the ideal state, all three classes – the productive, the soldier-guardians and the philosopher-rulers – are under the guidance of reason. But only the philosophers are directly ruled by rational deliberation: their physical appetites and passions, their desires and energies are specified and directed by reason. Of course production and military strategy also require a good deal of acute rational calculation. But the non-philosophic classes do not set their own ultimate aims, or determine their proper places in the polity. They must willingly consent to listen and to follow philosophic rulers.

Rulers must take all these psychological differences – and the necessity of constructing a just and harmonious unity from apparently incommensurable "parts" – into account in forming educational policies. The *nomoi* of most polities reflect, and also produce, social and psychological conflicts generated by the differences in the aims of distinctive psychological types and classes. They are likely to be unjust and to produce unbalanced and troubled, unjust citizens. Like the Demiurge of the *Timaeus*, ideal rulers must form a harmonious whole composed of distinctive parts. But rulers are more limited than Demiurge by their raw material: their task is constrained by the varieties of constitutionally fixed temperaments and mentalities, each with its distinctive aims and perspectives. Besides being an expression of his genetic endowment, a person's mentality – his ambitions, his reaction to authority, his capacity for moderation – is a function of his polity. As Plato describes the decay and fall of political systems in Books 8 and 9 of the *Republic*, an accidental failure in the policy of strictly controlled eugenics would disorder the ideal city, leading it to a timocratic state directed to honor rather than justice; and in a fixed sequence of a continued set of failures of family and civic education, the polity would fall to an oligarchy of wealth, then to the chaos of egalitarian democracy and finally to despotism (543a–566d). Reading Book 8, Plato's contemporaries would surely have vivid memories of the psychological and educational differences between oligarchies and democracies. They would be used to hearing, sometimes with admiration and sometimes with fear, about a Spartan timocratic education; and they might reflect on the way that recent Athenian political history affected the trial and condemnation of Socrates.[14] Constrained as they are by their political history and by genetic endowments of their citizens, even wise rulers with an ideal education might flounder and fail.

In setting the educational agenda for the ideal *politeia*, Plato is prepared to extend matters very far in order to minimize the effects of chance and history on civic harmony. In a way, ensuring a sound education of its citizens – doing everything that will make them as just as possible – is the primary aim of the *politeia* and its *nomoi*. The project of achieving the proper balance of distinctive mentalities leads to nothing less than the eugenic program of the *Republic*, supported by the myth of civic brotherhood. Population control – a well-formed eugenic reproductive policy – is central to preserving the order of a stable and just polity. Under the guise of a sacred (but actually fixed) "lottery," they are to arrange patterns of mating to attempt to retain the purity and to fix the proper numerical ratio among the three classes of (idealized) constitutionally-based psychological types: the "golden" philosopher-guardians, the "silver" auxiliary soldier-guardians, and the "iron" remainder. The purity and balance of the classes is the political analogue of justice in the soul: each part having its due measure and strength, its function doubly fixed by the contributions of its specialized nature *and* by its being ruled (over-ruled) by the needs and ends of the whole.

Eugenic control is supported by the myth of the brotherhood of the various psychological types, all of them children of Mother Earth. The common acceptance of this myth, with its implication that the *eudaimonia* of each class depends on the fulfillment appropriate to each of the others, is essential to the unity and harmony of the polis. If believed, it should bind citizens to one another in mutual flourishing (*Republic* 3.414–5).[15] Presumably it is among the basic myths that inform the play and education of all children. But Plato clearly thinks those myths are insufficient to maintain the purity and proper proportion of the classes required for a harmonious, just *politeia*.

The importance of eugenic control is marked by the fact that the pretence of a lottery of mating partners is the central ruling lie of the *Republic*. Curiously, commentators focus on the "golden lie" of the myth of brotherhood, a tale which is not, by Platonic standards, false. As I see it, concentration on the "golden lie" is a radical displacement of the real lie, the downright out-and-out lie of the marriage lottery. After all, Plato thinks the myth of the metals represents something true.[16] By contrast, the regulations covering the eugenic policy embed an outright falsehood, no myth at all. Policy, resting on a theory about how justice and necessity, rather than chance/accident (tuchē), should determine the outcome of the fake "lottery" of mating partners. No lottery at all, except as a very bad joke.

THE EDUCATION OF THE PHILOSOPHERS

Plato's views about the systematic character of belief, its dependence on the forms and reforms of civic life, and his proposals for the distinctive education of rulers, philosophers and various types of citizens, generate a formidable set of problems. Why do philosophers agree to leave contemplation of the eternal order among the Forms, and return to rule? They understand that human justice, like cosmic justice, involves each part playing its role, giving each his due, in maintaining the harmonious good of the whole. Even the most Form-entranced philosopher sees that a philosopher's "dues" to the polis requires his active participation in a just rule. Since the philosopher's nature is fully harmonious, since his knowledge guides his desires and actions, he consents to play his part in ensuring the justice of the polity. In doing so, he does not act from an abstract conception of "duty," but from his nature and habits, from what he sees, knows and wants. Far from becoming impartial and detached through philosophic contemplation, his erotic attachment to philosophy also carries over to the object of his contemplation, to the Good and its instantiation in Justice, and so to his proper activity in maintaining a just polity. Like all members of the community, he wholeheartedly accepts the myth of civic brotherhood, treating his own *eudaimonia* as connected with that of all the others. For all of that, the philosopher returns to the polis-cave reluctantly, setting aside his distinctive activity for the sake of the common good. Even when he consents to being checked by the claims of reason, the soldier-guardian remains spirited for honor: his contribution to the polity would be diminished if he did not. So too, the philosopher's contribution must retain his distinctive desires, even when he sees what justice requires of him. The distinctive natures and aims of each of the classes are necessary for the common good; and ideally each willingly, but with some reluctance listens to the claims of the dominant shared good. It is this feature of the *Republic*'s account of the education of the rulers that makes Plato seem more Chinese than neo-Platonists who counsel the ruler to leave politics behind.

How, then, do the philosopher-kings deliberate among themselves when they take their brief turns to rule? Do Socrates' conversations serve as models for the shared deliberations of the rulers of the ideal city? Do their deliberations include the method of taxonomic division? As contingencies arise (a drought, an earthquake) the rulers may have to make important policy decisions about which they could reasonably disagree. How should food be apportioned and distributed during a famine? What priorities should guide rebuilding the city after an earthquake? The daily routines of an ideal polity, however just and stable its organization, require decisions about which even mathematically minded, harmonically inclined philosophers may disagree. Plato leaves such questions unanswered. But good sense – no enemy to Plato – can help. Of course there will be no Thrasymachus or Alcibiades to create a fuss or diversion in the ideal state; and the philosopher-kings are, at a very general level, of one mind. They have had the same upbringing and education; and even more important, they have the same temperament, the same balance of faculties in the soul. The *nomoi* give general guidance: disturbing poets are to be exiled; and radically critical questions are to be suppressed. But it is no small matter to determine whether Socrates is a disturbance, or whether Homer should be outlawed or edited. In its most general form, Socratic inquiry provides one, and by no means the only one, model for deliberation. It is clearly the ancestor of Rawls's method of reflective equilibrium: a mutual and open-ended adjustment of considered judgments and general principles. "Moral philosophy is Socratic [It attempts to adjudicate and balance] all possible descriptions to which one might plausibly conform one's judgments together with all relevant philosophic arguments for them".[17] Fully developed, the method of reflective equilibrium encompasses the tasks of taxonomic division, the continual refinement of morally relevant distinctions. Even in the ideal polity, rulers need to differentiate cases requiring justice from those requiring equity. Distinguishing good myths from bad poetry surely requires a good deal of discussion among even the wisest philosopher-kings.

WHAT CAN WE LEARN FROM PLATO'S COUNSEL ON EDUCATION?

Can Platonic education serve as a model for education in any city, Renaissance Florence, Paris 1848, Beijing, Ottawa or Washington, DC, 1998? In one way it can; in another it cannot. Certainly the text does not provide conclusive answers. But evidence suggests that Plato projects the general structure of *paideia*, anywhere, any time. He certainly thinks that an ideal model provides the most general directions, as a universal heuristic and guide, which any polity would do well to emulate as best it can, under the constraints of its history and circumstances. Moreover, the psychological theory so richly developed in the *Republic* is presented as a perfectly general theory about the human soul; and the political and educational extension of that theory is in place. To be sure, that educational counsel is not identical for Everyman. On the contrary. But it is, in its full form as including the aims and structures of the polity, an education designed to serve as an ideal model for all political systems. But Plato's lesson is ultimately dark: even the best philosopher-ruler is, with the weight of history and circumstance checking his efforts, unlikely to succeed in turning a bad polity into a good one; a bad regime can lead a polity astray beyond repair. While there is no clear counsel for where to begin the reform of corruption (other than that of saying it must start with music, games and theater), it is, for all of that, better to follow a model than to allow oneself to be carried by the currents of corruption. We are (and this is the gleam of

Plato's hopeful light) in any case carried by a current towards what we conceive as good. And if there is anything foreshadowed by the myth/theory of recollection, that striving carries gleams of knowledge within it.

The most illuminating, and the most troubling, Platonic lesson is that a well-formed education involves nothing less than a well-formed *politeia*. ("It takes a whole village to raise a child.") If education is to promote *eudaimonia*, if it is to form sound habits of perception and thought, desire and action, it encompasses the smallest details of the political system. In short, the ethos and *nomoi* of a polity, its economic and family arrangements, its popular art and even its architecture are the fundamental educators of the city. About all this, Plato is surely right.

But this insight appears to have terrifying consequences. A political system that undertakes to promote the best lives for its members will assume control of the most minute details of social arrangements. Censorship, marriage regulations, eugenic control, the lot. How can we have our Platonic insight without what surely appears to us as intolerable Platonic intrusion?

But Plato's political counsel does not attempt to reach into the finest policy details for all time, all places. It does not, and cannot, claim to chart specific policy directives for philosopher-kings in Florence, Paris, Beijing or Washington, DC. A parallel: consider the difference between a detailed banquet menu that specifies the exact quality, ripeness, measure and temperature for the preparation of each dish, with a schematic architectural blueprint that can be instantiated in different ways. The latter can be further specified and realized in brick or wood, it can be painted grey or white, landscaped with deciduous trees or a Japanese sand garden. Plato's politically oriented educational counsel is a blueprint, a rough guide rather than a recipe. It is a schema for possible plans.

The history of Platonic interpretation is a history of controversy about the relative priority of the metaphysical and the political aspects of the philosophers' education. Platonic scholars, and would-be Platonists, profoundly disagree about Plato's solution to those problems; they even disagree about whether he resolved them. The history of Plato's influence on educational policy reenacts those differences in interpretation. It should come as no surprise that the history of interpretations and appropriations of Plato's complex and layered views on education range from left to right, politically. Critics and supporters alike have presented him as advocating totalitarian ideological control. But he is also read as a vigorous opponent of any power-hungry regime. He outlined a plan for the education of an enlightened class of self-critical civil servants, set to develop the potentialities, and promote the flourishing, of every type of individual.[18] We are the inheritors of all those views. Conflicted as they are, they form our practices. In the best Socratic spirit, we find ourselves interlocutors ready to begin a Socratic inquiry, wherever our polity permits. It is ironic to reflect that like some modern nation-states, the polis projected by the *Republic* may limit such inquiry to a selected few who have themselves undergone ideological purification and training. A question which troubles a transitional leadership in China: Would the guardians have joined the Athenians in condemning Socrates?

NOTES

Editorial note: The inclusion of an essay by a pseudonymous author requires a special explanation.

When, after three years' gestation, *Philosophers on Education* was at long last ready for publication, the contributor of the essay on Plato withdrew. What to do? In desperation, I called various friends and Plato scholars. Many of them had, in one way or another, been working on related topics: Did they have something on hand? Could they possibly extend themselves to cast their favorite ideas into an essay . . . now? With all the regretful good will in the world: no. Could they perhaps help me scout out something suitable, say from Jaeger, Grote, Nettleship, Annas, Reeve or Grube? We searched to no avail. What to do? It would be absolutely impossible to publish a book of this kind without an essay on Plato. And it would be absolutely impossible to delay publication further: the other contributors had been given a lead time of roughly two years; some had sent their essays promptly; others had generously taken extra time for revisions. It would be wholly unfair to ask them to wait any longer. Perhaps, just perhaps, this unfortunate turn of events could be used as an opportunity for an experiment in the exercise of intellectual empathy? Ever since teaching a course in the history of philosophy in the People's Republic of China in 1981, and finding students and colleagues there passionately interested in Plato, I had been trying to see him through their eyes, with their preoccupations. Bolstered by continued correspondence with my colleagues in the PRC, I thought of writing an essay on Plato . . . assuming the persona of a Chinese scholar who had studied ancient philosophy in Canada and the United States and who had returned to the PRC to teach in a Normal College of Education. Zhang LoShan is the pseudonym assigned to that fictional person. Although I wrote the essay, it is, in a perfectly straightforward way, not strictly speaking mine. I tried as best I could to limit my secondary references to those that would be available to Zhang LoShan, and to whatever articles and books colleagues in the West might have sent him. More importantly, I tried to see Plato's views on education through the experience and preoccupations of such a figure. It is an experiment I strongly recommend to all serious scholars: surprising features emerge from the exercise. Well, we had an essay on Plato, but could it, should it be published? I submitted it, for blind review, to two Sinologists and four eminent classical philosophers. I told the Sinologists I had received an essay purporting to be by a Chinese philosopher who had studied in the West. The style seemed suspiciously smooth for someone who was not a native speaker. Could it really have been written by a Chinese? Yes, they said, insofar as a brief essay can indicate an author's mentality and preoccupations, it might indeed have been written by Chinese. If the author had been able to find a knowledgeable translator and editor, nothing in the paper would rule that out. And while they predictably disagreed about some points of interpretation, the classical philosophers found the essay fresh and interesting. All four recommended publication. Since I was embarrassed at already having introduced a contribution of my own to the book, I briefly considered simply presenting the essay as by a Chinese philosopher who, for political reasons, wished to remain anonymous. I floated this idea to three friends, wise scholars whose judgment I trust. All three said I mustn't do it: it would be wrong. For my part, I am convinced it would be wrong to present the essay as mine: it is not what I would have written in my own voice. In the interest of guiding readers of this volume to further Platonic studies, I have added several bibliographical references that extend beyond the Grote and Jaeger commentaries that a figure like Zhang would be likely to find in his limited library. Sinologists have assured me that western correspondents would probably have sent (such a figure) xeroxed material. This essay is properly listed as by Zhang LoShan; but as editor, I offer you the story of its origins here. It grew out of discussions with Myles Burnyeat. I am grateful to him for detailed comments and counsel. Eva Brann and David Reeve added helpful reminders; Michel Oksenberg helped with the Chinese etymology; Jane Cohen, Catherine Elgin, and Lawrence Segar gave me wise advice.

1 The Chinese for education is *JiaoYu*, with each of the two characters that compose the word going back to antiquity. *Yu* roughly means: give birth, nourish, bring up. The character *Jiao* (to teach

or instruct) derives from the ancient word, *Xiao*, one of the words for filial piety. The word for learning, *Xue*, is also the word for "study"; the product and the process are identified: learning and studying are coalesced. The word for "university" is: *DaXue*, meaning, roughly, the Great Learning. The Japanese for education is *Kyolku* (teaching, nurturing). The Japanese correlate formal teaching with passive study: the word for both is *GakuShu*. *KunRen* refers to training; it is rule-bound, imposed from above, usually applied to vocational or military instruction, but unlike the English "training," never to animals or plants. English speakers may wish to see Donald Munro, "Egalitarian ideal and educational fact in Communist China," in John Lindbeck (ed.) *China: the Management of a Revolutionary Society* (Seattle, Wash., University of Washington Press, 1971); Donald Munro, *The Concept of Man in Early China* (Stanford, Calif., Stanford University Press, 1969); William de Bary (ed.) *Self and Society in Ming Thought* (New York, Columbia University Press, 1970); Mao TseTung, "Where do correct ideas come from?" in *Four Essays on Philosophy* (Beijing, Foreign Language Press, 1966); Burton Watson, *Early Chinese Literature* (New York, Columbia University Press, 1962); W. J. Peterson, Andrew Plaks, Ying-shih Yu (eds) *The Power of Culture: Studies in Chinese Cultural History* (Hong Kong, Chinese University Press, 1994); D. C. Buxbaum and Frederick Mote (eds) *Transition and Permanence* (Hong Kong, Cathay Press, 1972).

2 Although I believe we don't know, and won't ever know the actual sequence in which Plato wrote the dialogues, I shall, for the sake of convenience, refer to the conventionally accepted ordering of early, middle and late dialogues. I am both ill-equipped and disinclined to discuss the learned detailed controversies about the chronological order in which the dialogues might have been written. As a master stylist, Plato can vary his style to suit his theme. Arguments from one dialogue referring to another seem an unreliable indication of chronology. Even Plato or his editors might, as we all do, insert a later thought or discovery into the later editions of earlier works. Nor do arguments based on Socrates' age in any given dialogue provide convincing clues to the chronology of composition: his age is fixed to suit the thematic motif of each dialogue.

Although each of the Platonic dialogues is self-contained, with a distinctive central focus, most have indirect implications for the concerns that are at the forefront of other dialogues. For instance, though epistemological questions (e.g. what distinguishes knowledge from opinion?) are not at the forefront of the *Lysis*, *Laches* or the *Symposium*, those dialogues show how Socrates tries to move from opinion to knowledge; they provide examples of the investigations into the difference between the two that are the focus of the *Theaetetus*. Similarly, though the *Timaeus* appears to echo the *Republic*, the projects of constructing a well-ordered cosmos, forming a well-ordered *politeia* and achieving a harmonious soul inform one another, as different species of the same genus.

Be all that as it may, the sequence of the dialogues can nevertheless be rationally reconstructed as forming a train of thought, a staged investigation, with each phase raising questions and problems that press the inquiry forward. Independently of whether it is chronologically correct, the (accepted conventional sequence of) early, middle and late dialogues can be read as forming a single extended dialogue. The Platonic corpus, so ordered, exhibits the unfolding of a train of thought. Such a reading brackets, at least for the time being, questions about consistency. (A parallel: in principle, we could press questions of consistency on each individual dialogue, but in fact each dialogue is best read as exhibiting a train of thought, one thing leading to another.) I shall consider the dialogues as forming a continuous "argument" about what Platonic *paideia* involves: its structure, its social and political ramifications, its ontological presuppositions. Each stage of that sequence plays a crucial role in the unfolding of the whole; each adds a dimension to Plato's complex, considered counsel on education. It may well be – I have no opinion on the matter – that an investigation of the argumentative rationale of Plato's views on mathematics or pleasure or the Good might arrange the dialogues in a different sequence.

3 Sometimes, but not always, correction involves revolutionary change. The rhetoric of such transformations is, as no one knows better than our Chinese Plato, extremely complex. On the

one hand, the "reformer" must speak with the vulgar: he'd lose all hope of persuasion if he did not. On the other hand, he has a radically different conception of "what is to be done." And, as if this ambiguity were not burden enough, a *logos*-ridden, *agathos*-ridden philosopher like Plato also undertakes to *explain* the obscure object of all desire. In one way, the deflection of proper desire "just happens." But in another, it must be comprehensible: for if it were not, the world would be wayward, not properly a cosmos at all. *Republic* Books 8 and 9 testify to Plato's resolutely undertaking to explain both psychological and political waywardness.

4 The political motifs of the *Republic* move the investigation towards the *Statesman* and the *Laws*. The ontological motifs lead to the problems of the *Theaetetus* and *Parmenides*, which in turn lead the discussion to the *Sophist* and *Statesman*. On one reading, the *Timaeus* can be set with the *Republic* as an account of the construction of a unified harmonious system; on another, it can be read as a cosmological investigation of problems set by the epistemological/methodological trilogy. Similarly, the *Philebus* can be read as an ontological investigation of the relation between the indeterminate *apeiron* and logos-defined determinateness, or as an ethical investigation of the relation between intelligence and pleasure in the good life.

5 Because they are, as far as I can judge, irrelevant to Plato's considered views on education, I propose to ignore the contemporary discussions about the proper formulation and significance of the *elenchus*. Recent commentators have attempted to formulate a relatively formal rule for elenchic inquiry; they've also argued about whether positive conclusions can be drawn from elenchic discussions. See Gregory Vlastos' characterization: "a thesis is refused when, and only when, its negation is derived from the answerer's own beliefs. Respondents must undertake to say only what [they believe] that they believe" (Gregory Vlastos, "Elenchus and mathematics," *American Journal of Philology* 109 (1988), esp. nn. 14, 19, 30. Vlastos thinks that, at least in the *Gorgias*, the *elenchus* can reach positive ethical conclusions ("The Socratic elenchus," *Oxford Studies in Ancient Philosophy* 1 (1983). Also see Richard Robinson, *Plato's Earlier Dialectic* (Oxford, Clarendon Press, 1953); and Terence Irwin, *Plato's Moral Theory* (Oxford, Clarendon Press, 1977, pp. 63ff.); Hugh Benson, "The problem of the elenchus reconsidered," *Ancient Philosophy* 7 (1987) and "The priority of definition and the Socratic *elenchos*," *Oxford Studies in Ancient Philosophy* 8 (1990). Many of these essays are reprinted in William Prior (ed.) *Socrates*, vols 1–4 (London, Routledge, 1996).

To be perfectly frank, I think entirely too much has been made of this matter. Beyond his stricture that contradictions are an indication of confusion or error, Socrates would not attempt to formulate a rule for the argument. Properly understood, the *elenchus* reveals tensions and ambiguities among a person's beliefs and practices. It assumes that a person's budget of opinions and practices should form a consistent system; and that contradictions indicate ambiguity, confusion or error. Such apparent conflicts can in principle be reconciled by a new interpretation of commonplace opinions. Socratic questioning is contextual, open-ended, hospitable to tentative provisional positive conclusions, conclusions that may well be overthrown in the next turn of the discussion. His discussions exhibit an early ancestral version of Rawls's method of reflective equilibrium, with a focus on its first steps, those intended to show that there is a discrepancy between a person's specific considered judgments and the general principles (or definitions) he takes himself to believe. The actual work of adjustment and adjudication goes beyond (what has commonly been identified as) the *elenchus*. It is detailed, content-and context-bound. Unlike Aristotelian logic, the *elenchus* and the method of reflective equilibrium are heuristic guides, rather than rules for sound reasoning.

6 See A. O. Rorty, "Character, mind and politics: the Socratic case," in Jim Hopkins and Anthony Savile (eds) *Psychoanalysis, Mind and Art* (Oxford, Blackwell Publishers, 1992).

7 Students in an advanced seminar on Greek philosophy (given in the People's Republic of China in 1981 and in the United States in 1996) were asked to participate in a mock-trial of Socrates, using only the early dialogues as evidence in the prosecution and defense. Since the Chinese

judicial system was, in 1981, dramatically different from that of Athens or the States, it was difficult to get the students to carry out the assignment. But when they did manage it, their votes replicated those of the Athenian tribunal: they held Socrates guilty by a narrow margin. The American undergraduates were asked to make two judgments, first assuming themselves to be Athenians, and secondly in their own persons. As Athenians, they condemned Socrates by a slender majority; as Americans, they exonerated him by a strong majority.

8 "You can't look for what you don't know and don't need to look for what you know." I believe Diotima's speech (201e–204c). Diotima posits a *daimon* – an intermediary between the divine and the human, between knowledge and ignorance – that combines contraries and that strives for what is noble and beautiful. See C. D. Reeve, *Philosopher-Kings* (Princeton, NJ, Princeton University Press, 1988); Alexander Nehamas, "Meno's paradox and Socrates as a teacher," *Oxford Studies in Philosophy* 3 (1985); A. Sesonke and Noel Fleming (eds) *Plato's Meno* (Belmont, Calif., Wadsworth, 1965), and William Prior (ed.) *Socrates*, vols 1–4 (London, Routledge, 1996).

9 See Rorty, "Character, mind and politics."

10 Of course many of Socrates' interlocutors – Thrasymachus for example – did not want to pursue the truth. Did they nevertheless learn something? On the one hand, it seems they may have become worse, more entrenched in their eristic ways, through their encounter with Socrates. On the other hand, the very fact that they became angry suggests that Socrates had affected them, disturbed their confidence in their wayward views. Presumably Plato envisages the reader as the ultimate audience of Socrates' inquiries.

11 I realize this may not sit well with the principles of ranking offered in the *Philebus*. I cannot address, let alone solve that problem in this paper.

12 See G. E. R. Lloyd's admirable *Adversaries and Authorities* (Cambridge, Cambridge University Press, 1996).

13 Consider Plato's pervasive (and ambiguously ironic) use of genealogical motifs (of parentage and etymology) as a way of tracing significant similarities. *Euthyphro* 2a; *Laches* 178a; *Lysis* 204e; *Euthydemus* 271a–272a; as to origins of names: *Cratylus* 383a–384d; *Theaetetus* 14a–e; *Critias* 107d–108d. Although these motifs are often introduced in the dramatic opening byplay of the dialogues, that byplay expresses the common beliefs and practices that each dialogue explores. The heuristic role of genealogical and etymological motifs as a mode of recognition serves as an image of the deeper "logical" genealogical exercises of the *Sophist* (217a), the lineage of the taxonomic divisions in the *Statesman* and the Stranger's genealogical story (*Statesman* 270ff.).

14 See I. F. Stone, *The Trial of Socrates*, Boston, Little, Brown, 1988.

15 See George Grote, *Plato and Other Companions of Socrates* (New York, S. Franklin, 1974), vol. 4, ch. 35. Grote eloquently formulates something we Chinese have long understood: "It is indispensable . . . that this fiction should be circulated and accredited as the fundamental, consecrated, unquestioned creed of the whole city, from which the feeling of harmony and brotherhood among the citizens springs" (pp. 30–1).

16 Like the myth of the metals, the myth of Er – a tale of immortality, of the harmony of the spheres, the rule of the daughters of Necessity, and each soul's choice of its type of life – is presented by Plato as a moral lesson that, if believed, may enable souls to live justly. It is presented as an image because Plato can't, even in his Socratic persona, articulate the logos that would reconcile the rule of Necessity with his exhortation to *choose* a just life. That combination – the presumed compatibility of the rule of necessity with the reality of choice – seems incomprehensible. But nothing could be more shocking, more disturbing to Plato than a fundamental metaphysical truth that has an inconsistency at its core. It defies reason; and what violates *logos* cannot survive dialectical questioning. Yet Plato evidently thinks there is a shadow of truth in the tale, a truth that should be universally accepted. It must therefore be presented – it can only

be presented – as a story, one which embarrassingly seems to modify the rigorous conditions set on such tales in Book 2.

17 John Rawls, *A Theory of Justice* (Cambridge, Mass., Harvard University Press, 1971), p. 49.
18 See Myles Burnyeat's essay in this volume.

4

ARISTOTELIAN EDUCATION

C. D. C. Reeve

What should the goals of education be? And how are they best achieved? Because our manuscripts of the *Politics* break off in the middle of what is itself no more than a preliminary discussion of education (1336b24–7),[1] Aristotle's answer to both questions, especially the latter, is unfortunately somewhat incomplete. What we are told, however, together with what we can glean from other writings, provides us with a vivid, though not always incontrovertible picture. We shall first focus on goals, then on means. But, of course, the two are closely related.

Men, Aristotle famously says, are by nature political animals: animals with the natural potential for life in a *polis* or city-state (1253a7–18). Their happiness (*eudaimonia*), interwoven as it is with that of their wives, children, friends, and fellow citizens (*NE* 1097b8–14), is a communal achievement, requiring "household management and a constitution" (*NE* 1142a9–10). But it is also a communal achievement in another sense: it is only by being brought up and educated in a city-state that human beings can acquire virtue (*aretē*) – that state of character whose expression in action just is genuine happiness (*NE* 1098a7–17). The very thing that distinguishes a city-state from all other sorts of communities, indeed, is that it alone educates its citizens in virtue (1280a34–b15). Nature provides the potential for city-state life, then, while education helps to realize that potential, giving men the traits needed to perfect their natures as citizens and achieve happiness. Education is a part of politics for this reason.

Ancient Greek political thought distinguished three types of constitutions (*politeiai*): rule by "the one" (monarchy), by "the few" (oligarchy), and by "the many" (democracy). Aristotle adopts this classification, but introduces some important innovations of his own. First, he argues that differences in *wealth* are more fundamental than difference in numbers: oligarchy is really rule by the wealthy; democracy, rule by the poor. It just so happens that the wealthy are always few in number, while the poor are always many (1279b20–1280a6, 1290b17–20). This allows him to see the importance of the middle classes, who are neither very rich nor very poor (1295b1–3), and to recognize the theoretical significance of a constitution – a so-called republic or polity (*politeia*) – in which they play a decisive part (IV.11). A polity, which is a mixture of aristocratic, democratic, and oligarchic features, is not the absolutely ideal constitution, but it is the best one that can be achieved by "most city-states-states and most people" (1295a25–40). Second, Aristotle argues that each of the three traditional constitutions is of two sorts, one correct, the other deviant (1289b5–11), depending on whether its rulers aim at "the common benefit" or at their own "private benefit" (1279a26–31). Thus rule by "the one" is either kingship (correct) or tyranny (deviant); rule by "the few" is either aristocracy (correct) or oligarchy (deviant); and rule by "the many" is either polity (correct) or democracy (deviant).

The most important way in which these six constitutions differ is in their aims or goals (1289a17–28), that is to say, in their conceptions of happiness (1328a41–b2, *NE* 1095a17–1096a10). The goal of the correct constitutions is genuine happiness: that of the ideal constitution, which may be either a kingship or an aristocracy (1289a30–2), is blessed happiness of the most complete sort (1324a23–5) – "a complete activation or use of virtue" (1332a9–10); that of a polity is a more easily attainable level of that same happiness (IV.11). The goal of the incorrect constitutions, on the other hand, is what they mistakenly conceive to be genuine happiness: the goal of oligarchy is wealth; that of democracy, freedom. For oligarchs believe that happiness consists in wealth and the things money can buy (1280a25–32, 1311a9–10), while democrats believe that it consists in being free to live as one wishes (1310a29, 1317a40–41).

A second important difference between these constitutions, a consequence of the first, is that they embody different conceptions of justice (III.9). Their rulers all agree that a just share in ruling office and other political goods must be based on merit, and that a person's merit is determined by his contribution to achieving the goal of the constitution. But because they disagree about what that goal is, they disagree about what determines merit. Oligarchs hold that it is wealth, so that just shares must be commensurate with wealth or property; democrats hold that it is free status, so that all free citizens must have equal shares; those in a correct constitution hold that it is virtue, so that just shares should be commensurate with virtue (1283a24–6). Because justice "is complete virtue . . . in relation to another" (*NE* 1129b25–7), the different constitutions also have different conceptions of all the other individual virtues that together make up complete virtue (1309a36–9).

Aristotle distinguishes, however, between what the rulers typically think the virtues suited to their constitutions are and what these virtues actually are:

> being educated in a way that suits the constitution does not mean doing whatever pleases the oligarchs or those who want democracy. It means doing the things that will enable the former to govern oligarchically and the latter to govern themselves democratically.
>
> (1310a19–22; see also 1309b20–35)

The virtues truly suited to a constitution are those that enable it to survive for a long time, not those that represent its tendency in its most extreme form (1310a19–22, 1320a2–4). Possessed by citizens, these virtues invariably make the correlative constitutions more moderate and more inclusive: closer to aiming at the common benefit than exclusively at the benefit of the rulers themselves. But the goal of these more moderate constitutions, the conceptions of happiness they embody, are still different. Consequently, even the virtues that really do promote the achievement of their goals in the long term are distinct from one another. The justice that is truly suited to an oligarchy, for example, still distributes political office on the basis of wealth, it just sets the wealth qualification low enough to ensure that "the mass of those who want the constitution is stronger than the mass of those who do not" (1309b17–18).

Of these different conceptions of happiness, justice, and virtue generally, only one is correct, however, namely, the one *that accords with human nature*. This is the conception embodied in the correct or non-deviant constitutions. For only there do individuals really achieve what is genuinely their common benefit, namely, to fulfill their natures and achieve true happiness as parts of a city-state. Put another way, it is only in the correct constitutions that the virtues of a good *man* coincide with those of a good *citizen* (1288a37–9, 1293b5–6). Nonetheless, the conceptions embodied in the other constitutions, though deviant, are not simply wrong (*NE* 1134a24–30). For example, both democrats and oligarchs "grasp justice of a sort, but they go only to a certain point, and do not discuss the whole of what is just in the most authoritative sense" (1280a9–11). The same is true of their conceptions of virtue and happiness (*NE* I.5).

Because virtues differ from constitution to constitution, the education that inculcates them must differ as well (1337b1–4). However, in each case it must suit the constitution, furthering the stable, long-term achievement of its characteristic and defining goal (1260b8–20, 1337a11–21). To do this most effectively, Aristotle argues, it must, in the first place, be *public* – provided by city-states themselves:

> No one would dispute, therefore, that legislators should be particularly concerned with the education of the young, since in city-states where this does not occur, the constitutions are harmed. For education should suit the particular constitution. In fact, the character peculiar to each constitution usually safeguards it as well as establishing it initially (for example, the democratic character, a democracy, and the oligarchic one, an oligarchy), and a better character results in a better constitution in all cases. Besides, prior education and habituation are required in order to perform certain elements of the task of any capacity or craft. Hence it is clear that this also holds for the activities of virtue. Since the whole city-state has one single end, however, it is evident that education too must be one and the same for all, and that its supervision must be communal, not private as it is at present, when each individual supervises his own children privately and gives them whatever private instruction he thinks best. Training for communal matters should also be communal.
>
> (1337a10–27)

Moreover, public education should be provided to all the citizens, suiting them not just for their public, political functions but for their private, domestic ones as well:

> As for man and woman, father and children, the virtue relevant to each of them, what is good in their relationship with one another [1260b10] and what is not good, and how to achieve the good and avoid the bad – it will be necessary to go through all these in connection with the constitutions. For every household is part of a city-state, these are parts of a household, and the virtue of a part must be determined by looking to the

virtue of the whole. Hence both women and children must be educated with an eye to the constitution, if indeed it makes any difference to the virtue of a city-state that its children be virtuous, and its women too. And it must make a difference, since half the free population are women, and from children come those who participate in the constitution.

(1260b8–20)

So thoroughly does Aristotelian politics suffuse every aspect of community life, then, that the very natures of the relationships between husbands, wives, and children that constitute the household differ from constitution to constitution.

Just as the correct constitutions, embodying the correct conceptions of virtue and happiness, are those based on human nature, so too the correct sort of education must also be based on human nature, respecting its needs, abilities, and limitations (1337a1–3). Now, in Aristotle's view, human beings are psychophysical organisms, whose psyches or souls are responsible for their life and characteristic functioning. These souls have both a rational component, which is the locus of practical wisdom (*phronēsis*) and intellect (*nous*), and a non-rational component, which can yet be influenced by reason, and which is the locus of appetites and emotions. Hence Aristotelian education has three broad constituents: training for the body (*gymnastikē*); habituation for the appetites and emotions (*ethismos*); and instruction – or "education through reason" – for the rational part (1332b10–11, 1338b4–5). Their collective goal is to produce an harmonious, integrated person, one whose soul is organized so as to best promote his true happiness.

Training of the body begins in infancy, but that body is itself in part a social product, shaped for life in a constitution with specific values, ideals, and goals. For, like Plato before him, Aristotle argues that a constitution should regulate human reproduction so as to ensure a supply of children with the sorts of bodies it needs (VII.16). Ideally, these bodies are ones that physical training can bring into a condition "that promotes not just one thing, as the athletic condition does, but the actions of free people. And these should be provided to women and men alike" (1335b9–12). Evenly balanced, harmonious, graceful, and equipped for many activities, the body that results from such training is a resonant allegory, as we shall see, of the ideal Aristotelian human soul.

To understand Aristotle's views on the education of the soul, we need to set them in the context of a somewhat richer account of his psychology. An action or activity (*praxis*) expressing practical wisdom is paradigmatically (though not always) the result of a decision (*proairesis*), which is itself a desire based on deliberation (*bouleusis*) and wish (*boulēsis*); wish is a rational desire for happiness or what the agent conceives as such (*NE* 1113a9–14, 1139a31–b5, 1113a3–5). Before we begin to deliberate at all, however, we have to be presented with a practical problem to deliberate about. Sometimes it is our appetites that present us with such problems. We are hungry; we desire to eat; we wish for happiness. Should we order the poached sole (low fat, high protein) or the lasagne (high fat, high fiber)? We decide on sole with a salad, on the grounds that this combines low fat, high protein, *and* high fiber. For we believe that this is the kind of food that best promotes health, and that being healthy promotes our happiness. If our appetites are generally or habitually in accord with our wish, then (everything else being equal) we have the virtue of temperance (*sōphrosunē*). If the two are not generally in accord, we may be either weak-willed (appetite overpowers wish) or self-controlled (wish overpowers appetite). In either case, we experience painful inner conflict rather than the pleasurable inner harmony characteristic of virtue. For unlike the joylessly dutiful, Aristotelian virtuous agents take pleasure in doing what virtue demands of them – they positively enjoy the sole and salad and do not hanker after the lasagne.

Often, however, it is not our appetites that present us with practical problems but the situation in which we perceive ourselves to be. And one important way situations bring themselves to our attention is through our emotions or feelings. They may, for example, arouse our anger or fear, and these emotions, having motivational force, set us deliberating much as our appetites do. It is not bare, unconceptualized situations, however, that affect us in these ways. Fear and anger are triggered by situations perceived as threats or insults. Indeed, they help to interpret or compose the very situations to which they are responses. An overly fearful person tends to see situations as threatening; an overly angry person sees insults in every harmless utterance. For "we are easily deceived by our sense perceptions when we are in an emotional state . . . so that even a very slight resemblance makes the coward think that he sees his enemy . . . and the more emotional he is, the smaller is the similarity required to produce this effect" (*PN* 460b3–11). But these non-normal cases dramatize what is true of all of us: feeling anger or fear and seeing situations as insults or as threats go hand-in-hand.

The reason our emotions are modes of practical perception – or ways we perceive situations as requiring deliberation and action – is that, though they typically involve sensations and somatic disturbances, there is more to them than that: they also essentially embody beliefs and desires. Anger is "boiling of the blood around the heart" (*DA* 403a27–b2), but it also involves complex beliefs and desires about such ethically salient things as insults and revenge: it is "a desire accompanied by pain to take what is believed to be revenge because of what is believed to be an insult" (*Rh*. 1378a30–2). Now the virtues of character, as we have seen in the case of temperance, are concerned with our appetites, but they are also concerned with our emotions or feelings. Virtue is a matter of feeling the right things "at the right times, about the right things, towards the right people, for the right end, and in the right way" (*NE* 1106b21–3). So someone who possesses the virtues will have feelings that correctly interpret a situation, that are appropriately responsive to it.

What exactly do "right," "correctly," and "appropriately" mean here? Because emotions involve beliefs, they are potentially rational and educable. An overly fearful person can become less so through learning that the things he fears really pose no threat to him. But emotions also involve desires and somatic factors, and these are less easily changed by cognitive means: we may need time and experience with, say, garden snakes in order not to tremble or desire to flee when we see one. And this may continue to be so even after we have come to know coldly in the head that they are harmless. That is why habituation is typically needed to acquire the virtues. But habituation is not merely behavioral, it is also intellectual. In learning to fear correctly we are acquiring the capacity to see the right things as threatening or dangerous as well as gaining control of our trembling limbs and our desire to flee. What makes our fear correct in all these ways, however, is its relation to happiness. Our fear is correct, the beliefs involved in it are true, we possess the virtue related to it (courage), just in case fearing the things we do, to the degree we do, at the times we do really does promote our genuine happiness.

Our *habits* of desiring and feeling – especially those developed in early life (*NE* 1095b4–8) – largely determine how we will act, but they also do much to determine our very conception of the goal of action: happiness. We come to enjoy fatty foods, for example, and so come to associate eating them with living well and being happy, by being allowed to eat them freely when we are children and developing a taste for them (or perhaps by being forbidden to eat them in a way that makes them irresistibly attractive). If we had acquired "good eating habits" instead, we would have a different conception of that part of happiness that involves diet. If our upbringing has made us timorous, it will be difficult for us to experience the good things – such as fighting for justice – that require courage. If it has made us self-indulgent, so that we cannot postpone gratification, we will have difficulty experiencing the good things – such as playing the piano well or appreciating Proust or understanding Gödel's theorem – that take discipline and long training or study. But without the experience we will find it difficult even to *understand* an argument in favor of those goods: "someone whose life follows his feelings would not listen to an argument turning him away or even understand it" (*NE* 1179b26–8). Our habits thus limit our capacities for new experiences of what is good or valuable, and so lock us to some extent into our old values, making them seem the only genuine ones. To be sure, we should not overdo the metaphors of locks and chains: habits can be broken; bad habits replaced by better ones and vice versa. All the same, "it is not easy to alter what has long been absorbed by habit" (*NE* 1179b16–18).

What makes a certain conception correct, however, is not that it happens to emerge from our habits in this way, but that it is properly based on our nature. For it is our nature, and not what we happen to wish for or decide on, that determines what our happiness really is. Nonetheless, our habits do still largely determine what will look like happiness *to us*. So it is clearly of the greatest importance that we develop good habits of liking and disliking or desiring and rejecting – habits that will lead us both to conceive happiness correctly and to decide and do what will most promote it (1331b26–1332a10). That is why "it is hard for someone to be trained correctly for virtue from his youth if he has not been brought up under correct laws" (*NE* 1179b31–1180a3). But our need for such laws does not end with childhood: "to be under constraint, and not to be able to do whatever seems good, is beneficial, since freedom to do whatever one likes leaves one defenseless against the bad things that exist in every human being" (1318b38–1319a1). Moreover, this remains true no matter how virtuous we become, for "appetite is like a wild beast, and passion perverts rulers even when they are the best men" (1287a30–2). Our need to be under law, and the threat of sanction, is therefore lifelong.

Appetites and emotions are concerned with what Aristotle calls "external goods," that is to say, with both "goods of competition" – which include money, honor, and physical pleasure: things people tend to fight over – and with having friends, which "seems to be the greatest external good" (*NE* 1169b9–10). Consequently, the virtues of character are

56

themselves particularly concerned with external goods, since, as we saw, they ensure that our appetites and emotions are correct. For example, courage is concerned with painful feelings of fear and pleasant feelings of confidence; temperance, with the pleasures of taste and touch (*NE* 1118a23–b8); special justice, with acquisitiveness (*pleonexia*) – with wanting more and more of the external goods of competition (*NE* 1129b1–4); general justice, with friendship and community. It is our needs for these goods that lead us to form communities in the first place (I.1–2). But these same needs also bring us into conflict with one another. The single major cause of political instability, indeed, is competition – especially between the rich and the poor – for external goods such as wealth and honor (V.1). The political significance of the virtues is therefore assured; without them (or something like them) no constitution can long be stable. For "the law has no power to secure obedience except habit; but habits can only be developed over a long period of time" (1269a20–1).

The goal of an Aristotelian education of the appetites and emotions, then, is to produce citizens with the virtues and the conception of happiness suited to their constitution, citizens for whom acting in accord with the laws is second nature, it having seeped into their characters like dye into wool. If we have received such an education in a *correct* constitution, we will have all the genuine virtues of character; our feelings will be in harmony with our wish; our wish will be for genuine and not merely apparent happiness. Equipped with good habits and living in a good constitution, haven't we everything we need to ensure, as far as any human being can, that we will live happily?

It is certainly crucial to have been brought up with good habits "if we are to be adequate students of what is fine and just and of political questions generally" (*NE* 1095b4–6). But good habits, though necessary, are not sufficient. Ideally, we should also receive the sort of explicit instruction in ethics and politics, outlined in Aristotle's treatises on these subjects (VII.1–3, *NE* I.3), that will turn us into "adequate students." For ethics and politics are bodies of practical knowledge, like medicine, whose goal is "action not knowledge" (*NE* 1095a5–6). Ethics makes us "more likely to hit the right mark" (*NE* 1094a22–4) – genuine happiness – by providing us with a clear and explicit conception of what it is; politics, insofar as we may separate it from ethics, provides us with the knowledge needed to design constitutions in which such happiness is achieved as fully as circumstances permit (IV.1).

When instruction has done this work, and a clear conception of happiness is added to our properly habituated soul, we acquire practical wisdom (*phronēsis*) and statesmanship (*politikē epistēmē*). For these are pretty much the same capacity applied to different areas: practical wisdom primarily seeks the good of the individual; statesmanship seeks the same good for an entire city-state (*NE* 1094b7–10, 1141b23–4). Moreover, when we acquire practical wisdom we simultaneously acquire the full-blown virtues of character:

> Each of us seems to possess his type of character to some extent by nature, since we are just, prone to moderation, and courageous, or have another feature immediately from birth. However, we still search for some other condition as being full goodness and expect to possess these features in another way. For these natural states belong to children and to beasts as well, but without intellect they are evidently harmful. At any rate, this much would seem to be clear: just as a heavy body moving around unable to

see suffers a heavy fall because it has no sight, so it is with [natural] virtue. But if someone acquires intellect, he begins to act well; and the state he now has, though still like the natural one, will be full virtue.

(*NE* 1144b4–14, see also 1117a4–5, 1144b30–1145a2)

Before we acquire full virtue, then, we have only habituated virtue. We are disposed to listen to reason, but we do not yet have the kind of understanding of happiness – of our goal in life – that comes from instruction and the critical and reflective self-consciousness it makes possible.

A clear, self-conscious grasp of happiness is an important individual possession, obviously. It makes us more secure in our values and gives us the sort of self-knowledge that is intrinsically valuable and that promotes effective action in previously unencountered types of situations. But it is an even more important possession for a statesman. For he is charged with the legislative task of designing a system of laws for a city-state that will enable its citizens to achieve happiness. And this involves not just knowing which laws are best suited to the ideal constitution and circumstances, but which ones are best suited to a particular non-ideal constitution, given the character of its citizens and its actual circumstances (IV.1). Aristotle is witheringly critical of his predecessors, indeed, for focusing exclusively on ideal or inaccessible constitutions, to the neglect of the study of political realities (1288b35–1289a5). A statesman, he says, "ought to introduce the sort of organization that the people will be easily persuaded to accept and be able to participate in." But this very fact highlights the importance of his having explicit, and not merely habit-based, instinctual knowledge of what happiness is, so that he may be better equipped to design appropriate laws and persuade people to accept them. No doubt, this is at least part of the reason Aristotle claims that practical wisdom is the only virtue peculiar to a statesman (1277b25–6). It is not for this reason the exclusive possession of a few, however, for in many constitutions, such as an aristocracy or a polity, the statesmen may constitute almost the entire citizen body.

Instruction in ethics and politics is for the most part practical; it is directed largely to one of the components of the rational part of our souls, and aims to produce practical wisdom. But the rational part of our soul has another component, namely intellect (*nous*), which also requires instruction. Here the goal is to produce a generally educated (*pepaideumenos*) or free (*eleutherios*) person:

In every study and investigation, humbler or more honorable alike, there appear to be two kinds of competence. One can properly be called scientific knowledge of the subject, the other as it were a sort of educatedness. For it is the mark of an educated person to be able to reach a judgment based on a sound estimate of what is properly expounded and what isn't. For this in fact is what we take to be characteristic of a generally educated person. And we expect such a person to be able to judge in practically all subjects.

(*PA* 639a1–6; see also *NE* 1094b28–1095a2)

A generally educated person studies practically all subjects, then, not just one. Moreover, he does so not to acquire expert scientific knowledge in all of them (which would be impossible), but in order to become a good judge. Having studied medicine "as part of his general education," for example, he is as capable of judging "whether or not someone has treated a disease correctly" as an expert doctor (1282a3–7); having studied rhetoric, perhaps by attending the lectures that make up Aristotle's own *Rhetoric*, he won't mistake rhetorical skill for genuine political knowledge (*Rh*. 1356a27–9); having theoretical knowledge of all the various aspects of wealth-acquisition, he will have a good grasp of economics (1258b9–11, 33–5); having studied philosophy, he knows that logic precedes metaphysics (*Metaph*. 1106a5–11); acquainted with many subjects, methodologies, and areas of study, he knows "what we should and should not seek to have demonstrated" (*Metaph*. 1106a5–11) and "seeks exactness in each area to the extent that the subject-matter allows" (*NE* 1094b23–7).

Because he is able to judge the works and advice of experts, a generally educated person is free from the sort of intellectual enslavement to them that would otherwise be his lot. He knows who is and who isn't worth listening to on any matter and so can get good expert advice when he needs it. But he is also free from the inner enslavement that is all too often the lot of the narrow expert, whose imagination is strait-jacketed by the one thing he knows too well. For while he has indeed studied all the "sciences that are suitable for a free person," he has done so only "up to a point," and not so assiduously or pedantically as "to debase the mind and deprive it of leisure" (1337b14–17). He has drunk deeply enough from the Pierian spring of the various disciplines and branches of knowledge to lose the intoxication induced by shallow draughts, but not so deeply as to become newly intoxicated. Evenly balanced, harmonious, possessed of sound judgment, and equipped for many activities, a generally educated person's intellect is an analogue of the ideal Aristotelian body.

In a world of experts and pseudo-experts, in a world in which omniscience is impossible and there is a deep-going division of epistemic labor, it is clearly of enormous practical, political importance to have general good judgment. So even purely intellectual training brings practical benefits. But general education (as part of a broad program of physical training and habituation) also confers another benefit, to which Aristotle gives yet greater weight: it provides us with the capacity "for noble leisured activity" (1337b30–2). For leisured activity and happiness are closely tied:

> Leisured activity is itself held to involve pleasure, happiness, and living blessedly. This is not available to those who are working, however, but only to those who are engaged in leisured activity. For one who is working is doing so for the sake of some end he does not possess, whereas happiness *is* an end . . . It is evident, then, that we must learn and be taught certain things that promote leisured activity. And these subjects and studies are undertaken for their own sake, whereas those relating to work are necessary and for the sake of things other than themselves.
>
> (1338a1–13)

To value work (*ascholia*) more than leisure (*scholē*), or education more for its effects on the former than on the latter, is to value means more than ends. As the Spartans do, it is to think that education should promote only those virtues that are "held to be more useful and more conducive to acquisition" (1333b6–10).

59

Although we too sometimes think of leisure as peculiarly important to happiness, and of work or labor (properly so-called) as something we do more because we have to, we are still not likely to go all the way with Aristotle here. Work, not leisure, is what our lives are mostly built around. In part, this is a matter of necessity: we do not have the option of not working or of having slaves do the work for us. But it also expresses our values. We value work – at least genuinely "meaningful" work – as intrinsically rewarding, as something that can and ought to make a larger contribution to happiness than leisure does. Partly because we live in capitalist, consumer societies, indeed, we are all too inclined to make the Spartan error of thinking that leisure activities are valuable largely because of the contributions they make to work: relaxed by them we return to work sharper and more efficient. Rather than succumbing to this error, we should agree with Aristotle that "it is shameful to be unable to make use of good things . . . in leisure time." But by the same token, he should agree with us that it may be no more than equally shameful to be unable to make use of them "when working or at war" (1334a36–40). In any case, once we accept that there are intrinsically valuable things available both in work and in leisure, we are well on our way to accepting Aristotle's main point: that a legislator aiming to make his citizens genuinely happy (rather than, say, merely productive) must provide them with the education needed to achieve access to a reasonably wide range of both sorts of goods (see VIII.3).

So much for the goals of Aristotelian education. It will be well now to start over, ignoring the distinction between training, habituation, and instruction and their different targets in the individual soul, and focusing instead on the actual educational institutions and practices Aristotle recommends. Many of these are specifically designed for the free male citizens of an ideal constitution (characterized in Books VII and VIII of the *Politics*), though some seem to have much more general application. All the same, we should beware of assuming that they are the very institutions that Aristotle would recommend for a democratic society like our own (see 1322b37–1323a6).

Early education, up to age 7, takes place in the household (1336b1–2), and some of Aristotle's legislative proposals seem intended to ensure the stability of that institution and the harmony of life within it. What is remarkable about them, in contrast to Plato's much more revolutionary – if occasionally more enlightened – proposals, is their great sensitivity to the realities of human life and human nature. The age of marriage should be regulated so that couples avoid the "conflicts and differences" (1334b37–8) that mismatch in fertility (and so in sexual desire) causes; to avoid "conflicts over the management of the household," fathers should be old enough to secure their children's respect, young enough to aid and be aided by their grown children (1334b38–1335a4); husbands should be punished for adultery committed "during their childbearing years" (1335b38–1336a2); the health of pregnant women and children should be safeguarded by regulating their diet and exercise. Other legislation dealing with the household, by contrast, looks beyond it to the city-state of which it is a part. For example, infants should be habituated to the cold, not only because it is good for their health, but because it will better suit them for later military service (1336a9–21).

From infancy to age 5, children are not given any formal education, since it "would interfere with their growth" (1336a24–5). But much of what they do is informally educative and so ought to be controlled by legislation. The games children play "should not be unfit for free or civilized men or involve too much exertion or too little discipline" (1336a28–30); the stories and fables they hear "should imitate the serious occupations of later life and pave the way for their later practices" (1336a32–4). Children should spend very little time with household slaves, lest they "pick up some taint of servility from what they see and hear even at that early age" (1336b2–3). And they should neither hear nor see anything obscene or abusive, whether in art or in real life, until "their education has rendered them immune to the harm such things can do" (1336b22–3). Underlying all these legislative prohibitions is the often reiterated belief that "whenever it is possible to create habits, it is better to create them right from the start" (1336a18–19), since "whatever we encounter first we like better" (1336b33).

When children reach the age of 5, they should spend the next two years "as observers of the lessons they themselves will eventually have to learn" (1336b35–7). These are primarily lessons in reading and writing, physical training, drawing, and music (1337b24–6). The utility of the first three is plain enough. But their contributions to leisure are more important than their mere utility. Thus drawing should be taught "not in order to avoid being cheated when buying or selling products," but because it makes children "study the beauty of bodies" (1338b1–2); reading and writing should be taught "because many other areas of study become possible through them" (1338a39–40).

Education for leisure is so important, indeed, that Aristotle reserves his longest and most probing discussion, not for reading and writing, but for the one traditional component of education that seems to have no practical utility whatsoever: music (VIII.3, 5–7). One reason music should figure in education is somewhat utilitarian, nonetheless, namely, that it makes other studies more palatable to children, who have "a natural affinity for harmonic modes and rhythms." But its primary educational importance is ethical: it has "the power to produce a certain quality in the character (*ethos*) of our souls" (1340b10–18):

> everyone who listens to representations comes to have the corresponding emotions, even when the rhythms and melodies these representations contain are taken in isolation. And since music happens to be one of the pleasures, and virtue is a matter of enjoying, loving, and hating in the right way, it is clear that nothing is more important than that one should learn to judge correctly and get into the habit of enjoying decent characters and noble actions. But rhythms and melodies contain the greatest likenesses of the true natures of anger, gentleness, courage, temperance, and their opposites, and of all the other components of character as well. The facts make this clear. For when we listen to such representations our souls are changed. But getting into the habit of being pained or pleased by likenesses is close to being in the same condition where the real things are concerned.
>
> (1340a12–25)

The quality music produces in our souls, then, is the habit of being pained or pleased in the right way by the actual situations and circumstances of life. But what is distinctive about music among all the arts, in Aristotle's view, is that it alone contains direct representations of the emotions (1340a38–9). Painting or sculpture, by contrast, can do no more than represent people caught in their grip. Thus we can, as it were, directly study anger, gentleness, temperance, and the other virtues in music in a way that we cannot in any other subject. The cognitive component of our emotions, noted earlier, is therefore just as nourished and shaped by music as the affective or conative one.

For this reason, the kind of music children learn is of the greatest ethical and political significance. But should they learn to perform music or merely to listen to it? Aristotle's answer is rather surprising. Children should learn to perform music. But their goal is not to become good lifelong performers, least of all professional ones (1341b8–18), rather it is to become good judges. And the only way to achieve that goal is to learn to perform: "it is difficult if not impossible for people to become excellent judges of performance, if they do not take part in it" (1340b22–5). Once someone has become a good judge in adulthood, however, he should give up performance altogether:

> one should take part in performance in order to judge, for this reason they should engage in performance while they are young and stop performing when they are older, but be able to judge which melodies are noble and enjoy them in the right way, because of what they learned while they were young.
>
> (1340b35–9)

The following passage, though dealing specifically with the evils of professionalism in music, sheds some light on what lies behind this recommendation:

> We reject professional education in a musical instrument . . . For the performer does not take part in this kind of education for the sake of his own virtue, but to give his audience pleasure, and a boorish pleasure at that . . . That is precisely why we judge this sort of activity to be more appropriate for hired laborers than for free men.
>
> (1341b9–14)

When someone performs, he is aiming to please his audience, and to that extent he becomes subject to them and *their* characters and tastes; in extreme cases, indeed, his very body becomes misshapen as a result of the strange repetitive movements such performance requires, so that he no longer even has the kind of body appropriate to a citizen (1341b15–18). This sort of submissiveness to others is permitted in children, but not in adult male citizens (1333a7–16), who must never be even tinged with servility (*Rh.* 1367a32–3).

From age 7 to 14 education in reading, writing, music and the rest are accompanied by "easier gymnastic exercises" (1338b40–2). From 14 to 21 are three years of education in what are referred to only as "other studies" (1339a5), which are followed – at least in the case of male children – by four years of arduous physical training and strict diet (1339a5–7) in preparation for military service. These other studies presumably include whatever else is required for general education: training in medicine and in some aspects of wealth-acquisition are explicitly mentioned (1258b9–11). No period is earmarked for specifically ethical training, but that, presumably, is because the entire program of education is suffused with it.

At 21, a young man becomes an adult citizen allowed to "recline at the communal table and drink wine" with the other adults (1336b21–3). But here, too, his education continues.

For communal meals, ideally provided free by city-states to all citizens, are intended to serve many functions besides that of feeding them. For example, they enable the citizens to learn to know one another and to develop bonds of friendship and mutual trust – which is why tyrants outlaw them (1313a41–b6). Without this knowledge, the election of officials is bound, Aristotle thinks, to be largely arbitrary. Public meals also give young men the opportunity to observe virtuous older ones, and to see at close quarters and over long periods how they act and talk. But equally importantly they are also the occasion for that peculiarly Greek institution, the *symposium*, at which poetry was sung, music played, and important topics, including ethical and political ones, discussed. It may be at this stage in their lives that citizens begin to receive the more formal instruction in ethics, politics, and rhetoric that cannot begin in youth, because a young person "lacks experience of the actions in life which political knowledge argues from and about" (*NE* 1095a2–4). But it is also possible that such education does not begin until, in later life, they abandon military duties for judicial and deliberative ones (1329a2–17).

Aristotelian education continues to some extent even in adulthood, both at symposia, in the army, in the school of experience, in institutions of higher education, like the Lyceum, and in that other distinctively Athenian institution where music played a fundamental role. I mean the *theater*. For the Athenian theater was itself a political institution. One of the city's chief magistrates selected the three tragedians, whose plays were performed and judged at the great city-state-sponsored dramatic festivals, the Lenea and the Dionysia. The theater building was public. The actors were citizens, as were the judges, who were chosen by lot from the city's various constituent tribes. Attendance for poorer citizens was subsidized from public funds. The Assembly of all citizens met after the festivals to decide whether or not they had been properly conducted.

Yet, for all that, the theater stood in a complex relationship to the political culture of which it was a part. Comedy allowed public figures to be parodied and criticized (*Knights*), public institutions to be ridiculed (*Wasps*), public policies to be questioned (*Peace*), cultural practices to be inverted and explored (*Lysistrata*). Tragedy allowed the city-state to reflect collectively on its deepest fears, on conflicts with its ideals, on what it excluded or repressed, or represented as alien. Its themes, therefore, included the power of women in the household (*Oresteia*), the merit of enemies (*Persians*), the ruin of powerful and apparently virtuous rulers (*Oedipus*), the conflicts between household and city-state (*Antigone*), the terrifying way in which the deepest human bonds – those of parents and children, husband and wife – can lead to unspeakable horrors and cruelties (*Bacchae*, *Medea*).

By provoking powerful emotional responses in the citizens, tragedy allowed them not only to explore these fears in an imaginative and illuminating way, but to experience their community and shared values in a sustaining and reassuring one. Each member of the audience felt pity and fear at what he witnessed on the stage, but – aided by the very shape of the amphitheater – each also saw his fellow citizens, rich and poor, feel them too. The politically educative role of tragedy, again operating both cognitively and affectively, consisted to a large extent in its ability to facilitate this communal achievement on the part of the audience. The famous *katharsis* of pity and fear that Aristotle discusses as one of the important effects of tragedy in the *Poetics* and of music more generally in the *Politics*, needs itself to be seen as an achievement of this sort. Athenians were able to experience tragic emotions without being undone by them, first of all, no doubt, because they knew they were at the theater, but also because they saw that their feelings were shared.

We are back where we began, with Aristotelian politics and its intimate involvement with Aristotelian education at every stage. There is something exhilarating in the sense we get of the importance thereby accorded to education by this involvement. But there is also the fear that education buys that importance at too high a price, that habits so thoroughly instilled by so pervasive an institution as an Aristotelian constitution pose too large a threat to democratic freedoms. There is some basis for this fear, obviously: to be guided by the past in the form of habit without being stifled by it or forced to repeat its mistakes is hard to ensure. The problem of tradition and the individual talent has its political and ethical analog. It is important to remember, therefore, the vast resources for critical, imaginative and politically-transforming thought that general education, continued in symposia and the theater, opens up – if not in the ideal Aristotelian constitution, where perfection is supposed already to have been achieved, then certainly in any that we are likely to encounter in real life. But it is equally important to see, as Aristotle so vividly does, that there is no such thing as a culture that fails to habituate the appetites, emotions, and broader sensibilities of its citizens *in some way*; none that fails to inculcate something that at least plays the role of the virtues. The task of thinking out how and by what means a culture *should* shape these things so as to enrich people's lives by enabling them to experience the really valuable things already discovered, while at the same time equipping them to discover new ones, what is that but the task Aristotle helps and encourages us to undertake – the central task of philosophy as education?

NOTE

1 Quotations unaccompanied by an abbreviated title are from my translation of Aristotle's *Politics* (Indianapolis, Ind., Hackett, 1998). The abbreviations used for Aristotle's other works are as follows: *DA* (*De anima*); *Metaph.* (*Metaphysics*); *NE* (*Nicomachean Ethics*); *PA* (*Parts of Animals*); *PN* (*Parva naturalia*); *Rh.* (*Rhetoric*).

BIBLIOGRAPHICAL NOTE

F. A. G. Beck, *Greek Education* (London, Methuen, 1964) is a good general treatment, and includes a brief chapter on Aristotle. Werner Jaeger's classic, *Paideia* (Oxford, Clarendon Press, 1939–45) retains its interest, though it does not treat Aristotle specifically. The role of education in Aristotle's politics is discussed in Carnes Lord, *Education and Culture in the Political Thought of Aristotle* (Ithaca, NY, Cornell University Press, 1982) and in Steven G. Salkever, *Finding the Mean* (Princeton, NJ, Princeton University Press, 1990).

Specifically moral education is the topic of Myles Burnyeat's "Aristotle on learning to be good," reprinted with many other excellent papers on Aristotle's ethics, in Amélie Rorty (ed.) *Essays on Aristotle's* Ethics (Berkeley, Calif., University of California Press, 1980), and of much of my own *Practices of Reason* (Oxford, Clarendon Press, 1992). Fred D. Miller, Jr., *Nature, Justice and Rights in Aristotle's* Politics (Oxford, Clarendon Press, 1995) is the best recent book on the *Politics* as a whole. Richard Kraut's *Aristotle* Politics Books VII and VIII (Oxford, Clarendon Aristotle Series, 1998) is a useful guide to these important books. Many of the papers in Amélie Rorty (ed.) *Essays on Aristotle's Rhetoric* (Berkeley, Calif., University of California Press, 1996), including my "Philosophy, politics, and rhetoric in Aristotle," discuss rhetoric and its role in politics and education.

David J. Depew, "Politics, music, and contemplation in Aristotle's ideal state," in David Keyt and Fred D. Miller Jr. (eds) *A Companion to Aristotle's Politics* (Oxford, Blackwell Publishers, 1991), discusses Aristotle's views on music and leisure. The various aspects of the symposium are treated in Oswyn Murray (ed.) *Sympotica* (Oxford, Clarendon Press, 1990). Charles Segal, "Spectator and listener," in Jean-Pierre Vernant (ed.) *The Greeks* (Chicago, University of Chicago Press, 1995), is a brilliant essay on the role of the theater in Athens, to which my own very brief discussion is much indebted. Aristotle's views on tragedy and its role in education are discussed in Amélie Rorty (ed.) *Essays on Aristotle's Poetics* (Princeton, NJ, Princeton University Press, 1992), and in Martha Nussbaum's *The Fragility of Goodness* (Cambridge, Cambridge University Press, 1986).

Jonathan Barnes (ed.) *The Cambridge Companion to Aristotle* (Cambridge, Cambridge University Press, 1995), contains interesting essays on almost every aspect of Aristotle's thought, together with a superb bibliography.

ACKNOWLEDGEMENTS

I would like to thank Amélie Rorty for proposing this topic to me, for persuading me to rethink some early ideas, and for generous advice on the present version. Tamar Szabó Gendler and Teresa Robertson commented helpfully on the penultimate draft; I am grateful to them both.

5

AUGUSTINE ON WHAT WE OWE TO OUR TEACHERS

Simon Harrison

When Descartes sat 'by the fire, wearing a winter dressing-gown' holding his piece of paper in his hands, and set out 'once in the course of my life, to demolish everything completely and start again right from the foundations' (*First Meditation: CSM* II, 13, 12) the argument he used as his foundation immediately reminded his contemporaries of St Augustine. I wish to suggest in this essay that Augustine's encounter with education as a philosophical problem is greatly illuminated by Descartes's fire. Augustine, like Descartes, faces education – faces everything that he has been taught – as a philosophical problem which must be thought through 'right from the foundations'.

Augustine is among the first to conceive of his life as autobiography. He is among the first to sit down and write an intimate account of his own life. He does so in order to try and make sense of the question of the self, to try and rethink from fundamentals who he is, how he became what he is.

> I at least, Lord, have difficulty at this point, and I find my own self hard to grasp. I have become for myself earth tilled with much difficulty and the sweat of my brow. . . . Great is the power of memory, an awe-inspiring mystery, my God, a power of profound and infinite multiplicity. And this mind, this is I myself. What then am I, my God? What is my nature?
>
> (*conf.* 10.16.25–17.26, adapted from Chadwick)

It is this question that Augustine attempts, autobiographically and philosophically, to ask and to answer: autobiographically by examining the influences upon his life and the way they construct his identity and his knowledge of himself, philosophically by asking about the way such influences work – by asking about the nature of education and about what it imparts. Augustine encounters education as what makes us what we are. But what are we? How did we become what we are? Augustine goes about this question by telling his life story, and it is as an attempt to make sense of this story that he must rethink the nature of education.

Augustine's *Confessions* tells his autobiography from a certain standpoint: that of the convert. The narrative takes us from Augustine's birth to his conversion and baptism at the age of 32. It gives way to a philosophical inquiry into the nature of memory and the self (Book 10), and then to three books (11–13) which give an allegorical interpretation of the book of Genesis.

Augustine converts to Christianity in 386, only seventy-four or so years after the conversion of Constantine. Within his lifetime Rome will be sacked by Goths (410), and when he dies in 430 in North Africa, his city, Hippo, is besieged by Christian, but Arian, barbarians. Yet his upbringing and education was thoroughly classical, its aims and values far older than the Christian religion, and far removed from those of our own day. As a schoolboy he read Virgil, Terence, Sallust and Cicero (each of whom we meet in turn in the first three books of the *Confessions*). These authors were learnt by heart and dissected word by word. It was fundamentally a literary education and its aim was to produce successful speakers. Looking back at his youth Augustine spoke of it as an 'infernal river' into which 'the sons of men are thrown and fees are paid for them to learn these things. . . . The river of custom strikes the rocks and roars: "This is why words are learnt; this is why one has to acquire the eloquence wholly necessary for carrying conviction in one's cause and for developing one's thought."' (*conf.* 1.16.26). It was a narrow education, but it covered the entire Roman empire, and had, for centuries, created an elite with a unified identity across the Mediterranean world. For those who, like Augustine, excelled, it brought great benefits. Augustine works his way as a teacher of rhetoric ('I used to sell the eloquence that would overcome an opponent . . . the tricks of rhetoric' (*conf.* 4.2.2) to a publicly funded chair at Milan – then the capital of the Western Empire. His career prospects were good. 'We have plenty of influential friends. Provided that we are single-minded and exert much pressure, it should be possible to obtain the governorship of a minor province' he represents himself as musing in Milan (*conf.* 6.11.19). Not bad for the son of a father of relatively modest means from a small provincial town.

Looking back, in the *Confessions*, at his education Augustine contrasts form with content. The role models his education proposed for him 'would be covered in embarrassment if, in describing their own actions in which they had not behaved badly, they were caught using a barbarism or a solecism in speech. But if they described their lusts in a rich vocabulary of well constructed prose with a copious and ornate style, they received praise and congratulated themselves' (*conf.* 1.18.28). 'Veils hang at the entrances to the schools of literature; but they do not signify the prestige of elite teaching so much as the covering up of error' (*conf.* 1.13.22). But this is, of course, a retrospective view. It is a view, as Augustine is fully aware, made possible to a large extent by this very education. Augustine in thinking back on his schooling in his autobiography is trying to come to terms with the extent and nature of his debt to his teachers.

Such an education had little time or purpose for philosophy. Even Augustine's reading of Aristotle's *Categories* – a triumph, Augustine tells us, albeit an unprofitable one, of his own unaided abilities – seems surprisingly banal (*conf.* 4.16.28). So it comes as a great shock to Augustine when he reads Cicero's exhortation to philosophy, *Hortensius*, to find himself caught up by its content. Suddenly it is as if the entrance veils have been torn down:

> I was studying the textbooks on eloquence. I wanted to distinguish myself as an orator for a damnable and conceited purpose, namely delight in human vanity. Following the usual curriculum I had already come across a book by a certain Cicero, whose language (but not his heart) almost everyone admires. The book changed my feelings.

. . . Suddenly every vain hope became empty to me, and I longed for the immortality of wisdom with an incredible ardour in my heart. . . . 'Love of wisdom' is the meaning of the Greek word *philosophia*. This book kindled my love for it.'

(*conf.* 34.7–8)

This moment, this reading, marks for Augustine the first of his conversions, the first of his major stages of his conversion to Christianity. Conversion. Augustine lived in an age of conversions. (Augustine's *Confessions* tells of at least nine other 'conversions' of one form or another.) After Constantine the empire was becoming Christian. Even the anti-Christian reaction of the emperor Julian the Apostate (361–3) was defined precisely by its opposition to this transformation. It is Julian who highlighted a central point of conflict – education. He issued, in 362, an edict banning Christians from teaching the classics. Like Augustine he insists on the importance of content:

> I hold that a proper education results, not in laboriously acquired symmetry of phrases and language, but in a healthy condition of mind, I mean a mind that has under-standing and true opinions about things good and evil, honourable and base. Therefore, when a man thinks one thing and teaches his pupils another, in my opinion he fails to educate exactly in proportion as he fails to be an honest man.

(Julian, *Letter* 36 442A–B)[1]

Such sentiments remind one of Augustine's words 'For if a man is bad, he is not a teacher, but if he is a teacher, he is not bad' (*lib. arb*. 1.1.3). It also recalls images such as Plutarch's bee which 'discovers amid the most pungent flowers and the roughest thorns the smoothest and most palatable honey; so children, if they be rightly nurtured amid poetry, will . . . learn to draw some wholesome and profitable doctrine even from passages that are suspect of what is base and improper' (*How the Young Man Should Study Poetry*, 32E). 'One ought therefore to strip off the superfluity and inanity of style, and to seek after the fruit itself, imitating not women that make garlands, but the bees' (*On Listening to Lectures*, 41F).[2] Julian however seeks to mark this tension as the front line between Christianity and the ancient world:

> I give them this choice; either not to teach what they do not think admirable, or, if they wish to teach, let them first really persuade their pupils that neither Homer nor Hesiod nor any of these writers whom they expound and have declared to be guilty of impiety, folly and error in regard to the gods, is such as they declare. . . . If, however, they think that those writers were in error with respect to the most honoured gods, then let betake themselves to the churches of the Galilaeans to expound Matthew and Luke . . .

(*Letter,* 423B–D)[3]

Augustine's contemporary Jerome writes of a nightmare in which he had stood before a heavenly Judge and had been accused of being 'not a Christian but a Ciceronian' (*Letter* 22.30).[4] This conflict between Christianity and the world it was changing was felt by Augustine as well. Inspired by Cicero to 'love and seek and pursue . . . wisdom itself, wherever found' he turned to the sacred writings of the scriptures only to find unpalatable stories told in rebarbative, uneducated prose; 'unworthy in comparison with the dignity of Cicero' (*conf.* 3.5.9).

This then, is one way that Augustine encounters education as a problem: education as the creator of cultural identity. Augustine's education had made him what he was, a member of the ruling elite of the Roman empire. There was no other system of education. Everyone of this elite had read – even if that was all they had read – Virgil and Cicero. What then did it mean to become a Christian? What did it mean to reject the divinities and values promoted by the gripping poetry of Virgil? What did this mean for his attitude to the education to which he owed everything – not just worldly success, but everything: the ability to read, to think, to express himself – the encounter with Cicero, with men such as Ambrose, the powerful bishop of Milan whose sermons Augustine went to hear as examples of rhetorical finesse, only to find Ambrose finessing the Bible. I have already quoted Augustine critical of his education – but from what Archimedean point, as it were, could he criticize it? Augustine's every sermon, every word of the *Confessions* owes its brilliance to his rhetorical, classical education. How and in what sense could it be replaced or transcended?

This question does not present itself to Augustine simply as a problem about which texts to read, as if it would be sufficient to translate the gospels into hexameter, or even construct them from chopped up Virgilian lines (as does, for instance, Proba's Virgilian *Cento*). Education presents itself to Augustine as a problem for philosophy.

Augustine's world already possessed an educational and cultural critical perspective on itself – the life of philosophy. Immediately after his conversion Augustine retired to a villa in the country, rather as Cicero had spent time in his villa in Tusculum. There with some friends and pupils he set up a philosophical community, their aim to 'grow godlike in retirement' (*Letter* 10.2). They studied Virgil and Cicero. They discussed the nature of evil, the good life, the soul and truth. At this time Augustine embarked upon a massive and magisterial project: to write a complete series of books in the 'liberal arts': grammar, music, dialectic, rhetoric, geometry, arithmetic and philosophy. The project however was abandoned. Only the works on grammar and music were completed, and of the *de musica* only the first part, on meter. Augustine gives the aim of this project as 'to arrive at the incorporeal through secure stepping stones through the corporeal' (*retr.* 1.6: The *Retractations* is Augustine's own catalogue raisonné of his literary output, written towards the end of his life – another form of autobiographical examination). The *de musica* brilliantly exemplifies this philosophical method: five books of detailed analysis of the rules of meter, are followed by a sixth in which the discussion ascends from there to consider God 'who rules all and governs our intelligence' (*mus.* 6.1.1).

This approach to philosophy as advanced studies, as intellectual ascent, will remain with Augustine. It finds its most intricate expression in his massive fifteen-volume work *On the Trinity*, in which the mind progresses from the study of itself to an understanding of the three-fold nature of God. Yet as a 'liberal arts project' it is abandoned. Shortly afterwards Augustine is back in North Africa, and in 396 is ordained bishop of the busy port of Hippo Regius. Augustine abandons his way of life as a full-time seeker after truth, for the crushing burden of bureaucracy and petty strife – as well as the care of souls and preaching of sermons – of a bishop's life. In *de musica* he is careful to warn those who have not had the tremendous advantage of his advanced education from reading the sixth book: 'I warn those who have no special education for this science, but who are Christians, to pass it by; for by religion they can fly above a road which is hard for their feet' (*mus*. 6.1.1)

The educated understanding of God worked out in the *de musica* remains the preserve of the same narrow cultural elite. But what of the uneducated? What of those who by mere 'religion fly above'? Did real 'Christianity' really require education, or did it make Augustine's *de musica* an anachronistic irrelevance? There were certainly those who thought that Christianity offered something that pagan learning could not offer, and hence that such learning was a waste of time. Take, for instance, Arsenius, once tutor in Constantinople to the future emperor Arcadius, who found among the hermits of the Egyptian desert a new culture, a new kind of wisdom: 'I knew Greek and Latin learning. But I have not yet learned the ABC with this peasant' (quoted by Brown 1992: 73). In the prologue to his *de doctrina christiana*, Augustine speaks of

> Antony, the holy and perfect Egyptian monk, who is said to have memorized the Sacred Scriptures simply by hearing them, without any training in reading, and to have understood them through prudent thinking

and of a

> foreign Christian slave, about whom we have recently heard from serious and reliable people, who, although no one had taught him to read, prayed that the skill might be revealed to him, and after three days of prayer read a book which was handed to him, to the astonishment of those who were present.

> (*doctr. christ*. prologue 4)

Augustine's failure to complete his textbooks, and his becoming a bishop (expounding Matthew and Luke in the churches of the Galilaeans) do not imply rejection of his education. As he stresses in connection with Antony and the slave, people who think that they can simply read the Bible aided only by divine inspiration 'should remember that they have learned at least the alphabet from men'

> (*doctr. christ*. prologue 4)

Augustine ends the *Confessions* with three books of exegesis of the book of Genesis. The relationship between these books with the first ten is a familiar puzzle for scholars. Yet, as Brown notices, they are 'the most strictly autobiographical part . . . they show exactly what Augustine had come to regard as the essence of his life as a bishop' (1967: 262). The young man who had found the Bible so unreadable, who had resigned his chair in Milan, found himself again what he always was, a teacher. This time his 'classic', the text it was his duty to expound, was the Christian Bible. How did his role as a Christian educator relate to his role as a teacher of rhetoric? Had Julian been right – should Christians abandon classical literature for the uncouth and unpolished, barely readable, Bible? How could one brought up to be a thoroughgoing 'Ciceronian' come to terms with being a Christian?

One of the first books Augustine was to write after becoming a bishop (although he was to leave it uncompleted for another twenty years), and just before his *Confessions*, was his treatise 'On Christian education', *de doctrina christiana*. Along with his *City of God* (*de civitate dei*) this was to become one of the foundation texts of mediaeval Christendom. Yet, just as the *City of God* is almost anything but what one would expect a work of political theory to be, so Augustine's *Christian Education* does not aim to set up a programme or curriculum to rival the educational practice of his day. Just as Augustine's *civitas* is not constituted by detailed political, constitutional or social proposals, his *doctrina christiana* is not constituted by a curriculum based on the Bible. Augustine's *City of God* is an attempt to rethink and to reevaluate the nature of history and society. It is a work which situates the Christian both inside the Roman empire and inside history, and outside it. The City of God itself which gives the book its title is not, like say Plato's ideal city, a possible (if ambitious) political constitution. It is the society of all Christians arching across all time, and anchored in the eternal. Its membership is defined by an individual's desire, by an individual's ultimate values.

> Two cities, the earthly and the Heavenly, which are mingled together from the beginning to the end of their history. One of them, the earthly city, has created for herself such false gods as she wanted . . . The other, the Heavenly City on pilgrimage in this world, does not create false gods. She herself is the creation of the true God . . . Nevertheless, both cities alike enjoy the good things, or are afflicted with the adversities of this temporal state, but with a different faith, a different expectation, a different love, until they are separated by the final judgement . . .
>
> (*civ.* 18.54)

The *City of God* was written in response to a crisis: the sacking of Rome in 410. Anti-Christians blamed this almost unimaginable disaster upon the new religion, and the abandonment of the old. Augustine's reply is breathtaking in the breadth of its vision. He rethinks the writing of history. Rome, he argues at length, is simply one empire among many, its existence is merely a historical contingency, merely part of the 'one damn thing after another' of human life. 'Remove justice, and what', he asks, 'are kingdoms but gangs of criminals on a large scale?' (*civ.* 5.5). Or rather, its existence is due entirely to the providence of the God who controls history. The point, for Augustine, is not to replace the Roman empire with a Christian version, but for each individual to come to terms with the unpredictable and miserable course of history, to understand the workings of God's providence within it, and to learn to love what is truly of value within it. Thus the *City of God* is an attempt to look at history from another perspective, the perspective of truth and of the good. Augustine's Christian city is made up of those who desire God, whose ultimate value, and ultimate end is God. Augustine's educational programme for this City is about the education of that desire.

It is this ideal of education that lies behind Augustine's *de doctrina christiana*. At first sight this work looks very conservative. It belongs very much to its world, to the classical culture of late antiquity. 'There are', it begins, 'certain precepts for treating the Scriptures which I think may not inconveniently be transmitted to students, so that they may profit not only from reading the work of expositors, but also in their own explanation of the sacred writings to others' (*doctr. chr.* prologue 1). These precepts do not at first seem particularly groundbreaking. They apparently treat the Bible, rather than Virgil, merely as the core text of education. All the resources and techniques of classical learning are to be deployed in its elucidation. Thus, for instance, the reader of the Bible must know about logic: 'the science of disputation is of great value for understanding and solving all sorts of questions that appear in sacred literature. . . . Since correct inferences may be made concerning false as well as true propositions, it is easy to learn the nature of valid inference even in schools which are outside of the Church. But the truth of propositions is a matter to be discovered in the sacred books of the Church' (*doctr. chr.* 2.31.49).

Here again, however, it is the change in perspective that makes all the difference. Augustine rethinks hermeneutics, rethinks the study of the text from a perspective that puts his classical education in its place, just as the *City of God* puts the Roman empire in its place. 'However the truth of valid inference was not instituted by men; rather it was observed by men and set down that they might learn or teach it. For it is perpetually instituted by God' (*doctr. chr.* 2.32.50). Julian's edict claimed that education belonged to the pagan culture that had produced it. Augustine denies this claim. Classical education, or at least whatever it teaches that is good and true, does not belong to the pagans. It is not that Christianity has to work out its own peculiar way of constructing and teaching truth and value. Christianity is, for Augustine, the only correct way to the ultimate source of truth and value. Pagan learning like – to use Augustine's image – the gold the Israelites took from the Egyptians (Exodus 3: 22; 11: 2; *doctr. chr.* 2.40.60; *conf.* 7.9.15) belongs by right not to the pagans, but to the source of its value, to God, and hence to the Christian.

De doctrina rethinks education from its basic terms up. 'All teaching concerns either things or signs, but things are learned by signs' (1.2.2). The first book deals with things; that is, with what the Bible – as a collection of signs – is about. This leads him to determine what the Bible means in advance of having discussed how we are to interpret it.

> The sum of all we have said since we began to speak of things thus comes to this: it is to be understood that the plenitude and the end of the Law and of all the sacred Scriptures is the love of a Being which is to be enjoyed and of a being that can share the enjoyment with us . . . Whoever, therefore, thinks that he understands the divine Scriptures or any part of them so that it does not build the double love of God and neighbour does not understand it at all. Whoever finds a lesson there useful to the building of charity, even though he has not said what the author may be shown to have intended in that place, has not been deceived, nor is he lying in any way.
>
> (*doctr. chr.* 1.25.39–26.40)

This might appear as a mind-numbingly unscientific hermeneutics, an even narrower conception of learning and research than the torrent of human custom (*conf.* 1.16.26) that carried Augustine to a Chair of Rhetoric, and to the duties of delivering political panegyrics known by all present to be a pack of, albeit well-packaged, lies (*conf.* 8.6.9). What gives Augustine's *doctrina* its dynamic is his deployment of the distinction between 'use' and 'enjoyment'. 'Some things', Augustine says, 'are to be enjoyed, others to be used . . . To enjoy something is to cling to it with love for its own sake. To use something, however is to employ it in obtaining that which you love' (*doctr. chr.* 1.3.3.–4.4).

Augustine's *Christian Education* is the education of desire, it is the employment of all our available resources in the service of the love of God. God, the ultimate value, as the ultimate source of value is the only 'thing' to be 'enjoyed'. The point of reading the Bible, the point of expounding the text with all the ingenuity at one's disposal is to educate the natural longings and wishes of all humans. The point is not to construct another system of references, and allusions for the elite to deploy in their political intercourse. The aims and objectives of education, along with the aims and objectives of political engagement, are thoroughly 'internalized'; where Augustine had read Virgil for style, for form, where Augustine had taught his students the 'tricks of rhetoric' – now all these are acknowledged, only they are subordinated to a new and radical grasp of the content of education – of what education is about. 'Our heart is restless', as Augustine writes in the opening paragraph of the *Confessions* 'until it rests in you' (*conf.* 1.1.1).

It seems, again, that Augustine's hermeneutics still remains trapped in a vicious, and tedious, circle. Why bother to read the Bible if you already know what it means? Augustine lists what the Bible means in the first book: the 'things' that it signifies are the articles of faith of Christianity. Yet even here, even with the concept of faith – which appears in the passage quoted from *mus.* above as a kind of short cut – Augustine is still thinking in terms of education. In his work 'On the usefulness of belief' Augustine talks of 'faith' in terms of the kind of 'taking on trust' necessary in education:

> Who ever thought of having the obscure and recondite works of Aristotle expounded to him by an enemy of Aristotle? . . . If we hated Vergil, indeed if we did not love him, before we knew anything about him, because our seniors praised him, we should never derive any satisfaction from the innumerable Vergilian questions that are wont to excite and agitate teachers of literature. We should not be willing to listen to anyone who discussed these questions and praised the poet. We should be favourably impressed by anyone who tried to show that he was wrong or mad. But now, many teachers try to explain these questions variously according to the capacity of each; and those obtain the greatest applause by whose exposition the poet appears in the best light, so that even those who do not understand him at least believe that he was guilty of no error and that his poems are admirable in all respects. So if in any question the teacher fails to give an answer, we are angry with him, and do not attribute his dullness to the fault of Vergil. If he tried to defend himself by blaming so famous an author he would soon be without pupils or fees.

(*ut. cred.* 6.13)

Failure to take Virgil's genius 'on trust' would lead to failure to learn about good poetry. Likewise, failure to 'think the best of God' (*cf. lib. arb.* 1.2.4), to give God the benefit of the doubt, as it were, would lead to failure in Christian education, failure to learn about the good itself. But what this 'faith' achieves is precisely the kind of shift in perspective with which the *City of God* and the *Christian Doctrine* work. To explain the sack of Rome as a failure on God's part to protect the city, rather than as an exercise in humility (cf. *civ.* 1. pref.), is

73

to adopt a mistaken perspective similar to that which would discard Virgil rather than take a 'Virgilian question' as an opportunity to learn.

I began with Descartes, and with the resemblances his contemporaries noticed. Thus, for instance, Arnauld begins his (*Fourth*) *Set of Objections* by quoting Augustine:

> In Book II chapter 3 of *De Libero Arbitrio*, Alipius, when he is disputing with Euodius, and is about to prove the existence of God, says the following: 'First, if we are to take as our starting point what is most evident, I ask you to tell me whether you yourself exist. Or are you perhaps afraid of making a mistake in your answer, given that, if you did not exist, it would be quite impossible for you to make a mistake?' This is like what M. Descartes says: 'But there is a deceiver of supreme power and cunning who is deliberately and constantly deceiving me. In that case I too undoubtedly exist, if he is deceiving me.
>
> (*CSM* II, 139)

Arnauld says nothing more on the subject, and Descartes's *Reply* is entirely to the point.

> I shall not waste time here by thanking my distinguished critic for bringing in the authority of St Augustine to support me, and for setting out my arguments so vigorously that he seems to fear that their strength may not be sufficiently apparent to anyone else.
>
> (*CSM* II, 154)

The point is, of course, that Descartes's arguments can look after themselves. Indeed they are intended precisely to be arguments which can, which must, do without assistance from authority. What I want to suggest in this essay is that Augustine encounters and formulates education – his education, himself as an educator, everything that education has given and made him – as a philosophical problem in a similar way. It is not just the basic argument that Augustine shares with Descartes, but the attempt to rethink from fundamentals – and from fundamentals revealed by the *cogito* type of argument – everything that he has learnt and has taught. As Descartes, Augustine undertakes a first-personal inquiry, an inquiry that takes the nature of the inquirer as an 'I' seriously. Such an inquiry leads Augustine not only to write autobiographically, but also think through a family of arguments that resemble Descartes's *cogito ergo sum*. Augustine's calling into question of his education takes the form, moreover, of an inquiry into one of the fundamental questions of philosophy: the nature of knowledge.

Perhaps the best place to begin is with Augustine's earliest memory, his most original sense of himself, and with his analysis of the first thing he learnt. I will then go on to show how this analysis is itself dependent upon an analysis of the nature of teaching and of what is taught, knowledge. This will then lead me on to sketch briefly one of Augustine's '*cogito*-like' arguments.

Augustine's first memory of himself is as 'already a boy with the power to talk. This I remember' (*conf.* 1.8.13). His memory can take him no further back into his origins and provenance than a 'chattering boy': his earliest memory of himself finds a young Augustine already kitted out with a basic education. (Perhaps indeed his memory cannot go further back than language?) But how did he get this education? How did he learn to talk? Augustine answers this question in what is his first account of education in the _Confessions_, an account made famous by its partial quotation as the opening paragraph of Wittgenstein's _Philosophical Investigations_. Wittgenstein quotes the following:

> When they (my elders) named some object, and accordingly moved towards something, I saw this and I grasped that the thing was called by the sound they uttered when they meant to point it out. Their intention was shewn by their bodily move-ments, as it were the natural language of all peoples: the expression of the face, the play of the eyes, the movement of other parts of the body, and the tone of voice which expresses our state of mind in seeking, having, rejecting, or avoiding something. Thus, as I heard words repeatedly used in their proper places in various sentences, I gradually learnt to understand what objects they signified; and after I had trained my mouth to form these signs, I used them to express my own desires.
>
> (_conf._ 1.8.13: translation as quoted in the footnote to Wittgenstein,
> _Philosophical Investigations_ §1)

Wittgenstein uses this account to exemplify 'a particular picture of the essence of human language' (§1). Burnyeat (1987) – to which this paper is fundamentally indebted – has shown that readers of Augustine, and of Wittgenstein, miss much if they fail to see what Wittgenstein has omitted to quote: namely the passage that immediately precedes:

> I have since realized from what source I had learned to speak. For it wasn't that my elders had been teaching me, presenting words to me in a definite order of training as they did a bit later with my letters. Rather, I had been teaching myself with the mind which you, my God, gave me, when I tried to express the feelings of my heart by cries and different sounds and all sorts of motions of my limbs (in order to get my own way) but could not manage to express everything I wished to everyone I wished. I had been taking thought with the aid of memory: . . .'
>
> (_conf._ 1.8.13: Wittgenstein's quotation begins at this point;
> translation quoted from Burnyeat 1987)

What Wittgenstein's quotation risks obscuring (whether intentionally or not (see Burnyeat 1987: 24)) is that Augustine's analysis of his first education has as its focus the claim that he taught himself to speak. He was not taught to speak by anyone else. He owes his being able to speak not to his elders, but to 'the mind which you, my God, gave me'. This is at once a statement of his complete dependence upon God for everything that he has, and a statement of a theory of education.

In order to understand this 'theory of education' we need to turn to Augustine's marvellous dialogue 'On the teacher'. Here, in a sophisticated and playful work of dialectic, Augustine investigates the nature and possibility of learning. The dialogue reaches the apparently paradoxical conclusion that 'there is no teacher who teaches man knowledge except God, as it is in fact written in the Gospel: "One is your teacher, Christ"' (_retr._ 1.(11.)12).

It is paradoxical because it is offered as the conclusion taught us, in the course of the dialogue, by Augustine – and a conclusion which is taught by one of the interlocutors to the other. But how can Augustine teach us that no one can teach anyone else – if it is true that no one can teach anyone else? The key term of the statement is, of course, *knowledge*. Knowledge cannot be taught. Augustine in this dialogue thinks through an ancient approach to the nature of knowledge. Working within a tradition that can be traced through to Plato, Augustine seeks to distinguish knowledge from belief and opinion in terms of what Burnyeat (1987, 6) calls 'the mode of justification'.

'When we speak properly', Augustine says in a famous passage, 'we say we know only that which we grasp by firm reasoning of the mind.' Knowledge properly so called however does not extend to 'what we perceive by our bodily senses and what we believe on the authority of trustworthy witnesses' (*retr.* 1.14.3, quoted from Burnyeat 1987: 6). These last two may be true, and may have justification. But what justifies knowledge as knowledge is something else – the 'grasp of the mind's firm reasoning'. This Augustine can also call 'understanding'. What differentiates knowledge from belief, then, is understanding.

Plato illustrates the distinction by means of the example of the difference between the jury and the eyewitness (*Theaetetus* 201a–c): while the jury may reach the right verdict, they cannot know what happened, in the same way as the eyewitness can. Augustine will take up the use of direct first-hand vision in his accounts of what makes knowledge in his account of knowledge as 'illumination'. But for the moment it is sufficient to see that the burden of Augustine's claim that no human can teach another is that no one can impart understanding to another. This is because 'understanding' is something one has to do for oneself. This is not to deny that the teacher can help bring the student to understand. (Augustine's treatise 'On instructing the uneducated' – *de catechizandis rudibus* – is, for instance, full of insight into the practice of lecturing.) It is to assert that what we understand, what we make of our education, is in the last analysis, up to us. It is to make the claim that the teacher cannot do the understanding for the pupil. 'Knowledge, in the sense of understanding, cannot be taught or conveyed by words from one person to another. Every schoolboy is familiar with the fact that it is one thing to know in that external way *that* the connection holds (e.g. that these propositions constitute a proof of that theorem), and quite another to understand the connection, to see how the elements hang together. That is something one can only do for oneself' (Burnyeat 1987: 21).

This is a point well taken by Descartes: 'But, to follow the passage from St Augustine which you sent me, I cannot open the eyes of my readers or force them to attend to the things which must be examined to ensure a dear knowledge of the truth; all I can do is, as it were, to point my finger and show them where the truth lies' (*CSM* III, 168f.). To take a couple of quotations from Augustine:

> This much can words do, to attribute to them as much as possible. They merely prompt us to look for things. They do not show them to us so that we know them. He teaches me who puts before my eyes, or any bodily sense, or even my mind itself, those things which I want to know.

> (*mag.* 11.36)

And secondly a passage in which the same idea is given in rather more theological terms:

> But as for all the things which we understand, we do not consult someone speaking
> externally, but inwardly the Truth which presides over the mind, prompted, perhaps
> by the words. And it is he who is consulted that teaches, that is, Christ who is said to
> dwell inside a man, who is the immutable and eternal Wisdom of God. It is Wisdom
> that every rational soul consults, but Wisdom is available to each soul only as much as
> each soul is able – on account of its own good or bad will – to receive.
>
> (*mag.* 11.38)

Knowledge cannot be taught. It cannot simply be passed, like a common cold, or a piece
of news, from one person to another. In order for a piece of information to become
knowledge, those who would understand have to see how it fits with everything else they
know; in order to understand that it is, for instance, an answer to a question, the student has
to have asked the question and to recognize it as the answer. Knowledge, then as for Plato,
is something acquired at first hand, something acquired from the first person. Here, then,
Augustine finds his way to something that is 'all our own work'. Education is indeed what
makes us what we are, but there is also, for Augustine, a point from which I can see that what
I am depends on what I make of my education. This standpoint is that of the first person
singular.

I said above that Augustine shares an argument with Descartes – something commented
upon by Descartes's contemporaries. What they share is an argument that works in the first
person. Descartes's 'I think therefore I am' is in this respect similar to Augustine's 'if I am
deceived I am' (*civ.* 11.26) – or to take us back to Arnauld's quotation: 'I ask you to tell me
whether you yourself exist. Or are you perhaps afraid of making a mistake in your answer,
given that, if you did not exist, it would be quite impossible for you to make a mistake?' (*lib.
arb.* 2.3.7). While Descartes is right to insist that he and his predecessor put the argument
to different uses, I wish to suggest that the task in which Augustine employs his is as
fundamental and radical in its own way as that of Descartes: the rethinking from the
foundations of what one has learnt.

As Arnauld's quotation shows, the argument of *lib. arb.* 2.3.7 is to be employed as a
'starting-point' and as something 'most evident'. To characterize the argument as a proof of
God's existence, while correct, fails to capture its revisionary status. It is not just that the
interlocutors in the dialogue are to work to a proof of God's existence without any recourse
to 'authority', without relying on what they believe about God. Rather this working is to
re-educate the interlocutors about what they believe. It is to bring them to relearn for
themselves about their own selves and their relation to God. It is to give them that correct
Christian perspective upon which the political programme of the *City of God*, and the
hermeneutical rules of *Christian Education* depend. God's existence is proved; it is 'learnt',
by investigating the nature of truth, the standard by which we are able to judge whether
something is the case or not (*lib. arb.* 2.12.34;15.39). When Augustine in the passage from
On the Teacher quoted above, talks of 'consulting Truth which presides over the mind' he is
referring to the same feature of our mental life that he discussed in *de doctrina* under the
heading of logic ('the truth of valid inference', quoted above). What his '*cogito*-like'

argument reveals in the *lib. arb.* is a mind that depends for its ability to learn wholly upon truth – wholly upon God. The mind – when it understands, when it grasps something rationally – works along the laws of 'valid inference', or at least the laws of valid inference represent man's achievement in coming to terms with the nature of the universe. But the '*cogito*-like' argument also reveals that in order to come to understand its dependence upon God, in order to learn about the nature of itself, it must begin from the perspective of the first-person singular, from the 'I' that is inquiring and which desires to understand. It is this perspective that enables Augustine to rethink clearly the nature and role of education in his time. It is this perspective that Augustine uses to make sense of his own identity over against the education that made him what he was. And it is by philosophical reflection upon the nature of education that Augustine is able to look from this perspective.

Nabokov, in his novel, *Pale Fire* (1962), is able to conceive of 'Man's life as commentary to abstruse | Unfinished poem' (*ll.* 939–40).[5] It is Augustine's genius to have conceived of his life in terms of autobiography, to have been among the first to attempt to make sense of himself by telling his own life story. Augustine is well aware that he owes everything he is to what he has been taught. Indeed I would suggest that the heart of Augustine's theology is the claim that he owes everything he is to God. 'What do you have that you have not been given?' This biblical text (1 Cor. 4: 7) sums up for Augustine an insight fundamental to his theology, to his understanding of himself and his relation to God. He will repeat it continually in the Pelagian controversy, the great theological controversy over grace and predestination which dominates the later years of his life. He will refuse to concede any respect in which the human creature is not, in the last analysis, totally dependent upon God. Some have seen this insistence as a denial of human freedom. Reasons for thinking that this is not the case may be visible in this essay's exploration of the educational questions that drive Augustine's philosophy. Perhaps I could put it like this: where Nabokov's Shade and Kinbote tell their life, explore and expose their identities, in poem and commentary, Augustine's life story reads rather like – to take another literary model – the list of acknowledgements that open an academic book. The author thanks friends, colleagues, teachers ('the moon's an arrant thief | And her pale fire she snatches from the sun'), and claims full responsibility for all errors ('all errors are my own'). These two movements – the 'without whom, etc' and the 'all errors are my own' – capture the two senses of Augustine's title for his autobiography, 'Confession': *confessio in laude dei* – the praise of God, and *in peccatis nostris* – the acknowledgement of sins (Cf. *conf.* 10.2.2; O'Donnell 1992: ii. 3–4).

'*What do you have that you have not been given?*' In an essay of this scope I have not been able to do justice to what we might call Augustine's unoriginality. Just as the *de doctrina* simply puts to use hermeneutical tools which lie to hand, prepared by the work of centuries of educational practice and theory, just so Augustine's 'educational theory' must be regarded as the 'precipitate of some 800 years of Platonist philosophizing' (Burnyeat 1987, p. 2). These things lie before him, as the 'objects' and 'sounds' and 'expressions of the face' lie before the infant child (*conf.* 1.8.13). But Augustine's unoriginality, his debt to his education, is precisely what he is inquiring into, and trying to make sense of, by working back to, and back from, the 'I' from which we all begin – 'the mind which you, my God, gave me'.

BIBLIOGRAPHICAL INFORMATION AND NOTES

Translations quoted, and abbreviations

conf.   Confessions (*confessiones*)

Quotations, unless otherwise stated, are taken from the excellent translation by H. Chadwick, *Saint Augustine: Confessions* (Oxford, Oxford University Press, 1991). Chadwick's numbering, converted into arabic numerals, accompanies the quotations. There is a very helpful three-volume text with commentary by J. J. O'Donnell (1992) *Augustine: Confessions,* vol. 1: Introduction and text, vols 2–3: Commentary. (Oxford, Clarendon Press, 1992)

civ.   The City of God (*De civitate dei*)

H. Bettenson (trans.) *Saint Augustine: City of God* (Harmondsworth, Penguin Books, 1972).

doctr. chr.   On Christian Education (*de doctrina christiana*)

D. W. Robertson (trans.) *Saint Augustine: On Christian Doctrine* (New York, Macmillan, 1958)

mus.   On Music (*De musica*)

W. Jackson-Knight (trans.) *Saint Augustine's De Musica: a Synopsis* (London, Orthological Institute, 1949).

ut cred.   On the Usefulness of Believing (*De utilitate credendi*)

J. H. S. Burleigh (ed. and trans.) *Augustine: Earlier Writings*, Library of Christian Classics (London, SCM and Philadelphia, Pa., Westminster Press, 1953)

Other works cited

lib. arb.   On Free Choice of the Will (*de libero arbitrio*)

retr.   Retractations (*retractationes*)

mag.   On the Teacher (*De magistro*)

A general guide to texts and translations can be found in, for example, C. A. Kirwan, *Augustine* (London, Routledge, 1989, 225–33)

A. Di Beradino (ed.) *Patrology: Volume IV* (Westminster, Md., Christian Classics, Inc., 1991)

Descartes

CSM   Translations taken from *The Philosophical Writings of Descartes*, 3 vols, ed. and trans. J. Cottingham, R. Stoothoff, D. Murdoch (and for vol. III, A. J. Kenny), Cambridge, Cambridge University Press, 1984, 1985, 1991.

Secondary literature

Brown's biography remains the essential introduction:

Brown, P. R. L., *Augustine of Hippo: a Biography* (London, Faber, 1967).

    I have also quoted from his

Power and Persuasion in Late Antiquity: Towards a Christian Empire (Madison, Wis., University of Wisconsin Press, 1992).

Brown's chapters acknowledge the debt they owe to

Marrou, H. I. *Augustin et la fin de la culture antique*, 4th edn (Paris, de Broccard, 1958).

I have learnt most about Augustine on education from

Burnyeat, M. F. 'Wittgenstein and Augustine *De Magistro*', *Proceedings of the Aristotelian Society, Supplementary Volume* (1987), pp. 1–24.

and about the *De doctrina*, in addition to Brown's (1967) chapter, from

Williams, R. D. 'Language, reality and desire in Augustine's *De Doctrina*', *Journal of Literature and Theology* 3 (1989), pp. 138–50.

and about the classical traditions of educational theory and practice to which Augustine is so indebted from

Morgan, T. J., *Literate Education in the Hellenistic and Roman Worlds* (Cambridge, Cambridge University Press, 1998).

NOTES

1 From the Loeb Classical Library edition of Julian's works: *The Works of the Emperor Julian*, 3 vols, trans. Wilmer Cave Wright (London, William Heinemann and Cambridge, Mass., Harvard University Press, 1923), vol. 3, p. 117.

2 Both quotations are from the Loeb Classical Library: *Plutarch's Moralia*, 16 vols, trans. Frank Cole Babbit (London, William Heinemann and Cambridge, Mass., Harvard University Press, 1927), vol. 1.

3 Loeb, *Julian*, vol. 3, pp. 119–21.

4 Translation adapted from that in Loeb Classical Library: *Select Letters of St Jerome*, trans. F. A. Wright (London, William Heinemann and Cambridge, Mass., Harvard University Press, 1933).

5 *Pale Fire* (London, Everyman's Library, 1992), p. 67.

I would like in particular to thank, for their comments and assistance, Teresa Morgan and Malcolm Schofield. All errors, of course, are entirely my own.

6

AUGUSTINIAN LEARNING

Philip L. Quinn

How can people learn to understand the truth? Augustine of Hippo tries to answer this question about the education of the mind in *The Teacher* (*De magistro*). There he refutes the knowledge-transfer model of education, according to which a teacher transfers knowledge to a learner by means of speech or writing. The teacher transfers knowledge by encoding it into language and uttering the appropriate sounds; the learner, hearing the utterances and knowing the language, decodes language back into thoughts. Augustine formulates the transfer model as follows: "Nor is there any other reason for signifying, or for giving signs, except for bringing forth and transferring to another mind the action of the mind in the person who makes the sign" (*On Christian Doctrine* 2.2.2). Augustine's alternative view is that much, if not all, of what we know we learn from the teacher within, who is Christ. How can people learn to do the good? Augustine narrates in his *Confessions* an account of how his own heart was educated and he was brought to do the good. His story refutes the naïve view that knowing the good is sufficient for doing it. He holds that God had to convert him before he was able to commit himself firmly to doing the good.

In this essay I examine Augustine's answers to these questions about the education of mind and heart. I try to show that they are quite plausible within the framework of traditional Christianity. I also argue that even those who reject that framework should acknowledge that Augustine addresses important educational issues.

AUGUSTINE ON THE TEACHER WITHIN

The Teacher is a dialogue in which Augustine's interlocutor is his son, Adeodatus. It deals with problems in the philosophy of language: for instance, how does language connect with the world? Augustine and Adeodatus try to understand how we learn what is signified by signs that signify non-signs. They examine the hypothesis that ostensive teaching can exhibit the thing signified to the senses. They recognize that learning by ostension presents a problem. Suppose you ask me what the word "red" signifies, and I show you a red color patch. How do you learn that the patch's color rather than its shape is signified by the word and that the particular shade of the patch's color is not what is signified by the word? Augustine and Adeodatus agree that intelligent people somehow manage to learn ostensively despite such ambiguities. And so Augustine begins the monologue that takes up the last quarter of the

81

work by concluding that "some people can be taught some things without signs" (*The Teacher* 10.32.103). This conclusion is consistent with the further claim that some people can also be taught some things through signs, through the medium of language.

But Augustine argues for the stronger thesis that "nothing is learned through its signs" (*The Teacher* 10.33.115), and this thesis is inconsistent with the knowledge-transfer model of education. He initially presents the argument as a version of the learner's paradox. Signs can draw our attention to or prompt us to search for the sensible things they signify. But we do not know what they signify until we have sensed those things, and only then do we know that they are signs. Once we do know that they are signs, however, presenting them to us can only serve to remind us of something we already know. Augustine thus endorses the following argument for words signifying sensible things: "we either know what they signify or we don't; if we know, then it's reminding rather than learning; but if we don't know, it isn't even reminding, though perhaps we recollect that we should inquire" (*The Teacher* 11.36. 15–18).

Augustine divides the things we perceive into the sensible and the intelligible. He says: "Everything we perceive, we perceive either by one of the bodily senses or by the mind" (*The Teacher* 12.39.9). He also maintains that "someone who presents what I want to know to my eyes, or to any of my bodily senses, or even to my mind itself, does teach me something" (*The Teacher* 11.36.3–4). In other words, teaching consists in one person bringing it about that something is shown or presented to another person who desires to know. I can teach what the color red is because, by means of a color patch, I can show or present the color red to another's sense of vision. Though nature is not a person and hence, strictly speaking, not a teacher, we can learn from nature because it shows or presents things to our bodily senses. As Augustine notes, nature can and does "show and display to those paying attention, by themselves, this sun and the light pervading and clothing all things present, the moon and the other stars, the lands and the seas, and the countless things begotten in them" (*The Teacher* 10.32.110–14).

But neither nature nor I can show or present to anyone intelligible things that can only be perceived by the mind. I can, of course, utter the English word "two" or inscribe the arabic numeral "2," and this word and that numeral signify the number two. They do not, however, show or present the number two to the bodily senses; nor do they show or present it directly to the mind. So I cannot teach anyone what the number two is. Nature cannot do so either. Augustine thinks God can. He tells us:

> When we deal with things that we perceive by the mind, namely by the intellect and reason, we're speaking of things that we look upon immediately in the inner light of Truth, in virtue of which the so-called inner man is illuminated and rejoices. Under these conditions our listener, if he likewise sees these things with his inward and undivided eye, knows what I'm saying from his own contemplating, not from my words. Therefore, when I'm stating truths, I don't even teach the person who is looking upon these truths. He's taught not by my words but by the things themselves made manifest within when God discloses them.
>
> (*The Teacher* 12.40.29–37)

In short, God teaches us about intelligible things by showing or presenting them directly to our minds.

The suggestion that our understanding of formal logic and mathematics depends upon some sort of inner vision or illumination has considerable plausibility. Many of us have had the experience of going over the steps of a mathematical proof without understanding how the proof works; only after a flash of insight do we come to understand the proof. There is a cognitive difference between our situation before and after the flash of insight. Like Augustine, we often describe this difference with visual metaphors.

There is some reason to believe that Augustine intends this account of divine illumination to cover more than our knowledge of such subjects as logic and mathematics. In a famous passage, he boldly claims:

> Regarding each of the things we understand, however, we don't consult a speaker who makes sounds outside us, but the Truth that presides within over the mind itself, though perhaps words prompt us to consult Him. What is more, He Who is consulted, He Who is said to *dwell in the inner man*, does teach: Christ – that is, *the unchangeable power and everlasting wisdom of God*, which every rational soul does consult, but is disclosed to anyone, to the extent that he can apprehend it, according to his good or evil will.

> (*The Teacher* 11.38.44–51)

So apparently Augustine thinks that Christ, God the Son and the teacher within, explains how we understand any of the things we really do understand.

Some explanation is needed for Augustine's choice of Christ to play the role of the teacher within. Augustine believes that God is a trinity of persons. Hence he asks whether the teacher within is one of these persons acting alone, two of them acting together in the absence of the third, or all three acting in concert. Introspection yields no answer to this question. Augustine thinks scripture, which he takes to be revealed truth, points to the answer he favors. The scriptural texts from which he derives his answer are alluded to by the phrases emphasized in the passage quoted above. The first is Ephesians 3: 16–17: "I pray that, according to the riches of his glory, he may grant that you may be strengthened in your inner being with power through his Spirit, and that Christ may dwell in your hearts through faith, as you are being rooted and grounded in love." This suggests that the teacher within is the Holy Spirit, Christ or both. The second text is 1 Corinthians 22–4: "For Jews demand signs and Greeks desire wisdom, but we proclaim Christ crucified, a stumbling block to Jews and foolishness to Gentiles, but to those who are the called, both Jews and Greeks, Christ the power of God and the wisdom of God." It seems fitting that the wisdom of God personified should impart understanding to us, and so Christ's claim on the role of the teacher within has, as Augustine sees it, the support of scriptural authority.

How does Christ play the role of the teacher within? I think it would be a mistake to suppose that he does so by means of some inner analogue of human speech. Such divine speech would give the learner nothing more than signs for intelligible things that are only perceived by the mind. It could not guarantee that the learner understood what is signified by such signs. Such a supposition would merely replicate at the level of the divine teacher the problem Augustine believes human teachers confront. According to Augustine, humans teach by showing or presenting to the learner sensible things signified by signs for them. It seems to me best to think of the divine teacher as operating in an analogous fashion. Christ teaches by showing or presenting directly to the learner's mind, not signs for intelligible things, but the intelligible things signified by such signs. This is what seems to me to be suggested by the claim quoted above that we are taught about intelligible things by the things themselves made manifest within when God discloses them. In short, like human teaching, divine teaching is showing rather than telling. The difference is that the divine teacher can show the learner's mind intelligible things and human teachers cannot.

I am inclined to think that Christians can reasonably endorse Augustine's claim that Christ is the teacher within. It is not refuted by the fact that non-Christians often succeed in understanding things at least as well as Christians do, for Christ might operate within the minds of non-Christians unbeknownst to them. The doctrine of the teacher within is supposed to explain certain cognitive achievements. Like other explanatory theories, it is entitled to postulate unobservable occurrences in order to explain observable phenomena. Christ could be at work in any human person's mind without the person being introspectively aware of it.

There are, of course, rivals to Augustine's identification of the teacher within with Christ. According to Descartes, the role of the teacher within is played by the stock of innate ideas and the natural light of reason with which God endows people when he creates them. According to modern naturalists, the role of the teacher within could be played by hardwired cognitive dispositions that form part of our evolutionary legacy. So it is only to be expected that there will be disagreement about who or what the teacher within is even among those who agree that something must be postulated to play the role of the teacher within.

Is it plausible to suppose that we need to postulate an inner teacher of some sort in order to explain some of our cognitive achievements? I think that, by means of examples, it can be made at least somewhat plausible in cases where we understand non-sensible truths. Augustine provides an example in his *Confessions*, when he describes his struggles to interpret Genesis 1: 2: "The earth was invisible and without form [*Terra erat invisibilis et incomposita*]."

> I used to use the word formless not for that which lacked form but for that which had a form such that, if it had appeared, my mind would have experienced revulsion from its extraordinary and bizarre shape, and my human weakness would have been plunged into confusion. But the picture I had in mind was not the privation of all form, but that which is relatively formless by comparison with more beautiful shapes. True reasoning convinced me that I should wholly subtract all remnants of every kind of form if I wished to conceive the absolutely formless. I could not achieve this. I found it easier to suppose something deprived of all form to be non-existent than to think that something could stand between form and nothingness, neither endowed with form nor nothing, but formless and so almost nothing.
>
> (*Confessions* 12.6.6)

Unless he can interpret the sentence "The earth was invisible and without form" in a satisfactory fashion, Augustine thinks he cannot find within himself the truth it expresses. Although he can believe that the sentence "The earth was invisible and without form" is true, he cannot grasp its truth. He can get out of his predicament if he can figure out for himself, consulting the teacher within, what the sentence means or what proposition it expresses. Faithful to his own understanding of who the teacher within is, Augustine praises God for "all that you disentangled for me in examining this question" (*Confessions* 12.6.6).

Augustine concludes his assault on the knowledge-transfer model of education by pointing out cases in which speech does not convey to the hearer the thoughts of the speaker. They include lies and other deceptions, recitations of a memorized speech when the speaker's mind is on something else, slips of the tongue, misunderstandings and mis-hearings. But even if such cases are set aside and it is granted that the hearer grasps the thoughts of the speaker, Augustine argues, the hearer does not thereby learn whether what the speaker has said is true. Instead, he claims, "when the teachers have explained by means of words all the disciplines they profess, even the disciplines of virtue and of wisdom, then those who are called 'students' consider within themselves whether truths have been stated" (*The Teacher* 14.45.5–8). They do this by consulting the teacher within, and that is the point at which they learn. The illusion that students learn from their human teachers arises, Augustine suggests, because there is usually no delay between the time of speaking and the time of learning. "Since they are quick to learn internally after the prompting of the lecturer," he says, "they suppose that they have learned externally from the one who prompted them" (*The Teacher* 14.45.15–16).

Teachers of many subjects could learn a becoming modesty from Augustine's refutation of the knowledge-transfer model of education. For example, a mathematician who walks into a classroom and writes on the blackboard a proof of some theorem she knows should be aware that she is not thereby transferring her knowledge into the minds of the students who copy the proof into their notebooks. Even if the bright students understand the proof right away, others will have to pore over their notebooks after class before they see for themselves how the proof goes. All the students in the class will have to acquire for themselves an understanding of the proof. To be sure, our mathematician will typically provide some commentary intended to facilitate understanding along with her presentation of the proof. But she should also be aware that, though such commentary may prompt understanding, it is not by itself guaranteed to produce it. Understanding of the proof requires the cooperation of something within the learner, whether it be literally an inner teacher who is a divine person, as Augustine thought, or the activation of some cognitive disposition that is not itself a person, as others suppose. Of course good mathematics teachers are at least tacitly aware of these things. But perhaps some helpful conversations about how teachers can prompt and facilitate the learning of their students would ensue if this awareness were made more explicit in discussions of mathematical pedagogy.

I think the point I have tried to make in terms of the imaginary mathematician of my example can be applied to the teachers of quite a few other subjects. At any rate, I would apply it to teachers of any science that has a good deal of theoretical content and to teachers of any of the humanities that involve interpreting difficult texts. Much of what such teachers do is not imparting understanding; it is instead prompting students to acquire it for themselves. Once this point has been made explicit, I expect that it will seem almost blindingly obvious to those among my fellow philosophers who, year after year, work through with their students such texts as Plato's *Parmenides*, Aristotle's *Nicomachean Ethics*, Spinoza's *Ethics*, or Kant's *Critique of Pure Reason*.

AUGUSTINE ON THE RESTLESS HEART

In the discussion of teaching by preaching in *On Christian Doctrine* (*De doctrina christiana*), Augustine considers the problem of how to address those who know what ought to be done yet do not do it. For him, an important part of moral education involves persuading people to do what they ought to do, and merely instructing them about what they ought to do is not always sufficient to persuade them to do it. "And perhaps when the necessary things are learned," Augustine says, "they may be so moved by a knowledge of them that it is not necessary to move them further by greater powers of eloquence. But when it is necessary, it is to be done, and it is necessary when they know what should be done but do not do it" (*On Christian Doctrine* 4.12.28). He recommends a subdued rhetorical style for instruction and a grand style for persuasion, claiming that the teacher "persuades in the grand style that those things which we know should be done are done, although they have not yet been done" (4.25.55). When there is resistance to doing what ought to be done, teaching in the grand style is aimed at "moving an adverse mind to conversion" (4.19.38). But conversion cannot be achieved without divine assistance. Augustine tells us:

> Medicines for the body which are administered to men by men do not help them unless health is conferred by God, who can cure without them; yet they are nevertheless applied even though they are useless without His aid. And if they are applied courteously, they are considered to be among works of mercy or kindness. In the same way, the benefits of teaching profit the mind when they are applied by men, when assistance is granted by God, who could have given the gospel to man even though it came not from men nor through a man.
>
> (*On Christian Doctrine* 4.16.33)

Since an attempt at persuasion will succeed only if God assists it, anyone who engages in moral teaching "should pray that God may place a good speech in his mouth" (*On Christian Doctrine* 4.30.63). And when the speech of moral teachers does persuade, "for the profitable result of their speech they should give thanks to Him from whom they should not doubt they have received it, so that he who glories may glory in Him in whose hand are both we and our words" (4.30.63). According to Augustine, then, there is in many human lives a large gap between knowing what ought to be done and doing it, a chasm so wide that it cannot be crossed without the divine action needed to produce a conversion.

As his *Confessions* reveals, Augustine's awareness of this gap comes in large part from his own experience. Augustine thinks that we all do – and ought to – pursue happiness, which he equates with seeking to experience joy. As he sees it, all humans aspire to be happy. He remarks that if people "are asked whether they would like to be happy, each would at once say without the least hesitation, that he would choose to be so" (*Confessions* 10.21.31). For Augustine, the happy life consists of joy grounded in and caused by God, but he is well aware that many people are mistaken about where to find happiness: they do not want to find in God their source of joy. Before his conversion, he himself was such a person. But his view as a Christian convert is this: "The happy life is joy based on the truth. This is joy grounded in you, O God, who are the truth" (10.23.33). His conversion narrative relates how he came to hold this view and then to act on it.

Augustine begins his *Confessions* by addressing God, telling him that "our heart is restless until it rests in you" (1.1.1). His narrative is thus to be an account of the searchings of his own restless heart. Even as an infant, Augustine thinks, he was already sinfully separated from God, manifesting in his behavior the consequences of original sin. "Yet, for an infant of that age," he asks, "could it be reckoned good to use tears in trying to obtain what it would have been harmful to get, to be vehemently indignant at the refusals of free and older people and of parents or many other people of good sense who would not yield to my whims, and to attempt to strike them and to do as much injury as possible?' (*Confessions* 1.7.11). He describes himself when a schoolboy as dying because of his alienation from God. Augustine takes his youthful self to task thus: "I abandoned you to pursue the lowest things of your creation. I was dust going to dust" (1.13.21). He confesses that his education only encouraged him by bad examples to move away from God. "When one considers the men proposed to me as models for my imitation," he says, "it is no wonder that in this way I was swept along by vanities and travelled right away from you, my God" (1.18.28). Augustine the youth was, therefore, not at rest in God but in motion away from God.

Augustine the adolescent added sexual sins to his other offenses. He tells God: "I travelled very far from you, and you did not stop me. I was tossed about and split, scattered and boiled dry in my fornications. And you were silent" (*Confessions* 2.2.2). Yet God was not far from Augustine. "For you were always with me," he says to God, "mercifully punishing me, touching with a bitter taste all my illicit pleasures" (2.2.4). Nor was God really silent. Augustine's mother, Monica (who was a Christian), admonished him not to fall into fornication and above all not to commit adultery. At the time, Augustine regarded these warnings as womanish advice he would have blushed to notice. "But they were your warnings," he now confesses to God, "and I did not realize it. I believed you were silent, and that it was only she who was speaking, when you were speaking to me through her" (2.3.7). What most perplexed him about his adolescent behavior was an instance of evil-doing for its own sake. He stole some pears, even though he already had pears in plenty and of much better quality. "It was foul," he says, "and I loved it" (2.4.9). "What could I not have done," he asks himself, "when I loved gratuitous crime" (2.7.15). As an adolescent, he thinks, he became a region of destitution.

Augustine went to Carthage to study rhetoric. He was then still moving away from God. "My stiff neck took me further and further away from you," he says to God, "I loved my own ways, not yours. The liberty I loved was merely that of a runaway" (*Confessions* 3.3.5). Reading Cicero's *Hortensius* kindled in Augustine a love for philosophy. He says of this book that it "altered my prayers, Lord, to be toward you yourself" and that it "gave me different values and priorities" (3.4.7). So this event seems to Augustine to mark the beginning of his return to God. At the time, however, not much came of his new love for philosophy because he fell in with Manichees and adopted their errors. "While travelling away from truth," he says, "I thought I was going towards it" (3.7.12). He recounts one of Monica's dreams. In the dream, she was standing on a wooden rule and mourning Augustine's heretical commitments. A young man appeared and asked her to explain her grief. When she had done so, the young man told her to look and see that Augustine was also with her, where she was on the rule. Augustine proposed interpreting the dream as a prediction that Monica would become a Manichee. Monica immediately replied that she had not been told in the dream that, where he was, there she would also be, but that, where she was, there he would also be. Augustine confesses: "I was more moved by your answer through my vigilant mother than by the dream itself. My misinterpretation seemed very plausible" (3.11.20). At the time, of course, Augustine would not have acknowledged that God was answering him through Monica's reply, since he was then taken in by the apparent plausibility of his interpretation of her dream. So for a second time Augustine recounts that he failed to receive a message God tried to communicate to him through Monica.

Augustine remained a Manichee for several years. He confesses that he thought of God not as immaterial but as "like a luminous body of immense size and myself a bit of that body" (*Confessions* 4.16.31). He tells God: "I did not dedicate my courage to you, but I travelled away from you into a far country to dissipate my substance on meretricious lusts" (4.16.30). He laments that he had even departed from himself: "Where was I when I was seeking for you? You were there before me, but I had departed from myself. I could not even find myself, much less you" (5.2.2). Eventually he became disillusioned with the Manichees, in large part because of their arrogant pretense to have scientific knowledge of matters of which they were actually ignorant. He moved from Carthage to Rome and then to Milan, where he encountered Bishop Ambrose. Although Ambrose's preaching convinced him that Catholicism could be defended against the criticism of the Manichees, he was not ready to accept the Catholic faith. "Accordingly, after the manner of the Academics, as popularly understood," says Augustine, "I doubted everything, and in the fluctuating state of total suspense of judgment I decided I must leave the Manichees, thinking at that period of my skepticism that I should not remain a member of a sect to which I was now preferring certain philosophers" (5.14.25). Unwilling to entrust the care of his soul to these philosophers, he decided to follow the precedent of his parents and to become a catechumen in the Catholic Church.

His study of Catholicism led Augustine to think that he had previously been mistaken about its teachings. "Even if it was not yet evident that the Church taught the truth," he remarks, "yet she did not teach the things of which I harshly accused her. So I was confused with shame. I was being turned around" (*Confessions* 6.4.5). He describes himself as deeply conflicted, in a paradoxical state of motion both toward and away from God. Worldly ambition and fleshly lusts retained their grip on him; they were, he says, "pushing my heart to and fro" (6.11.20). He tells God: "I longed for the happy life, but was afraid of the place where it has its seat, and fled from it at the same time as I was seeking for it" (6.11.20). To express his fear in another vivid way, he says: "Fettered by the flesh's morbid impulse and lethal sweetness, I dragged my chain, but was afraid to be free of it" (6.12.21).

From the books of the neo-Platonists, Augustine got what was needed to overcome all intellectual obstacles to adopting the Catholic faith. He confesses to God: "I no longer had my usual excuse to explain why I did not yet despise the world and serve you, namely, that my perception of the truth was uncertain. By now I was indeed quite sure about it. Yet I was still bound down to the earth" (*Confessions* 8.5.11). Now Augustine knew what he ought to do, and now the stage was fully set for his conversion.

Augustine and his friend Alypius were staying at a villa in Milan. One day Ponticianus, a fellow North African and high imperial official, paid them a visit on some unspecified business. By chance he noticed a book on a table, picked it up and discovered it was the epistles of Paul. When Augustine indicated that he was very interested in the epistles, Ponticianus, who was a Christian, made some remarks about the Egyptian monk Antony, of whom Augustine and Alypius had never heard. Ponticianus went on to tell a story about how two of his colleagues had converted to Christianity after reading a life of Antony. While he was telling the story something extraordinary happened to Augustine. He tells God:

> You took me up from behind my own back where I had placed myself because I did not wish to observe myself, and you set me before my face so that I should see how vile I was, how twisted and filthy, covered in sores and ulcers. And I looked and was appalled, but there was no way of escaping from myself. If I tried to avert my gaze from myself, his story continued relentlessly, and you once again placed me in front of myself; you thrust me before my own eyes so that I should discover my iniquity and hate it.
>
> (*Confessions* 8.7.16)

It seems to Augustine that God is putting pressure on him to act on his knowledge of what he ought to do. But Augustine does not yet act.

When Ponticianus had left, Augustine, in torment, rushed out into the villa's garden, followed by Alypius. In the agony of his hesitation, Augustine made gestures of the kind people make when they want to achieve something but lack the ability to do so. He says: "I was twisting and turning in my chain until it would break completely; I was now only a little bit held by it, but I was still held" (*Confessions* 8.11.25). His struggle continued, and the pressure on him mounted. He describes the situation as follows.

> Inwardly I said to myself: Let it be now, let it be now. And by this phrase I was already moving towards a decision; I had almost taken it, and then I did not do so. Yet I did not relapse into my original condition, but stood my ground very close to the point of deciding and recovered my breath. Once more I made the attempt and came only a little short of my goal; only a little short of it – yet I did not touch it or hold onto it. I was hesitating whether to die to death and to live to life. Ingrained evil had more hold over me than unaccustomed good. The nearer approached the moment of time when I would become different, the greater the horror of it struck me. But it did not thrust me back nor turn me away, but left me in a state of suspense.
>
> (*Confessions* 8.11.25)

Even though he wanted to do it, Augustine was unable to decide to cross the gap between knowing what he ought to do and actually doing it. He portrays himself as lacking the wherewithal to reach his goal under his own steam.

Weeping, Augustine moved away from Alypius and threw himself down under a fig tree. He interrogated himself: "'How long, how long is it to be?' 'Tomorrow, tomorrow.' 'Why not now? Why not an end to my impure life in this very hour?'" (*Confessions* 8.12.28). And then a second extraordinary thing happened to Augustine. The part of the narrative most of us already know about deserves to be quoted at length:

> As I was saying this and weeping in the bitter agony of my heart, suddenly I heard a voice from the nearby house chanting as if it might be a boy or girl (I do not know which), saying and repeating over and over again "Pick up and read, pick up and read." At once my countenance changed, and I began to think intently whether there might be some sort of children's game in which such a chant is used. But I could not remember having heard of one. I checked the flood of tears and stood up. I interpreted it solely as a divine command to me to open the book and read the first chapter I might find. For I had heard how Antony happened to be present at the gospel reading, and took it as an admonition addressed to himself when the words were read: "Go, sell all you have, give to the poor, and you shall have treasure in heaven; and come, follow me" (Matthew 19: 21). By such an inspired utterance he was immediately converted to you. So I hurried back to the place where Alypius was sitting. There I had put down the book of the apostle when I got up. I seized it, opened it and read the first passage on which my eyes lit: "Not in riots and drunken parties, not in eroticism and indecencies, not in strife and rivalry, but put on the Lord Jesus Christ and make no provision for the flesh in its lusts" (Romans 13: 13–14).
>
> I neither wished nor needed to read further. At once, with the last words of this sentence, it was as if a light of relief from all anxiety flooded into my heart. All the shadows of doubt were dispelled.
>
> (*Confessions* 8.12.29)

The language of decision, which featured so prominently in *Confessions* 8.11.25, has disappeared from Augustine's account; the language is now the language of being overcome. Rejecting his former way of life and adopting a new one was not something Augustine decided to do but something he found himself doing. Augustine confirms that he was a passive participant in the event of his conversion when he says to God that "the effect of your converting me to yourself was that I did not now seek a wife and had no ambition for success in this world" (8.12.30). And he is even more explicit about this passivity when he later on says this to God: "You command continence; grant what you command, and command what you will" (10.29.40). Before, Augustine had failed to acknowledge that God was speaking to him through Monica's words and trying to communicate with him through her dream; now he takes it for granted that God is commanding him through the eerie childish chant, *tolle lege, tolle lege*, and through the sentence he reads from the book of epistles. An artful back reference to Monica's dream reminds us of the contrast. Augustine says: "I stood firm upon that rule of faith on which many years before you had revealed me to her" (8.12.30). The wooden rule of the dream has now been transfigured into the rule of Christian faith. God has enabled Augustine to do what he had come to know he ought to do. Augustine's restless heart has been brought to its place of repose.

What lessons about moral education are to be learned from Augustine's conversion narrative? Christians will recognize in it the familiar idea that Christian faith is a gift of grace and not something humans can bring about in themselves. They may also find attractive Augustine's suggestion that even moral virtues such as continence cannot be acquired without divine assistance. I am particularly struck by Augustine's conviction that God tried to communicate with him through Monica's words and her dream and succeeded in communicating with him through the childish chant he heard and the scriptural passage he read in the garden in Milan. If he is right about this, a properly Christian education would include training in being open to the possibility and sensitive to the prospect that God speaks to us through human discourse contained in such things as oral sermons and written scriptures. More generally, a theistic pedagogy should not start from the assumption that the only way God could speak is by means of a booming voice resounding from the heavens. It should also take seriously the idea that God communicates with humans through dreams, by means of the quiet inner voice of conscience, and in other ways as well.

If Augustinian Christians do take this idea seriously, they will want to find a way to identify genuine divine communications. They will face a problem that also confronts those who experience mystical visions and voices and wonder which of them come from God and which come from Satan or other sources. Spanish mystics such as John of the Cross and Teresa of Avila respond to this problem by proposing that visions and voices come from God just in case they cohere with scripture and tradition. I think Augustinian Christians can and should adopt this proposal. The coherence criterion will, of course, work best as a negative test for divine communication. There are clear cases of messages that are alleged to come from God but are inconsistent with the teachings of scripture or tradition. Positive coherence will be harder to establish. Christian tradition has many strands, and there are disagreements among Christians about the interpretation of scripture. Differences of opinion among Christians about which purported divine communications cohere well with scripture and tradition are therefore only to be expected.

There may, moreover, be a lesson of general interest in what Augustine has to say about what held him back from doing what he knew he ought to do in the period just before his conversion. He portrays himself as having a will divided against itself. When he reflects on his condition immediately before his conversion, he has this to say:

> In my own case, as I deliberated about serving my Lord God which I had long been disposed to do, the self which willed to serve was identical with the self which was unwilling. It was I. I was neither wholly willing nor wholly unwilling. So I was in conflict with myself and was dissociated from myself. The dissociation came about against my will. Yet this was not a manifestation of the nature of an alien mind but the punishment suffered in my own mind. And so it was "not I" that brought this about "but sin which dwelt in me," sin resulting from the punishment of a more freely chosen sin, because I was a son of Adam.
>
> (*Confessions* 8.10.22)

The words Augustine quotes are from scripture; they are part of a famous Pauline self-description. Paul says:

> I do not understand my own actions. For I do not do what I want, but I do the very thing I hate. Now if I do what I do not want, I agree that the law is good. But in fact it is no longer I that do it, but sin that dwells within me. For I know that nothing good dwells within me, that is, in my flesh. I can will what is right, but I cannot do it. For I do not do the good I want, but the evil I do not want is what I do. Now if I do what I do not want, it is no longer I that do it, but sin that dwells within me.
>
> (Romans 7: 15–20)

Augustine's ascription to himself of a pre-conversion state of inner conflict has scriptural backing. He believes that, like Paul, he had been in the post-Adamic fallen condition which blocks even those who know the good from doing it.

Perhaps we can better understand Augustine's plight if we put part of what he says in a different vocabulary. Before his conversion, Augustine regularly acted on first-order desires for pleasures of the flesh and worldly fame, but he had also acquired a second-order desire not to have those first-order desires. He was, however, not able completely to subdue or to uproot the first-order desires that he had renounced. After his conversion, he found himself without those first-order desires; he no longer desired a wife or worldly success. Because God had freed him from his unwanted first-order desires, he could act from his knowledge of the good. I think Christians can reasonably accept at least this much of what Augustine says about his conversion. I also tend to think they can reasonably believe that Augustine's pre-conversion condition is the normal condition of fallen humanity apart from divine assistance. After all, Christians need not hold the exclusivist view that God gives grace only to Christians, and so they need not be committed to the silly view that only Christians get across the gap between knowing the good and doing it. And even if non-Christians do not accept the theology in Augustine's account of his conversion, they could understand his description of the change in psychology it produces.

Is there an alternative to waiting for divine assistance in getting people across the gap between knowing the good and doing it? If we are honest with ourselves, I believe we must admit that we know little about how to empower those who know the good to act from their knowledge. Our schools seem increasingly to be failing to perform this task for us. All too often even a good family (or a good village) raises a child who seems to know the good without doing it. Augustine's Christian perspective is pessimistic about the hope of finding a naturalistic technique comparable to grace. Such a technique would involve exercising a great deal of control over human desires, reliably implanting desires for the good and extirpating contrary desires. The hope for a technique of this sort seems Utopian. And even if such control of first-order desires is possible, its exercise may be unacceptably manipulative or coercive. So perhaps the most humans can or should hope to be able to achieve by way of solving this particular problem of moral education is to furnish occasions on which divine action may close the gap between knowing the good and doing it. Or, in the absence of faith in divine assistance, maybe our best hope is to do what we can to convert knowers into doers and then trust to luck for its occasional aid.

If Christians are pessimistic about merely human endeavors
knowing and doing the good, they must then face a new form of
does God, who is perfectly good, not intervene more frequently
good into doers of the good? A simple answer is that, for all we
the good but does not do it has been offered and has freel
Christian tradition contains the resources to provide theolog
who, like Augustine, view the gap between knowing and doing
Adam's original sin can point out that God is not responsible
of the gap. They can also point to a providential connectio
Paul's statement of it goes as follows: "Therefore just as one man's trespass
condemnation for all, so one man's act of righteousness leads to justification and life for
all. For just as by the one man's disobedience the many were made sinners, so by the one
man's obedience the many will be made righteous" (Romans 5: 18–19). And in a remarkable
liturgical passage we find Adam's fall described as a happy fault (*felix culpa*) because it
merited Christ, who is God the Son, as its Redeemer. It is sometimes said, not wholly in
jest, that original sin is the one Christian doctrine that receives overwhelming empirical
confirmation from our ordinary experience of human affairs. But it should never be
forgotten that Christianity's grand narrative is a story of both sin and salvation.

There are, I think, two lessons to be learned from this essay's discussion of Augustine.
First, when we teach, we typically facilitate learning but cannot impart knowledge. Second,
getting people to cross the gap between knowing what ought to be done and doing what they
ought to do is an intractable problem for moral education. Augustine has something
significant to offer contemporary thought about educating the mind and the heart.

BIBLIOGRAPHY AND ACKNOWLEDGMENTS

I have not quoted from secondary sources in the body of this essay; nor have I cited them in notes.
Nonetheless I am indebted to the work of other scholars. So I now wish to acknowledge my debts
and to point readers in the direction of the bibliographical resources I have found most useful in
thinking about the topics of this essay.

Scriptural quotations are from the *HarperCollins Study Bible*. Quotations from Augustine are from
the following translations: Augustine, *On Christian Doctrine*, trans. D. W. Robertson, Jr.
(Indianapolis, Ind., and New York, Bobbs-Merrill, 1958); Augustine, *Confessions*, trans. Henry
Chadwick (Oxford, Oxford University Press, 1991); and Augustine, *The Teacher*, in *Against the
Academicians and The Teacher*, trans. Peter King (Indianapolis, Ind. and Cambridge, Hackett, 1995).

Peter Brown's *Augustine of Hippo: a Biography* (Berkeley and Los Angeles, Calif., University of
California Press, 1967) is required reading for those interested in Augustine's life. Frederick J.
Crosson's "Show and tell: the concept of teaching in St Augustine's *De magistro*," in *De Magistro di
Agostino d'Ippona*, ed. Giovanni Scanavino (Palermo-Rocca, Edizioni Augustinus, 1993) and Peter
King's "Introduction," in Augustine, *Against the Academicians and The Teacher*, trans. Peter King
(Indianapolis, Ind. and Cambridge, Hackett, 1995) provide helpful analyses of the arguments of *The
Teacher*. Christopher Kirwan's *Augustine* (London and New York, Routledge and Kegan Paul, 1989)
treats Augustine's thoughts about language in the context of modern philosophy of language. Gareth
B. Matthews's *Thought's Ego in Augustine and Descartes* (Ithaca, NY and London, Cornell University
Press, 1992) contains a chapter devoted to Augustine's doctrine of the teacher within. And Nicholas
Wolterstorff's *Divine Discourse: Philosophical Reflections on the Claim that God Speaks* (Cambridge,

University Press, 1995) emphasizes the role of divine speech in bringing about s conversion.

grateful to Kent Emery, Jr., for a timely reminder, to Fred Crosson for giving me a copy paper by him referred to in the previous paragraph, and to Amélie Rorty for tough but very pful criticism of my first and second drafts.

7

AQUINAS'S CRITIQUE OF EDUCATION: AGAINST HIS OWN AGE, AGAINST OURS

Alasdair MacIntyre

Against his own age? Standard histories of medieval philosophy give so much attention to Aquinas's thought that their readers may inadvertently conclude not only that Aquinas was an outstanding philosopher and theologian, but also that he was generally recognized as such by his contemporaries. Yet he was in important respects a marginal figure, an outsider. The ecclesiastical condemnation of 1277, three years after his death, was in part aimed at his opinions. The Franciscan theological tradition then and later viewed his writings as a source of error. In the perspective of some of the conservative Augustinians of his own time he must have seemed to be a more than usually evasive Latin Averroist. And to most of the Latin Averroists he would have appeared as someone unable to accept the full implications of Aristotelian philosophy. He had opponents even in the Dominican order and those Dominicans who after his death continued to study and teach the *Summa theologiae* too often understood it as a series of treatises, some more worth studying than others, so failing to grasp the overall structure and direction of Aquinas's thought. The issues that thus divided Aquinas from so many of his contemporaries extended beyond substantive questions of philosophy and theology to matters of the curriculum. And, as the curriculum changed, during and after Aquinas's lifetime, it was not in the direction that he would have taken it.

Against ours? It might seem that the quarrels between Aquinas and his academic contemporaries were so much a matter of issues peculiar to the thirteenth century in the Latin West that our interest in them could only be historical. But the same premises from which Aquinas argued against his thirteenth-century opponents put him equally at odds with the liberal academic culture of universities in late twentieth-century North America. That culture presents itself as tolerantly hospitable to many standpoints: positivist, pragmatist, Heideggerian, deconstructivist, libertarian, neo-Marxist – the list is indefinitely long. And it is prepared to find a place for all these standpoints within its curriculum. But it is not the least important fact about the Thomism of Aquinas – although not necessarily about all later versions of Thomism – that it cannot be added to this list, that it has to exclude itself from that culture by opposing itself to that culture's educational inclusiveness. To explain why is the task of this paper.

I

It would be all too easy to extract from Aquinas's writings a variety of passages on topics relevant to education – observations about the liberal arts, remarks about the order of the curriculum, theses on learning and on teaching – and to fabricate a collage with the title "Aquinas's philosophy of education." But it would be an act of gross misrepresentation, and this for more than one reason.

First, Aquinas had no philosophy of education. The works from which the materials for such a collage would have to be extracted contribute to a variety of philosophical disciplines: ethics, politics, metaphysics, theology. And it is from arguments whose concepts and premises belong to these disciplines that Aquinas derives his educational conclusions. Abstract those conclusions for the purposes of such a collage and you not only deprive them of justification, but remove them from the argumentative contexts which make them intelligible.

Second, with Aquinas's texts as with those of many philosophers a crucial question is always: Against whom is he writing here? Within what controversy is this or that particular contention to be situated? Philosophers characteristically invite us not simply to assert *p*, but to assert *p* rather than *q* or *r*, and we will often only understand the point of asserting *p*, if we know what *q* and *r* are. Aquinas from 1239, when at the age of 14 he first became a student of the liberal arts at the imperial *studium generale* in Naples, the earliest secular university in Europe, until the completion of his second period as a Regent Master at the University of Paris in 1270, had first as teachers and then as colleagues protagonists of a range of opposing views on whether and how the newly recovered works of Aristotle should be integrated into the established curriculum and what the implications for the reformation of that curriculum were. There was no way in which he, or any other university teacher, could have avoided taking sides.

The established curriculum, as it had emerged from the controversies of the twelfth century, was already open to question. On the one hand it represented a division of academic labor in which each of the disciplines of the *trivium* and the *quadrivium* and the hegemonic discipline of theology has been assigned its own territory. Each had its own modes of inquiry and its own body of authoritative texts. Each was thereby protected against interventions from without. On the other hand it had become difficult not to recognize that many of the inquiries of *philosophia* could not easily be accommodated within this scheme of the disciplines.

Theology in its development of a variety of *quaestiones* and of alternative solutions to the problems posed by them had drawn upon the resources of grammar and of dialectic. In so doing – in the work of Anselm, for instance – it had opened itself up to the possibility of questioning from the standpoint of dialectic. Controversies about universals, and about epistemology, whose participants drew upon a heterogeneous range of ancient sources, had a bearing on the concerns of various disciplines. When Hugh of St Victor (1096–1141) in the *Didascalion: de studio legendi* defended the study of the seven liberal arts as preparatory to theology, he already had to do so in the face of a variety of doubts and questions.

It is scarcely surprising then that the twelfth- and thirteenth-century recovery of Aristotle's metaphysical, ethical, political, psychological and natural scientific writings should have reopened older questions as well as posing new ones. How is the teaching of the *libri naturales* to be related to the teaching of Euclid's geometry, Boethius's arithmetic and Ptolemy's astronomy in the *quadrivium*? What are the implications of the teaching of the *Nicomachean Ethics* for theological ethics? What cognizance should theologians take of the *Metaphysics*? How is the study of dialectic to be extended to include the *Posterior Analytics* (translated by 1159, but only the subject of commentaries in the thirteenth century) as well as the other works of the *Organon*, already known in the translations of Boethius?

At Naples Aquinas's first university teachers had added Aristotle to the curriculum in a piecemeal way. Albert the Great, his teacher at the Dominican *studium generale* at Cologne, had expounded Augustinian theology in his classes, but also lectured on the texts of Aristotle, so making available to his students the knowledge that they needed to state the problems and difficulties posed by Aristotelianism, but without offering them any type of systematic resolution. In 1255, when Aquinas was still a *sententiarius*, a lecturer on Peter Lombard's *Sentences*, in the University of Paris – he was to become a Regent Master in Theology in 1256 – the arts faculty of that university adopted a new curriculum, prescribing the teaching of all Aristotle's known works. In so doing it put in question in a systematic way the relationship between its teaching and the teaching of the theology faculty.

There were two principal responses to that putting in question, that of conservative Augustinian theology and that of the so-called Latin Averroists. The most distinguished theologian among the conservative Augustinians at Paris, Bonaventure, admitted certain Aristotelian concepts into his theology, but in general opposed the influence of Aristotelianism and this because of his view of the relationship of Christian theology to philosophy. Without Christian theology philosophy is not merely incomplete, it inevitably leads to error. "Philosophical science is the way to other sciences, but to stop there is to fall into darkness" (*De septem donis spiritus sancti* 3,12). Philosophy therefore cannot be permitted the status of an independent form of inquiry. It is for theology to pass judgment on the claims of contending philosophies and Bonaventure invokes theological theses and arguments in order to adjudicate between the rival standpoints of Plato and Aristotle. Theology by reason of its grounding in revealed truth has hegemony over the other disciplines, since it alone points us to the one source of truth, the Word of God. And Jesus Christ, that Word incarnate, is the exemplar of a perfect human life.

The contrast with the Latin Averroists could not be sharper. Ibn Roschd, in his commentary on the *De anima*, had called Aristotle "the exemplar that nature found to manifest supreme human perfection" (III, 2). And the Paris Averroist Boethius of Dacia follows him in asserting that whoever does not lead the life of the philosopher does not lead the right life. "It is easier for a philosopher to be virtuous than anyone else" (*De summo bono sive de vita philosophiae*).[1] Among the Averroist propositions condemned by the Bishop of Paris in 1277 were that "Happiness is to be had in this life and not in another," that "Philosophers alone are the wise ones of the world" and that "The only good that can be achieved by human beings consists in the intellectual virtues."

So while the conservative Augustinians assert the dependence of philosophy on theology, the Averroists assert the independence of philosophy. And, while the conservative Augustinians assert that the end towards which human beings are directed by their nature is to be found only beyond this present world and can be known only from teaching that appeals to revelation, the Averroists assert that happiness, the ultimate end of human beings, is to be understood and achieved only through philosophical inquiry and that such happiness belongs to the life of this present world. It is in opposition to both that Aquinas redefines the relationship of theology to philosophy. And it is equally in opposition to both that he elaborates a unified conception of the human good, one that integrates Aristotelianism and Christian elements in its account of human powers, of the virtues needed for the development of those powers and of the social relationships through which human goods and the ultimate human good are achieved. It is this account of the human good that provides the premises for Aquinas's conclusions about the nature of teaching and learning and the kind of education that human beings need.

Human practices and activities are, on Aquinas's Aristotelian account, aimed at the achievement of a variety of heterogeneous ends: the goods that are ours by virtue of our animal nature and appetites, the goods that are specific to social animals capable of practical reasoning, the goods of particular theoretical inquiries that satisfy the desire for completed understanding, and the ultimate good to which all these other goods are ordered. We discover and identify – and sometimes go astray in discovering and identifying – those various goods through practical reasoning that afford expression and direction to our natural inclinations. It is first through practical reasoning and later by theoretical reflection upon practice that we discover and identify an ordering of those goods, such that each contributes to the complex unity of the kind of life that it is good and best for human beings to pursue.

Theology and philosophy, insofar as they give an account of human nature, human activity and human goods, in part address the same subject-matter. There is indeed that of which theology can speak about which philosophy can say nothing: truths known only from God's self-revelation, which provides faith with its object and theology with its premises. And there are types of question answers to which can be given only by philosophical inquiry in areas where theology has no competence. But there is also a range of central questions about human nature and the ends of human life that both theologians and philosophers need to address in order to carry through their respective inquiries. And on all these questions there is a single truth to be discovered and asserted, and not a truth-from-the-standpoint-of-philosophy asserted by reason and a truth-from-the-standpoint-of-faith, as at least one Averroist asserted (*De unitate intellectus* 123).[2] So theologians have to come to terms with philosophical arguments and not just with their conclusions, since they have to be assured both of the soundness of the philosophical arguments and of the consistency of the conclusions with their own interpretations of and deductions from revealed truth. But this is far from all.

Theologians cannot carry through their own work adequately who do not recognize that what they have to say about divine providence and human affairs, about divine law, human knowledge of it and human rebellion against it, and about redemption and grace can only be made intelligible in terms of an account of human powers, reasoning, will and choice and of the relationship of human beings to their ultimate good. But what theology needs in these respects can in large part only be supplied by philosophy. Theologians therefore have themselves to become philosophers and therefore have to engage systematically with the disagreements and debates of philosophers.

II

This integration of Augustinian theology with Aristotelian philosophy – so very much in conflict both with the spirit of conservative Augustinianism and with some of the central theses of the Averroists – is nowhere better exemplified than in the treatment of ethics in the two parts of the Second Part of the *Summa theologiae*, about which George Wieland has written, "The doctrine is unambiguously theological but philosophy is not discarded; on the contrary in the field of ethics philosophical thought is quite clearly determinative."[3] What are the philosophical arguments and conclusions that are thus determinative? They include not only Aquinas's account of the human good, of the nature of the virtues and of our rationally grounded knowledge of the natural law, but also his corresponding account of how human nature is directed towards that good, of the passions, will and intellect, of practical reasoning and of agency and choice.

Some features of that account need to be remarked. First, on the same grounds as Aristotle, Aquinas holds that there is one final end for human beings towards which they are directed by their nature as rational animals, that for the sake of which all else is done and which is itself a means to no further end (*Summa theologiae* Ia–IIae 1, 4). Good actions are those which direct us towards the achievement of that end. They are perfective, so that in performing them we become the kind of human beings able to achieve that end. Each individual, in achieving what she or he takes to be the goods of her or his life in this way rather than that, directs her- or himself to a single end, that of a life in which goods are so ordered (Ia–IIae 1, 5). But in so directing their lives individuals recurrently fail to direct themselves to their proper end as rational animals and they do so both by failing to recognize in what direction their good is to be found and by on particular occasions taking it to be good for them to perform some action that is in fact bad. What judgments or misjudgments they make and whether their actions are good or bad depends in the first instance on the relationship within each individual of intellect, will and passions.

Whether a particular individual judges and acts so as to achieve her or his good is a matter of whether and how far that individual has acquired the virtues of character, that temperateness which disciplines and educates the bodily appetites, that courage which orders our passions in their responses to threats of harm and danger, that justice which disposes the will rightly in relationship to others by giving to each her or his due, and that prudence which is the exercise of practical intelligence in relationship to the particulars of any given situation. Aquinas understands a range of other virtues as parts or aspects of these four cardinal virtues. The endurance involved in the exercise of patience is an aspect of courage. Untruthfulness is a failure in justice, since we owe to each other truth in our utterances.

What is indispensable to the acquisition of the virtues is the right kind of habituation. It is only in and through practice that the virtues can be acquired. Some individuals are more predisposed than others by their natural endowments to respond to training in habituation. And intellectual instruction concerning the virtues is only effective with those who already to some significant degree possess them (*Commentary on the* Nicomachean Ethics X, lect. XIV, 2139–47). Moreover without that directedness towards our good which results only from habituation in the moral virtues, so that they become stable and fixed dispositions, we lack the experiences that provide the subject-matter for moral inquiry. So it is relevant to ask of any philosopher who makes claims about the good what that philosopher's way of life is. Certainly we need to attend to that philosopher's arguments, but "in practical matters the truth of someone's assertion is tested more by deeds and way of life than even by argument" (*Commentary*, lect. XIII, 2132, a passage in which Aquinas not only quotes, but goes considerably beyond Aristotle). Theoretical understanding of goods and virtues requires prior practical formation in the kind of activity that is directed to our good, just because it involves the exercise of the virtues.

The happiness which is our final end is of course not just a matter of the exercise of the virtues. It can be attained only through a development of all our powers and, so far as the attainment of happiness in this-worldly terms is concerned, the actualization of our higher powers depends on and presupposes the actualization of our lower powers. In this area, says George Wieland, "the perfection of the lower faculties is a necessary condition for the perfection of the higher faculties."[4] It is "the whole human being," that in us which is animal as well as that which is rational, whose good has to be achieved (*Summa theologiae* Ia–IIae, 3, 3).

That good of the whole human being cannot be achieved by individuals in isolation and this for two reasons. First we need the aid and friendship of others at each stage in our lives, if we are to become able to perform the tasks of that stage. And second, the achievement of the good of each individual is inseparable from the achievement of the common good that is shared with those other individuals with whom she or he cooperates in making and sustaining a common life. That common good is always the good of some whole of which the individuals are parts and it is more and other than a summing of individual goods (*Summa theologiae* Ia–IIae 90, 2; IIa–IIae 58, 7). We are directed towards the common good by the precepts of the natural law, precepts of reason whose violation damages those relationships through which we can achieve the common good and so, each of us, our own individual good. And obedience to the precepts of the natural law both assists in our practical education into the virtues and requires on occasion the exercise of every one of the virtues (Ia–IIae 92,1, and 94, 3).

Aquinas has thus developed a scheme of the practical life defined in terms of goods, virtues, laws and the relationships between these three. This scheme is presupposed by and embodied in those activities directed by practical reasoning which exemplify good human practice. It is through reflection on such practice that the relevant set of truths about that scheme is discovered by the inquiries of theoretical reason. And nothing in that scheme, as I have outlined it so far, depends upon or derives from those truths of revelation that are matter for theology. From this an important conclusion emerges. Since it was that scheme – even if not only that scheme – which put Aquinas at odds with his contemporaries, both on substantive intellectual issues and consequently on questions of education, and since it is that scheme which nowadays puts Aquinas at odds with the liberal academic culture of North America, both on substantive intellectual issues and also on questions of education, we make a mistake, if we suppose that in either case it was and is only or primarily Aquinas's theological stances that involved and involves him in conflict. Aquinas's purely philosophical positions are by themselves sufficient to engender those conflicts.

Yet before we examine the implications of Aquinas's scheme for a critique of thirteenth- and twentieth-century education, it may be as well to reinforce this conclusion by considering briefly the relationship of Aquinas's theology to his philosophy.

III

What philosophers learn from theology, on Aquinas's view, is the incompleteness of their understanding, even at its best, and the limitations of their mode of inquiry. And philosophical understanding is not always at its best. Error and disagreement are endemic in philosophical inquiry (*Summa theologiae* IIa–IIae 2, 4) and even the best-founded of philosophical conclusions will always be open to further question. Yet philosophy can arrive at well-grounded conclusions about at least some aspects of its own inquiry. For it is such a conclusion that the ultimate end of human beings, their perfected happiness, cannot be any finite or created good, since no finite or created good could finally and completely satisfy human desire (Ia–IIae 2, 6 and 7). Only God could be that good, the God whose existence and goodness can be known through philosophical inquiry. But what we know from such inquiry, apart from and independently of God's self-revelation, about that perfect good is very little indeed. Philosophy can itself instruct us about that imperfect happiness which is our this-worldly end, but it can only instruct us about the limits of its own ability to instruct us, where the end of perfect happiness is concerned. To know what needs to be known about that relationship to God which is perfect happiness we first need the gift of faith.

It is by faith alone that we can understand the nature of our recurrent waywardness and willfulness in taking as our good, either in particular situations or in general, what is not our good and so falling into vicious habits. It is by faith alone that we can understand how only redemptive grace can rescue us from this sinfulness. It is by faith alone that we can understand that in addition to the moral virtues we need the theological virtues. And it is by faith alone that we can understand that charity is the form of all the virtues.

God summons us to acknowledge these and other truths of his self-revelation in the teaching of the Church. The teaching authority of the Church is owed recognition by secular political authority as well as by individuals. But from those who have not recognized the teaching authority of the Church or the truth of Christianity it cannot compel recognition. There is therefore a type of education that differentiates Christians from others, one that takes cognizance of the teaching of the Church concerning the supernatural end of human beings and how it is to be attained, and so goes beyond any education only directed towards the achievement of our this-worldly ends. But such a distinctively Christian education, while it complements, corrects, and completes a secular education, has to integrate into itself everything essential to an adequate secular education.

What Aquinas aspired to achieve and to a remarkable extent did achieve was then an integration of Aristotelianism into Christianity and not, as his opponents claimed, a revision of Christian doctrine designed to accord with Aristotelianism. But to achieve this he had at certain points to reinterpret and restate both Aristotelian and Augustinian theses and the way in which he did this often reveals a strong awareness of an internal tension between his philosophical and his theological positions, a tension that has to be creatively resolved. So it is for example in Aquinas's treatment of the virtues in the *Summa theologiae*, where a largely Aristotelian treatment of particular virtues is subsumed under a largely Augustinian account of the virtues in general, so that what at first seem at least different and possibly rival accounts of virtue each receive their due. It is true, as Mark Jordan says, that his attempt to synthesize the Aristotelian account with the Augustinian "succeeds . . . but only by subordinating Aristotle to Augustine."[5] Aristotle himself would have been surprised to discover that the moral virtues as he characterized them are incomplete virtues. But they remain, on Aquinas's account, virtues and virtues needed to achieve our natural ends. Here as elsewhere Aquinas's Christianity complements, corrects and completes, but does not displace his philosophical Aristotelianism. Some specifically theological issues were indeed central to his disagreements with his contemporaries and his theology, just because it is a theology of revealed truth, certainly puts him at odds with the academic culture of our own day. But in both cases the fundamental divisive issues, including those concerning education, are philosophical. What then were Aquinas's central theses on education?

IV

One issue needs to be faced immediately. Aquinas has what we are now able to see as an absurd view of the capacities of women, a view characteristic of his age and strengthened by his reading of Aristotle. What he says about education is therefore by intention only about the education of men, just as what he says about parental responsibility is usually framed only in terms of paternal responsibility. Were it not possible to excise these features from his work, it would indeed be badly flawed. But they are in fact accidental features and what he says about both education and responsibility for it can only be considered on its merits, if we consider it as having application for both women and men.

What happens, on Aquinas's view, when teaching and learning take place? A student by exercising her or his powers develops those powers. A teacher may initiate learning, but a good teacher follows the same order in teaching that the student would follow, if making the relevant decisions for her- or himself (*De veritate* ix, 1). So students are taught in such a way that they can become independent practical and, later, theoretical reasoners. The teacher, by introducing the student to this or that particular mode of practice or type of understanding, provides the occasion for the actualization of potentialities. Such teaching begins in the home where both parents are needed for adequate instruction (*Summa contra Gentiles* III, 122). Parents owe it to their children to begin educating them early (*De duobus praeceptis caritatis*), making use of what their children have "from nature, namely reason and hands" (*Summa theologiae* Ia–IIae, 95, 1).

Hands are put to good use in the skills of both the mechanical and the liberal arts. Aquinas draws what had become the conventional distinction between these: the mechanical or servile arts supply the necessities of bodily existence, while the liberal arts are those "ordained to knowledge" (*Commentary on* Metaphysics I, lect. 3, 59). But when Aquinas discusses the arts in general he is as likely to cite examples from the mechanical arts as from the liberal arts, and his emphasis is on how in both cases skills are taught that may be put to the service of the ends of higher types of activity.

The skills, including the argumentative skills, acquired through the liberal arts are a necessary first stage in a philosophical education. Aquinas's predecessors had generally believed that the place of philosophy in education was entirely within the scheme of the liberal arts. But "the seven liberal arts do not adequately divide theoretical philosophy" (*Commentary on Boethius's* De trinitate V, 1, ad 3) and they are now to lead on to a course of study in which the movement will be from logic to mathematics to the natural sciences to moral and political philosophy and finally to metaphysics. Logic is understood as comprising all questions of method in intellectual inquiry – the word *philosophia* is still used to name intellectual inquiry as such – and is therefore the point of departure. Mathematics is understood as an exercise in imagination, independent of experience, even though mathematical concepts are abstracted from experience. For scientific study of nature, reference to experience is indispensable. Inquiry into moral questions requires both experience in those who study and a maturity that frees the mind from the passions. And finally metaphysics and theology take us beyond the limits of imagination and require peculiar strength of intellect (*Commentary on* Nicomachean Ethics VI, lect. vii, 1209–11).[6]

This ordering of the curriculum was never adopted in any university. The expansion of the curriculum to include most of Aristotle's known works, at Paris and elsewhere from the mid-thirteenth century onward, added the three disciplines of natural philosophy, first philosophy (metaphysics) and moral philosophy, while the study of logic continued to expand its scope as one of the liberal arts. But from these developments Aquinas's conception of an ordering of the curriculum prescribed by the ordering of the development of human powers is notably absent. Aquinas's was and remained a Utopian proposal.

One crucial aspect of that proposal concerned the relationship between the goods to be achieved through the various types of intellectual inquiry and the ultimate human good. If children, adolescents and younger adults are to flourish as human beings, then it is of the greatest importance that they acquire not merely the skills needed for intellectual inquiry, but the habits needed to direct those skills to the achievement of genuine goods. Engagement in the kind of practice that issues in the acquisition of the virtues has to be inseparable both from one's earlier training in skills and from one's later education into inquiry. Consider an example of the former.

Aquinas in the prologue to his commentary on Aristotle's *De interpretatione* takes a preoccupation with language to be integral to all education[7] and what he says about the structure of language makes it clear what the teaching of the uses of language, first in the household, then in one's elementary schooling, such as Aquinas himself had with the

Benedictines of Monte Cassino, and finally in the disciplines of the *trivium*, would have to consist in. The basic units of language are those assertive utterances to which truth or falsity can and must be ascribed. Subordinate constituents of such utterances and other uses of language are to be explained in terms of these. But it is not just, of course, that truth or falsity can and must be ascribed to such utterances. The communication of truth about some particular *res*, some particular subject-matter, is what gives them their point and purpose. Communication of what is in one speaker's mind to another speaker is thus guided by shared norms of truth and shared expectations of truthful speech, an ordering of speech that is violated by a liar (*Summa theologiae* IIa–IIae 110, 1–4). What matters about lying is not primarily the intention to deceive, but the intention to utter as if true what is in fact judged by the speaker to be false, and thereby to violate the semantic rule governing assertive utterance. So no one can understand the nature of assertive utterance who does not also understand that a commitment to truthfulness is presupposed by it. Hence learning how to use and to understand language as part of one's training in letters is inseparable in a rightly ordered education from the acquisition of the habit of truthfulness. But characteristically this is the kind of habit that one has to bring with one from one's home.

When a student moves beyond skills to inquiry, in the progress that runs from logic to metaphysics and theology, the exercise of virtues of practice remains as important as the acquisition of intellectual virtues. The task of an inquirer, and so the task of a student of inquiry, is to find her or his way through a multiplicity of *aporiai*, of *causae dubitationis*, and of disagreements, of disputed questions, in the direction of finality of understanding. In order to achieve this she or he will have to combine singleness of intellectual purpose with an ability to understand how some particular set of *phenomena* or some particular problem appears from each of the points of view from which it has hitherto been understood. Inquiry is by its dialectical nature a dialogue between different points of view, in which the individual inquirer cannot arrive at a resolution without having understood each contending position from its own vantage point and in its own terms.

Knowing how to proceed thus in inquiry, that is, knowing how to achieve the goods of inquiry, is of a kind with knowing how to proceed in the achievement of any human good and of the human good. All the virtues are needed, but the exercise of each virtue also requires the exercise of *prudentia*, Aristotle's *phronēsis*, and in his account of the relationship of *prudentia* to the achievement of finality of understanding Aquinas follows Aristotle's account of the relationship of *phronēsis* to *sophia* in Book VI of the *Nicomachean Ethics*. But *prudentia* cannot be exercised without the exercise of the other moral virtues. Progress in genuine understanding cannot be independent of moral progress. And moral progress is not to be confused with progress in moral philosophy. For although moral philosophy is "directed to action, still that action is not the act of the science, but rather of virtue, as is clear in the *Ethics*" (*Commentary on Boethius's* De Trinitate V, 1 and 3, referring to *Nicomachean Ethics* VI 1144b 17–30). What then is the point of including moral and political philosophy in the curriculum? They are after all disciplines that it is useless to teach to those too young or too immature to have the relevant types of experience and the relevant moral qualities. And its students must already be to some significant extent virtuous to learn what moral and political philosophy have to teach them. So what is it that they have to learn?

The answer is: the theory needed to inform the practice of the legislator, the teacher, those responsible for the life of a household, the pastor. Richard Bodéüs has argued compellingly that Aristotle's intended audience for his ethical and political teaching was composed of legislators and others responsible for making and sustaining the civil and household environment in which the moral education of the young is to be carried on.[8] Those texts presuppose in those who are to learn from them a prior practical habituation in the virtues as a prerequisite for learning from those texts, and the possession of theoretical abilities that can be put to work in that learning. Aquinas's purposes in his philosophical and theological writings on morals and politics closely resembled Aristotle's. He too aimed at educating educators, although primarily pastors, confessors and teachers.[9] And part of what educators first learn and then have to teach is the indirect bearing of philosophical argument on practical activity, both positively and negatively. What such argument provides are the resources for the reflective evaluation of political and educative activities, a type of activity that itself presupposes some measure of virtue in those who engage in it.

Consider as an example the opening questions of the Ia–IIae of the *Summa theologiae*, which speak to a series of misunderstandings about the nature of the human good. These are types of misunderstanding that bear directly on those occasions when in contexts of practice we find ourselves arguing that this or that consideration cannot be a good reason for some proposed political or legislative or educational or pastoral course of action unless the ultimate human good is such-and-such; and that, since the ultimate human good cannot be such-and-such, the consideration in question cannot be a good reason for so acting.

Moral and political philosophy however also has its distinctive place in the curriculum for another reason. The student's movement through the curriculum as a whole is directed towards the good of comprehensive and completed understanding. Logic, mathematics, the natural sciences and the study in ethics and politics of human nature, human powers and human affairs are all a prologue to metaphysics, first philosophy. Metaphysics is not, as in much contemporary philosophy, one more specialized subdiscipline, but that without which other types of understanding remain incomplete. And part of what we learn from moral and political philosophy is the indispensability of the moral virtues and especially of prudence in achieving such completed metaphysical understanding.

Educational progress thus involves two distinct types of good. There are the goods of skill and understanding at which each type of art and inquiry and the whole sequence of arts and inquiries aim. And there are the goods of individuals, who happen at particular times in their life to be students or teachers or inquirers, those goods to which their activities are now directed, so that they may in the end achieve their ultimate good. An education is a good education only insofar as the pursuit of the goods of the arts and of inquiry enable those individuals who engage in such activities to achieve their own goods. And what is true of education in the liberal arts and in philosophy is true also of education in the mechanical arts. They too are activities with their own ordered goods and an education in farming or ship-building is a good education only insofar as it serves the proper ends of those individuals who receive it.

What is needed for a good education therefore cannot be supplied only by schools and universities. It requires the cooperation of family and household, school and the local political community, so that all three work together to involve individuals in those practices in which they become habituated in the exercise of the moral virtues and especially of prudence. Of these agencies the home comes first and not only chronologically. Educational authority belongs primarily to parents and secondarily to those whom parents authorize to act as their agents in educating their children. The authority of the parent, while the student is a child, cannot be displaced by that of the teacher. For "it would be contrary to *ius naturale* if a child, before coming to the use of reason, were to be taken away from its parents' custody, or anything done to it against its parents' wish" (*Summa theologiae* IIa–IIae 10, 12). Aquinas wrote this in defence of the rights of Jewish parents and we should note that this precept of the natural law, a precept of reason, is one that Christian authorities are required to respect universally. In any home of course, Christian, Jewish, Islamic, or whatever, the parents may not succeed in playing their part in educating their children, either because of their own failings or because they have peculiarly difficult children. When they do not succeed, it falls to the community outside the home to supply what is needed, if possible (Ia–IIae 92, 1 and 95, 1). So that what is required for a good education is not theological agreement between home, school and the local political community, but rather agreement in the practice of the virtues, an agreement that is independent of religious belief.

It is only at this point that Aquinas adopts positions that are significantly different from Aristotle's. He gives to the household a place that Aristotle denied it and his understanding of political community is much further from Aristotle's understanding of the *polis* than Aquinas himself recognized. But in this rewriting Aquinas not only corrected Aristotle, but did him a service, that of showing how Aristotle's texts could be made relevant to and in cultural and social contexts very different from those of fourth-century Greece, something in which Aquinas was to be followed by such later Thomists as Vitoria and las Casas.

That relevance is a matter of the truth or falsity of two theses: that it is generally and characteristically through the practices of households, schools and political communities that we are educated into those virtues without which we cannot identify, let alone achieve our goods, and that in turn the practices of households, schools and political communities depend for their flourishing upon the exercise of those same virtues, without which those who participate in their common life could not achieve their common good. For, as I remarked earlier, such practices need to be informed by the exercise of the virtue of prudence, that virtue which enables us in particular situations so to act as to achieve the end towards which we are directed by the moral virtues. It is prudence that enables us to apply our skills rightly, to discern which precepts of the natural law are those relevant in this or that situation, to know how to take into account this or that aspect of our relationship to others, and so to act well.

The rules to which we must conform in order to act rightly are never by themselves sufficient to specify what we must do, if we are to act well. And the ends for the sake of which we act are never such that we can simply read off from them what to do here and now; there is no algorithm by which we may connect our particular situation with the relevant aspects of those ends. This is why we need prudence.[10]

Aquinas followed Aristotle is distinguishing three kinds of prudence: that by which the individual directs her- or himself in her or his individual life; the domestic prudence needed for the affairs of a household; and the political prudence needed for those of a political community (*Summa theologiae* IIa–IIae, 47, 11). And part of what prudence contributes in all three spheres is a continuing recognition of the need to extend one's learning (49, 3). Education, especially self-education, is then not merely preparatory, something that terminates at a certain age. It is rather an aspect of the life of the virtues at every stage and it cannot be rightly understood except in the context of that life.

V

"*The* life of *the* virtues": "What could that be?" inquires the late twentieth-century American reader of Aquinas. Where for Aquinas education presupposes a background of shared moral beliefs, the dominant educational ideals of contemporary America presuppose a morally heterogeneous and divided society. Where for Aquinas the goal of education is the achievement of a comprehensive and completed understanding, in modern America what education offers are skills and knowledge designed to enable the student to pursue the satisfaction of her or his preferences, whatever – within certain very wide limits – they may be. And where for Aquinas what the individual is to be measured by, in education as elsewhere, is her or his success or failure in directing her- or himself towards *the* human good, the dominant culture of the American present takes it for granted that there is no such thing as *the* human good, but that each individual must at some point choose for her- or himself among a variety of different and rival conceptions of the good. A good education is then an education that prepares individuals for making such choices. And by that standard a Thomist education is a bad education.

What anyone who follows Aquinas is committed to asserting is that a conception of the good is not the kind of thing that can be *chosen*. The choices made by individuals, on particular occasions, together with their actions and their future-oriented plans and purposes, cannot but presuppose some more or less coherent conception of their good and of the good. But what a particular individual's choices, actions and plans are depends on that individual's habits of practice, on her or his virtues and vices, and mature rational choice is possibly for individuals only in those areas of their lives in which they have acquired the relevant set of virtues to some significant degree. So an education from which there emerge individuals capable of exercising an autonomous capacity for rational choice will be one already informed from the outset by a determinate conception of the good.

Does this mean that a Thomist education will be an education that ignores the facts of contemporary moral conflict and diversity and the range of conflicting conceptions of the good that are to be found in our social life? Nothing could be further from the truth. Aquinas's method of confronting the most fundamental disagreements at the outset of each inquiry committed him and commits modern Thomists to learn how to confront these disagreements in order to test their own conclusions as thoroughly as possible. So a good education will be one that prepares students adequately for systematic critical and self-critical debate between rival standpoints. Education now, as in Aquinas's own time, should be a preparation for constructive engagement in conflict.

NOTES

1 Quoted in N. Kretzmann, A. Kerry and J. Pinborg (eds) *The Cambridge History of Later Medieval Philosophy* (Cambridge, Cambridge University Press, 1982), p. 681.
2 On this and on the issues dividing Aquinas from the Averroists more generally, see Ralph McInerny, *Aquinas against the Averroists* (West Lafayette, Ind., Purdue University Press, 1993).
3 "The reception and interpretation of Aristotle's *Ethics*," in Kretzmann *et al.* (eds) *Cambridge History*, p. 661.
4 "Happiness: the perfection of Man," in Kretzmann *et al.* (eds) *Cambridge History*, p. 679.
5 "Theology and philosophy," in N. Kretzmann and E. Stump (eds) *The Cambridge Companion to Aquinas* (Cambridge, Cambridge University Press, 1993), p. 237.
6 For an extended discussion of Aquinas's view of the liberal arts, see Ralph McInerny, "Beyond the liberal arts," in D. L. Wagner (ed.) *The Seven Liberal Arts in the Middle Ages* (Bloomington, Ind., Indiana University Press, 1983).
7 See Mark D. Jordan, *Ordering Wisdom: the Hierarchy of Philosophical Discourses in Aquinas* (Notre Dame, Ind., University of Notre Dame Press, 1986), p. 10.
8 *The Political Dimension of Aristotle's Ethics*, trans. J. E. Garrett (Albany, NY, SUNY Press, 1993).
9 On this see Leonard E. Boyle, *The Setting of the* Summa theologiae *of Saint Thomas* (Toronto, PIMS, 1982).
10 Prudence, as characterized by Aquinas, is of course the virtue that Aristotle named *phronēsis*. Those like René Antoine Gauthier, who have thought otherwise, did so on the basis of a view of Aquinas's relationship to Aristotle that cannot be sustained. See Daniel Westberg, *Right Practical Reason: Aristotle, Action and Prudence in Aquinas* (Oxford, Clarendon Press, 1994), especially ch. 3.

FURTHER READING ON AQUINAS

Hibbs, Thomas S. (1995) *Dialectic and Narrative in Aquinas: an Interpretation of the* Summa contra gentiles, Notre Dame, Ind., University of Notre Dame Press.
Jordan, Mark (1986) *Ordering Wisdom: the Hierarchy of Philosophical Discourses in Aquinas*, Notre Dame, Ind., University of Notre Dame Press.
Kretzmann, Norman and Stump, Eleonore (eds) (1992) *The Cambridge Companion to Aquinas*, Cambridge: Cambridge University Press.
McInerny, Ralph (1992) *Aquinas on Human Action: a Theory of Practice*, Washington, DC: Catholic University of America Press.

FURTHER READING ON LATER THOMISTS

Vitoria, Francisco de (1991) *Political Writings*, edited and translated by Anthony Pugden and Jeremy Lawrance, Cambridge: Cambridge University Press.
Gutiérrez, Gustavo (1993) *Las Casas: In Search of the Power of Jesus Christ*, translated by Robert R. Barr, Maryknoll, NY: Orbis Books.

8

MAIMONIDES ON EDUCATION

Josef Stern

I

Toward the beginning of *The Guide of the Perplexed*, Moses Maimonides (1138–1204) recounts an "objection" raised by a "learned man" about the biblical story of Adam's sin. According to the "clear sense of the biblical text [Genesis 2–3]," we are told that the first human was created without an "intellect, without thought, and without the capacity to distinguish between good and evil."[1] Only as a result of disobeying the divine command was he rewarded with an intellect, his greatest perfection, and with knowledge of good and bad.

Maimonides replies to this "learned man" that he has three lessons to learn. First, he has mistaken the imagination for the intellect. The intellect is not the faculty that distinguishes good and evil; the intellect judges the true and the false, the subject-matter of physics and metaphysics. The capacities by which humans hold "generally accepted," or conventional, moral and political opinions about good and bad are the bodily faculties of desire and imagination: what is good or bad is what is good or bad *for* the community, i.e. what the members of the community collectively want or, more important, imagine they want for themselves.

Second, the learned man is wrong about human perfection. The highest good is not moral excellence, which is a matter of acting and acting in a way that is useful for everyone, or most people, in one's community. Instead the greatest human perfection – that in virtue of which humans are said to have been created in the "image of God" (I: 1: 22) – is to have, or to be, a fully actualized intellect that is constantly and solely engaged in apprehension of and reflection on the most noble subjects: the deity and the physical world whose natural processes and events are "divine acts." This state of perfection, contemplation, involves no actions, hence, no good or evil, and indeed anything bodily that would interfere with the cognition and concentration it demands. Moral perfection may be necessary for intellectual perfection, but too much attention to it can also come into tension with contemplation. On Maimonides' reading of Genesis 2–3, the story of Adam's sin is not a narrative about a particular individual whose moral is that crime pays. It is a philosophical parable about the natural and ultimate perfection of humanity, which consists in having a fully actualized intellect occupied in constant pursuit of knowledge, the state in which man was "created."

Conventional moral and political virtues only acquire value when we follow Adam, cease to be solely engaged in intellectual reflection, and become absorbed in sensual pleasures and what we imagine we desire, in short, with the corporeal. Better that man not be "engaged in any way in the consideration of generally accepted things" (I: 1: 25) like good and bad, but only in apprehension of the necessarily true and false.

The "learned man's" third error is that he reads the Torah, the Hebrew Bible, as if he were "glancing through a history or piece of poetry" and takes its *only* meaning to be the literal senses of its words. Maimonides counters that many biblical passages (like Genesis 2–3) are philosophical parables, bearing "external" and "internal" meanings in addition to their literal meanings. The literal meaning, the exclusive focus of the "learned man," is only how the vulgar, most unlearned members of the community, understand Scripture, but its literal content is sometimes a falsehood no reasonable person should believe, for example, when it describes God corporeally. On the other hand, both the external and internal meanings of the scriptural parables express kinds of wisdom. The external contains wisdom bearing on political and social flourishing; the internal (which Maimonides describes in much more awkward and circumlocutious terms), "wisdom that is useful for beliefs concerned with the truth as it is," i.e. not necessarily truths themselves but beliefs about truth or reality, namely, beliefs about physics and metaphysics. Not everyone (and, with respect to some topics, perhaps not anyone), Maimonides thinks, can and should be made to understand the external and internal parabolic contents of biblical texts. But everyone in the community without exception should know *that* these texts *are* parables and that their vulgar literal meaning is not their only meaning. Failure to recognize this only leads to the "perplexity" in the title of the *Guide*, a tug-of-war between one's intellect and religion or tradition. Unlike Aristotle's wonder, this perplexity is not the beginning of wisdom but, Maimonides says, of fear, difficulty, and heartache.

These three lessons the "learned man" has yet to learn correspond to three major motifs that shape Maimonides' conception of education. First, the ultimate goal of all education is intellectual and contemplative, not moral or practical – although moral excellence is necessary for intellectual perfection. Education inculcates this ideal both by enabling a small number of individuals to achieve it and by creating whole communities who value it as their ultimate goal – rather than simply material, political, and social welfare – even though many of their members will never realize the ultimate perfection. Second, the primary obstacle in the way of straightforwardly realizing the intellectual ideal is the body (or, in more metaphysical terms, matter), its needs, desires, and, most dangerous of all, its most potent faculty, the imagination. The job of education is to free the individual, or his intellect, from these fetters: to teach individuals to restrain and minimize their material desires and needs and not to confuse what they simply imagine with the demonstrably necessary, possible, and impossible. Third, perhaps the most common means by which the imagination exercises its hold on people is through words, especially the written word and, even more so, certain texts which readers, whole communities of readers, worship and to whose literal meaning they believe they owe unqualified obedience – even when the texts conflict with the demonstrations of their intellects. For Maimonides, the guide to correct belief is never the meanings of words but what the intellect represents to itself as true. The external meanings of these texts, on the other hand, are often the source of the worst falsehoods about the most important subject, the deity. Once again, the job of education is to break the hold of the literal meanings of these authoritative texts on readers; and chief among these texts is the Torah itself.

At a right angle to these themes, and cutting across them, Maimonides draws a sharp distinction between the education of a community as a whole and the education of particular individuals who have the capacity to achieve the highest humanly attainable intellectual perfection. He believes that the education of these two have distinct goals, require different instruments and methods, and present different obstacles. In the remainder of this essay, I shall discuss three examples of Maimonidean education in theory and practice. The first two focus on the education of a community, the third on the education of the individual.

II

The Hebrew word "Torah" (literally: teaching) is usually reserved for the Pentateuch, or Mosaic Law, but for classic rabbinic Judaism there actually exist two Torot (pl.), a Written Torah and an Oral Torah. In the Introduction to the *Mishneh Torah*, his seminal codification of rabbinic law, Maimonides presents the classic rabbinic account of the relation between the two Torot. The Written Torah, the Pentateuch, was "revealed," he says, with its "interpretation" to Moses at Mount Sinai.[2] This "interpretation" is the Oral Torah which lays out the detailed practices in which the Mosaic commandments are applied to everyday circumstances and the hermeneutic rules for justifying those practices in terms of the biblical text. According to our earliest sources, the Oral Torah was taught and transmitted by word of mouth by the sages and, later, rabbis (a title in rabbinic Judaism which came to mean "teacher") of Palestine and Babylonia, from roughly the beginning of the second Jewish commonwealth (538 BCE). Starting in the second century CE, it was edited, redacted, and put into writing in a number of authoritative texts. The first of these was the Mishnah (c. 200 CE), followed (during the fifth century CE) by the two Talmuds which consist of much longer, sprawling records of the oral teachings, interpretations, and debates revolving around the Mishnah that issued forth from the rabbinic academies of Palestine and Babylonia, respectively. In addition, a variety of other compositions of the Oral Torah were produced throughout this period, continuing into the early Middle Ages. These include both works of *halakhah* (literally: "the way in which one goes"), i.e. rabbinic law on topics including religious ritual, civil and marital relations, sacrifices, and the Temple cult, and collections of *aggadah* (literally: "narrative"), a rubric for everything else: non-legal scriptural exegesis, homiletics, moralistic writing, history, theosophy, and folklore. By the twelfth century, the written literature of the Oral Torah had become so voluminous that, in light of the precarious political situation of the Jewish people in the Diaspora, which threatened its religious survival, Maimonides tells us he decided to compose his own comprehensive code, the *Mishneh Torah*.

Three characteristics of the Oral Torah were especially important in the tradition of classic rabbinic education that Maimonides received. First, it was assumed that there was never a Written without an Oral Torah; therefore rabbinic Judaism always assumed that

111

interpretation was essential to the scriptural text. The Written Torah was never free-standing with a transparent fixed meaning that could be understood independently of the exegesis provided in the Oral Torah. Just the opposite: multiple conflicting interpretations of one text were not only a reality in practice but a normative, and valued, feature of rabbinic exegesis. Not that there aren't constraints on rabbinic interpretations. But the rabbinic tradition nurtured an active, creative relation to the sacred text that empowered the reader and emphasized his autonomous, self-confident capacity as a human interpreter of divinely revealed texts. Although this attitude does not explain Maimonides' negative view of the written word, it is the source of his own multi-leveled parabolic interpretations both of Scripture and of the rabbinic texts which themselves are interpretations of Scripture. His bold stance as an interpreter must be seen in light of his place in a long-standing interpretive tradition within rabbinic Judaism, and the skills of interpretation were a core of the curriculum in which he was educated.

There is also a second, different side of interpretation that figured in the educational curriculum Maimonides received. The interpreter is a commentator, and the role of the commentator is inevitably conservative: his task is not to stake out his own position or to reject others but primarily to explicate, elaborate, sometimes critically comment but, more frequently among the medievals, *harmonize* conflicting passages in his sources. This was true not only in the rabbinic tradition but also in the medieval Aristotelian (and specifically Arabic) philosophical traditions in which the commentary was a main vehicle of philo-sophical prose. Aristotle, no less than the Author of Scripture, was regarded as the last word on many subjects. In the Arabic world this attitude was also held, though to a lesser degree, toward Plato, the various pseudo-Aristotles, and, often for lack of a clear realization that they were different, the neo-Platonists. All that was left to the medieval philosopher, and student, was to explain and explain away problematic passages. Both the skills of textual harmonization and the attitude to the text it presupposes were staples of education in Maimonides' medieval world.[3]

Second, creation of the Oral Torah and its public instruction were intimately connected. The teaching situation – the interaction between teacher and disciple – was both the setting in which and the dynamic mechanism by which the Oral Torah was produced. Oral Torah was never first authored in isolation and only after it assumed its finished form taught and transmitted in the academy. It emerged from teaching. Conversely, the brunt of rabbinic education consisted in the Oral Torah, both mastering the detailed knowledge of rules governing all aspects of day-to-day life and training in its interpretive, justificatory techniques. Thus the Babylonian Talmud (BT) states: "One should always divide his years into three: devoting a third to Scripture, a third to Mishnah, and a third to the Talmud" (BT Kiddushin 30a). Here the Written and Oral Torah do not get equal time; the Written Torah is the stuff of elementary education; the more mature two-thirds of the person's life go to the rabbis and, specifically, to their specifically *halakhic*, or legal, compositions.

Third, classic rabbinic Judaism is focused on the act rather than creed, on what one should do rather than what one should believe, on the performance of the commandments applied to, or realized in, all aspects of day-to-day life. But the rabbis also make *study* of the Oral Torah, and especially of *halakhah*, how one should act, the supreme commandment of the Law, the paradigmatic activity by which one worships the deity. When the Talmud states that one should spend two-thirds of his time on Mishnah and the Talmud, it means that one should study the canonical texts on the basis of which one knows how to act as a Jew, not simply *in order to* know what to do, but because that study is itself the highest act of religious worship.

With this background, we are now in a position to appreciate the revolution in rabbinic education Maimonides sought to accomplish. Expanding on the talmudic quotation, Maimonides writes in the *Mishneh Torah*:

> One should divide the time of his study into three: a third to the Written Torah, a third to the Oral Torah, and a third [should be devoted to] reflection, deducing conclusions from premises, drawing implications of statements, comparing statements, and applying the hermeneutical rules by which the Torah is interpreted, until one knows the principles of these rules, and how to deduce the prohibited, the permitted, and similar things from what one has learned by tradition. This subject is called "Talmud." For example, if one is a craftsman, working at his trade three hours each day, and devotes nine hours to the study of Torah, three of those nine hours he should [spend] studying the Written Torah, three the Oral Law, and three reflecting using his own thought how to deduce one thing from another. The words of the prophets are included in the Written Torah, and their interpretation in the Oral Torah, and the subjects entitled "Pardes" are included within Talmud. When is [this plan] to be followed? At the beginning of one's studies. But when his wisdom has grown, and it is no longer necessary for him to study the Written Torah or to constantly occupy himself with the Oral Torah, he should read, at fixed times, the Written Torah and the statements of the tradition in order not to forget any of the rules of the Law, and he should devote all his days to Talmud exclusively, according to his breadth of understanding and the composure of his mind.[4]

Maimonides' lengthier formulation makes two major changes. First, the talmudic passage describes the curriculum for a lifelong educational career which progresses from easier to more difficult texts but whose subject-matter is clearly focused, like classic rabbinic Judaism, on *halakhah*. Maimonides subordinates *halakhah*, which he labels "Oral Torah," to second place at best. Unlike the rabbis who made study of the laws governing proper action the supreme commandment, and the noblest kind of study of Torah, Maimonides makes study of those laws purely practical and instrumental. Although one must know how to act according to the commandments in all their detailed applications, and, having once mastered those rules should review them periodically lest they be forgotten, there is no intrinsic value to their study. The highest object of study is what Maimonides here calls "Talmud," which refers not to a text, or even a body of discussions concerning how to act, but to a general activity: reasoning, drawing consequences, and deduction, whose aim is not, or not only, to know *what* is prohibited and permitted, the appropriate act for each circumstance, but *how to derive* the prohibited and permitted, the very exercise of reasoning that is required for justification or understanding. That is, Maimonides' use of the term "Talmud" now refers to dynamic, discursive contemplation and reasoning.

113

Maimonides' second revision of his Talmudic source consists in his addition of "the subjects entitled 'Pardes'" to Talmud. The term "Pardes" originally meant a cultivated garden but in the Talmud it refers to the story of four sages who engaged in esoteric studies. Although there were many earlier speculations about the nature of those subjects, Maimonides identifies the secret branch of knowledge those rabbis pursued with physics and metaphysics. He begins the *Mishneh Torah* with "Laws concerning the foundations of the Torah" – "laws" governing what every Jew must believe. This itself was novel: until then the Mosaic commandments extended only over actions, not beliefs, though, of course, certain shared beliefs were taken for granted. But this is not all. The first two chapters of these "Laws" sketch a basic course in neo-Platonized Aristotelian metaphysics (covering the necessarily existent-in-itself being who is also identified with the first cause, his unity, incorporeality, and timelessness; the figurative reinterpretation of anthropormorphic scriptural verses about the deity; the separate intellects and their identification with the scriptural angels; and divine knowledge). The third and fourth chapters are a brief course in Aristotelian celestial astronomy and sublunar physics (the nature and number of the spheres and stars; the explanation of their motions; the elements and their modes of composition; and the relation between matter and form). Maimonides concludes by identifying these two philosophical subjects with the subject-matter of two secret rabbinic doctrines: physics with the "Account of the Beginning," the interpretation of Genesis 1–3, and metaphysics with the "Account of the Chariot," the theosophical interpretation of the vision of a divine chariot in Ezekiel 1 and 10. Finally, these two "Accounts" and, thus, physics and metaphysics, are said to comprise "Pardes."

By including these philosophical subjects under the title "Pardes" in the study of the Talmud, Maimonides has done nothing less than incorporate Aristotelian metaphysics and physics into the study of the Torah. If Talmud is a contemplative activity, it is contemplation not only about *halakhah* but about all branches of wisdom.[5] And, within this expanded conception of Talmud, physics and metaphysics are not only two more sub-fields; Maimonides makes it clear that they are the most advanced and noblest of its subjects. He calls study of "what is forbidden and permitted" the "bread and meat" of the Law, socially necessary and pedagogically prior, but nonetheless a "small thing." Physics and metaphysics supplant them as the "great thing," the most elevated branch of the Torah and the end of a rabbinic education.[6] Insofar indeed as study of Torah is mandatory, philosophy is now a religiously obligatory subject of study.[7]

Maimonides' ruling in the *Mishneh Torah* is a programatic statement. It sets out a set of educational priorities and goals rather than their mode of implementation. But we know as a matter of historical fact that it served as the blueprint for actual educational programs that were put into practice by his contemporary and later followers. In a curriculum written by Joseph ben Judah ibn 'Aqnin (1150–220), a slightly younger Spanish contemporary of Maimonides, the child begins his education with the story of the Torah at age 5 and the Mishnah at age 10, both with a heavy dose of Hebrew grammar and poetry ("fit to develop in them all good qualities"). At 15 the student begins the study of the Talmud, at first emphasizing only the development of his technical skills, and at 18 he is given talmudic instruction "which lays emphasis on deeper understanding, independent thinking, and investigation." Finally, once the students' "mental powers have been strengthened, when the Talmud has become so much a part of them that there is hardly any chance of its being lost, and they are firmly entrenched in the Torah and the practice of its commands," they begin "philosophic studies," first logic, mathematics, astronomy, music, and mechanics; second, natural sciences, including medicine; and third, metaphysics, "that which Aristotle has laid down in his work, *Metaphysics*." "This," ibn 'Aqnin concludes, "is the first among sciences. All the other sciences, which are but the groundwork of philosophy, have this discipline in mind."[8]

Maimonides' legal ruling that philosophy is the highest of the aims of education is also part of his program to reconstitute the Torah as a philosophical religion and, hence, divine law. In the *Guide* he first *defines* a "divine law" as the law of a community whose commandments aim, not simply at the material and social soundness of its citizens, but also, and more important, at their intellectual soundness: as "a Law that takes pains to inculcate correct opinions with regard to God . . . and the angels, and that desires to make man wise, to give him understanding, and to awaken his attention, so that he should know the whole of that which exists in its true form" (II: 40: 384). In other words, what makes a law divine is not the identity of its author, but its content and its end, which is not only the practical but also the theoretical well-being of the community.

Having defined the conditions under which a law is divine, Maimonides then claims that the Mosaic Law in fact satisfies those conditions. It aims at both "the welfare of the soul and the welfare of the body," the latter, material, social, and political well-being; the former, community-wide correct opinions and sound beliefs. Now, Maimonides *asserts* this. But what is his evidence? How does he in fact know that the Mosaic Law indeed achieves the welfare of the soul of the Jewish community? The answer to that question is that he, Maimonides, *makes it true*. As we have seen, he *legislates* in the *Mishneh Torah*, his codification of the Law, that "Pardes," physics and metaphysics, is the end of the education based on the Law. Thus Maimonides *ensures* that the welfare of the communal soul is the end of the educational process based on study of the Torah as he reconstructs that education. Having defined in the *Guide* what a divine law must be, he rules in the *Mishneh Torah* in accordance with his definition to make the Torah such a divine law.[9]

Maimonides emphasizes that this communal intellectual welfare is not of the same kind as the intellectual perfection that can be attained by those individuals with the capacity to engage in true philosophical contemplation, who have undergone strict and lengthy training in the sciences and fully actualized their intellects. Throughout the *Guide* he warns of the "harm" that can befall the community at large if all its members are exposed to metaphysics, indiscriminately and immediately, without attention to their respective capacities and without leading them through a methodical, systematic training in the sciences with all the necessary but lengthy preliminaries. If a young member of the community "begins with the divine science," i.e. metaphysics, it "will not be a mere confusion in his beliefs that will befall him, but rather absolute negation" (I: 33: 71), i.e. loss of all belief. But, in the same breath – and, it should be added, in sharp contrast to his fellow Cordovan, the great Muslim philosopher-jurist Averroes – Maimonides emphasizes that this is "just at the outset"; with training everyone with the right capacities can and should be encouraged to achieve individual perfection. Furthermore, and again in contrast to Averroes, everyone in the community, including the multitude, should be "brought up" and "made to accept on traditional authority" specific beliefs, for example, that God is incorporeal, incomposite, and unique, that his knowledge is completely different in kind from humans', and that there can be no relation between him and anything else. These beliefs are the same metaphysical truths Maimonides lays out in the first chapters of the *Mishneh Torah*. They are the sound beliefs that must be taught to everyone in the community by any divine law that seeks the welfare of the soul as well as that of the body. The education of such a community is a divine education.

III

Maimonides' most detailed account of the pedagogical role of the Law is his historical explanation, in the *Guide*, of a wide range of Mosaic commandments; these were legislated to re-educate the ancient Israelites who were "brought up in the religious community of the Sabians" (III: 29: 514), believing in star-worship, idolatry, astrology, and magic.[10] The explanation illustrates how educational practice comes to assume particular institutional arrangements in order to meet conflicting educational needs and goals. It also highlights the problems posed for the Law insofar as it is claimed to be a potent educational instrument in Maimonides' day – and still in ours.

Abraham, whom Maimonides portrays as the first "Jewish" philosopher-teacher, attempted to refute the idolatrous beliefs of the Sabians by means of arguments and specu-lative proofs. Maimonides makes it clear that he failed: he did not educate a community, beyond his immediate household, that would deny Sabian star-worship and accept a divine law. Only Moses succeeded at this educational job: through the legislation of specific commandments, including sacrifices and the Temple cult, various agricultural laws, prohibitions against magic and idolatry, and the laws of ritual purity and impurity. These commandments "educated" by different strategies. Some, like purgative medicines, required the Israelites either to do an act opposite or contrary to the Sabian practice or to refrain from an action the Sabians performed or to do something they prohibited. A second class, using symbolic representations, attempted to inculcate in the Israelites new beliefs and attitudes as an alternative to Sabianism. But the pedagogically most subtle group of commandments is exemplified by certain sacrifices and the Temple cult.

Maimonides explains these commandments as the product of two "intentions" of the Law. The first intention was to "put an end to idolatry, to wipe out its traces, and all that is bound up with it" (III: 29: 517). Among the things bound up with idolatry was the institution of sacrifice: no one at that time could even imagine worship of a deity except by sacrifice. Given the first intention, it should therefore follow that *all* sacrifice should be prohibited. Yet, Maimonides explains, sacrifice was nonetheless legislated by the Mosaic Law because of its second intention: its aim to preserve and respect human nature and, in particular, human psychological necessities. In this case, the necessities were, one, the fact that "man has in his nature a love of, and inclination for, that to which he is habituated" (I: 31: 67) and, two, that "according to his nature, man is not capable of abandoning suddenly all to which he was accustomed" because "a sudden transition from one opposite to another is impossible" (III: 32: 526). In other words, man is a creature of habit and slow evolutionary development. So, given the Israelites' habituation to sacrifice as *the* mode of religious worship and their natural resistance to dramatic change, Moses adapted his first intention to fit the second. He did not "give us a Law prescribing the rejection, abandonment, and abolition of all these kinds of worship." Had he, Maimonides adds with a remarkable comparison, he would have been no more successful than a prophet "in these times, who calling upon the people to worship God, would say: 'God has given you a Law forbidding you to pray to Him, to fast, to call upon Him for help in misfortune. Your worship should consist solely in meditation without any works at all'" (III: 32: 526). Instead Moses let the institution of sacrifice remain in place, and "transferred" it to worship of the one God while "restricting" its practices to specific places, times, and persons (III: 32: 526–7).

Maimonides compares this model of Mosaic education to a "divine ruse" (ibid.) or the divine "wily graciousness and wisdom" (III: 32: 524f.) manifest in nature. Natural processes accommodate their teleological ends to the capacities, needs, and limitations of their materials.[11] Likewise, Moses accommodated the Law to the capacities, needs, and limitations of the Israelite community it was meant to educate. "The Torah speaks in the language of the sons of man," i.e. in the anthropomorphic and corporeal language of the multitude, because the slavish Israelites could not believe that anything immaterial, anything other than a body, could exist. The Law as an educational system is not, then, perfect in any absolute sense, as it would be if it were a pure, unaccommodating mechanism to achieve its first intention. It involves compromise for the sake of education. But this, Maimonides argues, is inevitable. Education, including divine education, could ignore or ride roughshod over human nature only if education could be accomplished by miracle. But if education could be by miracle, then "prophets and all giving of a Law would have been useless" (III: 32: 529), i.e. there would be no point to an *education*.

Maimonides' characterization of the education of the ancient Israelites as a "divine *ruse*," an expression of the deity's "*wily* graciousness," also hints at a second and nowadays unpopular theme that runs through his view of education. The good teacher must, at least out of necessity, be devious: at times speak falsely and not always openly. On occasion the teacher must introduce "deliberate contradictions" and "conceal" his primary intentions (1: Introduction, pp. 17–20), and Maimonides himself uses these devices, as he explicitly tells his reader, in writing the *Guide*. These characteristics of Maimonides' writing are often criticized, but they should be judged in the context of his theory of education. They are integral to the very process of accommodation, for in adapting one's ends to the available means one exploits those means however one can in order to achieve to the furthest extent possible the primary intention. By speaking the language of the sons of man, the Torah asserts falsehoods (e.g. that God is corporeal) to get its main point across (e.g. that there exists a deity). To explain an obscure, difficult matter,

> the teacher must be lax and, using any means that occur to him or gross speculation, will try to make that first matter somehow understood. He will not undertake to state the matter as it truly is in exact terms, but rather will leave it so in accord with the

listener's imagination that the latter will understand only what he now wants him to understand. Afterwards, in the appropriate place, that obscure matter is stated in exact terms and explained as it truly is.

(I: Intro.: pp. 17–18)

A similar point applies to Maimonides' advocacy of pedagogical concealment. The commandments like sacrifice that Maimonides explains were designed to combat the Sabian upbringing of the ancient Israelites were described by the rabbis of the Talmud as "statutes" that have either no reason or an unknown reason. Maimonides, who argues on metaphysical grounds that all divine commandments must have knowable reasons, reinterprets the rabbis' statement to say that the reasons for these commandments were (and remain) better off not *made* known, or revealed, to the community at large. For example, the reason for sacrifice had to be hidden because public revelation would have defeated its own success. If its point was to wean the people away from idolatry while and by using its external institutions, sacrifice would obviously not have been psychologically effective at this task if it was known that this was the only reason it was legislated.

The historical explanation of these commandments as tools of re-education to undo Sabian mis-education raises a difficult question, however. Why should these commandments continue to be valid and obligatory, or why perform them at all, if there is no continuing need for this kind of education, if the Sabian threat no longer exists? In different places Maimonides hints at different solutions to this problem, none of which are entirely satisfying. It is hard to see, in fact, how a problem cannot but arise given the dual use of a legal system as an educational system. Laws must be inflexible, universal, and irrevisable in ways that methods of education should not be. Perhaps the strongest of Maimonides' answers is that, despite undeniable progress in the education of the Jewish community, Sabianism still survives in the guise of astrology, magic, hermetic popular religion, and various superstitions; hence, the war against Sabianism is not yet won. Indeed sometimes Maimonides describes Sabianism, in Wittgensteinian terms, as a myth that continues to exercise an almost magical power, through people's imaginations and fantasies, over the way in which they think of the power of the stars and celestial world, their freedom to act, and their responsibility as agents. In these cases, it is not enough for the teacher simply to point out the error from which the false conclusions follow; he must free those caught in the grip of the myth. A crucial step in this process is exposing the Sabian origins of these present-day superstitions embedded in popular religion and culture. Only then do we see how an original idolatrous act was taken and perpetuated out of context, and only then can we disabuse ourselves of its magical hold. An equally important instrument in this struggle is offering a different way of life, like that informed by the Mosaic commandments, which were designed to combat and replace these same myths. In the first case, revealing the reasons for the commandments is now required; in the second, it may still be necessary to conceal them. In addition, some unsatisfied students may take the historical explanation of the Mosaic commandments as antinomian grounds to reject the educational system *in toto*; that alone may be reason why the teacher will want to conceal it from his student body at large.

IV

The individual who possesses the capacity to achieve the highest humanly attainable intellectual perfection requires a particular kind of education in addition to what he receives as an ordinary member of the community. This student must, first of all, display a "longing for speculative matters." But because his longing may exceed his ability, the teacher tests him with mathematics, astronomy, and logic to prove that he is worthy of having the contents of the "secrets of prophetic books revealed to him" (I: Dedicatory Epistle: 3). The worthy student then follows the rabbinic and philosophical curriculum in strict order, "elevated step by step" (I: 33: 71) through the natural sciences. He must also demonstrate the appropriate emotional and psychological temperament, "qualities of tranquility and quiet," and moral virtues. Students who by nature are angry, rash, reckless, agitated, or disordered or who have great sexual appetites can never go on to divine science, i.e. metaphysics. For this last, and highest, subject of study, Maimonides says that the student must be

> wise, I mean that he has achieved knowledge of the sciences from which the premises of speculation derive; and . . . he [must] be full of understanding, intelligent, sagacious by nature, that he divine a notion even if it is only very slightly suggested to him in a flash.
>
> (I: 34: 72)

Elsewhere he adds that the individual must also be "perfect in the varieties of political regimes as well as in the speculative sciences" and he must have "the gift of finely expressing himself in communicating notions in flashes" (I: 34: 78). Only when all these conditions are realized in an individual can the "mysteries of the Torah," especially metaphysics, be transmitted to him. Such an individual will then fully actualize the potentiality of his intellect by apprehending all potential intelligibles, everything that is in the capacity of a human to apprehend. In terms of Maimonides' medieval Aristotelian epistemology, this individual will be a pure intellect *in actu*, or acquired intellect, in a state of conjuction with the active intellect, the highest human intellectual condition.

Maimonides' descriptions of this ultimate intellectual state are ambiguous and qualified, and it is a live question in contemporary Maimonidean scholarship whether he indeed believed that it is possible for any actual human inquirer (in contrast to figures such as Moses who may be *just* figurative devices to articulate an unrealizable ideal) to have metaphysical knowledge, especially knowledge of the deity, without which it would be impossible to achieve fully actualized intellectual perfection. But even if he did not believe in the possibility of achieving metaphysical *knowledge*, he may have believed that metaphysical *inquiry* is inevitable insofar as inquirers are drawn to metaphysics from their study of natural science in search of the ultimate causes of sublunar phenomena. It is also possible that he believed that the study of metaphysical questions leads, not to knowledge, but to the recognition of antinomies in the face of which the inquirer suspends judgment and thereby, like the ancient skeptic, achieves a state of "dazzlement" that parallels the *eudaimonia* that the metaphysical dogmatist seeks to achieve through the highest state of knowledge, constant conjunction. In any case, the highest humanly attainable intellectual state is also of the deepest spiritual significance: to be either constantly conjoined with the active intellect or to be in a state of skeptical awe of the unknowable is the highest state of divine worship.

Without pursuing the epistemological question further, I want to focus on Maimonides' account of the last steps of education or training in metaphysical inquiry. Once again, Maimonides' source is a rabbinic statement:

> The Account of the Chariot [i.e. metaphysics] ought not to be taught even to one man, except if he be wise and able to understand by himself, in which case only the chapter headings may be transmitted to him.
>
> (BT *Hagigah* 11b, 13a; cited in *Guide* I: Intro.: 6; I: 34: 72)

"Chapter headings," Maimonides explains, are "glimpses of the truth" (*Guide* I: Intro.: 6), and the way these glimpses are given is not only by literal chapter headings, i.e. hints and allusions which are "scattered and entangled with other subjects," but also (and especially in written books where explaining the truths explicitly "would be teaching them to thousands") through the medium of "riddles and parables" (ibid., pp. 7–8). Now parables for Maimonides, as we explained earlier, are not only texts with a certain literary structure but passages – scriptural, rabbinic, and philosophical – with multiple levels of meaning. The level Maimonides is concerned with here is their internal meaning, the "wisdom that is useful for beliefs concerned with the truth as it is." While the philosophical subjects concerned with truth are physics and metaphysics, it may also be, as we said earlier, that he thought that the contents of these philosophical parables do not always express physical or metaphysical *truths*. They may only express their authors' beliefs about truths of physics and metaphysics or about their knowledge (or lack of knowledge) of these subjects.

The rabbis prohibited the public teaching of the Account of the Chariot in order to conceal it from a certain audience. For Maimonides, concealment is also one reason why the internal meanings of philosophical parables are expressed in their parabolic form. As we saw earlier, this concealment is mainly in order to protect those who are unprepared for metaphysics from the possible harm even a little knowledge may cause them. But it is also, Maimonides hints, in order to protect the philosopher from the possible harm that the vulgar may do to *him* for holding and teaching beliefs that he, the vulgar, does not understand and that oppose his familiar beliefs inculcated by the literal meaning of certain texts.

Both of these explanations for the educational use of parables concern the *teaching* or *dissemination* of their metaphysical content. Maimonides adds, however, a third, and for him more important, explanation which stems from the teacher's own knowledge of metaphysics. None of these "great secrets," he says, "are fully and completely known to anyone among us." The most we can grasp are "flashes of the truth," flashes that vary in their frequency and illumination according to the rank of the knower. That is, the prophet's or philosopher's *apprehension* of metaphysical truths is partial, fragmentary, unsustained, far from the complete understanding that would be necessary to articulate these truths in explicit discursive statements. And the same limited understanding that curtails his apprehension curtails his teaching:

whenever one of the perfect wishes to mention, either orally or in writing, something that he understands of these secrets, according to the degree of his perfection, he is unable to explain with complete clarity and coherence even the portion that he has apprehended, as he could do with the other sciences whose teaching is generally recognized. Rather there will befall him when teaching another that which he had undergone when learning himself. I mean to say that the subject matter will appear, flash, and then be hidden again, as though this were the nature of this subject matter . . . For this reason, all the Sages possessing knowledge of God the Lord, knowers of the truth, when they aimed at teaching something of this subject matter, spoke of it only in parables and riddles.

(I: Intro.: 8)

The rabbinic statement proscribing public, explicit discursive teaching of metaphysics is not, then, primarily a prohibition expressing the prudent practical wisdom of concealment. It reflects the limited nature of human knowledge of metaphysics, and prescribes how and to whom metaphysics can, insofar as it is possible, be transmitted: at best indirectly and elliptically, and only to properly prepared individuals who, with the slightest hints, can figure it out on their own. As Maimonides describes his own indubitable but, he admits, fallible understanding of the "Account of the Chariot":

I followed conjecture and supposition; no divine revelation has come to me to teach me that the intention . . . was such and such, nor did I receive what I believe in these matters from a teacher. But the texts of the prophetic books and the dicta of the [rabbinic] Sages, together with the speculative premises that I possess, showed me that things are indubitably so and so. Yet it is possible that they are different and that something else is intended.

(III: Intro.: 416)

In sum, metaphysics is unteachable; at best a worthy student can be guided to discover it by his own reason.

Maimonides' *Guide* is such a guide to metaphysics, like the Torah itself which Maimonides, playing on the Hebrew word for guide *moreh*, calls "that book which guides all those who seek guidance toward what is correct and therefore is called Torah" (III: 13: 453). Neither of them *teaches* metaphysics but, through various exercises, guides its philosophically trained reader toward an intellectual state in which he can discover, insofar as it is humanly possible, "wisdom that is useful for beliefs concerned with the truth as it is." By working through the *Guide* as an interpretive exercise, Maimonides means to train his reader to work through and interpret the internal meaning of the Torah. The commandments also function as exercises for the student of metaphysics. They no longer aim at the welfare of the community; instead their role is to "train [the student] to occupy [himself] with His commandments rather than with matters pertaining to this world" (III: 51: 622), i.e. to empty himself of all concern with this-worldly interests such as the needs and desires of his body. The philosophically trained student seeking metaphysical knowledge must learn to control his longing for metaphysical knowledge, curtailing it to the absolute limits of the human intellect. Where he discovers irresolvable disagreements, he must learn to "refrain and hold back," preventing himself from "pressing forward to engage in speculative study of corrupt imaginings" (I: 32: 70). Like the talmudic sage R. Aqiba, the only one of the four rabbis who "entered [Pardes] in peace and went out in peace," this student who "engages in the theoretical study of these metaphysical matters" to the furthest extent his intellect allows without being "overcome by imaginings . . . will have achieved human perfection" (I: 32: 68–9).

NOTES

1 Moses Maimonides, *The Guide of the Perplexed*, trans. Shlomo Pines (Chicago, University of Chicago Press, 1963), Part I, Ch. 2, p. 23. All in-text parenthetic references are to Book, Chapter, and Page in this edition, e.g. I: 2: 23. The unusual Arabic term translated by Pines as "learned man" literally means "man of the sciences," but Pines's translation captures better, I think, Maimonides' ironic intent.

2 Moses Maimonides, *Mishneh Torah* (Heb.), Introduction. The first book of the *Mishneh Torah* is translated into English by Moses Hymanson, *Mishneh Torah: The Book of Knowledge* (Jerusalem and New York, Boys Town Press, 1974), p. Ib.

3 I emphasize this point because Maimonides is often, misleadingly, described as a "synthesizer" of philosophy and religion. Harmonization need not be synthesis but, more important, harmonization was a leitmotif already *within* each of medieval philosophy and religion. Coming with that training, Maimonides' harmonization of Torah and Aristotle is not surprising.

4 *Mishneh Torah*, "Laws concerning the Study of the Torah" I, 11–12," p. 58a.

5 It is a further question, which I cannot explore here, whether Maimonides thought that all philosophical knowledge could somehow be "found in" the Talmud or in classical biblical and classical rabbinic texts.

6 *Mishneh Torah*, "Laws concerning the Foundations of the Torah," IV, 13, p. 39b.

7 For further discussion of these themes, see I. Twersky, *Introduction to the Code of Maimonides (Mishneh Torah)* (New Haven, Conn., Yale University Press, 1980); Herbert Davidson, "The Study of Philosophy as a Religious Obligation," in S. D. Goitein (ed.) *Religion in a Religious Age* (Cambridge, Association for Jewish Studies, 1974).

8 Joseph ben Judah Ibn 'Aqnin, *Tibb a-Nufus*, in Jacob R. Marcus (ed.) *The Jew in the Medieval World, a Source Book 351–1791* [1938] (New York, Harper and Row, 1965), pp. 374–77.

9 See Warren Zev Harvey, "Political philosophy and *Halakhah* in Maimonides" (Heb.), *Iyyun* 29 (1980); English translation in J. Dan (ed.) *Binah: Jewish Intellectual History in the Middle Ages*, vol. 2 (Westport, Conn., and London, Praegar, 1994), pp. 47–64.

10 Maimonides' knowledge of the Sabians, a star-worshipping idolatrous community in ancient Babylonia, was based on works such as Ibn Wahshiyya's *Nabatean Agriculture* which are now known to have been medieval fabrications. Without pursuing the topic here, it should be noted that Maimonides' use of historical-anthropological materials to explain the Mosaic commandments was itself revolutionary.

11 On this passage, and its source in Alexander of Aphrodisias' *On Providence*, see Shlomo Pines' classic discussion in "The philosophical sources of *The Guide of the Perplexed*," his Introduction to his translation of the *Guide*, pp. lxxii–lxxiv.

BIBLIOGRAPHICAL NOTE

Much of the best recent scholarship on Maimonides is still available only in Hebrew but, for readers unacquainted with his philosophy, the best general introduction to his thought in the context of his Greek and Arabic sources remains Shlomo Pines, "The philosophical sources of *The Guide of the Perplexed*," the Introduction to his translation of the *Guide*. Isadore Twersky's *Introduction to the Code of Maimonides (Mishneh Torah)* (New Haven, Conn., Yale University Press, 1980), ch. 4, "Law and philosophy," is a detailed source of information on the philosophical dimensions of Maimonides' legal writings. An insightful study of Maimonides which emphasizes his orientation as a teacher is David Hartman, *Maimonides: Torah and Philosophic Quest* (Philadelphia, Pa., Jewish Publication Society, 1976). Warren Zev Harvey's "Political Philosophy and *Halakhah* in Maimonides" (see n. 9) is possibly the most important paper in recent years on the relationship between Maimonides' legal and philosophical writings. On philosophical issues raised by Maimonides' historical explanation of the commandments (Section III), see chs. 2 and 6 of Josef Stern, *Problems and Parables of Law: Maimonides and Nahmanides on the Reasons for the Commandments (Ta'amei Ha-Mitzvot)* (Albany, NY, State University of New York Press, forthcoming). On Maimonides' views of human knowledge of metaphysics (Section IV), the locus classicus for recent discussions is Shlomo Pines, "The limitations of human knowledge according to Al-Farabi, Ibn Bajja, and Maimonides," reprinted in his *Studies in the History of Jewish Thought (The Collected Papers of Shlomo Pines*, vol. 4), ed. W. Z. Harvey and M. Idel (Jerusalem, Magnes Press, 1997) and, for a reply, Alexander Altmann, "Maimonides on the Intellect and the Scope of Metaphysics," in his *Von der mittelalterlichen zur modernen Aufklarung* (Tubingen, J. C. B. Mohr, 1987), pp. 60–129.

I wish to thank Amélie Rorty for comments on an earlier draft and the National Endowment for the Humanities for fellowship support while this essay was written.

9

DESCARTES, OR THE CULTIVATION OF THE INTELLECT

Daniel Garber

René Descartes (1596–1650) aimed to sweep away the past, and start philosophy anew. Much of what made Descartes important for his contemporaries, and for us as well, concerns the contents of his philosophy. Descartes's philosophy was directed squarely against the Aristotelian philosophy taught in the schools of his day. For the Aristotelians, all cognition begins in sensation: everything in the intellect comes first through the senses. Descartes's philosophy, on the other hand, emphasizes the priority of reason over the senses. Furthermore, Descartes substitutes a purely mechanical world of geometric bodies governed by laws of motion for an almost animistic world of Aristotelian substances with innate tendencies to different kinds of behavior. These original doctrines, together with his work in metaphysics, optics, mathematics, the theory of the passions, among other areas, made Descartes a central figure in his age.[1]

But in this essay I would like to concentrate on something different. Descartes opposed himself not only to the content of the philosophy of the schools, but to their very conception of what knowledge is and how it is to be transmitted. Connected with the new Cartesian philosophy is a genuine philosophy of education, a conception of the aims and goals of education very different than the one that dominated the school where Descartes himself had been educated as a youth. My project in this essay is to tease out some aspects of this philosophy.

REJECTING AUTHORITY

Let us begin with one of Descartes's most important texts, the *Discourse on the Method of Rightly Conducting One's Reason and Seeking the Truth in the Sciences*, published in 1637 as the introduction to three scientific texts, the *Geometry*, the *Dioptrics*, and the *Meteors*. The *Discourse* is presented as the autobiography of the author, outlining the path he took to the discoveries that he outlines later in the *Discourse* (parts IV and V), and selections of which he gives in the three treatises with which it appeared. But though presented as an autobiography, the *Discourse* is a kind of moral tale, "a history or, if you prefer, a fable" as Descartes puts it (AT VI 4 (CSM I 112)).[2] Let us leave aside the question of historical veracity and simply call the protagonist of the *Discourse* "RD."

Part I of the *Discourse* is largely concerned with RD's adventures in school; it gives an interesting account of what school might have been like for the young Descartes. (Descartes attended the Jesuit college of La Flèche.) The account begins:

> From my childhood I have been nourished upon letters, and because I was persuaded that by their means one could acquire a clear and certain knowledge of all that is useful in life, I was extremely eager to learn them.
>
> (AT VI 4 (CSM I 112–13))

The young RD was thus eager for learning, eager for school. The school he was sent to was "one of the most famous schools in Europe, where I thought there must be learned men if they existed anywhere on earth" (AT VI 5 (CSM I 113)). Furthermore, he thought himself among the best of the students there, and did not doubt that "the age in which we live [is] as flourishing, and as rich in good minds, as any before it" (Ibid.). But yet, all he found was disappointment:

> But as soon as I had completed the course of study at the end of which one is normally admitted to the ranks of the learned, I completely changed my opinion. For I found myself beset by so many doubts and errors that I came to think I had gained nothing from my attempts to become educated but increasing recognition of my ignorance.
>
> (AT VI 4 (CSM I 113))

Because of his dissatisfactions with the learning of the schools, RD decided to leave it all behind and travel the world:

> That is why, as soon as I was old enough to emerge from the control of my teachers, I entirely abandoned the study of letters. Resolving to seek no knowledge other than that which could be found in myself or else in the great book of the world, I spent the rest of my youth traveling.
>
> (AT VI 9 (CSM I 115))

Travel for RD ultimately led to contemplation; having put to one side what he learned in school, RD made the following resolution:

> But after I had spent some years pursuing these studies in the book of the world and trying to gain some experience, I resolved one day to undertake studies within myself too and to use all the powers of my mind in choosing the paths I should follow.
>
> (AT VI 10 (CSM I 116))

This is the project that Descartes then represents in the *Meditations*, published four years later in 1641. Descartes begins the first of the *Meditations* with the following observation:

> Some years ago I was struck by the large number of falsehoods that I had accepted as true in my childhood, and by the highly doubtful nature of the whole edifice that I had subsequently based on them. I realized that it was necessary, once in the course of my life, to demolish everything completely and start again right from the foundations if I wanted to establish anything at all in the sciences that was stable and likely to last.
>
> (AT VII 17 (CSM II 12))

As with the *Discourse*, the *Meditations* begins in rejection. The Meditator, to give the protagonist of the *Meditations* a name, begins by rejecting all former beliefs, doubting everything that can be called into doubt, from the most obvious deliverances of the senses to the simplest truths of arithmetic and geometry. The First Meditation ends with the hypothesis of the evil genius, "a malicious demon of the utmost power and cunning [who] has employed all his energies in order to deceive me" (AT VII 22 (CSM II 15)). By reflecting on this hypothesis, supposing it to be true, I can keep all my former beliefs and prejudices at bay, and maintain myself in this state of epistemic detachment. Unlike RD of the *Discourse*, who simply sets his former beliefs to one side, the Meditator uses the strongest arguments possible, arguments derived from the skeptical tradition to cleanse the mind of all former belief.

In this way, the rejection of the past, of tradition, of the authority of teachers seems central to the Cartesian philosophy. There is rejection at a number of different levels. First, there is the rejection of the senses. Descartes begins Meditation I with an explicit discussion of the senses, how they can and do deceive us, both while awake and while we are asleep and dreaming. Every schoolboy in Descartes's day was drilled in the Aristotelian dictum that "everything in the intellect comes first through the senses." While the senses return in Meditation VI, they never regain the full authority that they appear to have had before beginning the process of meditation; Descartes's final judgment is that they cannot tell us the way things really are, nor are they even completely reliable in the practical situations for which they were given to us. The point of the opening of the *Meditations*, then, is at least in part to lead the mind away from its dependence on the senses.[3]

But the rejection is more profound than that. The skeptical arguments in Meditation I attack not only the senses, but, more generally, everything which the Meditator had learned in the past. At the conclusion of the series of arguments, the Meditator admits that "there is not one of my former beliefs about which a doubt may not properly be raised" (AT VII 21 (CSM I 14–15)). Here the arguments of Meditation I join the comments Descartes made on his own education in the *Discourse on the Method*. Descartes lived in a learned intellectual culture, one that emphasized the importance of tradition and authority. St Thomas's *Summa theologica*, for example, still authoritative in the Jesuit college of La Flèche where Descartes studied from about 1606 to 1615 or so, is full of reasoned argument. But it is also grounded in the authority of Aristotle and the Church Fathers, whose opinions are constantly cited and discussed. Many of the other books to which Descartes would have been exposed at school were commentaries on Aristotle's texts, which regularly quoted and discussed the philosophers of the past, both ancient and medieval, contrasting their opinions, weighing their authority.[4] In the Renaissance, there were various reactions against the intellectual tradition of the schools, a diverse movement that went under the general name of Humanism. Descartes would have been exposed to Humanist trends in the Jesuit academy, along with the more orthodox scholasticism that was at the core of the curriculum there. But Humanism, too, was a learned tradition, grounded in new scholarship concerning the texts of Greek and Roman antiquity, seeking to introduce into the canon new texts, literary and philosophical. Like scholasticism, Humanism was grounded in a respect for the past. To be educated, then, in the early seventeenth century, was to know the wisdom of the past, to understand the different intellectual traditions.[5]

126

It is in this context that we must read part I of the *Discourse* and the opening of the *Meditations*. Descartes seems to be rejecting an entire intellectual tradition, scholasticism and Humanism, the idea that we must begin with the wisdom of the past, as well as the authority of those who teach the tradition. What Descartes seems to be telling his contemporaries (and us as well) is that the tradition and those who teach it are not relevant to real knowledge. It is significant here that an admiring disciple reports that Descartes gave all his books away when he left La Flèche.[6] While this is probably not true, it says something about the way in which some of Descartes's contemporaries read him. If there is a philosophy of education in Descartes this would seem to be it: true education must be done by the individual alone, outside of history, outside of tradition, outside of school.

But all of this is rather negative; it tells us something about what Cartesian pedagogy is *not*, but it tells us little if anything about what it *is*, what Descartes thinks the schools and their students *should* be doing. It is that to which we must turn.

INTUITION, DEDUCTION, AND KNOWLEDGE

Descartes's philosophy begins with a rejection of the past. But the first positive step is the affirmation of the self. In the *Discourse*, after rejecting the learning of the schools, RD takes off, alone, to experience the world, ultimately to reject that too, and to turn to himself. In the *Meditations*, after the skeptical arguments of Meditation I, the Meditator begins the reconstruction of the world with the famous Cogito Argument, "I think therefore I exist," building the world out of the self. For Descartes, the rejection of tradition and authority goes hand in hand with the view that knowledge, properly so-called, must be grounded in the individual and in the individual alone.

This view can be traced back to one of Descartes's earliest surviving writings, the *Rules for the Direction of the Mind (Regulae ad directionem ingenii)*. This work is a treatise on the method of finding truth, which Descartes probably wrote between 1620 and 1628, abandoning it incomplete approximately ten years before he published his *Discourse*, though it is summarized in part II of that work. The main focus of the book is the development of a procedure for investigation which, Descartes claimed, will lead us to genuine knowledge. As a preliminary to this investigation, Descartes begins with an account of the nature of knowledge, the goal of this inquiry. Rule 3 reads:

> Concerning objects proposed for study, we ought to investigate what we can clearly and evidently intuit or deduce with certainty, and not what other people have thought or what we ourselves conjecture. For knowledge can be attained in no other way.
>
> (AT X 366 (CSM I 13))

Intuition is defined as follows:

> By "intuition" I do not mean the fluctuating testimony of the senses or the deceptive judgment of the imagination as it botches things together, but the conception of a clear and attentive mind, which is so easy and distinct that there can be no room for doubt about what we are understanding. Alternatively, and this comes to the same thing,

127

intuition is the indubitable conception of a clear and attentive mind which proceeds solely from the light of reason.

(AT X 368 (CSM I 14))

Intuition is, for Descartes, supplemented by deduction. By deduction Descartes means "the inference of something as following necessarily from some other propositions which are known with certainty" (AT XI 369 (CSM I 15)). Strictly speaking, deduction is not entirely separate from intuition. As Descartes writes, "the self-evidence and certainty of intuition is required not only for apprehending single propositions, but also for any train of reasoning whatever" (AT XI 369 (CSM I 14–15)). In this way, a deduction is just a train of intuitions. Were our memory better, we could dispense with deductive reasoning altogether, and know by intuition alone. In this way it is fair to say that for Descartes, knowledge, strictly speaking, is grounded in intuition, the immediate operation of this faculty.

Descartes's view is that we are all blessed with an innate ability to see certain truths. The opening passage of the *Discourse* reads:

> Good sense is the best distributed thing in the world: for everyone thinks himself so well endowed with it that even those who are the hardest to please in everything else do not usually desire more of it than they possess. In this it is unlikely that everyone is mistaken . . . [T]he power of judging well and of distinguishing the true from the false – which is what we properly call "good sense" or "reason" – is naturally equal in all men.

(AT VI 1–2 (CSM I 111))

There is a touch of sarcasm in this, to be sure. But, at the same time, it is a good summary of one of Descartes's basic commitments: we all have reason, a faculty, given to us by God for distinguishing true from false. This is what he means when he talks of intuition in the *Rules*.

As Descartes conceives them, intuition and deduction are grounded in the experiences individuals have. Knowledge, for Descartes, does not reside in books or in authorities; for an individual to have genuine knowledge, he or she must actually have the experience that counts as an intuitive grasp of the truth of a proposition or the validity of an inference from one proposition to another. In this way, learning cannot be a spectator sport, a passive absorption of what the teacher has to tell. The student who does not have the actual experience itself has no knowledge, properly speaking. Descartes wrote in the *Rules*:

> And even though we have read all the arguments of Plato and Aristotle, we shall never become philosophers if we are unable to make a sound judgment on matters which come up for discussion; in this case what we would seem to have learnt would not be science but history.

(AT X 367 (CSM I 113))

True knowledge thus can come neither from teacher nor from tradition. This has obvious consequences for Descartes's conception of education. True education, then, must involve not the transfer of information, doctrine, or dogma, but simply the cultivation of the intellect.

THE CULTIVATION OF THE INTELLECT

The *Rules for the Direction of the Mind* is, in a very general sense, meant as a pedagogical work intended to teach us a way to use our native intelligence (the literal translation of *ingenium* in the Latin title of the work) as well as we can. As such it includes mental exercises to help prepare the reader to use the method for finding truth that Descartes there outlines. The idea of the cultivation of the intellect is basic to this regimen. In Rule 9, for example, Descartes suggests the following exercise:

> We must concentrate our mind's eye totally upon the most insignificant and easiest of matters, and dwell on them long enough to acquire the habit of intuiting the truth distinctly and clearly.
>
> (AT X 400 (CSM I 33))

He goes on to say later in the body of the Rule:

> Everyone ought therefore to acquire the habit of encompassing in his thought at one time facts which are very simple and very few in number – so much so that he never thinks he knows something unless he intuits it just as distinctly as any of the things he knows most distinctly of all. Some people of course are born with a much greater aptitude for this sort of insight than others; but our minds can become much better equipped for it through method and practice.
>
> (AT X 401–2 (CSM I 34))

This idea, that we need to practice having intuitions and making deductions before beginning the process of following Descartes's method and seeking knowledge in earnest, appears again in the *Discourse*, in only slightly different form. There the cultivation of the intellect is not a *preparation* for using the method. Rather, Descartes recommends in the voice of RD that we accustom our minds to having intuitions and making deductions by practicing *the method itself* in the domain of mathematics, where intuitions and deductions seem easier to come by. He writes:

> Reflecting, too, that of all those who have hitherto sought after truth in the sciences, mathematicians alone have been able to find any demonstrations – that is to say, certain and evident reasonings – I had no doubt that I should begin with the very things that they studied. From this, however, the only advantage I hoped to gain was to accustom my mind to nourish itself on truths and not to be satisfied with bad reasoning.
>
> (AT VI 19 (CSM I 120))

It is, thus, by practicing this method that RD trained his intellect to grasp truth through intuition and deduction. He writes, again in the *Discourse*:

> But what pleased me most about this method was that by following it I was sure in every case to use my reason, if not perfectly, at least as well as was in my power. Moreover, as I practised the method I felt my mind gradually become accustomed to conceiving its objects more clearly and distinctly.
>
> (AT VI 21 (CSM I 121))[7]

A view very similar to that of the *Discourse* and the *Rules* is also found in one of Descartes's latest and most self-consciously pedagogical texts. In the 1640s, after having published the *Discourse* and the *Meditations*, Descartes began to ruminate about how to get his own philosophy into circulation in the schools, and how to get it to replace Aristotle as the new master. It is with this in mind that he undertook to write a book, the *Principles of Philosophy*, published in Latin in 1644 and in French in 1647.[8] While it is not exactly like any textbook in philosophy then in use, it is a more systematic presentation of his philosophy than is found elsewhere in the corpus. For the French translation, Descartes composed a preface that addresses explicitly the question of how one ought to learn philosophy. The idea of the method as a kind of mental exercise for training the intellect is very prominent there as well. After providing for ourselves a code of behavior to govern our actions while we are rebuilding our beliefs, Descartes recommends that we study logic:

> I do not mean the logic of the Schools, for this is strictly speaking nothing but a dialectic which teaches ways of expounding to others what one already knows or even of holding forth without judgment about things that one does not know. Such logic corrupts good sense rather than increasing it. I mean instead the kind of logic which teaches us to direct our reason with a view to discovering the truths of which we are ignorant. Since this depends to a great extent on practice, it is good for the student to work for a long time at practicing the rules on very easy and simple questions like those of mathematics. Then, when he has acquired some skill in finding the truth on these questions, he should begin to tackle true philosophy in earnest.
>
> (AT IXB 13 (CSM I 186))

The true logic, he tells us later in the preface, is just the doctrine of method as taught in part II of his *Discourse*, itself a summary of the method as taught in the *Rules*. (See AT IXB 15 (CSM I 186)). In this preface to the *Principles*, as in the *Rules* and the *Discourse*, Descartes suggests that we begin by cultivating reason, practicing finding truth.

In recommending the cultivation of the intellect through practice in intuition and deduction, Descartes set himself squarely against two features of the scholastic educational regimen that were intended to exercise the intellect: the study of formal logic and the practice of disputation.

A course on logic, based on Aristotle's *Organon*, digested into simplified form and rules of thumb by many generations of pedagogues, was a central part of the arts curriculum (i.e. the course of studies preliminary to advanced work in law, medicine, or theology) in every school in Europe in the early seventeenth century.[9] As taught in the schools, Aristotelian logic was very formal and abstract. Learning logic was a matter of memorizing numerous rules to enable the student to recognize valid and invalid syllogisms.

While on occasion Descartes felt that he had to mute his public rejection of formal logic, just as he had to tone down his opposition to other aspects of scholastic doctrine and practice,[10] it is clear that Descartes thought little of formal logic as a part of the education of the young. First of all, Descartes argues, the kind of logic taught in the schools is of extremely limited utility. Unlike his method, which Descartes sometimes refers to as logic,

130

the Aristotelian logic of the schools cannot help us find new truths, but only to arrange truths that we have already discovered by some other means. He writes in the *Rules*:

> On the basis of their method, dialecticians are unable to formulate a syllogism with a true conclusion unless they are already in possession of the substance of the conclusion, i.e. unless they have previous knowledge of the very truth deduced in the syllogism. It is obvious therefore that they themselves can learn nothing new from such forms of reasoning, and hence that ordinary dialectic is of no use whatever to those who wish to investigate the truth of things. Its sole advantage is that it sometimes enables us to explain to others arguments which are already known.
>
> (AT X 406 (CSM I 36–7); cf. AT VI 17 (CSM I 119); AT IXB 13 (CSM I 186))

Furthermore, Descartes notes, the rules taught in logic are confusing and may lead the student astray. And so, he remarks in the *Discourse*:

> And although logic does contain many excellent and true precepts, these are mixed up with so many others which are harmful or superfluous that it is almost as difficult to distinguish them as it is to carve a Diana or a Minerva from an unhewn block of marble.
>
> (AT VI 17 (CSM I 119))

And so, Descartes suggests in his dialogue, *The Search after Truth*, we should set formal logic aside, and cultivate the light of reason directly:

> When this light operates on its own, it is less liable to go wrong than when it anxiously strives to follow the numerous different rules, the inventions of human ingenuity and idleness, which serve more to corrupt it than render it more perfect.
>
> (AT X 521 (CSM II 415); cf. AT X 439–40 (CSM I 57))

The practice of disputation was also a central element of scholastic education in the early seventeenth century. According to the Jesuit *Ratio studiorum*, or "Order of study", an overarching curriculum that governed Jesuit education at the time that Descartes attended La Flèche, students were to participate regularly in these exercises, in which they were expected to argue extemporaneously for and against theses that were posed.[11]

Again, as with his criticism of scholastic logic, Descartes sometimes mutes his criticisms of the practice. In the *Rules*, for example, he writes:

> Yet I do not wish on that account to condemn that method of philosophizing which others have hitherto devised, nor those weapons of the schoolmen, probable syllogisms, which are just made for controversies. For these exercise the minds of the young, stimulating them with a certain rivalry; and it is much better that their minds should be informed with opinions of that sort – even though they are evidently uncertain, being controversial among the learned – than that they should be left entirely to their own devices.
>
> (AT X 363–4 (CSM I 11))

But even in his apparent praise, there are criticisms of the practice. First of all, insofar as the aim of the disputation is to convince the listener of the truth of one side of the disagreement, the emphasis is generally not on certainty, but on the probable syllogisms used in rhetoric, syllogisms whose premises are not necessarily certain, but only plausible to the intended audience. This, Descartes argues in the *Discourse*, if anything only undermines the student's ability to discern the truth, unlike the kind of cultivation of the intellect that he proposes in its place. He writes:

> Nor have I ever observed that any previously unknown truth has been discovered by means of the disputations practiced in the schools. For so long as each side strives for victory, more effort is put into establishing plausibility than in weighing reasons for and against; and those who have long been good advocates do not necessarily go on to make better judges.
>
> (AT VI 69 (CSM I 146))

Furthermore, the student who considers argument a competitive sport will actually resist the light of reason if it appears to oppose a position he is obligated to defend. Descartes writes in the *Second Replies*:

> This is why I wrote "Meditations" rather than "Disputations" . . . In so doing I wanted to make it clear that I would have nothing to do with anyone who was not willing to join me in meditating and giving the subject attentive consideration. For the very fact that someone braces himself to attack the truth makes him less suited to perceive it, since he will be withdrawing his consideration from the convincing arguments which support the truth in order to find counter-arguments against it.
>
> (AT VII 157 (CSM II 112))

Finally, in contrast to his regimen, which leads to certainty, and thus to agreement, the practice of disputation leads only to conflict. Writing in the preface to the French *Principles*, Descartes notes:

> The truths contained in these principles, because they are very clear and very certain, will eliminate all ground for dispute, and so will dispose people's minds to gentleness and harmony. This is the opposite result to that produced by the debates in the Schools, which – slowly and without their noticing it – make the participants more argumentative and opinionated, and hence are perhaps the major cause of the heresies and disagreements which now plague the world.
>
> (AT IXB 18 (CSM I 188))

In an era very much aware of the religious wars that plagued France in the late sixteenth century and still plagued Europe during Descartes's lifetime, this was a powerful consideration. Descartes's hope was that in a world in which every student was taught to cultivate reason and seek only certainty, disagreement would end and harmony would reign.

THE ORDER OF REASONS:
STARTING ON A FIRM FOUNDATION

Cartesian pedagogy begins with the cultivation of the intellect, exercises designed to practice finding truth, accustoming the mind to settling for nothing less than the certainty of intuition and deduction. But after these exercises, one must "begin to tackle true philosophy in earnest," as Descartes advises the reader in the preface to the French *Principles* (AT IXB 14 (CSM I 186)). At this point the Cartesian pedagogy follows the Cartesian philosophy. We begin with the self, with the Cogito Argument establishing the existence of a thinking thing (Meditation II). From the self flows everything else. From the idea of God found in the self Descartes proves the existence of God external to the mind (Meditation III). From the existence of God, his benevolence, and certain features of the mind, Descartes is then able to argue that everything that he clearly and distinctly perceives is true (Meditation IV). On this he is able to ground his arguments for the real distinction between mind and body, and his proof of the existence of a real world of bodies, conceived without color or taste, heat or cold, a world of geometrical objects made real (Meditations V and VI). And with this his physics is off and running, leading him from the general laws of nature, through a cosmology to a biology, and eventually, he hoped, to an account of the human being sufficient to ground both medicine and an account of the passions, which, in turn, is to ground a truly scientific moral theory. In this way he offers a systematic mechanist alternative to the philosophy of Aristotle and the schools.

The full details of this story go far beyond the bounds of this essay, and constitute an account of the Cartesian philosophy itself. But there is one aspect of this story that is very important to note in this connection. Descartes's philosophy is clearly organized in a hierarchical manner. As he writes in the preface to the French *Principles*,

> The whole of philosophy is like a tree. The roots are metaphysics, the trunk is physics, and the branches emerging from the trunk are all the other sciences, which may be reduced to three principal ones, namely medicine, mechanics, and morals.
>
> (AT IXB 14 (CSM I 186))

This hierarchy has an obvious epistemological consequence for Descartes. If we are to have real knowledge, then we must study these sciences in the proper order, beginning with the metaphysical foundations in the self and God, progressing then to body and physics, before ending with the practical sciences. In an important letter to his friend Marin Mersenne, Descartes wrote the following explanation of his procedure in the *Meditations*:

> It should be noted that throughout the work the order I follow is not the order of the subject-matter, but the order of the reasoning. This means that I do not attempt to say in a single place everything relevant to a given subject, because it would be impossible for me to provide proper proofs, since my supporting reasons would have to be drawn in some cases from considerably more distant sources than in others. Instead, I reason in an orderly way from what is easier to what is harder, making what deductions I can, now on one subject, now on another. This is the right way, in my opinion, to find and explain the truth. The order of the subject-matter is good only

133

for those whose reasoning is disjointed, and who can say as much about one difficulty as about another.

(AT III 266–7 (CSMK III 163); cf. AT VII 155 (CSM II 110))

This attitude is central to Descartes's assessment of the science of Galileo (1564–1642), a rough contemporary who, like him, opposed the philosophy of Aristotle and the schools. He writes, again in a letter to Mersenne:

Generally speaking, I find he philosophizes much more ably than is usual, in that, so far as he can, he abandons the errors of the Schools and tries to use mathematical methods in the investigation of physical questions. On that score, I am completely at one with him, for I hold that there is no other way to discover the truth. But he continually digresses, and he does not take time to explain matters fully. This, in my view, is a mistake: it shows that he has not investigated matters in an orderly way, and has merely sought explanations for some particular effects, without going into the primary causes in nature; hence his building lacks a foundation.

(AT II 380 (CSMK III 124))

Approaching the study of nature in this way, Descartes thinks, takes us to new heights. In the preface to the French *Principles*, Descartes notes five levels of wisdom. The first includes self-evident truths "so clear in themselves that they can be acquired without meditation"; the second includes what we learn from the senses; the third involves what we learn by talking with others, and the fourth, what we learn by reading books "written by people who are capable of instructing us well." To these Descartes adds a fifth degree, which, he modestly claims, he is the first to attain:

This consists in the search for the first causes and the true principles which enable us to deduce the reasons for everything we are capable of knowing . . . . I am not sure, however, that there has been anyone up till now who has succeeded in this project.

(AT IXB 5 (CSM I 181))

In emphasizing the proper order of instruction, Descartes perhaps thought of himself as departing from his teachers. One suspects that in the practical world of the classroom, where one is told to do ethics one year, physics another, teachers were not nearly as careful about following the order of reasoning as Descartes would have liked to have been. But in a deeper sense, his concern with order and the interconnectedness of knowledge is connected with deeper strands in scholastic thought. Scholastic pedagogues worried considerably over the question of the order of the curriculum, what should be taught before what, and why. Furthermore, the more general point, that true knowledge is grounded in knowledge of first causes is something that teachers would have acknowledged, though they would have disagreed about the starting place of knowledge. In this way, perhaps, the insistence on starting with the most basic, and proceeding in order down from there would not have been such a radical idea.[12]

Indeed, on this score, the true radicals may have been those like Galileo and, later, Newton, who relaxed the Cartesian (and Aristotelian) insistence on starting with first principles and ultimate causes, and worked in the other direction, from phenomena observed, back towards the first causes. Galileo, for example, started with observations of balls falling down inclined planes and bobbing at the end of pendula, and arrived at mathematical accounts of the motion of heavy bodies. Newton (1642–1727), working later in the century, famously claimed to "deduce causes from effects," and in this way claimed to discover the theory of universal gravitation. Neither worried about the basic principles and ultimate causes with which Descartes insisted on beginning. Ironically enough, the freedom that came from this move may have allowed natural philosophers to come closer to penetrating the real first causes than Descartes himself did.

A FINAL QUESTION: A PLACE FOR BOOKS AND TEACHERS

In the beginning of this essay, I discussed the way in which Descartes begins in rejection, rejection of authority of all kinds, including the kind of authority represented by books and teachers. But this would seem to raise a special problem for Descartes; he would seem to be posing as an authority who is telling us to reject authority, an author who writes books telling us not to read books! To write a book whose message is not to read books – this book included – would seem to be self-contradictory; to stand up in front of a class as a teacher, teaching the lesson that one cannot learn from teachers, would seem to be self-defeating. How can Descartes set himself up as a teacher, even if it is a teacher who is teaching us this radical truth?

Descartes was very much aware of this paradox. His answer lies in the personae that he adopts to present his philosophy, the 'I' that weaves its way through his prose, the voice of the teacher. In Descartes's day, it was common for the teacher to stand in front of the class, his lectures carefully written out, and dictate them to the students, who would copy them word for word into their copy-books, to be carefully studied. In such a classroom, it was clear who was the master, and who was the student, who had the knowledge and wisdom, and who was receiving it.[13] The *Principles* is a text-book, written for the classroom in the hope of being used in teaching children, and it shares the didactic qualities of other textbooks of the era. But Descartes's personae in others of his writings, in the *Search after Truth*, the *Discourse*, and the *Meditations*, Descartes's stand-in Eudoxus, as well as RD and the Meditator, as I have called them, are not teachers of this sort.

In the *Search after Truth*, Descartes begins in his introduction to the dialogue with a discourse about how we should not judge opinions on the grounds of who it is that holds them. He writes:

> I hope too that the truths I set forth will not be any less well received for their not being derived from Aristotle or Plato, and that they will have currency in the world in the same way as money, whose value is no less when it comes from the purse of a peasant than when it comes from a bank. Moreover I have done my best to make these truths equally useful to everybody. I could find no style better suited to this end than that of a conversation in which several friends, frankly and without ceremony, disclose the best of their thoughts to each other.

(AT X 498 (CSM II 401))

The dialogue form is an ideal way of presenting philosophical ideas in a non-dogmatic way. Though it is clear from the beginning which position Descartes himself endorses (unfortunately, in his use of the form, Descartes is not the equal of Plato or Hume, or even Berkeley), it is through debate and the interchange of arguments that the reader is led to see the wisdom of the Cartesian point of view, and not through being told what to think.

While the dialogue is a very traditional form of philosophical instruction, in others of his works, Descartes experiments with different literary devices for presenting his thought in non-dogmatic ways. In the *Discourse*, Descartes's protagonist RD emphasizes that he does not have any special talents or wisdom that sets him above others: "For my part, I have never presumed my mind to be in any way more perfect than that of the ordinary man" (AT VI 2 (CSM I 111)). Rather, he claims, it was luck that led him to his discoveries, the method that he will outline in part II of the *Discourse* and the scientific discoveries that he will present in the three "essays" that the *Discourse* introduces:

> [T]he diversity of our opinions does not arise because some of us are more reasonable than others but solely because we direct our thoughts along different paths and do not attend to the same things. For it is not enough to have a good mind; the main thing is to apply it well. . . . I consider myself very fortunate to have happened upon certain paths in my youth which led me to considerations and maxims from which I formed a method whereby, it seems to me, I can increase my knowledge gradually and raise it little by little to the highest point allowed by the mediocrity of my mind and the short duration of my life.
>
> (AT VI 2, 3 (CSM I 111, 112))

Even this is not presented dogmatically; RD freely admits that he may be deceived here: "perhaps what I take for gold and diamonds is nothing but a bit of copper and glass" (AT VI 3 (CSM I 112)). And so, he tells the reader:

> My present aim, then, is not to teach the method which everyone must follow in order to direct his reason correctly, but only to reveal how I have tried to direct my own. One who presumes to give precepts must think himself more skilful than those to whom he gives them; and if he makes the slightest mistake, he may be blamed. But I am presenting this work only as a story [*histoire*] or, if you prefer, a fable in which, among certain examples worthy of imitation, you will perhaps also find many others that it would be right not to follow; and so I hope it will be useful for some without being harmful to any, and that everyone will be grateful to me for my frankness.
>
> (AT VI 4 (CSM I 112))

In another image that he uses, RD tells the reader that he is presenting his intellectual history "as if in a painting, so that everyone may judge it for himself" (ibid.). This may be something of a pose; I strongly suspect that the historical Descartes did think himself to be more intelligent than the common person, and that he had enormous confidence in his method and in the discoveries that he made with its help. But no matter. What is important is that he did not represent himself in that way: his persona RD does not see himself as transmitting truth to the reader, but as telling a story, providing an example, some aspects of which the reader may find worthy of following. If RD is a teacher, he is teaching by the example of his own life; he is not *telling* you to reject teachers, but *showing* you how *he* did, and hoping that you will agree that the results are worthy of imitation.

Descartes's Meditator, his persona in the *Meditations*, is somewhat different from RD. Though one can read the opening of the *Meditations* as a kind of continuation of the *Discourse*, RD sitting down to actually pursue the intellectual program that he prepares in parts I and II of the *Discourse* (and, in a preliminary version, outlines in part IV), the rhetorical strategy is not the same in the two works. Whereas RD is the companion at the tavern, telling you his life's story, the Meditator is a kind of guide. "Guide" is, perhaps, not quite the right word here. Descartes writes in the preface to the reader "I would not urge anyone to read this book except those who are able and willing to meditate seriously with me" (AT VII 9 (CSM II 8)). The point is that the *Meditations* is not simply a book to be read as an account of what its protagonist (the Meditator) happened to think on a particular occasion, as the *Discourse* represents itself. Nor is it a book whose conclusions we are supposed to believe simply because we are told that they are true by the author. Rather, we are supposed to enter into the arguments, and meditate *with* the protagonist. When we read the skeptical arguments of Meditation I, *we* are supposed to feel their force, and *we* must reject everything we formerly believed. When in Meditation II the Meditator discovers his own existence as a thinking thing through the Cogito argument, *we* are each supposed to discover *our own existence*. For the *Meditations* to work then, we must actually *identify with* the Meditator, and have, for ourselves, the experiences that lead toward intellectual enlightenment.[14] Again, Descartes is not telling you what to believe, but, in a way different than in the *Discourse*, showing you how you can come to the knowledge that he thinks that he has obtained.

In these ways, then, Descartes can play the teacher without violating his own philosophy of education, and lead us to reject authority, turn to ourselves, and discover, for ourselves, the truths that Descartes would have us learn. But a touch of irony still remains. Descartes, the fresh, new voice in the 1630s and 1640s, when he burst upon the scene, the philosopher who sought to liberate philosophy from the past, has over the years become one of the classics himself, one of the ancient authors from which we must liberate ourselves, if we are to follow his own advice.

NOTES

1 This is not the place to present a full picture of Descartes's philosophical and scientific accomplishments. For a recent overview of Descartes's thought, see John Cottingham (ed.) *The Cambridge Companion to Descartes* (Cambridge, Cambridge University Press, 1992).

2 The standard original-language edition of Descartes's writings is René Descartes, *Oeuvres de Descartes*, ed. Charles Adam and Paul Tannery, new edn (11 vols) (Paris, CNRS/Vrin, 1964–74). This will be abbreviated 'AT', followed by volume and page number. The best current translation is René Descartes, *The Philosophical Writings of Descartes*, 3 vols, ed. and trans. John Cottingham, Robert Stoothoff, Dugald Murdoch, and (for vol. III) Anthony Kenny (Cambridge, Cambridge University Press, 1984–91). This will be abbreviated 'CSM' for volumes I and II, and 'CSMK' for volume III, followed by the volume and page number. References to Descartes's writings will generally be given in the text of the essay, with the original language edition followed by the translation, in parentheses.

3 For an excellent treatment of Meditation I that emphasizes the rejection of the senses, see Harry Frankfurt, *Demons, Dreamers, and Madmen* (Indianapolis, Ind., Bobbs-Merrill, 1970), esp. chs 1–9.

4 On the place of Aristotle and Aristotelianism in the school curriculum in this period, see L. W. B. Brockliss, *French Higher Education in the Seventeenth and Eighteenth Centuries: a Cultural History* (Oxford, Oxford University Press, 1987) and Charles B. Schmitt, *Aristotle and the Renaissance* (Cambridge, Mass., Harvard University Press, 1983).

5 For a recent survey of the Humanist tradition, see Jill Kraye (ed.) *The Cambridge Companion to Renaissance Humanism* (Cambridge, Cambridge University Press, 1996).

6 The report is contained in the notes of Frans van Schooten the elder, given in AT X 646.

7 When Descartes here talks about mathematics as an appropriate subject for cultivating the intellect, he doesn't mean Euclidean geometry, the kind of mathematics taught in the schools. RD was no happier with the mathematics taught in school than he was with any other subjects. See AT VI 17–18 (CSM I 119–20). The kind of mathematics Descartes has in mind here is his own analytic geometry. For a discussion of Descartes's mathematics, see Stephen Gaukroger, "The nature of abstract reasoning: philosophical aspects of Descartes' work in algebra," in Cottingham (ed.) *Cambridge Companion to Descartes*.

8 On the conception of the *Principles* as a textbook for the classroom, see, e.g., Descartes to Mersenne, 31 December 1640, AT III 276 (CSMK III 167).

9 See Brockliss, *French Higher Education*, pp. 194–205 for the teaching of logic in France.

10 See, e.g., Descartes's answers to the Jesuit Father Bourdin's *Seventh Objections* to the *Meditations*, AT VII 522, 544 (CSM II 355, 371). Descartes at that moment was particularly keen to get the Jesuits, his old teachers, on his side, and bent over backwards not to offend them. This was not an isolated incident. In writing to his then disciple Henricus Regius in January 1642, Descartes explained his general policy of tempering his views in delicate situations so as not to cause unnecessary hostility; see AT III 491–2 (CSMK III 205). Regius had recently gotten in some trouble at the Protestant University of Utrecht for presenting his Cartesian views with too much boldness, and Descartes was trying to tell him how to avoid future troubles of this kind.

11 For the rules concerning disputations in the *Ratio studiorum* of 1599, which governed La Flèche while Descartes was studying there, see Edward A. Fitzpatrick (ed.) *St Ignatius and the Ratio Studiorum* (New York, McGraw-Hill, 1933), pp. 144ff.

12 On the relations between Descartes and the schoolmen on the question of starting with first causes and the order of knowledge and instruction, see Daniel Garber, *Descartes' Metaphysical Physics* (Chicago, University of Chicago Press, 1992), pp. 58–62.

13 Many such copy books survive, which provide a window into the early seventeenth-century classroom. A number of such books of notes are listed as "courses" in the bibliography of manuscripts in Brockliss, *French Higher Education*, pp. 486ff. For some excerpts from philosophy courses that particularly concern seventeenth-century scholastic reactions to Descartes's philosophy, see Étienne Gilson, *Études sur le rôle de la pensée médiévale dans la formation du système cartésien* (Paris, Vrin, 1975), pp. 316–33.

14 On the background to Descartes's use of the meditation as a literary form for his philosophy, see the essays by A. Rorty and G. Hatfield in A. Rorty (ed.) *Essays on Descartes' Meditations* (Berkeley, Calif., University of California Press, 1986).

10

HOBBES: TRUTH, PUBLICITY AND CIVIL DOCTRINE

Jeremy Waldron

Governments base their authority ultimately on popular acceptance of their legitimacy. So governments have an interest in what people come to believe about the basis of their legitimacy, and in the processes by which these beliefs are taught and developed. In a well-ordered society, however, the government also has an interest in the inculcation of true beliefs and in the avoidance of ideology and false consciousness. What, then, is the relation between the government's interest in civil education and its commitment to truth and to the principle of publicity – that is, the principle that government should be conducted in the open, and that the successful conduct of public business should not depend on the public being misled about the basis on which it is conducted? Early in our tradition, we find some consideration of these questions in the work of Thomas Hobbes. In *Leviathan* Hobbes devotes considerable attention to the topic of "Civill doctrine," that is, the body of theory, principle, value and understanding that needs to be taught in the schools and universities, and to be widely accepted in society, if the social and political structure is to survive and do its work.

> [S]eeing the Universities are the Fountains of Civill, and Moral Doctrine, from whence the Preachers, and the Gentry, drawing such water as they find, use to sprinkle the same (both from the Pulpit, and in their Conversation) upon the People, there ought certainly to be great care taken, to have it pure, both from the Venime of Heathen Politicians, and from the Incantation of Deceiving Spirits.[1]

The universities are the fountains of civil and moral doctrine; the clergy and the gentry, who in their youth attend the universities, draw water from these fountains and sprinkle it abroad in their sermons, in their little homilies from the magistrates' bench, and in their general conversation; and if social hydraulics works as it ought, this holy water eventually trickles down all over the common people, drenching them in doctrine, and teaching them their civic duty and – what's more – the true ground of their civic duty. Or, as Hobbes also puts it,

> They whom necessity . . . keepeth attent on their trades, and labour; and they, on the other side, whom superfluity, or sloth carrieth after their sensual pleasures (which two sorts of men take up the greatest part of Mankind), being diverted from deep meditation, which the learning of truth, not onely in the matter of Naturall Justice,

139

but also of all other Sciences necessarily requireth, receive the Notions of their duty, chiefly from Divines in the Pulpit, and partly from such of their Neighbours, of familiar acquaintance, as having the Faculty of discoursing readily, and plausibly, seem wiser and better learned in cases of Law, and Conscience, than themselves. And the Divines, and such others as make shew of Learning, derive their knowledge from the Universities, and from the Schooles of Law, or from the Books, which by men eminent in those Schooles, and Universities, have been published. It is therefore manifest that the Instruction of the people dependeth wholly, on the right teaching of Youth in the Universities.[2]

The distinctive features of Hobbes's social and political setting allow us to pose some hard questions about this approach that are relevant *for us*.

I don't want to discuss Hobbes's view that the political sovereign has a right to regulate and restrict what is taught in the universities, but not because that's unimportant for Hobbes. On the contrary, he regarded "appointing Teachers, and examining what Doctrines are conformable, or contrary to the Defence, Peace, and Good of the people" as one of the essential rights – indeed one of the essential duties – associated with the office of sovereign representative.[3] This aspect of Hobbes's view would take us off into a discussion and vindication of free speech and academic coercion and academic freedom that would be too quick and too easy, leaving behind and undiscussed *the important question for us* – to which the trickle down theory is also relevant – namely: How should we in the universities regard our role in the inculcation of values? Never mind what the state or the sovereign is doing, do we as professors, particularly those of us associated explicitly with the study of ethics and human values, have an obligation to orient our research and our teaching to the broader ethical needs of the society, to its liberal values, and to the formation of good citizens?

Now, so far as his own situation was concerned, Hobbes was convinced that contemporary universities in England in the middle of the seventeenth century were doing a very bad job of maintaining the fountain of civil doctrine. For one thing, it was only a hundred years or so since the English reformation, and the universities were permeated if not by Roman Catholicism then by the spirit or ghost of Roman Catholicism, which preached quite severe limits on the authority of the temporal state. "'Tis no wonder," said Hobbes, if the current generation of scholars "yet retain a relish of that subtile liquor, wherever they were first seasoned, against the Civill Authority."[4] For another thing, teaching in the universities, particularly the teaching of moral and political philosophy, was still so overwhelmingly dominated by Aristotle as to be unworthy of the name "philosophy" – "the nature whereof," said Hobbes, "depends not upon Authors." (Hobbes is an early and healthy critic of the idea of a philosophical *canon*.) What's presently taught, he said, should be called "Aristotelity," not philosophy![5]

What *should* they be teaching, if not Aristotle and Catholic natural law doctrine? Should they be teaching Hobbes's *Leviathan*? In Chapter 30 of *Leviathan*, Hobbes imagines an interlocutor asking, "Is it *you* will undertake to teach the Universities?" Hard question, responds Hobbes, and then he adds coyly, "it is not fit, not needful, for me to say either I

[sic], or No; for any man that sees what I am doing may easily perceive what I think."[6] Though at the end of the book – eighteen chapters later – in the passage we began with, the one about "trickle-down," he is brazen enough to say,

> there is nothing in this whole Discourse, . . . as far as I can perceive, contrary either to the Word of God, or to good Manners, or tending to the disturbance of the Publique Tranquility. Therefore I think it may be profitably printed, and more profitably taught in the Universities.[7]

We know, of course, that nothing would have filled his contemporaries with greater horror than Hobbism being taught in the universities as the basis of civic education.[8] He was widely regarded as an atheist, a materialist, and a subverter of everything that political, ecclesiastical and educational authority were properly based on. Hobbes believed that good and evil have no intrinsic meaning: they are either relative to the appetites of the person who uses them, or they are defined purely conventionally by a political sovereign. Most contemporary moralists thought that was false and pernicious. Hobbes believed that political authority was based, in the last resort, on rational self-interest. Most contemporary politicians thought that was false and subversive. Most important for our purposes, Hobbes believed that *if* any view like his was true, it could safely be taught to the people as the basis of their civic obligation. The people do not need and social stability does not require any belief in intrinsic good and evil, transcending either individual appetites or conventional stipulations: it is enough, for political purposes, if they recognize and embrace the relativist position that positive "Law determineth what is Honest and Dishonest; what is Just and Unjust; and generally what is Good and Evill."[9] Again, Hobbes thought that the people do not need, and political authority does not require, a mythology of natural aristocracy,[10] divine right or any other superstitious cult of royalty, or even any noble lie about the immemorial integrity of the ancient constitution. The people can bear the truth about politics as they can bear the truth about morality, even if the truth is Hobbesian. His contemporaries thought the best one could say about all this was that it was evidently false and socially and politically reckless.

Suppose they were right about that. That is, suppose the truth about morality and politics were really Hobbesian in character, but that, as a matter of political sociology, that truth – if taught abroad – would be disorienting and subversive. Suppose that were the case. *Then* what should be taught in the universities, on Hobbes's account? Worse still, suppose it turned out that there was no rationally acceptable ground for political obligation and obedience at all, not even a Hobbesian ground. Suppose that impartial, learned, rigorous and rational inquiry vindicated the view that justice is a sham, that talk of rights is mischievous nonsense, and that laws and constitutions are not worthy of the respect and dignity they purport to command. Suppose such views turned out to be true. *Then* what should be taught in the universities? The truth which undermines authority, or the lies and myths that sustain it?

Thomas Hobbes avoided this question, or rather he was adamant that it was our good fortune it did not need to be faced. He said,

And though in matter of Doctrine, nothing ought to be regarded but the Truth; yet this is not repugnant to the regulating of the same by Peace [*that is, by the Sovereign who keeps the peace*]. For Doctrine repugnant to Peace, can no more be True, than Peace and Concord can be against the Law of Nature.[11]

Now it is tempting to read this position ("Doctrine repugnant to peace cannot be true") as though it represented a pragmatic conception of truth: "true" in politics just is whatever conduces to peace; "false" is (maybe *inter alia*) whatever disturbs it or is likely to result in war. It is tempting in other words to say that this passage reveals a Hobbes who not only has no respect for value – good and evil, right and wrong – and who allows value to be endlessly manipulated by the sovereign allegedly in the interests of peace; but that it also reveals a Hobbes who has no respect for truth, and who either does not accept the vocabulary of objective truth and falsity, or (even if he does accept it *qua* philosopher) is perfectly willing to allow the sovereign to play fast and loose with truth and falsity for political purposes, affixing these labels where it seems most expedient from the point of view of peace and political stability. In other words, Hobbes is sometimes – I think wrongly – placed among those who thought that the independent claims of truth counted for very little in comparison with the basic survivalist imperatives of politics. (Hannah Arendt takes this view, for example, in her otherwise compelling essay, "Truth and politics.")[12]

I guess the appearance that Thomas Hobbes was, so to speak, Machiavellian about truth is also made plausible by his insistence that certain types of proposition which we take very seriously – for example, propositions about justice – have only conventional truth-values. What's more, he believed that anyone who denied this, and anyone who sought to make claims on the basis of the allegedly *intrinsic* truth or falsity of certain propositions about justice was, politically speaking, a menace. That can easily sound like a decision to suppress the truth about justice or to eliminate debate about what the true meaning of justice actually is, for political reasons.

Or, if it is not quite as Machiavellian as that, it certainly sounds (as I said) like a form of pragmatism: justice has if not the meaning, then at least *the sort of* meaning we need it to have, in the interests of peace.

I believe that either of these would be a serious misreading of Hobbes. Both views – the Machiavellian and the pragmatist – underestimate the power and distinctiveness of Hobbes's insistence in Chapter 30 of *Leviathan* that it is "against [the Sovereign's] Duty to let the people be ignorant, or mis-informed of the grounds, and reasons of . . . his essentiall rights."[13] He is not saying that the Sovereign has a duty to come up with a theory that can serve as a public ideology and do what is necessary to get that ideology believed. When Hobbes says that "the grounds of these Rights, have the rather need to be diligently, and truly taught; because they cannot be maintained by . . . terrour of legal punishment,"[14] he is not just preferring indoctrination to coercion. Instead he seems to be saying that civil doctrine is so much at the mercy of individual reason that an attempt to base public ideology on anything less than "the perspicuity of reasons"[15] – any attempt to base it on falsehood or myth or mystery – will leave it and political allegiance terribly vulnerable to individuals' abilities to figure things out for themselves and to spot a lie when they hear one. (This of course goes against Marxist or structuralist theories of the efficacy and hegemony of false consciousness, ideology, and mystification. But "[p]eople," as E. P. Thompson once remarked, "are not as stupid as some structuralist philosophers suppose them to be. They will not be mystified by the first person who puts on a wig."[16] For Hobbes, the political force of Enlightenment consists in the fact that it is too much of a risk to try telling lies to people who can reason about something they have reason to regard as important.

I don't mean of course to deny that Hobbes was a conventionalist about justice, property, honesty, honor, good and evil: he *does* maintain that all of these terms have the meaning, and only the meaning, that the sovereign assigns to them in a well-ordered society. But that is not an alternative to truth, on his account: that *is* the truth about these terms. Dispassionate enlightened inquiry in what we would call metaethics establishes that almost all moral vocabulary is relative either to the appetites and aversions of individuals in the state of nature, or to the stipulations and conventions of the sovereign in civil society. That's the truth in metaethics, not because we want or need it to be the case, but because of what philosophical inquiry reveals to be the case.

Moreover – and this is very important – I take it Hobbes is saying that *that* is what the people are to be taught. Once the sovereign has stipulated a meaning for justice, for example, the people are not to be taught (the falsehood) that that stipulation is the intrinsic meaning of the term. Instead they are to be taught that it is a purely stipulative, conventional meaning and that, on account of the truth in metaethics, in this area that is the best one can expect.

All of this makes Hobbes a more modern thinker than he is often presented as being, and in my view, a *liberal* thinker, if not in his political conclusions, then in his respect for individuals as reasoning beings and in the sense that his own determination to analyze politics and get to the bottom of human affairs resonates with the reasoning capacities of the ordinary individuals who are the subject-matter of his inquiry.

If Hobbes is regarded as a proto-Enlightenment philosopher, it is pretty clear that he is associated with the Cartesian foundationalist strand of Enlightenment thinking. And it may be thought that this strand of Enlightenment thinking, at least, has been unraveled by the critiques of Horkheimer and Adorno, and a thousand others. For nothing is clearer, it will be said, than that the sort of tight, axiomatically-organized epistemology to which Hobbes subscribed – under the influence of Galilean science, Cartesian rationalism, and Euclidean fantasy – is hopeless, at least in the realm of human, social and moral inquiry.

We need to say something more general about the idea of Enlightenment and the idea of a crisis of Enlightenment.

These remarks are necessarily sketchy, but I believe it is all too easy to exaggerate the rationalism, the scientism and the positivism of the Enlightenment approach to social and political justification. The claim is sometimes made, for example, that the Enlightenment cult of science requires valid knowledge to take the form of exact, exhaustively specifiable impersonal facts, established through linear reasoning by well-defined logical procedures. But there is no reason to narrow or constrain our conception of Enlightenment inquiry in that way. I suggest instead that we should understand it more in terms of giving free rein to human inquisitiveness, and more in the light of Immanuel Kant's admonition to dare to trust the activity of one's own understanding, and to be willing to follow inquiry and critique wherever they lead,[17] rather than to accept blocks on inquiry in the name either of someone else's authority or the exigencies of morality, religion, decency and order.

I stress this broader and more generous notion of inquiry, because I believe that a preoccupation with rational foundations, as the essence of the matter, also makes it possible to misunderstand and perhaps to underestimate the threat which Enlightenment thinking may actually pose to our cherished illusions about value, morality and politics. If we are obsessed with scientism and foundationalism, then – in the prevailing pessimism about the Enlightenment – we are likely to be obsessed with the failure of Enlightenment inquiry to provide secure foundations for morality and rights. We will tend to say, with critics such as John Gray[18] or Alasdair MacIntyre,[19] that rational foundations are what the Enlightenment promised and rational foundations are what the Enlightenment failed to deliver. But this lets us off the hook too easily. For if *this* is all the crisis of Enlightenment amounts to, then it seems open to us to say, as Richard Rorty urges us to say:

> So the Enlightenment has failed to provide rational foundations. So what? We can simply continue our liberal moralizing *without* foundations, resting our moral activity and practice not on objectively secured axioms, but on the solidarity of a certain sort of community – i.e. a bunch of participants in moral practice – and on their (our) joint determination to go on talking in this way and to imbue their (our) actions and institutions with such talk, whatever the scientists say.[20]

In other words, if this is all that the crisis of Enlightenment amounts to, then surely we can still talk proudly, with Rorty, of our moral and political commitments as "having no foundation except shared hope and the trust created by such sharing."[21]

That, as I said, underestimates the challenge. For the challenge is not just the lack of something positive (i.e. foundations), the challenge of enlightened critique is also negative, critical and potentially destructive of morality. The critical challenge is that moral judgments about goodness, justice and right might not only lack objective truth status, but they might also be revealed as nothing more than subjective expressions of emotion. What appear grammatically to be indicative propositions or judgments might turn out, in the light of serious inquiry into their function and operation, to be mere imperatives or avowals or projections of attitude. Or – worse still – once we take seriously the possibility that some such non-cognitivist view is correct, and that the function of judgments about goodness, justice and right is simply to express or elicit certain emotions in the speaker or audience, then an account of the origin and character of these attitudes or emotions – an account of the sort that Marx or Nietzsche or Freud offered, for example – may reveal things about them that make us much less comfortable about a social solidarity rooted in their orchestrated and institutionalized expression.

I am not saying that any of these accounts is correct. But *if* any of them is, then it may not be open to a Rorty to defy the lack of foundations by invoking moral solidarity, for that solidarity may be revealed as something much less pleasant, perhaps more chilling and more disturbing, than anything we would want to advertise openly as the flavor of our joint and shared commitments. The contrast with Hobbes is instructive. Hobbes did not flinch from taking scientific inquiry to the foundations of value, and Hobbes did not flinch either from what he found there. He did not flinch when inquiry revealed (as he thought) that value was for the most part subjective and that an adequate politics would have to build itself on that. Hobbes did not abandon Enlightenment in the face of what it threatened to show about morality.

For us, the issues in metaethics remain open, not only between realists and their opponents or between cognitivists and non-cognitivists in the analytic tradition, but also, more broadly, in the radical skepticism of postmodern and deconstructionist thinkers about morality, moral traditions and traditional moral vocabulary. These debates flourish, and it is a sign of our intellectual maturity that they do – that we will not be browbeaten out of critical inquiry by the afficionados of moral discourse.

Yet at the same time – and particularly in political philosophy – one can often detect a certain sense of *reproach* directed, for example, by liberal Kantians at moral skeptics and moral non-cognitivists. It is as though the skeptics and non-cognitivists are letting the side down. We expect nothing better from the postmoderns, it may be said, but those non-cognitivists who work within the broadly liberal analytic tradition are letting their own side down. It is as though everyone is supposed to know that we need it to be the case that there can be moral truth, moral knowledge and moral objectivity. We need to be able to condemn genocide or clitorectomy as objectively morally wrong. And this need is itself taken as a reason for doubting the truth or acceptability of moral non-cognitivism. How, we say, can we possibly condemn human rights abuses in the tones in which (and with the stridency with which) we want to condemn them, if non-cognitivism is countenanced among us as a serious metaethical alternative?

Our perseverance with universal truth-claims in the domain of morality is consistent with the idea of Enlightenment only if it is either sustained or permitted by what we find out in metaethics – only if, in other words, it is the upshot of the most searching critical inquiry in metaethics that we can undertake. It is not, however, consistent with the spirit of Enlightenment if it is the upshot of a pusillanimous refusal to pursue metaethical inquiry when it threatens to trouble or undermine moral discourse. And it is certainly not consonant with that spirit if the image we project is the one that Rorty suggests – of a bunch of liberals clinging together desperately to their moral commitments and political convictions, and timorously refusing to run the risks with our habits and practices that the challenge of Enlightenment requires us to run.

In all of this, I am not *assuming* a skeptical position about morality. But it is possible that the skeptics are right. It is possible that the non-cognitivist analysis is correct. The attractive thing about Hobbes's work is that he showed what it would be like to brave these possibilities and begin the challenging task of building a theory of politics on that basis – a theory that would not have to disguise itself from the critical intellects of the men and women whose lives it purported to order. Hobbes may or may not have succeeded in the task of establishing adequate foundations. But at least he respected the imperative of Enlightenment that we should never have to build our politics on assumptions, beliefs or presuppositions that we know to be false or questionable or that we are frightened to have questioned or falsified. We should never be in the business of having to shield our politics or our moral practices and convictions from inquiry or from inquiry's results.

Hobbes's concern for the truth of civil doctrine is accounted for in part by a desire on the sovereign's part not to make himself or his pretensions vulnerable to his subjects' reasoning. The sovereign thinks, "If I tell them lies, they may find me out. Better to tell them the truth about our respective positions." But I suspect that this is not just Hobbes's pragmatic political precaution. It is born also of a more principled and respectful sense that government and authority should no longer be in the business of insulting the intelligence of those who are subject to them. That period of human history – when we treated one another as intellectual infants – is over.

And liberal moral theory should not be in the business of insulting our intelligence either. We should not pretend that there are warrants or foundations for our views when there are not, and equally we should not pretend not to be worried by the absence of foundations when (or if) it is the clear upshot of Enlightened critique that we ought to be. We should be willing to face the reality of social order and moral discourse with a clear head and sober senses and above all a willingness to follow our critical understanding where it leads in the construction of social and political theory.

That is the demand of Enlightenment. And the principle of publicity is simply the requirement that in the specification and defense of principles governing social structure we should – at last – not have to put up with anything less.

NOTES

1 Thomas Hobbes, *Leviathan*, ed. Richard Tuck (Cambridge, Cambridge University Press, 1988), p. 491.

2 Ibid., ch. 30, pp. 236–7.

3 Ibid., ch. 30, pp. 231ff. See also ch. 18, pp. 124–5.

4 Ibid., ch. 30, p. 237.

5 Ibid., ch. 46, p. 462.

6 Ibid., ch. 30, p. 237.

7 Ibid., Review and Conclusion, pp. 490–1.

8 See Samuel Mintz, *The Hunting of Leviathan: Seventeenth Century Reactions to the Materialism and Moral Philosophy of Thomas Hobbes* (Cambridge, Cambridge University Press, 1962).

9 Hobbes, *Leviathan*, ch. 6, p. 461.

10 Hobbes (ibid., ch. 15) criticized Aristotle's view that some men are more fit to govern, others to serve.

11 Hobbes, *Leviathan*, ch. 18, pp. 124–5.

12 Arendt misleadingly groups Hobbes among those thinkers who believes that lies told to the people about the basis of political authority may actually serve the needs of authority. She says that Hobbes believed "that lying can very well serve to establish or safeguard the conditions for the search after truth" (Arendt, "Truth and politics," in *Between Past and Future* (Harmondsworth, Penguin Books, 1977), p. 229). She explains in a note (pp. 297–8) that she has in mind a passage from one of the later chapters – ch. 46 – of *Leviathan*. She writes:

> Hobbes explains that "disobedience may lawfully be punished in them, that against the laws teach even true philosophy." For is not "leisure the mother of philosophy; and Commonwealth the mother of peace and leisure"? And does it not follow that the

Commonwealth will act in the interest of philosophy when it suppresses a truth which undermines peace? . . . It never occurred to Hobbes that all search for truth would be self-defeating if its conditions could be guaranteed only by deliberate falsehoods.

13 Hobbes, *Leviathan*, ch. 30, pp. 231–2.
14 Ibid., p. 232.
15 Hobbes, *De Cive*, ch. XIII, sect. ix, p. 160.
16 E. P. Thompson, *Whigs and Hunters* (Harmondsworth, Penguin Books, 1977), p. 262.
17 Kant, "What is Enlightenment?" in Hans Reiss (ed.) *Kant: Political Writings* (Cambridge, Cambridge University Press, 1991), p. 54.
18 John Gray, *Enlightenment's Wake: Politics and Culture at the Close of the Modern Age* (London, Routledge, 1995).
19 Alasdair MacIntyre, *Whose Justice? Which Rationality?* (Notre Dame, Ind., University of Notre Dame Press, 1988).
20 This is not a quotation from Rorty but a fair statement, I think, of his position.
21 Richard Rorty, "Solidarity or objectivity?" in his collection, *Objectivity, Relativism and Truth: Philosophical Papers*, vol. I (Cambridge, Cambridge University Press, 1991), p. 33.

11

HOBBES ON EDUCATION

Richard Tuck

Thomas Hobbes belonged to a generation of Englishmen whose lives had been transformed, both for the better and (as he believed) for the worse, by the remarkable expansion in the English education system in the late sixteenth and early seventeenth centuries. Underlying many of Hobbes's most distinctive speculations about political life we can see reflections on the educational institutions that had made him, and that he believed had come close to destroying his country; his moral and political philosophy is in fact one of the most profound engagements with the facts of education which is to be found in the main body of western philosophy.

By the time Hobbes went to grammar school, at the very end of the sixteenth century, England (like much of Western Europe) was educating a remarkably high proportion of its boys (and a remarkably low proportion of its girls) to a very high standard. It can be calculated that in 1630, the chances of a boy going to university in England were not far off what they were to be in 1930, after sixty years of universal secondary education: about one in fifty boys went to Oxford or Cambridge in the early seventeenth century. This was in fact a rather low proportion by European standards; in Spain, for example, the figure was more like one in thirty. Given that only about 30 per cent of the male population in England was literate, a very high proportion of the literate population proceeded to higher education. For any boy whose parents could afford an education at all, the way was surprisingly clear to the universities and then on (he no doubt hoped) to a career in the professions (Church, Law or Medicine): most of the students at Oxford and Cambridge in this period worked their way in some fashion through college, acting as porters, waiters or (apparently) barbers, and many of them avoided the expensive colleges, living instead in the cheaper and now for the most part vanished hostels or halls.

This higher education was conducted entirely in Latin, which was still the universal language (spoken as well as written) of the educated classes across Europe; the high schools which fed the universities were therefore *grammar* schools, teaching in effect nothing but Latin as a modern language, learned from modern authors such as Erasmus as well as the classical texts themselves. At the universities, boys would still read some of the Roman authors, but much of their time would be spent (as in the Middle Ages) reading and commenting on the works of Aristotle, before they proceeded to one or other of the professional courses. To do well in this system thus required above all a mastery of languages: it was an intensely linguistic and literary education.

Hobbes fitted exactly into this pattern: his father was an ill-educated country clergyman, who abandoned his family, leaving Thomas's education to be paid for by an uncle, a shopkeeper in Malmesbury (Wiltshire). He early displayed great ability at languages (he could read English, Latin, Greek, French and Italian), and was sent by his schoolmaster to Magdalen Hall in Oxford, not to one of the colleges, no doubt with the expectation that his quick intelligence and linguistic abilities would lead to a profitable career. They did indeed do so, though in a rather unusual direction: on graduation in 1607 he was recommended by the Principal of the Hall to Lord Cavendish (shortly to become the Earl of Devonshire), one of the richest men in England, as someone who could act as tutor to Cavendish's eldest son (who was only a few years younger than Hobbes himself). From then until his death in 1679 Hobbes was essentially to live with the Cavendishes, serving as tutor to the young men of the family in each generation, and as their secretary or adviser when they grew up and took over the running of the estates and the exercise of the powerful political role accorded to a wealthy Earl. He also went with them into exile during the Civil War.

As a tutor in an aristocratic family, Hobbes was involved on a day-to-day basis with the education of boys of 16 to 21, not of young children (that was left to less intellectually powerful figures); his duty was to give them the equivalent of a university education, for aristocratic parents would send their sons to an actual university for only a nominal period, and then often with a resident private tutor.[1] A number of manuscripts and one or two minor printed works survive from the first thirty years of his employment in this fashion, and they show that the education he was giving to his pupils was a fine example of a late Renaissance course of study. It was centred on the practice of rhetoric, the essential technique for a young man who was going, through the accident of birth, to play a major role in the councils of the kingdom. In a summary of Aristotle's *Rhetoric* which he wrote for his pupils, Hobbes described the practice of rhetoric as resting on

> the *common Opinions* that men have concerning *Profitable*, and *UnProfitable*; *Just*, and *Unjust*; *Honourable*, and *Dishonourable* . . . For as in *Logick*, where certain and infallible knowledge is the scope of our proof, the *Principles* must be all *infallible Truths*: so in *Rhetorick* the *Principles* must be *common Opinions*, such as the Judge is already possessed with: because the end of *Rhetorick* is victory; which consists in having gotten *Belief*.[2]

The skilled orator or writer would thus manipulate the existing opinions of his audience in order to win them round to his own point of view, and Hobbes devoted a great deal of effort to showing his young charges how they could win victory at the council table or in Parliament. From his point of view, and no doubt theirs as well, this was a skill much like the skill at arms which aristocratic sons were also taught (the Cavendishes produced a number of notable soldiers, including the commander-in-chief of the King's army in the Civil War): verve in argument was like bravery in battle. Although Hobbes is often depicted as himself excessively timorous, and obsessed with the power of fear in human life, in fact he repeatedly praised courage and the other martial virtues.

Hobbes not only sought to educate his pupils in the techniques necessary to bring them victory, but was also quite prepared to use those same techniques himself in order to instruct and discipline them. We can see this strikingly in a long letter of moral advice which he wrote in 1638 to Charles, the 18-year-old brother of Hobbes's employer William, third Earl of Devonshire (William himself was only 21, and had just come of age). Charles was touring the Continent, and disturbing news had come to the former tutor about the young nobleman's behaviour in Paris: he had apparently challenged someone, or been challenged, to a duel. Hobbes responded with the following piece of pedagogy.

> First . . . I must humbly beseech you to avoyd all offensive speech, not only open reviling but also that Satyricall way of nipping that some use. The effect of it is the cooling of the affection of your servants, and the provoking of the hatred of your equalls. So that he which useth harsh languadge whether downeright or obliquely, shall be sure to have many haters, and he that hath so, it will be a wonder if he have not many just occasions of Duell . . . To encouradge inferiors, to be cheerefull with ones equalls and superiors, to pardon the follies of them one converseth withall, and to helpe men off, that are fallen into the danger of being laught at, these are signs of noblenesse and of the master spirit . . . Secondly I beseech you take no occasion of quarrell but such as are necessary and from such men only as are of reputation. For neither words uttered in heate of Anger, nor the wordes of youthes unknowne in the world, or not known for Vertue are of scandall sufficient to ground an honourable duell on. When two boyes go out of the Academie to Pre aux clercs, no man but thinks them boyes as before. Nor is their Act Valour. For having engaged themselves rashly they are forced to the feild with shame, and expect their adversary with cold hartes, and prayers that he may be prevented. Does the world call this valour?
>
> Lastly, I think it no ill Counsell, that you professe no love to any woman which you hope not to marry or otherwise to enjoy. For an action without designe is that which all the world calles Vanity.[3]

Here, the "common opinions" of "the world" are used as the basis upon which Hobbes sought to persuade Charles not to do the conventionally "valorous" act, but instead to withdraw from the duel – a fine example of the subversive power of effective rhetoric.

This letter was written in 1638, and at about the same time Hobbes had begun to reflect more deeply on the implications of these techniques. There is an ancient and obvious anxiety about the power of rhetoric: if it can successfully induce beliefs in people, such that they do not know that they are the victims of a skilled practioner, how can we be confident about the objective basis of any of our beliefs? Any of our convictions may simply be the result of an effective piece of manipulation by someone else. Moreover, if there are people who possess this skill, are they not extremely dangerous fellow citizens, who can covertly control the rest of us? Plato (whom Hobbes admired more than any other ancient philosopher) had voiced these anxieties about the sophists of his own day, and his conclusion, that orators should be driven out of the republic, was often echoed by later writers – in Hobbes's time, most strikingly by Montaigne:

> Those common-wealths, that have maintained themselves in a regular, formal, and well-governed estate, as that of *Creete* and *Lacedemon*, did never make any great

esteeme of Orators . . . It is an instrument devised, to busie, to manage, and to agitate a vulgar and disordered multitude; and is an instrument imployed, but about distempered and sicke mindes, as Physicke is about crazed bodies. And those where either the vulgar, the ignorant, or the generalitie have had all power, as that of *Rhodes*, those of *Athens*, and that of *Rome*, and where things have ever beene in continuall disturbance and uproare, thither have Orators and the professors of that Art flocked . . . [4]

The power of rhetoric might incline one to conclude that *no* well-founded belief is possible, and this indeed seems to have been Montaigne's view. But Hobbes's view, as he developed it in the late 1630s, was more cautious. It was true, he argued, that almost everything which has been thought to be objectively true was in fact a matter of subjective conviction, and was open to debate: there was continuous disagreement about (for example) "what is to be called right, what good, what virtue, what much, what little, what *meum* and *tuum*, what a pound, what a quart, &c."[5] He even went so far as to argue, in a work from this period, that as soon as there was any disagreement between people about an issue, we could have no confidence in the veracity of any of the views expressed.

> The infallible sign of teaching exactly, and without error, is this: that no man hath ever taught the contrary; not that few, how few soever, if any. For commonly truth is on the side of the few, rather than of the multitude; but when in opinions and questions considered and discussed by many, it happeneth that not any one of the men that so discuss them differ from another, then it may be justly inferred, they know what they teach, and that otherwise they do not. And this appeareth most manifestly to them that have considered the divers subjects wherein men have exercised their pens, and the divers ways in which they have proceeded; together with the diversity of the success thereof. For those men who have taken in hand to consider nothing else but the comparison of magnitudes, times, and motions, and their proportions one to another, have thereby been the authors of all those excellences, wherein we differ from such savage people as are now the inhabitants of divers places in America . . . Yet to this day was it never heard of, that there was any controversy concerning any conclusion in this subject . . . [6]

This passage elides truth and universal agreement: what is to count as true is whatever is universally acknowledged. Judged by this criterion, mathematics and geometry ("the comparison of magnitude, times, and motions") are well founded, since they do not evince the kind of disagreement which other areas of human life display. But as Hobbes had argued when writing about rhetoric, successful persuasion in all aspects of human life proceeds by finding the area of agreement among the audience (the "common opinions" which are the basis of rhetorical arguments) and then showing the auditors how those common opinions might lead them in a new direction. The common opinions can function as truths for the audience, and a well-founded political or moral philosophy should therefore start from the most widely-held opinion possible, and move outward to show how a particular political or ethical vision might follow from it. The very techniques of rhetoric thus contained a method for counteracting the vertiginous disagreement which successful oratory might be thought to induce, since in the last analysis the successful orator was dependent on *agreement* within the community he was addressing – though the agreement might be of an extremely slender kind.

The best example of this is the particular opinion which Hobbes took as his starting-point in all his political works: the idea that someone cannot be blamed for defending his life. As he put it in a work from the end of the 1630s, the *Elements of Law*,

> Forasmuch as necessity of nature maketh men to will and desire *bonum sibi*, that which is good for themselves, and to avoid that which is hurtful; but most of all that terrible enemy of nature, death, from whom we expect both the loss of all power, and also the greatest of bodily pains in the losing; it is not against reason that a man doth all he can to preserve his own body and limbs, both from death and pain. And that which is not against reason, men call RIGHT, or *jus*, or blameless liberty of using our own natural power and ability. It is therefore a *right of nature*: that every man may preserve his own life and limbs, with all the power he hath.[7]

We do not have to suppose that Hobbes's theory here turns on the claim that men *actually* always avoid death (as various commentators have noted, this is clearly not true, and was not even thought by Hobbes himself to be true); instead, it turns on the claim that it is always *justifiable* or *understandable* to avoid death, and that all men will recognize this fact (or, more strictly, that their universal acceptance of this description constitutes it a "fact").

However, this "common opinion" was not in itself sufficient to prevent radical moral disagreement within a society, any more than the common opinion from which the rhetorician started was sufficient to lead, without his manipulation, to a consensus among his audience. Hobbes had a vivid example of that in the English politics of the 1630s. The royal government, during a period in which the King was trying to rule without calling a Parliament, decreed that England was at risk from the power of the Dutch navy, and it tried to levy a special tax (the infamous "Ship Money") in order to pay for the expansion of the English navy. Opponents of the tax argued that, while they would have paid had there been a genuine emergency, there was no evidence that England was threatened by the Dutch, who were traditional allies of the English; the case was argued in court, and the victorious opinion was that the King as sovereign was the sole judge of what constituted danger to the nation.[8] Here, there was consensus about the fundamental point – the duty to pay if the nation was genuinely in danger – but a complete absence of consensus about the empirical question of whether in this instance the condition was fulfilled.

In order to achieve this further agreement, Hobbes argued that men had to recognize the fallibility of their own judgements in cases where there was any disagreement, and accept that the only way to construct consensus was to erect a common source of judgement, whose opinions on any disputed matter had to stand in for the opinions of everyone else. This is the Hobbesian sovereign, whose power is therefore fundamentally *epistemic* in character, and whose prime responsibility is to prevent ideological strife by determining how any matter in dispute is to be regarded by the citizens. As he put it in a stunning passage of the *Elements of Law*,

In the state of nature, where every man is his own judge, and differeth from other concerning the names and appellations of things, and from those differences arise quarrels, and breach of peace; it was necessary there should be a common measure of all things that might fall in controversy; as for example: of what is to be called right, what good, what virtue, what much, what little, what *meum* and *tuum*, what a pound, what a quart, &c. For in these things private judgements may differ, and beget controversy. This common measure, some say, is right reason: with whom I should consent, if there were any such thing to be found or known *in rerum natura*. But commonly they that call for right reason to decide any controversy, do mean their own. But this is certain, seeing right reason is not existent, the reason of some man, or men, must supply the place thereof; and that man, or men, is he or they, that have the sovereign power . . . ; and consequently the civil laws are to all subjects the measures of their actions, whereby to determine, whether they be right or wrong, profitable or unprofitable, virtuous or vicious; and by them the use and definition of all names not agreed upon, and tending to controversy, shall be established. As for example, upon the occasion of some strange and deformed birth, it shall not be decided by Aristotle, or the philosophers, whether the same be a man or no, but by the laws.[9]

This, then, is Hobbes's fundamental political theory: that a sovereign is created by men who (in a "state of nature") are conscious of the fallibility and contentiousness of their own opinions, in order to have a common source of judgement in disputed matters, and thereby to avoid civil strife. Because of the strongly epistemic character of the sovereign, the chief enemies of civil order are (on Hobbes's account) any persons who seek to persuade their fellow citizens of the truth of *anything* disputable, without the permission of the sovereign. Since an education system looks precisely like a mechanism for persuading people of certain things, his theory required in principle an extremely close management by the sovereign of what was taught in both schools and universities, just as it required a close management of what was taught by churches.

But to put the matter as baldly as this is to risk misrepresenting Hobbes's actual sympathies. One of the striking facts about Hobbes's biography is that for the last twenty years of his life he was in fact engaged in a strenuous campaign to establish the limits of state power in religious matters: *Leviathan*, the great work on politics which he published in 1651, contains a notable plea for religious toleration, and in the 1660s and 1670s Hobbes wrote a series of works designed to show that under the existing English constitution there were no penalties for heretical opinions, and that none should be introduced. The reason for this is clear: the danger to civil order and therefore to human existence came from the claim by churches to the sole possession of truth, and their consequent wars of conquest over the minds of the citizens. An ecclesiastical regime which acknowledged the provisional character of religious doctrines, and did not use its religious principles to call into question the judgement of the sovereign on political matters, should be tolerated by the sovereign; the sovereign himself (or itself) ought to have no specifically religious commitment, since its authority rested solely on its role as the arbiter of conflicts over what conduced to the preservation of the lives of its citizens.

The best example of such an ecclesiastical regime, Hobbes believed, was one in which there was little or no priestly authority at all; if the members of the congregation conscientiously and independently pursued their own line of inquiry, they would not be led by the rhetorical power of the professional priesthood into a dangerous doctrinal arrogance. As he said in *Leviathan* about the destruction of unified church government by Cromwell and his followers after their victory in the English Civil War,

> we are reduced to the Independency of the Primitive Christians to follow Paul, or Cephas, or Apollos, every man as he liketh best: Which, if it be without contention, and without measuring the Doctrine of Christ, by our affection to the Person of his Minister, (the fault which the Apostle reprehended in the Corinthians), is perhaps the best: First, because there ought to be no Power over the Consciences of men, but of the Word it selfe, working Faith in every one, not alwayes according to the purpose of them that Plant and Water, but of God himself, that giveth the Increase: and secondly, because it is unreasonable in them, who teach there is such danger in every little Errour, to require of a man endued with Reason of his own, to follow the Reason of any other man, or of the most voices of many other men; Which is little better, then to venture his Salvation at crosse and pile [tossing a coin]. Nor ought these Teachers to be displeased with this losse of their antient Authority: For there is none should know better then they, that power is preserved by the same Vertues by which it is acquired; that is to say, by Wisdome, Humility, Clearnesse of Doctrine, and sincerity of Conversation; and not by suppression of the Naturall Sciences, and of the Morality of Naturall Reason . . . [10]

Consistently, Hobbes assimilated the universities to the Church; indeed, in his eyes the universities were simply agents of the established Church – first, in the Middle Ages, the agents of the papacy, and later, after the Reformation, the agents of the Protestant Church of England. Or, in a sense, the churches were the agents of the universities: in *Leviathan* Hobbes sketched out a history of the corruption of religion by philosophy which he returned to in a number of later works, and in which he argued that the universities were the heirs to the philosophical schools of antiquity: "That which is now called an *University*, is a Joyning together, and an Incorporation under one Government of many Publique Schools, in one and the same Towne or City."[11] The Church became contaminated with the taste for philosophy which characterized the pagans of antiquity, and the universities, continuing the disputations of the ancient schools, reinforced this taste. They also corrupted the laity, for students were exposed to the ancient political and moral writings which extolled republicanism to the exclusion of other forms of government – so that, in one of his most striking phrases, Hobbes could say that "there was never any thing so deerly bought, as these Western parts have bought the learning of the Greek and Latine tongues."[12]

Notoriously, Hobbes's solution to the problem of this corruption was to prescribe his own works as texts in the universities.

> There is nothing in this whole Discourse [*Leviathan*] . . . as far as I can perceive, contrary either to the Word of God, or to good Manners; or tending to the disturbance

of the Publique Tranquillity. Therefore I think it may be profitably printed, and more profitably taught in the Universities, in case they also think so, to whom the judgement of the same belongeth. For seeing the Universities are the Fountains of Civill, and Morall Doctrine, from whence the Preachers, and the Gentry, drawing such water as they find, use to sprinkle the same (both from the Pulpit, and in their Conversation) upon the People, there ought certainly to be great care taken, to have it pure, both from the Venime of Heathen Politicians, and from the Incantation of Deceiving Spirits . . . [13]

But to suppose that this is the end of the matter is to make the same mistake as supposing that the sovereign's power over churches means simply that it determines the doctrine taught in them. First, the essence of Hobbes's doctrine is that the authority of the sovereign is *known by the citizens* to be wholly conventional in character, and to make sense only against a background of multiple and competing beliefs. So the first thing in which the people would be instructed, on this account, would be that the sovereign did not have special access to the truth, because no one has. Second, it is far from clear that Hobbes's vision was in practice one of the dogmatic delivery of doctrine *ex cathedra*. Hobbes was challenged by various professors at the University of Oxford over this passage, and he replied with an interesting alternative proposal.

How would you have exclaimed, if, instead of recommending my *Leviathan* to be taught in the Universities, I had recommended the erecting of a new and lay-university, wherein lay-men should have the reading of physics, mathematics, moral philosophy, and politics, as the clergy have now the sole teaching of divinity? Yet the thing would be more profitable, and tend much to the polishing of man's nature, without much public charge. There will need but one house, and the endowment of a few professors. And to make some learn the better, it would do very well that none should come thither sent by their parents, as to a trade to get their living by, but that it should be a place for such ingenuous men, as being free to dispose of their own time, love truth for itself . . . [14]

In other words, the ideal university (for Hobbes) would have something of the same character as the ideal ecclesiastical regime: independent people pursuing their inquiries, just as in the Church the best arrangement is "to follow Paul, or Cephas, or Apollos, every man as he liketh best."

There is an interesting parallelism in what Hobbes says about education and the Church, and what he says about the legal system. In chapter XXIII of *Leviathan*, he draws a strict analogy between the Ministers of the Sovereign for teaching, and the Ministers of the Sovereign for judging; but he then goes on to argue that the Ministers for Judging are not in fact the royal judges, but *juries*; for the principal qualification for being a judge is knowledge of the laws of nature, and ordinary people know those better than do professional lawyers whose minds have been warped by their studies. He does not explicitly draw the same conclusion as far as teaching is concerned, but his remarks point in the same direction as his later thoughts about the ideal university — that any organized and policed system of teaching is a threat to human freedom.

Hobbes had confidence that if the practice of human reflection and inquiry were to be freed from the dominance of a philosophical profession, his own teachings would appear entirely reasonable; for alone among philosophical positions (he believed), his gave due weight to the multiplicity of human beliefs and treated each of them equally. The paradox is of course that they could only be accorded equal treatment by each renouncing its own right to set the public agenda, and being willing to see that agenda set by a common sovereign; but that is close to the familiar paradox of any liberal or pluralist philosophy, that the framework of toleration in which competing beliefs encounter one another is something which is itself to be defended in absolutist terms. Oddly enough, and despite their wildly different political conclusions, the modern writer on education whom Hobbes most resembles is probably Ivan Illich.

NOTES

1 Hobbes indeed took up this role with his new pupil for a few months at St John's College, Cambridge, immediately on appointment.

2 John T. Harwood (ed.) *The Rhetorics of Thomas Hobbes and Bernard Lamy* (Carbondale, Ill., Southern Illionois University Press, 1986), p. 41.

3 Hobbes, *The Correspondence*, ed. Noel Malcolm (Oxford, Clarendon Press, 1994), pp. 52–3.

4 Montaigne, *Essayes* (Modern Library, n.d.), pp. 263–4 (I.1i "Of the Vanitie of Words").

5 Thomas Hobbes, *Elements of Law*, ed. F. Toennies, 2nd edn by M. M. Goldsmith (London, Cass, 1969), p. 188 (II.10.8).

6 Ibid., p. 65 (I.13.3).

7 Ibid., p. 71 (I.14.6).

8 Hobbes refers to this case in *Behemoth* in the following terms. "When [the people] have laid the burthen of defending the whole kingdom, and governing it, upon any person whatsoever, there is very little equity he should depend on others for the means of performing it; or if he do, they are his Sovereign, not he theirs" (*Behemoth; or, The Long Parliament*, ed. Ferdinand Toennies, re-edited Stephen Holmes (Chicago, University of Chicago Press, 1990), p. 37). He also hangs a long theoretical discussion of law and obedience on the case, on pp. 37–59.

9 Hobbes, *Elements of Law*, p. 188 (II.10.8).

10 Thomas Hobbes, *Leviathan*, ed. Richard Tuck (Cambridge, Cambridge University Press, 1996), pp. 479–80 (1651 edn, p. 385).

11 Ibid., p. 462.

12 Ibid., p. 150.

13 Ibid., p. 491.

14 Hobbes, *English Works* VII, ed. W. Molesworth (London, 1845), p. 345 ("Six lessons to the Professors of the Mathematics," Lesson VI).

12

SPINOZA AND THE EDUCATION OF THE IMAGINATION

Genevieve Lloyd

We live in continuous change, and . . . as we change for the better or worse, we are called happy or unhappy. For he who has passed from being an infant or child to being a corpse is called unhappy. On the other hand, if we pass the whole length of our life with a sound mind in a sound body, that is considered happiness. And really, he who, like an infant or child, has a body capable of very few things and very heavily dependent on external causes, has a mind which considered solely in itself is conscious of almost nothing of itself, or of God, or of things. On the other hand, he who has a body capable of a great many things, has a mind which considered only in itself is very much conscious of itself, and of God, and of things.

In this life, then, we strive especially that the infant's body may change (as much as its nature allows and assists) into another, capable of a great many things and related to a mind very much conscious of itself, of God, and of things. We strive, that is, that whatever is related to its memory or imagination is of hardly any moment in relation to the intellect.

(*E* VP39S)

To live well, in a condition of continuous change: that is the ideal for human life articulated in Spinoza's *Ethics*. Spinoza insists that there are things more important than a long life; that to change from an infant body to a corpse is not the epitome of "unhappiness"; that a long life spent without knowledge of self, of God and of things, may be a more unhappy outcome than early death. Spinoza equates virtue with a joy that centres – even in its highest form – on the present. This joy is a transition to greater activity: the transformation of inadequate modes of knowledge into more adequate ones. The idea of virtue as residing in increased power of reason is of course neither novel in itself nor surprising in a seventeenth-century philosopher so strongly associated with rationalism. What is more unusual – and perhaps more surprising – is the firm grounding of this rationalist ideal in the strengthening of bodily powers.

Our opening quotation evokes the transformation of the powerless infant body into a vibrant unity of mental and physical capacities. Apart from this quotation, there is little explicit discussion of education in Spinoza's writings; and even here the connection is not

157

straightforward. As with many of the most important and interesting insights of the *Ethics*, the formulation of the point about the transformation of the infant body is ambiguous in the original Latin – an ambiguity preserved in Curley's English translation. Is it our own infant body that we are to transform? Or are the bodies of infants here construed as objects of adult intervention? Is it self-transformation or the education of others that is at stake here?

The text does not resolve the issue. But if what we are about is the appropriation of Spinoza's philosophy to the task of thinking through our own contemporary understanding of the processes involved in education, we should not try too hard to resolve the ambiguity. For the shift between the two ideas goes to the heart of Spinoza's radical revision of the relations between self and others, between the individual and the group, which makes his philosophy both an enigma and a source of illumination to modern readers. At the core of this challenge to our own thought patterns is Spinoza's treatment of imagination. The ambiguities between selves and others are not accidental but central to Spinoza's treatment of the nature and operations of the imagination. It is in his thoughts on imagination – its hazards and its enormous potential for ethical pedagogy, in relation to both individual and social life – that we find what can be most fruitfully appropriated from his philosophy for rethinking educational objectives and practices in the present.

Read out of context parts of our quotation may seem hostile to imagination. The developing child, it seems, is supposed to be trained to set aside "all that is related to memory or imagination", in favour of intellect. It all sounds a familiar refrain: the cultivation of autonomous intellect should replace rote memory of dogma: and the vagaries of imagination should give way to the rigours of reason. The figure of Spinoza finds its natural place among the portraits of the founding fathers of the project of enlightenment. But there is in fact a great deal more going on here than a familiar affirmation of the supremacy of reason. A fuller understanding of the distinctive version of rationalism which frames Spinoza's evocation of the transformation of the infant body yields educational ideals centred less on the supremacy of reason than on the cultivation of the powers of the imagination.

The key to a Spinozistic approach to education is that we strive that the infant body may change into one capable of a great many things. The emphasis is on bodily change. But Spinoza insists that the goal is not just "a sound mind in a sound body" for the whole length of a life. A prolonged state of mere "soundness" of mind and body is not Spinoza's ideal of happiness; in fact "soundness", with its normative connotations, is not a Spinozistic ideal at all. The desired outcome is rather a flourishing of bodily powers which cannot be determined in advance of the flourishing. As Gilles Deleuze puts the point in his *Spinoza: a Practical Philosophy*, we do not know ahead of time the affects of which we are capable. 'That is why Spinoza calls out to us in the way he does: you do not know beforehand what good or bad you are capable of; you do not know beforehand what a body or a mind can do, in a given encounter, a given arrangement, a given combination' (1988: 125). The powers of bodies are manifested in their characteristic joys; and the capacity for joy arises from the dynamic momentum of a body as a unity of component individuals, all affecting, and being themselves affected by external bodies in a multiplicity of ways. This idea of distinctive joys is so important for Spinoza that he identifies it with the individual soul: 'though each individual lives content with its own nature, by which he is constituted, and is glad of it, nevertheless that life with which each one is content, and that gladness, are nothing but the idea, or soul, of the individual. And so the gladness of the one differs in nature from the gladness of the other as much as the essence of the one differs from the essence of the other' (*E* IIP37S).

The mind, as "idea" of a human body, undergoes its own transitions in activity and passivity, clarity and confusion, according as the body's activity is enhanced or obstructed. ('The human mind is capable of perceiving a great many things, and is the more capable, the more its body can be disposed in a great many ways' (*E* IIP14).) These transitions to lesser or greater activity – lesser or greater perfection – are Spinoza's version of joy and pain. The goal then is the transformation of the infant body into a body capable of a great many things; and the mark of success in this project is the pleasure in living. ('It is the part of a wise man, I say, to refresh and restore himself in moderation with pleasant food and drink, with scents, with the beauty of green plants, with decorations, music, sports, the theater, and other things of this kind, which anyone can use without injury to another. For the human body is composed of a great many parts of different natures, which constantly require new and varied nourishments, so that the whole body may be equally capable of all the things which can follow from its nature, and hence, so that the mind also may be equally capable of understanding many things at once' (*E* IVP45S).)

A well-functioning intellect is undoubtedly part of this Spinozistic ideal. As the body becomes more capable of 'doing many things at once, or being acted on in many ways at once', the mind becomes capable of 'perceiving many things at once'. And as the actions of the body become capable of 'depending more on itself alone', so the mind becomes more capable of 'understanding distinctly' (*E* IIP3S). What is less obvious is that for Spinoza this achievement of reason, far from being at the expense of imagination, depends on the cultivation of a lively capacity for images and on understanding the constructive interplay between the power of imagination and the power of emotion.

It is this central role of imagination in Spinoza's philosophy which gives it its potential for enriching cultural self-understanding in the present. It is relevant not only to how we think about educational practices in schools but also to the broader understanding and critique of social ideals and of the processes through which they are formed and passed on between generations. We can draw from Spinoza insights into the integration of imagination, reason and emotion that is at stake in the formation and legitimation of social practices and institutional structures. His remarks about the transformation of the infant body, understood in the context of his philosophy as a whole, open up space for the elucidation and transformation of the prevailing images and fictions through which we understand ourselves.

SPINOZA'S VERSION OF IMAGINATION

The imagination has for Spinoza an unavoidably social dimension which is grounded in his treatment of the relations between bodies, and between minds and bodies. The mind is the 'idea' of the body; and the complexity of the human body makes possible both the confusions of the imagination and the higher forms of knowledge. Spinoza's treatment of individuality and of sociability is grounded in his brief remarks on the physics of bodies between Propositions 13 and 14 of Part II of the *Ethics*; and so too is his treatment of imagination and memory. Here we see the basis for Spinoza's insistence that the good life must be one that accommodates the reality of change: that accommodation is fundamental to the very idea of an individual.

Bodies, Spinoza explains, communicate motion to one another, and their synchronization – the unions of bodies – is what makes an individual. The simplest bodies are distinguished from one another by 'motion and rest, speed and slowness'; but these simple bodies come together as synchronized centres of the communication of motion. The nested orderings of these composite individuals reach up to the 'whole of nature', conceived as one individual whose parts may vary in infinite ways without any change in the whole. The human body is thus a composite individual, a union of parts acting as a centre of communicating and communicated motion. Each individual exerts a causal force on others, and each is in turn constantly impinged on by others. Each needs for its preservation 'a great many bodies, by which it is, as it were, continually regenerated' (*E* IIP19D). The account of the individuality of bodies – and hence of the minds, which are ideas of them – already has overtones of unavoidable sociability.

These social dimensions of imagination, interacting with the operations of the passions, play an important role in Spinoza's philosophy, connecting his metaphysical concerns in the *Ethics* with the more socially oriented political writings. It is misleading to think of the *Ethics* as about happiness and virtue as they unfold in individual lives, while the political writings address issues of the well being of collectivities. The relations between individuals and wider collectivities are fundamental to the *Ethics*; and the treatment of the imagination is fundamental to how Spinoza conceptualizes those relations.

Imagination is for Spinoza a form of bodily awareness. That is not novel in the history of philosophy. But in conjunction with the treatment of mind as idea of body, and the treatment of the relations between bodies as integral to individuality, it yields a new way of thinking of the imagination in relation both to reason and to sociability. The mind's ideas of the modifications of the body of which it is the idea, he stresses, involve both the nature of the human body and, at the same time, the nature of external bodies. There are implications here both for the relations between individuals and for the relations between imagination and reason.

For Spinoza the being of a singular, finite thing consists in its being a particular determination of the power of substance. Each finite thing mediates the power of substance, and is itself acted upon and changed by the power mediated through other finite things. The distinction between self and other here becomes something different from what we are accustomed to in more familiar models of incidental interaction between independently existing individual substances. To be an individual is, for Spinoza, to be determined to act through the mediation of other modes and to likewise determine others: to act and be acted upon within the totality of finite modes of substance. All this involves imagination.

In sensation our minds perceive the nature of a great many bodies together with the nature of our own. In other words, our perceptions are confused; and the confusion is carried over into imagination and memory. But although sensation is a source of confusion, it also makes possible knowledge that is not tied to the constant presence of the object known. As long as the human body is affected, the mind will have the idea of an actually existing external body. Our bodies retain traces of the changes brought about in them by the impinging of other bodies. So the mind will again regard external bodies as present even when they no longer exist (*E* IIP17D and C). Paul's mind will continue to regard Peter as present to it, even after Peter's death, when the idea of Peter which constitutes Peter's own mind no longer exists. These ideas of affections of the body which present external bodies as present to us are Spinoza's version of 'images'; and the mind's regarding bodies in this way is his version of imagining.

On this co-presence of things to mind, arising from the structural complexity of the human body, rests the world delivered to us by imagination and memory, the world of ordinary consciousness. Spinoza defines memory as the connection of ideas involving the nature of things outside the human body: 'a connection that is in the mind according to the order and connection of the affections of the human Body'. But these orderings of ideas according to the connections of affections of individual human bodies are affected by the more anonymous orderings of ideas that operate in the social world.

Spinoza's account of imagination, as we have seen, involves awareness of other bodies at the same time as our own. In Part II of the *Ethics*, the emphasis is on the impinging of other bodies – not necessarily human – in sensation. But in the later parts of the work he turns his attention to the social dimensions of human bodies, to interactions where a human body is affected by other bodies like itself. Here imagination and affect come together, reinforcing one another in patterns of association that can be subjected to rational investigation.

> The affects, therefore, of hate, anger, envy, and the like, considered in themselves, follow with the same necessity and force of Nature as the other singular things. And therefore they acknowledge certain causes, through which they are understood, and have certain properties, as worthy of our knowledge as the properties of any other thing, by the mere contemplation of which we are pleased. Therefore, I shall treat the nature and powers of the affects, and the power of the mind over them, by the same method by which, in the preceding parts, I treated God and the mind, and I shall consider human actions and appetites just as if it were a question of lines, planes, and bodies.
>
> (*E* III Pref.)

It is in the social dimensions of Spinoza's version of imagination that we can find the most illuminating applications of his philosophy to education and social critique. There are two strands in Spinoza's treatment of the imagination, which can be aligned with two kinds of contemporary stance towards the relations between reason and imagination. They appear at first sight to be in conflict. But by understanding the tensions between them and the ways in which they can come together we can gain insight into our own contemporary attitudes to ideals of reason.

On the one hand, it is clear that Spinoza regards the connections of images that follow the disparate affections of individual human bodies as an inferior mode of thought. The affections of individual bodies, he tells us, lay down widely divergent associational paths.

161

From traces of a horse seen in the sand, the soldier passes to thought of horsemen and war, the farmer to ploughs and fields (*E* IIP18S). But it is important to notice that these variations are not a product of the affections of an individual human body in isolation from others. The different associational paths reflect different social roles organized around the salience of different practices, different relations to environment: farming and military activity.

In Spinoza's discussion of imagination in the *Theologico-Political Treatise*, he emphasizes again the variations in how things are imagined, which reflect context and the related intellectual character of the imaginer. Spinoza's discussion of imagination in that *Treatise* is framed by a discussion of prophecy. The power of prophecy implies 'not a peculiarly perfect mind, but a peculiarly vivid imagination' (1951: 19). And the deliverances of prophecy vary according to the disposition, and the preoccupations, of the individual prophet.

> If a prophet was cheerful, victories, peace, and events which make men glad, were revealed to him; in that he was naturally more likely to imagine such things. If, on the contrary, he was melancholy, wars, massacres, and calamities were revealed; and so, according as a prophet was merciful, gentle, quick to anger, or severe, he was more fitted for one kind of revelation than another. It varied according to the temper of imagination in this way: if a prophet was cultivated he perceived the mind of God in a cultivated way, if he was confused he perceived it confusedly. And so with revelations perceived through visions. If a prophet was a countryman he saw visions of oxen, cows, and the like; if he was a soldier, he saw generals and armies; if a courtier, a royal throne, and so on.
>
> (1951: 30)

This inherent multiplicity in the operations of imagination are for Spinoza, as we might expect from his status as arch rationalist, a source of limitation and mutilation of knowledge. The limitations of the imagination are carried over into the operations of language. Images come to be organized into structures which are the product, not of any rational ordering activity, but rather of social practices. Language involves the organization of representations in ways which do not yield an adequate guide to the natures of things outside the individual body. Language provides a common space for communication, transcending the erratic associational paths traced by individual bodies. But words are to be distrusted as a vehicle of thought. Their meanings rest on associations between bodily affections – between sounds and images – which are themselves subject to variable social influences.

Our ideas of bodily affections are confused ideas, 'like conclusions without premises' (*E* IIP28D). So long as it perceives 'from the common order of Nature', the mind has only a 'confused and mutilated knowledge of itself, of its own body, and of external bodies' (*E* IIP29C). There is a different and higher kind of knowledge which escapes this mutilation. It too involves a perceiving of things 'together', but in a different way. When it perceives 'from the common order of nature' the mind is 'determined externally, from fortuitous encounters with things, to regard this or that'. When it knows according to reason, in contrast, the mind is 'determined internally, from the fact that it regards a number of things at once, to understand their agreements, differences, and oppositions' (*E* IIP29S). Despite these expected warnings about the limitations of imagination, there is a great deal more to

Spinoza's treatment of imagination – and of the world of the 'common order of nature' which it delivers to us – than an affirmation of the supremacy of reason. The mind's capacity to know in accordance with reason depends on that same bodily capacity to retain traces of sensation which gives rise to imagination. It is only because human minds are ideas of complex bodies that they are capable of forming the 'common notions' of reason.

The errors of imagination and the truths grasped through reason thus have their origins in the same facts of complexity of bodily structure. And although Spinoza thinks the imagination is flawed as a source of knowledge, he also insists that it is not of itself a source of error. ('The imaginations of the mind, considered in themselves contain no error . . . the mind does not err from the fact that it imagines, but only insofar as it is considered to lack an idea which excludes the existence of those things which it imagines to be present to it. For if the mind, while it imagined nonexistent things as present to it, at the same time knew that those things did not exist, it would, of course, attribute this power of imagining to a virtue of its nature, not to a vice – especially if this faculty of imagining depended only on its own nature, that is . . . if the mind's faculty of imagining were free' (*E* IIP17S).

Spinoza's insistence that the imagination, despite its limitations, is not a source of error poses difficulties for a common interpretation of Spinoza, made popular by Hegel, according to which Spinoza sees the world as it is delivered to imagination as an unreal world. The 'real' world, for Hegel's Spinoza, is the world as it is apprehended by reason – a world in which all particularity is consumed in the all-embracing unity of the one substance. It is a world without confusion, but also a world without individuality, a timeless world of universals. On this way of thinking of the relations between imagination and reason, the two stand in a hierarchical relation. The illusions fostered by imagination in individual minds and in the social world give way in well-functioning minds to the supremacy of reason.

The task of education, as reconstructed to fit this Hegelian interpretation of Spinoza, would be to inculcate the power to make the transition between the two ways of knowing. The transformation of the infant mind would be an ascent from the illusions of the imagination to the truths of reason. The play of imagination would be seen as the play of the infant mind, to be indulged perhaps as a retreat from the responsibilities of maturity, but not part of well-functioning, mature, enlightened consciousness. But Spinoza's commitment to the superiority of reason does not have to be read as a Platonic ascent in which the deliverances of imagination are left behind as the mind moves on to higher truth. Spinoza's treatment of the imagination and its 'fictions' is double-edged. Even if we do accept the Hegelian interpretation, we can see a distinctive role emerging here for the imagination as a powerful ally of reason. And, as we shall see, there are in any case alternatives to the Hegelian reading.

Christopher Norris, in *Spinoza and the Origins of Modern Critical Theory* argues that Spinoza made a lasting contribution to the enlightenment project of the rational critique of illusion through his distinctive approach to the status of 'fictions', the activity of 'feigning'. Norris stresses the importance of Spinoza's earlier work *The Emendation of the Intellect*, where Spinoza offers an account of 'feigning' as a 'mixed method' of knowing. Fictions – feigned ideas – partake of imagining; but through being criticized by reason they become a source of improved understanding. Fictions belong in the realm of cognitive values. They involve

163

untruths that are not mistaken for adequate ideas but are knowingly entertained. They rework the experience of minds initially held captive by inadequate knowledge. Without themselves being adequate knowledge, they give access to it. Although partial or mutilated, fictions have their own distinctive cognitive role. The capacity to feign is a positive mental capacity, although one that can be ascribed only to fallible minds. We can feign only because we are ignorant; an omniscient being would be unable to feign. But it is a capacity with its own strengths, a positive response to our limitations as knowers. We have here a cognitive activity which belongs to the imagination rather than the intellect.

Reason, on Norris's reading of Spinoza, retains a vantage point from which it is able to judge the inadequacy of imagination, subjecting its fictions to a rigorous scrutiny. Fictions offer a cognitive surrogate, improvable through the critical reflections of reason. In this border zone between error and truth, inadequate ideas can be reworked into better, more truthful representations, even if not all thinkers can individually make the full transition into the light of reason. Fictions facilitate reason's transformation of inadequate ideas. Rather than dragging the mind back into error, fictions facilitate its transitions into the clarity of reason. The rationalist commitment to the supremacy of reason is tempered by allowing a carefully monitored, complementary role for imagination.

Other readings of Spinoza go further in upgrading the status of Spinozistic imagination. In his book *The Savage Anomaly*, Antonio Negri presents Spinoza as offering a more radical revaluing of imagination. For Spinoza, he stresses, imagination is caught up in the realities of the social world; it has a constitutive role in the contingent forms of ordinary experience. Imagination here becomes active and constitutive, rather than merely a passive source of confused representation; and the emphasis shifts to the social, rather than the individual dimensions of imagination. The imagination ceases to be just an inferior faculty, which the mind must shed if it is to see the world truly. In understanding the fictions of the imagination, the mind, rather than transcending a realm of illusion, gains access to the real social world in all its confusions. In reflecting on imagination, the individual mind reflects not on its own inadequacies, but on the socially constituted world of ordinary experience. The imagination here shifts over from the side of the individual knowing subject to the social world as object of critical reflection. Reason can criticize and transform the fictions of imagination. But the imagination is never really left behind. So, in the later sections of the *Ethics*, as Negri stresses, Spinoza does not hesitate to take as his object of inquiry, 'the very world of delirium or the most fantastic or crazy dimensions of opinion' (Negri 1991: 36).[1] Rational investigation now traverses the totality of the world, 'pressing towards both the great outside of adventure and discovery and the sublime inside of consciousness' (ibid.).

On this more radical interpretation of Spinoza, reason and imagination are not in an ascending hierarchy, as in Plato's famous ascent from the world of appearances to the world of the forms. The imagination has here a resilience which allows it to coexist with reason in a unified perception of the world. As Michèle Bertrand puts the point in her book *Spinoza et l'imaginaire*, the movement of knowledge is supported by that of the imagination. The two can be separated; but they are not two worlds, but rather two ways of being and thinking. We do not cease to imagine, just because we begin to know (Bertrand 1985: 67–8). The constitutive operations of imagination are part of the reality reason confronts, rather than an inferior mechanism of knowledge that must give way before the supremacy of reason.

These readings of Spinoza invite us to move beyond thinking of reason and imagination as different ways of encountering a mind-independent world. We are to think rather of a distinctive kind of object of knowledge: amalgams, structured patterns of imagination, emotion and common beliefs embedded in social practices. We can then think of reason as manifesting itself especially in the capacity for social critique, the capacity for critical reflection on, and transformation of, those patterns. Reason, in this context, involves the capacity to distance and detach ourselves from the immediacy of social practices in order better to reflect on the contingent structuring of the social world in which our own self-consciousness is formed. The aim is not to transcend the fictions or illusions of the imagination, but to gain insight into their operations, and where appropriate to refine or replace them.

For Spinoza then the capacities for the higher kinds of knowledge – reason and what he calls 'intuition', the understanding of things with reference to the idea of God – depend on the capacity to imagine. Reason depends on the multiplicity of traces that makes possible comparisons, thus making possible the discovery of conformities, differences and oppositions between things which allow us to come to 'common notions'. It is from this perspective that in the final stages of the *Ethics*, where he moves on to consider the highest achievement of knowledge, freedom and virtue, Spinoza insists on the importance of the transformation of the infant body. We endeavour to change the infant body, then, not with a view to stopping the child from imagining, but on the contrary in order to increase and enhance that power.

To bring this interpretation of Spinoza's version of imagination to bear more directly on the processes involved in education, we need now to get into the picture another important dimension of Spinoza's philosophy: the concept of *conatus*.

IMAGINATION, *CONATUS* AND EMOTION

For Spinoza the term *conatus* means the endeavour or struggle to persist in being. *Conatus* in this sense is for Spinoza the very essence of finite individuals. To be an individual, as we saw earlier, is to be determined to act through the mediation of other finite modes and to likewise determine those others. Since imagination is by definition the awareness of our own bodies together with others, this interaction between bodies essentially involves imagination. But it is also closely bound up with *conatus*.

Both bodies and minds, as finite individuals, struggle – of their nature – to persist in being. Our bodies are not just passively moved by external forces. They have their own momentum, their own characteristic force for existing. But this is not something that any individual exerts of its own power alone. For an individual to preserve itself in existence, as we have seen, is precisely for it to act and be acted upon in a multiplicity of ways. The more complex the individual body, the more ways in which it can be affected and affect other things. The power to imagine is thus integral to the continued existence and flourishing of the individual. To define imagination in terms of bodily awareness, within the context of

Spinoza's philosophy, is to move imagination to the very centre of the story of the development of human beings into the fullness of human flourishing.

How then are we to reconcile the story of imagination as the source of illusion with the story of imagination as human flourishing? For Spinoza the tendency to illusion is not a matter of ideological distortion of a truth which would otherwise be accessible to un-obscured intellect. There will always be fictions governing the contingent structures of social life. The challenge is not to transcend them, but to use reason to see through, improve and replace, destructive, oppressive fictions with others judged better able to sustain individual and collective *conatus*.

Reason is involved in this process of transforming fictions. Spinoza's clearest illustrations of the process concern religious superstitions. People, 'in their folly', he observes in his discussion of miracles in the *Theologico-Political Treatise*, have no 'single sound idea concerning either God or nature' (1951: 82). They confound God's decrees with human decrees, conceiving nature to be so limited that human beings are its chief part. The *Theological-Political Treatise* discussion of the illusions of religious constructions of the vengeful or benign God parallels the diagnosis of superstition in the appendix to Part I of the *Ethics*. While they sought to show that 'Nature does nothing in vain (i.e. nothing not of use to men)', Spinoza says there, they seem to show only that 'Nature and the gods are as mad as men.' But Spinoza does not envisage any real possibility of leaving the realm of illusion. What must happen rather is a schooling of the imagination, so that its fictions do not lead us astray.

In the concluding sections of the *Ethics*, where Spinoza takes his readers into the highest reaches of knowledge – the understanding of themselves in relation to the idea of God as the substance of which they are finite modes – the mind still proceeds through 'fictions'. Our opening quotation, from these final sections, tells us that 'what is related to memory and imagination', are to become of 'hardly any moment' in relation to the intellect. But this process itself involves making use of highly sophisticated exercises of imagination: fictions through which we grasp the eternity of the mind and the intellectual love of God. To understand the eternity of the mind – which, in our less enlightened state, we think of, through a naïve imagination, as a kind of continued existence after death – we are to engage in an exercise of feigning. We are to 'consider it as if it were now beginning to be, and were now beginning to understand things under a species of eternity'. We may do this without danger of error, Spinoza says, provided we are careful to draw our conclusions only from evident premises (*E* VP31S).

The objective then is to increase the powers of the mind to discriminate between the inferior superstitious fictions of 'the multitude' – the belief in a purposeful God, the belief in an after-life – and the preferred fictions, which better serve the mind in its pursuit of freedom, wisdom and virtue. The imagination thus contributes to the mind's self-interest and thriving. The connections between *conatus* and the illusions of the imagination are illuminatingly discussed by François Galichet in a paper 'Le Problème de l'illusion chez Spinoza'. Galichet stresses that for Spinoza illusion must no longer be simply denounced but explained – and not explained away. In this philosophy, illusion has a 'paradoxical positivity'. He brings out the point by distinguishing two kinds of illusion. On the one hand there are illusions consisting in 'pure privation', illustrated by Spinoza's famous diagnosis of the belief in free will. Here the illusion consists in the coexistence of a presence and an absence: the consciousness of action together with ignorance of the causes of action.

It is important to keep in mind here that Spinoza is not denying that there is a difference between things done freely and things done under compulsion. What he is about is clarified in a letter to Tschirnhaus, where Spinoza illustrates the point by invoking an explicit fiction. Think, he says, of a stone in flight and conceive of it as thinking of its movement. The stone, aware of its motion but unaware of the external causes of that motion, will think of itself as moving because it so wills. 'And this is that famous human freedom which everyone brags of having, and which consists only in this: that men are conscious of their appetite and ignorant of the causes by which they are determined.' To believe in one's own free will then is to be subject to illusion. 'The infant believes that he freely wants the milk; the angry boy that he wants vengeance; and the timid, flight' (1994: 268).

In the fuller development of the diagnosis in the *Ethics*, Spinoza identifies the supposed freedom of the will with the mind's awareness of its own striving, in the lack of any awareness of the surrounding causal force of bodies other than its own. 'When this striving is related only to the mind, it is called will; but when it is related to the mind and body together, it is called appetite. This appetite, therefore, is nothing but the very essence of man, from whose nature there necessarily follow the things that promote his preservation; and so man is determined to do those things' (*E* IIIP9S). In contrast to those consisting in 'pure privation' are illusions that involve something more, which Galichet describes as the 'search for utility'. Beliefs in the benign or vengeful God, discussed by Spinoza in Part I of the *Ethics*, are illusions of this kind.

This second kind of illusion is less immediate than the first. Whereas the belief in human will is generated out of 'pure privation', the belief in the will of God takes on, in the appendix to Part I, the form of a more solid fiction – the 'asylum' or 'sanctuary' of ignorance. This kind of illusion develops in a system of connected representations, which substitutes another order for the 'order of nature'. Such illusions, Galichet observes, demand a different kind of criticism from those which consist in pure privation. For power is exerted through these constructions of the imagination. They involve the organization of emotions; they arise in contexts of domination and subjection. Such illusions feed on fear and oppression. They call for replacement, rather than coexistence.

The difference between the two kinds of illusion reflects their relative distance from the immediacy of bodily awareness. In another illusion of the first kind, Spinoza calls attention to the way our judgement of the true distance of the sun can coexist with our imagining it as much closer. Here knowledge derived from intellect does not drive out the direct, illusory experience. The imagined closeness is an immediate reflection of the constitution of our bodies. We could not modify this 'illusion' without an impossible modifying of the organization of our bodies and hence of our imaginings. We cannot modify the infant body in such a way that it will directly experience the true distance of the sun. The idea of the benign or vengeful god, in contrast, is not a direct reflection of the given constitution of our bodies. Such illusions are changeable; they can be destroyed through criticism and replaced by alternative ordering fictions. These new fictions will themselves, however, be embedded in organizing frameworks of *conatus*, and power.

167

It is in this domain of changeable illusions that Spinoza's version of imagination bears most directly on education. We are not urged to change the infant body by interfering with its bodily structure. The transformation, as Spinoza stresses, must respect the integrity of the body. We are to change the body only 'as much as its nature allows and assists'. Changing its sensations of the sun clearly lies beyond those limits. In other cases the limits will be harder to determine. The body itself, in its dynamic interactions with others – acting and being acted upon – guides our interventions. And we must remember here that on Spinoza's picture those 'interventions' themselves do not come from entirely outside the nature of the body we attempt to change. Educators and educated alike are caught up in the exchange of powers in which individuality is constantly re-formed. The changes Spinoza envisage are nonetheless envisaged as real bodily changes – changes in our powers of imagining.

This changeability of body that is at the centre of a Spinozistic conceptualization of educational processes does not stop with childhood. The changeability of the illusions embedded in social practices can be seen as continuous with the narrower forms of education associated with what happens in schools. The education of the imagination is a never-ending process. Again, what is important about reason is not the power to drive out illusion; indeed for Spinoza reason has of itself no such power. 'No affect can be restrained by the true knowledge of good and evil insofar as it is true, but only insofar as it is considered as an affect' (E IVP14). The role of reason is rather to understand the operations of imagination and their interactions with the passions, interactions which have a typical pattern that is amenable to rational understanding. Here again it is important to see that the operations of imagination become the object for reason's understanding, not just an inferior form of knowledge that it leaves behind.

We do not find in Spinoza, Galichet stresses, a story of 'progressive purification', a gradual passage from appearance to true knowledge. Illusion is for Spinoza not located just at the beginning of the passage into virtue and wisdom – as its point of departure. Illusion persists into the state of wisdom. But the wise know that they are in the state of illusion and are able to forge fictions for themselves. The ignorant, in contrast, receive their fictions from others intent on domination through manipulating emotions of fear and hope. The generation of new and better illusions – that is, illusions which better serve the struggle for persisting in being as a thriving mind–body unity – is an important part of Spinoza's version of the virtuous life. Imagination persists into the highest phases of virtue. But always the stories of individual transition to virtue are interwoven with stories of social transformation.

IMAGINATION AND 'THE IMAGINARY'

Two aspects of imagination come together in Spinoza's treatment: imagination as activity – as a power of the mind – and imagination as object of the mind's critical analysis. The first is more readily accessible to us than the second. But this more elusive aspect of imagination has affinities with the concern with what has come in recent social theory from a range of sources to be called 'the imaginary'. In the use of the term that is relevant here, the connotations of 'the imaginary' are not 'the unreal' as distinct from the real 'perceived'.

When modern social theorists talk of 'the imaginary' they mean, rather, a loosely connected set of images embedded in social practices, or throughout literary or philosophical texts.

The term 'imaginary' is used in this extended way in the translated title of Michèle le Doeuff's study of philosophical imagery, *The Philosophical Imaginary*. It occurs also – in a different, but related sense derived from the work of Jacques Lacan – in the work of Luce Irigaray. And as 'the social imaginary' it is a central concept in the work of Cornelius Castoriades. Although this sense of 'the imaginary' is in many ways a product of modern social theory, it has continuities with the shifts in Spinoza's treatment of imagination between a way of knowing and, on the other hand, the imagery which becomes lodged in social practices and institutional structures in ways that make it an anonymous feature of collective mental life.

Spinoza's treatment of imagination moves between consideration of the powers of the individual human mind, the collective interactions that strengthen those powers, and the stabilized upshots of those operations – integrated with *conatus* and with the passions – which yield appropriate objects of rational understanding.

Spinoza's version of the 'imaginary' clearly has a social dimension. It is, Michèle Bertrand says, the space of representations we form of our bodies, our minds and of others. It expresses, or indicates, the power and limits of our body. It is also the space where conflicts can appear between the different affects associated with representations by different people and within the same mind at different times. The imaginary occupies, as Bertrand puts it, a middle place between 'interior isolation', in which the mind follows the course of its own idiosyncratic associational paths and the 'total transparency' of the rational order (Bertrand 1958: 104). Because each mind is the idea of a different body, it is inevitable that there are divergent associational paths between representations. But because those different and reciprocally impinging bodies have nonetheless commonalities, there is also the possibility of communication. Intersubjectivity here rests on the connections between minds grounded in the impinging of bodies which are both alike and different, giving rise to affects of joy and sadness, loves and hates and all the emotions derived from them. Parts III and IV of the *Ethics* map the complex interactions of imagination and affect which yield this common space of intersubjectivity, and the processes of imitation and identification between minds which make the fabric of social life. In civil society the understanding of these processes are themselves represented in constitutions, laws, religious rituals and the wide ranging social fictions, which give a unity to those clusterings of images and affects through which we think, however inadequately, ourselves, others and the social wholes we form with them.

Emotions cluster around images – traces of previous bodily modifications, as Spinoza saw them. The power of these images is strengthened or diminished by the dynamic social collectivities formed or disrupted by the associations our bodies form with others. These underlying 'passive' images and their powers to organize our affects underpin the social critic's creative articulation of images and 'fictions'. The identification and confrontation of the fictions that structure our individual behaviour and social practices here become, on a Spinozistic approach, not just one educational aim – the cultivation of critical intelligence – but the very core of education.

Intellect, imagination and emotion come together in Spinoza's philosophy of mind. And it is their functioning in a unity that make possible the insight into 'the imaginary' which sets free the powers of bodies. To see this aspect of the educational force of the identification of fictions, it is helpful to turn from Spinoza to an example of this educational process at work. In her essay, 'Professions for women', Virginia Woolf brings to conscious articulation a fiction governing the interaction of men and women: the 'angel in the house'. The exercise is located somewhere between the creation of a fictional character and a direct description of social practice. The 'angel in the house' is a 'phantom', the shadow of whose wing falls on the page whenever the author tries to write her book reviews. The angel, she tells us, is sympathetic, charming, utterly unselfish and self-sacrificing. If there is a chicken, she takes the leg; if there is a draught, she sits in it. 'In short she was so constituted that she never had a mind or a wish of her own, but preferred to sympathise always with the minds and wishes of others.' The writer rids herself of the shadow of the angel on her page by throwing the inkpot at her.

> She died hard. Her fictitious nature was of great assistance to her. It is far harder to kill a phantom than a reality. She was always creeping back when I thought I had dispatched her. Though I flatter myself that I killed her in the end, the struggle was severe; it took much time that had better have been spent upon learning Greek grammar; or in roaming the world in search of adventures. But it was a real experience; it was an experience that was bound to befall all women writers at that time. Killing the angel in the house was part of the occupation of a woman writer.
>
> (Woolf 1942: 151)

What makes Woolf's exercise in the identification and confronting of a fiction work is that we recognize her as capturing something we know to be there: embedded, though not clearly visible without the work of the imagination, in our social practices. Although giving such fictions form is often the achievement of individual imagination, they answer to something already present in a collective and more anonymous social imagination. Good fiction, and good uses of fictions, allow us to see more clearly the social practices for what they are. The 'angel in the house' is not a product of any one mind but of a collective social imaginary. It is there independently of the efforts of the writer. Woolf's achievement is to give form to the phantom, to make the angel visible so that, from our familiarity with the social practices, we can say 'Ah, yes, that's how it is.' What makes that recognition possible is that the 'angel in the house' is not just an intellectual construct. It is the violent emotions which surround the phantom, the 'real experience' of frustration with invisible obstacles, that allows us to recognize the angel.

The Spinozistic transformation of the 'infant body' goes on at many levels: the increase in powers of individual bodies; the creation of intersubjective spaces in which those powers can be enhanced; the critical reflection on the settled associations of images around which affects are organized; the creation of new fictions. All this counts, in a Spinozistic approach to education, as the transformation of bodily awareness – the education of the imagination.

170

There is no firm distinction here between the education of the young and the ongoing processes of social critique and collective self-reflection which respond to the 'constant change' within which minds, as ideas of bodies, move between passivity and activity, ignorance and wisdom.

The individual and the social dimensions of Spinoza's version of imagination come together in an ideal of education as centring on the processes through which we transform the fictions through which we live our lives. In times of social transition it is inevitable that there will be clashes between the different phantoms to which social critics give form, in their efforts to articulate the contingency and changeability of our social practices. And there are unresolved, and perhaps unresolvable, tensions too between the implicit, unarticulated figures of the collective social imagination itself. We can learn here from Spinoza's treatment of the relations between reason and imagination without endorsing the implicit elitism of Spinoza's distinction between the unenlightened fictions of the multitude and the more rational fictions of the enlightened. The aim, again, is not to transcend the fictions of imagination, but to get a better insight into their operations and to learn to use them effectively in social critique. The engagement is not with an external and inferior 'multitude' in the grip of illusion, but with ourselves as participants in the contingent social practices and operation of symbols which make us what we are.

NOTES

Spinoza quotations are from *A Spinoza Reader* (1994), ed. and trans. Edwin Curley and *A Theologico-Political Treatise* (1951), trans. R. H. M. Elwes. References to the *Ethics* follow the abbreviations used by Curley: E = *Ethics*; P = Proposition; D = Demonstration; C = Corollary; S = Scholium; Pref = Preface; App = Appendix. Thus '*E* VP39S' refers to *Ethics*, Part V, Scholium to Proposition 39.

1 I discuss the contrasts between Norris's and Negri's interpretations more fully in *Spinoza and the Ethics* (London and New York, Routledge, 1996), pp. 55–70.

BIBLIOGRAPHY

Bertrand, Michèle (1985) *Spinoza et l'imaginaire*, Paris: Presses universitaire de France.
Curley, Edwin (1994) (ed. and trans.) *A Spinoza Reader: the* Ethics *and Other Works*, Princeton, NJ: Princeton University Press.
Deleuze, Gilles (1988) *Spinoza: a Practical Philosophy*, trans. Robert Hurley, San Francisco: City Lights Books.
Elwes, R. H. M. (1951) *The Chief Works of Benedict de Spinoza*, New York: Dover.
Galichet, François (1972) 'Le Problème de l'illusion chez Spinoza', *Revue de Metaphysique et de Morale* 1.
Hegel, G. W. F. [1840] (1974) *Lectures on the History of Philosophy*, trans. R. S. Haldane and Frances H. Simson, London: Routledge and Kegan Paul; New York: Humanities Press.
Le Doeuff, Michèle (1989) *The Philosophical Imaginary*, trans. Colin Gordon, London: Athlone.
Lloyd, Genevieve (1996) *Spinoza and the* Ethics, London and New York: Routledge.

Negri, Antonio (1991) *The Savage Anomaly: the Power of Spinoza's Metaphysics and Politics*, trans. Michael Hardt, Minneapolis, Minn.: University of Minnesota Press.

Norris, Christopher (1991) *Spinoza and the Origins of Modern Critical Theory*, Oxford: Blackwell Publishers.

Woolf, Virginia (1942) *The Death of the Moth and Other Essays*, London: Hogarth Press.

13

LOCKE: EDUCATION FOR VIRTUE

John W. Yolton*

John Locke, medical doctor, psychologist, economist, biblical exegete, naturalist, amateur scientist, may also with some careful qualification be called an 'educationalist'. He published a book, *Some Thoughts concerning Education* in 1693; he had been writing on the subject of education from at least 1684. [. . .] The title of the published version, *Some Thoughts*, indicates Locke's view of that work. Many of his books carry similar modest titles: *A Letter concerning Toleration* (1689), an *Essay concerning Human Understanding* (1690), *Some Considerations of the Consequences of the Lowering of Interest and Raising the Value of Money* (1692). His political work was more definite: *Two Treatises of Government* (1690).

Some Thoughts [occupies] a central place in his thought and writing. The themes of the origin and growth of knowledge, the development of awareness, the formation of character, virtue, and social responsibility: these themes span much of his writing. The links between *Some Thoughts* and *Two Treatises* are especially important; the former provides a training and educational programme for the development of a moral person, the latter places that person in the political arena. The rationale of Locke's civil society is the protection of property: the possessions, the life, the individuality of the person. The list of virtues praised by Locke in *Some Thoughts* includes some individual-oriented properties (e.g. kindness, generosity, civility). The individualism of his philosophy is nicely balanced by his twin concepts of the community of mankind and the civil polity. The person as a moral being belongs to both communities; both communities set the standards for and preserve the values of Locke's morality. Locke's person is, in short, a socialized and Christianized individual. The *Essay* guides us through the distinction between man and person, *Some Thoughts* gives parents a very specific manual on how to guide and mould their children into moral, social persons. Seen in this light, Locke's work on education acquires the significance and importance it deserves.

[. . .]

* © Oxford University Press 1989. Reprinted from *Some Thoughts concerning Education* by John Locke, ed. by John W. and Jean S. Yolton (1989), by permission of Oxford University Press. Material omitted within or between paragraphs is indicated by ellipses in square brackets: editor.

Most of Locke's writings were the result of some question, problem, or concern which arose from his own experience. What are the limits of our knowledge? How do ideas arise in the mind? How can we formulate the knowledge that experimental scientists are acquiring of the world? What can we say about the nature of things themselves? How can the acquisition of private property be accounted for and our right to it defended? What is the relation between parental and political power? What will motivate men to pursue virtue? These are the kinds of specific questions to which Locke addresses himself in different writings, the bases from which he carried on his careful and detailed analyses of related concepts. He does not, in other words, start with a systematic philosophy and then fit his thoughts on government, society, or education into that framework.

[. . .] A close examination of *Some Thoughts*, of his recommendations for working with children so that they acquire the virtue and wisdom necessary for living in the world nevertheless reveals a complex and detailed set of beliefs about adults and children. There are some important continuities between this aspect of that work and his account of civil society in *Two Treatises*.

[. . .]

METAPHYSICAL PARTICULARS AND CIVIL PERSONS

There is one concept fundamental to Locke's general thought which is found in the *Essay* and in *Some Thoughts*: the concept of particulars. Locke accepted the principle that 'all that exists is particular'. What this expression means within his general system was that there are no natural classes. He did not mean there are no similarities between objects; it was the observable qualities which provide the bases for forming classifications of use. Classes are, on this account of reality, man-made. Locke's commitment to particularity has many forms, including the disavowal of talk of a common human nature shared by all men. There is no property or characteristic that I have which is *essential* to me, or more strictly, the *Essay* says, all my characteristics are equally essential: essential for me as an individual, the particular being that began to exist at a specific time, that has had the experiences I have had, that is shaped and formed as I am. Locke does not take this particularist view of man to the extreme of saying (as Leibniz did later) that the loss or alteration of any single feature would result in a different particular individual: the time and place of the beginning of my existence fixes my identity as *this* man. Along with the individuating beginning of existence there also goes a functioning biological and physiological mechanism. So long as the same continuous life unites the parts of this mechanism together, I am the same man.

The centrality given by Locke to particulars in his metaphysical system is reflected in his account of persons and in his work on education. Each child is to be dealt with individually; children have particular traits, biases, humours, tempers, a bent and tendency of their minds. Locke urged the tutor and the parents to pay careful attention to these natural dispositions, for they must be reckoned with in rearing children. Some can be altered to some extent, others can perhaps be replaced, but by and large the tutor must work around them. Thus a child may be gay, pensive, modest, timorous, confident, obstinate, or curious.

It is not clear whether Locke considered these qualities to be born with the child, but that is how he tends to talk about them. Just as we have certain faculties which can be used later, so we have certain traits which will be manifested in behaviour. They are not especially good or bad, although some of them pose more of a problem than others for the objective of moral education.

Despite the stress upon particularity, Locke's notion of man did contain some common elements. Each of us has a set of psychological or mental faculties (reason, understanding, sensation, memory), and every human being has certain desires and aversions: the desire for pleasure and the aversion to pain are explicitly described as innate practical principles. Locke does not pay much attention to desires and emotions, save to urge their control by reason. Present desires may close future options, the desire for immediate pleasure may stand in the way of future (and especially of eternal) happiness. Reason was for Locke the preferred faculty, rationality the urgent goal. Rationality and morality were closely linked, in part because he viewed reason as natural revelation and revelation as 'natural *Reason* enlarged by a new set of Discoveries communicated by GOD immediately' (*Essay*, 4.19.4). What is important about natural revelation (other writers used the phrase 'light of reason' or 'of nature') is that it can (so Locke hoped) reveal God's moral laws, the laws of nature or of reason. The faculty of reason does not, however, play its role of natural revelation unaided and untrained. Education helps to shape the psychological and motivational structure of the child, enabling him to attain rational control of his life.

Locke's *Essay* contains a developmental psychology, the infant is traced from its first experiences of warmth in the womb to its first post-natal sensations, and to its first ideas and truths. The adult of the *Essay* is the scientific observer, careful and precise in recording experiences and uniformities, Locke's objective being to systematize experience so as to understand and control his environment. Locke sketches for us the dangers and pitfalls of careless attention to objects and events, and to imprecise and confused use of language. We are urged to be as careful in our use of language as we are in our scientific endeavours. Control of language and experience is the goal. The acquisition of ideas and knowledge of ourselves and our world is traced from infancy to adulthood. The child begins without any information of self or world, but possessed of the necessary faculties and tendencies to learn about the world and to form a responsible self.

Locke's political work, *Two Treatises of Government*, contains a move parallel to the child's transition from innocence to knowledge or from man to person, the move from pre-civil to civil society. There are in that work two components in this social maturation: one from the state where there is no private property, no 'private dominion' over land and what it produces or the beasts it feeds to ownership of land and possessions, the other from the state of nature or the community of mankind to the civil society. This latter component is especially important for an understanding of Locke's views on education. His objective in *Two Treatises* was in part to explain political power, its nature, jurisdiction, and origin. For an understanding of its origin we must, Locke says,

> consider what State all Men are naturally in, and that is, a *State of perfect Freedom* to order their Actions, and dispose of their Possessions, and Persons as they think fit,

within the bounds of the Law of Nature, without asking leave, or depending upon the Will of any other Man.[1]

Almost every phrase in this passage is important for the context of education: the notions of (a) ordering our actions, (b) disposing of our possessions and persons, (c) the law of nature, and (d) freedom from the will of others.

The skill and knowledge needed to order our actions in accordance with the law of nature, to treat our possessions and persons responsibly, and to avoid coming under the absolute control of others (a particularly frightening state for Locke in its threat to personal freedom) are major objectives for education. The particularity of Locke's metaphysics is echoed in his strong emphasis upon individual liberty in his political philosophy, but liberty for him is always correlative with law and order, the law and order of God's laws, of God's will. The state of liberty is not '*a State of Licence*', and the state of nature 'has a Law of Nature to govern it, which obliges every one' (TII: 6). The child born into this world has all the equipment and potential to become a member of the community of mankind. Membership in that community must, however, be earned. Training for membership is conducted by the family; the rearing of children is guided by that objective. The consequence of failing to meet the standards of that community are a slide down the chain of being to the ranks of the beasts.

There are some stark passages in Locke's discussions of the failure to conform to the norm of humanity, that norm being conformity to the law or laws of nature. The exact content of the law of nature is not always specified by Locke, but it clearly contains most of the Christian moral values and injunctions, as to honour one's parents, help those in need, recognize God and ourselves as his workmanship. To transgress the law of nature is, Locke declares, to 'live by another Rule, than that of *reason* and common Equity, which is the measure God has set to the actions of Men, for their mutual security' (TII: 8). To do so makes such a man dangerous to mankind, 'a trespass against the whole Species', it turns him into, and he can be treated as, a wild savage beast. Such a transgressor of the law of nature can 'be destroyed as a *Lyon* or a *Tyger*' (TII: 11). So fragile is the boundary between man and beast, when that boundary is not secured by meticulous attention to moral education, the education which will prepare us for entry into the community of mankind, that Locke even says we have a right to kill a thief, since stealing my purse may only be a step towards the attempt at absolute dominion over me.

The value of civil society lies in the greater security and order provided by explicit laws, as well as the understanding and consent of its members. The state of nature is not a disorderly state, is not, as it was depicted by Hobbes, a war of all against all. The state of nature, whatever its status (whether real, imaginary, or conceptual), cannot quite be compared with the state of infancy, but there are some instructive parallels. Civil laws in the political society, based as they are on the laws of nature, provide a more secure environment for the acquisition of private property and the development of moral persons. The use of the term 'person' in the passage cited from *Two Treatises* about the state of nature had for Locke a special importance. He was careful to distinguish in his *Essay* between man and person. In discussing the nature of identity, person-identity (the identity of persons) is distinguished from the identity of man. The latter is the sameness of life in a biological organism, but identity of a person is an identity acquired through awareness of one's actions and thoughts, through a concern one takes in one's life, in one's rationality and morality. The term 'person' is, says Locke,

> a Forensick Term appropriating Actions and their Merit; and so belongs only to intelligent Agents capable of a Law, and Happiness and Misery. This personality extends it *self* beyond present Existence to what is past, only by consciousness, whereby it becomes concerned and accountable, owns and imputes to it *self* past Actions, just upon the same ground, and for the same reason, that it does the present.[2]

Not only do we own (or 'own up to') our actions, if we are to be morally responsible; we also own and have property in our person: 'Though the Earth, and all inferior Creatures be common to all Men, yet every Man has a *Property* in his own *Person*' (T11: 27). Since the protection of private property is one of the main functions of civil society, the protection of the person, of the morally responsible person, comes under that function as well.

If civil society has the task of *protecting* the person, education has the task of *producing* persons. As with Aristotle, so with Locke, education and politics go closely together. One of the ways these are linked is revealed in the account of property given in *Two Treatises*, an account founded on the premise that we all have property in our persons. Education takes place within the family; it consists primarily in turning children into persons, into persons who embody natural laws and the rationality on which civil society and civil laws (as well as the community of mankind) are based. How is this transformation accomplished?

MORAL EDUCATION: MOTIVATING AND PRODUCING PERSONS

It would be only a slight exaggeration to say that Locke's *Some Thoughts* is mainly a treatise on moral education. Virtue is the health of the soul, the aim of education is to produce a healthy, virtuous person. While Locke writes about educating the son of a gentleman, his treatise is less about gentlemen than it is about developing a moral character. Morality was not limited to gentlemen, although there is greater importance for such persons to be virtuous. The connection between virtue and being a gentleman was clear for him: if those in 'the Gentleman's Calling' are 'by their Education once set right', that is, are 'vertuous, useful, and able Men', then they will 'quickly bring all the rest into Order' ('Epistle Dedicatory'). Locke's concept of man and his views about right conduct are most strongly revealed in this work. *Some Thoughts* is in effect a manual on how to guide the child to virtue. Close to half of its total sections are concerned with this topic.

The notion of *moral man* was an important one in the *Essay*, linked as it was with Locke's novel account of 'person' as a forensic term, in other words as a term for identifying the locus of responsibility. The morality assumed in the *Essay*, and clearly cited in several places, was that of natural law, God's laws. Those laws also play a role in *Two Treatises*. One can build up some of the specific content of those laws, of that morality, from what Locke says in those works (and also, of course, from what he says in the *Reasonableness of Christianity* and his

JOHN W. YOLTON

Paraphrases of the Epistles of St Paul; cf. the early unpublished *Essays on the Law of Nature*), but it is his *Some Thoughts* which gives us the most particular and detailed account of Locke's concept of morality and of a virtuous person. There is no other work in the seventeenth century that gives such a detailed account of moral man, and of how to develop that man into a responsible person. Locke works with the metaphor of children as 'Travellers newly arrived in a strange Country, of which they know nothing' (§ 120). Like strangers in any country, these new arrivals must learn the customs and habits of the country. In time, they will become citizens. Another revealing metaphor is found in Locke's advice on how to waken a sleeping child:

> great Care should be taken in waking them, that it be not done hastily, nor with a loud or shrill Voice, or any other suddain violent Noise. This often affrights Children, and does them great harm. And sound *Sleep* thus broke off, with suddain Alarms, is apt enough to discompose any one. When Children are to be waken'd out of their *Sleep*, be sure to begin with a low Call, and some gentle Motion, and so draw them out of it by degrees, and give them none but kind words, and usage, till they are come perfectly to themselves, and being quite Dressed, you are sure they are throughly awake.
>
> *(Some Thoughts, § 21)*

Helping the child move from being an individual, a man, to being a person requires the same kind of care and skill specified in this passage for waking him. The objective of a tutor is

> to fashion the Carriage, and form the Mind; to settle in his Pupil good Habits, and the Principles of Vertue and Wisdom; to give him by little and little a view of Mankind; and work him into a love and imitation of what is Excellent and Praise-worthy; and in the Prosecution of it to give him Vigour, Activity, and Industry.
>
> (§ 94)

Love of virtue must be instilled in the child. Outward behaviour is insufficient, acting in accordance with virtue is only a start: 'he that is a good, a vertuous and able Man, must be made so within' (§ 42). Locke is very clear about the role of education in that process.

> And therefore, what he is to receive from Education, what is to sway and influence his Life, must be something put into him betimes; Habits woven into the very Principles of his Nature; and not a counterfeit Carriage, and dissembled Out-side, put on by Fear, only to avoid the present Anger of a Father, who perhaps may dis-inherit him.
>
> (§ 42)

The child enters both a family and a nation (as well as what Locke calls in *Two Treatises* the community of mankind), the family's duty being slowly to awaken the child to virtue. Each of these communities should be guided by moral laws, laws derived from the laws of nature which are God's laws. Some of these are cited in *Two Treatises*, a few in the *Essay*, but Locke nowhere gives any systematic list of them. He is emphatic, though, that the true touchstone and standard for morality is God's laws (*Essay*, 2.28.8). A basic principle for civil society (for government) is that it must be consistent with natural law. What is the content of that law?

If there is no list of moral rules, and no firm set of natural laws, how are we to know what we ought to do? How are we to identify moral actions? There are sufficient examples of rules or laws labelled 'natural law', 'laws of nature', 'law of reason', or 'God's laws' (which are all the same thing) to indicate that the content of that law speaks of more than self-preservation. The examples turn out to be rather familiar moral rules from the Christian and even classical traditions. It was symptomatic of Locke's partiality to reason and rationality that he suggested in his *Essay* that a demonstrative morality was possible,[3] but it was also indicative of his belief in the limitations of human reason that in the end he tells us to look to revelation in the Bible for our moral rules. It is even more typical that Locke insists that, just as one cannot learn a language by first learning the rules, so we become moral, as Aristotle said, through custom and habit.

The aim of education is identified as 'Vertue . . . direct Vertue', the 'hard and valuable part', harder to be acquired than 'a Knowledge of the World' (§ 70). To set the mind of the child right is to set it through training to be 'disposed to consent to nothing, but what may be suitable to the Dignity and Excellency of a rational Creature' (§ 31). Locke does not overlook the non-rational side of human nature, for it is most important for the tutor to be able to work with the emotions and desires of children. The non-rational side of children is part of human nature.

> We must look upon our Children, when grown up, to be like our selves; with the same Passions, the same Desires. We would be thought Rational Creatures, and have our Freedom; we love not to be uneasie, under constant Rebukes and Brow-beatings; nor can we bear severe Humours, and great Distance in those we converse with.
>
> (§ 41)

Passions and desires, however, are defects, or at least forces which must be controlled, though they can be used and manipulated in moral education. Perhaps Locke wished we did not have passions and desires, but since we do, and since this is God's world and we are his workmanship, they have a purpose: 'the great Principle and Foundation of all Vertue and Worth, is placed in this, That a Man is able to *deny himself* his own Desires, cross his own Inclinations, and purely follow what Reason directs as best, tho' the appetite lean the other way' (§ 33). He did not rule out the possibility that reason might authorize the satisfaction of some desires, but 'the Principle of all Vertue and Excellency lies in a power of denying our selves the satisfaction of our own Desires' (§ 38). The importance for Locke of this principle is indicated by his repetition:

> He that has not a Mastery over his Inclinations, he that knows not how to *resist* the importunity of *present Pleasure or Pain*, for the sake of what Reason tells him is fit to be done, wants the true Principle of Vertue and Industry; and is in danger never to be good for any thing.
>
> (§ 45; cf. § 52, 200)

The time to begin mastering our desires is infancy: 'Children should be used to submit their Desires, and go without their Longings, even *from their very Cradles*' (§ 38). Locke admits that the denial of desires is 'contrary to unguided Nature' (§ 45), but the tutor and the parents

179

should guide the child in learning how to modify his basic nature so that reason will take control. Reason and morality are closely connected. One positive result of denying children's appetites is to teach them modesty (§ 107) but it is clear that the greater virtue lies in acquiring mastery over our desires: that is a first step towards becoming virtuous. Reason is not and should never be, as Hume was to call it, the slave of the passions. Morality for Locke lies in reversing this relation.

At the same time, Locke recognized the power of desires, they have a power which can be turned to good, in motivating us to action. Our unguided nature will not help us pursue virtue: 'I grant, that Good and Evil, *Reward* and *Punishment*, are the only Motives to a rational Creature; these are the Spur and Reins, whereby all Mankind are set on work, and guided, and therefore they are to be made use of to Children too' (§ 54). But we must choose motivating desires carefully, using those that work on the intellect, not the body. Children 'are to be treated as rational creatures'. Not rewards such as sweets and punishments or threats and bodily blows, but *esteem* and *disgrace*, these are 'the most powerful incentives to the Mind' (§ 56). Children are to be shamed out of their faults (§§ 58, 60, 78). While Locke is very clear that the true principle and measure of virtue is 'the Knowledge of a Man's Duty, and the Satisfaction it is to obey his Maker, in following the Dictates of that Light God has given him', he sees reputation, the reputation the child has in the eyes of parents and tutor, as a help to virtue because it is 'the Testimony and Applause that other People's Reason, as it were by common Consent, gives to vertuous and well-ordered Actions' (§ 61).

Some Thoughts is filled with very specific suggestions for bringing the child's behaviour and character into harmony with what reason, the reason of adults, approves. A very ingenious method for moral education is suggested in an earlier section, the use of case studies: 'Especially in Morality, Prudence, and Breeding, Cases should be Put to him, and his Judgment asked' (§ 98). The tutor and the parents will also set the example by their behaviour and by the way they treat the child. Locke also gives illustrations of ordinary situations, and of others designed by the tutor, which show how dealing with the child in the way Locke recommends will, over time, produce some particular virtue. How many of these situations Locke depicted were witnessed by him, or whether he actually was able to apply, or to get parents to try, the methods he recommends, we do not know. That his account of child behaviour was in many cases based on first-hand observation has been indicated above. It is clear that Locke's own notion of morality and gentlemanly virtues is put to work in his examples. That morality was the common one accepted by most of Locke's acquaintances, based on Christian notions, with a strong conviction in the good of self-denial. A quick search through the sections of *Some Thoughts* will confirm this fact.

Praiseworthy Traits	*Negative Traits*
civility § 145	captiousness § 143
feeling of humanity § 117	censoriousness § 143
generosity §110	clownish shamefacedness §142
gracefulness of voice and gestures §143	contempt § 43
honour § 56	craving § 39
humility § 145	cruelty §116

Praiseworthy Traits	*Negative Traits*
industry §§ 70, 94	domineering § 103
kindness § 139	hasty judgement § 122
love of God § 136	hypocrisy § 50
love of study §128	indolence § 123
modesty § 70	lies §§ 131, 133
politeness § 117	malice § l00
prudence § 91	negligence § 141
reverence § 44	rashness § 115
self-control § 48	sheepish bashfulness §141
self-denial § 45	stubbornness §§ 111, 112
self-restraint §§ 38, 39	timidity § 115

MORAL MAN

The list of virtues culled from *Some Thoughts* is very traditional. Few of Locke's readers would have rejected any on this list. Where some disagreement might have entered was about two questions: (1) were any of these virtues innate; (2) was man by nature inclined towards virtue rather than towards vice? To the first question, Locke had given a comprehensive 'no', but in returning that answer he was careful to specify just what was being denied.

> I deny not, that there are natural tendencies imprinted on the Minds of Men; and that, from the very first instances of Sense and Perception, there are some things, that are grateful, and others unwelcome to them; some things that they incline to, and others that they fly: But this makes nothing for innate Characters on the Mind, which are to be the Principles of Knowledge, regulating our Practice.
>
> (*Essay*, 1.3.3)

Nature, not custom, 'has put into Man a desire of Happiness, and an aversion to Misery'. These desires 'do continue constantly to operate and influence all our Actions, without ceasing'. The role of custom and habit in the breeding of children is to use those desires as motives, as well as to free the faculty of reason from the control of those desires. Thus, Locke's answer to the second question is also 'no': a tendency or inclination towards happiness but not towards virtue.

[. . .]

Locke's concept of human nature was firmly planted in the midst of his acceptance of a traditional doctrine of natural law and right, of laws and rights stemming from God. More than once in his writings, natural inclinations are linked with rights. In *Two Treatises*, self-preservation is both an inclination we all have and a right. *Some Thoughts* links love and duty: 'They love their little ones, and 'tis their Duty' (§ 34). 'Honour thy Father and Mother' is an eternal law prescribing this parent–child relation (TI: 64). Children have a right to inherit the goods and possessions of their parents; that right is one aspect of the natural law that commands parents to provide for their children (TI: 88). The correlative right for children is that they should be 'nourish'd and maintained by their Parents' (TI: 89). In these passages Locke was speaking specifically of 'Possessions and Commodities of Life valuable by Money', not of 'that Reverence, Acknowledgment, Respect and Honour that is always due from Children to their Parents' (TI: 90). A man also has a right to be cared for and maintained by his children when he needs it. In contrast to Filmer, Locke emphasized that 'All that a Child has Right to claim from his Father is Nourishment and Education, and the things nature furnishes for the support of Life: But he has no Right to demand *Rule* or *Dominion* from him' (TI: 93). Locke also declares that 'a Father cannot alien the Power he has over his Child, he may perhaps to some degree forfeit it, but cannot transfer it' (TI: 100).

Locke's concept of freedom and law linked them together; a lawless man is not free. 'For *Law*, in its true Notion, is not so much the Limitation as *the direction of a free and intelligent Agent* to his proper Interest' (TII: 57). The virtuous man is a free man. The child is an apprentice to freedom and reason. While children are not born in 'the full state of *Equality*', they are nevertheless born to it (TII: 55). The natural right children have for tuition and guidance gives parents the obligation to educate their children. 'He that *understands* for him, must *will* for him too; he must prescribe to his Will, and regulate his Actions' (TII: 58). After the child has reached the age of reason, he is free and equal: 'after that, the Father and Son are equally *free* as much as Tutor and Pupil after Nonage' (TII: 59). Age and education generally bring reason and the ability to govern oneself (TII: 61). One of the criteria for the age of reason is understanding 'that Law he is to govern himself by', meaning the law of nature or reason or, derivative from this law, civil law. Parental power (and educational or tutorial power) is 'nothing but that, which Parents have over their Children, to govern them for the Childrens good, till they come to the use of Reason' (TII: 170). To guide one's self by the law of nature and reason is not merely to live an orderly and virtuous life: it is to have the very essence of humanity. To turn the child 'loose to an unrestrain'd Liberty, before he has Reason to guide him, is not the allowing him the privilege of his Nature, to be free; but to thrust him out amongst Brutes, and abandon him to a state as wretched, and as much beneath that of a Man, as theirs' (TII: 63). Education literally humanizes the child by bringing him to reason and virtue, the defining marks of man and of that community of mankind which was so important for Locke.

When we remember that Locke described reason as 'natural revelation', we get a reinforcement of his strong views on the need for a careful training of the child in the ways of reason and virtue. The 'naturalness' of reason is not independent of training and culturation. We must learn how to make use of the faculties God has given us. The significance of training for virtue in *Some Thoughts* has not always been placed in the context of Locke's concept of reason and the community of mankind. The 'moral man' of the discussion in the *Essay* of personal identity and the forensic term 'person' reinforce the point that the consciousness which for Locke constitutes identity of person is meant to include a strong moral content. That moral awareness has to be cultivated and inculcated by education; that is what good breeding does. Locke was, it could be argued, more moralistic, more prescriptive, than his more traditional contemporaries, who were content to settle for innate moral truths and religious dictates. The traditional morality which Locke also accepted was placed in an even more compelling context, what it is to be human. Moreover, Locke not only insisted upon the importance of virtue, he set to work in *Some Thoughts* to chart the ways of helping children become moral persons. It was the negative aspects of Locke's response to the traditional morality – no innate idea of God, no innate moral truths, not even a natural inclination to virtue – which his contemporaries saw as a secularization of human nature. Without those built-in moral components, how was man to become moral, how was he to recognize the obligation which even Locke stressed to obey God's laws?

Locke's answer to the question, 'How is man to become moral?', was 'through education'. Some readers of Locke interpret his emphasis upon reason and rationality as an attempt to discover through reason alone how to be moral. Even if that could be done for each individual, we must recognize that Locke's reason is closely linked with revelation: it is natural revelation. Locke's answer to the question, 'How am I to recognize the obligation to obey God?', is that reason tells us we are God's creatures and hence should obey his laws. Revelation supports reason (being indeed described as 'natural reason'), and the prospect of eternal punishment or reward gives an incentive towards virtue. Locke may be seen as a transition figure from the traditional belief in innate truths implanted by God to the various secular views of man in the eighteenth century, secular views which struggled to explain how self-interest was compatible with concern for others. After Locke, attention was focused on human nature. With the theological basis for morality weakened, but with a strong concern to reject the Hobbesian view that all the desires of the person reduce to self-love, eighteenth-century writers talked of a moral sense as part of man's nature (Hutcheson, Hume, Shaftesbury), of a natural fittingness of things and actions (Samuel Clarke, Wollaston), or of a natural sympathy for others (Hume). To what extent the moral sense, or Hume's 'sentiment common to all mankind, which recommends the same object to general approbation',[4] were products of education induced in each generation from considerations of utility, is a question some of these writers discussed. Whatever the answer, the dominant account of human nature in eighteenth-century Britain and France leant towards finding that nature essentially good, inclined towards virtue, at least open to being formed into a virtuous person. The 'malleability of man' (Passmore's phrase) characterizes the eighteenth-century concept of man, a malleability which education and society can pervert from its 'natural' proclivity towards virtue, but which, in the fashion of Rousseau, education freed from the distortions of society can develop properly.

Locke's education of children is rooted in his civil society: he saw no need to break out of the social mould and rear children outside the traditional norms. Locke was in this respect very tradition-oriented especially with respect to virtue. With his strong prescriptive instruction on moral education, with his definition of man as both rational *and* moral, the amoral aspect of his concept of man is greatly reduced in significance. What is important is that the child is malleable, that he can be trained to be virtuous. Thus, while Locke may have disagreed with the claims made later by Rousseau – that 'il n'y a point de perversité originelle dans le cœur humain', that 'les premiers mouvemens de la nature sont toujours droits'[5] – the main difference between Locke and Rousseau (and many other eighteenth-century writers on education and morality) lies in the primary role given by these writers to

183

the passions, to sentiments, rather than to reason. Hume's extended discussion of the source of morality – whether it is reason or the passions[6] – deals with most of the answers to that question. Hume does not tell us how to train the passions, how to allow the sentiment of humanity to surface, other than advising us not to be bewitched by reason and the claims of philosophers. Rousseau's *Émile* attempts to chart some of the ways in which a tutor can guide the child away from the perversions of reason and bad education. Locke, too, writes with a firm understanding of the different tempers and passions of children, trying to suggest to parents and tutors various ways in which they can be harnessed and used in the moulding of a virtuous character. The apparent opposition between Locke and other writers on education and morality in the eighteenth century may be less than we first believe, since all these authors (Locke included) gave attention to the non-rational side of human nature. They were interested in the moral man, and with ways in which the morality of man was linked with and supported society. In one way or another, moral education was believed to be possible.[7]

PRINCIPLES OF LEARNING

In his specific comments on teaching and learning in *Some Thoughts*, Locke is more concerned with general methods and rules of thumb than with subject-matter and curriculum. He is never far from his constant stress upon virtue in the education of children. Virtue is a more important aim of education for Locke than specific instruction in subjects, and he never tires of stressing this point. In § 70 he suggests that parents have 'a strange value for words, when preferring the Languages of the Ancient *Greeks* and *Romans*, to that which made them such brave Men', and warns against hazarding 'your Son's Innocence and Vertue, for a little Greek and Latin'. Foreign languages and the contemporary teaching techniques for learning languages typified for Locke the wasteful preoccupation by tutors and parents with subject-matter rather than with the training of character. Some of Locke's de-emphasizing of particular subjects clearly arises because of the seventeenth-century notion of a young gentleman. The studies to which he is set are more designed as 'Exercises of his Faculties, and Imployment of his Time, to help him from Sauntering and Idleness' than for specific instruction (§ 94). No one expects the young gentleman to become 'an accomplished Critick, Orator, or Logician' or be a master of science or history. But along with these socially determined ideas of a gentleman's education, Locke's remarks show a more general appreciation of the importance of good character and a recognition that the learning of a method of study related to what each person's own industry can achieve is of greater value than factual knowledge. The tutor's goal 'is not so much to teach him all that is knowable, as to raise in him a love and esteem of Knowledge; and to put him in the right way of knowing, and improving himself, when he has a Mind to it' (§ 195). One of the reasons Locke was opposed to large classes (a school in the seventeenth-century sense) was that these goals depend upon personal tuition: 'The forming of their Minds and Manners requiring a constant Attention, and particular Application to every single Boy' (§ 70). In a school or class of fifty or one hundred, the only successful instruction is book learning.

Locke may have been too pessimistic about what can be accomplished in large classes.

What he has to say about teaching – his commonsense psychology of learning – has value beyond the small context he had in mind for the Clarkes.* The constant stress upon and the priority given to virtue and good character has, so Locke claimed, even a practical pedagogic value. 'The more this Advances, the easier way will be made for all other Accomplishments, in their turns. For he that is brought to submit to Vertue, will not be refractory, or resty, in any thing, that becomes him' (§ 70). If once a 'right disposition' has been acquired, 'though all the rest [specific subjects] should be neglected', that right disposition 'would, in due time, produce all the rest' (§ 177). A virtuous character, carrying with it all the proper tempers of mind, is not only a condition for humanity: it is a condition for learning as well.

Just as there are some general principles for Locke's account in the *Essay* of the order of acquiring ideas, so there are a few advisory rules that he recommends to the teacher and tutor. The right way to teach children specific subjects is 'to give them a Liking and Inclination to what you propose to them to be learn'd' (§ 72). What is to be taught should not be presented as a task or burden or duty. Even play can become hated if children are made or forced to play (§ 73). The notion of forcing children to play is almost contradictory, force and play being incompatible. Similarly, Locke is suggesting that if not incompatible, the notion of forcing children to learn is at least impracticable. Another rule is not to attempt to get children to do even the things for which they have an inclination except when they 'have a Mind and *Disposition* to it' (§ 74). The changes of temper in children should be carefully studied so that instruction can fit the 'favourable *Seasons of Aptitude and Inclination*' (ibid.). More can be learnt in this way, and less time spent; in addition, more time for play can be allowed. Locke criticized contemporary educational methods for ignoring this psychological fact, as he thought it was. The rod is no substitute and should be used only in very special and recalcitrant cases, and then in careful and limited ways. Following these two rules of instruction, Locke thought, would enable teachers to make learning as much recreation as children's play is, thereby creating a motive to learn. Men will not follow virtue out of a knowledge of it; and, similarly, children will not learn without an activating motive. Pleasure and pain (more the former than the latter) function in both the acquisition of virtue and the learning of specific subject-matter. The goal of teaching is to get the child to ask to be taught.

Along with these two rules, Locke mentions two cautions. First, we may miss the seasons of aptitude through carelessness and inattention, or those seasons may not occur as often as they should in some particular child. We may in consequence confirm a child in habitual idleness. Second, we can help the process of learning if we are able to teach the student how to gain mastery over himself, how to be able, upon choice, to study some subject (§ 75). Control and even alteration of our desires is necessary for both virtue and learning. This sort of training or guidance in how to learn to study may be part of the psychology of learning, since it is not instruction in a particular subject but training for learning. For this, we should sometimes try to make the child 'buckle to the Thing proposed' when he is 'by Laziness unbent, or by Avocation bent another Way' (ibid.).

Locke does not give much specific advice on how to bring out these learning tempers, though he does offer a few suggestions. In § 76 he points out the effectiveness of the example of others whom the child esteems; in § 148 he cites the case of a boy whose reluctance to learn to read was overcome by the parents and Locke talking among themselves in the child's presence of 'the Privilege and Advantage of Heirs and Elder Brothers, to be Scholars; . . . And that for Younger Brothers, 'twas a Favour to admit them to Breeding', but that they could, if they pleased, 'be ignorant Bumpkins and Clowns'. Envy and a feeling of exclusion from privilege seem to have operated in this instance. The natural curiosity of children can also be used to lead the child to want to learn: it is nature's device for removing ignorance. As a way of cultivating this natural curiosity, Locke cites a few simple rules: do not check the child's questions, do not laugh at his questions, explain in his own terms, and never give deceitful answers (§§ 118, 120). Commending the child and frequently bringing strange and new things to his attention are other ways to encourage and use curiosity (§§ 119, 121). Whether or not these suggestions for bringing the child to want to learn are useful, they at least show that Locke's principles of learning were not meant to lead the tutor to stand idly by and wait for the seasons of aptitude to come. Learning is not to be permissive, but the guides and controls ought to be child-centred: they ought to arise from the child's own character and motivational structure, subtly manipulated by the tutor.

Another more general learning principle is that 'Care must be taken with Children, to begin with that, which is plain and simple, and to teach them as little as can be at once' (§ 180). In this passage Locke is speaking specifically of teaching astronomy, but I think he would take this principle as having a wider use, as the alternative formulation in the language of ideas clearly indicates: 'Give them first one simple Idea, and see that they take it right, and perfectly comprehend it before you go any farther, and then add some other simple Idea which lies next in your way to what you aim at, and so proceeding by gentle and insensible steps.' The natural temper of children is that their minds wander, but also think about one thing at a time (§ 167). Just as the order of time (the chronology) must be followed in studying and teaching history and the order of nature carefully observed and recorded in physical science, so there is an order of learning and knowledge natural to the mind (§ 195). That order is 'from the knowledge it stands possessed of already, to that which lies next, and is coherent to it, and so on to what it aims at, by the simplest and most uncompounded parts it can divide the Matter into' (ibid.). The notion of one piece of knowledge or idea being 'coherent' with another is important. Locke's notion of demonstration set out in the *Essay* was that of showing the conceptual relations of ideas. What the teacher does is to demonstrate the connections one idea has with another within any given subject-matter. More importantly for Locke's conception of a curriculum, the connection of ideas is carried over into the relations between one subject and another. One of the most interesting features of Locke's account of the curriculum – a feature I do not think was stressed by other writers at this time – is the careful use he makes of the interconnection of subject-matter. Just as there is an order of acquiring ideas, both a temporal and a conceptual one, so there is for Locke an order in learning. The order in learning across the curriculum is not only a temporal one, though he does specify the order of instruction in this way: the curriculum order is also a *content* order.

THE CURRICULUM

The standard curriculum of spelling, reading, writing, and foreign languages was integrated, in that reading and writing skills were to be exercised by copying and reading the material in Latin or French. Locke follows the latest trend in language learning by downgrading grammar and stressing oral instruction.[8] He also testifies from his own experience that having a child read from a Latin Bible, where the syllables have been marked for pronunciation, will in a short time produce some understanding of the Latin. The same technique, together with the use of interlinear Latin and English, can be used with Aesop's *Fables* and other books of interest (§ 177).[9] Skill in reading one's native language is thus put to use and paired with reading another language. That process is also aided by having the child copy the interlinear books which he had been reading (§ 167). Skill in writing can also be enhanced by drawing, which is therefore to be encouraged in the child (§ 161). Facility in Latin or French can in turn be used for learning geography, astronomy, chronology, anatomy, history, and other sciences (§ 166). In this way, the child will improve his knowledge of those languages and acquire some knowledge of those specific disciplines as well (§ 178).

Within the specific disciplines, Locke recommends a definite order of learning based upon natural connections of subject-matter. Geography is the first of these disciplines to be taught. 'For the learning of the Figure of the *Globe*, the Situation and Boundaries of the Four Parts of the World, and that of particular Kingdoms and Countries, being only an exercise of the Eyes and Memory, a child with pleasure will learn and retain them' (§ 178). Locke believed that 'Children may be taught any thing, that falls under their Senses, especially their sight, as far as their Memories only are exercised' (§ 181). That is why geography comes first in this order. The study of geography is not exhausted by the knowledge of the main physical divisions and characteristics of the globe, but this will be the child's first learning in this field. He learns these geographical facts by sight and by rote, rather than reasoning. Arithmetic, the next subject in Locke's order, introduces the child to abstract reasoning (§ 180). With the rudiments of counting, addition, and subtraction, further progress can be made in geography by teaching the child '*Longitude* and *Latitude*, and by them be made to understand the use of Maps, and by the Numbers placed on their Sides, to know the respective Situation of Countries, and how to find them out on the Terrestrial Globe' (ibid.). From them, the tutor can progress to the figure and position of the constellations, to the nature of our solar system, and then to an outline of the Copernican system. By this progressive and interdisciplinary process, the child can be prepared 'to understand the Motion and Theory of the Planets, the most easy and natural Way'.

Geometry is a natural step after the child has acquired some knowledge of the globe, the equator, and the meridians. The first six books of Euclid can be taught at this stage. Another closely related subject to geography is chronology. These subjects go hand in hand (§ 182). They are prerequisites for history, the next subject in Locke's integrated curriculum. Without these prerequisites, 'History will be very ill retained, and very little useful; but be only a jumble of Matters of Fact, confusedly heaped together without Order or Instruction' (ibid.). Latin can also be put to use by giving the child some Latin history, starting with the easiest and going to 'the most difficult and sublime', Cicero, Virgil, and Horace (§ 184). Ethics and civil law will emerge from some of this historical reading, and English law can also be easily introduced at this point (§§ 185–7).[10]

Locke's curriculum goes on to include rhetoric, logic, and natural science, as well as art and dancing. It was a typical gentleman's education. What is of interest is his attempt to show how learning in one area can aid and be used in other areas. While he does not assign ages to the features of his curriculum, he clearly worked with a notion of development. The rudimentary developmental psychology of the *Essay* is matched by his commonsense recognition of the ways in which the child's interest and skills in one area can be stepping stones for another. He saw and stressed the difference between learning by heart (as the child should learn languages, his first geography, the Lord's Prayer, the Creeds, and the Ten Commandments, §§ 157, 177–8), learning to read (which requires understanding), and learning to reason (as he begins to do in arithmetic). Throughout his outline of the curriculum, Locke illustrates the learning principles that he accepted. The general principle – to make learning play and recreation – is stated in his discussion of reading (§ 148). Some methods of carrying out this principle are the device of putting letters, syllables, and pictures of animals on the child's toys (§ 151–3), and encouraging the child to read by giving him books that will catch his interest (§ 156). The device of using pictures of objects for teaching their names was urged as a way of making sure that when the child hears visible objects talked of he has clear ideas of those objects, 'those Idea's being not to be had from Sounds; but from the Things themselves, or their Pictures' (ibid.).[11] The constant stress in Locke's account of the science of nature in the *Essay* was laid upon the same way to clarity of ideas, on going to the things themselves and observing and recording precisely and carefully. The move away from scholastic verbiage and from sounds without meaningful ideas – a move characteristic of the century – is reflected in *Some Thoughts* by injunctions for making sure that children acquire clear and distinct ideas of the objects discussed in the various disciplines.

[. . .]

NOTES

1 *Two Treatises of Government*, ed. P. Laslett (Cambridge, Cambridge University Press, 1960), TII: 4.

2 *Essay Concerning Human Understanding*, ed. P. H. Nidditch (Oxford, Clarendon Press, 1975), 2.27.26.

3 Sometimes the demonstrative morality suggestion is taken to be a claim for a deductive derivation of moral rules. The more likely meaning is simply the demonstration of conceptual connections between moral ideas.

4 David Hume, *An Enquiry concerning the Principles of Morals*, ed. L. A. Selby-Bigge, 3rd edn, rev. P. H. Nidditch (Oxford, Clarendon Press, 1975), § IX, pt. i (p. 272).

5 J. J. Rousseau, *Émile, ou de l'éducation*, in *Œuvres complètes*, ed. B. Gagnebin and M. Raymond (Paris, Gallimard, 1959–69), iv. 322.

6 Hume, *A Treatise of Human Nature*, ed. L. A. Selby-Bigge, 2nd edn, rev. P. H. Nidditch (Oxford, Clarendon Press, 1978), bk. III, pt. i, § I.

7　Among the less well-known 18th-century writers on education who carry forward these themes of moral education, many either using Locke or showing his influence, are John Clarke, *The Foundation of Morality in Theory and Practice* (1726?) and *An Essay upon the Education of Youth* (1720); I. Watts, *A Treatise on the Education of Children and Youth* (2nd edn, 1769); Thomas Sheridan, *British Education: Or, The Source of the Disorder of Great Britain* (1756); James Burgh, *The Dignity of Human Nature* (1754); J. P. de Crousaz, *Traité de l'éducation des enfans* (1722). For a discussion of the knowledge of most such works, including Locke's *Some Thoughts*, in America, see Jay Fliegelman, *Prodigals and Pilgrims: The American Revolution against Patriarchal Authority, 1750–1800* (Cambridge, Cambridge University Press, 1982).

*　Edward Clarke (MP for Somerset) and his wife were close friends of Locke: editor.

8　'After the Restoration the practice of talking Latin, always difficult to enforce, was dying out, although some educationists like Charles Hoole, John Locke and John Aubrey advocated that boys should learn Latin by speaking the language and hearing others speak it' (W. A. L. Vincent, *The Grammar Schools: their Continuing Tradition, 1600–1714* (London, Murray, 1969), p. 76).

9　For an account of Locke's role in the publication of just such an edition of Aesop, see James Axtell, *The Educational Writings of John Locke* (Cambridge, Cambridge University Press, 1968), p. 271, n. 2. See also Robert H. Horwitz and Judith B. Finn, 'Locke's Aesop Fables', in *The Locke Newsletter* 6 (1975), pp. 71–88.

10　Ethics as a subject in the curriculum must be distinguished from the moral training that Locke emphasized as a preliminary to any learning and as the way to lead students to become moral. The training of the child in virtue seeks to habituate him to right conduct, in accordance with the laws of nature. It is hoped that along with these habits will go some beliefs about what is right and wrong. The study of ethics would be the examination of previous systems of laws and beliefs about right and wrong. There is no suggestion that Locke intended the study of ethics to make the student moral.

11　A prospectus for a school at Tottenham High Cross in Middlesex promised that, among many other useful ideas, 'Repositories for Visibles shall be immediately provided, out of which may be produced, Herbs, Drugs, Seeds, Mineral Juices, Metals, precious Stones, Birds, Beasts, and Fishes, that cannot be produced in Specie, shall be shewed in their Pictures' (Quoted by Vincent, *Grammar Schools*, p. 200). Comenius, of course, stressed the value of pictures in teaching, but not before 1649; about 1635, John Frooke criticized his *Janua Linguarum*, suggesting that its defects 'might be overcome if an "Encyclopaedia of Sensuals" was combined with the *Janua*, complex pictures being particularly valuable as showing both physical characteristics and relationships, operations and degrees of phenomena' (Charles Webster (ed.) *Samuel Hartlib and the Advancement of Learning* (Cambridge, Cambridge University Press, 1970), p. 20). Cf. Locke's suggestion for a natural history dictionary with little pictures, *Essay*, 3.11.25.

14

LOCKE ON THE EDUCATION OF PAUPERS

Peter Gay

Locke addressed his little book on education to a gentleman, on the subject of the education of that gentleman's son and in the hope that other gentlemen would read it. It never occurred to him that every child should be educated or that all those to be educated should be educated alike. Locke believed that until the school system was reformed, a gentleman ought to have his son trained at home by a tutor, and he devoted some lengthy paragraphs of his *Some Thoughts Concerning Education* to the proper qualifications of such a tutor. As for the poor, they do not appear in Locke's little book at all, and we have to gather his ideas from a document he wrote in 1697. In his capacity as a commissioner of trade and plantations, Locke drafted a plan for the revision of the Elizabethan Poor Law in light of the almost overwhelming problem of pauperism in England.[1] The increase of the poor, he wrote, meant an increase in the burden of local taxation designed to provide for them. One way out was to prevent their debauchery by closing down taverns; another was to compel beggars to do hard labor at soldier's pay. But the most burdensome question was the children. Here Locke suggested some drastic remedies, remedies which seem oddly out of place with his general humanitarianism and which demonstrate that to seventeenth-century thinkers, even to radicals, the poor were barely human: "If any boy or girl, under fourteen years of age, shall be found begging out of the parish where they dwell . . . they shall be sent to the next working school, there to be soundly whipped and kept at work till evening, so that they may be dismissed time enough to get to their place of abode that night."[2] Since most of the children of the poor lived in vicious idleness, Locke proposed that "working schools be set up in every parish, to which the children of all such as demand relief of the parish, above three and under fourteen years of age, whilst they live at home with their parents, and are not otherwise employed for their livelihood by the allowance of the overseers of the poor, shall be obliged to come."[3] This would give the mothers liberty to work and the children better food than they would obtain at home: "If . . . care be taken that they have each of them their belly-full of bread daily at school, they will be in no danger of famishing, but, on the contrary, they will be healthier and stronger than those who are bred otherwise."[4] This diet, Locke thought, should be supplemented "in cold weather, if it be thought needful," with "a little warm water gruel."[5] Since the children would be earning their way with what they produced, Locke added thoughtfully, the education of paupers would cost the parish nothing. I need hardly point out that these working schools did not offer such subjects as

French or Latin, but confined themselves to teaching the little paupers such manual skills as "spinning or knitting, or some other part of woollen manufacture" and such edifying matters as "some sense of religion."[6] That was all; those who counted needed a knowledge of geography and French, some dancing ability, and much skill in conversation, but the poor did not count – not yet.

NOTES

1 Locke's proposals are reprinted in H. R. Fox Bourne, *A Life of John Locke*, 2 vols (New York, 1876), II, pp. 337–91.
2 Ibid., p. 381.
3 Ibid., p. 383.
4 Ibid., p. 384.
5 Ibid.
6 Ibid., p. 385.

15

LEIBNIZ AS A THEORIST OF EDUCATION

Patrick Riley

INTRODUCTION

Leibniz wrote only one substantial piece on education, the *Lettre sur l'éducation d'un prince*, though he took this essay seriously enough to rewrite it four times between its original composition in 1685 (the year before the "Discourse on Metaphysics") and 1710 (the year in which the *Theodicy* was published).[1] There is nothing surprising in this princely focus; after all, Leibniz spent his adult life – having rejected a professorship and an academic career at the age of 21 – in the service of the princely courts of Mainz (beginning in 1668) and of Hanover (from 1676 to 1716), and believed that "it is principally for the great, to whom God has given the means to contribute effectively to the advancement of the general good" to be "the main instruments of divine glory."[2] It was thus natural for Leibniz to think that "the education of princes" (and of princesses, such as his former pupil Queen Sophie Charlotte of Prussia) should be his central educational concern, that suitably "enlightened" rulers might be willing to found (for example) academies of arts and sciences, such as the one of Berlin, of which Leibniz was the first President (1700).[3]

Even when, exceptionally, Leibniz discussed the reform of education in "schools," as against the formation of academies to rival the Royal Society (London) and the Académie des Sciences (Paris), his focus was still overwhelmingly *political*. In the *Grundriss eines Bedenckens von Aufrichtung einer Societät in Deutschland* of c. 1671 he insists that, in "improving" schools, the focus of the curriculum should be *Richtigkeit* (rightfulness), and that "youth" should be steeped not in "poetry, logic and scholastic philosophy" so much as in "*moralia et civilia studia.*"

To be sure, in the space between "the great" and "the common man" Leibniz found himself (and a number of other middle-class intellectuals including Newton, Hobbes, Locke and Huygens); but while near the end of his life he wrote important letters to the French Platonist Remond, in which he discussed his own early education in Leipzig,[4] he never wrote a substantial essay on the education of that class of intellectuals that (he thought) should give enlightened counsel to those among "the great" who are more "powerful" than "reasonable": "Those to whom God has given reason without power . . . have the right to be counselors [while the powerful] must listen patiently, and not throw good counsels to the winds."[5] Since Leibniz was (or viewed himself as) largely self-taught, he may have thought that the education of independent thinkers was too individual and idiosyncratic to permit useful generalization. Whatever the reason, he focused his educative efforts on enlightening those who have the capacity to affect (or even effect) *le bien général*:

> The greatest and most efficacious means of augmenting the general welfare of men, while enlightening them, while turning them toward the good and while freeing them from annoying inconveniences, in so far as this is feasible, would be to persuade great princes and [their] principal ministers to make extraordinary efforts to procure such great goods and to allow our times to enjoy advantages which, without this [extraordinary effort], would be reserved for a distant posterity. And it is certain that besides immortal glory, they will derive great utility from this, and will be working even for their own perfection and satisfaction; for nothing is more worthy of great souls than the knowledge and the execution of that which produces human happiness, and which displays the greatness of God, which gives us admiration and love for him.[6]

But the Leibnizian title, *Lettre sur l'éducation d'un prince*, tells us only whose education matters, not what is to be imparted or learned or known. The first thing to be said, therefore, about Leibniz as a theorist of (usually princely) education, is that everything depends on the degree to which Leibniz was a Platonist, and above all on the degree to which he was a Platonist in the sphere of education. This is true for five closely-linked reasons:

1　Leibniz was concerned principally with the education of rulers who must care for the general good ("since almost all important things which concern the common good consist in exact inquiry, it is better to deal with one head [*Haupt*] and a few high officials than with a community, which is incapable of reflection").[7]
2　Leibniz thought that rulers must above all have "great sentiments of piety, of justice, and of charity."[8]
3　Leibniz thought that justice itself should be defined as "wise charity," *caritas sapientis* (a fusion of Pauline "charity" and Platonic "wisdom").[9]
4　Leibniz thought that justice was an "eternal verity" enjoying universal geometrical necessity (as in Plato's *Phaedo* and *Euthyphro*).
5　Leibniz thought that knowledge of eternal moral verities was innate or a priori, more or less in the manner of Plato's *Meno*, and therefore not imparted by sense impressions or teacherly instruction; he thought this was so, at least, if Platonism could be suitably chastened, and stripped of the notion that knowing is reminiscence or recollection of prenatal psychic states ("in order that knowledge, ideas or truths be in our mind, not necessary that we have ever actually thought of them; they are only natural capacities").[10]

If, then, the Leibnizian prince must be just or wisely charitable above all, and if justice *qua* "eternal verity" is (in effect) a quasi-Platonic "idea," and if Platonic ideas are simply there, waiting to be drawn out by Socratic probing (rather than "taught" or imparted), then "Leibniz on education" will be equivalent to "Leibniz as chastened Platonist" for whom the essential thing is, in some sense, reminding potentially just princes of what they potentially know. Hence Leibniz's insistence in the *Lettre sur l'éducation d'un prince* that the final, adult phase of princely education must rest not on perception or "imagination" but on "the things which the mind alone can know," especially "the art of reasoning in moral philosophy, in politics and in law."[11] (And law itself, he asserts in the *Elements of Law and Equity*, "belongs to those sciences that are not built on experiments but on definitions, not on the senses but on demonstrations according to reason . . . mathematical and jurisprudential sciences do not take their point of departure from the senses, but from a clear and distinct intuition, or, as Plato calls it, Idea."[12])

Leibniz the "philosopher of princely education" is Leibniz the chastened Platonist, or perhaps (better still) the enlarged Platonist who insists that "wise" or ordered or measured charity is the essence of justice, and that the benevolent rulership of the enlightened prince is our only hope for social betterment: "True politics consists in justice and in charity, and a great prince cannot be better served than when the happiness of the people makes up his own."[13]

A final introductory remark: Leibniz's practical thought, including his views on education, reflects a division or a tension within Platonism itself. In the *Republic* the "wise few" (who are not "appetitive") rule justly; in the *Meno* even an uneducated slave ("Meno's slave") can have astonishing quasi-geometrical a priori knowledge of virtue. In the *Meno* "eternal moral verity" seems to be "in" all persons, awaiting emergence through Socratic interrogation; in the *Republic* by contrast there are dominant psychological types (gold, silver and brass men), and eternal verity seems to be beyond (or above) the "brave" and the "appetitive."[14] In the *Meno* Plato is a psychic egalitarian for whom all are potentially wise (even Meno's slave); in the *Republic* only a few are wise and they justly rule. This same division or split appears in Leibniz as well: for him moral truths are universally available, but the "common man" is "heavy with shadows"[15] (as in Plato's cave) and it is mainly the (principally princely) beneficiaries of "enlightenment," and their enlightened counselors who actually know and rule. Leibniz's Christian egalitarianism (the equality of souls in the sight of God) set some limits to his Platonism; but if a benevolent prince is wisely "charitable," that salvages everything which Leibniz most admired in Christian ethics anyhow. For Leibniz, like Augustine, was a Christian Platonist; and from his Christian Platonism flowed a general "universal jurisprudence" of which princely education was a particular part. (Here Leibniz is best compared with Pascal, a Christian but assuredly no Platonic rationalist. Since for Pascal reason is weak, à la Montaigne ("le coeur a ses raisons que la raison ne connaît point") charity is supernatural ("of another order"), and politics is the realm of "illusion," force and *divertissement*, Pascalian education cannot mean bringing enlightened statesmen to be "wisely charitable"; Leibniz's highly political conception of education differs from Pascal's "education of the heart," which lies in a purely private inner sphere divorced from a "carnal" politics in which "force is Queen." Leibniz's demi-Platonism bent his Christianity in a way that Pascal would have found completely unacceptable, not least in notions of education; and the illuminating differences between Leibniz and Pascal will be brought out fully in the final section of the present essay.

LEIBNIZ'S "EDUCATION" AS PART OF "UNIVERSAL JURISPRUDENCE"

Since Leibniz's "global Platonism" ties together his views on justice, enlightened princely government, and education, the best course will be to see Leibnizian education as a facet or outgrowth of that global Platonism.[16]

The central idea of Leibniz's "universal jurisprudence," which aims to find quasi-geometrical eternal moral verities equally valid for all rational beings, human or divine, is that justice is "the charity of the wise (*caritas sapientis*),"[17] that it is not mere conformity to sovereign-ordained "positive" law given *ex plenitudo potestatis* (in the manner of Hobbes), nor mere "refraining from harm" or even "rendering what is due" (the *neminem laedere* and *suum cuique tribuere* of Roman law). The equal stress on "charity" and "wisdom" suggests that Leibniz's practical thought is a kind of fusing of Platonism, in which the wise know the eternal truths such as absolute goodness (*Phaedo* 75d), which the gods themselves also know and love (*Euthyphro* 93–10e), and therefore deserve to rule (*Republic* 443–e) – and of Pauline Christianity, whose key moral idea is that charity or love is the first of the virtues ("though I speak with the tongues of men and of angels, and have not charity, I am become as sounding brass or a tinkling cymbal"[18]).

If one decomposes *caritas sapientis* into its parts, charity and wisdom, the provenance of both elements is clear enough: charity or love is the very heart of Christian ethics (St Paul's "the greatest of these is charity" or St John's "a new commandment I give unto you, that ye love one another");[19] and the notion that justice requires the rule of the wise is famously Platonic. How charity and wisdom relate, how they might modify each other, is not just a historical but a philosophical problem, since love is "affective," wisdom "cognitive"; but the really grave difficulties in Leibniz's universal jurisprudence lie elsewhere. For it is not clear that a wisely charitable God would create a world which, though it may be "best," is not simply good; an *être infiniment parfait* might sooner contemplate his own perfection, *ad infinitum*. And whether Judas or Pontius Pilate could have acted better, been more benevolent, is notoriously problematical given Leibniz's ideas of "substance" (or monad) and of pre-established harmony.[20] Since however, Leibniz is a supremely architectonic thinker who wants to relate everything to "first philosophy," one cannot just cordon off his moral and political thought (from which his theory of education flows) from his metaphysics and theology: that is precisely what he himself did not do.

It was characteristic of Leibniz to try to reconcile apparently conflicting ideas, to take from each kind of thought that which was soundest and to synthesize it with the seemingly incommensurable truths of other systems; thus he struggled throughout his life to fuse Platonism, Cartesianism, Augustinian voluntarism, Christian charity, scholasticism, Hobbesian mechanistic materialism, and a number of other doctrines into a plausible whole whose apex would be a rational theology – indeed a "theodicy" or justification of God. Given this desire for reconciliation, for harmony, for synthesis – which he applied to political and moral philosophy (and to education) as much as to any other philosophical question – it should come as no surprise that Leibniz wanted to establish, or rather discover, a "universal jurisprudence," a system of justice and law common to God and man (and generally to any rational "substances"); anticipating Kant, Leibniz urged that justice and injustice "do not depend solely on human nature," but on "the nature of intelligent substance in general." As substances linked by intelligence, God and man exist for Leibniz in a "society or universal republic of spirits" which is "the noblest part of the universe," a moral realm within physical nature, a realm in which "universal right is the same for God and for men."[21] Or, as Leibniz put it near the end of his life, in the *Monadology*:

> the totality of all spirits must compose the City of God, that is to say, the most perfect state that is possible, under the most perfect of monarchs.
>
> This city of God, this truly universal monarchy, is a moral world in the natural world, and is the most exalted among the works of God.[22]

For Leibniz, the difference between divine and human justice was one of degree, not kind; God's justice is simply infinitely more perfect than men's, and "to say . . . that God's justice is different from men's is like saying that the arithmetic or the geometry of men is false in heaven." It is erroneous, Leibniz insisted, to say that we must not judge God in terms of the common concept of justice, for it must be the case that one has "an idea or a notion of justice when one says that God is just, otherwise one would only attribute a word to him." Just as the arithmetic and geometry of men and of God differ only in the degree of their perfection, so too "natural jurisprudence and every other truth is the same in heaven and on earth."[23] "As for the order of justice," Leibniz wrote in 1696, "I believe that there are universal rules which must be valid as much with respect to God as with respect to intelligent creatures." Intelligible truths "are universal, and what is true here below with respect to us is also such for the angels and for God himself." The eternal truths "are the fixed and immutable point on which everything turns," such as "the truths of numbers, of arithmetic, and those of motion or weight in mechanics and in astronomy."[24]

What is important is that Leibniz used the notion of objectively certain "eternal verities" politically and morally to attack the idea of justice as bare superior power; the "formal notion" of justice, he observed in a commentary on Hobbes, has nothing to do with the mere "sovereign" command of authorities: "it does not depend on the arbitrary laws of superiors, but on the eternal rules of wisdom and goodness, in men as well as in God."[25] And he hoped that his own "education of princes" might help to draw out those "eternal rules," and even "translate them into fact."

For Leibniz it was merely an empiricist prejudice to see justice as "unreal" if it did not consist of tangible commands backed by power and threats. "The qualities of mind are not less real than those of body. It is true that you do not see justice as you see a horse, but you understand it no less, or rather you understand it better; it is no less in actions than directness or obliqueness is in motions."[26] And if justice were simply derivative from the possession of power, "all powerful persons would be just, each in proportion to his power"; if an "evil genius" somehow seized supreme universal power, Leibniz insisted, he would not cease to be "wicked and unjust and tyrannical" simply because he could not be successfully "resisted." Those who derive justice from irresistible power, he thought, simply confuse "right" and "law": the concept of right cannot (by definition) be unjust, but law can be because it is "given and maintained by power";[27] only in God is there an absolute coincidence of right and power which produces just law.

Perhaps the finest mature statement of Leibniz's view is contained in the *Opinion on the Principles of Pufendorf* (1706),

> Neither the norm of conduct itself, nor the essence of the just, depends on [God's] free decision, but rather on eternal truths, objects of the divine intellect . . . Justice follows certain rules of equality and of proportion which are no less founded in the immutable nature of things, and in the divine ideas, than are the principles of arithmetic and of geometry . . . Divine justice and human justice have common rules which can be reduced to a system; and they must be taught in universal jurisprudence.[28]

Leibniz understood "justice," however, not just as "wisdom" and Platonic "eternal verity" (which is known without being taught) but also as charity and benevolence. And this is why he always defined justice as "the charity of the wise." "The proper treatment of justice and that of charity cannot be separated," he urged in one of his earliest writings. "Neither Moses, nor Christ, nor the Apostles nor the ancient Christians regulated justice otherwise than according to charity . . . [and] I, too, after having tried countless definitions of justice, finally felt myself satisfied only by this one; it alone I have found universal and reciprocal." Charity is "a universal benevolence, which the wise man carries into execution in conformity with the measures of reason, to the end of obtaining the greatest good."[29] Charity, a "habit of loving" (with love defined as a "feeling of perfection" in others[30]), necessitated voluntary action; it was to be regulated by wisdom, which could provide a knowledge of what men deserved through their "perfections."

What is essential for Leibniz, is that Christian "charity" and Platonic "wisdom" be in equilibrium: "General benevolence is charity itself. But the zeal of charity must be directed by knowledge so that we do not err in the estimation of what is best: since in consequence wisdom is the knowledge of the best or of felicity, we cannot perhaps better capture the essence of justice than if we define it as the charity which resides in the wise."[31]

While Leibniz was not a Platonist in any doctrinaire sense – his clinging to Pauline charity and to Augustinian "good will" would have made that difficult – nonetheless he did agree with Plato on many points of fundamental importance. "I have always been quite content, since my youth," he wrote to Remond in 1715 (in a letter describing his own early self-education), "with the moral philosophy of Plato, and even in a way with his metaphysics; for those two sciences accompany each other, like mathematics and physics."[32] Leibniz, indeed, was Platonic not only in the way he conceived the concept of justice, but even in some of his more practical political opinions: he always urged, for example, that "following natural reason, government belongs to the wisest."[33] And it will soon be clear that Leibniz's theory of education is basically Platonic as well.

With the possible exception of the *Republic*, the Platonic work that Leibniz admired most was the *Euthyphro*, which he paraphrased almost literally in his most important work on justice, the "Meditation on the common concept of justice." In the *Euthyphro*, which deals with the question whether "the rules of goodness and of justice are anterior to the decrees of God" (in Leibniz's words), Plato "makes Socrates uphold the truth on that point."[34] That Leibniz was much affected by Plato is evident in his "Meditation" on justice, which merely converts Platonic dialogue into straightforward prose:

It is agreed that whatever God wills is good and just. But there remains the question whether it is good and just because God wills it or whether God wills it because it is good and just: in other words, whether justice and goodness are arbitrary, or whether they belong to the necessary and eternal truths about the nature of things, as do numbers and proportions.[35]

LEIBNIZ'S PLATONISM IN "EDUCATION": A FULLER CONSIDERATION

Given Leibniz's visible devotion to Plato and Platonism, which runs like a red thread through his whole moral and political philosophy, early and late, it is worthwhile to consider a little more fully the exact sense in which Leibniz was (and was not) a Platonist. For among Leibniz's intellectual ancestors, the one who comes closest to the Leibnizian project of establishing a universal jurisprudence which is (like mathematics) equally valid for finite and infinite "minds" in any logically possible cosmos is surely Plato.

It is a standard Platonic method (and one much appreciated by Leibniz) to throw light on morally problematical and elusive notions, such as "justice" and "virtue," by attempting to relate them to (or sometimes indeed to equate them with) the "necessary" truths of mathematics and geometry which all rational beings see in the mind's eye, and certainly do not learn from the empirical observation of mere phenomena. That is the clearest in *Phaedo*, where all "absolute" ideas are placed on a footing of logical equality: "absolute goodness," "absolute beauty," and "absolute [mathematical] equality" are mentioned in one single breath.

> If we obtained [knowledge] before our birth, and possessed it when we were born, we had knowledge, both before and at the moment of birth, not only of equality and of relative magnitudes, but of all absolute standards . . . [such as] absolute beauty, goodness, uprightness, holiness, and, as I maintain, all those characteristics which we designate in our discussion by the term "absolute."[36]

But in some ways the most striking example of the Platonic method is in the *Meno*, where a discussion between Socrates and Meno over the nature of "virtue" gets bogged down until Socrates takes aside Meno's utterly uneducated slave and shows (in effect) that any rational being has within him what we would now call a priori knowledge of mathematical and geometrical truth which cannot be "learned," but which can be drawn out and brought to full consciousness by Socratic probing.

Socrates: What do you think, Meno? . . . These [geometrical] opinions were somewhere in him, were they not?

Meno: Yes.

Socrates: . . . At present these opinions, being newly aroused, have a dreamlike quality. But if the same questions are put to him on many occasions and in different ways, you can see that in the end he will have a knowledge on the subject as accurate as anybody's . . . This knowledge will not come from teaching but from questioning. He will recover it for himself.[37]

After Socrates draws this pure rational knowledge from Meno's slave, the conversation turns from geometry back to virtue; and we now learn (*Meno* 89aff.) that "virtue is wisdom" – much as mathematics and geometry are knowledge. The structure of the *Meno* – first virtue, then geometry, then virtue again – makes no sense at all unless Plato is trying to suggest that moral knowledge is logically like mathematical-geometrical knowledge: necessary, universal, eternal, not subject to Heraclitean flux, loved by the gods (who do not "cause" it in time), and so on. And if the first of the virtues is justice, and if justice is a psychic-cosmic "harmony" or equilibrium, and if harmony is (in effect) "mathematics made audible," then justice will be a kind of "participation" in the beautiful mathematical order, known a priori, which links the well-tuned, consonant *psyche* to an equally non-dissonant *polis* (or *psyche* "writ large"), and then to "the harmony of the spheres" – as in *Republic* 443d–e: "Justice . . . means having first attained to self-mastery and beautiful order within oneself, and having harmonized these three principles [reason, spirit, appetite], the notes or intervals of three terms quite literally the lowest, the highest and the mean, and having . . . made of oneself a unit, one man instead of many, self-controlled and in unison".

Leibniz's "Platonism" is clear throughout his life, for example in the *Elements of Law and Equity*, which he wrote at the age of 23:

> The doctrine of law belongs to those sciences that are not built on experiments but on definitions, not on the senses but on demonstrations according to reason; it deals with questions, as we say, of law and not of fact [*juris non facti*]. Since justice consists in a certain harmony and proportion, its meaning remains independent of whether anybody actually does justice to others, or conversely, is treated justly. The same holds for numerical relationship . . . Hence it is not surprising that the propositions of these sciences possess eternal truth.

And these mathematical and jurisprudential "sciences," he adds, "also do not take their point of departure from the senses, but from a clear and distinct intuition or, as Plato called it *Idea*, a word which itself signifies discernment or definition."[38] In his *Discourse on Metaphysics* (1686), proposition 26, Leibniz writes:

> The mind at every moment expresses all its future thoughts and already thinks confusedly of all that of which it will ever think distinctly. Nothing can be taught us of which we have not already in our minds the idea. This idea is as it were the material out of which the thought will form itself. This is what Plato has excellently brought out in his doctrine of reminiscence, a doctrine which contains a great deal of truth, provided that it is properly understood and purged of the error of pre-existence, and provided that one does not conceive of the soul as having distinctly known at some other time what it learns and thinks now.

Plato, Leibniz goes on to say, has confirmed what is true in his position by "a beautiful experiment": he introduces a boy, Meno's slave, "whom he leads by short steps to extremely difficult truths of geometry bearing on incommensurables, all this without teaching the boy anything, merely drawing out replies by a well-arranged series of questions." A purged and chastened version of the *Meno* shows, Leibniz concludes, "that the soul virtually knows those things, and needs only to be reminded (animadverted) to recognize the truths."[39]

In his *Art of Discovery* (1685), to be sure, Leibniz laments, demi-Platonically, that reason and truth are not as triumphant in ethics and jurisprudence as they are in mathematics and geometry: "the reason why we make mistakes so easily outside of mathematics (where geometers are so felicitous in their reasonings) is only because in geometry and the other parts of abstract mathematics," we can submit to tests or trials "not only the conclusion but also, at any moment, each step made from the premises, by reducing the whole to numbers." But in "metaphysics and ethics" matters are "much worse" because we can test conclusions only in "a very vague manner."

The only way to "rectify our reasonings" in the practical sphere, Leibniz then suggests, is to make them "as tangible as those of mathematics," so that "we can simply say: let us calculate, without further ado, to see who is right." Such a procedure could work "if words were constructed according to a device that I see as possible": namely, using "characters," as mathematicians do, to "fix our ideas" by "adapting to them a numerical proof."

> For by this means after reducing reasoning in ethics . . . to these terms or characters, we shall be able at any moment to introduce the numerical test in such a way that it will be impossible to make a mistake except willfully.[40]

How could this *calculemus* work best in "ethics?" Plainly if the gap between ethics and mathematics were as small as possible, or even successfully bridged: if (for example) justice were a matter of "proportion," "order," and (mathematics-based) "harmony," or if at least our love, the basis of *caritas sapientis*, were truly "proportional" to the degree of perfection found (and felt) in the loved object or subject. Hence Leibniz uses the mathematical language of degree and proportion whenever he can, and bemoans the fact – in the *True Method in Philosophy and Theology* (1686) – that others do not do so.

> Geometry clarifies configurations and motions; as a result we have discovered the geography of lands and the course of the stars, and machines have been made which overcome great burdens, whence civilization and the distinction between civilized and barbaric people. But the science which distinguishes the just man from the unjust . . . is neglected. We have demonstrations about the circle, but only conjectures about the soul . . . The source of human misery lies in the fact that man devotes more thought to everything but the highest good in life.[41]

Why then, given so much Platonism in Leibniz's thought – including what he says about "knowing" and "learning" – should Leibniz not be, more than any modern philosopher, a "footnote to Plato"? Simply because Leibniz, as a Christian descended partly from Augustine, needs to place "good will" or *bona voluntas* somewhere in his universal jurisprudence; not only does he "place" it, however, he makes it equal to wise charity itself. And a pure Platonist would never equate the sublimated *eros* of the *Phaedrus* (which wisely ascends to *philosophia*) with "will," whether "good" or not. For Plato's *Protagoras* rules out a "will" which is independent of knowledge and "wisdom." There are simply parts of Leibnizian ethics that Platonism cannot accommodate at all; for *caritas sapientis* contains Plato and St Paul, Athens and Jerusalem.

LEIBNIZ TO THE QUEEN OF PRUSSIA:
Lettre sur l'éducation d'une princesse

Sometimes Leibniz uses "Platonism" to defeat the Lockean notion that there is nothing in the understanding which has not come from the senses; that, for Leibniz, is almost as bad as the "Hobbism" which treats mind as an epiphenomenon of matter, and "conceptions" as caused by the "pressure" of objects. He makes that clear in his celebrated 1702 letter to the Queen of Prussia (his former pupil) which is sometimes given the title, "On what is independent of sensation in knowledge," and which is central to his demi-Platonic notion of knowledge and of "learning."

"This thought of 'I'" Leibniz urges, "who distinguishes himself from sensible objects, and of my own action which results from it, adds something to the objects of the senses," such as the idea of moral necessity, which the senses will never "see." And since, he continues, "I conceive that other beings can also have the right to say 'I' (or one could say it for them), it is by this that I conceive what is called substance in general"; and it is also "the consideration of myself which furnishes me with other notions of metaphysics, such as cause, effect, action, similitude, etc., and even of logic and of morality." Thus, Leibniz insists, one can say that "there is nothing in the understanding which has not come from the senses, except the understanding itself, or he who understands."[42]

With that last sentence, which sums up the main thrust of the *New Essays Concerning Human Understanding* (written a year later), Leibniz at once reaffirms an adequate notion of rational substance: as a being who has the "right" to say "I" (a moral entitlement) and who does not just passively receive "impressions" in the manner of a plant, and justifies Greek antiquity against English modernity.

"Being itself, and truth, are not entirely learned through the senses," Leibniz goes on to say. "For it would not be impossible that a creature have long and ordered dreams, resembling our life, such that all that one believed to perceive through the senses would only be pure appearances" (what he elsewhere calls "well-founded phenomena"). It is for this reason that "we need, then, something beyond the senses, which distinguishes the true from the apparent." But here, Leibniz hopes, "the truth of the demonstrative sciences" such as mathematics, logic, and ethics may "serve to judge the truth of sensible things." For as "able philosophers both ancient and modern" have correctly remarked, even if "all that I believe that I see should be only a dream," it would nonetheless "remain always true that 'I' who think while dreaming would be something, and would think effectively in many ways, for which there must always be some reason."[43]

It is for these reasons, Leibniz continues, that "that which the ancient Platonists have remarked, is quite true and very worthy of being considered," namely, that "the existence of intelligible things and particularly of this 'I' who thinks and which is called mind or soul is incomparably more certain than the existence of sensible things," and that, therefore, "it would not be impossible, speaking with metaphysical rigor, that there should be at bottom only these intelligible substances, and that sensible things are only appearances." But, Leibniz complains, our "lack of attention" makes us "take sensible things for the only true ones." And this is exactly the demi-Platonic language of the *New Essays*: "You do not see justice as you see a horse, but you understand it no less, or rather you understand it better."[44]

Very radically, Leibniz goes on to assert that one need not even be awake to see that the "English" view of knowledge (including moral knowledge) and of learning cannot be right:

It is also good to notice that if I found some demonstrative truth, mathematical or otherwise, while dreaming (as can indeed happen), it would be just as certain as if I were awake. Which makes it clear how much intelligible truth is independent of the truth or existence of sensible and material things outside of us.[45]

Leibniz then, having stressed the necessity of mathematics, insists that the necessity of morality is "seen" through extrasensory *lumière naturelle*: "for example, one can say that there are charitable people who are not just, which happens when charity is not sufficiently regulated . . . for in justice is comprised at the same time charity and the rule of reason. It is by *lumière naturelle* also that one recognizes the axioms of mathematics."[46] As usual, Leibniz as demi-Platonist uses, back to back, moral and mathematical examples of what rational "substances" know – a priori, though not prenatally – through "natural light," independently of sense impressions. The Plato of *Meno* and *Phaedo* is again supported, Locke again criticized. And in the end Locke is subjected to a weaker version of the criticism that Leibniz had leveled against Hobbes: that British "empiricism," with its passive notion of a material substance which is only receptive, cannot account for (a) the conceivability of moral ideas; (b) the notion of a self with the "right to say 'I'"; (c) the self-determining activity (going beyond passive receptivity) of a self-so-conceived. This shows again (if further proof were needed) that for Leibniz an adequately conceived substance or monad is the substratum of all further reasoning about morality, justice and education. Thus the "monadology" is the foundation of *caritas sapientis*: only a rational substance can know the idea of what ought to be, and strive to bring it about.

THE IMPORTANCE OF EDUCATION IN LEIBNIZIAN POLITICS

Given Leibniz's insistence on *caritas sapientis*, the charity of a wise being, it is not surprising that he was centrally concerned not just with better public education, but with the better education of those who have the public in their care: most often, "benevolent" princes. This is plain in the *Lettre sur l'éducation d'un prince* (1685–6), a piece which Leibniz esteemed enough to rewrite four times, but which was never fully published until the 1980s.[47] In this characteristic essay, Leibniz insists that while it is merely "useful" for the prince to know *la politique et l'art militaire* (so much for Machiavelli), it is "necessary" that a prince "be a man of good will, a courageous man, a man of judgment, and an honorable man," for the *homme de bien* will have "great feelings of piety, of justice and charity, and will apply himself strongly to his duty." These moral qualities, for Leibniz, matter more than the "useful," and much more than the "ornamental." He would prefer a simple but pious and just ruler to "the cleverest prince in the world," a prince who

should know to perfection all theories and practices, who should speak all languages, who should have acquired all the fine manners of foreigners, who should shine in conversation, but who, neglecting the care of public affairs and the care of those whom God has committed to him, should stop up his ears to the cries of the miserable in order not to interrupt his pleasures and, in not being moved by the disapproval of his nation and by the views of his family and of posterity, should let the state sink into decadence.

Of all this, Leibniz adds, a "deplorable example" has just died (1685) – in the shape of Charles II of England.[48]

Leibniz must have known that while Charles was exiled as Prince of Wales (in the 1640s), his tutor was none other than Hobbes; but Leibniz's program for the education of a prince is more like a royalist *Émile* than it is like anything in English thought. While "natural goodness" is the foundation of all successful education, Leibniz argues, a tutor must understand what is psychologically suitable for a young person: "a child must be neither intimidated nor chagrined, neither deceived nor rebutted – but one must also not accustom him to being opinionated by giving him everything he wants." The way to turn him away from a "not very reasonable" desire, Leibniz goes on, "consists in the variety of pleasures." One can divert him "through pleasant actions and spectacles, which will soon begin to become instructive." At the age of 4, he continues, one can begin real education, "but always under the appearance and pretext of games." Finally, however, fully adult study arrives, ushered in by a Platonic insistence on geometry reminiscent of the *Republic*, Book VII:

> Up 'til now reason has taken advantage of the imagination as an escort. But little by little one must make it go beyond this, to the things which the mind alone can know . . . It is necessary to exercise the reason first of all in geometry and the neighboring sciences . . . [then] the prince must be led to exercise the art of reasoning in moral philosophy, in politics, and in law . . . History will furnish cases and unusual examples, and the young prince will be a member of the Councils of ancient emperors and kings, in order to preside over his own.[49]

In this same vein Leibniz goes on to say that when princely education has passed from childish "imagination" to "the things the mind alone can know," the time has arrived to acquaint the future prince, "little by little (in proportion as he advances)," with "the most important of the laws, of the Canon laws, of the public laws of his state" – with "the whole thing clarified by the memorials of modern history." At the same time the future prince should be provided with "knowledge of religions, which have so much influence on politics," together with "a little system of theology based on solid reasons as well as on Holy Scripture and on ecclesiactial history." (That subordination of scripture and of church history to "solid reasons" is what one would expect from the author of the *Théodicée*, which offers a kind of "religion within the limits of reason alone," in which even charity itself is "given" by reason, not just by the revelation of the Gospel according to St John. And Leibniz characteristically adds that "belief without foundations" – without "solid reasons" – "degenerates into libertinage or into hypocrisy."[50])

But while he stresses the prince's being reminded of "the things the mind alone can know," Leibniz does not recommend extensive immersion in "speculative" philosophy: "as for philosophy, one has already provided for that, in the most real way. Moral philosophy is comprised in politics and in law." And that is what matters in the education of a future prince, for "the most important and the most serious matters in life are justice, the quiet and the good of the state, human health, and even religion."[51]

The moral qualities of a ruler are, of course, crucial to Leibniz, who – no democrat – thought that "enlightenment" and the general good must descend from the top down. In *Des Controverses* (1680) he characteristically insists that "we must work above all to achieve something considerable for the glory of God and for *le bien public*," but that the public has comparatively little to do with that good, since "it is principally for the great," to whom God has given the means to contribute effectively to the advancement of the general good, to be the main "instruments of divine glory."[52] Leibniz hoped for little from "the common man" (*der gemeine Mann*), lamenting in *Ermahnung an die Deutsche* (1679) that ordinary people are "without excitement or fire," and it seems that they are "made of Adamic earth, but the spirit of life has not been blown into them."[53] Still, he did not confine education to "princes" entirely; in a letter to Joachim Bouvet (December 1697) he insisted that "true practical philosophy (*vera, non simulata philosphia*, as our Roman jurisconsults say) consists sooner in good arrangements for education, and for the conversation and sociability of man, than in general precepts about virtues and duties."[54] And this appears to be true for *der gemeine Mann*, not just for future rulers.

At the end of the *Lettre sur l'éducation d'un prince*, Leibniz takes care to insist, one more time, that "above all" the prince's education must "form his mind and his manners [*moeurs*]: the mind to sentiments of virtue, of generosity, and of charity, and manners to gentleness and agreeableness."

> I come back, then, to recommending above all that one inspire good sentiments in the young prince, in preference to all kinds of knowledge. If he has an upright mind and the will to do good, he will govern better than the most knowledgeable and able man on earth who lets himself sink into dissoluteness.[55]

In that paragraph, "princely education" and justice as "wise charity" draw very close together: since Leibniz defines justice as *caritas sapientis seu benevolentia universalis*, "the charity of the wise, that is, universal benevolence," charity and good-willing are one and the same, and it is the prince's "will to do good" that must be brought out above all. (Here one should recall that in *De bono unitatis et malis schismatis* (*c.* 1691), Leibniz makes *perfectio voluntatis*, "the perfection of the will," exactly equivalent to *perfectio caritatis*, "the perfection of charity."[56]) There is nothing offhand or inadvertent in the fact that Leibniz ends his only extensive treatment of education with "good will," and that for him *bona voluntas* and *caritas sapientis* are perfectly equivalent. He ended his sole essay on education (viewed as a branch of universal jurisprudence) with what he most wanted to stress.

The radically political and justice-colored character of Leibniz's "education of princes" can best be brought out through a comparison with Blaise Pascal. For Pascal men live in three "orders" simultaneously; the lowest order, that of the "flesh," is miserable and requires constant *divertissement* to allay reflection and despair; the middle order, that of mind or *esprit*, encompasses intellectual activities (including Pascalian geometry); the highest order is that of charity or *la volonté* and is "infinitely" separated not just from

204

"mind" (which at least knows its finite misery) but even more decisively from the flesh (which is mindless matter).

> The infinite distance between body and mind is a symbol of the infinitely more infinite distance between mind and charity; for charity is supernatural . . . All bodies, the firmament, the stars, the earth and its kingdoms, are not equal to the lowest mind; for mind knows all these and itself; and these bodies are nothing. All bodies together, and all minds together, and all their products, are not equal to the least feeling of charity. This is of an order infinitely more exalted. From all bodies together, we cannot obtain one little thought; this is impossible, and of another order. From all bodies and minds, we cannot produce a feeling of true charity; this is impossible, and of another and supernatural order.[57]

Pascal consigns politics wholly to the lowest, fleshly order: it is simply a matter of power, force, and useful illusions ("three degrees of latitude overturn the whole of jurisprudence"); but love is saved for the saved, a body "full of thinking members" held together by the spiritual gift of *la charité*. Jurisprudence can hardly be "universal," à la Leibniz, if three degrees of latitude "overturn" it altogether. Pascal drives to brilliant extremes fleshly politics and supernatural *caritas*: they are separated by a fearful infinity ("the eternal silence of these infinite spaces terrifies me"), and Christian love has no effect on a carnal sphere in which "force is Queen." Politics is part of a fallen nature, but supernatural grace is needed for the infinite ascent to charity: when Pascal called himself an "Augustinian," as did all Jansenists, he knew whereof he spoke. For Pascal charity has no political "place" at all, and hence a Leibnizian princely education – converting "wise charity" into policy and social institutions – is simply inconceivable. Pascalian education must concern itself with the individual "heart," which reason "does not know."

By contrast Leibniz strives to close up the "infinite distance" separating politics and charity: politics, "mind," and *caritas* converge in a kind of synthetic middle. No doubt this accounts for Leibniz's collapsing of everything that Pascal tried to keep infinitely distanced, as one of Leibniz's letters to Thomas Burnett (from *c*.1696–7) shows clearly:

> the fine accomplishments of M. Pascal in the most profound sciences [mathematics and geometry] should give some weight to the *Pensées* which he promised on the truth of Christianity . . . [But] besides the fact that his mind was full of the prejudices of the party of Rome . . . he had not studied history or jurisprudence with enough care . . . and nonetheless both are requisite to establish certain truths of the Christian religion.[58]

Evidently Leibniz either missed Pascal's point altogether, or (more likely) thought it wholly misconceived. For Leibniz universal, latitude-crossing jurisprudence and universal religion are grounded in the same demi-Platonic rational eternal verities, while for Pascal the impotence of reason (as revealed by Montaigne in the *Essais*) drives one to fideism: "God of Abraham, God of Jacob, God of Isaac, not of the philosophers and the theologians." For Pascal, St Paul was right to ask, "where is the wise?" and to cling to "faith, hope, charity, these three." Leibniz had an equal reverence for Greek philosophy and for Pauline charity, but his synthetic moderation made him incapable of appreciating Pascal's tortured extremism.

Indeed Leibniz, who maintained that "men usually hold to some middle way,"[59] would have approved Apemantus' remark to the protagonist of Shakespeare's *Timon of Athens*: "The middle of humanity thou never knewest, but the extremity of both ends." The Leibnizian fusion of Greek *philosophia* and Christian *caritas*, linking Athens and Jerusalem, comes out in a characteristic paragraph which Leibniz wrote for the *Journal des Sçavans* in 1696:

> Our perfection consisting in the knowledge and in the love of God, it follows that one advances in perfection in proportion as one penetrates the eternal verities, and as one is zealous for the general good. Thus those who are truly enlightened and well intentioned work with all their power for their own instruction and for the good of others; and if they have the means they strive to procure the increase of human enlightenment, Christian virtue, and the public happiness. This is the touchstone of true piety.[60]

The final Leibnizian fusion of "human enlightenment," "Christian virtue," and "the public happiness" would be, for Pascal, an obvious collapsing of "the three orders" into one another; for Christian virtue is isolated in the charitable sphere of *la volonté*, the "public happiness" is just gratified "flesh," and enlightenment is simply *esprit*. It is as if Leibniz were consciously knocking out of the supporting walls that sustain Pascal's ascending hierarchy.

Leibniz's concern with a "universal," Christian-Platonist, eternally-true justice – which led him to crown his whole philosophy with a theodicy ("the justice of God") – also led him to see education wholly in the light of that justice: wisely charitable and benevolent princes might actually be at the helm. For Pascal that was inconceivable, and therefore education had to retreat privately into the heart: "The sole cause of man's unhappiness is that he does not know how to stay quietly in his room."[61] If for Pascal, le coeur a ses raisons que la raison ne connaît point, Leibniz was an enlightened and enlightening courtier for whom la cour a ses raisons que la raison connait à merveille.

ABBREVIATIONS

Acad. Ed.	G. W. Leibniz, *Sämtliche Schriften und Briefe*, edition of the Berlin-Brandenburg (formerly Prussian) Academy of Sciences (Berlin, Darmstadt, Leipzig, etc., 1923–). Cited by Reihe (series), Band (volume), and page number; for example, Acad. Ed. IV, 3, p.3, refers to the fourth series (*Politische Schriften*), vol. 3 (1987), p. 3.
Dutens	Louis Dutens, *God. Guil. Leibnitii . . . Opera Omnia* (Geneva, 1768)
Ger.	C. I. Gerhardt, *Die Philosophischen Schriften von G. W. Leibniz* (Berlin, 1875–90)
Latta	Robert Latta (ed.) *The Monadology and Other Philosophical Writings* (Oxford, 1898)
Loemker	Leroy Loemker (trans. and ed.) *Leibniz: Philosophical Papers and Letters*, 2 vols (Chicago, University of Chicago Press, 1956); 2nd edn, Dordrecht, 1969 (cited as Loemker, 2nd (edn)
NE	Leibniz, *New Essays Concerning Human Understanding*, trans. and ed. Peter Remnant and Jonathan Bennett (Cambridge and New York, Cambridge University Press, 1981), (cited by book, chapter, and part, for example, *NE* IV, iii, pt. 1)
Riley	Patrick Riley (trans. and ed.) *Leibniz: Political Writings*, 2nd edn (Cambridge University Press, 1988)
Textes inédits	Leibniz, *Textes inédits*, ed. G. Grua (Paris, Presses Universitaires de France, 1948)

NOTES

1 Leibniz, *Lettre sur l'éducation d'un prince*, in Acad. Ed. IV, 3, pp. 542–57.

2 Leibniz, *Des Controverses*, in Acad. Ed. IV, 3, p. 211.

3 R. Ariew, G. W. Leibniz, "Life and works," in N. Jolley (ed.) *The Cambridge Companion to Leibniz* (Cambridge, Cambridge University Press, 1995), pp. 18ff.

4 Leibniz, letters to Remond (1713–16), in Ger. III, pp. 599ff.

5 Leibniz, *Grundriss eines Bedenckens von Aufrichtung einer Societät in Deutschland*, in Acad. Ed. IV, 1, pp. 530–1.

6 Leibniz, *Memoir for Enlightened Persons of Good Intention*, in Riley, pp. 107–8.

7 Leibniz, *Einige Patriotische Gedancken* [1697], in *Politische Schriften*, ed. H. Holz (Frankfurt, Germania Verlag, 1960), p. 90.

8 Leibniz, *Lettre sur l'éducation d'un prince*, in Acad. Ed. IV, 3, p. 546.

9 See Patrick Riley, *Leibniz' Universal Jurisprudence: Justice as the Charity of the Wise* (Cambridge, Mass., Harvard University Press, 1996), pp. 4ff, 141ff.

10 Leibniz, letter to Simon Foucher (1686), in Ger. I, p. 380.

11 Leibniz, *Lettre sur l'éducation d'un prince*, in Acad. Ed. IV, 3, p. 553.

12 Leibniz, *Elements of Law and Equity*, in P. Wiener (ed.) *Leibniz Selections* (New York, Scribners, 1951), p. 1.

13 Leibniz, letter to Queen Sophie Charlotte of Prussia, in André Robinet, *Le Meilleur des mondes* (Paris, Vrin, 1994), p. 309.

14 Plato, *Republic* 417a.

15 Leibniz, *Grundriss*, p. 532.

16 René Sève, *Leibniz: le droit de la raison* (Paris, Vrin, 1994), p. 8, n. 1.

17 Riley, *Leibniz' Universal Jurisprudence*, pp. 4ff., 141ff.

18 St Paul, Corinthians 13: 1 (Authorized version).

19 Gospel according to St John, 13: 34 (Authorized version).

20 Riley, *Leibniz' Universal Jurisprudence*, ch. 2.

21 Leibniz, *Theodicy*, trans. E. Huggard (New Haven, Conn., Yale University Press, 1952), "Preliminary dissertation," pt. 35, p. 94.

22 Leibniz, *Monadology*, in Latta, props. 85–86, pp. 267–8.

23 Leibniz, letter to Landgraf Ernst of Hessen-Rheinfels, in *Textes inédits* I, pp. 238–9.

24 Leibniz, letter to Electress Sophie (1696), in *Textes inédits* I, p. 379.

25 Leibniz, "Reflections on . . . Hobbes's 'Liberty, Necessity and Chance,'" in *Theodicy*, trans. Huggard, p. 403.

26 Leibniz, *NE* III, v, pt. 12.

27 Leibniz, *Observationes de principio juris*, scc. ix, in Dutens IV, iii, p. 270ff.

28 Leibniz, *Monita quaedam ad Samuelis Pufendorfi principia*, in Dutens IV, iii, p. 275.

29 Leibniz, *Elementa juris naturalis*, in Acad. Ed. IV, 1, p. 481; Leibniz, letter to Arnauld (1690), in Loemker II, p. 360.

30 Leibniz, *Meditation on the Common Concept of Justice*, in Riley, pp. 45ff.

31 Leibniz, *De justitia et novo codice*, in *Textes inédits* II, pp. 621–2.

32 Leibniz, letter to Remond (1715), in Ger. III, p. 637.

33 Leibniz, letter to Thomas Burnett (1699), in Ger. III, p. 264.

34 See E. Cassirer, *Leibniz' System in Seinen Wissenschaftlichen Grundlagen* (Marburg, 1902), pp. 428ff.

35 Leibniz, *Meditation on . . . Justice*, in Riley, p. 45.

36 Plato, *Phaedo*, 75d.

37 Plato, *Meno*, 85bff.

38 Leibniz, *Elements of Law and Equity*, in Wiener (ed.) *Leibniz Selections*, p. 1.

39 Leibniz, *Discourse on Metaphysics*, Loemker, 2nd edn, sec. 26, p. 320.

40 Leibniz, *The Art of Discovery*, in Wiener (ed.) *Leibniz Selections*, pp. 50–1.

41 Leibniz, *True Method*, in Wiener (ed.) *Leibniz Selections*, p. 59.
42 Leibniz, *What is Independent of Sensation*, Ger. VI, pp. 502–3.
43 Ibid., p. 503.
44 Leibniz, *NE*, III, v, pt. 12.
45 Leibniz, *What is Independent of Sensation*, in Ger. VI, p. 503.
46 Ibid.
47 Leibniz, *Lettre sur l'éducation d'un prince*, in Acad. Ed. IV, 3, pp. 542ff.
48 Ibid., pp. 556–7. (This is not a reference to Louis XIV, as some have mistakenly urged.)
49 Ibid., p. 553.
50 Ibid., p. 554.
51 Leibniz, letter to Thomas Burnett (1697), in Acad. Ed. I, 13, p. 555.
52 Leibniz, *Des Controverses*, in Acad. Ed. IV, 3, p. 211.
53 Leibniz, *Ermahnung an die Deutsche*, in Acad. Ed. IV, 3, p. 805.
54 Leibniz, letter to Joachim Bouvet, in Acad. Ed. I, 14, p. 830.
55 Leibniz, *Lettre sur l'éducation d'un prince*, in Acad. Ed. IV, 3, p. 556.
56 Cited in Riley, *Leibniz' Universal Jurisprudence*, p. 32.
57 Pascal, *Pensées*, no. 792, in L. Brunschvicg (ed.) *Oeuvres* vol. xiv (Paris, 1914).
58 Leibniz, letter to Thomas Burnett (1696–7), in Ger. III, p. 196.
59 Leibniz, *Caesarinus Fürstenerius*, ch. xi, in Acad. Ed. IV, 2, pp. 58ff.
60 Leibniz, letter to Étienne de Chauvin (1696), in Acad. Ed. I, 13, p. 232.
61 Pascal, *Pensées*, no. 139, in Brunschvicg (ed.) *Oeuvres*.

16

CONDORCET AND ADAM SMITH ON EDUCATION AND INSTRUCTION

Emma Rothschild

The idyll of universal public instruction has been justified, at least since the educational projects of the French Revolution, by recourse to the principles of political economy. Talleyrand, in a parliamentary report of September 1791 on educational reform, wrote that 'one should think of society as an enormous workshop', in which the greatest of all economies was 'the economy of men', and where education could be considered 'as a product of society, as a source of goods for society, and as an equally fertile source of goods for individuals'.[1] For Lakanal, the educational theorist of the Jacobin period, in a parliamentary report published in December 1794, the value of educational 'establishments' was to be judged by their 'utility': 'the famous Smith gave lectures in Edinburgh on commerce, of which the sum and the total formed *The Essay on the Wealth of Nations*, perhaps the most useful work for the peoples of Europe'.[2]

My concern, in what follows, will be with the use and misuse of economic ideas in disputes over universal instruction, and in particular with the ideas of Adam Smith and Condorcet. Smith's observations on education were a continuing standard for successive programmes of educational reform of the revolutionary period, both in England and in France. Condorcet invoked Smith in his first plan of universal public instruction of 1788, and he referred to Smith repeatedly in his great, extended work of 1791–2 on the principles and organization of public instruction. It is these projects, or the intertwining, in the disputes of the 1790s, of Smith's and Condorcet's economic, philosophical and educational ideas, with which I will be principally concerned.

Smith's and Condorcet's ideas about public instruction are remote, as will be seen, from the political economy implicit in the policies of Talleyrand, Lakanal, and most other contemporary (and subsequent) exponents of educational reform. Neither Smith nor Condorcet argued for public instruction on the grounds that it would increase prosperity, or the 'goods' of society; both were sceptical about the value of occupational training or apprenticeship; both saw universal instruction as something which is good in itself, a condition in which individuals are able to amuse themselves, to think about interesting questions, to avoid being bored. Their writings on education offer some insight, I will suggest, into a *laissez-faire* political economy which is quite unlike the 'cold' economic thought – utilitarian, materialist, rationalist, determinist – depicted in much recent intellectual

209

history. They also provide insight into a dilemma, over instruction in morality, which is still at the heart of the philosophy of education. The great object of education, for both Smith and Condorcet, is to be able to live in a mild and discursive or conversational society. 'The good temper and moderation of contending factions seems to be the most essential circumstance in the public morals of a free people', Smith wrote in his account of education in the *Wealth of Nations*; it is this ideal, I will suggest, which is both the prize and the omen of liberal political economy.[3]

Smith's only extended description of education comes in the final, political section of the *Wealth of Nations*, the Book V of which Smith's acquaintance, the conservative critic Alexander Carlyle said that it has 'the air of being occasional pamphlets . . . On political subjects his opinions were not very sound'.[4] Smith is bitterly critical of established institutions for the education of young men, and especially of the English universities, which he describes as 'sanctuaries [for] exploded systems and obsolete prejudices'. He finds no good reason that the public should pay for educational endowments, or for the great ecclesiastical corporations, which were exempt from competition between private and public teachers, and 'exempted from the civil jurisdiction'. But he is strongly in favour, by contrast, of public support for the education of the 'common people'. This is indeed especially important, he says, in the most civilized or developed societies. For the effect of the division of labour – of the very principle, that is, which has led to commercial progress – is to induce a sort of torpor or psychological mutilation in the population of rich countries. An individual who is obliged to do little more, all day, than attend to one simple, repetitive task, becomes incapable of 'conversation', 'sentiment', 'judgement' and 'courage'.[5]

Smith describes a strikingly unequal distribution, in rich countries, of the experience of what he calls 'variety'. There is certainly a great deal of variety within the society as a whole, and for some individuals, there is an 'almost infinite variety of objects'. But for others, there is virtually no variety at all. Smith concludes that the education of ordinary or common people is a matter of far greater public concern than the education of people 'of rank', whose employments seldom 'harass them from morning to night'. The lack of education is indeed a principal source of the inequality which develops in the early years of children's lives. Smith's proposal is that the children of the common people should learn 'to read, write and account' before they have to start work, and that this system of universal instruction should be supported, or at least facilitated by the public. He is opposed, as ever, to the privileges of established orders (including teachers, whose tendency, especially in universities, is to gain 'protection' by 'obsequiousness'.) His model of common education is based on the parish schools of Scotland; he would prefer that the state impose educational requirements, presumably by examination, rather than itself establishing schools. But the desired outcome is clear. It is that everyone, without exception, should be more 'instructed', and that no one should be in the grip of 'gross ignorance and stupidity'.[6]

Condorcet's plan of public instruction was read to the French parliament in April 1792 (where it was interrupted by Louis XVI's declaration of war against Austria.) Like Smith, Condorcet was resolutely opposed to all government interference with the freedom of commerce, which he considered to be unjust, or useless, or both. But even in his earliest economic writings, published shortly before the *Wealth of Nations*, he identified 'public education', together with the impartial administration of justice, as acceptable objects of government expenditure. His first major writing on education comes in his work on provincial assemblies of 1788. He cites the *Wealth of Nations*, and Smith's description of the effects of the division of labour, in support of his proposal for 'a true public instruction'; he concludes that universal public instruction, 'as Smith says', is the 'only effective remedy' for the ills of modern commercial societies.[7] In the *Bibliothèque de l'Homme Public* which he edited early in the Revolution, he published a 200-page summary of the *Wealth of Nations*, which is described as 'one of the works which does most honour to Great Britain'.[8] In his memoirs on public instruction of 1791–2, he again quotes Smith's warning about the consequences of the division of labour: 'Instruction is the only remedy for this ill, which is the more dangerous in a particular state to the extent that the laws of that state have established a greater degree of equality . . . The laws proclaim an equality of rights, and only institutions for public instruction can make this equality real.'[9]

Condorcet remained committed to the principles of free competition in education throughout his revolutionary career, which ended with his death in 1794 as a victim of the Jacobin Terror. His political ideal, quite generally, was of a 'virtual non-existence' (*cette presque nullité*) of government, in which people need 'laws and institutions which reduce to the smallest possible quantity the action of government'.[10] In his work on education, he distinguished between public institutions which should be provided directly by public funds (such as courts and police), those where competition is possible but unlikely (such as city lighting and street cleaning), and those 'where competition must be respected'. He put public instruction, together with the services of doctors and midwives, in the last category, and insisted that public funds should not be spent to 'make competition impossible'. One reason was 'to preserve for parents a real freedom of choice in the education they owe their children'; another was to prevent the 'exclusive influence' of government on instruction.[11]

Universal public instruction, both for Smith and for Condorcet, was one of the few reasons for governments to deviate from the principles of *laissez-faire*. But their arguments were strikingly different from those put forward by contemporary exponents of education as a 'public good'. In the first place, neither Smith nor Condorcet argues for public instruction principally on the grounds that it will increase national prosperity or the productivity of labour. Such arguments were certainly familiar throughout the eighteenth century. The advice of Mentor or Minerva, in Fénelon's *Télémaque*, is that the sovereign should 'establish public schools, to teach fear of the gods, love of country, respect for the laws', and should also ensure that young men are trained to be good carpenters or oarsmen, 'industrious, patient, hard-working, clean, sober, and cautious'.[12] Smith's contemporary, the economist James Anderson, urged Scottish landlords in 1777 that 'instead of spending your time in futile attempts to ascertain the value of your soil, or unavailing efforts to improve your fields, turn your attention to improve your people'.[13] Herder, in 1779, called for 'plans for the encouragement of industry', competing 'academies of economics', and efforts to encourage the 'practical, mechanical side' of the sciences, such that better links would be established between universities and 'our schools, academies, seminars, business activities and public administration'.[14]

There is virtually nothing of this instrumental justification for education as an economic good in either Smith's or Condorcet's writings. Smith at no point argues that universal education will lead to an increase in national wealth. His concern is rather that the very change – in the division of labour – which has brought an increase in prosperity is itself a source of social impoverishment. Education is needed as a consequence of economic development, and not as a cause of future development. He is critical of existing schools on the grounds that they teach skills which are of little or no use to their pupils (and he contrasts the education of boys disobligingly with that of girls, who are at least instructed in such 'useful' concerns as domestic economy).[15] But his arguments about utility, such as they are, are concerned very largely with the utility to be derived by individuals. He is sharply critical of vocational training, and in particular of the apprenticeship system for craft and manufacturing workers. His opinion, in any case, was that the poor tended to be *too* sober and *too* industrious; to 'over-work themselves', or to err on the side of 'excessive application'.[16]

In the view of contemporary critics, Smith was indeed opposing a system of education to a system of training. 'To free youth from the shackles of apprenticeship, and to subject infancy to the authority of schoolmasters, is the present bent of political economists', William Playfair wrote in 1805, in his augmented edition of the *Wealth of Nations*. 'Whether or not it contributes to the comfort and happiness of the working man, to read and write, is a question not necessary to decide, and probably not very easy,' Playfair says; 'reading frequently leads to discontent, an ill-founded ambition, and a neglect of business . . . it is at least clear, that habits of industry, and a trade, are the most essential parts of the education of the lower order of people. But Dr. Smith is an enemy to apprenticeships.'[17] In 1813, describing the attentions of Smith's admirer Samuel Whitbread 'to the education of poor children', Playfair concludes that 'perhaps we do not agree with him and many others, in regard to the advantage of men doomed to industry and privation being excited to read and write'.[18]

Condorcet, like Smith, says very little about the benefits to be expected from education for industry, trade or national wealth. He is sceptical, in general, of arguments from national utility. The object of policy, he wrote in his *Life of Turgot*, should be to promote the enjoyment of natural rights and not 'the greatest utility of society, a vague principle and a fertile source of bad laws'.[19] Every occupation is useful to the people who are employed in it, and to those who employ them. But it is no part of the duty of public authorities to prepare individuals for future employment; their obligations 'in no respect consist in opening schools' to train people in particular occupations.[20] He is opposed to 'the utilitarian interpretation of the division of labour', the modern editors of his memoirs on education conclude; 'public instruction is not concerned in the first instance to prepare for a trade, but to prepare everyone in such a way that they have no need, in their future trade, to give up their own selves'.[21]

Both Smith and Condorcet say very little about even the most general and synoptic arguments for education as an economic public good. One widely discussed benefit of

212

education was that individuals would become more industrious and efficient. Another, more subtle benefit was that the economic system, or the sum of individual efforts, would itself be more efficient. Education was expected to facilitate the working of the overall economic system because educated people would be more likely to move from one employment to another, to take risks, to free themselves of a superstitious regard for old customs and regulations, and in general to behave in the independent manner which was associated with modern commercial relations. The effect of education would also be to make people more enlightened about their own self-interest; they would see more clearly wherein their interest lay. If the economy is an enormous, interconnected system – a system, connected by 'principles', in Smith's words, or an order discovered by the imagination in the apparent chaos of millions of individual, self-interested transactions – then it could function only under conditions of both institutional and psychological flexibility (or in societies which have transportation, a jurisprudence of contracts, and universal public instruction).[22]

The idea of psychological preconditions for economic efficiency – of the mentality or *Denkart* of commercial society – was the subject of intense debate in the period of Smith's and Condorcet's proposals for public education. The 'great art' of political economy, for Sir James Steuart, was to concern itself with 'the spirit, manners, habits, and customs of the people'; the business of the statesman was 'to model the minds of his subjects'.[23] On the one hand, it was suggested, individuals must be law-abiding and obedient to authority (much like the carpenters in Mentor's Salentum). 'Good order is the foundation of all good things,' Edmund Burke wrote, against the policies of the National Assembly in France; 'to be enabled to acquire, the people, without being servile, must be tractable and obedient . . . The body of the people must not find the principles of natural subordination by art rooted out of their minds.'[24] On the other hand, individuals should be independent, busy, knowing with respect to their own self-interest, uninhibited in the way of life described by Smith as 'their universal, continual, and uninterrupted effort to better their own condition'.[25] There was indeed some tension between the two objectives, of an intermittently comic sort. As Kant wrote in the *Critique of Practical Reason*, 'Suppose some one recommends you a man as steward, as a man to whom you can blindly trust all your affairs, and, in order to inspire you with confidence, extols him as a prudent man who thoroughly understands his own interest, and is so indefatigably active that he lets slip no opportunity of advancing it . . . you would either believe that the recommender was mocking you, or that he had lost his senses.'[26]

For both Smith and Condorcet, the condition of understanding one's own interests, of being independent and indefatigably active, was of evident economic importance. One of the many defects of statutory apprenticeships, in Smith's description, was to obstruct workers from moving from one industry to another.[27] The effect of the extreme division of labour – in which people 'only know how to do one single thing, or even one part of a single thing', as Condorcet wrote – was to prevent workers from finding new employment when technical change led to the decline of old industries.[28] Individuals were seen as restless and flexible, always searching for new opportunities. The objective of policy should be to facilitate these yearnings; it is necessary, Condorcet wrote during the debates over revolutionary fiscal reforms, to 'regulate progressive taxation in such a manner that it should not become useless, for an individual, to acquire a new piece of land, or to invest a new capital sum'.[29] 'The only difficult question' for economic policy, he wrote as early as 1776, consisted in the prejudices of public opinion. Individuals were not 'led by reason', or by 'the voice of [their] true interests'. They remained prejudiced against 'capitalists' and corn merchants, and believed that their interests could best be served by 'bad laws'.[30]

The incidence of enlightened self-interest was thus essential to Smith's or Condorcet's idea of an enormous, efficient, interdependent economy. If individuals pursue their own self-interest by being obsequious or venal – if artisans do well by ingratiating themselves with the masters of apprenticeship guilds, and merchants by giving emoluments to Members of Parliament – then the invisible hand of the commercial economy will be little more than a guide to decline. But there is virtually no suggestion, in either Smith's or Condorcet's writings on education, that economic self-interest should itself be the object of public instruction. Their recommendation, above all, was for change in legal institutions: the reform of corporate regulations, for example, or of parliamentary procedures. It was the constraints on individual choices, far more than the tractability or liveliness of individuals, which was the proper concern of policy.

The second characteristic of Smith's and Condorcet's arguments – a second difference from arguments about education as a public good – is that they are concerned with public instruction as an end in itself, more than as a means to national prosperity. They are about individual amusement, more than about economic utility. All children, Smith suggested at the beginning of the *Wealth of Nations*, have the capability to become philosophers; the difference 'between a philosopher and a common street porter' is a matter of 'habit, custom, and education' rather than of 'genius and disposition', and they were 'perhaps, very much alike' until they were 6 or 8 years old. All children also share the natural disposition to curiosity, to wonder, and to conversation. The lack of education is thus for the children of the poor 'one of their greatest misfortunes'. They are deprived of 'subject for thought and speculation', Smith said in his *Lectures on Jurisprudence*. A boy who starts work when he is very young finds that 'when he is grown up he has no ideas with which he can amuse himself'. Children who have little education, and who grow up to do uniform, repetitive jobs, lose the use of their intellectual faculties, and are thereby 'mutilated and deformed' in an 'essential part of the character of human nature'. They become 'not only incapable of relishing or bearing a part in any rational conversation, but of conceiving any generous, noble, or tender sentiment, and consequently of forming any just judgement concerning many even of the ordinary duties of private life.'[31]

Condorcet is close to Smith, once again, in his account of the eventual objective of public instruction. To be instructed in science, he says, is to have 'an inexhaustible resource' in one's later life, a source of infinite variety and endlessly renewed interest. This is not a matter of the 'direct and physical utility' of the natural sciences. Instruction in science should be seen 'as much as a means of happiness for individuals as of useful resources for society'; it should encourage a use of time which 'although limited, even, to simple amusement', is not thereby 'a frivolous occupation'.[32] Instruction in the principles of geometry, Smith said, while it can be of practical use to virtually all children, is 'the necessary introduction to the most sublime as well as to the most useful sciences'. Condorcet, too, envisaged that all children should be instructed in geometry towards the end of their second year of public school (or at the age of about 10); it was essential, he said, to 'insist a lot on principles of theory', and on the 'reasons' for mathematical operations, such that they should remain a source of interest later in life.[33] Even for very young children, numbers were an amusement, and should be something that mothers talk about to their small children: 'numbers and lines speak more than people think to their incipient imaginations'.[34]

Natural philosophy and moral philosophy, Smith says in his account of education, correspond to two universal dispositions of individuals. One is the disposition to wonder and curiosity; to think about and try to connect the apparently disjointed phenomena of nature (or of human contrivance). The other is the disposition to moral reflection: 'in every age and country of the world, men must have attended to the characters, designs, and actions of one another', and they must also have tried to connect their observations into general maxims, principles or rules.[35] These natural dispositions, or needs, are also the principal objects of Condorcet's system of public instruction. Curiosity, he says, is not a 'factitious sentiment' from which children are to be protected, but rather something which teachers should make every effort to excite. It is a recourse without which people are at risk of falling into 'a stupid lethargy'. Instruction, or the development of the intellectual faculties, is a source of 'reflective pleasure', and at the same time a protection against 'that painful disquiet which is associated with being aware of one's own ignorance, and which produces the vague fear of not really being in a position to defend oneself against the ills by which one is threatened'.[36]

The disposition of reflecting on one's own and other people's moral sentiments is the other object of public instruction. Condorcet was strongly opposed to education in morality, in the form of any 'sort of catechism'. 'Maxims of morality' or general 'rules of conduct' are not something that people should be made to 'learn by heart', but rather something that they should learn 'to form for themselves'. Even very young children should read or listen to 'short moral stories'; like Smith, who thought that 'the poets and romance writers', including 'Richardson, Marivaux and Riccoboni', were often 'much better instructors than Zeno, Chrysippus, or Epictetus', Condorcet believed that to read novels is the best way to understand how our actions influence 'the people who surround us', which is in turn 'the most important and the most neglected part of morality'. The object of instruction for young children should be not 'to give them principles of conduct or to teach them truths, but to dispose them to reflect on their sentiments'.[37] It is not a matter, Condorcet says, of 'attaching a philosopher to the cradle of every child'. But children should learn to analyse, acquire, and understand the limits of moral ideas, rather than simply learning how the ideas are defined; 'the man and the philosopher should not be in some sense two separate beings, each with a different language, different ideas, and even different opinions'.[38]

Instruction should be taken to a point, in Condorcet's description, where 'one has both the desire to take it yet further, and the capacity to do so without external help, and without too much effort'. Almost everyone, that is to say, would have acquired the 'taste for an intellectual occupation', or would have come to experience the 'pleasure attached to the exercise of the intellectual faculties'. This is in turn a most powerful protection against two of the great ills of life, which are 'fear' and 'boredom'.[39] In orderly and secure times, Smith wrote in his *History of Astronomy*, 'the curiosity of mankind is increased, and their fears are diminished'. The prosperous 'can fill up the void of their imagination' in no other way than by reflecting on the world around them; they turn to philosophy, and they 'pursue this study for its own sake, as an original pleasure or good in itself, without regarding its tendency to procure them the means of many other pleasures'.[40] This idyll is for Condorcet quite general. Public instruction is to be for girls as well as boys, for adults as well as children, for mothers and for labourers. The object of adult instruction is to make possible for everyone the desires of the 'man of enlightenment'; 'taken up with the education of his family, with the details of domestic administration', and 'filling up the void of his life with pleasures worthy of a thinking being'. It is not a 'useless and almost shameful life', Condorcet says, to 'remain quietly in the bosom of one's family, preparing the happiness of one's children, cultivating friendship, exercising benevolence', and thinking about one's ideas and one's sentiments: this quiet life is the object of universal instruction.[41]

The third argument for public instruction, for Smith and Condorcet, is different yet again from contemporary justifications for education as a public good. Universal public instruction is indeed a means to the ends of society, as well as an end in itself. These social ends are however political far more than economic. Smith concludes his bitter indictment of 'civilized society' – of the 'mutilation, deformity and wretchedness', worse even than the mutilation of cowardice, which is a consequence of the division of labour – by urging governments to address themselves to education as a good in itself: 'Though the state were to derive no advantage from the instruction of the inferior ranks of people, it would still deserve its attention that they should not be altogether uninstructed.' But he goes on, immediately, to describe universal education as a means to governments' own ends: 'The state, however, derives no inconsiderable advantage from their instruction.' The advantage, above all, consists in political security. People who are instructed, Smith says, are less liable to 'the delusions of enthusiasm and superstition'. An 'instructed and intelligent people' are 'always more decent and orderly than an ignorant and stupid one'. 'They feel themselves, each individually, more respectable', and they 'are more disposed to examine, and more capable of seeing through, the interested complaints of faction and sedition'.[42]

The outcome is a version of the extended conversation – the correction of sentiments and judgements – which is at the heart of Smith's, as of Hume's, philosophical thought. If one is more instructed, and spends more of one's time having conversations about political and moral ideas, then one is a milder, more reflective, and more reasonable person. A little later in the *Wealth of Nations*, Smith urges governments to counteract the 'unsocial' austerity of religious sects by encouraging 'the study of science and philosophy' and 'the frequency and gaiety of public diversions', including 'all sorts of dramatic representations and exhibitions'. These activities were intended, to a great extent, for people of 'middling or more than middling rank and fortune'. But the causal process is much the same in relation to universal instruction. 'Science is the great antidote to the poison of enthusiasm and superstition', Smith says; public diversions induce a 'gaiety and good humour', a 'temper of mind', a disposition to see the ridiculous in political projects, which wards off 'that melancholy and gloomy humour which is almost always the nurse of popular superstition and enthusiasm'.[43]

For Smith, a secure political society is much like Hume's 'easy and sociable' age, in which 'profound ignorance is totally banished, and men enjoy the privilege of rational creatures, to think as well as to act', knowledge 'naturally begets mildness and moderation', science, conversation, and good humour vanquish superstition, and 'factions are then less inveterate . . . seditions less frequent'.[44] The 'most essential part of education', Smith said in his *Lectures on Jurisprudence*, or at least of education within families, is that the child should learn 'to bring down its passions' and accommodate to others. Even 'philosophical education' in universities, he says in the *Wealth of Nations*, should tend 'to improve the understanding, or to mend the heart'. It is this good temper and moderation which is important to political security as well. The disposition to mild-humoured political discussion, or 'seeing through', is to be encouraged quite generally: 'In free countries, where the safety of government depends very much upon the favourable judgement which the people may form of its conduct, it must surely be of the highest importance that they should not be disposed to judge rashly or capriciously concerning it.'[45]

Condorcet's more elaborate project of public instruction has much the same objective. Everyone, in a secure political society, will be instructed and intelligent, and everyone will be disposed to examine, discuss, and come to slow and reflective judgements about political projects. For Condorcet, as for the other proponents of educational reform in France in the 1790s, public instruction (or national education) was an essential constituent of revolutionary politics. France was no longer simply a 'free country', where government is dependent on the judgement of the people. It was now a country which was actually governed by the people, or at least by their representatives. The *Bibliothèque de l'Homme Public* thus recommended the study of political economy – 'this study will become that of all good spirits' – on the grounds of political utility: 'according to the new constitution, there is no one who cannot be called to discuss and to defend the interests of their canton, their province, and even of the entire kingdom'.[46] If most people remain ignorant, Condorcet said, if they are in a 'state of servile dependence' where they have to hand themselves over blindly to 'guides whom they can neither judge nor choose', then 'liberty and equality can be no more than words that they hear read in their codes, and not rights that they know how to enjoy'.[47] 'Would the constitution really exist,' Talleyrand asked in his report on public instruction, 'if it existed only in the legal code?'[48]

Smith's prospect of an epidemic of stupidity is for Condorcet especially insidious in the new circumstances of the French constitution. Instruction, which is the only remedy for this ill, is also the only way of ensuring that the principle of equality of rights is not 'in contradiction' with the other great political principle, that people should only enjoy those rights of which the exercise does not inflict harm on the rights of others. If people are subject to the 'authority of ignorance, always unjust and cruel', then one can only maintain 'this ghostly imposture of equality by sacrificing property, freedom, security, to the caprices of the ferocious agitators of a stupid and disorderly multitude'.[49] Public instruction should be universal for all children, although it should be restricted to fairly simple lessons, and should never, by imposing a residential or Spartan 'national education', be such as to restrict 'domestic happiness' and the 'rights of parents'. It should be common to girls and boys; if it were not, Condorcet says, then it would lead to a marked inequality, 'not only between husband and wife, but between brother and sister, and even between son and mother', and thus to destruction of the 'equality which is everywhere, but above all in families, the first element of happiness, peace and virtue'. Public instruction should also be available for adults as well as for children. No one should have to say that though he had once been instructed, he was now dependent on everything which surrounded him: 'obliged to work in order to survive, these early ideas were soon worn away, and all that is left to me is the pain of sensing, in my ignorance, not the will of nature but the injustice of society'.[50]

What is notable, even in this new world of universal politics, is that Condorcet's view of political instruction, or of instruction for a secure political society, is still very close to Smith's. 'Enthusiasm' and 'superstition' are conditions to be warded off, as dangers to public security; the ideal is of open and critical public discussion. Even the constitution of one's own country is something which should be taught in public schools only as a matter of information, or 'if one is speaking about a fact'. To teach it as 'a doctrine which conforms to the principles of universal reason, or to excite in its favour a blind enthusiasm which makes citizens incapable of judging it', would be 'to violate freedom in its most sacred rights, under the pretext of teaching how to cherish it', Condorcet wrote. Children should not be made 'to admire a constitution, and to recite by heart the political rights of man'; there should be 'no sort of catechism'. The example of England, here, is a warning for other countries, in that 'a superstitious respect for the constitution' has become 'part of education', a 'sort of political religion' of which the effect is to prevent improvements in the constitution itself. The object of the new public instruction should rather be to set out for individuals 'the discussions which are of interest to their rights or their happiness, and to offer them the help they need so that they can decide for themselves'.[51]

It is of evident use to society, in Condorcet's view, that virtually everyone should be well-informed, respectable, and disposed to political discussion. Universal public instruction is indeed the only reliable protection, he asserts, against the subversion of a free country by a 'conspiracy' of bold and self-interested tyrants.[52] But this sort of security, of 'seeing through' projects and ridiculing political enthusiasm, was for most of Condorcet's revolutionary contemporaries only a most flimsy recourse. It is interesting that Talleyrand, who was far more insistent than Condorcet on the economic utility of public instruction (for the 'enormous workshop' of society), also had a very much more authoritarian view of its political utility. Principles, for Talleyrand, are to be imprinted or engraved in people's minds, more than to be discussed or examined. The new constitution would not exist, he wrote, 'if it did not spread its roots in the soul of all citizens, if it did not imprint, for ever, new sentiments, new morals, new habits'. Morality was 'the first need of all constitutions; it should not only be engraved in all hearts by means of sentiments and conscience, but should also be taught as a true science'; 'the declaration of rights and the principles of the constitution should in future make up a new catechism for childhood, which will be taught in even the smallest schools of the kingdom'.[53]

For the Girondin theorist Rabaut Saint-Etienne, in yet another project of 1792, public instruction, which was a matter of 'schools, colleges, academies, books, instruments for calculating, methods', was to be distinguished from national education, which required 'gymnasia, arms, public games, national festivals'. Instruction was a source of enlightenment, and education of virtue; only education could provide society with 'consistency and force'. Rabaut's ideal was of institutions modelled on those of the 'ancients', in which 'at the same instant, for all citizens, of all ages and in all places, everyone would receive the same impressions by the senses, by the imagination, by memory . . . and by that enthusiasm which one could call the magic of reason'. Society should protect itself by 'taking hold of man from the cradle, and even before he is born'. The principles of the constitution should 'be edited in the form of a catechism, and every child of fifteen will be obliged to know it by heart'.[54] The magic of reason was a religion of politics. As Joachim Murat said some years later, at the opening ceremonies for the first Italian Republic, 'If some peoples recognised the Sun as their God, this was no doubt because it appeared to them in all its brilliance, in all its splendour, everywhere spreading life and fertility, and it is thus that, in order to inspire love for the Constitution with which the Italian people have just endowed themselves, you will present it as always beautiful, always benevolent.'[55]

Condorcet's discursive political society was in such times the object of contemptuous derision. The idea of instruction in discussion was indeed deplored both by the theorists of revolutionary education and by their greatest enemies. Robespierre's famous speech of May 1794 in favour of national festivals, residential education, and the 'sublime enthusiasm' for liberty was in part a denunciation of Condorcet. The supporters of 'moderatism', Robespierre said, favoured a 'domestic federalism' of public instruction, in which children were 'isolated' in their families; the duty of 'society' should rather be to create, as its 'chef d'oeuvre', 'a rapid instinct which, without the belated support of reason' will decide the moral and political choices of men.[56] With the separation of 'religion from the state', or 'morality from policy', Edmund Burke wrote, 'conscience will lose all 'coactive or coercive force' in politics. The prospect that 'every thing is to be discussed' will make people indifferent to the constitution of their own state: governments will feel 'the pernicious consequence of destroying all docility in the minds of those who are not formed for finding their own way in the labyrinths of political theory, and are made to reject the clue, and to disdain the guide'.[57] 'What is this trembling light which we call reason', Joseph De Maistre asked, this 'deceiving cloud' which is all we have left when we have added up 'all probabilities' and 'discussed all doubts and all interests?'[58]

Adam Smith's earlier ideas of public instruction and public judiciousness were themselves vilified as subversive. Smith's critic Alexander Carlyle imagined that Hume and Smith would be punished for their contributions to the dire state of the world in the 1790s: 'the one, by doing everything in his power to undermine Christianity, and the other by introducing that unrestrained and universal commerce, which propagates opinions as well as commodities'.[59] William Playfair wrote, against Smith, that public instruction was an impediment both to wealth – 'the education of the middling and lower ranks is one of the things that principally tends to limit the prosperity of a trading nation' – and to political security: some 'working people', 'very fortunately for themselves', 'never learn to read sufficiently well to understand the words they do read, whilst others . . . find they are led to wish for things they cannot enjoy, or to discuss questions they cannot understand.' Smith's arguments in favour of public support for science and for philosophy, Playfair added, were 'entirely contradict[ed]' by the events of the French Revolution, and 'a smattering of either is a very dangerous thing'.[60] Smith's first biographer, Dugald Stewart, was denounced in Edinburgh for having referred favourably to Condorcet, whom he identified as 'one of the ablest' supporters of 'the economical system', and in particular to his (pre-Revolutionary) views on public instruction; he was obliged, ignominiously, to describe his comments as derived 'not from a wish to encourage political discussions among the multitude, but from an anxious desire to prevent the danger of such an evil . . . I shall ever regret that I dishonoured some of my pages by mentioning with respect the name of Condorcet.'[61]

The political economy of education, in all these disputes, is quite unlike a cold calculation of public goods. Universal instruction, for Smith and for Condorcet, was a source of individual enjoyment, and of the political security which is the outcome of endless and judicious public discussion. The men and women and children they describe are remote from the busy, calculating, and resolutely self-interested individuals who are supposed to be characteristic of the political economy of the enlightenment. Children and their parents are described as curious and full of wonder, they amuse themselves with ideas, they would like to have time to speculate about the origins of the universe, or to go to performances of tragedies, or to have conversations about their moral sentiments. They particularly enjoy trying to impose order on the disjointed events of life. They would particularly like to be respected by the people around them. Smith speaks, even, of parents having respect for their children. He is in favour of 'domestic education', and urges parents to keep their children at home: 'Respect for you must always impose a very useful restraint upon their conduct; and respect for them may frequently impose no useless restraint upon your own.'[62]

To be instructed is to be prepared for one's public life, in the sense of judging the projects of governments, for one's private life with one's friends and one's family, and for one's public life in private enterprise, or in the economy. But economic life is itself a disorderly and discursive business. It is much like the world of which Hume said, in his essay 'Of Commerce', that when someone 'forms schemes in politics, trade, economy, or any business in life, he never ought to draw his arguments too fine, or connect too long a chain of consequences together. Something is sure to happen, that will disconcert his reasoning, and produce an event different from what he expected.'[63] It is the world in which 'capitalists', in the description of Smith's and Condorcet's common friend Turgot, are occupied with judging 'the course of events' and 'the debates of commerce', 'the risk or the opinion of risk which the capital must run', which varies from moment to moment and 'from one man to another', and the consequences of an 'arbitrary and fluctuating jurisprudence, which changes with public opinion'.[64] People make errors, even about their own interests, and they are in the sway of their passions in every part of their lives. Their most insidious errors arise, in fact, in the frontier region between their public lives as citizens and their lives in the economy; when they try to promote their interests by influencing the regulation or the jurisprudence of their own enterprises.

The public instruction to which Smith and Condorcet looked forward is an introduction to these different, disconcerting lives. Philosophical thought, both for Smith and for Condorcet, consists in a mild, discursive, and occasionally awe-struck scepticism: Hume's sort of scepticism, in which sentiments and reasons jostle together, and which is itself an amusement. The natural disposition, in different parts of one's life and in different sorts of philosophy, is to try to impose order on crowds of impressions, to be filled with doubt, to correct one's original orderings. This is the posture of even the most sublime reflection; as when one dwells, Smith says, on 'the very suspicion of a fatherless world . . . the thought that all the unknown regions of infinite and incomprehensible space may be filled with nothing but endless misery and wretchedness'.[65] It is the posture, certainly, of moral thought. It is also the posture of a reasonable political economy. To prescribe determinate laws – an 'exact regimen of perfect liberty and perfect justice' – was for Smith the great error of the French economists or physiocrats; for Condorcet it was to have presented their system in 'too absolute and magisterial a manner', and to have alarmed people with the 'generality of their maxims, the inflexibility of their principles'.[66]

The discursive political society is itself, above all, a society of individuals who have been brought up to be mild and good-tempered sceptics. This was indeed one of the principal charges against what Benjamin Constant described in 1796 as the 'political Pyrrhonist' of the Revolution, going here and there 'collecting doubts, weighing probabilities, and endlessly asking of the majority whether they still prefer present forms'.[67] But it was also, and in particular for Constant himself, a heroic society. It was the society, in fact, of the 'modern liberty' of the nineteenth century. Condorcet in his first memoir on public instruction – arguing against a 'national education' which seeks to 'take hold of rising generations', dictating to them what they are to think – describes the liberty and diversity of opinions as a characteristically modern good. He contrasts it to the liberty of the ancients: 'The ancients had no conception at all of this sort of liberty; they seem in fact to have had no object, in their institutions, except to destroy it. They would have liked to leave men with nothing but the ideas, the sentiments, which entered into the system of the lawmaker.'[68] This passage was later the inspiration for Constant's famous distinction of 1819 between ancient and modern liberty. Constant takes 'individual rights' as the synonym of Condorcet's 'sort of liberty': he writes that 'the ancients, as Condorcet said, had no conception of individual rights', and that the 'education' of antiquity, in which the government must 'take hold of rising generations, to shape them as it wishes' has no place in the society of the 'moderns'.[69]

Constant's opponents, in the essay on ancient and modern liberty, were to a considerable extent the conservative theorists of education in the Bourbon restoration. His rhetoric consists (as in his writings of the 1790s, against the revolutionary overthrow of revolutions) in pointing to what is common in the policies of the revolutionary 'left' and the ultra-monarchist 'right'. Mably, like Rousseau, admired the education of Sparta, and was full of regret that the law could only extend to people's actions, where 'he would have liked it to extend into their thoughts, their most fleeting impressions'. But the ultra-conservatives of the 1810s, too, were admirers of Sparta and ancient Egypt; they too wished to take hold of people's thoughts through education, their words through censorship, and their beliefs through religious laws. 'We are moderns', Constant retorts, and this is not for us. The moderns want to be independent in their private lives, busy with their speculations, their enterprises and their enjoyments, unimpeded by government in their thoughts or in their commerce. They want to develop their own faculties, and to take charge themselves of 'the development of these faculties' in their children, dependent on authority only for the 'general means of instruction', much as they travel on the public highways without being directed as to where they should go.[70]

Condorcet's idyll of open-minded public instruction, here, is at the heart of post-Revolutionary liberal politics. Constant's use of Condorcet in the disputes of the 1810s can indeed cast some light on Condorcet's and Smith's arguments about education; on the ways in which these arguments differ, at least, from more utilitarian justifications for universal education as an economic public good. For Smith and Condorcet were in favour of *laissez-faire* in economic policy, and also of *laissez-faire* with respect to people's thoughts and opinions. Their enemies, in the generation after the French Revolution, were on the political 'right' even more than on the political 'left'. 'One of the principles of the new system is not to prescribe any belief to the child. Out of respect for his reason, one declines to concern oneself with it,' Lamennais wrote sarcastically in 1818.[71] Instruction does no more than give knowledge, in Bonald's description, while education consists in 'everything that tends to form habits'. But the system of *laissez-faire* political economy, and most insidiously of Adam Smith, had the effect, for Bonald, that governments are 'distracted from the morality of society, which does not work by itself . . . the administration of things has made them lose sight of the direction of men'.[72]

It is the *laissez-faire* of reason, among prudent, self-respecting, discursive individuals, which was the great promise of enlightenment thought for nineteenth-century liberals. John Stuart Mill told John Morley 'that in his younger days, when he was inclined to fall into low spirits, he turned to Condorcet's life of Turgot; it infallibly restored his possession of himself'.[73] Mill believed, like Smith, that governments should support public instruction by imposing examinations, rather than by organizing schools; like Condorcet, he believed that the examinations should 'be confined to facts' in matters of religion or politics, such that 'the rising generation' can form their own opinions of 'disputed truths'. The freedom of reason was thus a good in itself. But it was also a good for society. It was indeed the condition for a free society, in Mill's famous, constricting introduction to *On Liberty*: 'Liberty, as a principle, has no application to any state of things anterior to the time when mankind have become capable of being improved by free and equal discussion'.[74]

For Morley, Condorcet's work on public instruction – his 'admirable and most careful remarks upon the moral training of children' – was a lasting monument to the political thought of the enlightenment. Education, in Condorcet's work, 'consists in such a discipline of the primitive impulses as shall lead men to do right, not by the constraint of mechanical external sanctions, but by an instant, spontaneous, and almost inarticulate repugnance to cowardice, cruelty, apathy, self-indulgence'. An education of this sort, Morley wrote, was in turn the foundation of future politics: 'It was to a society composed of men and women whose characters had been shaped on this principle' that Condorcet looked in his hopes for humanity. 'The freedom of reason was so dear to him' that he was opposed not only to 'anything like official or other subordination', but also to the efforts of parents to instil their own convictions in the 'defenceless minds' of their young children: 'this religious scrupulosity, which made him abhor all interference with the freedom and openness of the understanding as the worst kind of sacrilege, was Condorcet's eminent distinction'.[75] Condorcet described Socrates, who always 'expresses himself with the modesty of doubt', as the victim of the same Athenian 'priests' who made education into an instrument of politics, and sought in their 'institutions' to exalt the state.[76] For Morley, Condorcet was himself an adept of the examined life: 'His cardinal belief and precept was, as with Socrates, that the *bíos anexétastos* is not to be lived by man'.[77]

Sainte-Beuve, in a disobliging review written in 1851, said that people would die of boredom in Condorcet's idyllic future society. Everyone would live in a condition of 'universal mediocrity', they would turn imperceptibly into 'reasonable and rational philosophers', there would be no place 'for great virtues, for acts of heroism'.[78] This charge, of an idealization of the unheroic, was something that Condorcet himself accepted, even before the Revolution. He was ready to defend the softness or sweetness of modern life; to look forward to the 'easy virtues' of a time in which improvements in education and laws would have made 'the courage of virtue almost useless'.[79] Like Hume, he thought that it was people in 'the middle station of life' who were most 'susceptible of philosophy', most secure in their virtues, most suited to the virtue of friendship (a virtue that seems to 'lie among equals', and is thereby 'chiefly calculated' for the middle classes).[80] But he also thought that through universal public instruction, these middling virtues could be the universal endowment of almost everyone. There would in the future be peasants who live surrounded by 'a thermometer, a barometer, a hygrometer', who would have been instructed in the 'means of instructing themselves', and who would keep registers in which they wrote down their own observations of the weather. They would discuss politics with their friends. They would talk to their children about moral sentiments, and about being kind to animals. They would help children not to be frightened by other people's suffering, and not to turn away: this would not be a 'useless and almost shameful life'.[81]

There is a more serious charge against Condorcet's heroism of the unheroic. It is boring, and it is also flimsy. It provides only a tenuous security against political oppression. Hippolyte Taine, another of Condorcet's nineteenth-century critics, described the educational projects of the early years of the Revolution as eclogues, much like the pastoral prints in which the children of shepherds declare their feelings of brotherly love. But the eclogues turned out to be no more than dreams: 'it is sad, when one falls asleep in a pastoral ode, to find when one wakes up that the sheep have turned into wolves'.[82] The discursive society of free and equal discussion can be seen (in Mill's terms) as a necessary condition for political liberty. But it is not thereby a sufficient condition. It offers only the most doubtful protection, with its mild and more or less universal virtue, its more or less universal instruction, its judicious public discussion of political projects, against bold and confident despotism.

Condorcet's own response was that public instruction, and moral reflection even by very young children, was the best political security that he could think of. He believed that people can learn to be good, not by learning the rules of how to be good, but by a long, recursive process of feeling sympathy, and disliking cruelty, and thinking about one's feelings.[83] It would help, undoubtedly, to live in a society with enlightened institutions. 'It may be natural to want to win when one is in the position of being compared to someone else, but is it natural always to put oneself in that position?', he asks. Is it natural to take pleasure, or pride, in 'making children quarrelsome'?[84] But it also helps not to be afraid, and to be instructed. None of this, and nothing in the moral and political sciences, can give one a very powerful sense of confidence in the political future. But then a powerful sense of confidence, for Condorcet as for Adam Smith, is itself something to be disconcerted by, and examined with the greatest judiciousness.

NOTES

1 M. Talleyrand-Périgord, *Rapport sur l'instruction publique, fait au nom du Comité de Constitution* (Paris, Assemblée Nationale, 1791), pp. 7–8.

2 'Rapport de Lakanal', 16 December 1794, in C. Hippeau, *L'Instruction publique en France pendant la révolution* (Paris, Didier, 1881), p. 432.

3 Adam Smith, *An Inquiry into the Nature and Causes of the Wealth of Nations* (henceforth *WN*), ed. R. H. Campbell and A. S. Skinner (Oxford, Clarendon Press, 1976), p. 775.

4 Alexander Carlyle, *Autobiography of the Rev. Dr Alexander Carlyle* (Edinburgh, William Blackwood and Sons, 1860), p. 281.

5 *WN*, pp. 765, 772, 782–5.

6 *WN*, pp. 762, 783–8. On Smith's writings on education, see Mark Blaug, 'The economics of education in English classical political economy: a re-examination', in *Essays on Adam Smith*, ed. Andrew S. Skinner and Thomas Wilson (Oxford, Clarendon Press, 1975), and Andrew Skinner, 'Adam Smith and the role of the state: education as a public service', in *Adam Smith's Wealth of Nations*, ed. Stephen Copley and Kathryn Sutherland (New York, St Martin's Press, 1995).

7 *Oeuvres de Condorcet* (henceforth *OC*), ed. A. Condorcet O'Connor and M. F. Arago (Paris, Didot, 1847–9), VIII, pp. 476–7, XI, pp. l67, 191–4. On Condorcet's writings on education, see Keith Baker, *Condorcet from Natural Philosophy to Social Mathematics* (Chicago, University of Chicago Press, 1975), pp. 285–303, and Catherine Kintzler, *Condorcet: L'instruction publique et la naissance du citoyen* (Paris, Minerve, 1984).

8 *Bibliothèque de l'Homme Public; ou Analyse raisonée des principaux ouvrages françois et étrangers*, ed. M. de Condorcet, M. de Peysonel, M. Le Chapelier (Paris, Buisson, 1790–1), I, p. iv, III, p. 108.

9 *OC*, VII, p. 192.

10 'De la nature des pouvoirs politiques dans une nation libre' [1792], in *OC*, X, p. 607.

11 *OC*, VII, pp. 320–1.

12 Fénelon, *Les Aventures de Télémaque* [1699] (Paris, Garnier, 1994), pp. 166, 169, 348.

13 James Anderson, *Observations of the means of exciting a Spirit of National Industry; Chiefly intended to promote the Agriculture, Commerce, Manufactures, and Fisheries of Scotland* (Edinburgh and London, C. Elliott and T. Cadell, 1777), p. 424.

14 'Dissertation on the reciprocal influence of government and the sciences', in F. M. Barnard, *J. G. Herder on Social and Political Culture* (Cambridge, Cambridge University Press, 1969), pp. 242–3.

15 *WN*, p. 781.

16 *WN*, p. 100.

17 *WN*, pp. l39–52; 'Supplementary chapter', in *The Wealth of Nations*, ed. William Playfair (London, T. Cadell and W. Davies, 1805), III, pp. 243–4, 251; see Emma Rothschild, 'Adam Smith, apprenticeship and insecurity' (Cambridge, Centre for History and Economics, 1994).

18 William Playfair, *Political Portraits in the New Aera* (London, Chapple, 1813), II, p. 450.

19 *OC*, V, p. 187.

20 *OC*, VII, pp. 249, 382.

21 Charles Coutel and Catherine Kintzler, 'Présentation', in Condorcet, *Cinq Mémoires sur l'instruction publique*, ed. Coutel and Kintzler (Paris, Flammarion, 1994), pp. 47–8.

22 *WN*, pp. 768–9.

23 Sir James Steuart, *An Inquiry into the Principles of Political Oeconomy*, ed. Andrew S. Skinner (Edinburgh, The Scottish Economic Society, 1966), I, pp. 16–17.

24 Edmund Burke, *Reflections on the Revolution in France* [1790] (Harmondsworth, Penguin Books, 1982), p. 372.

25 *WN*, p. 345.

26 *Kant's Critique of Practical Reason*, trans. Thomas Kingsmill Abbott (London, Longmans, Green, 1889), pp. 124–5.

27 *WN*, pp. 151–2.

28 *OC*, VIII, pp. 458–9.

29 *OC*, XII, p. 632.

30 *OC*, XI, pp. 197, 201, 207–8.

31 *WN*, pp. 28–30, 782, 788; Adam Smith, *Lectures on Jurisprudence*, ed. R. L. Meek, D. D. Raphael and P. G. Stein (Oxford, Clarendon Press, 1978), p. 540.

32 *OC*, VII, pp. 284–5.

33 *WN*, pp. 785–6; *OC*, VII, pp. 249–50.

34 *OC*, I, p. 479.

35 *WN*, pp. 767–9; see also, on the changing propensity to wonder and imagination of the artisan, Adam Smith, *Essays on Philosophical Subjects*, ed. W. P. D. Wightman and J. C. Bryce (Oxford, Clarendon Press, 1980), p. 44.

36 *OC*, VII, pp. 258–9.

37 *OC*, V, p. 175, VI, pp. 568, 579, VII, p. 234; Adam Smith, *The Theory of Moral Sentiments*, ed. D. D. Raphael and A. L. Macfie (Oxford, Clarendon Press, 1976), p. 143.

38 *OC*, VI, p. 548, VII, p. 247.

39 *OC*, VI, pp. 593–4.

40 Smith, *Essays on Philosophical Subjects*, pp. 50–1.

41 *OC*, VII, pp. 193, 324–6.

42 *WN*, pp. 787–8.

43 *WN*, pp. 796–7.

44 'Of refinement in the arts', in David Hume, *Essays Moral Political and Literary*, ed. Eugene F. Miller (Indianapolis, Ind., Liberty Classics, 1985), pp. 271–4.

45 Smith, *Lectures on Jurisprudence*, pp. 142–3; *WN*, pp. 772, 788.

46 *Bibliothèque de l'Homme Public*, I, pp. iv–v.

47 *OC*, VII, p. 172.

48 Talleyrand, *Rapport*, pp. 4–5.

49 *OC*, VII, pp. 191–3.

50 *OC*, VII, pp. 200–1, 218–19, 452.

51 *OC*, VI, pp. 549, 579, VII, pp. 211–15; see Emma Rothschild, 'Condorcet and the conflict of values', *Historical Journal* 39, 3 (1996), pp. 677–701.

52 *OC*, VII, pp. 226–8.

53 Talleyrand, *Rapport*, pp. 1–12.

54 J.-P. Rabaut Saint-Etienne, 'Projet d'éducation nationale', in Bronislaw Baczko (ed.) *Une éducation pour la démocratie* (Paris, Garnier, 1982), pp. 296–8, 301; see also Baczko, 'Introduction', pp. 30–6.

55 *Foglio Officiale della Repubblica Italiana* (Milan, 14 February 1803), year I, no. I, p. 3.

56 *Oeuvres de Maximilien Robespierre* (Paris, Presses Universitaires de France, 1967), X, pp. 452, 458, 461.

57 Burke, *Reflections on the Revolution*, p. 188; Edmund Burke, *An Appeal from the New to the Old Whigs* (London, J. Dodsley, 1791), p. 133.

58 Joseph De Maistre, *Considérations sur la France* [1797] (Paris, Complexe, 1988), p. 121.

59 Carlyle, *Autobiography*, p. 547.

60 Playfair, 'On education', in *The Wealth of Nations*, III, pp. 239, 251; note, p. 203.

61 Sir W. Hamilton (ed.) *The Collected Works of Dugald Stewart* (Edinburgh, Thomas Constable, 1857), II, pp. 236–7, X, pp. lxxiii–lxiv.

62 Smith, *Theory of Moral Sentiments*, p. 222.

63 Hume, *Essays*, p. 254.

64 A. R. J. Turgot, *Oeuvres de Turgot et documents le concernant*, ed. G. Schelle (Paris, Alcan, 1913–23), III, pp. 168–9, 174–9, 191–2.

65 Smith, *Theory of Moral Sentiments*, p. 235.

66 *WN*, p. 674; *OC*, I, p. 567, VI, p. 191.

67 Benjamin Constant, *De la force du gouvernement actuel* (Paris, Flammarion, 1988), pp. 41–2.

68 *OC*, VII, pp. 201–2.

69 Benjamin Constant, 'De la liberté des anciens comparée à celle des modernes' [1819], in Constant, *De l'esprit de conquête et de l'usurpation* (Paris, Flammarion, 1986), pp. 270, 284.

70 Constant, 'De la liberté', pp. 269, 273, 278–9, 284–5.

71 F. De Lamennais, 'De l'éducation du peuple' [1818], in *Réflexions sur l'état de l'église en France* (Paris, Tournachon-Molin, 1819), p. 420.

72 L.-G.-A. de Bonald, 'De l'éducation et de l'instruction', in Bonald, *Oeuvres complètes*, ed. J.-P. Migne (Paris, Migne, 1864), III, p. 1237; 'Sur l'économie politique', in *Oeuvres complètes*, II, p. 299.

73 John Morley, *Recollections* (London, Macmillan, 1918), I, p. 57.

74 John Stuart Mill, *On Liberty* [1859] (Harmondsworth, Penguin Books, 1974), pp. 69, 177–8.

75 John Morley, 'Condorcet' [1870], in Morley, *Critical Miscellanies* (London, Macmillan, 1886), II, pp. 252, 254–5.

76 *OC*, V, pp. 66, 73.

77 Morley, 'Condorcet', p. 254.

78 C.-A. Sainte-Beuve, 'Oeuvres de Condorcet', in *Causeries du Lundi* (Paris, Garnier, 1868), III, pp. 345–6.

79 'Discours de réception à l'académie française' [1782], in *OC*, I, p. 395.

80 'Of the middle station of life', in Hume, *Essays*, pp. 546–7.

81 *OC*, VI, pp. 545–8, VII, pp. 360–1.

82 Hippolyte Taine, *Les Origines de la France contemporaine* (Paris, Hachette, 1876), I, p. 311.

83 See M. F. Burnyeat, 'Aristotle on learning to be good', in Amélie Oksenberg Rorty (ed.) *Essays on Aristotle's Ethics* (Berkeley, Calif., University of California Press, 1980).

84 *OC*, VI, pp. 534, 565.

17

HUME ON MORAL SENTIMENTS, AND THE DIFFERENCE THEY MAKE

Annette C. Baier

Moral sense and moral sentiments came into philosophical vogue in the modern period with Shaftesbury, Hutcheson, Hume, and Smith, but we also find them discussed in passing by Locke, and doubtless by many others before him. Locke, when discussing 'moral relations' in the *Essay*, takes the main moral idea to be that of an action being in accordance with or contrary to some authoritative law, and speaks of three sorts of laws: the laws of God, of the civil magistrate, and of 'Opinion or Reputation'. Speaking of the last, he writes 'Nor is there one in ten thousand who is stiff and insensible enough, to bear up under the constant Dislike and Condemnation of his own Club. He must be of a strange, and unusual Constitution, who can content himself, to live in constant Disgrace and Disrepute with his own particular society . . . He must be made up of irreconcilable contradictions, who can take pleasure in Company, and yet be insensible of Contempt and Disgrace from his Companions' (*Essay* II, 28, 12). Nor is it only others' bad opinion that hurts – since one's own opinion about what is disgraceful is unlikely to differ greatly from that of one's companions, when they hold one in contempt one will be likely to feel shame, which Locke describes as an 'uneasiness of the Mind upon the thought of having done something which is indecent, which will lessen the valued Esteem that others have for us' (*Essay* II, 21, 17). Locke writes that without pleasures and pains, man would be 'a very idle unactive Creature' and would 'pass his time only in a lazy lethargick Dream'. It has, he says, pleased our wise creator to rouse us out of such stupor by 'annexing' pleasure and pain to certain sensations and thoughts. The thought that we ourselves have done something that, had another done it, we would condemn, is just such a thought, and awareness of the link between the thought and the pain it brings are cases of Lockean 'reflection', of what happens when 'the mind turns inward upon itself'.

Shatesbury exploits the literal meaning of 'reflection' more explicitly than Locke does; reflection becomes a reflex act of the mind, a flexing back on itself. It can do this by thinking about its thoughts, and also by being pleased or pained by its pleasures and pains. (Also, presumably, by fearing its fears, feeling proud of its pride, and so on.)

> not only the outward beings themselves that offer themselves to the senses, are the
> objects of the affection; but the very actions themselves, and the affections of pity,
> kindness, gratitude, and their contraries, being brought into the mind by reflection,

become objects. So that, by means of this reflected sense, there arises another kind of affection towards those very affections themselves which have already been felt, and are now become the subject of a new liking or dislike.[1]

This new liking and disliking is what Shaftesbury equates with a sense of virtue and vice. Hutcheson speaks of a 'superior sense' of the beauty or depravity of actions, affections desires, and intentions, and this of course is 'the moral sense'. So when Hume speaks of a moral 'sentiment', he introduces it in a section entitled 'Moral distinctions deriv'd from a moral sense'. The sense in question is that 'superior' sense Hutcheson had spoken of, that meta-sense or reflective sense that Shaftesbury had spoken of.

The positive Humean moral sentiment, like its Shaftesburian and Hutchesonian ancestors, is a *pleasure*. 'No enjoyment equals the satisfaction we receive from the company of those we love and esteem . . . to have the sense of virtue is nothing but to *feel* a satisfaction of a particular kind from the contemplation of a character' (*Treatise*, 470–1). It is quite striking that, after describing this special reflection-derived pleasure, neither Shaftesbury nor Hutcheson nor Hume make the desire to be its object the appropriate motive to virtuous action; indeed Hutcheson argues strenuously against this,[2] since if one behaved apparently benevolently only in order to feel pleasure, and to get pleasure from giving others pleasure in one's own benevolence, then the disinterested benevolence would be only apparent – one would really be motivated by desire for approval or self approval, by what Shaftesbury terms 'self-enjoyment'. Hume does not take the fact that some course of action would elicit approbation to provide the morally approved motive for that action – the difficult discussion he gives (in *Treatise*, III, II, I) of the impossibility of the virtuousness of just action providing the motive for such action parallels Hutcheson's argument about benevolence. (Hume says that the principle he is applying is an 'undoubted maxim'.)[3] Just as one could scarcely be recognizing a motive as pleasingly benevolent if one knew the motive in fact to be *to please*, which in this case requires being benevolent, so one could scarcely be recognizing, as the pleasingly *honesty-motivated* person, the one who just wants to please, which in this case happens to require behaving honestly. The moral pleasure positively must not provide the motive for morally approvable actions. When its object is an action, it adds a benediction to already motivated action, or, as Aristotle says in *Nichomachean Ethics*, book X, ch. 4, it 'completes' an activity which already has is own approvable goal.

When however we turn to Adam Smith, we find that he emphasizes the desire to have pleasing virtues as a natural consequence of the fact that virtues do please those who recognize them. That we try to please, and to avoid blame, Smith takes as obvious. What may not be so obvious is that: 'Man naturally desires not only to be loved, but to be lovely . . . He dreads not only blame, but blameworthiness' (*TMS*, ch. II). He likens the desire to please human moral judges to the desire to please God. In both cases, of human and divine judge, 'they are taught by nature to acknowledge that power and jurisdiction which have been conferred on him [the moral judge], to be more or less humbled and mortified when they have incurred his censure, and to be more or less elated when they have obtained his applause' (*TMS*, ch. II). Smith sees this God-given desire to please our fellows (as well as to please 'the all-wise Author of Nature' and the inner spokesman for both, 'the man within') as a sort of hidden hand that ensures that virtues do get produced to satisfy the demand for them. Although he is to some extent, in these discussions, following Hume's account of the close association between virtue and the concern for reputation (especially Hume's essay 'Of the dignity and meanness of human nature'), Smith goes further than Hume in supposing that the very fact that virtue will normally be recognized by the expressed pleasure of approbation (and self-approbation) gives us a proper and morally commendable desire to give (and receive) such special pleasure. There is no trace left in Smith of that Ciceronian established maxim that there must be a *natural* motive as the object of moral approbation, that the wish to secure approbation will not do as the approved motive, and, if Hutcheson is right, positively disqualifies the action for approbation.

What does it matter whether moral sentiments are seen as themselves providing appropriate motives or as merely giving a blessing to activity that is already finely motivated? Is it that there is a substantive difference of opinion between Smith and, say, Shaftesbury, Smith admiring the higher-minded hedonist, the amasser of a secular version of treasures in heaven, more than Shaftesbury does? And, if there is a difference between Smith and his moral sense predecessors, is it of any concern to any except philosophers and historians of moral philosophy? Well, it is fairly easy to see that there would be a difference between the person who, because she is pleased by pleasing, aims to please, so cultivates all and only the character traits that do please, and another one who in fact pleases, but not because she set out to. Not that she will not be pleased to receive approbation rather than censure, and self-approbation rather than self-censure, but she can welcome the pleasure which thus comes her way without having set out to get it.[4]

It would yield a different developmental story if we saw morality as a variant of the desire to please those who can give us pleasure or pain (parents, school teachers, the powers that be, God), than if we took it as the earlier philosophers of moral sentiments did, as a development of a sort of shareable taste in personal characteristics – a preference for one sort of company over others, with oneself eventually included as a limit case of company, and as normally bringing an increase of self-consciousness about why one prefers one sort of person to another, a recognition of what variation in such taste is reasonably to be expected, and of when one could reasonably expect one's tastes to be shared. Different plans of moral education would emerge, one aimed at leading the young person to want to please the 'right' judge, the other cultivating the young person's own powers of judgment, and her delicacy of taste, and helping her towards an understanding of what could count as a standard of taste. Smith's variant of a sentiment-based view is closer to the Christian view, that morality is a matter of choosing whom to serve, what judge to look to for feared punishment or hoped-for reward. Smith's version of an internalized judge is not so different from Butler's version of conscience – in both morality makes demands primarily on the will, or power of choice, and the authority with which it does so is a close descendant of divine authority. By contrast, the Humean moral sentiment's authority (and, Hume tried to persuade Hutcheson, also the Hutchesonian), is entirely human, and is not the sort of authority respect for which takes the form of obedience. For it issues few commands; what it provides are complex standards of excellence in human character, not or not primarily demands made on the will. Where the Christian morality came as a specification of Christian virtues or perfections, along with the demand 'Be ye therefore perfect', and where Smith's version too highlights conscience, duty, and virtuous choice,[5] Hume's is a realistic morality, and one for determinists or even for fatalists, one which insists that 'sentiments are every day experienced of blame and praise, which have objects beyond the domain of the will or choice' (*Enquiry*, App. IV, p. 322). Smith's voluntarism contrasts with Hume's minimalization of the role of will, and makes him much closer to Butler and to Kant.

One of the dangers of putting the emphasis on the motive of trying to please moral judges, once these are seen as human judges, even if supposedly spokesmen for the divine judge, is that what Locke called the law of opinion can be a fickle law, shifting in what it requires, as power shifts and as the opinions of the powerful or the majority shift. If the decision on what is morally lovely is determined by what in fact is loved by those whom one aims to please, then morality becomes reducible to the questions Hume puts during the low point of the conclusion of Book One of the *Treatise*: 'whose favour I must court, whose anger must I dread?'. And one must keep updating one's answers. There are fashions in what gets the stamp of public approval. Wit, for example, which Shaftesbury and Hume (but not Smith) include in their list of approved traits, was according to Hume in his *History* (ch. 63) 'proscribed' under Cromwell, and Shaftebury's vigorous defence of it shows it to be still a fairly beleaguered virtue in his lifetime. Shaftesbury has to take various extreme measures to defend it from the attack of 'Lancashire noddles', 'provincial head-pieces', and 'morose bigots'. He equates reason with what enables one to engage in reasoning together in company where there is 'a freedom of raillery, a liberty in decent language to question everything, and an Allowance of unravelling or refuting any argument without offence to the Arguer' (*Characteristicks I, Sensus Communis*, sect. IV). These are the terms on which conversation can count as reasoning, and 'make a Reasoner'. In *Characteristicks III, Miscellaneous Reflections*, he undertakes to show not only that wit and reason are inseparable, but that the God of the Judeo-Christian religion is the supreme joker, so that wit and humour have the authority of divine example. (It is God's dealings with Jonah, discussed also by Spinoza, which prompts this playful suggestion.) But irreverent humour is *not* reliably pleasing to those who are the butt of such humour, so a version of morality which makes it a matter of pleasing our fellows by showing the character traits which please them will be a variable and, if one can use the word in this context, heteronomous version of it. Dubbing the one to be pleased 'the inhabitant of the breast, the man within', will not avoid the heteronomy, if that man is attempting to see himself as others see him.

It might be objected that any view which rests morality on human sentiment is resting it on shifting sand, and that the Smith version, where the desire to be approved of assumes a more dominant role than it does in his predecessors, is no more open to the charge of making the moral life a popularity competition, where whims of popular taste vary what counts as excellence from group to group, and from period to period, than are the accounts of Shaftesbury, Hutcheson and Hume. For they all, surely, require consultation with other people at the very least to confirm one's moral judgment, of one's self or of others. The appeal has to be to what pleases from what Hume calls the 'general point of view'. So if, say, irreverent wit displeased the puritans and pleased the court of Charles II, then its moral status shifts, as the puritan influence wanes in England. It was easier for Shaftesbury than, say, for Hobbes to praise the contribution that witty parody makes to cultural life, since the times had changed. The Restoration had, among other things, restored wit and merriment to cultural legitimacy.

This charge, that a sentiment-based morality has no more stability than human sentiments have constancy, whether or not a desire to get the blessing of approbation is postulated as the definitive moral motive, is closely related to the charge that such accounts have no satisfactory story to tell about apparent moral disagreement. For someone like Hume, living in his youth in a puritan hold-out province of an on the whole wit-tolerant eighteenth century Britain, the question is not just of shift over time in the public appreciation of irrelevant wit, but of appreciation in some quarters along with fierce denunciation in others. There seems to have been a real discrepancy between the character traits that pleased the Calvinists in Edinburgh and Chirnside, and those that pleased the more relaxed Anglicans in London, let alone the self-proclaimed atheists of the Paris salons. Even if Hume did not see setting out to please any of these groups as the point of morality, let alone postulate the impossible goal of setting out to please them all, surely the mere existence of such diverse reflective attitudes to, say, his own *Natural History of Religion* (which pleased the Parisians, but upset the Anglicans just as much as it upset the Church of Scotland), shows that we cannot appeal to the *actually expressed* approbation of any group of people to give us a stable standard of moral acceptability.

This of course is precisely the issue that Hume faced in *A Dialogue*, and addresses later, not primarily for moral standards but for aesthetic standards, in 'Of the standard of taste'. How can appeals to universal validity for normative standards be reconciled with the empirical fact that different judges reach clashing decisions, each claiming to speak from a general and impartial point of view? Hume's first answer, in *A Dialogue*, is that the disagreement is only apparent. When we allow for difference of historical circumstance, and for a certain amount of inevitable arbitrariness in the details of social artifices, then differences in the toleration of, say, different sorts of killing of human persons (suicide, tyrannicide), or of sexual activity (homosexuality), in different times and social conditions, need not show any real shift in moral standards. Every society has to regulate sex and killing, and the details of how they do it may be a matter of moral indifference. *However* they do it, some people will feel unfairly pressured into conformity, and others will find the existent regulations too lax. This Humean defence of the compatibility of the unchangingness of moral standards with the known variety of human customs, in respect to sex and to killing, depends heavily on his own account of the 'artificiality' of some virtues, and the inevitable arbitrariness in the details of any actual human artifice and seems to make any 'right to life' as convention-dependent as property rights. He claims, in *A Dialogue*, that there will not be the same social variation in approbation of the 'natural' virtues. Pride and wit are 'natural' by his classification, yet have varied dramatically in social acceptability (or in forms of it that were acceptable), not just between ancient Athens and Edinburgh, 'the Athens of the North', but in Hume's own society in his own and his parents' and grandparents' time. So his attempt, in *A Dialogue*, to write off apparent moral disagreement as merely apparent, is not very successful.

He does in that piece have another possible explanation of the monkish virtues and the whole puritan movement in Britain (and elsewhere) – namely that, like Pascal, all the self-deniers and puritans are choosing to live unnatural or 'artificial' lives, and are deliberately masochistic, attempting to deny expression to a normal part of human nature. But be speaks of Pascal (and, at the other extreme, Diogenes) as aberrant individuals, not as representatives of whole possible cultures. He knew well enough, however, that whole cultures had been tried on the Pascal model, so his dismissal of such standards as 'artificial', in the sense of 'unnatural', denying true irrepressible human needs, seems disingenuous.

Of course one tradition in moral philosophy sees morality's task precisely to be to serve as a counterforce to our sinful natures, so that an 'unnatural' morality is just what is needed. Many rationalist accounts, before and after Hume, distinguish the voice of morality (and of reason, and of God) very sharply from the voice of human inclination and take it for granted that much immorality will occur. But Hume's version of morality is resolutely non-Utopian, and naturalist. It avoids sharp dichotomies between the evil and the good components of our nature and requires that virtues be commonly attained human traits. The only fairly sharp good/bad contrast he draws among the forces affecting motivation and affecting character is that between sympathy as a natural communication of passions from person to person and 'the principle of comparison', which makes us wish to fare better than others, so blocks sympathy, giving us, on the contrary, pleasure in another's pain and pain from their pleasure. Moral judgment for Hume depends upon the free unhindered workings of sympathy, even though these have to be corrected for natural selectivity and partiality to those close to us, so the principle of comparison is a hindrance to the point of view of morality, as well as an object of unfavourable judgment from those who do achieve that viewpoint. Whatever else the Humean moral sentiment approves, it has to approve of what makes its own existence possible: that is to say of unblocked and wide sympathies; of intelligent fact-gathering; of the ability to listen to others' viewpoints, to correct for one's own ignorance or biased sympathies; of the diplomatic skill of finding areas of agreement; and the ability to make reasonable compromises to achieve agreement. One of the reasons why Hume does not see moral judgment as a matter of rank ordering people for merit, or handing out greater and lesser rewards and punishments, is that such activities inevitably employ comparison, so work against the animating spirit of morality itself. They invite envy of the 'winners', or even malice towards all fellow competitors. It is no accident that Hume takes such pains to divorce his version of morality from the notion of a law, obedience to which is differentially rewarded, and wrote scathingly, in 'Of the immortality of the soul', of the supposed possibility of separating out the meritorious 'saved' from the unworthy 'damned'. Humean morality discriminates the better from the worse traits within each person, and need not sort the better persons from the worse persons. (In his *History* Hume finds both good and bad traits in almost everyone he evaluates.)

Why is Hume confident that he has described a version of moral excellence that is universal? On what grounds can he dismiss the puritan pseudo-virtues as not *really* virtues, rather than simply admitting that there is no moral agreement about their value? As I suggested in *A Progress of Sentiments*,[6] it is in part at least the reflexivity of the moral sentiment, on Hume's version of it, that gives him confidence that its deliverances will be fairly stable, agreed-on by different human moral judges in different times and places. How could a sentiment that requires sympathy for its own workings ever approve of cold insensibility to others' joys and sufferings? How could it *not* treat intelligent attention to the consequences of actions as desirable in a person, when sound moral judgment itself presupposes such attention? How could it fail to approve communicative skills, including the ability to listen to others, and imaginative powers, since its own point of view requires a transcending of particular personal viewpoints, so that there can be an expectation of agreement between moral judges? One core group of approved traits will be those needed for more judgment itself. Hume writes at the end of his *Treatise* account of morality that, given his view of it, 'not only must virtue be approv'd of, but also the sense of virtue' (*Treatise*, p. 619) and agreement in approving a particular version of that sense will bring at least some agreement about the virtues. I think we see the same principle at work in 'Of the standard of taste,' where the strategy is to use the more easily achieved agreement about the qualifications of competence in a critic to get derivative agreement about what such qualified critics are judging, namely art works. Critics who themselves need 'strong sense, united to delicate sentiment, improved by practice, perfected by comparison, and cleared of all prejudice' (*Essays*, p. 241) are not likely to give high aesthetic marks to works of literature expressing crude rather than delicate sentiments, or given over to the venting of 'prejudices'. They may recognize more sorts of literary merit (inventive imagination, a way with metaphors for example) than the merits needed to function as a minimally competent critic but those they will certainly recognize. (The 'comparison' Hume thinks a critic needs to engage in is not so much a rank ordering of art works as a 'comparing of the different kinds of beauty', and included in this will be comparing the beauty of, say, a good novel or good epic poetry, with that of well written literary criticism.)

Hume thinks, perhaps too optimistically, that we do agree, and agree across cultures and across generations, on the needed qualifications for being a literary critic, and that it is largely a matter of fact, not of possibly varying sentiment, who has such qualifications. People may indeed disagree about whether some particular would-be critic really is, say, free of prejudice, and then, Hume says, they must do what we do in other disputed questions — see who produces the better arguments, and 'have indulgence to such as differ from them' in appeals to what each takes to be 'a true and decisive standard'. The difficulty of getting an agreed standard is, he claims, 'not as great as it is represented', especially when the sought standard is one *for critics*, rather than for what it is that they are evaluating.

Does the same strategy of moving to the meta-level work for moral criticism? Is a virtuous character trait simply one which a competent critic of character traits (that is to say, any one of us who assumes the moral point of view) takes to be good, where the criteria or competence as a critic, that is the defining features of the moral point of view, are fairly easily agreed upon? Could Hume seriously think this, given how much time he has to spend knocking the claims of rationalist moralists, that reason alone is the proper discerner of true virtue? But the philosophically controversial parts of his account of moral judgment lie more in his use of the labels 'sentiment', 'peculiar pleasure', etc. for what pronounces the final judgment, than in his substantive characterization of the moral point of view, or even of the proper objects of moral evaluation. He did not take it to be controversial to claim that moral judgment judges inner character more than outward action, nor controversial to claim that,

233

in such judgments, self-interest has to be 'over-looked' (not ignored, but looked beyond), that 'steady and general' point of view has to be obtained, from which we can 'converse together on reasonable terms' with our fellow judges, fixing together on standards of merit and demerit 'that do not admit of so great variation'. For rationalists could agree with all those claims. Some of the details of Hume's view about *how* we fix on our standards (for example the role of sympathy), or about how much moral centrality is to be given to evaluation of what is voluntary, 'may often be the subject of dispute', as will the proper applicability of the terms 'reason' and 'sentiment' to the human capacities at work in different phases of the complex activity of reaching a moral judgment. For Hume really has usurped, for this special sentiment, most of the formal features that have been taken to be defining of 'reason' – impartiality, universality, successful reflexivity. So it is not surprising that in his later works Hume is content to call the complex of capacities exercised in moral judgment, and indeed virtue itself, the habit of living by moral standards, 'simply a more enlarged and more cultivated reason' (*History of England*, App. I). The difficulty of agreeing on the qualifications for the competent moral judge may not be as great as it has been represented.

Still, there surely are disagreements among apparently equally competent moral judges, such as that about the value of pride and of wit. Hume's spelling out of the sort of freedom from prejudice the literary critic should show includes religious but not moral toleration. 'Where a man is confident of the rectitude of that moral standard by which he judges, he is justly jealous of it, and will not pervert the sentiments of his heart for a moment, in complaisance to any writer whatsoever' he writes (*Essays*, p. 247). The 'justly' makes this not just a report on how reluctant we are to 'change our judgment of manners', but an apparent endorsement of such reluctance. So moral standards, including intolerance of bigotry, are to constrain the sort of toleration shown in aesthetic appreciation. This suggests that the claims of taste in morals have, for Hume, greater authority and a securer confidence in their own objectivity and constancy than have the standards of aesthetic taste, which are to be subordinated to the moral standards.

Rightly or wrongly, then, Hume is confident that moral judgment, as he has analyzed that, not only will aspire to constancy and the agreement of all qualified moral judges, but will eventually achieve that constancy and that agreement. The only good reason he could have, to be sure of this, is that moral judgment incorporates not just the input of all moral judges (and extensive sympathy ensures this input) but is itself the outcome of a conversation, conducted in reasonable terms, among such judges (or among representative members of such divergent views as can be expected to be heard among them). The *social* nature of the Humean moral sentiment, and the mutual correction of sentiments that goes into it, gives it its confidence in its verdicts. As with Rousseau's general will, it is the inclusiveness of its input, and the generality of its procedures, that helps ensure the general acceptability of its outcome. As not the case with Rousseau's general will, general discussion and exchange of view complete the generality. So there must be some sense in which Hume sees his confident demotion of the monkish traits into vices as itself the outcome of a conversation with monks, a conversation in which their case has been heard, and in which they have in theory seen the error of their ways, after conversing with the Humeans.

But what *are* the reasonable terms for such normative conversations? Hume may have 'gravelled' the monks of La Flèche with his arguments about miracles, but did he convert them from their monkish 'virtues'? He may have felt reasonably sure that, in his own life, puritan ways had indeed been tried (in his childhood) and that his move away from Calvinism was not itself an exercise of bigotry, but a reasonable move, not dependent on refusing to listen to the case for puritanism. (He had heard that plenty times over, at obligatory sermons in Chirnside kirk.) Still, one person's not unreasonable change of mind and manners after some dialogue with mother, preacher, and friends, and plenty dialogue in the soul, is not easily translated into the terms of public reason, the terms by which a culture can reasonably settle the differences between different factions within it on an issue such as abortion. (In Hume's time that of suicide was comparable in intractability.) Sincere moral disagreement, and disagreement about what counts as reasonable mutual correction of sentiments purporting to be moral, remains a grave problem for any version of morality which claims objectivity for its standards (where this means 'valid for all human persons') and also strives not to be authoritarian in its decision procedures.

Hume, as much as any other proponent of moral standards claiming universal validity, has a problem with intractable moral disagreement. But his problems are no worse, and may be less severe, than those of his rationalist opponents in moral theory. For not only do those who appeal to Kantian practical reason disagree on abortion or suicide as much as do those who appeal to calm mutually corrected sympathy-based moral sentiment, but they have slenderer resources for explaining the disagreement. Unless Kantian reason can be seen to be a social capacity, requiring the sort of listening to other parties' point of view which Humean 'reasonable conversation' does, then we cannot explain discrepant (mutually contradictory) outcomes of Kantian practical reasoning as due to some failure in the social setting of the debate, or in its faulty agenda, as in principle we can for disagreement between Humeans. Nor can the Kantian appeal to the possible inadequacy in capacity for wide sympathy, and in imagination-employing capacity to grasp the situation of people very differently placed from oneself, in order to explain apparent disagreements, say on pornography. All the Kantian can pretend to check is the reasoner's will to find universalizable maxims, her ability to recognize contradiction in a maxim, and possibly the sources of supply of suggested maxims. Even that check has to be done by each person for herself; it is not an interpersonal activity. For Humeans, however, it is a matter of public fact whether or not a given person suffers from 'cold insensibility' or has normal capacities for sympathy, public fact whether they can listen as well as preach and pronounce, publicly ascertainable fact how well they have done their moral homework in ascertaining relevant facts. Since the moral sentiment pronounces its verdict only after wide sympathies have been felt and corrected for bias, only after due reasoning with others gone on, 'nice distinctions made, just conclusions drawn, distant comparisons formed, complicated relations examined, general facts fixed and ascertained' (*Enquiry*, §1, p. 173), all these prerequisites have to be checked as possible explanations of failure to get agreement between moral judges before we need to worry that the final 'internal feeling' which gives the Humean verdict might not really speak with one voice, be 'universal in the whole species' (ibid.). It is too soon to say whether or not the Humean moral sentiment could yield agreement

235

between moral judges, since few of us could plausibly claim that we have, on any issue, done all the moral homework that Hume stipulates. The best we can do is approximate in competence as moral judges,[7] and so, if Hume is right, improve our chances of resolving disagreements.

The initial idea of the proponents of the moral sentiment was that of reflexivity, of using a human capacity not just on 'outward' objects but on ourselves. That our faculty of understanding could be used to understand itself was an old doctrine. Lockean reflection tries for an empiricist version of this, in the idea of an inner sensing of the mind's activities in relation to what the outer senses have yielded. But neither in its rationalist nor its Lockean version were our reflexive cognitive activities seen to yield specifically normative outcomes. We do, for Descartes as for Locke, need to be aware of our cognitive and passionate natures before we can discern what norms should guide us, but the reflexive turn, if it is purely cognitive, is not enough to yield moral insight. For reflexivity to yield normative outcomes what is turned inward has to be itself by its nature evaluative, having the good – not merely the true – as its proper object. In Shaftesbury it is pleasure and affection whose reflexive capacities are taken to yield normative conclusions. In Kant it is will which is to be turned on itself, to get 'objective' deliverances about the right and the good. In Smith it is a mixture of Shaftesburian affections (to get judgments about 'propriety') and will (to get judgments about duty). Hume's version of how our evaluative capacities can turn upon themselves to yield more stable and more fully considered evaluations seems to turn *more* of our evaluative capacities on themselves than do most of the other modern philosophical experiments with reflexivity, and yields, or purports to yield, reflexivity-grounded evaluations over a larger range of matters. Since pleasure can be taken in strength of will as well as in intelligence and kind-heartedness, in civilized conversations and enlightened institutions as well as in good people, then making the chief reflexive capacity pleasure is itself a move in the direction of breadth of evaluative scope. But unless conversations, intelligence, and will, as well as passion and pleasure, are themselves playing a part in the reflexive evaluation, then the reflexivity will be fully present only when it is not them, but passions and pleasures, that are evaluated. (In Kant, reflexive individual will is limited in its verdicts to what is in the scope of individual will, and this is in a sense proper in accord with the 'logic' of reflexivity.)

Hume's rich characterization of the moral point of view, of the prerequisites for any felt sentiment having the right to take itself to be a *moral* sentiment, his incorporation into his account of what has to be done in order to be a competent moral judge not merely of sympathy with others but of conversation with them, of listening to their views, his enlistment of intelligence and reasoning as well as concern for 'the party of human kind' into his full description of just what human capacities have to be involved, in order for any sentiment to count as a moral sentiment – all this gives a fine coherence to his whole normative theory, and makes the notoriously wide scope of what gets evaluated by the Humean moral sentiment perfectly in order. If good humour and verbal skills have to be employed in the reasoning together that must 'pave the way' for the moral sentiment, then of course they count as among the Humean virtues. Since some strength of will is bound to be needed, to stick the course of preparing ourselves for moral judgment, will's strength also gets included in the evaluation. Since some self assertiveness is required, especially for oppressed groups to get themselves heard in the moral conversation, then lack of a sense of what is one's due, and lack of any anger at its being denied one, will count as weaknesses (*Treatise*, p. 605).

Whether or not there will still be some disagreeing 'factions' within 'the party of humankind' if we ever all become competent moral judges of each other's character traits, of our customs, our styles or conversation, our ways of setting moral agendas, our educational and other institutions, it is much too early to predict. 'We are still in too early an age of the world [or at any rate of the world of morality] to discover any principles which will bear the examination of the latest posterity . . . ' (*Treatise*, p. 273).

NOTES:

1 Shaftesbury, *Characteristics of Men, Manners, Opinions, Times*, vol. II, book I, part II, §III, in D. D. Raphael (ed.) *British Moralists*, vol. I (Oxford, Clarendon Press, 1969), p. 172.

2 Francis Hutcheson, *An Inquiry Concerning Moral Good and Evil*, Sect. II, in Raphael (ed.) *British Moralists*, vol. 1, p. 270ff. For a discussion of Hutcheson's views, see also Adam Smith, *A Theory of Moral Sentiments*, ed. A. L. Mackie and D. D. Raphael (Indianapolis: Liberty Classics, 1982) (henceforth *TMS*), p. 302ff.

3 It was Cicero, not Hutcheson, whom Hume saw to have conclusively established that maxim. Indeed, in his letter of 17 September 1739 to Hutcheson, Hume writes that Hutcheson does not assent to the maxim that to every virtuous action there must be a motive distinct from the virtue, and recommends the fourth book of Cicero's *De Finibus* to Hutcheson's attention. Hutcheson, of course, found only one sort of motive to be virtuous, namely benevolence, and so could be read as identifying virtue with benevolence, rather than seeing the essential thing to be the pleasingness of benevolence to our moral sense. Hume, who recognizes a great variety of motives, including some forms of self-interest, as virtuous, can give no such monolithic account of the substance of virtue, but defines it as whatever pleases us from the moral point of view. Both he and Hutcheson agree that virtue does not consist in the desire to obtain or to provide this higher pleasure. Hume, Shaftesbury, and Cicero, but not Hutcheson, believe that a great variety of different motives are morally pleasing.

   References to Hume are to the following editions: *Enquiry Concerning the Principles of Morals (Enquiry)*, ed. L. A. Selby-Bigge (Oxford, Oxford University Press, 1975); *A Treatise on Human Nature (Treatise)*, ed. L. A. Selby-Bigge (Oxford, Oxford University Press, 1978); and *Essays, Moral, Political and Literary (Essays)*, ed. Eugene F. Miller, rev. edn (Indianapolis, Ind., Liberty Classics, 1987).

4 I have discussed this topic in 'The ambiguous limits of desire', in *The Ways of Desire*, ed. Joel Marks (Chicago, Precedent Publishers, 1986).

5 Cf. *TMS*, p. 137: 'It is not the soft power of humanity . . . that is thus capable of counteracting the strongest impulses of self love. It is a stronger power . . . It is reason, principle, conscience, the inhabitant of the breast, the man within, the great judge and arbiter of our conduct.'

6 Annette C. Baier, *A Progress of Sentiments* (Cambridge, Mass., Harvard University Press, 1991).

7 Geoffrey Sayre-McCord, in 'Why Hume's "General Point of View" isn't ideal and shouldn't be', *Social Philosophy & Policy*, vol. II, no. 1 (Winter, 1994) pp. 202–28, argues that Hume makes the moral point of view 'accessible' to every would-be moral judge, so does not make it an ideally impartial standpoint. I have taken Hume to make it more 'ideal' than it is on Sayre-McCord's version of it. There has to be some trade-off between ease of accessibility and expectation of agreement, and Hume certainly demands the latter.

18

ROUSSEAU'S EDUCATIONAL EXPERIMENTS

Amélie Oksenberg Rorty

What, according to Rousseau, is the aim of education? Who should be its ultimate beneficiary? How should it be designed? The aim is set by our natures: we are active, independent beings who are transformed (and readily malformed) by culture and social hierarchies; but we are also capable of autonomous critical rationality in the service of civic harmony. Education should be designed to preserve that activity, to bypass a natural tendency to dependency and the ills it produces. It should enable us to be freely and rationally self-legistating, actively participating in the construction of the political arrangements that form our character, our sentiments and motives. Education is in the first instance moral education: that is, education of a person's active psychology: his fundamental needs, the habitual direction of his imagination and sentiments, his ability to reason and to act from reason.

"Our passions are psychological instruments," Rousseau says, "with which nature has armed our hearts for the defense of our persons and of all that is necessary for our well-being. [But] the more we need external things, the more we are vulnerable to obstacles that can overwhelm us; and the more numerous and complex our passions become. They are naturally proportionate to our needs."[1]

Education is directed to the proper formation and direction of the passions: but since these encompass his social life, his relation to his fellows, a person's passions indicate his conception of what is essential to him, of his boundaries and what endangers or supports them.[2] They reveal the power politics of the faculties of the mind, the relative empowerment of reason, the imagination and fantasy. It is not surprising that the passions serve as clues to a person's self-conception: they are direct functions of what he takes himself to be. But there is also a basic fact of the matter about a person's identity, a level of identity that affects passions and actions independently of a person's self-conception. Rousseau sees the passions as more than red-dye tracers of a person's self-conception; they also indicate some constitutionally based directions of his actions, even when he attempts to distance himself from them. Even someone who discounts his embodiment and identifies himself as a spiritual or intellectual being is nevertheless standardly afraid of serious physical dangers. He may use his self-conception to overcome his fears, or at least to distance or detach himself from them. But the fears are initially there, to be overcome, whatever his self-identification may be.

Who then is the rational self – the *we* – who is served by civic harmony, whose passions must be properly formed and who is endangered by their malformation? What are the self's real needs and vulnerabilities? How can the passions serve us, and how, transformed as sentiments, do they endanger us? Rousseau believes that there is a distinction between what we really are, and what, through corrupt societies, we might think ourselves to be. If our conceptions of ourselves are justly coordinate with what we really are, our passions will serve us well. But when our conceptions of our vulnerabilities are mistaken, when we become dependent and passive, our passions are likely to be directed to things we do not in truth really need, and that harm us. Rousseau develops an important addition to his Stoic inheritance: he takes us to be sufficiently plastic so that there is a sense – or rather a level – in which we become as vulnerable and as needy as we believe ourselves to be. The concept of need is tethered to a description: needs point to what is necessary to the survival of an entity of a certain kind. In nature, mankind needs little; in society, he has become a different being, one who is aswirl with fanciful needs. To the extent that we are motivated to sustain whatever we fancy ourselves to be, the scope of the passions that serve our "needs" can become quite extensive. Yet norms govern even self-defining persons: individuals can be mistaken about aspects of their identities, and to that extent, they, and their needs, can be divided and divisive. Some of that discomfort derives from the tension between the individuals' vital real needs – those that arise from their basic natures – and the needs they define for themselves. Passions are destructive when they are at the service of a self-conception that standardly renders the individual passive and vulnerable. Liberation from such passions requires correcting our self-understanding. But whether we succeed in such correction is not merely an intellectual matter, if only because there is nothing which is merely an intellectual matter. A person's mode of knowing, the way his knowledge affects his actions and reactions, is a function of his whole psychology. True self-knowledge does not depend wholly on us as individuals: it depends on our early education and our social environment.

Because he contrasts an individual's real needs with his conception of his needs, Rousseau is obsessed with the question: what is the truth of the matter? What are the proper boundaries and needs of the self? What is essential to an individual, and in particular, what is his proper relation to his fellows?

Rousseau attempts to provide a finely atuned account of the natural and the social contributions to the coordination between the self and the passions. There is, first, natural man as he might exist in a pre-social world, the raw material, so to say, of the fully developed citizen that he can become. As society develops, natural man becomes a socially formed, self-conscious subject focused on issues of domination and subservience. By Rousseau's lights, society provides the necessary but disastrous transitional stage from natural man to his fulfillment as a rational, autonomous citizen, capable of acting on generalized social sentiments.[3] Each of these stages marks a distinctive mode of coordination between the self and the passions, as well as distinctive forms of rationality, imagination and desire. Nevertheless, although we are, so to speak, radically different persons with quite different psychologies as we find ourselves primarily defined by distinctive social and political environments, some aspects of our basic natural endowment and well-being remain constant. They provide the grounds for evaluating social and political systems, and for diagnosing their failures.

NATURAL MAN: THE RAW MATERIALS OF EDUCATION

In *The Discourse on the Sciences and the Arts* (1750) and in *The Dtscourse on the Origins and Foundation of Inequality* (1755), Rousseau projects a story about the origins and the corruptions of society. By providing a diagnosis of what he sees as the diseases of the self, that story is also meant to indicate the moments for educational intervention. With an entirely different metaphysics and moral, Rousseau returns to the classical primary contrast between activity and passivity: we are constitutionally independent, active sentient creatures, whose well-being consists in our actively engaging in those activities that constitute the best development of our natures. But Rousseau modifies the classical understanding of the role of rationality in our constitutional structures: rationality is an achievement rather than a starting-point. Until he becomes a fully developed autonomous citizen, natural man reacts instinctively to what is present, without forethought, choice or precautions for the future. The constitution of the species defines a set of natural activities: no motives are required to develop or exercise them and individual thriving consists in their appropriate exercise. If – hypothetically – we could exist in a pre-social state of nature, we would have an unselfconscious somatic *amour de nous-même*, a non-comparative sense of our own individual existence and well-being, a pleasurable sense of our own natural activity. *Amour de soi* is an unreflective *être bien dans sa peau*. In primitive activity, we have not yet taken ourselves as objects for our own scanning. The exercise of our proper activities – running, leaping, climbing trees, eating – carries unselfconscious delight.[4]

Pre-social natural life is difficult but healthy; it is solitary but not instinctively aggressive. It involves neither an innate disposition to social trust nor one of distrust. Human encounters, including sexual encounters and partuition, are brief and casual. Sexual passion is commanding but neither discriminating nor bonding. Unlike animal sexuality, human sexuality does not, at least in the state of nature, set males in competition over the female. There is no enduring affective bonding. Infants are attended for the sake of the female's comfort and from an immediate sense of *pitié*, but children go their own way as soon as they become independently able to forage for their food (1986: 160ff.) Despite the natural sense of *pitié* – a preconceptual responsiveness to the vulnerability and suffering of other sentiment creatures that we share with animals – there is no affective bonding. Alone, without the necessity, or the consequences, of bonding relations to others of his kind, pre-social man does not develop language. His actions are unmediated impulsive responses to immediate needs; he does not yet have desires whose formation requires an active imagination for future contingencies or future possibilities. Since there is no thought for the future, there is no need for property, no need to regulate entitlement, no need for a formal political organization.

Besides the basic sentiment of his own existence, presocial natural man is endowed with *pitié*, a sympathetic responsive awareness of the suffering of other sentient creatures.[5] An unmediated pre-reflective sentiment that impels assistance without yet being a fully

240

developed dispositional motive, *pitié* provides the raw materials for the developed civic sentiments and the possibility of identifying with our fellow citizens. Because men do not naturally define themselves by comparison or competition, natural marginal physical inequalities do not generate the debilitating passions that accompany psychological and social inequality. Though pre-social man is not malformed or corrupt, he is also not yet genuinely himself, neither autonomously rational, nor capable of genuinely moral – that is, principled – sentiments. Bound to his impulses, he is only negatively free in not being subject to the will of another.

THE MALFORMED SOCIAL SUBJECT

There is nothing in the state of nature, and nothing within our own natures that impels us to form societies. Because we are basically naturally self-sufficient there is no press towards the division of labor that generates dependency. Still, as Rousseau sees it, "Man was born free yet everywhere we see him in chains." So why and how did free men enchain themselves, and in what do their chains consist?

Rousseau speculates that the events that brought men together in society were in a way accidental.[6] A series of geological accidents (an earthquake that enclosed a small valley, a flood or glacier that narrowed the scope of natural wandering) brought men into continued and close contact with one another in an environment that was sufficiently harsh to make survival an unending task and yet not so brutal as to set them desperately against one another. He supposes that the accidental discovery of the preservation and utility of fire brought individuals closer together for the warmth and security it provides. Accidentally but not surprisingly, they discovered the benefits of cooperation; by combining their efforts, they built better and more enduring shelters, secured their food and comfort more efficiently. A crude technology brought a simple comparative idea of species superiority and pride. It also introduced a "sort of property": warmer, more secure dwellings (pp. 172–3). Although the crepuscular beginnings of inequality engendered quarrels, they did not yet harden into continuing combat. Instead of plotting for revenge, the weaker went to fend for themselves as best they could (p. 173). The random mating that took place in nature was replaced by a more permanent affectionate bond between male and female in the care of their offspring. The relatively early separation between mother and child was replaced by a stronger and more protracted familial grouping. Sociability and language developed coordinately. The earliest form of the arts, arising from clustering around the hearth – story telling, singing and dancing – all appeared together. Men began to compare and to rank one another's talents and skill. The minimal inequality of talents brought differential attention and admiration. Instead of singing expressively, men began to *perform*, and to measure themselves by their success or failure in impressing or moving (what had become) an audience.

As they begin to live more closely together, and to become increasingly dependent on their cooperation, men develop an informal division of labor, along with the specialization of talents that normally follows it. They must learn their skills from others instead of from experience. As apprentices, they become dependent on their masters; as dependent, they need to acquire a whole new set of skills and talents, the social arts of pleasing their superiors and controlling their inferiors. Because the social arts that secure cooperation have little to do with the basic self-reliant skills of practical life, men begin to re-construct themselves – to acquire those skills and attributes – to conform to the patterns that they believe will gain them the esteem, and therefore the cooperation of others. But the emphasis on social talents further weakens the self-reliant skills of simple survival. Natural animal activity gives way to reactive attitudes, physical strength gives way to canniness; the ability to solve practical problems gives way to the tactics of manipulating others. The division of labor introduces a vicious circle of increasingly debilitating dependence: the loss of self-sufficiency is inseparable from the loss of a well-grounded sense of self.

And it is this, the dependency that develops from a reliance on the division of labor, that enchains us in a vicious cycle of increasing passivity. The ills of social man are a function of the structures of dependency and the patterns of domination and subservience, along with the strategies of defence and offense that they bring. Gradually, *amour propre* replaces *amour de soi*: men come to evaluate themselves by comparison to others and by reference to the esteem that others accord to them. Because their self-consciousness is mediated by the regard that others have of them, men develop a divided consciousness, objects of their own subjectivity. Natural man has become a subject capable of taking himself as an object; in society, his sense of himself is now mediated through others. Gradually the individual is transformed into the social subject, increasingly dependent on the perception, cooperation and good will of others. Alternately servile and defiant, grateful and resentful, proud and abject, social man is thoroughly ambivalent about those on whom his self-esteem depends. Ironically, the most social of men cannot have true, steadfast social sentiments.[7]

As self-moving agents become mutually constituting spectatorial selves, the imagination is transformed. Indeed all faculties and abilities are redirected and restructured. Always at the service of the satisfaction of needs and desires, the natural imagination had been a simple immediate activity of direct imaging. In society, it becomes fantasy, still linked to the satisfaction of desire, but now constructing and exploring remote possibilities, whose conceptualization generates more desires, and whose satisfaction creates even more refined possibilities. Men who live in a world defined and articulated by imagined fictions and hypothetical futures have been essentially transformed; individuals have become selves attended with a host of new "needs" and passions. The pre-social individual, who had been content with a simple life, becomes feverish, perpetually dissatisfied, reactively busy without being genuinely – that is, independently – active. He is complicit in the process of his malformation. Instead of learning from nature, he is educated by culture, by the theater, the arts, fanciful music.

Full of anxious forethought, beset by ever shifting, never satisfiable desires that he falsely believes represent his needs, the social subject is a creature of his fantasy-imagination, fashioning himself as social fashions change. His language becomes increasingly fanciful and metaphorical. The arts – and particularly drama – command him. The theater inflames the imagination in such a way as to enlarge imagined possibilities of self-definition: it engenders a whole range of new passions.[8] A calculating form of prudential rationality directed to satisfying desires develops in an uneasy relation to the fantasy-imagination. It is allied with them to plot the most effective means – often devious social stratagems of flattery – for fulfillment. In principle, it could check them by marking those which cannot be fulfilled by even the cleverest of stratagems. But Rousseau notes a startling pathology: the unsatisfiable desires of social man are inflamed rather than dampened by frustration and opposition. Because social man does not identify with his rationality, prudential reasoning is insufficient to correct malformed, harmful passions. Once the fantasy-imagination rules desire, calculations of the probability of satisfaction do not always effectively counsel the passions. It is here, and nowhere else, that the philosophically fashionable opposition of reason and the emotions is in play. In nature – and, as we shall see, in a rational polity – thought and the sentiments are coordinate, indeed interfused. And even for the corrupt social subject, the alleged opposition of reason and the passions is perspicuously construed as a paired set of oppositions. Narrowly prudential calculation directed to the satisfaction of subjective interest – interests that rest on a misconception of the true nature of the individual person – can be at odds with true self-critical, universalizing rationality. Similarly, the narrow passions of the pre-political self are tensed against the socially informed sentiments that serve the citizen-person. In a corrupt polity, what is commonly thought of as the opposition between prudential reason and the passions reflects what Rousseau sees as the deeper divisions between merely narrowly prudential and generalized, self-critical rationality, between the passions of the social subject and the sentiments of civic citizen.

An uneasy alliance between the fantasy-imagination and prudence combine to invent the idea of property as a form of security. But property readily becomes detached from its initial function of satisfying basic needs: it is absorbed into the materials for comparative *amour propre*. The marginal inequalities of nature are magnified by the institution of property, which in turn produces new forms of dependency and its consequences: servility, resentment, malice, jealousy. Competition, greed and envy become the dominant social passions. Men are no longer free: they are enchained to ever-multiplying passions that cannot be satisfied. Whatever public institutions such a society might develop to protect lives and their property reflect, and augment, the inequalities and inequities of social life. In such circumstances political institutions reproduce and solidify rather than correct social ills. Property gives rise to fundamental, dangerous conflicts: without some agreement on the rules for its legitimation and transmission, it generates the sorts of conflicts that Hobbes believed to be the natural condition. Initially, it is the need for recognized and authorized arbitration that impels the movement to properly civic, political life. But once that need is acknowledged, it also becomes clear that much more than security and property are at stake. Man is not yet fully himself until he has become a citizen.

THE SELF AS AUTONOMOUS CITIZEN: THREE EDUCATIONAL EXPERIMENTS

Having diagnosed the ills of our condition and traced their origins to dependency and to our plastic susceptibility to social formation, Rousseau conducts several thought-experiments to investigate the fundamental sources of education. There are basically three modes for the transformation of the debased social subject: the political solution is sketched in *The Social*

Contract (1762); the psychological and educative solution is sketched in *Émile* (1760); and the domestic/affectional solution is explored in *La Nouvelle Héloïse* (1760). All three educational experiments have the same directions: to bring men to the fulfillment of their real natures by assuring their independence and blocking the formation of the structures of dependency; to reunite the subject and object in autonomous activity; to promote equality; to strengthen true universalizing rationality over the calculations of personal prudence; to replace the tumultuous and fortuitous passions with stable, generalized benevolent sentiments. And all three educational strategies have the same problems: they presuppose the conditions they are meant to achieve; they depend on the intervention of a benign, paternalistic, unflawed Legislator-Tutor; and they introduce elements and structures that undermine the primary aims and directions of education.

The polity whose origins and organs are analyzed in *The Social Contract* is meant to furnish the solution to the fundamental problem of constructing a form of political association that unites individuals into a single body with a single voice and force, while nevertheless also preserving the autonomy and liberty of each of its members (I. vi. 40).[9] The force of Rousseau's solution rests on the special connection that the contract creates between the will of each individual and the General Will.[10] It is this, the transformation of the social subject into a principled and autonomous citizen, that differentiates Rousseau's solution from other contractarian theories. Political institutions are to be defined and designed in such a way as to enable men to regain a sense of their own activity and liberty, reuniting the self as subject and the self as object. Each individual voluntarily and without any conditions or reservations undertakes to turn over all his rights – indeed his entire person – to the community as a whole. Because the contract moves the power and the will of each individual to rest with the Body Politic as a whole, no individual has acquired power over any other. As a Sovereign member of the Body Politic, the individual is an autonomous legislator: he is only subject to laws to which he has in principle actively consented. Whether this solution is more than a verbal tour de force entirely depends on whether the psychology of the subject has, by virtue of his active and voluntary engagement in forming the civil state, been transformed into the psychology of the citizen. Only if the individual actually in fact identifies his own interests with those of the Body Politic taken as a whole, only if he has bound himself without qualifications and without reservations, does he remain free, despite having transferred his person and his power to the State. It is not enough for him to recognize, in an abstract way, that in obeying the laws of the State as a Subject, he is also legislating those laws as a Citizen. For subject and object to be effectively reunited, it is also necessary that the individual's interests as a Citizen – his interests as expressed in the General Will – genuinely coincide with his private interests as an individual, even when (as might sometimes happen) his inclinations and desires are thwarted. Rousseau recognizes that "each individual may, as a man, have a particular will that . . . diverges from the General Will" (I. vii. 53). Even when it is done voluntarily, acceding to the General Will may sometimes be more of a burden to an individual than his taking part in the activities of the polity. And so the original contract includes a proviso, to which each individual voluntarily agrees, that whoever refuses to follow the General Will shall be forced to do so by the Body Politic acting as a whole. It is then a practical fact, and not a verbal formula, that it is to the

244

interest to every individual to align his will with the General Will, if only because he has voluntarily accepted the general dictum that *whoever* disobeys the Sovereign is accountable for his deviation. He will, as Rousseau puts it, "be forced to be free." In granting the Sovereign the general power of coercion, the individual appears to have done what Rousseau thinks impossible to do: voluntarily alienated his person and power. Rousseau thinks he has solved the problem of retaining autonomy by arguing that in a just polity, the individual has only alienated his powers to himself under another name, his left hand has shifted himself to his right hand. But legerdemain is nevertheless still at work. For the individual has shifted his power from himself to the Sovereignty of which he is but a part, sometimes a very small, swayable part. That his original consent was fully and freely given does not by itself assure that it must remain always freely accorded.

The problem of understanding the reasoning that brings men to the contract remains. Is it merely prudential reasoning, weighted by the recognition of the beneficial consequences of the contract, one that gives the Body Politic authority and power to levy sanctions against any and every individual? But surely a prudential person would reserve to himself the right to attempt secret disobedience if the cost of consenting to the Contract should ever become too large to himself. If the subject's acceptance of the Contract is motivated solely by prudential reasoning, Rousseau's claim that the contract is entered "without qualification or reservation" seems hollow. Only if the subject already honors that phrase in all its force – acceding the right, as well as the benefit of the Contract – does his participation in the contract carry full weight. But if he does honor it, then he is already acting from principle. In that case, the Contract only makes explicit what is already implicitly in place, with the addition that every individual legitimizes the Sovereign's use of force against himself. It remains an open question whether the Contract fully succeeds in uniting the subject and the object self, the private individual and the citizen. It is clear that the unification of force makes it prudentially beneficial for every individual to obey the Sovereign and the Sovereign's magistrates, at pains of being coerced to do so. But Rousseau wanted a better unification than one which might still leave resentment and subjective alienation in its wake. Yet it is only if the individual wholeheartedly endorses the right of the law, cost him what it may, that the individual and the citizen are genuinely unified, without remainder or resentment. But nothing about the Contract can by itself assure this genuine unity. Only if the individual has acquired a new psychology, one that can wholeheartedly act from principle, from a rationality that goes beyond prudence, will he succeed in fully reconciling his private and his civic sentiments.

The individual who has objectively identified his interest with those of the Body Politic, in such a way that he accedes to the General Will without in each case calculating the private losses and gains of doing so is a New Man with a new psychology. He has become a moral being, one whose actions are directed by general principles rather than by the immediate impulses of natural man or the self-serving calculations of the social subjects. "Justice has been substituted for instinct" (I. viii. 55). This change expresses transformations in the operations of reason, imagination and the passions. As Rousseau saw it, instinctual actions are always particular: they are immediate responses to particular situations. In their own way, the actions of social subjects are always also particular: they are directed to satisfactions

245

that the agent calculatively imagines for himself. The motives that prompt action are not generalizable to secure benefits to others; nor can they be rationally projected to the individual's future actions. But once the citizen has become capable of acting from principle on behalf of the General Will, he is capable of general thoughts and motives.

The intentional objects of the General Will are general and universal. Any individual who recognizes himself as a Sovereign member of the Body Politic and who has internalized the principle of acting from General Will, has therefore learned to think and to act in a new way. The self-consciousness which the social subject suffered to be defined by his dependency on the whims and moods of others is transformed into genuinely corrective self-criticism: in opening himself to rational reflection, the individual does not subject himself to others. Because true rationality is, in the nature of the case, universalizing, the rationality of one individual coincides with the rationality of every other. In agreeing with others, the individual agrees to nothing that is alien to himself. Nowhere is Rousseau's Stoic inheritance more forcibly stated: man fulfills his true nature by identifying himself with rational law, recognizing that his freedom – that is, his acting from his deepest nature – can only be achieved by that identification.[11]

The shift from desire-oriented prudential reasoning to generalizable critical rationality is coordinate with the shift from the passions of the social subject to the civic sentiments of the citizen. Although Rousseau does not give a precise definition of the differences between passions and sentiments, the entries under *Passions* and *Sentiments* in *L'Encyclopédie des sciences et des arts* can help sketch something of his intentions.[12] Both *passions* and *sentiments* are characterized by a cluster of distinctive strands. None are sufficient, nor are all of them necessary. Passions are typically intensely felt in such a way as to absorb an individual's attention; they are strongly and impulsively motivating or at least action-guiding; they center on self-preservation and sexuality; their immediate objects tend to be relatively specific and immediate, uncritically and even unreflectively described. With some exceptions – pre-social unreflective sentiments like *pitie* and *le sentiment intime de son propre existence* – sentiments are closely related to beliefs and attitudes.[13] By contrast to passions, they are gentler and less dominating on attention and on action; they are not ultimately directed to organic self-preservation; they are implicitly forms of evaluative judgment; because it takes considerable reflection to specify the actions they motivate, they are subject to rational scrutiny. (So, for instance, it requires examination and reflection to determine how the sentiments of familial affection or civic benevolence are best expressed in particular circumstances. And so too, crucially, an individual's *sentiment intime de son existence* does not, in contrast to the passion for self-preservation, by itself dictate any specific actions.) It is this susceptibility to critical examination that allows Rousseau to think of the sentiments as general. The person's stance towards the objects of his sentiments allows for some distance; he thinks of them under a general description, one that is, in the nature of the case, open to objective scrutiny.

The development of civic sentiments, and the corresponding freedom from dominating passions, requires a shift in the education of the imagination. Instead of being at the service of generating ever new possibilities, objects of fear and delight, the imagination must be refined and curbed. In order to sustain the new psychology, citizens must voluntarily agree to legislation that effectively restrains and re-educates the fantasy-imagination: they agree to censor the arts, to curb luxury, to limit an expansive economy. The feverish imagination of religious fanatic superstition is to be replaced by a grave and decorous civic-nature ritual.[14] In short, *The Social Contract* is an egalitarian transformation of Plato's *Republic*, one that substitutes the ideal of rational individual autonomy for the ideal of a philosophically determined rational order.

But the account of the just polity is riddled with manifest difficulties. It is a contractual account whose detailed elaboration in actual legislation depends on the counsels of a semi-divine external Founder and legislator.[15] While the individual citizen can think of himself as part of the Sovereign Body Politic, still it is the Sovereign's designated Magistrate, rather than the Sovereign as such who legislates particular substantive statutes, laws that could sometimes have adverse effects on the individual subject. In consenting to the General Will, the individual cannot thereby promise not to suffer and resent the harm that the agents of the General Will can effect on him. It is a "social" contract that nevertheless deliberately minimizes the social interaction of its citizens; its citizens suffer Janus-faced allegiances to the polity on the one hand and to their families on the other; it proclaims an egalitarian polity that excludes some of its members (women as the nurturing mothers) from the rights and obligations of citizenship; it is a thoroughly rationalized and secularized polity that nevertheless institutes the ritual observances and sentiments of civic-nature religion.[16] Moving from consent to the General Will of the Sovereign Body Politic – agreements that are accepted by universal consent – to accepting a Magistrate's particular, substantive legislative decisions depends on an exceptional level of mutual trust. But how is this trust grounded and developed? Must the working assumption of the just polity be that distrust only appears in corrupt societies? The hidden implication of *The Social Contract* is that the best and most just political solution of social ills, the solution that restores (a rational and consensual version of) *amour de soi* is, at best, precarious. The formation of the social contract presupposes the very conditions it is meant to establish.

And Rousseau acknowledges this: it is no argument against his account of the best type of State that corrupt social subjects cannot achieve the psychology of truly civic citizens without having had a sound moral education in childhood, and that under normal circumstances such a childhood typically requires the support of just institutions. Nor is it an argument against a particular conception of political life that its best functioning presupposes a certain kind of civic psychology – whose development in turn presupposes just political structures. This bootstrap problem does not mark a problem within Rousseau's theory: it is a practical problem that faces any program of reform.

Although Rousseau describes the contrast between the social subject and the autonomous citizen in dynamic terms, as if it could be effected by a deliberate decision to participate in the Social Contract, it is not always clear that this is the picture that he has in mind. His version of the contractarian account of justice suggests a discontinuity between the two mentalities: it suggests that rational consent at least begins, even if it does not fully effect an individual's transformation to a genuinely civic mentality. But Rousseau's understanding of the processes of psychological formation – his analysis of childhood moral development and the role of the arts and social institutions in that development – moves in another direction. It suggests that only those with a well-formed psychology are capable of rational consent. Some of the problems about the motivation that prompts an individual to enter the contract suggests that the contrast between the pre- and the post-contractarian psychology is not meant to represent a temporal sequence; it is, rather, a dramatization of an analytic contrast. Rousseau recognizes that someone who is capable of understanding the import of the contract, and to undertake to abide by it, is someone who is in effect, already a New Adam. If he has not had exactly Émile's education, he is at least a person in the position of Émile after his travels, having to choose where to establish his home and family.

A just polity requires not only just principles but just citizens to fulfill them. The polity described by *The Social Contract* depends on the educative program sketched in *Émile*, one that traces the education of a truly well-formed human being, one who could become a free and rational citizen. In principle, no special social or historical conditions are required to carry on the experiment of Émile's education; in principle, his education should not presuppose the benign political conditions fixed by *The Social Contract*. Rousseau claims that his investigation will take men as they are to be found, anywhere and everywhere. In a sense this condition is met: Émile is a healthy but ordinary child; he is isolated in the countryside, but any countryside in a relatively temperate climate will do. And since he does not come into contact with political institutions, no particular political conditions are presupposed.

Nevertheless Émile's education is placed in a specific and highly controlled social setting: he has no siblings; there are servants; there are peasants and gentry; there is property; the institution of promising is strongly in place. The peasants are manifestly not serfs but autonomous persons, and although the servants take their orders from the Tutor, they regulate the performance of their tasks in much the same way that the Tutor himself does. Still, so far as possible, the political basis for these conditions is not to affect Émile's development. Although Émile must acquire an understanding of promising and the proprieties dictated by property, no particular system of legislation or of inheritance is presupposed.[17]

Émile is in many ways like natural man, and it is the Tutor's task to keep him that way as long as possible. He is independent and active; his sense of his existence is formed by a natural non-comparative sense of *amour de soi*. He has no passionate or idle curiosity, but inquires only when he has a particular practical need; and he is satisfied when that need is satisfied. Initially, he has no bent to generalizing for its own sake. He is to learn from experience, by the consequences of his actions rather than from persons or books. If he were directly taught by the Tutor, the complex relations of power and dependence would be set in motion. He would become passive, anxious to please, secretly rebellious, biding his turn for tyranny. And if he were to learn from books, his "thought" would consist of ill-digested phrases that he prates without understanding. When he learns from his experience, he remains free and active. The development of the proper joys of thought, those of appropriate generalization and invention, are to be delayed as long as possible, until Émile is a genuinely self-reliant and self-sustaining person. The Tutor's maxims give the clearest account of Émile's psychology: never tell Émile anything he doesn't ask about. Never tell him anything beyond his experience that he cannot actively use. Make things rather than persons his mode of education. Maximize self-determination and minimize self-consciousness. Postpone emotional development. Like natural man, Émile has an instinctive sense of *pitié*. Unlike natural man, he also has a primitive sense of indignation, the key to a primitive and unarticulated sense of injustice. In a natural imitation of the peasants around him, Émile begins a little garden. After Émile had thoughtlessly harvested some of his neighbors' melons, the Tutor has the peasants uproot some of his beans. Sensing himself wronged, he is outraged. By a series of lessons that connect his indignation with his experience of the indignation of others, he develops an understanding of the rights of property that labour brings.[18]

All goes well until adolescence and the wild host of passions that the appearance of sexuality brings. Émile encounters Sophie; he is of course enamoured of her. The hope of his development as a free and independent citizen depends on his surviving that turmoil. It is at this point, and only at this point, that the Tutor presents himself as a commanding authority. He must call on Émile to leave Sophie for a time, to postpone their life together. He sends Émile off on his *wanderjahre* to explore the world. Sophie cannot, of course, accompany him. To begin with, if Émile is to come to a sound understanding of the world, he and Sophie must postpone their sexuality. At so early an age, it would so dominate them that their proper development would be arrested. Émile must now develop a capacity to form his own judgment, to compare ways of life, to think in general terms. If the Tutor has done his job well, it is now even safe for Émile to go to the theater.

There is another crucial reason that Sophie cannot accompany Émile on the journeys that will prepare him for the last stage in his self-development. Sophie is not another Émile. She must be educated to tend to the welfare of others, and to define her self through her capacity to nourish and to nurture. Far from having a sense of active independence, Sophie is to focus her life on her relation to Émile and to their children. Although Rousseau assigns her a life of sweet service, rather than one of rational autonomy, he believes he has accorded her a certain sort of superiority. In time, Émile will not only depend on her sentiments, but must, in certain instances, be guided by them. But Rousseau's account of Sophie's moral development contains several conflicting strands. While her life is meant to accord with, and to fulfill, her nature, she does not choose her mode of life. At best, she chooses the husband who will set the guidelines and principles of her life. Although she is the Nurturer, it is Émile, and indeed the Tutor, who gives her the general principles which are to guide her children's education and the running of the household. Although Rousseau claims that she is Émile's moral equal, she is not, by Rousseau's lights, capable of choice, and so, by Rousseau's lights she is not a moral being at all.

Like *The Social Contract*, the educational experiments presented in *Émile* presuppose conditions which, on Rousseau's theories, they are meant to produce. As the social contract presupposes a semi-divine legislator, so the Tutor appears to be a new sort of autonomous divinity, simultaneously devoted and detached. Without relations or affectional ties of his own, he has the education of Émile as his primary project. For all his devotion to his educative task, he cannot become dependent on his relation to Émile. And yet the education of Émile is his primary, and it seems his only achievement.

There are other oddities. Because Émile must not compare himself with others, he is to have no siblings. To the extent he has companions of his age, they are the children of peasants and servants. How could he fail to observe significant differences between them and himself? He must understand equality without having grown up among equals. Since he is not to learn by being taught, the circumstances that lead to his discoveries must be contrived. But he must not guess that he has been deceived or even manipulated. Although Émile is clearly not given to psychological observation or speculation, and although everything is done to avoid his developing the habits – even the ideas – of domination and subservience, he would surely become aware of the Tutor's orders to the servants and peasants. It is virtually impossible to imagine that Émile would remain wholly unaware of the theatricality of his condition.

But it is Sophie who presents the real problem for Rousseau's educational experiments. If Émile is the New Adam, Sophie is the new Eve in the Garden of Eden. She must be, and yet she cannot be, a citizen. The future mother of free men is nevertheless obedient or at any rate compliant, relatively ignorant of the world, educated for domestic economy and for the particular nurturing sentiments of motherhood – and thus unsuited to the disinterested universalizing rationality of citizenship. She is to have ribbons and she must learn to be coy. To maintain Émile's ardor for her, she must learn to refuse her favors. Vanity – innocent vanity, but vanity nevertheless – is introduced. In any case, Émile's relation to Sophie introduces an internal division within himself, an obstacle for the unification of his subjectivity and his objectivity. His familial life, a life that is essential both to his welfare and that of his polity, leaves him with divided loyalties and a divided mind. As an adult citizen and *père de famille*, Émile must work through the contrast between the particularized interests of his devotion to Sophie and their children on the one hand and the generalized interests he develops as a citizen identified with the General Will on the other. In principle rationality should enable Émile to see the interconnection and perhaps the ultimate identity of these spheres. But he nevertheless initially experiences a distinction between his own initial responses and those which common life require. Émile must express his private interest in order for the General Will to be formed: the particularity of his perspective is constitutively necessary for the formation of general policy. But to the extent that his sense of himself is particular and perspectival, it is not – at least initially – identical with the civic decisions to which he gives his rational consent. The contrast between familial sentiments and rational General Will remain, even though they are marked as contrasts between the psychology of Sophie and that of Émile.

The question arises: could a person with Émile's psychology be formed without the peculiarities of Émile's education? What would be the childhood and youth of those who might be capable of being parents to a sound citizen? If *The Social Contract* must be supplemented with an account of the education of a sensible citizen, *Émile* must be supplemented with an account of naturalized domestic life. In its own way, *La Nouvelle Héloïse* explores the possibility of a familial, affectional solution of the corruptions exposed in the *Discourses*. Like Rousseau's other educational experiments, it depends upon the direction of a benevolent, paternal figure. Like the Legislator and the Tutor, Monsieur de Wolmar is Olympian: he sets the frame for the actions of the other characters. He gives his wife Julie and her former lover Saint-Preux the perfect freedom of intimacy; and his wholly benevolent trust in their virtue is precisely what constrains that freedom.

La Nouvelle Héloïse explores the contrast between the passions and sentiments. "Passion," Rousseau says, "expresses itself more effusively than forcibly. It does not think of being persuasive; it does not suspect that anyone may question it. It expresses itself in order to comfort itself . . . . But sentiment has no past or future. [It is] a gentle ecstasy [that] fills the whole duration, converges time into a single point."[19] Speaking of how readers might react to *La Nouvelle Héloïse*, he adds, "All [its] sentiments will [seem] unnatural for those who do not believe in virtue." The novel traces the differences between the power of the passionate love of Julie and Saint-Preux and the gentler, more diffuse sentiments of friendship of the Wolmar household. Passions are exclusive, sentiments are inclusive; the impetuous urgency, the focused attention, of passionate love endangers the welfare and virtue that is normally protected through the sentiments of affectionate friendship. Even perceptions of Nature are distinguished: passion is overwhelmed by the grandeurs of Nature, while the sentiments are charmed by its harmony and fertility.

But the educational experiment of *La Nouvelle Héloïse* fails: the illicit harmful passionate love that Julie and Saint-Preux had hoped to transform into the enduring sentiments of friendship was never fully eradicated. Despite the regimen of the Wolmar ménage, the shared architectural and agricultural projects, despite Julie's devotion to her husband and her wholehearted attachment to her children, she found she could not overcome her longing for Saint-Preux. Her virtue remained unshaken, but at the cost of a constant struggle. Once passion has been aroused, neither the wisdom of Wolmar nor the most resolute virtue can eradicate it. Even the most virtuous person, under the care of the wisest man, remains torn by passionate attachments. To save her from a life of inner struggle, Rousseau had to devise a fortunate death for Julie, a lingering illness that overtakes her after she heroically rescues one of her children from the danger of drowning. Like the political and psychological modes of education, that of domestic and affectional attachment is successful only for characters that are already well-formed.

Taken independently of one another the educational experiments – the political, the psychological and the social – will be likely to fail. The psychological reforms of *Émile* need to be supported by those growing out of the political contract. But these in turn require the kinds of citizens formed by Émile's education. An attempt to naturalize and domesticate the education of Émile is likely to introduce conflicts between the sentiments of virtue and the kinds of passion that any social life, no matter virtuous, are likely to raise. Each of the educational modes appears to reintroduce the very diseases it was meant to avoid. The educational projects cannot succeed in returning us to the unconflicted joys of our pre-social condition.

Ironically, the kind of self-awareness that reading Rousseau brings reintroduces the very disharmony, the internal division, it was meant to overcome. None knows better than he that the good fortune of reading the best of books is insufficient to change the ills for which they provide the clearest diagnosis. At best, such reading produces an interesting conflict between deep-seated habits and new insights. Reforms are only as good as the reformers. Unlike the Tutor and the Legislator, we suffer malformed passions fed by imaginations excited by corrupt relations of dependency. Whether any aspects of the three educational strands – the political, psychological and social – can be appropriately combined will be a matter of historical accident. We are left in doubt and darkness, for it is not at all clear that the three domains can be combined. Superficially at any rate, there are barriers to the promised harmony of the inner and the outer man, of the familial and civic affections.

Rousseau's diagnosis of our ills and his analysis of educational directions express his divided mind, and his struggles to unite it. He is metaphysically and morally committed to individual natural autonomy. Yet it is he who most stresses the social formation of an individual's conception of his freedom, his rationality, even his desires. He is a passionate egalitarian, and yet the social structure that he idealizes depends on women's political inequality. Sensitive to what he conceives to be the dangers of the power of language in forming the imagination, he nevertheless indulges in rhetorical outbursts, using the very methods he hopes to overcome, in the full realization that the processes of learning and transformation remain immanent in the outcome.

Rousseau speaks with many tongues. In one sense, he has returned us to our Stoic selves, fully ourselves only when we have achieved rational autonomy, identified our interests with those of the General Will, and transformed our passions into generalized and impartial civic sentiments. Rousseau answers the question that he poses for himself: what is the connection between the self and any particular idea of the self? In a corrupt society, there is no relation; in a benign polity, they are identical. Nevertheless, Rousseau leaves us more conflicted, more divided than ever. Even setting aside the alleged miseries of the debased social subject – miseries which might seem delightfully interesting to those not burdened by Rousseau's longing for unity and harmony – the autonomous citizen remains layered and conflicted. There is the natural creature who persists through his social and political formation/ transformation. There is the private, familial man, and there is man as rational citizen. It would be a piece of false consciousness to deny any of these aspects; none can be transcended.

Nevertheless, while Rousseau recognizes that his educational experiments cannot assure immunity against corruption, he believes that they will promote whatever little health our complex plasticity allows. Although we can never be well, we can diminish our malaise. Like Plato, Rousseau is skeptical about whether we can succeed in constructing a harmonious form of life immune from damaging conflicts; and like Plato, he thinks that he can describe a polity that could in principle serve us well, a mode of education that could in principle develop us well, a mode of affectional and domestic life that would sustain us well. Like Plato's thought-experiments, Rousseau's projections contain strands that show the impossibility of their perfect realization or implementation. Still for all of that, his three educational experiments sketch the directions that Rousseau thinks could promote our greatest and least fettered activity.[20]

NOTES

1 Rousseau, *Fragments for Émile*, *Oeuvres Complètes*, vol. IV, Gallimard, Editions Pleiade, 1969, p. 873. My translation.

2 In discussing Rousseau's account of the relation between the self and its passions and sentiments, it is appropriate, indeed necessary, to use the masculine pronoun throughout. Despite their presumed moral equality, women are disqualified from citizenship. But Rousseau holds that only autonomous, rational citizens qualify as fully developed persons.

3 It is a vexed question whether these "stages" mark a temporal sequence. Certainly the state of nature is a projected thought-experiment, a set of speculations about what life might be like for men physically constituted as we are, if – hypothetically – we did not live in social groups. But Rousseau also seems to believe that men might once have lived in social groups without having consciously, explicitly formed and consented to a set of rules, procedures for settling disputes and authorizing a system of legislation.

4 "Second Discourse," in *The First and Second Discourses*, edited and translated by Victor Gourevitch (New York, Harper and Row, 1986), p. 170. All references will be to this edition.

5 Cf. *Discourse on the Origins of Inequality* and *Émile*, ed. A. Bloom (New York, Basic Books, 1979), pp. 17ff. Because it connotes a sharp distinction between subject and object, because it presupposes a comparative judgment, "pity" is a poor translation of *pitié*.

6 *Second Discourse*, pp. 174ff. in Gourevitch. Rousseau claims that Hobbes's description of men in the state of nature is in fact a description of man in society. If Hobbes were right, he argues, the political contract could never have been formed. But Rousseau may not be entitled to make this criticism. His own account of the contractual institution of the state is as hypothetical and ahistorical as Hobbes's. If the social subject were as deformed as Rousseau suggests, he would be incapable of the kind of rational deliberation required to form the political contract.

7 In the *Confessions* and in the fourth *Reverie d'un promeneateur solitaire*, Rousseau deliberately reveals himself as the prime example of such a malformation. But his corruption is often more clearly revealed in his unselfconscious accounts of his adventures, as in the story of his role in the dismissal of his fellow servant Marion, than it is in his dramatic self-consciously confessional proclamations. It is evident that although he was the cause of her unjust dismissal, he never attempted to help her find another position. While he (melo)dramatically blames himself for his cowardice in lying, it never occurs to him to blame himself for the harm he has done or for his callousness in not rectifying her situation.

8 In the *Essay on the Origins of Languages* and in *Lettre à d'Alembert*, Rousseau analyzes the complicity of the arts and letters in the processes of that corruption.

9 References will be made to book, chapter and paragraph number. The abbreviated title, *Le Contrat social*, is a misnomer. The full title of the work is: *Du contrat social, ou Principes du droit politique*. It is, after all, Rousseau who develops the contrast between society and the polity, between the informal psychological relations that grow without a person's explicit consent and the political relations founded on principles to which an individual has freely consented. Although in Book 1, i–viii, Rousseau speaks loosely of the transition from "the state of nature" to the civil state, it is clear that those who enter the Sovereign compact are already social beings: they live in families, they have a developed language and property.

10 Despite his attempt to spell out the steps by which the General Will is the rational expression of each individual's own interest, Rousseau's conception of the relation between the General Will and private interest remains obscure. That obscurity is marked by the fact that almost no two commentators agree about how best to interpret it.

11 Cf. *Social Contract* I. vii. 55.

12 Those entries reflect a strong Stoic and Cartesian influence. Rousseau's distinction between passions and sentiments echoes Descartes's distinctions between *passions* and *habitudes* (*Passions of the Soul*, III). Both articulate the Stoic distinction between *pathé* and *eupathé*. Like *eupathé*, sentiments are dispositional, presumptively rational and benign.

13 *L'Encyclopédie* treats *sentiment*, *avis* and *opinion* as modes of judgment, differentiating *sentiment* by its sincerity.

14 But interestingly enough, the summary of *The Social Contract* that appears in *Émile*, V does not include any reference to the Legislator or to civic religion.

15 *Social Contract* II. vii.

16 *Social Contract* IV. viii. 440 ff.

17 But the Tutor nevertheless introduces a normative account of initial property entitlement: the control of property is explicitly linked to labour.

18 *Émile*, Book II. It is difficult to resist comparing this passage with Augustine's account of his reflections on the consequences of his childish theft of pears (*The Confessions*). Augustine argues that the guilt that followed his theft revealed God's mark, an innate sense of right and wrong. Rousseau suggests that Émile's outrage is the natural beginning of a sense of justice. Despite the interesting differences between them, both Augustine and Rousseau hold that the emotional consequences of moral infraction express an innate sense of morality. Both echo the *Genesis* story: in eating the forbidden fruit, Adam and Eve acquired a knowledge of good and evil, expressed in their subsequent shame.

19 Preface to *La Nouvelle Heloise*, *Oeuvres complètes*, vol. II (Paris, Gallimard, Edition Pleiade, 1964), p. 5.

20 An ancestor of this paper appeared in *Philosophy* (Vol. 66, No. 258, 1991, pp. 413–434); it was delivered at a conference on "The Self and Symbolic Expression" at the East–West Center at the University of Hawaii in Honolulu, 1992. Victor Gourevitch first introduced me to Rousseau. I am grateful for his patient and painstaking tutorials; like Émile, I find myself returning to him again and again for further counsel. I also benefited from discussions with Sissela Bok, Fred Neuhouser and Tom Wartenberg.

19

TRAINING TO AUTONOMY: KANT AND THE QUESTION OF MORAL EDUCATION

Barbara Herman

Kantian moral theory does not seem to provide a comfortable environment for thinking about moral education. Education is about development and change. Moral education, where it is something beyond inculcating a list of "dos and don'ts", involves the creation of a sense of self and other that makes shared moral life possible. But the Kantian moral agent, *qua* rational agent, is one whose capacity for morality, for good willing, comes with her autonomous nature. We *are* rational agents; insofar as we are rational, we are autonomous: able to act as morality requires – "from duty." Apart from training to make moral life easier, there does not appear to be much room to *form* or *develop* anything.

Nonetheless, Kant's interest in moral education is not peripheral to his understanding of the conditions of autonomous moral agency. The impediment to seeing this comes from interpretive confusion about the place of empirical conditions of agency in a theory that looks to a noumenal fact about rationality as the necessary *and* sufficient condition of good willing. As a way of sorting some of this out, I want to develop a very different line of thought: although autonomy is an essential property of individual rational wills, for human beings, autonomous moral agency is realized in and through a certain form of social life with others. It is this fact that sets the task for moral education, though it is a different task, taking place in a different venue, than the orthodox view of Kant's moral theory suggests.

To show this will require several stages of argument and attention to some non-standard texts. I will begin with a brief review of the official account of moral education. Some of its limitations will point us towards the underexplored subject of empirically conditioned practical reason. Understood, as it often is, in an essentially Humean way, empirical practical reason[1] is the rational faculty in the service of self-love, inevitably at odds with the demands of morality: something that needs to be overcome in the moral activity of an autonomous agent. I want to argue that, to the contrary, the real problem is the *incompleteness* of empirical practical reason exacerbated by its pretensions to be a wholly adequate determining ground of the will. Moral education is about securing the completion of empirical practical reason, a process necessary for the real possibility of pure practical reason in human agents. It is a process that turns out to be, surprisingly, a social one.

I

The official view: Kant has many sensible and interesting things to say about moral education as usually understood. He thinks that early education needs to be catechistic (*KpV* 152ff.; *DV* 477ff.), and that the rote lessons, given in terms of examples and stories, are chiefly directed at inculcating a feeling for action "from duty": its possibility, its motivational distinctness, and its awe-someness. After catechism comes the "erotetic method" – of question and answer – by which a young person's natural pleasure in sharpening her ability to make distinctions is deployed in the service of sorting out real from false virtue. Puzzles and hard cases, rather than fueling moral skepticism, challenge ingenuity and stretch newly acquired conceptual skills. As Kant shrewdly notes: "We ultimately take a liking to that the observation of which makes us feel our powers of knowledge extended" (*KpV* 160). This knowledge is to be supplemented by vivid examples that bring the student to experience the possibility of her own powers of freedom as preparation for taking the moral law as her highest-order regulative principle of action (*KpV* 165).

Much of this is obvious. Children need to be taught to recognize their duties (the content of obligations) and to understand the distinctive nature of moral action. Their recognitional abilities need to be honed and their character strengthened. From his official pronouncements, we should conclude that Kant's distinctive contribution to moral education is a method for learning about acting from duty alone. Through modeling, imaginative exercises, self-criticism, and so forth, we come not only to recognize the separateness of moral and nonmoral incentives, but also to achieve a reorganization of our dispositions so that, when appropriate, one has immediate and reliable access to the moral motive. One will come to have a particular kind of strength of character, able to "refuse" the pretensions of nonmoral incentives: one learns to "exclude the principle of self-love from the highest practical principle" (*KpV* 74). Refusal should not be confused with renunciation. Refusal is a choice we make, supported on the one hand by respect for the moral law and esteem for oneself as its source, and, on the other, by the reciprocal humiliation of the pretensions of the feelings to be the ultimate determining ground of the will (self-conceit). We do not thereby renounce our interest in the satisfaction of desires. However, the ability to refuse the pretensions of inclination in general also makes it easier to ignore specific contrary-to-morality inclinations, thereby enhancing the effectiveness of the moral motive.

Moral education is thus, as one would expect, propadeutic to virtue, "the product of pure practical reason insofar as it gains ascendancy over such [opposing] inclinations with consciousness of its supremacy (based on freedom)" (*DV* 478). Beyond the "dos and don'ts", it provides the training needed to remedy the misfortune of our natures: that we are "finite beings" strongly and naturally motivated by concern for happiness and well-being (most often our own). For most of us, once we learn how to refuse the pretensions of self-love, it provides well-person care for a morally decent life. Should it do more?

One might think not – that there is nothing more for moral education to do. If we take one strain of his thought, Kant follows Rousseau in the idea that even the "ordinary man" exhibits the basic elements of sound moral conscience. Thus the *Groundwork* can argue "from the ordinary rational knowledge of morality to the philosophical" (*G* 393). And, at a key moment in the *Critique of Practical Reason*, Kant appeals to the "order of concepts" in a man who asserts that "lust is irresistible" to show that even he is aware that in the face of the moral law, he could resist after all (*KpV* 31). This makes sense because we have, by nature, a "predisposition to personality": a "capacity for respect for the moral law as in itself a sufficient incentive of the will" (*R* 23). The predisposition reveals itself in the virtue of ordinary persons, and can be elicited from even those who are degraded or corrupt. If this is the whole story, the point of moral education is to protect us from the latter condition and provide stability and a sound foundation for the former.

However, an account of moral education as basic training for morally worthy action and stability of good character misses something fundamental. Training to virtue must include training to *value*: what value is, where in action it lies. This is not a point about purity of motive or the degree of conformity of action to morality. Failure to appreciate the connection of moral requirement to unconditioned value leads to errors in judgment; even when right action is taken, it will not be done in the right way. Actions that are only accidentally right, even if reliably so, are not responsive to moral concerns. At the extreme, moral legality – the outward conformity of action to moral principle – can be a vice. A person whose actions were governed by attention to the outward sign of dutifulness would not do what she ought. She would not correctly read the nature of moral facts even though her actions conformed to law.

The proper arena for legality is one where the task is conformity to rules. There one needs training in judgment: whether the rules apply, and if they do, about the range of freedom within a rule's domain of regulation. But Kantian moral reasoning is not in the service of rule-following. We are not in a primary moral sense required to avoid this or that *kind* of action; we are to acknowledge, in action and judgment, rational agency as a higher-order regulative value.[2] Moral judgment must thus be responsive to detail of circumstances, institutions, character: how rational nature is expressed, where it is vulnerable, how it may be made effective.

The reasons why we act morally – help when there is need, refrain from harming – establish basic structures of moral connection with others, as well as our conception of ourselves as moral agents. If I see your need as a source of frustration and pain for you, which I am drawn to alleviate, then I see you as a vulnerable sentient creature, and myself as provider of a benefit. If, by contrast, I see your need as an obstacle to your effective agency, as making a claim on me that derives from the value of rational agency *per se*, then it is not just your need that I see differently, but you, and so myself in relation to you. Moral action expresses the sense of relation. This in turn affects how we go on: how we act when intentions go awry, or what we do if we discover, for example, that the need in question is chronic, or a source of dependency.

If this is the nature of moral action, the curriculum of moral education cannot consist of rote learning and motivational discipline. Training in value requires the acquisition of a distinctive orientation towards the practical world, including the domain of possible actions and objects of action. The powers of the virtuous person not only make visible a different world (or different elements of the world), as *practical* powers, they also have as their object "to confer on (*zu erteilen*) the sensuous world the form of a system of rational beings" (*KpV*

43). The point of moral education must then be to produce an empirical character capable of autonomous judgment and action. How empirical autonomy is possible when consistent with the laws of nature is another matter, but *that it is* seems plainly to follow from the nature of the moral law and its commands. Moral pedagogy will therefore require a different kind of investigation of the empirical conditions of rational moral agency, and of nonmoral empirically conditioned practical reason, than would be needed if its task were only the provision of rules and stability of motive or character.

II

With all this in mind, we would do well to re-think the starting place of the account of moral education. Suppose we ask: what does Kant think we are like? what is the "nature" that moral education trains? Human beings are not by nature moral agents – in the following sense. We do not see moral facts in the direct way that we perceive colors and shapes. We do not grasp the moral truths about things by being informed of their names and natures. We require certain experiences – moral experiences – and interpretations of the experiences (instruction) to become aware of and responsive to a moral world. We may have an innate predisposition to morality: a capacity to act from duty and for the sake of the moral law. But if the moral capacity is natural, its actualization in our lives is not; it must be produced (*R* 23).

The conjunction of interpreted experiences with the acquisition of elements of a virtuous character presents the world as a moral world and establishes in us a "second nature." It is not a *new* nature; that would be impossible. It involves a construction of a conception of self and the development of innate possibilities by which we would be able, if only ideally, to become fully moral persons. What stands in the way of this is not as clear as traditional readings of Kant would suggest.

Construction proceeds from something and is directed towards something else. Accurate accounts of both ends are essential. About nonmoral human nature, Kant is often regarded as a crude hedonist: by nature, we pursue happiness; happiness is about pleasure or the satisfaction of desires. About the goal, morality, he is taken to be a strict deontologist. Neither view is right. The mistakes about happiness need to be sorted out first, for they stand in the way of understanding the empirical (nonmoral) side of the development of practical reason.

Consider the standard picture. Whether Kant is a simple hedonist about happiness, or allows for a multiplicity of ends pursued for the various reasons we pursue things, in either case, the state of happiness is some kind of contentment, the desire for happiness, roughly, the desire for an orderly and complete satisfaction of our desires. The role of reason in the pursuit of happiness is instrumental. We have desires; we set ends; reason points to means which we follow, insofar as we are rational. Discerning the connection between means and ends is a bit of technical or theoretical reasoning, as is the more complex task of timing and coordination that is necessary when ends are complex or of long duration. The normative grip of instrumental reasons on the will is secured through the end we desire: happiness.[3]

But this leaves a problem. The end, happiness, is indeterminate (*G* 418–19, *KpV* 25–7). It marks a practical challenge, not a discrete goal. As finite, that is, not self-sufficient beings, we have needs, and then desires for things that will meet or satisfy them (*KpV* 25). But needs are different, agent to agent, and for an agent, from time to time. Not all desires can be satisfied; some, we may think, should not be satisfied. Part of the project of happiness for each of us is to figure out what "our" happiness amounts to. The concept or idea of happiness provides little guidance. There are various reasons for this: the limitations of our own insight; the fact about desires that the satisfaction of some brings on others; the linkage between pain and the possibility of pleasure; and so forth. The technical diagnosis of the problem is that happiness is an ideal of imagination: "an absolute whole, a maximum of well-being in my present and in every future condition" (*G* 418). But an ideal of imagination can provide no rule of action. We would need Leibnizian omniscience – knowledge of all the possible lives we might live – to see a clear path (*G* 419).[4] In addition, Kant is close enough to stoic thought to regard the state of happiness as one in which we might approximate the condition of non-finite rational beings: a state of *Seligkeit*: blessedness, or bliss (*KpV* 25); a state of not wanting anything. Clearly, then, neither the idea of the end, nor the state we would be in if we reached the end, can be the source of determinate practical guidance.

If happiness is the region in which empirically conditioned practical reason has its own work to do, it is hard to see what work that is. There is one rational principle in the area – the hypothetical imperative – that instructs us to take sufficient means to our ends. But it applies indifferently to moral ends, trivial ends, and ends of happiness. It cannot, by itself, tell us what to do. Missing is any *non*moral rational guidance, theoretical or practical, about *ends*. Each of us is left to muddle along, to form an ordered set of ends from a happenstance stock of desires and interests plus some precepts drawn from accumulated human experience about which sorts of lives work well, and which do not.[5] There is no basis in the principle of self-love to say that not just any order of ends is an adequate conception of happiness. But if one can't even say *that*, then Kant's worry that empirically determined practical reason has pretensions to advance *its* principle to be the sole determining ground of willing makes no sense: its pretensions would be empty or futile, not wrong-headed. We therefore do not seem to have a notion of the nonmoral or empirical work of practical reason in terms of which one could understand the project of moral education as the task of developing the rational faculty *from* its "natural" state of concern for one's own well-being *to* a fully moral power.[6]

In fact, Kant has a fuller view of nonmoral practical reason.[7] It is, as it ought to be, a view about *value*: the object of rational action. To discern the content of nonmoral practical reason, Kant follows Rousseau. The key pieces of his view are therefore to be found in texts where he has Rousseau on his mind. I want to look at parts of two of these: one is the *Religion*, the other is the short, slightly satiric essay, "Conjectural beginning of human history." It may seem strange to rely on sources away from the critical philosophy for elements of Kant's view of *practical reason*, but once we have the view in sight, I think it will be evident that it is not unique to these texts.

"Conjectural beginning" offers a philosophical "reading" of *Genesis* as a history of the *emergence* of reason in the human species. The conceit may be strange, but the detail is instructive. The history is presented in four stages. Here, in summary, is what they are. The human animal begins as a creature of instinct, following that one sense tuned to discern in a general way the fitness or unfitness of things to be used for food, and so for survival: the sense of smell. The initial emergence of reason is provoked by the deployment of a second sense, sight, by means of which one could compare foods that are similar in look to those selected by smell, thereby extending "knowledge of sources of nourishment beyond the limits of instinct" (CBH 111). Human beings go beyond their animal nature as soon as they can ask whether a "this" that they are drawn to by one sense is comparable to a "that" that they are drawn to by another. Two things about this "moment" stand out. The awakening of reason comes from *comparison*, and the power that reason confers to alter the order of experience: "an ability to go beyond those limits that bind all animals" (CBH 112). Even so limited a deployment of reason brings problems. With the aid of imagination, reason generates new desires, desires for things for which there is no natural urge (even a natural urge to avoid), opening us to an "abyss" of choice: an infinitude of possible objects of desire. But note that the first distinctive act of reason is not taking means to ends, it is a comparative, *evaluative*, judgment.

The second stage of the emergence of reason belongs to the sexual instinct. The transformative moment in this domain is the discovery that by controlling the instinct (covering the genitalia), by interjecting the imagination between desire and its object, the possibilities of enjoyment can be greatly enhanced. If in the first stage the possible *objects* of desire are extended by comparison, in the second, *instinct itself* is reshaped by "making a propensity more internal and obdurate by removing [covering] the objects of the sense" (CBH 113). This is the discovery of "refusal": "the feat whereby man passed over from mere sensual to idealistic attractions, from merely animal desires eventually to love, from the feeling for the merely pleasant to the taste for beauty . . . " (CBH 113). Forsaking something that we immediately want, we come to want something we *imagine* would be better. Kant views this as laying the foundation for "true sociability": for moral agency and for culture. This is because, as a stage in the development of reason, it is about the redirection of the instincts, away from their natural objects and towards objects that reflect a constructed ideal. It is a first move in the construction of non-desire-based value. Not only does the redirection of instinct create new desires, the refusal of immediate sense attraction for the sake of an "idealistic attraction" establishes the possibility of *rational desires*.

The first and second stages of reason bring on a third: the capacity to think about one's life in terms of distant or possible ends. This is the fruit of knowledge. Once one can imagine an ideal and come to desire it, one is open to desires for things one does not have. This gives reason to plan, to construct an ideal of what will make life good. But the rational, constructive, and evaluative activity also reveals our limits as agents. One foresees a life of endless care, and its inevitable end, death. That is a source of despair; it is also a route to attachment to family and society, to living on through one's descendants and one's creations. In the third moment of reason, we are led to the introduction of the idea of *a human life*: the idea that different ways of living are worthwhile, not because of any amount of desire or satisfaction, but because they fulfill an ideal and enable us to resist despair through the extension of our lives into love and work.

"The fourth and final step that reason took in raising mankind altogether beyond the community of animals" concerns our sense of ourselves as a special kind of thing, different from and superior to animals (CBH 114). In this moment, human beings gain a sense of entitlement of use with respect to the nonhuman world, and, correlatively, of other persons as inappropriate subjects of command and involuntary exploitation. This sense of self and others as equal members of a kind – rational being – is the condition that makes distinctly human social life possible. We may be drawn together by instinct (self-interest or love), but we have true social relations as a function of reason – reason that identifies the value of humankind by distinguishing it from the use-value of the nonhuman.[8]

It is this complex development of reason, one that alters the very nature of the natural being – giving rise to new desires, new powers, endless travail, and imagined bliss – that characterizes what we are like as rational or reasoning beings. This is the rational nature that morality at once emerges from, constrains, and completes. The contrast between pure and empirical rational nature, then, is not captured by the pure rationality of the moral law, on the one hand, and, as we might have thought, "reason insofar as it is considered merely to be a tool for satisfying . . . many inclinations" (CBH 114), on the other.

The next piece of the account of the nonmoral development of practical reason comes from the discussion of human "predispositions" in the *Religion*. Though introduced there to help address the problem of evil, it provides key elements of the explanation of the incompleteness of the nonmoral rational will.[9]

The *Religion* divides the will into three parts, by function, "considered as elements in the fixed character and destiny of man" (R 21). Kant calls them predispositions to *animality*, *humanity*, and *personality*.[10] All are predispositions to *the good*, both in the sense that they do not of themselves prompt action contrary to morality, and in the sense that they (together) predispose "*towards good*," that is, "they enjoin observance of the moral law" (R 23). It is the second predisposition, to humanity, that tells us a bit more about comparative nonmoral practical reason. Again, let me give a quick summary.

The predisposition to *animality* is human physical nature; Kant describes it as "purely mechanical self-love, wherein no reason is demanded" (R 22). Its concerns are for self-preservation, for the propagation of the species (through the sexual impulse and the care of offspring), and "for community with other men, i.e., the social impulse" (R 22). Though no reason is required to explain the fact that human beings have these interests, as "original" elements of human nature, they organize the faculty of desire, giving a direction or point to desire that is independent of our will or wish.

At the other extreme is the predisposition to *personality*: "the capacity for respect for the moral law as *in itself a sufficient incentive of the will* (R 22–3). The point of calling this a predisposition is to point out that although good character needs to be acquired, it could not be acquired unless the human will had an interest in the moral law as a natural principle of its possible organization. Reason here is pure practical reason: a reason "which dictates laws unconditionally" (R 23).

In between the animal and the moral, as it were, is the predisposition to *humanity*. It involves practical reason, but a reason "subservient to other incentives" (R 23). However, it is subservient to nonrational incentives *not* because it is a deployment of instrumental reason; rather, practical reason serves nonrational incentives by making possible *comparative* assessments of happiness. The predisposition to humanity is an original (i.e. necessary) feature of human nature to "judge ourselves happy or unhappy only by making comparison with others" (*R* 22). We have a *physical* impulse to sociality; we come to have a *reason-supported* desire, given that we live with and among others, to make comparisons. The initial comparative impulse seeks equality with others (that no one be superior to me); but having no independent measure of worth, it is converted into an inclination to "acquire worth in the opinion of others" (*R* 22): no one should be in a position to judge me less worthy.

Suppose we describe the task of moral education as making the human predisposition to personality actual. On the traditional picture of our nonmoral natures and of empirical practical reason, we are end-seekers who strive for the maximal satisfaction of our desires. Nonmoral rationality is about means, either directly for the object of a desire, or about strategies to maximize desire-satisfaction of different kinds over a lifetime. If this were right, a moral educator's primary task would be to teach restraint: to increase the power of refusal and to restrain the pretensions of self-love to practical priority in agents' maxims. This is the familiar lesson-plan of morality versus self-interest. However, if the project of desire-satisfaction does not capture our nonmoral rational natures, the lesson-plan needs to be revised.

Morality, as the expression of pure practical reason, completes and perfects what we are as rational agents.[11] This completion project must connect with the distinctive features of nonmoral rational nature. Two things have moved to center stage. One is that the evaluative principle of empirical practical reason is comparative. The other is the deeply social orientation of rational agency. The instinct to sociality insures that we do not live our lives in isolation, while the comparative principle leads us to a sense of our own well-being that is continuously measured against the well-being of others. This suggests a different picture of the ways in which we are incomplete and likely to be imperfect. If reason's employment gives us a sense of the open-endedness of choice and freedom from the press of instinct, a merely comparative measure of value gives us no sense of direction; it is incomplete. But this is not the whole of the problem. In the context of our inherently social lives, the wish not to be or seem worse off than others gives way to an "arms race" for defensive superiority. Jealousy and competition become the motivational bases that give a shape to our lives. Prompting vice and wrongdoing, it is clearly an imperfect solution to the indeterminateness of our concept of happiness. Where the highest goal is to be comparatively best, the requirement that we give priority to moral over nonmoral incentives is likely to be reversed.[12]

These are the concerns that the curriculum of moral education needs to address. But there are limits on what it can include. The classical eudaimonist's move to a normative account of happiness is unavailable: for Kant, the concept of happiness *is* indeterminate. Kant also holds that the exaggerated Stoic ideal of restraint and renunciation makes human agents vulnerable to despair. We just do seek happiness; the satisfaction of desires is an ineliminable element of our practical orientation as finite rational beings with needs. Morality brings order – a final end; it creates the rational unity of a system of ends (under the moral law) that the principle of self-love cannot provide. But order may not be bought at the cost of ignoring happiness. The demand for happiness is ineradicable in us, and when made subordinate to the moral law, good. But the limited efficacy of human agency in bringing about its ends, combined with the moral indifference of nature, leaves a gap between morality and (deserved) happiness. This lack of fit between virtue and worldly reward cannot be set aside on rational grounds, since it is reason itself that disposes us to seek a whole that fully exhibits order.[13]

One response to this problem is the doctrine of moral faith (*KpV* 107ff.). Belief in the immortality of the soul and the existence of God can give us confidence in the extension of the place and time, as well as the cause, of eventual moral order: of everything turning out for the best. There is, however, another response that Kant offers that is more directly concerned with the idea of moral education and the curricular needs of social agents whose imperfect rational natures are comparative. It looks to social or civic life of a certain sort as a kind of "finishing school" for moral development. I want to consider two elements of this – two "moments" of moral education, if you will – one drawn from the idea of interpreting history from a cosmopolitan point of view and the other, an odd argument about voting. It will turn out that the instruction they give is much better suited to completing the nature of social beings whose rational nature seeks unconditioned goodness, than to some Hobbesian project of restraining unbridled self-interest. Moreover, they provide something that rational faith cannot: a means of ameliorating the competitiveness and conflict that comparative judgments provoke.[14]

III

To make room for this "public classroom" for moral education, the first thing we need to do is to dispel some myths about the aprioristic austerity and individualism of Kant's ethics. The moral life of a Kantian moral agent takes place as anyone's life does, within a specific social setting. One has various duties and obligations, invariantly, Kant thinks, concerned with norms for property and promises, truthfulness, vulnerability to needs, and some story about the development and training of the capacities we make use of in rational action. These duties and obligations to self and others have specific and local forms. We make promises this way, or in these contexts; we take care of basic human needs through private charity or the institutions of the welfare state; we have specific norms of civility and respect, and reciprocal sensitivities to insult and offense; and so on. Although the moral law under-determines specific moral requirements, it is of course not neutral with respect to the ways things get worked out. In addition to providing the foundation for any claim of ultimate normative authority, it sets limits on the range of things that can have moral authority (or at least on the range of arguments that can be deployed to establish duties), and provides formal conditions that putative duties have to meet.

Though this way of thinking about morality is superficially at odds with the classical story of Kantian moral judgment – individual agents separately determining the permissibility of their actions through use of the Categorical Imperative test procedure – it is in fact necessary if the classical story is to make sense. The Categorical Imperative is a rule of form for maxims of action. For an agent's action to be morally justified (permissible), her maxim of action must be a real instance of a possible universal law for rational nature. Context specificity comes with the agent's maxim: a principle that describes an action as it is taken to be choiceworthy, containing, therefore, the local descriptive and evaluative concepts an agent uses in making her choice. Further, moral judgment will have no purchase on a maxim unless it is described using morally salient concepts *prior to* any use of the Categorical Imperative. And these concepts, like the others an agent uses, will be social and local.[15]

We might say: moral life takes place within a community of moral judgment. The rules of salience that identify the features of our circumstances that require moral attention, as well as the regulative principles of deliberation, are social rules acquired through participation in a moral community. Even the most basic moral facts – what counts as a harm that sets a moral claim, what counts as conditions for a valid agreement – are functions of social practice. Neither agents' moral circumstances nor their obligations can be understood without locating them within a social setting. This is not in any way an aberration or something ideal moral theory might avoid.

The social nature of moral concepts is not merely an external fact about them: that they are taught or acquired in social contexts. The moral concepts that agents use to describe a moral world are ones they reason with, by themselves and with others. The terms of reasoning must be ones that can be shared. Nor are moral concepts merely names for states of character, objects, or events of certain kinds – "vicious," "laudable," "murder." In using a moral concept, an agent accepts a rationale that alters a range of attitudes and judgments. If deceit is judged impermissible as a routine means because it subverts the conditions of respect for rational agency, then I am drawn to think about my communications with others in different ways than I would if I viewed deceit as ruled out because it causes harm. In the latter case, carefully paternalistic deceit could be justified, as might partial truths that saved feelings, to say nothing of lies that promote the greater good. None of these survive according to the former rationale. But this is not all. The different rationales alter the way we think about speech, and about those to whom we speak. In one case words have effects that need to be assessed on a calculus of benefits and harms; in the other, our words belong to a grid of connection with others like us, whose very ability to act *as rational agents* is partly dependent on what we say. Consider the different terms one would use when apologies were necessary – what one would be sorry for doing. A community of moral judgment is the context that makes such normatively governed activity intelligible.

Local moral concepts support *objective* moral judgments just in case the local concepts themselves are expressions of moral principle (i.e. if they can be shown to express the value of rational agency). Thus one of the tasks of moral education is to provide the conceptual resources through which we can construct objectively valid values. We may be brought up to respect our elders; the right kind of moral education puts us in a position to evaluate and then re-found the practice as its value is commensurate with the moral regard all are owed. Getting it right – distinguishing, say, respect for experience from deference to status-authority – is something we rarely figure out entirely on our own. This kind of developmental dependence is quite general. Consider the movement of desire from appetite to value. For any X we desire, it is (in the beginning) natural to want more of it. Natural satiety responses school us to the value of "enough" for some desirable things. For others, we may need to wait on the social lessons about acquisitiveness and greed to understand when and why more is too much. For still others, it may only be within the space of a critical public culture that we can come to see that something whose accumulation seemed to us natural and right is in fact a product of morally suspect social institutions. In all of these cases, what we require are lessons in value.

If it is in and through the creation of a community of moral judgment that practical reason develops, then the primary work of moral education is not about the repression of the errant dispositions and impulses of its trainees. That would fit a view of us as susceptible to moral imperatives, but lacking the full power of practical reason – as if we had moral ends, but only instrumental reason. But we are not like that. Moral education for us is about the creation of the right sorts of desires and ends within institutions that support and enhance them *as* the desires and ends of practically rational agents.

IV

Suppose this is all reasonable. There is a practical puzzle. Moral education comes in part through social institutions. The institutions themselves are not typically based on principles that are morally well-founded. They arise and change through various forces, only some of them intentionally directed. Not all change and not all institutions are good. How, morally speaking, are we to make sense of this? Moral education, though dependent on the institutions in place, must also provide tools of criticism. Bad institutions need re-formation, others need to be re-founded to give them the moral content that their "natural" histories do not provide.

In the essay "Idea for a universal history from a cosmopolitan point of view," Kant provides an approach to these issues through a slightly different, but related question: How is empirical change for the better possible when most agents of change are not themselves good, nor even striving to be good? He responds this way. Social change is caused by a natural mechanism of – in Kant's terminology – "unsocial sociability." It is a background process, bringing persons into conflict with one another that they cannot resolve through social separation, but can resolve through further and more complex social connection. This would not be the case if the conflict was driven by greed (which might allow vanquishing or eliminating competitors), but is possible because the conflict is about status and excellence: something one wants more of, but wants it *from* others.[16] Agents are thus led by their deeper needs to adjust and readjust their social order, moving without intention towards more interesting moral possibilities.

On Kant's view, though the possibilities are created by the mechanism of unsocial sociability, their realization is not similarly determined. He holds that the causes of change need to be seen as, understood as, causes for some good. The idea of a progressive history provides a moral-teleological interpretation of the causal story: it makes sense of historical events. But *why* would a moral agent (an *autonomous* moral agent) need to have a progressive view of history? Suppose there were no such view? And what "good" can having such a view do for an agent? Is it just a palliative – a further requirement of moral faith – giving hope to those trying to do the right thing while all around them evil flourishes? How could agents' locating themselves within an historical narrative of moral progress provide a condition necessary *for* moral progress? (IUH 22–4).

From either a historical or contemporary sociological perspective, the dense complexity of social life resists any univocal empirical interpretation. Whether we take the "meaning" of history to be progressive or to reveal cycles of hegemonic oppression, we do take it to mean something: something worth contesting. Actions have intentional and social meaning (typically both, though this can come apart). Whether one is honored as "fighting the good fight" or accused of being a "running dog of capitalism" is a function of a reading of the social context of action. Not every period of history can be interpreted to mean what one likes, but the inaccessibility of causes and the complexity of effects leave room for some debate about what is going on. Where a progressive interpretive narrative is possible, it can establish a social context that allows agents an expanded range of effective moral meaning for their actions and efforts, making possible further developments of institutions and of moral character.

Kant develops this idea by means of an interpretation of the rise of republican constitutionalism and the end of "wars of violent self-expansion" as a stage in the development of empirical moral character. He argues that to create a true culture of morality requires "a long internal working of each political body toward the education of its citizens" in circumstances of lawful freedom and international peace (IUH 21). Equality of citizenship and maximal liberty constrained by rights, on the one hand, and economic well-being and public education, on the other, provide the conditions in which the exercise of moral autonomy could be most fully realized in a community of persons. Given that these are multi-generational ambitions, realizable through "no one's" good intentions, and given that progress of this sort tends not to be visible through any indisputable markers (the path to stable peace and constitutional democracy was to be through war, industrial oppression, imperialism), how one looked at things from within the process would matter. It could make a difference to how events developed, and *would* make a difference to the sort of person one became as events unfolded. Belief that one's actions occur within a course of change for the better gives one access to resources of endurance, tolerance, generosity, even forgiveness. These are not merely the sort of things that make one a better person, though they do that; they also serve to promote continuing moral progress. If we believe that our actions can, over time, amount to something positive, then we may adopt ends and endorse institutions that support the direction of change, even if doing so involves some sacrifice or risk. In the absence of such belief, we lose important reasons to act in concert, to take risks together. There may then seem to be better reasons for risking little, for conserving whatever we have, and if we have little, conditions for nihilism or despair. A shared progressive narrative makes possible a kind of boot-strapping: a sense of the direction of history helps give history direction; it is a way of taking hold of impersonal events that brings them into the sphere of autonomous action.

There is of course no guarantee that a direction of history endorsed by an interpretation gets things right. Supporters of all sorts of millenarian ideals see their faith as creating the conditions for the "new beginning." The Kantian picture is therefore no better than its portrayal of the moral possibilities of constitutional democracy and world peace – the former for its commitment to equality of persons, the latter for the liberation of resources, material and human, for securing welfare and the public culture of reason. If that still leaves too much room for injustice, racism, or sexual oppression, or if it turns out, for reasons we cannot imagine, to be the condition for the loss and not the gain of moral culture, then Kant is wrong about the circumstances in which the rational and moral capacities of human beings can be most fully developed.

The possibility of a progressive history can make a difference even where institutions are unjust. Growing up in an unjust culture that presents itself as natural or inevitable, one might take oppressive social roles for granted and so justified; one may view gross inequalities as unfortunate, but deserved; one may see oneself as injured, but without moral standing to complain or resist. If a progressive history can include these institutions, it can support reform.[17] By providing an account of a culturally available moral ideal in a framework that represents it as a real possibility – that is, connected to an ongoing direction of historical change – the progressive history offers a transformed mode of action and expression. Victims do not need to see their injuries as deserved; the virtue of unwilling "oppressors" need not be limited to kindness, charity, or even self-sacrifice.

A moral culture that contains an historically progressive moral story (of itself) does not by itself turn moral persons into agents of change; nor does it (necessarily) give them revolutionary or even social reformist goals. This is for two reasons. First, the mechanism of change is not the individual moral action. The effect of individual action is limited; most of what most agents do does not reach beyond a small sphere of local interactions. It makes no moral sense to oblige agents to make attempts where they cannot succeed. Second, individual agents act within a framework of institutions that constrain what their actions can do or signify (I can give away what property I have; I cannot make it the case that what I give away is not itself property). On the other hand, recognizing the natural limitations on the possible end-related effects of individual action does not sanction a moral posture of passivity. If, for example, moral change occurs largely through change in institutions, then moral agents may be obliged to support and promote those institutions which support the possible realization of progressive moral culture. The promotion of and participation in democratic institutions would be an instance of such an obligation.

When public moral education locates us in a progressive historical narrative, we have two views of ourselves as moral agents. As individuals, our primary task is one of responsible integrity: good willing. As persons sharing the world with other persons, we try to see our activity as promoting and sustaining moral culture. In times of moral regression or catastrophe, infertile virtue may be all that is available. But if we can plausibly tell ourselves that we live in morally interesting times, concern for our own integrity is only part of the story.

Kant's view is neither strongly teleological nor at odds with rational autonomy. The mechanism of historical progress, our "unsocial sociability," is not a process akin to erosion, moving us into ever increasing connection until our "irritation" is resolved with the arrival of the liberal state and the end of wars of international aggression. Rather, we are constituted "by nature" to respond to certain kinds of difficulty with reason-responsive creativity and ingenuity. In similar fashion the inevitable frustrations of childhood are experienced as goads to development and learning, background features that encourage us to increase the scope of our autonomy. We are no less fully autonomous agents in the historical-social context for the fact that we might be goaded by difficulties in our "natural" interactions with others to develop and endorse increasingly effective means of living together – something we might do if we are given a sense of direction by a philosophical, morally informed sense of our history.

Participation in a political order of the right sort – a republic of equal citizens under law with a progressive public culture – thus completes the process of moral education. "By nature," human sociality is driven to competition; if not the numbing Hobbesian "power after power," still a ceaseless Rousseauian quest for public esteem. The missing element is an independent conception of the good that could give order and meaning to a human life. It can be found in a form of social life where esteem is a function of moral respect, and well-being is secured through free action under law. Republican citizenship (with peace) provides the next step in moral education, bringing empirical practical reason to completion through individual experience of an order of persons under self-given law.

To illustrate the way this is supposed to work, I want to take a brief look at Kant's discussion of the morally edifying role of *voting*. According to Kant, through participation (voting) in a constitutional republic, citizens get to experience the *form* of moral autonomy: freedom *and* constraint under law of their own making.[18] It is a kind of modeling, and, quite plausibly, a step in grasping the essence of moral agency. But suffrage is limited. Not every one who lives under the law is qualified to make it: only those who are economically independent can have the right to vote. Although Kant's argument for this is impossible to defend in all its detail, the rationale for the limit nonetheless points to, and does not undermine, the heart of the moral lesson political participation is to provide.

Kant argues that although "all men [including women and children] are free and equal *under* public law as already enacted . . . they are not equal with respect to the right to *enact* law" (*TP* 294). There is nothing very strange in distinguishing the class of persons under the law's protection from those who can vote; non-citizens, children, prisoners, are routinely held to lack requisite standing or qualifications. The odd feature is the particular qualification Kant uses: that a voter must be "his own master (*sui iuris*): that he own some sort of property – among which may be counted any skill, craft, fine art, or science that supports him" (*TP* 295).[19] Mere laboring for a wage does not count; one is then, Kant holds, acting as a servant. Kant allows that the distinction between skilled making and mere laboring is difficult to draw. And it is hardly clear, even if we grant the distinction, why offering one's labor for hire would make one like a servant. But why should being, or being like, a servant disqualify one from voting? What in the distinction between producing and laboring, and between self-mastery and economic dependency, could be construed as vital to the moral status of voting in a constitutional republic?[20]

Perhaps one might argue this way: a servant is someone who is under the rule of another. If one's life-preserving activity (what one does to secure food and shelter) is directly dependent on the direction of others, then one's life is under their rule, and not one's own. But if, as Kant says (*RL* 315), dependence of this sort does not touch one's "freedom and equality as a human being," why does it disqualify one from making law? However difficult

Kant thinks it is to make the maker/worker distinction, he thinks the conclusion about voting, given the distinction, is obvious.

We might consider whether Kant could think there is some relation that the skilled artisan has to the law – and so to law-making – that an unskilled laborer (in this way like a servant) does not. Kant unhelpfully suggests that the artisan, but not the laborer, has something to sell: a product whose transfer requires the law of contract (*TP* 295n; *RL* 314).[21] A better argument might point to the fact that the day-laborer needs the law primarily for protection: it secures his rights and prevents his exploitation. His *activity* does not require the environment of law, it can take place under any law that protects him. By contrast, the work of the independent artisan is facilitated and enhanced by laws that promote liberty (free contract, freedom of movement, etc.). Where there is liberty, the artisan not only can develop his distinctive kind of activity, he is encouraged by the free activity of others to do so. He is in a position to acquire a civic personality, recognized and respected as such by other citizens. This, at least, is an argument of the right form.

The independent artisan can thus regard the law as an expression of his own activity and will, not merely as a source of command and protection.[22] Because of his social role, he understands what law is; and *that* is what qualifies him to vote. Moreover, since his relation to the law in voting resembles the relation of the moral agent to the moral law – the law he submits to is a law of his free activity – voting is training in autonomy. It provides the voter with an experience of himself and his co-citizens that models moral personality. By contrast, the day-laborer's relation to the law is heteronomous; the law is a means for his survival, not an expression of his freedom. He therefore lacks an understanding of what the law is, which makes him unfit to make law. The training to moral personality that republican civil life can provide is unavailable, given the limits of his social circumstances.

Making law for himself and with others who are free and equal citizens, a voting citizen not only experiences autonomy, he gains insight into the form of a kingdom of ends. Voting is thereby training for moral culture. Moreover, because citizens understand what law signifies for autonomous agents, the laws made by them will keep the possibility of ownership and independence open to all (*TP* 296). Free and independent citizens also support peace. War and the "never remitting preparation for war" drain resources that could be put to public education, education that would train all persons to be independent agents and citizens in their ways of thinking. In short, voting citizens come to respect the moral autonomy of all, and read their history in a progressive way.

This brings home the force of the claim that insofar as Kantian moral education is a training to autonomy, it is not just a lifelong task for individuals, but a task of culture. The right social institutions are the background of sound moral judgment: institutions that are just and whose rational foundations are deliberatively accessible. But beyond this, participation in a kind of civic life wherein one can see oneself as having a role in an historically progressive process is necessary for the full development of practical reason, in oneself and also, Kant thinks, in the species. This re-ordering of the psychic and social world is not a second-best approximation of the way things would be if only pure moral autonomy were not interfered with by the empirical morass of desire and social disorder. The completion of moral education brings into being what Kant calls the "ectypal world"

– nature transformed by reason "determining our will to confer on the sensuous world the form of a system of rational beings" (*KpV* 43). Training to autonomy makes autonomy empirically real.

NOTES

References to and citations of Kant's works are given parenthetically in the text, using the abbreviations below, citing the page number of the relevant volume of *Kants gesammelte Schriften* (published by the Preussiche Akademie der Wissenschaft, Berlin). The translations of works quoted from are listed below.

KrV   *Critique of Pure Reason* [lst edn (A), 1781; 2nd edn (B), 1787], trans. N. Kemp Smith (New York, St Martin's Press, 1965).

KpV   *Critique of Practical Reason* [1788], trans. Lewis White Beck, 3rd edn (New York, Library of Liberal Arts, 1993).

G   *Grounding of the Metaphysics of Morals* [1785], trans. James W. Ellington (Indianapolis, Ind., Hackett, 1981).

CBH   "Conjectural beginning of human history" [1786], in *Perpetual Peace and Other Essays*, trans. Ted Humphrey (Indianapolis, Ind., Hackett, 1983).

IUH   "Idea for a universal history from a cosmopolitan point of view" (1784), in *Perpetual Peace and Other Essays*.

RL   *Rechtslehre*, part I of *The Metaphysics of Morals* [1797], trans. Mary Gregor (Cambridge, Cambridge University Press, 1996).

DV   *Tugendlehre*, part II of *The Metaphysics of Morals*.

R   *Religion within the Limits of Reason Alone* [1793], trans. Theodore M. Greene and Hoyt H. Hudson (New York, Harper Torchbooks, 1960).

TP   *On the Old Saw: That May be Right in Theory But it Won't Work in Practice* [1793], trans. E. B. Ashton (Philadelphia, Pa., University of Pennsylvania Press, 1974).

A   *Anthropology from a Pragmatic Point of View* [1797], trans. Mary Gregor (The Hague, Martinus Nijhoff, 1974).

1 This locution, while familiar, is strictly speaking inaccurate. The reference is not to some separate kind of practical reason, but always to "empirically conditioned practical reason."

2 It is *reasoning* because it is deriving a particular from the universal, not judgment, strictly speaking, which is "discovering the particular as it is an instance of . . . rules" (A199). This use of reason, also called judgment, is creative.

3 Helpful discussions of these and related issues may be found in Christine M. Korsgaard, "The normativity of instrumental reason," in G. Cullity and B. Gaut (eds) *Ethics and Practical Reason* (Oxford, Oxford University Press, 1997) and Andrews Reath, "Hedonism, Heteronomy and Kant's Principle of Happiness," *Pacific Philosophical Quarterly* 70 1 (March 1989), pp. 42–72.

4 To the extent that an ideal of the imagination is like an "ideal of reason," it is not a concept of a totality, but a representation of it via a particular (*KrV* A567/B596–A571/B599). It gives an "archetype" of a happy life: a person of the right (ripe) age who is content with her life; someone without impossible-to-satisfy yearnings or age-inappropriate projects or health-impairing vices; a person whose life contained a good balance of activity, rest, enjoyment, friends, work, and so forth. Practical indeterminacy comes not so much from lack of omniscience as from the ineluctable particularity of any copy of the archetype. When we imagine a happy life, we can recognize its form; we know what elements to look for. How to go about living such a life remains a problem. An ideal of imagination is unlike an ideal of reason in being "blurred" or "shadowy" and, most importantly, in furnishing no rule (*KrV* A570/B598).

5 These are the *Groundwork*'s "counsels of reason" (*G* 418).

6 This is not to say that advancing the interests of the self makes no sense. The point about the claim is that these interests have nonmoral, rational support.

7 What makes it seem that he does not is mainly a function of his parsimony of argument. Where Kant is concerned to argue that neither the principle of self-love nor the end of happiness can yield practical *necessity*, he needs to argue no more than to the indeterminateness of happiness as an end. Where the issue is the determining ground of volition, setting the object of the will, the only relevant fact is the passivity of the will with respect to any empirically given object (the heteronomy of its principle). Both arguments assume the contrast: that morality requires law or autonomous willing. It is not part of the argument structure of the *Groundwork* or *Critique of Practical Reason* to make anything of the fact that without morality, practical reason's ambitions to provide a complete order of ends cannot be realized. For unless morality is possible, the apparently self-defeating ambition of empirically determined practical reason would show no more than the truth of Hume's view.

8 This view of other human beings is "early preparation for the limitations that reason would in the future place upon him in regard to his fellow man and which is far more necessary to establishing society than inclination and love" (CBH 114).

9 In order to represent the inaccessible ground of free choice, Kant offers an hypothesis about a "property of the will which belongs to it by nature": what he calls "the original predisposition to good in human nature" (*R* 21).

10 Kant indicates that we might have other predispositions, but only these have "immediate reference to the faculty of desire and the exercise of the will" (*R* 23). What might others be? Sub-volitional physical processes, perhaps, such as digestion (patterns of hunger, satiety, and rest). Perhaps also certain aesthetic predispositions: that we will experience disinterested pleasure from certain forms. Perhaps even the systematic impulses of Reason.

11 The Categorical Imperative is the unique principle of unconditioned goodness that provides closure to the valuing activities of agents. It offers a final end – rational nature as an end-in-itself – that both sets a limiting condition on our ordinary pursuits, and, more profoundly, gives meaning to our actions *as* the actions of a self-consciously rational agent.

12 This is argued explicitly in *Religion* 24–5.

13 If we set aside religious explanations, it is not obvious *why* reason should demand that virtue be rewarded with happiness. There is the argument from order: the combination of vice with happiness or virtue with suffering offends against one's sense of things happening for a sufficient reason. But that sense begs the question. Why should there be this connection between moral character and happiness at all? Only if the connection has been already made does it make sense to talk about being *rewarded for* one's virtue or about having earned it. In fact, the connection is already present in the actions of both the virtuous and the vicious agent. Each, by nature, pursues happiness; not in the same way, to be sure, and not with the same substantive end (the happiness of the virtuous agent is different from the happiness of the vicious one). But only the happiness-seeking actions of the virtuous agent are, from the point of view of reason, fully justified. The happiness that a virtuous person has rational warrant to have is not some extrinsic gift of heavenly bliss, but the success of her actions and plans. That is why, if reason had control over nature, the gap between virtue and happiness would be closed. (The proportional thesis introduces complexities I cannot take up here, as does the idea that virtue should protect against unhappiness that results from external bad luck.)

14 The passions that are aroused in comparative contest – "the manias for honor, for power, and for possession" – both require and enslave practical reason. Their insatiability makes those in their grip passive, and because they are directed to other persons, they incline judgment to consider "the mere opinion of others about the value of things as equivalent to their real value (A266–70)."

15 These arguments are developed in chapters 4 and 10 of my *The Practice of Moral Judgment* (Cambridge, Mass., Harvard University Press, 1993), and in my essay "Pluralism and the community of moral judgment," in D. Heyd (ed.) *Toleration: an Elusive Virtue* (Princeton, NJ, Princeton University Press, 1996).

16 Of course this only works if the others are those whose respect means something – not slaves.

17 Of the Rousseauian emergence of social life, characterized by competition, pride, *amour de soi*, Kant says: "Thus are taken the first true steps from barbarism to culture, which consists in the social worth of man; thence gradually develop all talents, and taste is refined; through continued enlightenment the beginnings are laid for a way of thought which can in time convert the coarse, natural disposition for moral discrimination into definite practical principles, and thereby change a society of men driven together by natural feelings into a moral whole" (IUH 15).

18 "In this way [entering civil society], the first true steps from barbarism to culture, in which the unique social worth of man consists, now occur, all man's talents are gradually developed, his taste is cultured, and through progressive enlightenment he begins to establish a way of thinking that can in time transform the crude natural capacity for moral discrimination into definite practical principles and thus transform a *pathologically* enforced agreement into a society and, finally, into a *moral* whole" (IUH 21).

19 Women are of course disqualified before the argument gets going; they, like children, cannot be their "own master." That Kant lacks the moral imagination or will to resist this idea is hardly news.

20 It is possible that Kant is merely an apologist for traditional privilege. It does not seem to me the most interesting assumption. It is in any case not so traditional to give artisans and large landowners equal political rights (*TP* 296).

21 Kant seems to lack the distinction between making one's will available and selling one's labor power.

22 The feudal artisan, by contrast, must submit himself to the authority of master or guild.

20

JEFFERSONIAN AMBIVALENCES

Eva T. H. Brann

Toward the end of the nineteenth century "the canonization of Jefferson the Educator" (Peterson: 240) had, after a half century's eclipse, been pretty well completed, especially in the South. Three ideas were especially ascribed to him: the duty of the state to educate its citizens for its own and their well-being; a unified, merit-selective system from elementary school to university; the specifically American character of an education on republican principles: practical, locally controlled and as free as possible from needless discipline.

Nowadays Jefferson is still thought of as that one among the founders who was most interested in education, and, more concretely, he is known as the father of the University of Virginia. His writings on education, consisting of legislative draft bills, reports, one tract, reading lists, and many private letters, are readily accessible in collections of his writings. The most significant of these are: the Bill for the More General Diffusion of Knowledge (1779) and its revised revival of 1817; Queries XIV and XV from the *Notes on the State of Virginia* (1785); the "Report of the Commissioners Appointed to Fix the Site of the University of Virginia," known as the "Rockfish Gap Report," the founding document of the University of Virginia (1818); the letter to Peter Carr, with a reading list (1787); and the "natural aristocracy" correspondence with John Adams (1813).

Jefferson's expressions on this as on all topics are forceful and crystalline; irony and ambiguity are not among his literary modes. And yet, a reader of these documents is unlikely to come away with unequivocal answers to the following ten questions, answers to which would specify more closely the implications of his three main educational ideas:

1 Was Jefferson an egalitarian or an elitist?
2 Did he take a utilitarian or a liberal view?
3 Did he support indoctrination or free inquiry?
4 Was he anti-clerical or tolerant?
5 Was he for or against moral instruction?
6 Were his educational schemes modern or classical?
7 Was he successful as an innovator?
8 Was he influential?
9 Did he have a theory of education?
10 Does he offer lessons for the present?

To the question why the marble definition of his written opinions and the force of his public activities should leave so much of his thought in doubt, I might venture a very general answer, whose exposition is beyond the scope of this article: Jefferson was first by temperament and then by habit a man of the Enlightenment, of which finished surfaces and clouded depths are characteristic. More specifically, Jefferson had an ever-active mind, stocked, as he himself would have put it, with information and ideas, but he had little zest – had even an antipathy – for coherent foundations and any sort of metaphysics. Consequently he felt no urgency to harmonize all his opinions, as long as they could be brought under the general aegis of reason and republicanism. I might add that Peterson (pp. 244–5) gives a vivid account of the well-defined yet totally opposite impression Jefferson's person made on different observers.

Using the ten questions above as rubrics, I shall sketch out some of the evidence for an answer on either side.

1 WAS JEFFERSON AN EGALITARIAN OR AN ELITIST?

The quandary presents itself most sharply in one and the same document, the "Bill for the Diffusion of Knowledge," to be read with its expositions in Query XIV of the *Notes*. The bill introduces a comprehensive selective system of education for the state. Every county was to be divided into "hundreds," each of which was to establish and support an elementary school to be attended gratis by all male *and female* children of the locality for three years (or longer at private expense). Each year one poor boy "of the best and promising genius and disposition" was to be chosen by the overseers to go to one of the twenty "grammar schools" of the higher districts. After a year or two of trial "the best genius" was again to be selected to attend for four more years, and "the residue dismissed." Finally half the remaining seniors "of most hopeful genius" would attend the College of William and Mary for three years for free. The selections at each state were to be made by overseers and visitors eminent for learning, integrity and "fidelity to the commonwealth," by impartial and diligent examination, and by inquiry.

This selection by merit was somewhat more complicated than here reported, and included several stages at which "those thought to be of the least promising genius and disposition" were to be discontinued. The phrase that has given most offense and has been thought to expose Jefferson's elitism occurs in Query XIV: "By this means twenty of the best geniuses will be raked from the rubbish annually . . . "

There is no gainsaying the fact that this system is severely meritocratic: literally meritocratic because the selection is for republican *leaders* and, as we will see below, their education is sharply distinguished from that of mere citizens. The preamble of the bill also makes it clear that Jefferson is more preoccupied with preventing tyranny by illuminating "as far as practicable, the minds of the people at large" than with giving every child a chance to develop its abilities.

On the other hand, the bill, in addition to its largest aim, "to diffuse knowledge more generally through the mass of the people," evinces if not a democratic faith in the sense of trust in the "mass" as republican rulers, certainly a demophilic disposition in the sense of belief in the improvability of the people through elementary learning. The "diffusion of knowledge among the people" is the instrument of progress (letter to Dupont de Nemours, April 24, 1816).

Note the incessant mention of "genius," that is, innate talent. The ground for Jefferson's ambivalence is to be found in his notion of a natural aristocracy, as communicated by letter to John Adams (October 28, 1813). The democratic element of this doctrine is the opposition of the naturally best to an artificial aristocracy "founded on wealth and birth" rather than "virtue and talents." Furthermore, in the same letter, instead of a national mass democracy, Jefferson proposes a state of "little republics" to which would be confided all the functions of self-government for which these are best qualified. These divisions he called *wards*, the very same term he substituted in the bill of 1817 for the *hundreds* of its antecedent bill of 1779. There is probably no way around the fact that Jefferson was, in most moods, a republican (small "r") rather than a democrat, who insisted on differential dispositions and endowments with respect to virtue and talent.

When I say in "certain moods," I mean especially in matters of education. One must not forget that the foundational statement of America, "that all men are created equal" was formulated by him. He meant in the Declaration as elsewhere that human beings were equal with respect to rights. He wrote, for example, about Negroes:

> Whatever their degree of talent, it is no measure of their rights. Because Sir Isaac Newton was superior to others in understanding, he was not therefore lord of the person or property of others.
>
> (letter to Henri Grégoire, February 25, 1809)

These sentiments are echoed fairly exactly by Lincoln, a much warmer believer in the common people.

Again, in a letter to John Taylor (May 18, 1816) he expressed his faith in a strong republicanism – which he defines as having the greatest element of popular elections and control – because "the mass of citizens is the safest depository of their own rights."

The battle about Jefferson's egalitarian or elitist propensities, which is mainly about the question whether a commitment to democracy is a matter of love or of judgment, is very much alive today (Edmondson: 66; Koch: 165; Peterson: 246). It is therefore worth highlighting some remarkably prescient aspects of his proposed educational system.

It was within certain limits, a free public system. The significance of "free" coupled with "public" is greater than appears at first, for it meant that rich and poor were enabled – though of course not required – to attend school *together*, without any invidious means test and removed from the inequalities of private tutoring. This universality of access made the bill, as we shall see, unacceptable in its time; the legislature begrudged public money for the non-poor. The other feature, equally unviable, was the local control of the schools; the legislature preferred to have unified oversight. Add to these elements the absence of a religious test and the required impartiality of the examinations, the notion of a system through which a student could rise by merit, and the modern nature of the curriculum – and the picture of a daring initiative in popular education emerges, egalitarian in opportunity, selective in effect. And finally, there is the startling innovation of public elementary education for girls – perhaps not so surprising from one who could devote a large part of an affectionate letter to his 15-year-old daughter Patsy to gently chiding her into "conquering her Livy," since "it is a part of the American character to consider nothing as desperate" (March 28, 1787).

2 DID JEFFERSON TAKE A UTILITARIAN OR A LIBERAL VIEW OF EDUCATION?

I assume here the strict sense of liberal education, as learning done for its own sake, that is, contemplatively and for the self-perfection of the learner. Jefferson often expressed himself on the pleasure and happiness of study and reading, and he had no doubts about the formative force of education. The "improvement of the mind," the acquisition of knowledge, he says, "is a desirable, a lovely possession" (letter to Thomas Mann Randolph, August 27, 1786). The education of those chosen "to guard the sacred deposit of the rights and liberties of their fellow citizens" is specifically called "liberal" in the bill of 1779.

Simultaneously, Jefferson's view of education is unabashedly utilitarian. To be sure, few would-be legislatures would dare, then or now, to argue for pure self-development at public expense. But Jefferson was a most willing participant in the thoroughgoing utilitarianism of the Enlightenment expressed in the dictum "knowledge is power," political and scientific (e.g. letter to Joseph C. Cabell, January 22, 1820). Every writing of his on education or study emphasizes their uses, particularly but not only their public uses. Science is applied science; correct philosophy is "an anodyne," a pain-killer for the mind (letter to John Adams, August 15, 1820). Perhaps the most telling testimonial to this intellectual utilitarianism is a negative one: Jefferson managed to "read seriously" Plato's *Republic* and to dismiss it in terms of consummate scorn (letter to John Adams, July 5, 1814) without noticing that here was presented a contemplative education that might be instructive as a counterpart and foil to his own system: a progressive, highly selective curriculum, including the latest in science, and designed to educate leaders devoted to the public good.

Jefferson's positive statements of the purposes of education (through all grades) are set out most clearly in the Rockfish Gap Report (1818), which establishes the place and plan of his university. The lower schools are to give a citizen the information necessary to transact his own business and the ability to calculate his accounts and express his ideas; they are further to improve his morals and to help him to understand his duties to his various communities and to know his rights and how to exercise them. The upper schools are intended to shape the public officials on whom the general happiness depends, to expound o them the principles, structures and limits of government which are conducive to eedom, to teach them the political economy necessary to the free scope of public ustry, to introduce them to the mathematics and science useful to human comforts; and, erally, to form them to habits of reflection and correct action, rendering them examples tue to others and happiness within themselves."

feature that first leaps to the eye is the well-defined difference in the education of ple and its leaders (Brann 1979: 54ff.). The actual curriculum, which will be summarized below, was very modern but also quite theoretical, although Jefferson had written earlier concerning agriculture as a university subject:

> It is the first in utility, and ought to be first in respect . . . In every College and University a professorship of agriculture, and the class of its students, might be honored as the first, . . . closing their academical education with this, as the crown of all sciences.
>
> (letter to Joseph Priestley, November 14, 1803)

This is going pretty far in introducing applied science into a university curriculum, clearly farther than Jefferson was willing to go in his own foundation, whose studies are, though modern, not so determinedly vocational. Thus in the university it is chemistry, a *genuine* science, which "is meant . . . to comprehend the theory of agriculture."

Jefferson is a deep-dyed utilitarian, to be sure. Education is primarily for effective action in the economic and public realm, and the pursuit of truth is for the eradication or confining of error; his Bill for Establishing Religious Freedom (1779) says that: "Truth is great and will prevail if left to herself; that she is the proper and sufficient antagonist of error . . . "

This is noble utilitarianism, and moreover it is, as his public positions occasionally were, somewhat at odds with his private disposition: he took endless delight in the most varied sorts of knowledge. Nonetheless, this utilitarianism is also ultimate, for it is grounded in Jefferson's views of the nature of knowledge as this-worldly: always for a practical purpose, with no *intrinsic* object.

3 DID HE SUPPORT INDOCTRINATION OR FREE INQUIRY?

There can be no question about Jefferson's faith in free thought, such as is expressed in the quotation above from the Bill for Religious Freedom. In a letter advising his nephew Peter Carr on his education, he goes so far as to say: "Question with boldness even the existence of a god." And later: "Do not be frightened from this enquiry by any fear of consequences."

As for secular inquiries, Jefferson gave his future students, in the day of totally prescribed curricula, great freedom of choice. Contrasting his university's plan with the regulation of students at Harvard, he says:

> We shall, on the contrary, allow them uncontrolled choice in the lectures they shall choose to attend, and require elementary qualifications only, and sufficient age.
>
> (letter to George Ticknor, July 16, 1823)

The object was not only to allow for each student's bent, but to promote an "inquisitive mind" and independent judgment.

There is, however, an area in which Jefferson was candidly doctrinaire: the inculcation of republicanism, and republicanism of the right stripe. In a university in which the professors were, contrary to custom, allowed to choose their own textbooks, "heresies" in politics were to be prevented by prescribing the texts to be used. The poison whose diffusion Jefferson names is "quondam federalism" (letter to Joseph C. Cabell, February 5, 1825). Thus the minutes of the March 5 meeting of the Board of Visitors of the University provide that no principles incompatible with the Federal and State constitutions be taught. Besides works by Locke, Sidney, the Declaration, *The Federalist*, and Washington's Valedictory Address, it lists Madison's 1799 Resolutions of the Virginia Assembly on the Alien and Sedition Laws, which, whatever may have been their function at the time, became a founding document of the states' rights faction.

Jefferson was not alone in his intolerant zeal for the republic (Edmondson: 87). Several tracts on education of the period tend to take this tone. (See Smith, *passim*.) Destutt de Tracy in particular (Koch: 159), whose thought Jefferson admired, argued for a large literature of "propaganda" on behalf of republicanism.

Even taking account of the worries of the day, there does remain something paradoxical about a *norma docendi* (Jefferson's term), a course of indoctrination, on behalf of freedom.

4 WAS JEFFERSON ANTI-CLERICAL OR TOLERANT?

Under the previous question, Jefferson's encouragement of his nephew in absolutely free inquiry has been noted. But what if "Dear Peter" had decided to take orders? The suspicion arises that Jefferson would have been appalled, and that his passion for religious freedom had a strong admixture of a desire for deliverance from the clergy and the Church. He scarcely loses an opportunity for excoriating one or the other. In the very founding paper of his university he inveighs, somewhat gratuitously, against the resistance to progress of a Church allied to the state and afraid of having its usurpations unmasked (Rockfish Gap Report, 1818).

And yet, on the side of generous toleration, there are the novel and prescient arrangements he made for a religious presence in his university. As a public establishment the university could not offer religious, i.e. sectarian, instruction (as Jefferson noted with satisfaction) and had no professorship of Divinity, which was itself a novel situation. Jefferson therefore provided that the sects might be encouraged to come on campus to use the facilities, and might maintain professors there. Although he expected that "proximity might neutralize their prejudices" and meld their doctrines into a "general religion of peace, reason, and morality," the offer was made in good faith and was expected to be taken up (letter to Thomas Cooper, November 1, 1822). The arrangement was as genuinely liberal as it was cunningly politic.

5 WAS JEFFERSON FOR OR AGAINST MORAL EDUCATION?

Moral education is an ever-present element of Jefferson's plans for learning. But he is not referring to moral philosophy. It is "lost time to attend lectures in this branch" (letter to Peter Carr, August 10, 1787). The reason is his adherence to the notion of a "moral sense," which he learned from Lord Kames's *Essay on the Principles of Morality*. This sense is inborn. It might be naturally stronger or weaker, but it can be improved by exercise and good books; Jefferson recommends especially the writings of Sterne, which exercise this sense imaginatively.

Thus moral education, really moral training, consists not in reflection but in the absorbing of precepts of virtue (*Notes*, Query XIV), in cultivating the sentiments, and in emulating living exemplars (letter to Thomas Jefferson Randolph, November 24, 1808). Thinking about virtue is not a way to virtue; it may be a hindrance.

And yet, for himself, Jefferson reflected at unusual length on moral questions, especially in a letter to Thomas Law (June 13, 1814). His project here is to reject in turn truth, the love of God, beauty, and egoism as bases of morality. He takes most trouble about the last, because he wishes morality to be an impulse, though of course a good one: "The Creator would indeed have been a bungling artist had he intended man for a social animal, without planting in him social dispositions."

To meet the argument that a common moral sense is incompatible with the variety of mores, Jefferson falls back on utilitarianism: "nature has constituted *utility* to man, the standard and test of virtue." What is useful in one country is not so in another; thus the virtues differ, but the moral sense is universal.

It would seem that as so often stated, doctrine and personal practice were somewhat at odds: his announced view was that morality was the province of a sense rather than of the intellect, yet he felt compelled to clarify his mind about its basis.

It has been suggested, evidently in the light of the letter to Thomas Law, that Jefferson later became more amenable to the possibility of formal moral education (Smith: 314). But late in life he was still advising his daughter Martha (the Patsy who was to study her Livy) that attendance at ethical lectures would be time lost to her son (Edmondson: 72 ff.). To be sure, there was to be a professor of ethics in his university to whom were assigned certain duties of the discarded professor of divinity: to give proofs of the being of a God who is the author of all the relations of morality and to develop those moral obligations on which all sects agree. The impression is left that this ethicist is an incapacitated theologian, not a moral force.

6 WAS JEFFERSON'S EDUCATIONAL SCHEME MODERN OR CLASSICAL?

Even Jefferson's earliest scheme for higher education, the proposal to reform his own College of William and Mary, was novel in its day, with its strong language curriculum, which included oriental, northern and modern languages. The legislature refused this plan, but under Jefferson's influence the Board of Visitors instituted a reform at once even more radical and more practical. The two old schools of divinity went by the board (*nota bene*: without the handy pretext of constitutional compulsion). Instead there were professorships of public administration, medicine, physics and mathematics, moral philosophy (which subsumed international law and the fine arts!), and of modern languages; a sort of forerunner of the Indian Bureau, devoted to ethnographic studies, was also established (Adams: 41).

Four decades later the new university was not dissimilar in plan. (It has been observed that Jefferson's ideas on education remained fairly fixed over time.) The professors' subject-matters — each professor constituted a one-man department — were, however, more closely specified. There were again professorships in ancient and modern languages, but non-linguistic disciplines were preponderant. There were professorships in pure mathematics (including algebra and calculus), in mathematical physics, in chemistry, botany, medicine, government, and law, with allied subjects. Then there was a catch-all professorship for "ideology" (Jefferson's favorite philosophy, derived from Destutt de Tracy), "general grammar," the above-mentioned ethics, rhetoric, literature and fine arts (Rockfish Gap Report, 1818). Jefferson, who knew his way around the sciences, especially the empirical and applied ones, had produced a thoroughly modern curriculum. It would do a contemporary college honor.

What is remarkable is that a man who was fairly insouciant about jettisoning outdated institutions was so conservative with respect to classical learning. Classical reading was not only a private pleasure; he regarded the study of Greek and Latin as ideal for the proper development of young minds from age 8 to 15, in developing the memory without forcing the intellect:

> The learning of Greek and Latin, I am told, is going into disuse in Europe. I know not what their manners or occupations may call for: but it would be very ill-judged in us to follow their example in this instance.
>
> (*Notes*, Query XIV)

Consequently the grammar schools of his state system (equivalent to our high schools) were to teach Greek and Latin. Greek and Roman (together with English and American) history was to be taught in the elementary schools, albeit with the motive of forestalling Bible study at an immature age (Query XIV).

In this classical allegiance Jefferson was, for once, in the rear rather than the vanguard of American education, though no less wise for that.

7 WAS JEFFERSON SUCCESSFUL AS AN INNOVATOR?

Yes and no.

Jefferson's Bill of 1779 for reforming William and Mary failed in the legislature, though the college was modernized by its own board under his influence.

His Bill of 1779 for the More General Diffusion of Knowledge failed, though he never gave up, drafting a slightly altered version of a bill for a statewide progressive free public system as late as 1817 (Conant: 122).

Jefferson's proposal to the legislature of 1794 that the whole faculty of the College of Geneva be translated to Virginia was turned down as too grand and expensive (Adams: 45). His proposal, delivered in his sixth annual Presidential Message (1806), for a national university died in committee. (Each of the first six presidents advocated a national university, in vain.)

His University of Virginia alone succeeded. It was not the first functioning state university (that honor went to the University of North Carolina), but it was the first non-sectarian and publicly funded one. Jefferson regarded it as one of the three accomplishments that he wished to have commemorated on his tombstone: that he was author of the Declaration of Independence, author of the Virginia Statute for Religious Freedom, and father of the University of Virginia; they represent, it appears, his labors for Independence, Freedom and Enlightenment.

8 WAS JEFFERSON INFLUENTIAL IN SHAPING AMERICAN EDUCATION?

The subsequent history of public education in the Virginia legislature brought out clearly why Jefferson kept failing: the legislators were not ready for a system free to all on principle, not just for the poor, supported by local taxes, and not under centralized control. Jefferson had gotten two hundred years ahead of his fellow citizens. And that is the story of his influence in a nutshell: it lapsed with his death; Virginia made no progress toward free and truly public education. Conant reports (p. 37) that he could find no references to Jefferson in the writings of proponents of public schools between 1830 and 1860. When he emerged from this eclipse, in the late nineteenth century, Jefferson was lauded not for past accomplishments in education but for the blessings a future realization of his ideas might bring. These ideas, which now seem timely, were those mentioned in the beginning: the duty of the state to educate its citizens; a unified system from grammar school to university, universal at the bottom, merit-selective at the top; an education in harmony with American principles, secular, practical, locally controlled and non-coercive. But it does seem that those who now canonized Jefferson the Educator had been not so much influenced as anticipated by him. The story of his somewhat strange revivification is told by Peterson (pp. 238ff.).

9 DID JEFFERSON HAVE A THEORY OF EDUCATION?

The difficulty in determining Jefferson's concrete influence on education is surely related to that of delineating his theory of education. In many human activities, practical plans are more useful than ideal designs, but in education coherent theory is the *sine qua non* of long-range effectiveness.

Now Jefferson's mode of thought was far more suited to devising an educational system than to thinking out its intellectual foundations. His conception in its main features was, as we have seen, a brilliant innovation that became more timely with the passage of time. There were besides many incidental notions that are perfectly viable now: the extracurricular activities projected for the students at the university, such as training in the handling of tools (and, for that matter the appearance of religion as an extracurricular activity), the kindly relations envisaged between tutors and pupils together with the introduction of a disciplinary system based on "reason and comity," the encouragement to read more original authors and the wide choice permitted in attending lectures, the public education of girls.

All these add up to a powerful educational environment but not to a systematic theory of education. Nor was Jefferson interested in the kind of epistemological inquiry that leads to a theory of learning. In fact he had a deep aversion to speculation, expressed most keenly in the letter to Adams mentioned above, in which he reports that his first reading of a whole Platonic dialogue, the *Republic* was "the heaviest task work I ever went through," and how he

281

found it full of "whimsies, puerilities, and unintelligible jargon" (July 5, 1914). Consider that, whatever one may think of Platonic philosophy, the *Republic is* the founding work of western liberal education. The fact of the matter is that Jefferson was an extreme "particularist":

> Nature has, in truth, produced units only through all her works. Classes, orders, genera, species, are not her work.
>
> (letter to Dr John Manners, February 22, 1814; also in Koch: 111)

These categories are, instead, of our making; we throw together individuals by resemblances to aid the memory. He had no patience with deliberate abstractions, essences and generalizations (though of course, his writings abound in them). Consequently – setting aside his tolerance for inconsistencies – he could hardly have been interested in engaging in the sort of reflection that issues in a theory of learning.

This absence of a coherent grounding for his educational views does not mean that one might not produce one for him. It would be similar to any that might serve an experimental and progressive positivist; it would be in short some version of Enlightenment philosophy. In particular, Jefferson is, in his educational utilitarianism, a proto-pragmatist, and in a circumscribed sense a forerunner of Dewey, though the comparison requires a dictionary that translates Jefferson's brisk language of "republicanism" into the more diffuse talk of "society" (Edmondson: 156ff.). In any case, Jefferson is not cited in Dewey's *Democracy and Education* and he played no discernible role in Dewey's reform movement.

10 DOES JEFFERSON OFFER LESSONS TO THE PRESENT?

Jefferson offers us lessons, though in two opposed ways. On the one hand, through reading his educational writings we meet in bright and pristine form a number of ideas which had become worn commonplaces of American education and which are due for review. On the other, Jefferson's writings present in a crisp and confident tone certain other ideas that we have allowed to lapse and that are due for revival.

Here, first, is a list of some entrenched Jeffersonian ideas that are now under challenge:

- The idea of a mandatory state system supported by local taxes;
- The rigid division into primary, secondary and higher education;
- The viability of one publicly supported system for rich and poor;
- The necessarily secular character of elementary education;
- The delivery of specialized subject-matter by professional lectures;
- The vocational rationale for education.

Here, next, is a list of some Jeffersonian ideas that are due for recall:

- The function of the schools in forming a citizenry knowledgeable in American principles;
- The project of universal literacy. Jefferson once proposed that no person should be a citizen of the state who cannot "read readily in some tongue, native or acquired" (Education Bill of 1817, in Conant: 123).

- The localization of responsibility – for Jefferson in his beloved "small republics," the wards (Koch: 164), for us in neighborhoods – helped by burden-equalization across the districts (Bill of 1817).
- The reintroduction of access through a merit system;
- The return to required language and mathematics study (which Jefferson recommended, for the development of memory and reason respectively (letter to Thomas Mann Randolph, August 27, 1786)) in elementary schooling; the rescue of history, ancient and modern, from the social sciences; the use of original texts rather than textbooks; and finally even the study of ancient languages.

The timeliness of Jefferson on education might be seen in yet a third and wider way: as a case study. Now is a moment when the Enlightenment project with its ambivalent legacy of shallow rationalism and of humane reason is undergoing avid scrutiny. Jefferson himself is a most splendid exemplar of this movement, and his views on education are the most telling expression of his enlightened mind.

BIBLIOGRAPHY

Adams, Herbert B. (1888) *Thomas Jefferson and the University of Virginia*, Washington, DC: Government Printing Office.

Anastaplo, George (1994) Chapter 9, "Education in the New Republic," in *Amendments to the United States Constitution: a Commentary*, Baltimore, Md.: Johns Hopkins University Press.

Boorstin, Daniel (1948) *The Lost World of Thomas Jefferson*, Boston, Mass.: Beacon Press.

Brann, Eva T. H. (1979) *Paradoxes of Education in a Republic*, Chicago: University of Chicago Press.

Brann, Eva T. H. (1992) "Was Jefferson a philosopher?" in *Law and Philosophy: the Practice of Theory, Essays in Honor of George Anastaplo*, II, Athens, Ohio: Ohio University Press.

Conant, James B. (1962) *Thomas Jefferson and the Development of American Public Education*, Berkeley, Calif.: University of California Press.

Lee, Gordon C. (ed.) (1961) *Crusade against Ignorance: Thomas Jefferson on Education*, Classics in Education, no. 6. New York: Teachers College, Columbia University.

Edmondson, H. T. (1990) "Thomas Jefferson, John Dewey and Education for Public Affairs," Dissertation for the University of Georgia, Athens, Ga.

Koch, Adrienne (1943) *The Philosophy of Thomas Jefferson*, New York: Columbia University Press.

Lehmann, Karl (1947) *Thomas Jefferson: American Humanist*, Chicago: University of Chicago Press.

Mercer, Gordon E. (1993) "Thomas Jefferson: a bold vision for American education," *International Social Science Review* 68: 19–25.

Peterson, Merrill D. (1960) *The Jefferson Image in the American Mind*, New York: Oxford University Press.

Smith, Wilson (ed.) (1973) *Theories of Education in Early America 1655–1819*, Indianapolis, Ind.: Bobbs-Merrill.

Rudolph, Frederick (1962) *The American College and University: a History*, New York: Vintage Books.

21

A ROMANTIC EDUCATION

The concept of *Bildung* in early German romanticism

Frederick C. Beiser

SOCIAL AND POLITICAL CONTEXT

In 1799 Friedrich Schlegel, the ringleader of the early romantic circle, stated, with uncommon and uncharacteristic clarity, his view of the *summum bonum*, the supreme value in life: "The highest good, and [the source of] everything that is useful, is culture" (*Bildung*).[1] Since the German word *Bildung* is virtually synonomous with education, Schlegel might as well have said that the highest good is education.

That aphorism, and others like it, leave no doubt about the importance of education for the early German romantics. It is no exaggeration to say that *Bildung*, the education of humanity, was *the* central goal, *the* highest aspiration, of the early romantics.[2] All the leading figures of that charmed circle – Friedrich and August Wilhelm Schlegel, W. D. Wackenroder, Friedrich von Hardenberg (Novalis), F. W. J. Schelling, Ludwig Tieck, and F. D. Schleiermacher – saw in education their hope for the redemption of humanity. The aim of their common journal, the *Athenäum*, was to unite all their efforts for the sake of one single overriding goal: *Bildung*.[3]

The importance, and indeed urgency, of *Bildung* in the early romantic agenda is comprehensible only in its social and political context. The young romantics were writing in the 1790s, the decade of the cataclysmic changes wrought by the Revolution in France. Like so many of their generation, the romantics were initially very enthusiastic about the Revolution. Novalis, Schleiermacher, Schelling, Hölderlin and Friedrich and Dorothea Schlegel celebrated the storming of the Bastille as the dawn of a new age. They toasted the ideals of liberty, equality and fraternity, and they swore that humanity would blossom only in a republic. Their enthusiasm was much more intense and persistent than many of their older contemporaries, such as Schiller, Herder and Wieland, who became disillusioned in 1793 after the execution of Louis XVI, when it became clear that France would not become a constitutional monarchy. The romantic fervor glowed unabated throughout the September massacres, the execution of the royal family, the invasion of the Rhineland, and even the terror.

By the late 1790s, however, the romantic ardor began to dim. The constant instability in France, the readiness of the French to invade and conquer, and the onset of Napoleon's military dictatorship, disillusioned them, as so many of their generation. The romantics became especially troubled by the anomie, egoism, and materialism of modern French society, which seemed to undermine all ethical and religious values. Their political views grew more conservative in the final years of the decade. They asserted the need for some form of elite rule, for a more educated class to direct and control the interests and energies of the people. Although they continued to affirm their republican ideals, they believed that the best state was a mixture of aristocracy, monarchy and democracy.

The political problems in France soon crossed the Rhine, posing a serious crisis for the old Holy Roman Empire. It had become clear that Germany could not follow the path of France: the French attempt to introduce wholesale political reforms, without any prior change in attitudes, beliefs and customs, had proven itself a failure. But it was also plain that there could be no going back to the past: the Revolution had raised hopes and expectations among the people that could no longer be satisfied by the old alliance of throne and altar. The people wanted to participate in the affairs of the state, to have some control over their own destiny, and they no longer could be appeased with the reassurance that their prince loved them and ruled in their name. Yet how was it possible to satisfy the widespread demands for social and political change *and* not to slide down the path of perpetual chaos, as in France? That was the question. Every intelligent observer of the Revolution pondered it, and the romantics were no exception.

The romantics' solution to this crisis lay with education. If all the chaos and bloodshed in France had shown anything, they argued, it is that a republic cannot succeed if the people are not ready for it. A republic has high moral ideals, which are worthless in practice if the people do not have either the knowledge or the will to live by them. For a republic to work, it must have responsible, enlightened and virtuous citizens. If the people are to participate in public affairs, they have to know their true interests and those of the state as a whole; and if they are to be responsible citizens, they must have the virtue and self-control to prefer the common good over their private interests. But such knowledge and such virtue are possible only through education, and indeed by a very deep and thoroughgoing one. Somehow, it was necessary to transform the obedient, passive and benighted subject of an absolute monarchy into an autonomous, active and enlightened citizen of a republic.

The romantic argument on behalf of education seems like common sense, and it had been advanced by almost every moderate thinker in the 1790s. Nevertheless, it was still controversial. The argument presupposes a classical doctrine that they inherited from Montesquieu: that 'the principle' of a republic is virtue.[4] In his famous *Esprit des lois* Montesquieu had written, with the models of ancient Rome and Greece in mind, that the stability of a republic depends upon the virtue of its citizens, their willingness to sacrifice their self-interest for the sake of the common good. This doctrine had been countered by no less than Kant himself, who contended in his essay *Zum ewigen Frieden* (*On Eternal Peace*) that a republic would be possible "even for a nation of devils." Kant's point was that even if everyone acted solely on their self-interest, they would consent to live according to a republican constitution, because it alone ensured that everyone could pursue their self-interest with a minimum of interference from others. Hence the diabolic Kantian republic required no education at all.

The romantics believed that education was indispensable, however, because they questioned one of the central premises of Kant's argument: that self-interest can be socially cohesive. To build a true community from the separate self-interests of individuals, they argued, is to square the political circle.[5] A self-interested agent would forever take advantage of the rules when they could not be enforced, so that the only form of social control of a nation of devils would be repressive and authoritarian rule, a true Hobbesian Leviathan. There was no recourse, then, but to turn to education, which provided the only foundation for the state.

EDUCATION AS THE HIGHEST GOOD

Although the social and political context explains why education became such a pressing issue for the romantics, it still does not account for why they regarded it as the highest good, the supreme value in life. To understand why they put it at the very pinnacle of their hierarchy of values, it is necessary to reconstruct their philosophical position regarding a classical philosophical problem.

The question of the highest good, of the supreme value in life, had been a central philosophical problem since antiquity, and indeed a major source of controversy among all schools of philosophy. This issue had lost none of its relevance and importance in eighteenth-century Germany, where it was a popular theme of religious and philosophical writing. Kant had posed it anew in his *Kritik der praktischen Vernunft* (*Critique of Practical Reason*), and Fichte had made it a central issue of his influential 1794 lectures *Über die Bestimmung des Gelehrten* (*On the Vocation of the Intellectual*). The romantics simply continued with the tradition; the problem of the highest good appears often in the unpublished writings of Schlegel, Novalis, Hölderlin and Schleiermacher. There can be no doubt that, when he wrote his aphorism, Schlegel was taking a stand on this ancient question.

In the classical sense, first defined by Aristotle and then reformulated by Kant, the highest good has two meanings. First, it is a *final* end, a goal that does not derive its value from being the means to any other end. Second, it is a *complete* end, a goal that comprises all final ends, so that nothing can be added to it to give it more value.[6]

Prima facie the romantic view that education is the highest good appears very paradoxical, not to mention implausible. Surely, it seems, education cannot be the supreme value, since it is only the means for something else. After all, someone might well ask, what do we educate people for?

The paradox disappears, however, when we reconsider the German term *Bildung*. This word signifies two processes: learning and personal growth. They are not understood apart from one another, as if education were only a means to growth. Rather, learning is taken to be constitutive of personal development, as part and parcel of how we become a human being in general and a specific individual in particular. If we regard education as part of a general process of *self-realization* – as the development of all one's characteristic powers as a human being and as an individual – then it is not difficult to understand why the romantics would regard it as at least a plausible candidate for the title of the highest good.

The romantics regarded self-realization as the highest good in both its classical senses. Self-realization is the *final* end, because it does not derive its value as a means to some higher end, such as the common good or the state. Although the romantics stressed the importance of education for the state, they did not value it simply as a means to that end; on the contrary, they insisted that self-realization is an end in itself, and they argued that the whole purpose of the state is to promote the lives of all its citizens, so that ultimately the state is a means for self-realization rather than the converse. Self-realization is also the *complete* end, since an individual who attains it lacks nothing, having achieved everything of value in life. In other words, a person who achieves self-realization attains the end of life itself, the very purpose of existence.

These were broad and bold claims, to be sure, yet they were rarely defended explicitly in the writings of the young romantics.[7] Nevertheless, we can begin to reconstruct their position when we consider their attitude toward the two competing theories of the highest good in the late eighteenth century. One of these theories was the hedonism of the English utilitarians and the French *philosophes*, who defined the highest good in terms of pleasure. The other theory was the moral stoicism of Kant, who regarded virtue as the final good, and happiness in accord with virtue as the complete good.

The romantics rejected hedonism because it did not encourage the development of those capacities characteristic of our humanity or individuality. Pleasure by itself cannot be the highest good since, in immoderation, it even harms us. If it has any value at all, then that is when it is the result of, or integral to, acting on our characteristic human powers.[8]

The romantic critique of hedonism is most explicit and emphatic in Schlegel's and Novalis' indictment of the lifestyle of modern bourgeois society. They use a very redolent term to characterize this way of life: *philistinism*.[9] The philistine, Novalis says, devotes himself to a life of comfort. He makes his life into a repetitive routine, and conforms to moral and social convention, just so that he can have an easy life. If he values art, it is only for entertainment; and if he is religious, it is only to relieve his distress. In short, the sin of philistinism is that it robs us of our humanity and individuality.

If the romantics found hedonism too morally lax, they regarded Kant's ethics as too morally severe.[10] They saw two fundamental difficulties to the Kantian ethic. First, Kant had stressed reason at the expense of sensibility, ignoring how our senses are just as much a part of our humanity and just as in need of cultivation and development. It is not simply a purely rational being who acts morally, the romantics held, but the *whole* individual, who does his duty not *contrary to* but *from* his inclinations. Second, by emphasizing acting according to universal laws, Kant had failed to see the importance of individuality. The Kantian ideal of morality demanded that we develop a purely rational personality, which we all share simply as intelligent beings, and so it endorsed uniformity. While such an ideal might be a sufficient analysis of morality, it could not be regarded as an adequate account of the highest good, which also demands the realization of individuality, that which makes me just this person rather than anyone else.

The romantic ideal of *Bildung* was meant to rectify these shortcomings of Kantian ethics. A romantic education had two fundamental goals, each compensating for one of these flaws. One, it would unite and develop *all* the powers of a human being, forging all his or her disparate capacities into a *whole*. Two, it would develop not only our characteristic human powers – those shared by everyone as a human being – but also our individuality – those

287

unique aptitudes and dispositions peculiar to each individual. These goals were, of course, closely linked: to develop all one's powers as a whole was inevitably and naturally to realize one's individuality, for individuality emerges in that unique synthesis, that special unity, of all one's human powers.

AESTHETIC EDUCATION

To describe the romantic ideal of education in terms of human perfection, excellence or self-realization, as we have done so far, is insufficient. This gives only its genus, not its *differentia specifica*. Perfection was not an ideal characteristic of romanticism alone, but it can be found in many strands of eighteenth-century German thought. The pietists (P. J. Spener and Johann Arndt), the classicists (C. M. Wieland, Goethe, Herder), and the Leibnizian-Wolffian school (Moses Mendelssohn, Alexander Baumgarten, and Christian Wolff) all had their ideal of perfection. It is necessary to be more precise because, in basic respects, the romantics were critical of the ideals of their predecessors and contemporaries.

We come closer to a more accurate account of the romantic ideal if we describe it as *aesthetic* education. The term was first given currency by Schiller in his famous 1795 *Über die Ästhetische Erziehung des Menschen in einer Reihe von Briefen* (On the Aesthetic Education of Mankind in a Series of Letters), a work of seminal importance for the romantics. Much of the aestheticism of the romantic movement – its belief in the central role of art in cultural renewal – can trace its origin back to this work. The romantics followed Schiller in seeing art as the chief instrument for the education of mankind, and in viewing the artist as the very paragon of humanity.

Why did Schiller and the romantics give such importance to art? Why did they see it as the key to *Bildung*? We can reconstruct their reasoning only if, once again, we place it in their social and political context, and more specifically the social and political crisis of the 1790s.

Well before the 1790s, the leading thinkers of the *Sturm und Drang* – J. G. Hamann, J. G. Herder, Justus Möser, and eventually Schiller himself – had criticized the traditional *Aufklärung* for failing to provide a proper education for the people. The *Aufklärer* of the Leibnizian-Wolffian school had defined enlightenment in terms of imparting knowledge, of spreading clear and distinct concepts, among the public, as if education were only a matter of cultivating the intellect. But such a program of education (so it seemed to Herder and Möser as early as the 1770s) suffered from two serious shortcomings. First, it did not encourage thinking for oneself, spontaneity of thought, because it presupposed that someone else had already done all the thinking for one; the public were made into passive and unquestioning recipients of knowledge already acquired and concepts already clarified. Second, and even more problematically, it assumed that if people did understand the principles taught to them that they would be willing and able to *act* according to them; but such fatuous intellectualism ignored the classical problem of *akrasia*: that even if we know the good, we might not act according to it.

For all these thinkers, the Revolution provided striking confirmation of this diagnosis. The *philosophes* in France had been preaching the principles of reason to the people for decades, and they had proclaimed constitution after constitution. But all to no avail. The people were not ready for such high principles and lofty ideals. Rather than acting according to the principles of reason, they gave free reign to their interests and passions. The result was plain for all to see: France was tumbling, sinking further into the abyss of chaos, strife and bloodshed.

The lesson to be learned from the failure of the Enlightenment, and the chaos of the Revolution, Schiller argued, is that it is not sufficient to educate the understanding alone. It is also necessary to cultivate feelings and desires, to develop a person's sensibility so that he or she is *inclined* to act according to the principles of reason. In other words, it was also essential to *inspire* the people, to touch their hearts and to arouse their imaginations, to get them to live by higher ideals.

Of course, in the past there had been a remedy for this problem. That was religion, with its powerful myths and seductive mysteries. They had provided a popular incentive to morality because they could appeal directly to the heart and the imagination of the people. There was nothing like the image of a suffering Christ, a resurrected Lazarus, or an angry Jehovah to edify the virtuous and to chasten the vicious. But, by the late 1790s, this traditional support of morality was on the wane, and indeed on the verge of collapse. Here the *Aufklärung* had been only too successful. Its ruthless and relentless criticism of the Bible, of the traditional proofs for the existence of God, and of the authority of the clergy, had left little standing of the old religion, which was now condemned as prejudice, superstition and myth. Clearly, there was an enormous vacuum to be filled. The obvious failure of Robespierre's contrived and artificial cult of reason had made this all the more apparent.

Art became so important to Schiller and the romantics because they saw it as the only means to resolve this crisis. They argued that philosophy cannot stimulate action, and that religion cannot convince reason, but that art has the power to inspire us to act according to reason. Because it so strongly appeals to the imagination, and because it so deeply affects our feelings, art can move people to live by the high moral ideals of a republic.

Ultimately, then, the romantics want art to replace the traditional role of religion as the incentive and stimulus for morality. Hence they developed ideas for a modern mythology, a new Bible, and a restored church. Now the artist will take over the ancient function of the priest.

This case for the power of art to educate humanity was first put forward by Schiller, but it soon became a *leitmotif* of the romantic movement. It is a central theme of Novalis' *Heinrich von Ofterdingen*, of Friedrich Schlegel's *Ideen*, and of Wackenroder's *Herzensergie-ßungen eines kunstliebenden Klosterbruders* (*Effusions of an Art-Loving Friar*). Nowhere does it emerge with more simplicity and clarity, however, than in a later work of High Romanticism, Heinrich von Kleist's short story *Heilige Cäcilie oder die Macht der Musik* (Holy Cecilia or the Power of Music). In the story, which takes place during the early Reformation in Holland, four brothers, who are fanatical Protestants, organize a mob to attack a convent; its despairing and defenseless nuns appeal to Saint Cecilia, the patron saint of music, who inspires them to sing. Such is the beauty of their *Gloria* that the plunderers fall on their knees, confess their sins, convert, and then finally go mad, spending the rest of their days in a sanitorium, singing every evening the *Gloria*. Of course, this was a myth all of its own; but there can be no doubt that it expresses the highest hopes, and most fervent wishes, of the romantic soul.

THE ROLE OF ART

But it seems the romantics have only traded one form of naïveté for another, the enlightenment confidence in reason for their own faith in art. Both beliefs seem quixotic because they ascribe exaggerated power to the realm of culture. It is very idealistic, to say the least, to assume that we can become better people simply by listening to music, reading novels, and watching plays. If art does have that effect, one is tempted to say, that is probably because people are already predisposed to it, and so already educated for it. But then the whole case for art is caught in a vicious circle: art educates humanity only if people are already educated.

The charge of naïveté is one of the most common objections to Schiller's argument, and the reputation of the romantics for hopeless idealism is largely based upon it. But this criticism rests upon a very superficial understanding of the role of art in romantic education. When the romantics write of aesthetic education they are not simply referring to the effect works of art have upon moral character. They have something more in mind. But what is this?

It becomes clear from a close reading of Schiller's *Briefe*. It is striking that, in the tenth letter, Schiller virtually concedes the whole charge of naïveté.[11] He admits that art will educate only the virtuous, and he notes that the periods when art flourished were also those when morals declined. But, after accepting these points, Schiller then turns his argument in a new direction. The question for him is not whether art has an effect upon moral character, but whether beauty is an essential component of human perfection itself. Schiller's argument is that if we perfect ourselves – if we form our different powers into a whole – then we will become like works of art. To perfect ourselves is to unify the form of our reason with the content of our sensibility; but the unity of form and content is what is characteristic of beauty itself. Hence aesthetic education does not consist in having our characters formed by works of art but in making our characters into works of art.

Schiller's most detailed account of how a person can become a work of art appears in his treatise *Anmut und Würde* (Grace and Dignity).[12] Here he puts forward his ideal of "the beautiful soul" (*die schöne Seele*), the person whose character is a work of art because all his or her actions exhibit grace. For Schiller, a graceful action is one that shows no sign of constraint – whether that of a physical need or a moral imperative – and that reveals the spontaneity and harmony of a person's whole character. Such an action does not stem from sensibility alone, as if it were the result of natural need, and still less from reason alone, as if it were the product of a moral command, but it flows from the whole character, from reason and sensibility acting in unison. The beautiful soul does not act from duty contrary to inclination, or from inclination contrary to duty, but from inclination according to duty. Such a spontaneous inclination is not, however, the product of the desires and feelings that are given by nature, but the result of our moral education, the discipline and training of virtue. In a graceful action, then, our desires and feelings are neither repressed according to

290

reason, nor indulged according to sensibility, but refined and ennobled, or, to use a modern term, "sublimated."

Schiller's ideal of the beautiful soul gives a completely new perspective on how art motivates moral action. It is not that contemplating works of art inspires us to do good deeds, but that there is an aesthetic pleasure inherent in human excellence, which serves as an incentive to attain and maintain it. The stimulant to moral perfection does not derive from any work of art but simply from the pleasure involved in the exercise of characteristic human activities. Like most moralists, Schiller maintains that virtue brings its own reward, a unique kind of pleasure; he simply adds that this pleasure is essentially aesthetic, because achieving human perfection is like creating a work of art.

Schiller's argument on behalf of aesthetic education ultimately depends upon a theory of beauty as perfection. Such a theory could easily be generalized and extended to whatever is capable of perfection, whether it is an object in nature, an individual person, or the state and society itself. This was a temptation that neither Schiller nor the romantics could resist. They broadened their case for the primacy of the aesthetic in human life by also applying it to the state and society. They argue that the perfect society or state is also a work of art. In the final letter of the *Briefe*, for example, Schiller wrote of his Utopia as an *aesthetic* state (*ästhetischen Staat*), which, like a work of art, unites the different members of society into a harmonious whole.[13] In his *Glauben und Liebe* (Faith and Love) Novalis imagined a *poetic* state, in which the monarch is the poet of poets, the director of a vast public stage in which all citizens are actors.[14] And in his early manuscript *Versuch einer Theorie des geselligen Betragens* (Essay on a Theory of Social Conduct) Schleiermacher imagined an ideal society in which individuals form a beautiful whole through the free interaction of personalities and the mutual exchange of ideas.[15] Schiller, Novalis and Schleiermacher all assume that the perfect society or state is like a work of art because there is an organic unity between the individual and the social whole, which is governed neither by physical nor moral constraints but only free interaction.

The early romantic ideal of Utopia was therefore the creation of a social or political work of art. This aesthetic whole would be a *Bildungsanstalt*, a society in which people would educate one another through the free exchange of their personalities and ideas. Their *salons*, in Berlin and Jena, were fledgling attempts to put this ideal into practice. If life were only one grand *salon*, one long learning experience in which everyone participated, the romantics believed, then society would indeed become a work of art, and this life "the most beautiful of all possible worlds."

EDUCATION AND FREEDOM

We come closer to the *differentia specifica* of romantic education when we describe it as aesthetic. Yet we are still far from our goal. The problem is that even the ideal of aesthetic education – though central to the romantics – was not unique to, or characteristic of, them. There were many thinkers in eighteenth-century Germany who described human perfection in aesthetic terms, and who stressed the need to cultivate human sensibility as well as reason. This line of thought can be found in the Leibnizian-Wolffian school, and especially in the writings of its most outstanding aesthetician, Alexander Baumgarten.[16] By the early eighteenth century the connection of virtue with beauty had already become a venerable tradition: it was a favorite theme of Shaftesbury and Hutcheson, who had an enormous influence in Germany. Schiller's theme of the beautiful soul also had a proud ancestry, which could trace its origins back to pietism and that 'German Voltaire', C. M. Wieland.[17]

This raises the question: What, if anything, is characteristic of a *romantic* aesthetic education? How, if at all, did it differ from the forms of aesthetic education so prevalent in the eighteenth century?

Although there are clear points of continuity between the Leibnizian-Wolffian tradition and the romantics, there is also a drastic and dramatic break between them. That break is made by Kant's critical philosophy, which had sundered the link between virtue and beauty so carefully forged and crafted by the Leibnizian-Wolffian school. In the *Kritik der praktischen Vernunft* Kant had argued that the basis and incentive for moral action must derive from pure reason alone, independent of all considerations of pleasure, aesthetic or otherwise. And in the *Kritik der Urteilskraft* (*Critique of Judgment*) he stressed that the pleasure of beauty is completely disinterested, having its characteristic qualities independent of all moral and physical ends. When we experience an object as beautiful, Kant contended, we take pleasure in the sheer contemplation of its form, and we do not consider whether it conforms to moral or physical purposes.[18] In both these works Kant attacked the worth of the concept of perfection – the keystone of the ethical and aesthetic thought of the Leibnizian-Wolffian school – as a criterion of morality or beauty.

The sheer prestige of the critical philosophy in the 1790s in Germany would seem to be sufficient to bury, once and for all, the seductive equation of virtue and beauty, morality and aesthetics, which had entranced so many thinkers in the eighteenth century. But the very opposite is the case. Paradoxically, Kant's critique led to Schiller's reformulation and transformation of this equation, which gave it a new lease of life. In his unpublished but seminal 1793 *Kallias oder über die Schönheit* (Kallias or concerning Beauty) Schiller resynthesized on a new basis the realms of art and morality, of beauty and virtue, which had been so disastrously divided by Kant.[19] Schiller endorsed some of the negative conclusions of the Kantian critique: that art must be autonomous, serving neither moral nor physical ends, and that the concept of perfection, understood in the classical sense as unity in multiplicity, is insufficient to explain beauty. Nevertheless, Schiller argued against Kant that beauty is more than simply a subjective quality, such as the pleasure of contemplation, and he insisted instead that it is an objective feature of an object itself. Whether or not an object is beautiful, Schiller contended, depends upon whether it is *self-determining*, that is, whether it is free from external constraint and acts according to its inherent nature alone. Since self-determination is equivalent to freedom, and since a beautiful object presents, exhibits or reveals this quality to the senses, beauty is nothing more nor less than *freedom in appearance*.

In thus defining beauty, Schiller intended to give a new foundation to Kant's concept of aesthetic autonomy, its independence from moral and physical ends. But, ironically, such a definition also provides a new connection between art and morality. For the self-determination of the aesthetic object – its independence from all forms of constraint, whether

292

moral or physical – means that it can serve as a symbol of freedom, which, according to the critical philosophy itself, is the fundamental concept of morality. Hence Schiller, quite self-consciously and deliberately, rejoins the realms of art and morality, though now the connecting link between these domains is provided by the concept of freedom rather than that of perfection.

This does not mean that Schiller completely rejects the old concept of perfection, which he continues to use and to describe in the traditional terms as a unity in multiplicity; but it is important to see that this concept now has a new underpinning: the concept of freedom itself. Perfection is now defined in terms of self-determination, acting according to the necessity of one's nature independent of all constraint.

The romantic concept of aesthetic education has its roots in Schiller's redefinition of the moral role of art. What is central to and characteristic of the romantic concept is the Schillerian thesis that the end of aesthetic education is freedom. Like Schiller, the romantics maintain that to become an aesthetic whole, to make one's life a work of art, it is necessary to realize one's nature as a spontaneous and free subject. Since beauty consists in freedom in appearance, we attain beauty only when our moral character expresses freedom itself.

That *Bildung* consists in the development of freedom is a point much stressed by both Friedrich Schlegel and Novalis. Schlegel simply defined *Bildung* as "the development of independence" (*Entwicklung der Selbständigkeit*), and he had famously argued that what is characteristic of *Bildung* in the modern world, in contrast to the ancient, is precisely its striving for freedom.[20] The purpose of our lives, he maintained, is to realize our nature as self-determining beings, where self-determination consists in constantly attempting to determine what one is, and then realizing that one is nothing but the activity of constantly attempting to determine what one is.[21] Novalis was no less emphatic and explicit than Schlegel: "All education (*Bildung*) leads to nothing else than what one can call freedom, although this should not designate a mere concept but the creative ground of all existence".[22]

It is this emphasis upon freedom, then, that separates the romantic account of aesthetic education from its historical antecedents in the Leibnizian-Wolffian school. But is this not what we should expect? The rallying cry of anyone who came of age in the 1790s was freedom. The problem with the old *Aufklärer* of the Leibnizian-Wolffian school, the romantics complained, is that they had abandoned their freedom by compromising with the social and political status quo. A romantic education would be one fitting for the 1790s: the liberation of the spirit from all forms of social and political oppression.

THE AWAKENING OF THE SENSES

The chief aim of aesthetic education, whether in the romantic or Leibnizian-Wolffian tradition, was the cultivation of sensibility. Normally contrasted with reason, sensibility was defined in a very broad sense to include the powers of desire, feeling and perception. The underlying premise behind the program of aesthetic education was that sensibility could be developed, disciplined and refined no less than reason itself. Long before the 1790s, the *Sturmer ünd Dränger* had complained that the *Aufklärung* had failed to educate this faculty. Since their main task was to combat superstition, prejudice and enthusiasm, the *Aufklärer* had naturally devoted most of their attention to the development of reason. But, the *Sturmer und Dränger* objected, this was to neglect one half of our humanity.

The romantics shared this criticism of the *Aufklärung*, and in this regard their concern with sensibility is continuous with the tradition of the *Sturm und Drang*. Like Schiller and the *Sturmer und Dränger*, the romantics wanted to cultivate sensibility as an *aesthetic* faculty. Their aim was to educate the senses, their power to perceive the beauty of the world. This faculty could be made more sensitive, refined and acute, they believed, so that a person's life could be greatly enriched and ennobled.

It is important to see, however, that there was something else unique to, and characteristic of, the romantic program of aesthetic education, and that in an important respect they went beyond even Schiller and the *Sturm und Drang*. What is distinctive of their program is not *that*, but *how*, they wanted to educate sensibility. Their aim was, in a word, to *romanticize* the senses. But what does this redolent word mean?

The best clue comes from Novalis. To romanticize the world, he explained in an unpublished fragment, is to make us aware of the magic, mystery, and wonder of the world; it is to educate the senses to see the ordinary as extraordinary, the familiar as strange, the mundane as sacred, the finite as infinite.[23] The romantics want us to break outside the confines of our ordinary and mundane perception of the world, where we automatically categorize everything according to common concepts, and where we see things only as objects of use. Their goal is to develop our power of *contemplation*, so that we can see things anew, as they are in themselves and for their own sakes, apart from their utility and common meaning.

The romantics want to romanticize not only our external senses — our powers of perception of the external world — but also our internal ones — our sensitivity to the world within. They attempt to direct our attention to our inner depths, to the hidden recesses of the self, no less than to the world without, the realms of society and nature. For the romantics, self-realization was essentially self-discovery, an exploration of one's inner depths. As Novalis put the point:

> We dream of a journey through the universe. But is the universe then not in us? We do not know the depths of our spirit. Inward goes the secret path. Eternity with its worlds, the past and future, is in us or nowhere.[24]

It was this conviction that later inspired Novalis to write *Heinrich von Ofterdingen*, the major *Bildungsroman* of the romantic school, as an antipode to Goethe's earlier work in the same genre, *Wilhelm Meisters Lehrjahre*. While Wilhelm's apprenticeship consists in his adventures in the wider world, his encounters with extraordinary characters and difficult situations, Heinrich's education comes from unraveling the secret of his own dreams. There were two ways to educate the soul, Heinrich explained, one of them "the path of experience," which was very indirect and led to only worldly wisdom or prudence, while the other was "the path of inner contemplation," which was very direct and resulted in spiritual self-realization.

There was a grand ambition behind this program for the reawakening of the senses, whether internal or external. The romantics' aim was to *reunify* man with himself, nature and others, so that he would once again feel at home in his world. According to the romantic philosophy of history, early man had been at one with himself, with others, and with nature; this unity was purely natural, given to him by no efforts of his own. Inevitably and tragically, however, this primal harmony had been torn apart by the development of civilization. Man had become alienated from others as a result of the increasing competition of civil society; he had become divided within himself with the rise of the division of labor; and he had become estranged from nature after the sciences had demystified it, making it into an object to be dominated and controlled for human benefit. The task of modern man was to *recreate* on a self-conscious and rational level that unity with ourselves, others and nature that had once been given to early man on a naïve and intuitive level.

Such indeed was the vocation of the romantic poet, who would attempt to revive our lost unity with ourselves, with nature, and with others. The key to recreating that unity consisted in the *remystification* of the world, in romanticizing the senses, because only when we were reawakened to the beauty, mystery and magic of the world would we reidentify ourselves with it.

Not surprisingly, this demand for a reawakening of the senses led to the reappraisal of mysticism among the romantics. This sympathy for mysticism appears in many works of the early romantic school, in Novalis' *Die Lehrling zu Sais*, Schleiermacher's *Reden über die Religion*, Friedrich Schlegel's *Ideen*, and Schelling's *System des transcendentalen Idealismus*. All these works argue that we have a spiritual sense, a power of contemplation or intellectual intuition, which transcends our discursive reason, and which brings us into direct contact with ourselves, others and nature itself. They all praise the power of the artist to express these intuitions, and to revive our slumbering powers of contemplation.

Naturally, this new mysticism went hand-in-hand with a revival of religion in the romantic circle, which becomes especially apparent after the publication of Schleiermacher's *Reden* in 1799. Rather than regarding religion as a primitive form of metaphysics or morality, as the *Aufklärung* had done, the romantics saw it as a specific form of contemplation or perception of the universe. The essence of religion, Schleiermacher argued in his *Reden*, is the intuition of the universe. This religious reawakening has often been criticized as a relapse into the ideology of the *ancien régime*, but it is important to see it in the context of the romantics' general concern with *Bildung*. They valued religion chiefly as an instrument of aesthetic education, as a means of reawakening the senses.

THE POWER OF LOVE

The romantic program for the education of sensibility involved not only the cultivation of the senses, but also, more importantly, the development of "the faculty of desire." Its aim was to educate not only our powers to perceive, but also those to feel and desire. For the romantics, to educate feeling and desire meant essentially one thing: to awaken, nurture and refine the power of love.

What especially inspired the early romantics – what, more than anything else, gave them their sense of purpose and identity – was their rediscovery of the lost power of love. It was their view that this vital source of our humanity had been forgotten, repressed or ignored for far too long, and that it was now time to remember, reclaim and revive it. Owing to the rationalism of the *Aufklärung*, and owing to the legalism of the Kantian-Fichtean ethics, love had lost its once pivotal role in ethics and aesthetics, the pride of place it once held in the Christian tradition. The romantics saw it as their mission to restore the sovereignty of love to the realms of morals, politics and art.

The central concept of romantic ethics is love. The romantics gave it all the stature that reason once held in the *Aufklärung* and Kantian-Fichtean ethics. It is now love, rather than reason, that provides the source and sanction of the moral law. Love, Schlegel tells us,[25] is to the law as the spirit is to the letter: it creates what reason merely codifies. The power of love indeed transcends all moral rules: while love inspires, the law represses; while love forgives, the law punishes. Love is also a much more powerful "determining ground of the will" (as Kant would call it), a much more effective stimulant to moral action, than reason. The bonds that tie the individual to the community and state are not the universal norms of reason but the affection and devotion of love.

Love had a no less pivotal place in romantic aesthetics. It is the spirit of love, Schlegel wrote, that must be "invisibly visible" everywhere in romantic art.[26] The artist could romanticize our senses only through the inspiring power of love. We can remystify the world, we can rediscover its lost beauty, mystery and magic, only if we see all things in the spirit of love. It is through love that we see ourselves in nature and others, and so re-identify with the world and become at home with it again.

The romantic program of *Bildung*, of aesthetic education, stressed the cultivation of love, the development of the capacity of every individual to give and receive affection. This was essential to self-realization, to the development of our humanity and individuality, the romantics believed, because love is the very core of our humanity, the very center of our individuality. "Only through love, and the consciousness of love," Friedrich Schlegel wrote, "does a human being become a human being."[27] Love was indeed the key to reconciling and unifying the two warring sides of our nature, the intellectual and physical, the rational and the emotional. It was not simply a physical urge, but a much deeper spiritual desire: the longing to return to that golden age when we were at one with ourselves, others and nature.

Although the romantic rediscovery of love was based upon a reappreciation of its spiritual significance, it is important to see that they never neglected or debased its physical roots. The education of desire meant arousing and cultivating not only our spirituality, but also our sensuality. That we must learn to accept and enjoy our sexuality, that we must see sexuality as part of love, and that we must love someone sexually to be fulfilled human beings, were the central themes of Friedrich Schlegel's novel *Lucinde*, which shocked the public of his day. Schlegel protested against repressive social norms that saw sexuality as legitimate only in marriage, and that regarded marriage as a matter of domestic convenience. He could see nothing wrong with divorce and a *menage à quatre* if it led to the development of one's individuality and humanity, and he could see nothing right with a marriage and chastity if it resulted in repression and indignity.

An essential theme of Schlegel's campaign for sexual liberation was his attack upon sexual stereotypes. He criticized the prevalent sexual norms that limited men to an active and aggressive role and women to a passive and submissive one. To better enjoy our sexuality, he advised couples to switch these roles. There was no reason within human nature itself that men could not develop their passive, tender and sentimental sides, and that women could not develop their active, dominant and rational ones. Thus, masculinity and femininity were properties of each person, regardless of their sex.

A FINAL PARADOX

The romantic philosophy of education ends with a paradox. We have seen that there was nothing more important to the romantics than *Bildung*, the education of humanity. This was the central theme and goal of their ethics, aesthetics and politics. But, from a more practical perspective, there seems to be nothing less important to the romantics than education. When it comes to concrete suggestions about how to educate humanity, about what specific institutional arrangements are to be made, the romantics fall silent. There is very little in the writings of the romantics about the social and political structure to be created to ensure the education of humanity.

Such silence, however, is more the result of principle than negligence. The reason for their taciturnity is their deep conviction that the self-realization of the individual must derive from his freedom, which must not be impaired by social and political arrangements. It is for this reason that Friedrich Schlegel wrote:

> Humanity cannot be inoculated, and virtue cannot be taught or learned, other than through friendship and love with capable and genuine people, and other than through contact with ourselves, with the divine within us.[28]

The paradox of German romanticism is utter commitment and devotion to the education of humanity, and yet its recognition that it cannot and ought not do anything to achieve it. We are left, then, with a striking gap between theory and practice, which we cannot in principle overcome.

NOTES

Editions cited

Kant, Immanuel, *Schriften, Preussischen Akademie der Wissenschaften*, ed. Wilhelm Dilthey (Berlin, de Gruyter, 1902).

Novalis, *Werke, Tagebücher und Briefe Friedrich von Hardenbergs*, ed. Richard Samuel, Hans-Joachim Mähl (Munich, Hanser Verlag, 1978).

Schiller, Friedrich, *Werke, Nationalasugabe*, ed. L. Blumenthal and Benno von Wiese (Weimar, Bühlaus Nachfolger, 1943–67).

Schlegel, Friedrich, *Kritische Friedrich Schlegel Ausgabe*, ed. Ernst Behler *et al.* (Munich, Shöningh, 1966). Cited as *KA*.

Schleiermacher, Friedrich, *Friedrich Schleiermacher Kritische Gesamt Ausgabe*, ed. Günter Meckenstock *et al.* (Berlin, de Gruyter, 1984). Cited as *KGA*.

Translations

Behler, Ernst and Struc, Roman, *Friedrich Schlegel: Dialogue on Poetry and Literary Aphorisms* (University Park, Pa., Pennsylvania State University Press, 1968).

Beiser, Frederick, *Early Political Writings of the German Romantics* (Cambridge, Cambridge University Press, 1992). Cited as *EPW*.

Firchow, Peter, *Friedrich Schlegel's Lucinde and the Fragments* (Minneapolis, Minn., University of Minnesota Press, 1971).

1 Friedrich Schlegel, *Ideen* no. 37. Cf. no. 65 and the statement in his *Vorlesungen über die Transcendentalphilosophie*, *KA* XII, p. 57: "According to the highest view of man, the concept to which everything must be related is that of education [*Bildung*]." Cf. *EPW*, pp. 127, 131.

2 My subject-matter here will be the early romantic circle, which flourished from 1797 to 1802. The membership of this circle was fluid, and other figures could be included within it, such as Friedrich Hölderlin, Wilhelm von Humboldt and A. L. Hülsen.

    Romanticism is commonly divided into three distinct periods: *Frühromantik* from 1797 to 1802, *Hochromantik* from 1803 to 1815, and *Spätromantik* from 1816 to 1830. On this periodization, see Paul Kluckhohn, *Das Ideengut der deutschen Romantik*, 3rd edn (Tübingen, Niemeyer, 1953), pp. 8–9.

3 See the "Vorerinnerung" to the *Athenäum* I (1798), pp. iii–iv. Cf. *Athenäum* III (1800), p. 236. The contributors of the journal swore to devote themselves to the realm of *Bildung* according to the following lines: "Der Bildung Strahlen All in Eins zu fassen, Vom Kranken ganz zu scheiden das Gesunde, Bestreben wir uns treu im freien Bunde."

4 Montesquieu had an influence in Germany as great as Rousseau. On the history of his reception in Germany, see Rudolf Vierhaus, "Montesquieu in Deutschland: Zur Geschichte seiner Wirkung als politischer Schriftsteller im 18. Jahrhundert," in *Deutschland im 18. Jahrhundert* (Göttingen, Vandenhoeck & Ruprecht, 1988), pp. 9–32.

5 This argument is explicit in Novalis' *Glauben und Liebe* (Faith and Love) §36, in *Werke*, II, pp. 300–31. Cf. *EPW*, pp. 45–6.

6 See Aristotle, *Nicomachean Ethics*, Book I, chs 1 and 5, 1094a and 1997b, and Kant, *Kritik der praktischen Vernunft* V, pp. 110–11.

7 The most explicit treatment is in Friedrich Schlegel's lectures on transcendental philosophy. See *KA* XII, pp. 47–9, 85–6. Cf. *EPW*, pp. 146–7.

8 Friedrich Schlegel explicitly rejected hedonism on such grounds in his early essay "Ueber die Grenzen des Schönen," *KA* I, 37.

9 On the romantic critique of philistinism, see Friedrich Schlegel's novel *Lucinde*, *KA* VIII, pp. 41–50, and Novalis, *Blütenstaub* §77, *Werke*, II, pp. 261–3. Cf. *EPW*, pp. 24–5.

10 For the romantic critique of Kant's ethics, see Schleiermacher's *Monologen*, *KGA* I/3, pp. 17–18 (*EPW*, pp. 174–5), and Friedrich Schlegel's *Ideen*, §39 and lectures on transcendental philosophy, *KA* XII, pp. 48, 72. Cf. *EPW*, p. 128. The source for the first criticism of Kant ultimately goes back to Schiller, and especially his treatise *Über Anmut und Würde*, which will be discussed below.

11 Schiller, *Werke*, XX, pp. 336–41.

12 Schiller, *Werke*, XX, pp. 251–89. The entire first part is relevant to the argument reconstructed above.

13 Schiller, *Werke*, XXI, pp. 410–12.

14 Novalis, *Glauben und Liebe*, no. 39, *Werke*, II, pp. 303–4. Cf. *EPW*, p. 48.

15 Schleiermacher, *KGA* I/2, pp. 169–72.

16 See A. G. Baumgarten, *Aesthetica*, which was first published in 1750.

17 On the history of the concept of the beautiful soul, see Robert Norton, *The Beautiful Soul* (Ithaca, NY, Cornell University Press, 1995).

18 See *Kritik der Urteilskraft*, §4–7, §15, V, pp. 207–12, 226–9.

19 Schiller, *Werke*, XXVI, pp. 174–229.

20 On the definition of *Bildung*, see Schlegel's *Vorlesungen über Transcendentalphilosophie*, in *KA* XII,

p. 48. On the account of modern *Bildung*, see the early essays "Vom Wert des Studiums der Griechen und Römer," in *KA* I, pp. 636–7, and "Ueber das Studium der Griechischen Poesie," in *Die Griechen und Römer: Historische und Kritische Versuche über das klassische Alterthum*, in *KA* I, pp. 232–3.

21 Such was Schlegel's remarkable formulation in the section entitled "Eine Reflexion" in his novel *Lucinde*, in *KA* V, pp. 72–3.

22 Thus spake Novalis' hero in *Heinrich von Ofterdingen, Werke*, I, p. 380.

23 See "Vorarbeiten 1798," no. 105, *Werke*, II, p. 334. Cf. *EPW*, p. 85.

24 See *Blütenstaub* no. 16 (*EPW*, p. 11).

25 See *Ideen* no. 39.

26 See Schlegel's *Brief über den Roman*, *KA* II, pp. 333–4.

27 *Ideen* no. 83. Cf. *EPW*, p. 132.

28 *Ueber die Philosophie* VIII, pp. 44–5.

22

HEGEL ON EDUCATION

Allen W. Wood

Hegel (1770–1831) spent most of his life as an educator. Between 1794 and 1800, he was a private tutor, first in Bern, Switzerland, and then in Frankfurt-on-Main. He then began a university career at the University of Jena, which in 1806 was interrupted by the Napoleonic conquest of Prussia, and did not resume for ten years. In the intervening years, he was director of a Gymnasium (or secondary school) in Nuremberg. In 1816, Hegel was appointed professor of philosophy at the University of Heidelberg, then abruptly ascended to the chair in philosophy at the University of Berlin in 1818, where he remained until his sudden death from cholera in 1831.

As a university professor of philosophy, Hegel viewed his most important activity as classroom lecturing, and all the major philosophical texts of his maturity after 1816 took the form of manuals to be read by students and to be lectured upon. After Hegel's death, the first comprehensive edition of his writings prominently included additions to his texts on logic, philosophy of nature, philosophy of spirit and philosophy of right drawn from his lectures, as well as transcriptions of entire lecture series on the philosophy of history and on aesthetics, philosophy of religion and the history of philosophy.

Hegel was the friend of Immanuel Niethammer (1766–1848), an important administrator and reformer in the Bavarian educational system. Niethammer occasionally used his influence to help Hegel's career, and the two men sometimes corresponded about matters relating to pedagogy, either at the secondary school or the university level.[1]

Education is not only a prominent but also a fundamental theme in Hegel's philosophy. But perhaps surprisingly in view of his career, Hegel does not usually deal with this theme primarily in terms of a theory of pedagogical practice or method.

He does occasionally discuss the education of children (*EL* §140A; *PR* §§173–5); he also criticizes Rousseau's theory of education in *Émile*, along with some of the projects and practices that derived from it, such as those of J. B. Basedow and J. H. Campe (*Werke* 11: 283; *VA* 1: 384; *TJ* 26; *VPR* 1: 306; *EG* §396A; *PR* §175).[2] And while director of the Ägidien-Gymnasium in Nuremberg, Hegel did give annual year-end addresses which dealt with pedagogical theory – defending various aspects of the curriculum, such as religious, natural scientific or military instruction, and defending Niethammer's view that the secondary school curriculum should be grounded on a classical education in Greek and Latin language and literature (*Werke* 4: 305–402). During the same period Hegel also wrote short treatises to Niethammer and Friedrich Raumer on the teaching of philosophy in secondary schools (*Werke* 4: 403–25). But nowhere does Hegel develop a pedagogical theory comparable to that advanced by Rousseau or in Locke's treatise on education, or even in Kant's university lectures on pedagogy.

THE CONCEPT OF *BILDUNG*

What is a fundamental theme of Hegel's philosophy is *Bildung*. This term might be translated as "education," but it could also be rendered, more appropriately in many contexts, as "formation," "development" or "culture." For Hegel, the term refers to the formative self-development of mind or spirit (*Geist*), regarded as a social and historical process. *Bildung* is part of the life process of a spiritual entity: a human being, a society, a historical tradition. It occurs not primarily through the imparting of information by a teacher, but instead through what Hegel calls "experience": a conflict-ridden process in the course of which a spiritual being discovers its own identity or selfhood while striving to actualize the selfhood it is in the process of discovering.

Bildung is to be distinguished from the "upbringing" (*Erziehung*) of a child by its parents or pedagogues. But for Hegel the essential end of both processes is the same. For the principal achievement of upbringing is to overcome immediacy, simplicity or natural crudity (*Rohheit*), to deepen spirit through *thought*, of the *universal*. Hegel emphasizes that the early stages of this process require some kind of external constraint or discipline, the frustration of immediate desires and the growth of a capacity, consequent only on this experience of conflict and frustration, to direct one's own agency through a self-conception and rational principles. The aim of education as upbringing, Hegel says, is therefore to enable the child to be consciously or for itself, what it already is in itself or for adults: namely, a rational or spiritual being (*EL* §140A). But since the child is already essentially or in itself a rational being, the entire process of *Bildung* is fundamentally an inner or *self-directed* activity, never merely a process of conditioning through environmental stimuli, or the accumulation of information presented by experience.

What is merely learned (*gelernt*) is made the possession of everyone through their becoming acquainted with it as something already familiar (*bekannt*) (*PhG* ¶13). But for this very reason, Hegel says, what is familiar is not rationally cognized (*erkannt*) (*PhG* ¶31). For rational cognition, it is required first that the object lose its familiarity, become separated or estranged from the rest of what is given, which happens through the operation of the analytical understanding (*PhG* ¶32). This, however, is only one aspect of *Bildung*; the more decisive step occurs when the thinking mind is reunited with the object in a new or rational form, that of the *concept* (*PhG* ¶33). In true cognition, the otherness of the object is overcome through a struggle with it, and the mind is reconciled to the given through acquiring a rational understanding of it. What was given immediately as familiar at the start of the process is now an otherness overcome; the object is no longer present in its immediate form, but is now grasped by means of a universal concept produced by the mind, which therefore recognizes itself in the object.

This new relation to the object is what Hegel also calls "being with oneself in another," which is his definition of spirit's actualized *freedom*: "Only in this freedom is the will completely *with itself*, because it has reference to nothing but itself, so that every relationship of *dependence* on something other than itself is thereby eliminated" (*PhG* ¶23). *Bildung* is therefore also a process of *liberation*, in which the freedom of spirit is vindicated over the mere positivity of what is given in nature.

Further, because in cognition what was merely accepted as given is now seen as the product of a process of thought, the mind's relation to it is free because it is self-supporting or justified through its own thinking. Education (*Bildung*) is therefore the "laborious emergence from the immediacy of substantial life," the acquisition of the "universal principles" or the "thought of the thing" (*Gedanke der Sache überhaupt*). When this occurs, one is able "to support and refute the universal thought with reasons" (*PhG* ¶4). *Bildung* is simultaneously a process of self-transformation and an acquisition of the power to grasp and articulate the reasons for what one believes or knows. Acquiring a genuinely rational comprehension of things goes hand in hand with a process of liberating maturation through a struggle involving selfhood and the overcoming of self-conflict.

BILDUNG IN THE *PHENOMENOLOGY*

Hegel's first major work, *The Phenomenology of Spirit*, takes as its theme "the long process of education (*Bildung*) toward genuine philosophy, a movement as rich as it is profound, through which spirit achieves knowledge" (*PhG* ¶68) or the "education (*Bildung*) of consciousness up to the standpoint of science" (*PhG* ¶78). In Hegel's use of this term, there may be more than a mere allusion to the contemporary literary genre of the *Bildungsroman*, such as *Hyperion* (1798), by Hegel's friend Friedrich Hölderlin, or Goethe's *Wilhelm Meister's Apprenticeship* (1796) which portrays the coming to maturity of a young man involving conflicts over self-identity and the aims of life. M. H. Abrams has even suggested that the *Phenomenology* itself is a *Bildungsroman* whose subject is not a particular person but rather the human spirit, especially since it has seen itself as coming into something like a state of adulthood in modernity, and especially in the ages of the Enlightenment and post-Enlightenment.[3]

The complex organization of the *Phenomenology*, which has been the topic of endless controversy,[4] involves both a systematic and a historical presentation of this educational process. The opening chapters appear to deal with pure philosophy, in abstraction from any historical process, but beginning with Chapter 4, there are increasing allusions to historical phenomena, formations, philosophical movements and events, until Chapter 6 appears to trace the entire history of western culture from the Greeks down to the French Revolution. The main controversy, which I do not intend to address here, is whether the *Phenomenology* is governed by a single philosophical aim or theoretical conception or whether Hegel fundamentally altered what he was doing in the course of writing the work.

Hegel begins with the "natural consciousness," and attempts to present it in a series of shapes or formations (*Gestalten*), each of which undergoes a dialectical process of experience, transforming itself into the succeeding shape. As Hegel outlines this process in the Introduction to the *Phenomenology*, each shape of consciousness is characterized by two fundamental features or "moments," which Hegel characterizes as (1) "the being of something for consciousness, or *knowing*" and (2) "the *being-in-itself*" of this same thing, which is called "*truth*" (*PhG* ¶82). In other words, consciousness has a conception of what it is to know reality, and also a conception of the nature of the reality that is to be known. When, as in many of the shapes Hegel describes, natural consciousness is presented as a self-conscious agent striving to realize itself, these two aspects could also be thought of respectively as conceptions of the state or condition it is trying to attain to, and also a conception of the worth it will achieve by attaining to it. Whichever way the matter is conceived, there is for each shape of consciousness a determinate "moment of knowledge" and a determinate "moment of truth"; each shape of consciousness has its own specific conception of what reality is and how it is known. Further, the natural consciousness involves (or even simply *is*) the comparison of its two moments, and the criterion of truth for each shape of consciousness is their agreement (*PhG* ¶84).

To attain to genuine knowledge, then, all that a shape of consciousness must do is ascertain that its own moment of knowledge agrees with its own moment of truth. It need not appeal to any criterion outside itself. If it is in agreement with itself, it has found the truth; but if its own proper conceptions are in disharmony with one another, then spirit is impelled to go beyond it and to seek the truth in a different shape.

The method of the *Phenomenology* is to examine each shape of consciousness in turn, and in particular to scrutinize its process of comparing its moment of knowledge with its moment of truth. Hegel's startling claim is that for every shape of consciousness (short of the "absolute knowing" with which the system of shapes of consciousness comes to a close), the two moments always necessarily fail to agree. The *Phenomenology* is therefore a record of a long series of *failures* (it traces, as Hegel says, "a path of *doubt*, or more precisely, a path of *despair*" (*PhG* ¶78); and the title of the work refers to the fact that it is supposed to be a complete record of all the false or merely apparent (hence phenomenal) forms that spirit's knowledge can take (*PhG* ¶89). At the same time, however, it is supposed to be a record of the "becoming of science as such or of knowledge" (*PhG* ¶27), since the end result of the process is supposed to be to reach a knowing that does not contradict itself.

This happens because the series of shapes of consciousness are supposed to be arranged in such a way that as each one breaks down internally, it leads necessarily to a new shape, which solves the previous incoherence (before, however, breaking down in an incoherence of its own). The breakdown of each shape of consciousness, in other words, takes the form of a "determinate negation," it results in a specific new shape which appears in this way as higher or deeper, one step closer to the truth, than the one which has gone before (*PhG* ¶79).

This process of *Bildung* is depicted in the *Phenomenology* as an ideal course of philosophical method leading up to genuine science; but through allusions of varying specificity and explicitness, it is also seen as the course the human spirit has taken in history. A key stage in the development of consciousness, for example, is the well-known master–servant dialectic in Chapter 4. Consciousness at this stage is presented as attempting to confirm its self-worth through conquest and appropriation of the external world. It comes to see that a genuine confirmation of its worth can be had only in the form of its *recognition* (*Anerkennung*) by another self-consciousness. The relation of self-consciousness to its objects, however, has thus far been the appropriation of external things, and following this model, the quest for recognition is the attempt to subjugate another self-consciousness, to have one's self-worth or independence recognized by it without having to recognize it in turn. Hegel supposes this to be achieved by the master consciousness, which (using the threat of death) subjugates another self-consciousness, the servant consciousness. Both consciousnesses understand the master as the independent and the servant as the dependent consciousness. In relation to external things, this means that the master's only relation is that of enjoyment, while the servant's sole relation is one of labor. The master appropriates the world without doing anything; the servant labors on the world, but the will it impresses on things is solely an alien will, that of the master (*PhG* ¶¶188–92).

The irony in this relation, as Hegel depicts it, is that each self-consciousness is in reality exactly the opposite of what it is understood to be. The master, who relates to things only through the labor of the servant, is in fact the dependent consciousness, which needs the other's recognition in order to be what it is, and does nothing to appropriate the world and whose will is therefore idle in relation to it. The servant, on the other hand, is the one whose will is truly expressed in labor, and it is further the only genuinely independent consciousness in the relation, since it does not receive recognition from the other consciousness (*PhG* ¶¶192–5). The frustrating and self-alienating process of being reduced to a condition of servitude turns out in the end, therefore, to be one which is liberating, once the servant consciousness attains to a comprehension of what it truly is. This happens, on Hegel's account, when it comes to see that the will which appropriates the world through its labor is really its own will, yet not its particular will, but a universal or rational will, and it sees its independence as the unconditional validity of this will. With this the servant consciousness, in Hegel's portrayal, attains to the standpoint of ancient Stoicism, which views its own rational and universal comprehension of things as liberating (*PhG* ¶¶196–9).

The course of the master–servant dialectic illustrates Hegel's general conception of *Bildung*. For it is a process of liberation achieved only by means of initial frustration, struggle, and an altered conception of oneself. The aims of the master self-consciousness, in their original form, are doomed to frustration because they rest on a false conception of the self whose aims they are. In this way, the specific goal of the master consciousness (to dominate another self-consciousness) fails to correspond to its own concept (that of achieving independence in relation to that other). This goal is achievable only when it is reconceptualized and transformed, as is done by the servant consciousness when it attains to a Stoic sense of itself as universal rationality, and independence as the comprehension of things from the rational or universal standpoint.

Bildung is also the central theme in one phase of the *Phenomenology*'s account of the history of spirit: This is the emergence of modern self-consciousness out of the self-alienation of the Christian Middle Ages (*PhG* ¶¶484–526). Hegel views the transition from the culture of the Greek city-states to that of the Roman empire as involving a loss of a sense of community, and along with it, a sense of self. No longer at home in a spiritual world on earth, people turn to an otherwordly religion that promises them citizenship in a kingdom of God, or as Hegel calls it, a "beyond" (*PhG* ¶485).

The earthly side of Christian culture, however, remains one of self-alienation: individuals live with a sense of separation between their merely natural being and their universal or rational essence. Self-actualization for them therefore is constituted by the "cancelling (*Aufheben*) of the natural self"; the "end and substance" of the individual will "belongs only to the universal substance and can be only a universal" (*PhG* ¶489). This universal substance is, on the one hand, identified with the state power, and the culture of individuals consists in their devoting themselves to the ends of the state (*PhG* ¶494). The self-alienation of culture is exhibited in the fact that the state power confronts them as something other, and its interests are "good," whereas their individual power, characterized as the power of private wealth, is something "bad." Culture consists in putting one's private wealth in the service of the universal good, through a "noble" disposition, as distinct from the "ignoble" disposition, which obeys the sovereign only reluctantly and in a spirit of revolt (*PhG* ¶¶499–503).

In this discussion Hegel portrays with considerable subtlety the mind-set of the early modern monarchical state, in which a modern centralized monarchy is arising out of a power structure dominated by semi-independent feudal nobles, the chief one of which lays claim to the universal authority of state sovereignty. He calls upon the obedience and devotion of the others, which often takes the form less of the structured subordination of a genuinely organized state than of the giving of counsel or even the language of flattery (*PhG* ¶¶508–11). The real meaning of all this, however, is the cultivation of a self which identifies its own worth with the vindication of what is rational or universal in itself as distinct from what is merely particular. In this way, his discussion of early modern *Bildung* leads into his account of the Enlightenment and modern moral self-consciousness. As Terry Pinkard has recently emphasized, *Bildung* in the *Phenomenology* is a process through which modern culture forms the modern self, whose aim is the actualization of its own freedom. This is a process through which a human being becomes not merely a self but a particular kind of self, deriving a sense of self-worth from a self-chosen way of life and from living according to self-given rules or principles.[5] Or to put it in the language Hegel was to use later in the *Philosophy of Right*, early modern culture (*Bildung*) was to shape the "moral subject" which finds its self-actualization in "subjective freedom" (*PR* §106).

CIVIL SOCIETY

At the time he wrote the *Phenomenology*, however, Hegel still had not conceptualized the social world that corresponds to the moral self who is the product of modern culture. He did this only after the ten year hiatus in his university career, first in the *Encyclopedia of Philosophical Sciences* composed to be lectured upon when he took up his professorship at the University of Heidelberg in 1817, then (more intensively) in his last major work, *Elements of the Philosophy of Right* (1821).

Pre-modern society was "ethical" (*sittlich*) in Hegel's technical sense of that term, organized around two principal institutions: a private, particular and natural society, associated with religion (the family); and a public, universal or political society, a secular world fashioned by human intelligence (the state).[6] Both institutions display the charac- teristic Hegel associates with "ethical life" (*Sittlichkeit*), namely, that there is a direct and immediate identity of the interests of society and that of the individual. Ethical life, as Hegel puts it, is spirit in its immediacy: "I that is we and we that is I" (*PhG* ¶177) or "the individual that is a world" (*PhG* ¶441). "Ethical" institutions are those which directly harmonize the interests of individuals with those of society; "ethical" dispositions are those which reflect this state of affairs psychologically: they experience a direct identity between their interests and that of the social whole (*PR* §146). In the family, this takes the form of feeling or sense (*Empfindung*): family love is "spirit's feeling of its own unity" (*PR* §158); in the state, it is "patriotism" or "the political disposition" which is "the certainty, based on truth . . . that my substantial and particular interest is preserved and contained in the interest and end of . . . the state" (*PR* §268). In modern society, however, ethical life is complicated by a third sort of institution, in which this unity is not directly present, a "stage of difference" or "world of ethical appearance" (*PR* §181) in which "ethical life is lost in its extremes" (*PR* §184). Hegel's name for this institution is "civil society" (*bürgerliche Gesellschaft*).

Historically, Hegel identifies "ethical life" with the beautiful and harmonious civilization of ancient Greece, and he sees modernity as arising out of the long historical process following upon its dissolution. In the *Phenomenology*, the downfall of the Greek polis is analyzed in terms of a conflict between the two institutions: the family and the state (*PhG* ¶¶444–76). Free individuality does not emerge directly, but appears as an indirect result of a conflict between two ethical forms. (Hegel views the traumatic and tragic conflict between family and state as portrayed most purely in Sophocles' *Antigone*, where Antigone represents the principle of the family, and Creon that of the state: *PhG* ¶¶457–66). The disruption of Greek ethical life leads to the alienation of the Roman empire and the long self-alienation represented by the dominance of Christian religion, leading to the educative culture (*Bildung*) of the early modern period. Implicit in this analysis is that if the original harmony of Greek society is again to be achieved, but this time on a higher and more reflective plane, it will have to be through new forms of social institution not reducible to these earlier forms. Yet in 1807 Hegel still had no name for such a society and no conception answering to the demand.

The *Philosophy of Right* conceptualizes objective spirit or the social order as "ethical life" (*Sittlichkeit*). It is society conceived as an actual world in which the self exists concretely. Hegel analyzes the ethical life of modern society in terms of three phases or institutions: the family (*PR* §§158–81), civil society (*PR* §§182–256) and the state (*PR* §§257–329). The self or the will is also conceived in two other ways, which are seen as abstractions from the concreteness of ethical life: it is regarded as a *person*, under the heading of Abstract Right (*PR* §§34–104), and as a *subject*, under the heading of Morality (*PR* §§105–41). What is most striking in this is that these two abstract conceptions, which Hegel regards as definitive of the modern conception of the self, relate in their concrete form chiefly to the character-istically modern addition to the social structure: the institution of civil society.

As Riedel has pointed out,[7] before Hegel "civil society" (and its cognates, *societas civilis*, *société civile*, *bürgerliche Gesellschaft*) was used interchangeably with "political society" or "state." Hegel effected a revolution in social theory by using the term to designate a *public* institution, created and sustained by human will and reason, but distinct from the state, and in which individuals appear not as citizens acting on behalf of the universe but as private persons and self-conscious subjects pursuing their own private ends. The paradoxical newness of this institution is indicated by the name which had recently been devised for the new science devoted to its study: "political economy." For this name indicates simultaneously the universal character of the society (as "political") and yet also its private character, since *oikonomia* is the Greek word for the management of the family or household (*oikos*), regarded as the social institution in which labor, production and exchange were carried on (particularly in a society dominated by agriculture). Political economy began to treat entire states as units of production, to be managed like families, while at the same time acknowledging that through a system of production and exchange standing outside the political state, individuals were acting as persons and subjects in an extra-political capacity, and yet as members of a genuine *society*, which Hegel also characterized (in a paradox converse to the one involved in the term "political economy"), as a "universal family" (*PR* §239).

Hegel's conception of civil society is grounded on that of the modern market economy, or what he calls the "system of needs" (*PR* §§189–208). But it is important to recognize that this is only the *foundation* of the institutional structure of civil society (*PR* §188), whose higher phases are the legal system protecting the rights of individuals (*PR* §§209–29) and the network of both state and private institutions, which are seen as both protecting the economic realm (*PR* §§230–49) and developing it into a genuine social home in which individual freedom may flourish (*PR* §§250–6). It is in civil society, as we shall see, that Hegel locates the function of *Bildung* in the modern state, whether considered as the *education* of individuals or the larger *culture* of spirit.

THE EDUCATIVE FUNCTION OF CIVIL SOCIETY

Civil society, Hegel tells us, has two main principles: that of the individual, and that of universality (*PR* §182). Civil society, as an economic reality, is made up of private persons engaged in self-seeking activities. But civil society is to be treated as a social institution, and constitutes a genuine form of *society* at all only because behind the mere appearance of universal self-seeking, there is implicit a spiritual or ethical principle of social or collective interest, in which the aims and interests of individuals are finally brought into harmony or identity. In the "system of needs" (the market economy) this process of socialization goes on silently, behind the backs of individuals, who do not recognize what they are really doing and what is really happening to them. This is what Hegel means when he says that in civil society the principle of universality assumes the form of an "external necessity" and hence of an "appearance" (*PR* §184). The principle of universality first emerges in the public system of justice protecting the rights of private individuals, and is finally made an explicit *aim* of action in the state functions which regulate the economy and in the institutions outside the state through which the common interests generated within the economic realm take the form of collective aims. But within the economic system itself, the universal first makes its appearance in the form of the *Bildung* individuals undergo as part of their life-activities.

Individuals, as citizens of [the "necessity state"], are *private persons* who have their own interest as their end. Since this end is mediated through the universal, which thus *appears* to the individuals as a means, they attain their end only insofar as they themselves determine their knowledge, volition and action in a universal way and make themselves links in the chain of this *continuity*.

(*PR* §187)

When individuals act as members of civil society their conscious motivation is typically self-interested. When they think of things with the economic mind-set of civil society, they regard the entire society to which they belong in the way Hegel would describe using the term *Notstaat*,[8] the "necessity state," and – like liberal social theorists – they regard this state not as a universal end in itself but as merely a means to the satisfaction of their ends and those of other, similarly active and similarly motivated, individuals. But this, Hegel tells us, is only the way things *appear* to them. For in reality, when they participate in civil society, they turn themselves objectively into links in a chain, or means to an end which is universal in scope and content. Yet their activity not only means something different objectively from what it means to them subjectively, but it also subtly transforms them. Through it they are shaped, cultivated and educated (*gebildet*), so that they too come subtly to have a consciousness which is directed not merely at selfish or particular aims, but acquires universal and rational aims as well:

> In this situation, the interest of the Idea, which is not present in the consciousness of these members of civil society as such, is the *process* whereby their individuality and naturalness are raised, both by natural necessity and by their arbitrary needs, *to formal freedom* and formal *universality of knowledge and volition*, and subjectivity is *educated* (*gebildet*) in its particularity.

(*PR* §187)

The modern market economy had already been attacked by both conservatives and radicals, as promoting moral corruption and disordered relationships between human beings based solely on self-interest. Hegel, on the contrary, sees it as subtly promoting a deepened interdependence between people and ways of life which, even prior to reflection, are oriented systematically to a common good. Critics such as Rousseau had, on the one hand, attacked modern society for its endless refinement of human needs and desires, its catering to whims, caprices and luxuries, and the way it promotes "artificial" needs. Hegel, on the other hand, finds in this an "aspect of liberation"; those who reject modernity in favor of what they see as natural simplicity, are like the ancient Cynics, who recommended a way of life that was really unfree, because its rejection of civilization was "merely a consequence of these same social conditions, and in itself an unpreposessing product of luxury" (*PR* §194, A). On the other hand, when modern civil society expands people's needs, this is a sign that individuals are being encouraged to value their own opinion, even their own arbitrariness, and this is the social medium through which they also develop the inner life of moral subjectivity, and the subjective freedom which is the proper contribution of the modern world to the development of spirit (*PR* §185, R, A).

Through the refinement of people's needs, moreover, they are brought into an ever greater interdependence, as they labor to acquire the means to satisfy these needs. In order to do this, they must acquire the skills needed to work in civil society, and also both the theoretical and practical education required to be productive. To live successfully in modern society, one must cultivate one's intellectual capacities, one's capacity to analyze and to perform mental activities with flexibility, agility and rapidity, and also one's capacity to articulate these mental operations in language:

> This involves not only a variety of representations and items of knowledge, but also an ability to represent and to pass from one representation to another in a rapid and versatile manner, to grasp complex and general relations, etc. – it is the education of the understanding in general, and therefore also includes language.
>
> *(PR §197)*

Beyond this cultivation of purely *theoretical* abilities, participation in the work of civil society builds a certain habitual *practical* orientation toward a life of cultivated activity, in place of the idleness and lethargy which in Hegel's view, has been characteristic of earlier (agricultural or pre-agricultural) social forms. "The barbarian is lazy and differs from the educated man in his dull and solitary brooding, for practical education consists precisely in the need and habit of being occupied" *(PR §197A)*. The practical education of civil society for Hegel also consists in "the limitation of one's activity" to suit both the nature of the objects of one's labor and the human needs to be satisfied, "a habit, acquired through discipline, of *objective* activity and *universally applicable* skills" *(PR §197)*.

The critics of modern civil society, of course, see in both the increased refinement of needs and the increased specialization and intellectualization of labor the increasing servitude of modern humanity to a corrupt and unnatural system. Hegel is aware of their standpoint, which is based on "notions of the *innocence* of the state of nature and of the ethical simplicity of uncultured (*ungebildeter*) peoples" *(PR §187, R)*. From this standpoint, he notes, *Bildung* itself appears as a kind of corruption. He is equally aware of the reply to these critics which takes the form of defending *Bildung*, conceived as the cultivation of our intellectual and practical capacities, as "merely a means to . . . the satisfaction of needs, and the pleasures and comforts of particular life" *(PR §187R)*. Hegel rejects both views, because they fail to recognize "the nature of spirit and the end of reason."

> Spirit attains its actuality only through internal division, by imposing this limitation and finitude upon itself, through the continuum of natural necessity and, in the very process of adapting itself to these limitations, by overcoming them and gaining its objective existence within them. The end of reason is consequently neither natural ethical simplicity nor the pleasures as such which are attained through education. Its end is rather to work to eliminate natural simplicity . . . i.e. to eliminate the immediacy and individuality in which spirit is immersed. . . . *Education* [*Bildung*], in its absolute determination, is therefore *liberation* and *work* toward a higher liberation; it is the absolute transition to the infinitely subjective substantiality of ethical life, which is no longer immediate and natural, but spiritual and at the same time raised to the shape of universality.
>
> *(PR §187R)*

309

THE INFINITE VALUE OF *BILDUNG*

By regarding the education afforded by civil society as expressing "the nature of spirit" and fulfilling "the end of reason," Hegel is saying that this education is not to be defended as a means to other ends (to pleasure or the satisfaction of particular needs) but it is rather an *end in itself*. "This is the level at which it becomes plain that education is an immanent moment of the absolute, and that it has infinite value" (*PR* §187R).

The limitations it involves are not hindrances on freedom, but in fact constitute a *liberation* from "immediacy and natural simplicity." Those who complain about the corruption of modern culture, Hegel thinks, are taking the standpoint of "ethical simplicity"; what they praise as "innocent" and "natural" is simply the unreflectivity of the customs of a pre-modern social order, which for that very reason is sunk in unfreedom. Hegel's liberal critics have often tried to depict his defense of "ethical life" as praise for this sort of unreflectively traditionalist disposition, but the passages we are looking at here are only a small part of the textual evidence indicating how totally they have misunderstood him on this point. In the above reply to the "Cynical" critique of civil society, Hegel emphasizes that ethical life is an "infinitely subjective substantiality, which is no longer immediate and natural, but spiritual and at the same time raised to the shape of universality." In other words, true ethical life is not unreflective habituation, but instead a rational self-harmony achieved after, and precisely by means of, the inner self-division which is essential to the process of *Bildung*. Ethical life, properly understood, is never opposed to education. In fact, the liberation of education leads precisely to an "absolute transition to the infinitely subjective substantiality of ethical life" (*PR* §187R).

The issue for Hegel is not whether people are happier or more contented when they remain in a state of crude simplicity than when they develop their capacities to master nature and satisfy their needs and desires. This issue, focused on by both the critics of modern society and its defenders, cannot be settled because the very terms in which it is posed rest on a misunderstanding of the meaning of the presupposed human ends, even the end of happiness itself. For the very idea of happiness, conceived as a total or comprehensive satisfaction of needs or desires, presupposes a standpoint in which the simplicity of natural needs and their satisfaction has already been reflected upon, and judged in the value it has for a free and rational being. In Hegel's view, people can be concerned about such a thing only after they have forever left behind the innocent simplicity whose loss the Rousseauian bemoan and to which the Cynic confusedly wants to return us. Socially and historically speaking, people can begin to measure things from the standpoint of happiness only after they have achieved "milder mores [*Sitten*]" and a certain level of culture (*VPR* 3: 144; *PR* §123; *EG* §§395A–396). Philosophically speaking, the value of happiness or contentment can be measured only from the standpoint of reason, and from that standpoint the principal value possessed by the pursuit of happiness lies precisely in the fact that this pursuit requires us to stand at a distance from our desires, weighing their value, and disciplining them through consideration of the way their satisfaction will contribute to our welfare on the whole.

> When reflection applies itself to the drives, representing them, estimating them and comparing them with one another and then with the means they employ, their

consequences, etc., and with a sum of satisfaction – i.e. with *happiness* – it confers *formal universality* upon this material and purifies it, in this external manner, of its crudity and barbarity. This cultivation of the universality of thought is the absolute value of *education* [*Bildung*] (cf. §187).

(PR §20)

It makes no sense, therefore, to estimate the value of education by its contribution to happiness; for the value of happiness itself consists precisely in the role it plays in the process of education.

EDUCATION AS PEDAGOGY: ITS SOCIAL FUNCTION IN MODERN ETHICAL LIFE

Hegel's conception of *Bildung* is clearly broader than our usual conception of "education," which has to do with the activities of schools and their pupils, teachers or tutors (including parents) and their students, whether they are children, or adolescents, or adults. Hegel, as we noted at the outset, did express himself on these topics occasionally, especially while he was engaged in directing a secondary school during the long period in which his university career was interrupted. But we can understand the full import of his remarks on education in the narrower and more familiar senses of "upbringing" (*Erziehung*) and "pedagogy" (*Pädagogik*) only when we see them in light of his larger theory of modern society and the crucial role of *Bildung* in achieving freedom as the actualization of spirit and absolute end of reason.

In relation to his theory of modern society, Hegel locates education in these narrower senses in the individual's transition from the family into civil society (*PR* §175). Hegel rejects the "play theory" of education proposed by the followers of Rousseau because it does not acknowledge that the characteristics of family life – the immediate unity with others through the feeling of love, the innocence of childhood, the comfort and contentment of immaturity and *Unmündigkeit*, in which one is cared for by others and one's thinking is done by others – are not good in themselves, but are rather conditions with which it is healthy and proper to be *discontented*. Children's need for upbringing is present precisely as "their own feeling of discontent with themselves at the way they are – as the drive to belong to the adult world whose superiority they sense, or as the desire to grow up" (*PR* §175R). The period of infancy is the only one in which the primary concern of parents for children should be care and love (and therefore the only period in which, characteristically, Hegel thinks the primary caregiver should be the mother) (*PR* §175A). The aim of parents in bringing up their children should not be to keep them contented with what they are, but rather to develop their capacities, through discipline, to rise above their arbitrary will and to appreciate the values that govern the adult world. "Upbringing also has the negative determination of raising the children out of natural immediacy in which they originally exist to self-sufficiency and freedom of personality, thereby enabling them to leave the natural unit of the family" (*PR* §175).

Hegel's view of the role of schools in education is also determined by his conception of it as a transition between the family and civil society. "*The school stands between the family and the real world* . . . It is the middle-sphere which leads the human being from the family circle over into the world" (*Werke* 4: 348–9). This is why he regards the responsibility for the education of children as a delicate matter, which must be shared between parents and civil society. "It is difficult to draw a boundary here between the rights of parents and those of civil society" (*PR* §239A). But because the true end of education lies outside the family in the larger world of civil society, Hegel appears to give the final say in matters of pedagogy to civil society rather than to the family: "Society has a right to . . . compel parents to send their children to school" (*PR* §239A). "In the face of arbitrariness and contingency on the part of parents, civil society has the duty and the right to supervise and influence the upbringing of children insofar as this has a bearing on their capacity to become members of society" (*PR* §239).

Hegel emphasizes the practical training schools must give children in matters which will equip them for life in civil society (*Werke* 4: 327–35). But even more fundamental, in his view, is teaching young people to think rationally, and to articulate their thoughts in ways that will make them part of the public world. Defending Niethammer's emphasis on classical education, Hegel argues that learning languages and grammar, and even the admittedly burdensome learning of Latin, is a valuable training for the young mind (*Werke* 4: 312–16, 322–4). Classical literature, he insists, provides us with the common matter on which to put to work our minds and our skills at communication. "Education [*Bildung*] must have an earlier material and object, upon which it labors, which it alters and forms anew. It is necessary that we acquire the world of antiquity, not only so as to possess it, but even more in order to have something that we can work over" (*Werke* 4: 320–1).

In many of his better-known remarks on moral education, Hegel appears to endorse the rather authoritarian idea that it is of first importance to break down the self-will of the child through stern discipline (*PR* §174, A). Hegel also rejects the Enlightenment pedagogical doctrine, advocated by both Locke and Rousseau, that moral education must appeal to the pupil's reason, and that children should not be taught substantive moral principles until they are capable of understanding them (*Werke* 4: 347). But Hegel's position on these issues must be understood as expressions of his larger conception of *Bildung*. The remarks about breaking the child's self-will should be understood as corollaries of the Hegelian doctrine that *Bildung* requires the development of one's self-conception in response to conflict and frustration: for example, the development of the concept of a free, rational self historically required the discipline of the servant self-consciousness and the overcoming of its condition of servitude. And Hegel's objection to the Enlightenment principle is that keeping children ignorant of moral principles while they are immature is counterproductive to the Enlightenment aim of encouraging rational moral reflection:

> In fact, if one waits to acquaint the human being with such things until he is fully capable of grasping ethical concepts in their entire truth, then few would ever possess this capacity, and these few hardly before the end of their life. It is precisely the lack of ethical reflection which delays the cultivation of this grasp, just as it delays the cultivation of moral feeling.
>
> (*Werke* 4: 347)

Hegel's views on moral education are in fact far from authoritarian. He applauds the more lenient attitude toward school discipline which he sees emerging in pedagogical practice, and justifies this change by appealing to the *liberating* function of school education in leading the pupil from the family into civil society.

> The concepts of what is to be understood by discipline and school discipline have altered very much with the progress of education [or: of culture (*Bildung*)]. Since upbringing has increasingly been considered from the correct standpoint that it requires essentially more support than suppression of the awakening self-feeling, that it must be a cultivation [*Bildung*] of self-sufficiency, the upbringing in families as well as institutions has increasingly lost the manner of inculcating in young people a feeling of subjection and unfreedom, and of making themselves obedient more to another than to their own will even in matters which are indifferent – demanding empty obedience for the sake of obedience, and reaching through hardness what more properly belongs merely to the feeling of love, respect and the seriousness of the subject matter . . . From this liberality follows also the setting of boundaries on the discipline which the school can exercise.
>
> (*Werke* 4: 350–1)

BILDUNG AND THE UNIVERSAL

If there is a central, and also controversial, thesis underlying Hegel's general theory of education, it is probably that education or culture consists fundamentally in disciplining what is particular or individual in the human personality so that it conforms to what is universal. As with many of the central theses in Hegel's philosophy, the verbal statement of this thesis is used by Hegel to express several distinct doctrines, and also to imply that there is a close connection among them. The "universal" for Hegel means, in the first place, the conceptual, that which belongs both to the analysis of the understanding and the reconciling comprehension of reason, that which can be explicitly articulated in thought and language. The thesis thus means that education aims at developing the capacities to rise above mere feelings and intuitions, to think in conceptual terms which can be articulated and rationally defended in discourse.

Secondly, the "universal" for Hegel also means the social, or what is rationally recognized as valid and binding in the social order. *Bildung* is therefore also the development of the capacity and disposition to conform to the rational demands of social life. This is closely related to Hegel's own philosophical project of reconciling us rationally with the demands of modern social life, so that we may regain the harmony between universal and particular which characterized Greek ethical life, but this time not at the level of immediacy but through reason or philosophy.

Thirdly, and related to the first two points: what is "universal" is what we have in common with others, as distinct from what distinguishes us from them or makes us unique among them. In this sense, Hegel's thesis means that education aims not at cultivating or indulging arbitrariness, personal peculiarity and idiosyncrasy, but in developing a character which values itself for what it has in common with other people. Hegel is at the opposite pole here from the Romantics, who equated the full development of individuality with an attitude of irony, vanity and eccentricity, particularly in art, but also in personal life-style. He declares: "The rational is the high road which everyone follows and where no one stands out from the rest. When great artists complete a work, we can say that it *had* to be so; that is, the artist's particularity has completely disappeared and no *mannerism* is apparent in it. Phidias has no mannerisms; the shape itself lives and stands out. But the poorer an artist is, the more we see of himself, of his particularity and arbitrariness" (*PR* §15A). Hegel intends the metaphor of the classical artist also to apply to ethical conduct and life-style: Exceptional excellence of character is found not in those who indulge in all sorts of eccentric experiments in living, but rather in those who take over a recognized role in society and master it in the way that a sculptor like Phidias mastered his craft.

The aim of education, then, even of the recent liberality in education which Hegel praises, should not be to indulge people's "individuality," to encourage them to social nonconformity or rebelliousness, but rather to make them into rational citizens of a rational society, who are capable of taking their place beside fellow citizens whom they recognize and respect as equals, and to whom they can articulate the rational principles of the society in universal terms that all can understand and whose validity everyone must rationally acknowledge.

SUMMARY AND ASSESSMENT

The strengths and weaknesses of Hegel's philosophy of education are those of his ethical and social theory generally. He views education, in the narrower senses of upbringing and pedagogy, as playing a determinate role in a modern rational society which is the outcome of a larger historical process of education or culture (*Bildung*). This vision involves an enlightened confidence in the progressive direction of history and in the rationality of the institutions of modern society. To the extent that we now question the vision, it is because we also question that confidence.

Hegel may be right in rejecting a theory of education which values childlike innocence, and correct in arguing that the tendency in modern society to make such innocence an ideal merely exhibits one symptom of the loss of innocence. But Hegel's conception of *Bildung* takes for granted modern society's conception of a whole series of oppositions, which are now often questioned. Among these are: underdevelopment/cultivation and backwardness/progress. Such questioning may arise from a recognition of the way in which the practical application of these distinctions has led to the brutal destruction of non-European cultures in many parts of the world, whose wisdom, art and social institutions surely had much to contribute to the *education, cultivation and progress* of the human species. And their barbarous suppression in the name of those very values has surely been a serious step backward. But as we question Hegel's implicit confidence in the values and ideals of modern European culture, we need also to acknowledge that it is only the ideas of Enlightenment modernity which enable us to recognize and deplore the destructiveness which has been carried on in their own name. We cannot reject Hegel's conceptions of *Bildung* or reason or progress — as is frequently done at present by well-intentioned but fatally confused critics of modernity – without undermining our own grounds for objecting to the abuse of those conceptions. In other words, we can expect to appreciate what has been lost and desecrated through the destruction and marginalization of non-western and "pre-modern" civilizations only by fully appropriating the enlightened standpoint of modernity in its authentic form. Thus in the end, Hegel's argument remains correct even for us: the value of innocence can be appreciated only from a standpoint which has come to terms with its loss of innocence.

Also controversial, no doubt, is Hegel's insistence on the educational ideal of rational universality: the cultivation of a stance of rational reconciliation with modern society, rather than an attitude of radical revolt, ironic detachment or self-protective flight. Contrary to false images of it which have been promoted by its ideological critics, Hegel's social theory does not rest on the quietistic assumption that everything in society is as it ought to be. When Hegel defends the rationality of the actual, he at the same time insists on distinguishing what is *actual* from what merely *exists*, and acknowledging that it is obvious that what exists is seldom wholly rational or as it ought to be (*EL* §6; *PR* Preface; *Werke* 7: 25). But Hegel is committed to the philosophical project of reconciling us to what exists through the comprehension of the actuality of the existent.[9] In other words, he holds that we can practically relate to the existing social world in a rational way by comprehending this world *as it is supposed to be*, that is, in terms of the rational relationships which are inherent in it, even if these are sometimes marred or perverted by accidents or human misconduct (*PR* §258A). Education is to develop our capacities to harmonize with the social world in its essence or actuality; they may include the capacity to perceive defects in the existing world and take the steps to correct them that are provided by the institutions of modern society.

Hegel's project of reconciliation does assume that the existing social world is *fundamentally* or *essentially* rational, and not in need of radical revolutionary change before it can become fundamentally or essentially rational. Hegel's project of reconciliation is therefore unacceptable to some of his revolutionary followers, who think that social relationships need to be fundamentally changed before they can be rationally accepted. Here again, however, Hegel's conception of what it is to achieve rational understanding and reconciliation with one's society seems to underlie even the radical vision of many who reject the view that modern society at present is fundamentally and essentially rational.

Hegel's vision on this point could be *radically* rejected only by some of his Romantic contemporaries (and their later spiritual heirs) who think that human beings are not destined *ever* to be rationally at home with their worldly condition. It is dubious, though, whether the characteristically modern forms of anti-rationalism (whether they should be called "fascism" or "fundamentalism" or "post-modernism") can in good faith claim to reject the values of modernity merely by striking the pose of doing so. Often they thereby merely exhibit themselves to be the purest modernists of all, since what they become is often simply an abstractly negative mirror image of modernity, usually in the shape of some grotesquely distorted caricature of it.

The chief aim of Hegel's philosophy was always to find a way of embracing otherness, including and reconciling his thought with whatever conceptions present themselves as opposed to his own. His critics most typically fail by underestimating the degree to which he was successful in achieving this basic goal.

NOTES

1 Niethammer's projects, and Hegel's correspondence with him, are documented in *Hegel: the Letters*, trans. Clark Butler and Christiane Seiler (Bloomington, Ind., Indiana University Press, 1984), pp. 171–233.

2 Hegel's published writings will be cited according to the following abbreviations:

Werke   *Hegel: Werke: Theoriewerkausgabe* (Frankfurt, Suhrkamp, 1970). Cited by volume: page number.

EL   *Enzyklopädie der philosophischen Wissenschaften: Logik, Werke* 8. Cited by paragraph (§) number. "A" means "Addition."

EG   *Enzyklopädie der philosophischen Wissenschaften: Philosophie des Geistes, Werke* 10. Cited by paragraph (§) number. "A" means "Additions."

PhG   *Phänomenologie des Geistes, Werke* 3. Cited by paragraph (¶) number in the A. V. Miller translation (Oxford, Oxford University Press, 1977).

PR   *Grundlinien der Philosophie des Rechts, Werke* 7. Cited by paragraph (§) number; "R" means "Remark"; "A" means "Addition."

TJ   *Theologische Jugendschriften* (1793–1800), *Werke* 1. Cited by page number.

VA   *Vorlesungen über Ästhetik, Bd* 1–3, *Werke* 13–15. Cited by volume and page number.

VPR   *Vorlesungen über Rechtsphilosophie*, ed. K-H. Ilting (Stuttgart: Frommann Verlag). Cited by volume and page number.

3 M. H. Abrams *Natural Supernaturalism: Tradition and Revolution in Romantic Literature* (New York, Norton, 1973).

4 See Robert Pippin, "You can't get there from here: transition problems in Hegel's *Phenomenology of Spirit*," in F. Beiser (ed.) *The Cambridge Companion to Hegel* (New York and Cambridge, Cambridge University Press, 1993), especially pp. 52–8.

5 Terry Pinkard, *Hegel's Phenomenology: the Sociality of Reason* (New York, Cambridge University Press, 1994), pp. 302, 324, 325.

6 See Manfred Riedel, *Zwischen Tradition und Revolution: Studien zu Hegels Rechtsphilosophie* (Stuttgart, KIett-Cotta, 1982); English translation by Walter Wright: *Between Tradition and Revolution: Hegelian Transformations of Political Philosophy* (Cambridge, Cambridge University Press, 1984).

7 Ibid., ch. 6.

8 The term *Notstaat* was taken over by Hegel on the basis of earlier usage. Friedrich Schiller equates the *Staat der Not* with the "natural state" which is based on force rather than right, and is contrasted with the *Staat der Vernunft* or *Staat der Freiheit*, founded on a "moral unity." In Schiller's view, it is the task of humanity to exchange the former (existing) state for the latter, which is at present only a political ideal (Schiller, *Werke* (Frankfurt, Insel, 1966), 4: 202). Fichte too identifies the *Notstaat* with the existing state and hopes for gradual progress toward the "rational state" (Fichte, *Sämtliche Werke*, ed. I. H. Fichte (Berlin, De Gruyter, 1971), 4: 238–9). Hegel's use of the term suggests that he thinks the earlier philosophers had wrongly identified the existing state with civil society, seen only from the limited standpoint of one of its members. He regards the rational state as the existing state (or the "actual state," of which the existing state is an imperfect version in the transitory empirical realm), but in order to recognize this, philosophers must look at what exists in a rational way, so that the state can be seen in its true actuality and not confused with civil society.

9 See Michael Hardimon, *The Project of Reconciliation: Hegel's Social Philosophy* (Cambridge, Cambridge University Press, 1993).

I wish to thank John McCumber for helpful bibliographical advice pertaining to this essay.

SELECTED BIBLIOGRAPHY

Beyer, Wilhelm Raimund (ed.) (1982) *Die Logik des Wissens und das Problem der Erziehung*, Hamburg: Meiner.

Hinchman, Lew (1984) *Hegel's Critique of the Enlightenment*, Gainesville, Fl: University Presses of Florida, chs 4, 9.

Inwood, Michael (1992) "Culture and education," in *A Hegel Dictionary*, Oxford: Blackwell Publishers, pp. 68–70.

Krautkrämer, Ursula (1979) *Staat und Erziehung*, Munich: J. Beichmann.

Lauer, Quentin (1983) "Religion and culture in Hegel," in L. Stepelevich and D. Lamb (eds) *Hegel's Philosophy of Action*, Atlantic Highlands, NJ: Humanities Press, pp. 103–14.

Reuss, Siegfried (1982) *Die Verwirklichung der Vernunft*, Frankfurt: Max Planck Institut für Bildungs-Forschung.

23

A NIETZSCHEAN EDUCATION: ZARATHUSTRA/*ZARATHUSTRA* AS EDUCATOR

Richard Schacht

> To educate educators! But the first ones must educate themselves! And for these I write.[1]

In *On the Aesthetic Education of Man*,[2] written as a series of letters a half-century before Nietzsche's birth, Friedrich Schiller saw "aesthetic education" as the key to the attainment of a richer and more complete humanity than had been attained even by the Greeks – who, however, were seen as showing the way. Through such an education, according to Schiller, the "sensuous" impulses of our natural natures may be transformed, the cultivation of the "formal" impulses of our rational nature is made possible, and then the opposition between them can be overcome as a new impulse comes to the fore: a "play" impulse, joining elements of both of these other impulses as our higher (artistic/authentic) nature emerges, with a sensibility attuned to beauty and abilities employed creatively.

In this picture, as well as in the critique of the impoverished humanity produced by the operation of the modern world, much that we find in Nietzsche from *The Birth of Tragedy* (henceforth *BT*) to *Thus Spoke Zarathustra* and beyond is anticipated. With Schiller in mind, Nietzsche's Apollonian–Dionysian distinction becomes a variation and deepening of a familiar theme. The employment of the idea of "play" in connection with the culminating stage of spiritual development identified in Zarathustra's very first speech "On the three metamorphoses" (when one expects to find something like artistic creativity) becomes readily understandable. The ideas of an enhancement of life and an attainable higher humanity, contrasting with the quality of life that leaves so much to be desired in the modern world and throughout so much of history, become easily recognizable. And even the seemingly odd central thesis of *BT*, that "it is only as an aesthetic phenomenon that existence and the world are eternally justified" (*BT* 5 and 24),[3] loses its strangeness.

What is even more to the point for present purposes is Schiller's explicit use of the notion of "education" (*Erziehung*) as the key to the enhancement of life, and his equally explicit indication that the kind of education meant has above all to do with the two-fold cultivation of an aesthetic sensibility and artistic-creative powers. Nietzsche does more than merely echo Schiller; he deepens and extends these ideas in ways placing him well beyond Schiller and his early-romantic naïveté. But in seeking to understand what Nietzsche is trying to do in *Zarathustra*, one does well to recall his Schillerian inheritance. Nietzsche's project too may be characterized as a version of Schiller's idea of the need for a further aesthetic education of humanity that might bring about a higher form of humanity – and *Zarathustra* was his greatest contribution to this campaign.

In this essay I shall develop this idea, attempting at once to bring out what I take to be the heart of Nietzsche's thinking with respect to education and to make sense of *Zarathustra* and the extraordinary importance he attached to it. The key to both, I believe, is to be found in the third of his *Untimely Meditations*, written nearly a decade earlier: *Schopenhauer as Educator* (henceforth *SE*). In and by means of Zarathustra and *Zarathustra* (both the figure and the work itself), I suggest, Nietzsche sought to provide posterity with something capable of performing the kind of "educating" function he had discussed and called for with urgency and passion in that essay, and considered Schopenhauer to have performed for him. This is a special kind of education, requiring a special kind of educator. And Nietzsche was convinced that the experience of encountering such an educator is quite essential, if one is to find one's way to a new Yes to life that does not depend upon buying into the various forms of illusion he began (in *BT*) by thinking were the only means of avoiding Schopenhauerian pessimism and the calamity of dead-end nihilism.

I

Nietzsche's first great case-study of this kind of education and call for a new aesthetic education of humanity was *The Birth of Tragedy*. He may not have thought of it in precisely these terms at the time; but the central theme of the entire first half of the book is that, thanks to their artists, the Greeks received an extraordinary aesthetic education that was the key to both their kind and quality of culture and their ability to relish life as greatly as they did – despite their acute awareness of "the terror and horror of existence" (*BT* 3), and in the absence of anything like Christian other-worldly consolation.

More specifically, Nietzsche regarded the Greeks' artists as their educators in the most important sense, cultivating their sensibility and transforming both their sense of themselves and their sense of their world in such a way that they were unsurpassed in their life-affirmation.[4] The Greeks' tragedians had educated their sensibility and self-consciousness, and had shown them a way of coming to terms with the harsh realities of life without succumbing to nausea and despair. They were the educators through whose efforts the wondrously affirmative and creative tragic culture of the Greeks achieved extraordinary heights. In *BT* Nietzsche looked to Wagner to serve as such an educator to modern European humanity. Wagner was to be their latter-day European counterpart, through whom a new tragic culture – no less affirmative and creative than that of the Greeks – was to be attained.

It was not long, of course, before Nietzsche's enthusiasm for Wagner-as-educator began to wane; and he soon (by the time of *SE*, two years later) settled upon Schopenhauer as being better suited to that role, at least in his own case. In *SE* Wagner still looms large as the unnamed epitome of the "genius" through whom the flourishing of culture that is the locus of higher humanity can occur (if enough of the rest of us will play our supporting roles). But now the true educator – the one through encounter with whom we are transformed and impelled in the direction of at once "becoming those we are" and contributing to the enhancement of life – is depicted more as a stimulus than as a leader to be followed or a paradigm to be imitated. Such an educator may be a kind of exemplar; but this type of educator is anything but an instructor, from whom information is received or rules and procedures are learned. The most important things to be learned have to do more with admirable traits to be emulated and standards to be aspired to than with specific ideas and values to be accepted. So in *SE* Nietzsche celebrates Schopenhauer as his educator without even discussing any of Schopenhauer's views.[5]

Even in *SE*, however, Nietzsche did not suppose that Schopenhauer could or should be everyone's educator, and was already worrying about where the educator(s) needed – to do for others what Schopenhauer had done for him – would come from.

> Where are we, scholars and unscholarly, high placed and low, to find the moral exemplars and models among our contemporaries, the visible epitome of morality for our time? . . . Never have moral educators been more needed, and never has it seemed less likely they would be found.
>
> > (*SE* 2, pp. 132–3)[6]

Nietzsche's intended audience here is all those "young souls" with the need, the courage and the ability to heed the call to "become yourself" – understood not self-indulgently, but rather in the sense that "your true nature is not concealed deep within you but immeasurably high above you, or at least above that which you usually take yourself to be" (*SE* 1, p. 129). For their sake he raises a question and poses a challenge that he subsequently took up himself in a variety of ways:

> Who is there, then, amid these changes of our era, to guard and champion humanity, the inviolable sacred treasure gradually accumulated by the most various races? Who will set up the *image of man* when all men feel in themselves only the self-seeking snake and the currish fear and have declined to the level of the animals or even of automata?
>
> > (*SE* 4, p. 150)

Nietzsche's prototype of the "free spirit" in *SE* is the "Schopenhauerian" type of humanity he goes on to sketch, in distinction not only from the all-too-human type of social-animal humanity he considers to be the human rule, but also from two alternative "images" or paradigms of a more genuine humanity he calls by the names of their most prominent representatives: Rousseau and Goethe. "Rousseauian man" for him represents naturalized humanity, renewed and revitalized through emancipation from the shackles of society and restoration to its basic instincts. "Goethean man" is the image of contemplative humanity, cultivated and sophisticated but detached from active involvement in life. "Schopenhauerian man" combines elements of both and also (for Nietzsche) supersedes both as the image of a "truly active" creative humanity, at once vital and spiritualized, and so most fully and truly human.

The significance of these images for Nietzsche in *SE* is that they have the power to liberate, stimulate and inspire – in short, to educate. Because of the diverse sorts of human development involved and the shortcomings associated with the first two of them, however, he takes them to differ not only in kind but also in value. Only the one he calls "Schopenhauerian" expresses and evokes the promise of an alternative form of humanity healthy and vital enough to be enduringly viable in this world, and sufficiently creative and spiritualized to justify itself – and human life and the world along with it. Cultural life is its domain; and so it is to the celebration and service of culture that Nietzsche looks in his response to the challenge he sets for himself when he writes:

> The hardest task still remains: to say how a new circle of duties may be devised from this ideal and how one can proceed towards so extravagant a goal through practical activity – in short, to demonstrate that this idea *educates* . . . And so we have seriously to ask the definite question: is it possible to bring that incredibly lofty goal so close to us that it educates us while it draws us aloft?
>
> (*SE* 5, p. 156)

Nietzsche's answer, of course, is affirmative; and it is of no little relevance to observe his elaboration upon it: "We have to be lifted up – and who are they who lift us? They are those true men, those who are no longer animal, the philosophers, artists and saints" (*SE* 5, p. 159). This is a veritable prescription projecting ahead to that "higher educator" we encounter in the pages of *Thus Spoke Zarathustra*, in whom there is something of each of this trinity of exceptions to the human rule. But *Zarathustra* was still years away, in conception as well as execution. Meanwhile Nietzsche could only observe that "The difficulty . . . lies for mankind in relearning and envisaging a new goal" (*SE* 6, p. 175). He was convinced that "the goal of culture is to promote the production of true human beings and nothing else" (*SE* 6, p. 164); but at this point he was clearer about the end than he was about what might be done to advance its achievement.

II

Nietzsche's concern with the inadequacies of what passed for education (and education of the highest quality at that) in his own time is reflected in his severe critiques, most notably in *SE* and his earlier series of lectures "On the future of our educational institutions." These critiques had as one of their recurring themes the contention that existing higher and lower forms of education alike were detrimental to intellectual as well as personal and human development, stultifying the minds and spirits of those submitting to them through over-specialization and regimentation. This concern did not fade away in the years that followed. On the contrary, Nietzsche's aphoristic volumes from *Human, All Too Human* (*HH*) to the first edition of *The Gay Science* (*GS*) may be regarded as an initial if tentative series of efforts on his part to fill this need himself. Thus he wrote of these works, on the back of the original edition of *The Gay Science*, that their "common goal is to erect a new image and ideal of the free spirit."[7] Here Nietzsche, as heir of Voltaire and the Enlightenment, sought by way of this "new image and ideal" to provide a beacon of enlightenment and inspiration. This "free spirit" series constituted a kind of experimental effort to contribute to and promote a different type of education.[8]

This series is educational in several respects. Through the hundreds of aphoristic reflections of which these books consist, Nietzsche was educating himself as well as his readers, working his way toward the kind of philosopher, thinker and free spirit he himself was becoming, while providing others with assistance in moving in the same direction themselves. And it is no system of doctrines that is set out here for the instruction of the reader, nor even a set of arguments advanced with the aim of compelling the reader's agreement. Rather, a variety of intellectual abilities and dispositions are being cultivated, with a view to fostering the emergence of the sort of human being realizing Nietzsche's conception of the "free spirit."

This involves a transformation of the way in which one understands oneself and relates to life and the world, along lines that Nietzsche clearly regarded as desirable. An indication of his underlying motivation is provided in the famous penultimate section of the original four-part edition of *GS* in which the idea of the eternal recurrence of every moment and episode of one's life is set forth with the question: "how well disposed would you have to become to yourself and to life to crave nothing more fervently than this ultimate confirmation and seal?" (*GS* 341). An education capable of bringing that about, without sacrificing the intellect, would be an education indeed!

Having reached this point, however, Nietzsche seems to have concluded that something more was needed than the kind of thing he had been doing in his "free spirit" series. One of the limitations of this series is that this extraordinary experiment in consciousness-raising was far stronger critically than it was constructively. The "free spirit" did not itself fill the bill, or suffice for this purpose. In the fourth and (at that time) final "book" of *GS*, however, and just prior to its concluding invocation of Zarathustra, a number of themes are sounded that point in the direction of this larger task.

These themes might be thought of as so many variations on a larger theme: the artistic transformation of our lives in ways endowing them with value sufficient to warrant their affirmation. Learning to "'give style' to one's character" (*GS* 299); learning to "live not only boldly but even gaily, and laugh gaily, too" by learning to savor such forms of "war and victory" as life affords – the pursuit of knowledge among them (*GS* 324); learning to love – for "love, too, has to be learned" (*GS* 334); wanting and learning "to become those we are, human beings . . . who give themselves laws, who create themselves" (*GS* 335); learning to glimpse and move toward "the 'humaneness' of the future" (*GS* 337); and learning to become capable of dealing with the challenge posed by the idea of existence conceived as subject to "eternal recurrence" (*GS* 341) – these are some of the variations on this theme with which this prelude to *Zarathustra* resounds. It was left to *Zarathustra*, however, to take up the challenge of this aesthetic education.

III

Nietzsche had begun in the early 1870s by thinking, or hoping, that someone – the Greeks, Wagner, Schopenhauer – could be found to serve as exemplars, mentors and educators for those like himself for whom neither reason nor revelation would suffice. Ten years later he had become disillusioned with all of those he formerly had revered. He had come to be convinced that not only traditional modes of philosophical and religious thought but also the available alternatives, both ancient and modern (including the natural sciences and historical scholarship), all fell radically short of educating our aspirations and valuations in a manner conducive to human flourishing in a postmodern world in which all gods have died. Indeed, he had come to see them not only as all-too-human and inadequate but as positively detrimental to that flourishing, having effects that boded ill rather than well for the future, and requiring something serving as both an antidote and an alternative. The kind of galvanizing educator that was needed was nowhere to be found; and while his efforts to promote a "new image and ideal of the free spirit" might be necessary steps in the right direction, they were far from sufficient.

What more could Nietzsche do? He could write *Thus Spoke Zarathustra*. I suggest that Zarathustra and *Zarathustra* were conceived to meet this need, "for all and none" – for none, if none were ready for the encounter, but for all who might (come to) be up to it. A work capable of making such a difference on such a scale would indeed be a great gift to humanity, particularly if nothing remotely comparable were anywhere else to be found. In this light, Nietzsche's subsequent extravagant estimation of the work becomes at least comprehensible. It was no mere work of literature, scholarship or philosophy, but rather a unique educational device capable of making a real and great difference in human life.

In *Zarathustra* Nietzsche undertook to meet head on the challenge of Schopenhauer – not the "Schopenhauer" of *SE*, but the Schopenhauer whose radical pessimism led him to champion the negation of life, and whom Nietzsche took to foreshadow the advent of nihilism. How can one affirm life – not merely endure it but relish it – if Schopenhauer was fundamentally right about the conditions of existence in this world (and the absence of any other, or any redeeming God beyond it), and if one refuses to sacrifice honesty and truthfulness?

Zarathustra is predicated upon the conviction that radical disillusionment, uncompromising truthfulness and unqualified life-affirmation are all humanly possible together, even under these circumstances. But it also proceeds from the recognition that this human possibility is not easily realized, and in fact requires the attainment of a new sensibility through an educational development that has free-spirited enlightenment as but its point of departure. To come to be capable of confronting what Nietzsche in *Ecce Homo* refers to as "the fundamental conception of this work, the idea of eternal recurrence, this highest formula of affirmation that is at all attainable" (*EH* III: Z: 1) with exhilaration rather than horror and despair, even the Zarathustra of the first parts of the work must undergo a major transformation. And Nietzsche shows us his education in a way that is designed to help effect ours as well, in the same direction and to the same ultimate effect.

But who, or what, is the educator here? Neither Zarathustra nor even Nietzsche himself at the outset, for both themselves had much to learn. The real educator, I suggest, is neither of them, but rather the work itself. What Nietzsche wrought in this work is the means of a remarkable possible educational experience and transformation that may reach into and affect the fundamental character of our humanity: a kind of spiritual *Bildungsroman*, akin perhaps both to Goethe's *Faust* and to Hegel's *Phenomenology*, but more radical than either of them. It is to *Zarathustra* rather than simply to Zarathustra that Nietzsche would above all have us respond. Zarathustra too has to be educated; and it is his education, as well as what he says and various other things about him, that is meant to serve ours.

IV

The Nietzschean educator is closer to the Socratic "midwife," and perhaps closer still to something like a catalyst of change and transformation. The basic concern of his desired kind of education is not simply to increase our knowledge of the world as it merely is, or even of ourselves as we already are. Those kinds of knowledge – of which Nietzsche had acquired and conveyed a great deal in his "free spirit" series – are at most only points of departure. What matters more to him is to raise our sights and awaken us to possibilities we will have to reach out and exert ourselves to realize. The object of such education is to "draw us out," as the terms *erziehen* and "educate" both fundamentally mean. Nietzsche would draw us out, beyond what we and the world already are, toward what we have it in us to become, and what we might make of ourselves and our world. And for him in *Zarathustra* as in *SE*, that calls for creativity rather than mere receptivity. Its general arena, beyond the empty abstractions and false dichotomies of the mental and the physical, the subjective and the objective, and the individual and the social, is the sphere of cultural life – Zarathustra's wilderness proclivities notwithstanding.

Zarathustra is not only the presentation of an educator who attempts to educate by free-spirited and wholesomely naturalistic enlightenment and counsel, doing a good deal of vivid debunking and reinterpreting and revaluing along the way – even though that is some of what we find, particularly in the First Part of the work (written more than two years before its final Fourth Part). It also is the presentation of the educator's education – and further, the vehicle and record of its author's education. And beyond that, it is the occasion and means of our own possible education. It is at these levels that the work does its real work, and serves to perform its larger and deeper educative function.

Zarathustra thus is not only Nietzsche's answer to the *New Testament*, but also his version of *Pilgrim's Progress*; and it is the whole multi-level phenomenon by which we are to be educated in the sense of *Erziehung*, being drawn out and up, toward becoming those we are. Zarathustra's speeches and reflections are part of it; but his transformations matter more, and the transfiguration of the picture of humanity to which all that transpires in the work contributes matters most of all. We are not taught what to think, or how to live, but we are shown the prospect of a possible humanity and the way toward a manner of life that Nietzsche believes can sustain us beyond all disillusionment.

As it is pursued in *Zarathustra*, Nietzsche's educational endeavor at once reflects and transcends the kinds of educating that had previously figured importantly in his thinking, in *BT*, in *SE*, and in the "free spirit" series. But it continues to undergo development in the course of the four parts of the work, in each of which something crucial is added, without which the kind of humanity attained would be seriously lacking. The successive transformations of sensibility that are explored supersede rather than negate previously attained forms; but the subsequent transformations are important. The sensibility of the First Part is still basically that of the Nietzschean "free spirit"; and it is still some distance from that which is barely envisioned in the penultimate section of *GS*, in which the idea of the "eternal recurrence" is invoked to assess one's disposition to oneself and to life (*GS* 341). In a large sense, the task of *Zarathustra* may be said to consist in the educational project of cultivating a sensibility capable of passing this "recurrence test," and so of affirming life under what Nietzsche considers to be the most daunting of possible descriptions.

The basic educational function performed by these many speeches elaborating upon the ideas of "faithfulness to the earth" and of the *Übermensch* as the "meaning of the earth" does not reduce to the specific points advanced in the various speeches. Rather, I would suggest, it consists in their use to give one a feeling for a genuine alternative to what Nietzsche elsewhere calls the "Christian-moral" scheme of interpretation and evaluation that we have come to take largely for granted – and that he believes is bound to collapse in the aftermath of "the death of God." What might it mean to achieve a reorientation of the way in which we think about ourselves that would make this life in this world the locus of meaning and value, and that would link them to considerations of differential quality of life and possible enhancements of life?

It is important to observe that, while Nietzsche retains the rubric of "tragedy" in connection with this new sensibility (Zarathustra is introduced in *GS* 342 under the heading *Incipit Tragoedia*[9]), he departs markedly and very significantly from the standpoint of *BT* in rejecting recourse to illusion as the key to life-affirmation. He makes much of this point in subsequent remarks about the figure of Zarathustra. Life-affirmation may require more than "truthfulness"; but the kind of life-affirmation Nietzsche associates with Zarathustra also requires nothing less. For nothing short of uncompromising truthfulness is immune to the threat of disillusionment in the aftermath of the severest critical scrutiny. Nietzsche does insist upon the importance of learning to appreciate and esteem surfaces, appearances, creations and even fictions as a part of the new sensibility he envisions; but in this sensibility such appreciation and esteeming are conjoined with truthfulness and honesty rather than indulged at their expense. So, in *Ecce Homo*, Nietzsche makes much of the point that "Zarathustra is more truthful than any other thinker" and "posits truthfulness as the highest virtue" (*EH* IV: 3).

But that is not the whole story, as Nietzsche makes clear in going on to state "what Zarathustra wants" in the following striking passage, which was nearly (and might well have been) his last word:

> this type of man that [Zarathustra] conceives, conceives reality as it is, being strong enough to do so; this type is not estranged or removed from reality but is reality itself and exemplifies all that is terrible and questionable in it – only in that way can man attain greatness.
>
> (*EH* IV: 5)

Truthfulness may be the "highest virtue"; but what Nietzsche here calls "greatness" is the highest goal. And much of *Zarathustra* has to do with the cultivation of a new sensibility appropriate to this revalued valuation of human life and possibility.[10]

The educational task of *Zarathustra* may thus be said to be that of confronting the "death of God" and rising to the challenge Nietzsche had sketched in *GS* a year earlier: "God is dead.

. . . And we – we still have to vanquish his shadow too" (*GS* 108). "When will we complete our de-deification of nature? When may we begin to 'naturalize' humanity in terms of a pure, newly discovered, newly redeemed nature?" (*GS* 109).[11] This is a kind of crisis Nietzsche had already been addressing in his "free spirit" series; but here he gives life to his belief in the possibility of an alternative to the "nihilistic rebound" from the death of God.

V

The lesson Nietzsche had learned from the Greeks, and the lesson of *BT*, has to do with the role the arts – and tragic art in particular – can play in effecting a transformation of our consciousness in such a way that not only our experience but our lives and the very aspect of existence are transformed, in a manner enabling us to affirm life and the world despite all. He may have given up on Wagner in this respect; but he did not abandon the very idea of what in *BT* he had called the "justification" of "existence and the world" as an "aesthetic phenomenon." *Zarathustra* was to do what Wagner had counterfeited, and so succeed where he had failed, in achieving a rebirth of tragedy (*Incipit tragoedie*), as a sensibility attuned to our finitude and yet infused with a fundamentally Dionysian affirmative spirit.

The educational task of Zarathustra is to assist those capable of doing so to attain this sensibility, and the associated forms of aspiration and valuation. Hence the "greatest weight" and recurrence test; for this is the education called for by Nietzsche's question, "how well disposed would you have to become to yourself and to life to crave nothing more fervently than this ultimate eternal confirmation and seal?" (*GS* 341). Hence also Nietzsche's characterization in *Ecce Homo* of "what Zarathustra wants" (*EH* IV: 5, cited above).

This kind of education may be conceived as Nietzsche's version of what in an earlier time had been called the cultivation of an "aesthetic sensibility"; and the need for it had already been intimated in *BT* in his contention that "it is only as an aesthetic phenomenon" that life and the world can ultimately be "justified" and so esteemed and affirmed. His advocacy of such education further may be regarded as an attempt to understand and work out the implications of his conviction that we must learn to sustain and nourish ourselves in the manner to which he alludes in the section of *GS* on "Our ultimate gratitude to art." He there has in mind "art as the good will to appearance," and writes:

> As an aesthetic phenomenon existence is still bearable for us, and art furnishes us with eyes and hands and above all the good conscience to be able to turn ourselves into such a phenomenon.
>
> (*GS* 107)

Nietzsche recognizes we may well need an education of the right sort to come to appreciate and find this not only a sufficient but also an invigorating diet. If we are to come to be able to relish life on the only terms it offers without the veils of illusion the Nietzsche of *BT* had deemed indispensable, we must learn not only to accept but also to love and cherish it under some possible interpretation or attainable configuration.

It is the educational task of *Zarathustra* to enable us to do so. To this end, like the tragic literature and culture whose earlier birth and demise Nietzsche had contemplated in *BT*, it must provide us with a way of facing and coming to terms with what he then had called "the terror and horror of existence" (*BT* 3) under the worst and bleakest of descriptions without being devastated by the encounter – and with a way of emerging from this encounter in a non-naïve but nonetheless exhilarated and affirmative manner. Indeed, it is of the utmost importance for Nietzsche in *Zarathustra* (and beyond) that one get beyond all naïveté and disillusionment. and leave behind not only despair, nausea, vengefulness, resentment and pity (including feeling sorry for oneself as well as others), but also all optimistic illusions, idealistic fantasies and the foolish belief in the sufficiency of fine sentiments and lofty principles.

This project by no means reduces to the inculcation of the secular-humanist maxims and principles one so often finds coming out of Zarathustra's mouth, especially in the first two parts of the work. Nietzsche may subscribe to the latter as far as they go; but one of the most important points of the work, brought out by Zarathustra's own transformation and abandonment of that mode of discourse, is that the "free spirit" mentality they express is far from sufficient as a way of thinking by which one might live. I see no reason to think Nietzsche does not mean us to take seriously the counsel Zarathustra offers in the first parts of the work. Quite clearly, however, he does at least mean to suggest that such rhetoric needs supplementing, by way of a fundamentally modified outlook; and that without the needed supplement this free-spirited enlightenment is incapable of carrying the day and sufficing to get one through the "dark night of the soul" by which Zarathustra himself is subsequently – if only temporarily – overwhelmed.

The enlightened humanistic outlook expressed in Zarathustra's early speeches and on a number of occasions thereafter is all very well and good as far as it goes; and it would be a most welcome thing if it could be much more widely attained. But Nietzsche did not stop there, and has Zarathustra venture further; for the attainment of this outlook is only a step in the right direction, and must be followed by others Nietzsche uses Zarathustra and *Zarathustra* to enable us to see – and to try to prompt us to take. These steps lead from the sunny Apollinian heights Zarathustra loves and evokes at the outset (in the First Part) through the dreary all-too-human swamps into which he descends (in the Second), and into the dark Dionysian depths underlying all of human existence, which give way to the strange and problematic brightness that is the other face of Dionysian reality (in the Third); and at length (in the Fourth Part) back into a human world in which we can recognize ourselves again – but with a difference.

This last part of the journey and educational process is absolutely essential, in my view; and for me this endows the Fourth (and final) Part of the work with a significance that is seldom appreciated. The outlook initially attained, both by Nietzsche at the time he wrote the First Part (1883) and by the Zarathustra it features, is only the beginning; and its insufficiency is soon brought home (in the Second Part, written within the year). Another crisis looms that the resources of aesthetic-naturalistic enlightenment are not adequate to meet. Zarathustra and his wisdom (and so Nietzsche as well) had to "ripen" further before he can either comprehend it or meet it. The crisis reaches a climax in the Third Part – the last part Nietzsche published, written a year later (1884) – in which that "ripening" proceeds far enough that Zarathustra has the resources to be capable of coming through it with a more profound wisdom, rooted in what might be called an aesthetically transfigured "ecstatic naturalism."

That climax is followed by another, however, or rather by a kind of anti-climax. The educator's education – and Nietzsche's, and ours – is far from complete at that point. A great gulf has opened up between the soaring height attained at the Third Part's end and the solid (or at any rate mundane) ground of daily life and human reality. A "Monday morning Dionysianism" may not be a human (or even a conceptual) possibility; but in the privately printed Fourth Part (written in 1885), we find that there is a way of bringing it all down to earth that is not entirely a descent from the sublime into the ridiculous. The all-too-human remains, and indeed is very much in evidence in the bizarre array of specimens of "higher humanity" Zarathustra collects. But by the end one can begin to understand what it actually can mean to go on without illusions and false hopes, yet undeterred by the circumstances that might inspire pity and warrant talk of tragedy, and sustained by a life-sized reaffirmation of life as the very ambiguous thing it is.

It is particularly important, in this connection, to recognize that Nietzsche employs both the figure of Zarathustra and such notions as the *Übermensch* ("overman," human and yet more than merely human) and Eternal Recurrence as devices in the context of his educational project of transforming our sensibility, rather than literalistically. In the language of *BT*, the image of the *Übermensch* represents his version of the Apollinian moment in this process, while the notion of the Eternal Recurrence represents the Dionysian – and neither, by itself, is enough.

The *Übermensch* may be regarded as an image introduced and employed to provide the (re-)education of our aspirations and our thinking about the enhancement of life with a kind of compass, enabling us to gain a sense of direction even if not a clear description of our goal (which would be impossible). Its upshot for our lives is the notion of attained and attainable "higher humanity." (The relation of these two images may usefully be conceived as somewhat analogous to the relation between the Greeks' Olympian deities and their heroes.) The notion of the Eternal Recurrence, on the other hand, is an idea Nietzsche appropriates and employs in connection with a larger and more fundamental (re-)education of our sensibility, as the touchstone of the transformation of our basic disposition toward ourselves and our lives and world. It is basically the idea of what transpires in the world as ever the same old story (which for Nietzsche is a matter of power-relationships), rather than any sort of linear development. Translated into its upshot, it becomes Nietzsche's conception of the affirmation of life, with *amor fati* ("the love of fate") as its insignia.

If there is any such counterpart figure to the third (tragic) moment in *BT* in which these other two moments come together and are *aufgehoben*, I would suggest that it can only be the figure of Zarathustra himself. And by this I do not mean simply the Zarathustra we encounter in the First Part, but rather the Zarathustra who begins as a well-meaning enlightened humanist, and winds up far wiser and more human by the end of the work. The upshot for us and our lives, in this case, is the newly and more truly human "future humanity" Nietzsche had recently envisioned and described (*GS* 337), possessed of what he went on (a year after completing the Fourth Part) to call the "great health" (*GS* 381).[12] Here one would be neither preoccupied with the dream of the *Übermensch* nor obsessed with the vision of the Eternal Recurrence, but rather concerned to get on with one's life and work – in the spirit of Zarathustra's parting lines at the end of the Fourth Part – as the only meaningful way of "becoming who one is": "My suffering and my pity for suffering – what does it matter? Am I concerned with *happiness*? I am concerned with my *work*" (*Z* IV: 20).

At this point mythic imagery gives way to actual human life as it must and can be lived – but now finding or working out one's own way ("This is my way; where is yours?"), in a spirit of transformed aspiration and sensibility. Neither the "meaning of the earth" associated with the image of the *Übermensch* nor the "affirmation" and *amor fati* associated with the Eternal Recurrence remain the talk of the town, or become the elements of a new creed and catechism; for their work is done when they have supplemented the "free spirit" and seen the latter-day pilgrims through their educational progress and childhood's end.

In a work the purpose of which is to educate our aspirations, valuations and sensibility, Nietzsche considers it fair to make use of ideas that serve to reorient our thinking regardless of their mere "truth-value" (or lack thereof). The notion of the *Übermensch* is one, and the image of the Eternal Recurrence is another. Indeed, the very figure of Zarathustra "himself" is a third. They are neither the literal truth nor illusions, nor are they even "noble lies," but rather something like the salient forms of imagery figuring centrally in myths. Their "truth" or justification is a matter of their value as means of enabling us to come to understand something important about life and the world that they do not literally describe or designate. Nietzsche does not tell us things about Zarathustra, and have Zarathustra proclaim and "teach" things about the *Übermensch* and the Eternal Recurrence, in order to have us "learn" them. Rather, he does so in the course of (and as part of) his effort to prompt us to the sort of response that may foster and further the enhancement of our lives.

The *Übermensch*, Eternal Recurrence and Zarathustra himself thus all have their places within the educational process Nietzsche crafts for us, rather than at its end, as its results. They are among the materials of a ladder that is to be dispensed with once it has been climbed. If we become fixated upon them, we have made the mere means of this education into its end; for their role is not to capture and hold our attention, but rather to aid us in reaching the developmental point at which we can go on without them – as Zarathustra himself suggests often enough.

Nietzsche earlier (in the time of *BT*, and even in *On the Uses and Disadvantages of History for Life*, written in 1874, just before *SE*) had been much concerned with the role of myth in making life possible, worth living and capable of flourishing; and he had been persuaded that, for better or worse, its efficacy in this respect depended upon illusion. As was earlier observed, however, he subsequently had second thoughts on this matter. While he continued to make much of the ubiquity and indispensability of fictions, lies and errors in human life, I believe that he came to understand that he had been guilty of a number of oversimplifications here, and that in particular it is a mistake to suppose that everything in the entire domain of human thought must be either "true" (in some impossible absolute sense) or "false." This is a false dichotomy; and what is important about the contents of myth and art alike is something else altogether – namely, their power to shape our dispositions and ways of thinking, feeling and esteeming.

Nietzsche subsequently (after *BT* and the *Meditations*) moved away from the celebration of myth, and during his "free spirit" years flirted with the idea that we may have to learn either to get along without it or to resign ourselves to the inescapability and necessity of all-too-human forms of untruth. He retained or soon regained the conviction that no healthy and vital culture and humanity can be attained and sustained without something of the sort. But he would seem to have come to the realization that the "something of the sort" need not be either myths of the kind by which we long have lived or the newer myths of scientism, nationalism and Wagnerianism. Something like *Zarathustra* might do the job, in a way that does not exact too high a price, does not entail the sacrifice of honesty and intellectual integrity – and does not self-destruct when the truthfulness it promotes is brought to bear upon itself.

To do the kind of job that myth has done, compelling images and representations of alternative interpretations are still required. Something on the order of the fare Nietzsche serves up in *Zarathustra* is needed, if our thinking is not to remain confined to the dead end of mere critique. It is a myth-substitute for the modern world, intended for a humanity (or at least for its vanguard) in transition, ready to be weaned away from its dependency upon myths, and yet still not fully mature, being either too cavalier or too desperate at the prospect of having to make do without them. This myth-substitute engenders a new enthusiasm, and then provides its own antidote (in the form of the Fourth Part) to ensure that the new enthusiasm does not congeal into a new dogmatism. For Nietzsche understood that we must be able eventually to distance ourselves from the means of our education, even if we must initially be seduced and induced to engage with it and take it seriously enough to be affected by it. As in the case of myth, literal truth is not what it is all about; and a fundamentalist turn of mind with respect to the "teachings" of Zarathustra would have been no more welcome to Nietzsche among would-be disciples than among detractors.

The Fourth Part makes it clear, if the first three do not (and as Nietzsche may have feared after writing them that they did not), that these teachings are not intended to be embraced as gospel truth. Its irony, parodies, grotesqueries and humor are more than sufficient for this purpose. But the whole of the work shares in this double effect, as a kind of self-parodying quasi-myth that we are expected both to take seriously and to see for what it is. It is offered to us as no mere self-parody, however, as Nietzsche's hyperbolic hype with respect to it in *Ecce Homo* renders obvious. He realized that it would take something approaching a miracle to enable humanity to get from where it is to where it needs to go without meeting one or another of the sorry fates he envisions – and *Zarathustra*, he believed, is that miracle.

But it can do its work only if it is taken seriously. Getting anything of the kind taken seriously, however, especially by the very readers Nietzsche wanted most to reach (with their modern and perhaps nascently postmodern sophistication), might seem to be a virtual impossibility. But this is a part of the genius of the work he came up with: its self-parodic character is neither what it is all about nor a hopeless stumbling block to sophisticated readers. Rather, it is the very device that enables such readers to take it seriously. We bear witness to that ourselves.

By the time of *Zarathustra*, Nietzsche both felt the need for something more than the ever-increasing sophistication of the "free spirit" series, and knew better than to think that anything on the order of Wagner's new mythology – or any of the older ones around, including that to which Wagner had returned – could be embraced by anyone like himself. He therefore sought to come up with something that would incorporate the means of coming to discern and attain an appropriately transformed and promising sensibility, in a form that protects it as well as possible against dismissal for reasons of intellectual integrity. *Zarathustra* is the result. We can take it seriously precisely because it is made clear that we are not expected to believe it. What is to be taken seriously in and about it is not the cognitive content of the images and ideas by means of which our attention is attracted and our thinking is engaged (let alone the story-line). Rather, it is the human possibilities that are reconfigured and opened up to us as the work unfolds, and as we respond.

VI

Zarathustra may fall short of deserving Nietzsche's claims for it, and may have fallen short of his hopes for it as well; and as a literary vehicle for his philosophical ideas it may leave a good deal to be desired, as anyone who has tried to use it to "teach Nietzsche" in a philosophy course can attest. Yet regarded as an educational device of the kind I have been describing, and assessed by any more modest standard of success than Nietzsche's own, it would seem to me to be a truly remarkable accomplishment. Most of humanity has been and is likely to remain untouched by it (for better or worse); and it has lent itself to uses and abuses both silly and sinister, as well as to others it is less awkward to acknowledge. Yet it does have the power to do – at least for some – the sort of thing Nietzsche attributed to his encounter with Schopenhauer; and it can have a great and profound educational effect upon the sensibilities of kindred spirits.

Zarathustra may deal in consciousness-raising and attitude-adjustment; but it is almost in a class by itself among efforts of this kind in the philosophical literature after Plato. Anecdotal evidence suggests that it not only is what first attracted many of us to Nietzsche, but also has figured importantly in the attraction of many others to philosophy who have long since left Nietzsche behind. And it has at least rocked the boats of countless students and others who have happened upon it.

This may be a far cry from saving humanity from the Scylla and Charybdis of fanaticism and nihilism, on whose rocks we may yet founder. But I do believe that the kind of education one can get from *Zarathustra* can enable those who worry about such things to navigate through and beyond those straits at least as well as anything else around. For those who do not worry about such things, however, it is perhaps better dead than read. It is, after all, 'a book for all and none'. (But what if they offered an education and nobody came?)

NOTES

1 Nietzsche, manuscript source uncertain. Cited elsewhere as "VII: 215."

2 Friedrich Schiller, *On the Aesthetic Education of Man*, trans. Reginald Snell (New York, Frederick Ungar, 1965).

3 I shall follow the common practice of identifying Nietzsche citations whenever possible by the initials of the English titles of the works or other volumes from which they are taken, in the translations indicated below, and of using Arabic numerals to identify Nietzsche's numbered

sections. In the case of citations from *Ecce Homo*, the roman numerals identify the main parts of the work, and the internal initials identify the writings he is discussing in the third part, "Why I write such good books." In the case of citations from *Thus Spoke Zarathustra*, "P" refers to the Prologue to the First Part, roman numerals refer to the four main parts of the work, and the first arabic numerals refer either to the numbered sections of the Prologue or to the numbers of the speeches or sections of the four main parts of the work. (While not numbered in print, the speeches and sections can easily and usefully be given numbers.) Subsequent arabic numerals refer to numbered subsections within these speeches or sections.

BT *The Birth of Tragedy*, with *The Case of Wagner*, trans. Walter Kaufmann (New York, Vintage, 1967)

EH *Ecce Homo*, with *On the Genealogy of Morals*, trans. Walter Kaufmann (New York, Vintage, 1967)

GS *The Gay Science*, trans. Walter Kaufmann (New York, Vintage, 1974)

SE *Schopenhauer as Educator*, in *Untimely Meditations*, trans. R. J. Hollingdale (Cambridge, Cambridge University Press, 1983)

Z *Thus Spoke Zarathustra*, in *The Portable Nietzsche*, trans. Walter Kaufmann (New York, Viking, 1954)

4 See my *Nietzsche* (London, Routledge & Kegan Paul, 1983), ch. VIII.

5 See my Introduction to *Schopenhauer as Educator* in *Unmodern Observations* (an alternative translation of *Untimely Meditations*), ed. William Arrowsmith (New Haven, Conn., Yale University Press, 1990), pp. 147–61.

6 Page numbers in quotations from *SE* refer to the page numbers in Hollingdale's translation. They are given, as well as Nietzsche's section numbers, because the sections are quite long.

7 See the Kaufmann translation of this work (New York, Vintage, 1974), p. 30.

8 See my Introduction to the 1996 edition of R. J. Hollingdale's translation of *Human, All Too Human* (Cambridge, Cambridge University Press).

9 "The tragedy begins." This is the heading Nietzsche gave to the final section of the last part of the original edition of *The Gay Science*, which consists in a version of the opening of the Prologue to the First Part of *Zarathustra*, published the next year but obviously already well under way.

10 See my *Nietzsche*, chs V and VI, esp. pp. 326–40 and 380–94.

11 See my "Nietzsche's Gay Science, or, How to naturalize cheerfully," in Robert C. Solomon and Kathleen M. Higgins (eds) *Reading Nietzsche* (New York, Oxford University Press, 1988), pp. 68–86.

12 It is well worth noting that Nietzsche returned to the project of *The Gay Science* after finishing the four parts of *Zarathustra* and writing *Beyond Good and Evil*, publishing an expanded second edition with a new Fifth Book and a new Preface in 1887, just prior to *On the Genealogy of Morals*. *Zarathustra* thus did not mark the end or abandonment of that project, but rather only an extended intermission in it – albeit a very important and perhaps necessary one for Nietzsche.

24

JOHN STUART MILL: DEMOCRACY AS SENTIMENTAL EDUCATION

Elizabeth Anderson

The only school of genuine moral sentiment is a society between equals.

John Stuart Mill, *The Subjection of Women*

UTILITARIANISM, DEMOCRACY, AND ELITISM IN EDUCATION

American universities usually introduce students to utilitarianism through the work of John Stuart Mill. This choice makes pedagogical sense: John Stuart Mill is a vastly more interesting, accessible, and readable author than Jeremy Bentham, the acknowledged founder of utilitarianism. Yet the choice is apt to lead to confusions, both about Mill, who departed in significant ways from orthodox utilitarianism, and about mainstream utilitarianism, which never accepted Mill's innovative departures. Mill thought that orthodox utilitarianism expressed important truths, but not the whole truth, about politics and morals.

The creative tensions in Mill's life work between enduring doctrines of utilitarianism and sophisticated emendations are particularly evident in Mill's philosophy of education. Utilitarians have always viewed education as a key tool for moral progress. To orthodox utilitarians, progress consisted in bringing happiness to the masses, not just to elites. A democratic temperament pervades utilitarian thought. From the conservative, elitist perspective of the day, this democratic temperament threatened the highest values of civilization. Mill's philosophy of education can be viewed as attempting to reconceive the conflict between democracy and elitism. There are significant elitist strands in Mill's thought. But this elitism reflects Mill's attempt to perfect and advance rather than restrain democracy, by paying attention to the intellectual and sentimental prerequisites of successful democratic practice.

Orthodox utilitarianism identified important relations between democracy and education. Utilitarianism was originally proposed as a theory of legislation. It directs legislators to pass laws that tend to produce the maximum happiness or pleasure of the members of society. To this end, we need legislators who are motivated to pursue the maximum happiness, and who have the knowledge of what means will produce this end. Periodic democratic elections provide the motive: if politicians don't give the people what will make them happy, the majority will elect someone else to exercise power. Scientific education provides the knowledge: legislators and civil servants must be trained in the principles of logic and empirical investigation through mathematics and the natural sciences, and study the modern social scientific disciplines of economics, psychology, sociology, and law. Science is the key to determining what policies would be effective in promoting happiness.

Utilitarianism is democratic not simply in advocating the political structures of democracy, such as the universal franchise, majority rule, and periodic elections. It is also, in an important sense, *culturally* democratic. The aim of government is to maximize pleasure, regardless of who enjoys it. One unit of pleasure counts the same, whether it is enjoyed by a noble aristocrat, a refined aesthete, or a lowly worker. Furthermore, orthodox utilitarianism treats all tastes as equal. One unit of pleasure counts the same, regardless of its source. Bentham insisted that so long as the quantities of pleasure were the same, "pushpin is as good as poetry." Since no pleasures are intrinsically superior to any others, there is no sense to be made of trying to improve or uplift people's aims. Orthodox utilitarianism therefore seeks only to satisfy people's given desires. It is anti-elitist, both in the sense of disparaging the usefulness of elites and in downgrading elite conceptions of value. Orthodox utilitarians regarded elites with distrust, as people who tried to maintain their privileges by keeping the masses ignorant and submissive.

These two democratic themes in utilitarianism – one about governance, the other about culture – inspired revolutionary changes in education. The vast expansion of mass education, and the dominance in modern universities of schools of applied sciences such as medicine, engineering, and business, owe much to the influence of utilitarian thinking. Utilitarianism also inspired the dramatic reversal, over the past century, in the relative standing of the liberal arts disciplines. Consider the prestige hierarchy of liberal arts disciplines currently entrenched in most modern universities. Mathematics and the natural sciences stand on top, holding the greatest authority in virtue of their unmatched rigor, empirical success, and technological applications. The social sciences stand in the middle, seeking greater prestige by trying to copy the methods and thus the empirical and practical successes of the natural sciences. The arts and humanities lie on the bottom, held in suspicion as useless luxuries, thought to be lacking either intellectual rigor or a coherent rationale for their pursuit, but hanging on out of a vague sense that something would be missing if their study were not continued. Theology has suffered even worse ignominy, having been expelled from most public universities and marginalized in divinity schools.

This hierarchy of liberal arts reflects utilitarian sensibilities. It is evident that the natural sciences, and hoped that the social sciences, can dramatically advance human happiness, by improving medicine, economic policy, and the like. Empirical knowledge of causal connections helps us achieve our aims more effectively, and thereby increases happiness. It is less clear how the arts and humanities increase human happiness. Notoriously, undergraduates tend to regard the humanities as impractical, a humanities degree as imparting no valuable skills. Of what use are the humanities? Once tastes are democratized, one can no longer say that they uplift us. Perhaps, then, they entertain and divert us. But if, as Bentham claimed, poetry is no better than pushpin, then why make poetry an object of serious study rather than discretionary indulgence? And how many people really do get much happiness out of studying medieval literature, say? An orthodox utilitarian justification of the arts and humanities is not easy to find. But perhaps it is not impossible. Theology, however, has virtually no chance of finding a utilitarian rationale. Most utilitarians regarded theology as nothing more than pernicious superstitions propagated by elites to keep the masses subdued.

This utilitarian hierarchy of liberal arts fundamentally challenged the conservative nineteenth century hierarchy in England. At that time the Church of England controlled most universities. Theology was the most prestigious discipline. Classical studies came next, with a peculiar emphasis on drilling students in composing Greek and Latin verse. Mathematics followed. Finally, England's top universities treated the study of the natural and social sciences with disdain. In contrast with the educational policies of France and Germany, which supported university-based science and engineering programs, England relied to a surprising degree on its tradition of independent invention, tinkering, and amateur science to promote industrial progress.

Like the utilitarians, English conservatives based their hierarchy of liberal arts on dual theories of governance and culture. But their theories were elitist ones, borrowed partly from classical sources, partly from Christian ones. Consider first governance. The ends of government were determined not by surveying the given wants of the masses, but by consulting the supposedly higher, eternal values supported by the Church and the classics. The tiny aristocratic elite comprised the only people fit to rule because only they could be trusted to uphold such noble values. Legislative skill depended on rhetoric, the art of persuasion, rather than social science. Theology and the humanities, especially Greek and Latin rhetoric and verse, were therefore most important for those destined to govern.

Consider next elite cultural values. The liberal arts were originally contrasted with the servile arts: they were the arts that fit a man for freedom rather than servitude. Freedom here referred to a particular class standing open only to propertied men. Free men were men whose independent wealth freed them from the burdens of toiling for a living so that they could pursue nobler ends at leisure. Where the servile arts taught workers how to supply the basic needs of life, the liberal arts taught free men the higher ends of life. The humanities enjoyed special prestige as the disciplines that taught men such uplifting values. This class-based ideology also ranked the theoretical or "pure" sciences over the practical or applied sciences. Workers pursued the applied sciences such as engineering for merely instrumental reasons connected to the necessities and conveniences of life. By contrast, men of leisure pursued the pure sciences for their own sakes.

In nineteenth-century England, this conservative model of education was fairly decrepit. It suffered from the obsolescence of the rationale for learning classical languages. Latin was once the common language of all educated Europeans, obviously indispensable to any person aspiring to higher learning. Now it was a dead language, of no use in communicating fresh ideas. Yet English universities stressed Latin and Greek composition, at the expense of reading great works of ancient literature and studying ancient history and philosophy. This distorted emphasis was due in part to the contradictions between classical and Christian values. The ancient Greek philosophers pursued reason freely where it led them, which was nowhere near Christianity. The Church suppressed free inquiry in the universities, and showed little interest in developing students' critical and analytical skills. Anglican doctrine was taught as dogma, insulated from critical scrutiny. Serious study of ancient Greek and Roman philosophers and statesmen would have raised questions that the Church would rather were not entertained. Students did learn some mathematics, although rarely at an advanced level. And math classes were valued more for the discipline and obedience they instilled through boring drill and rote exercises, than for their potential to sharpen students' analytical reasoning skills or to enable them to understand the basis of physical laws.

In this controversy between English educational traditions and orthodox utilitarian theory, where did John Stuart Mill stand? Consider his 1867 "Inaugural Address delivered to the University of St Andrews."[1] Here Mill stood squarely with the utilitarians in stressing the centrality of the modern empirical sciences to higher education, the importance of advanced mathematics and logic, and the dangers of dogmatically enforcing theological and moral views at the expense of free inquiry. Today's reader might find Mill's lengthy defense of these ideas tedious, for they express what we take to be obvious truths today. What modern university could take itself seriously that did not devote considerable resources to teaching the natural and social sciences? But Mill was fighting an ossified system of education that hardly recognized the value of these disciplines.

A closer reading of the "Inaugural Address" answers a question many humanities students have asked themselves: granting that universities ought to offer courses in the natural and social sciences, why must every student be required to take them? What is the utility to an English major of taking physics? Mill offered two arguments. First, the physical sciences offer the most successful examples of the use of observation and reasoning to attain truth. They therefore stand as models for the other disciplines. This methodological argument has had lasting influence on the social sciences, with mixed results.

Mill's second argument is more interesting. The curricular battle between utilitarians and conservative elites was framed as a conflict between modern science and ancient arts, between technical education and the cultivated intellect. Democracy needs technically trained experts who know how to determine effective means to satisfy people's wants. Many utilitarians could see less need for a democracy to have a class of broadly educated intellects. Mill disagreed. The fundamental purpose of a university is not to train professionals or experts but to produce cultivated human beings. An enlightened public is necessary to democracy, to prevent an otherwise credulous population from being duped by charlatans posing as experts and promoting absurd or destructive policies. The class of broadly educated people needn't acquire expertise in all the sciences. But they should know enough of the leading principles of each to be able to tell the difference between a charlatan and a real expert, and thereby to know where to turn when expertise is needed. Mill thereby turns the elite ideal of the liberally educated, cultivated intellect to the service of democracy, rather than against it.

Thus Mill rejected the alternatives presented by both the reforming, utilitarian scientific moderns and the conservative, humanistic traditionalists. Universities did not have to choose between a scientific curriculum and one centered on classical studies. They could teach both. Mill was not merely proposing to meet each educational camp halfway. In important respects, he stepped outside their debates altogether. Although classical studies retained a prominent position in Mill's scheme, he mercilessly criticized the absurd waste of forcing students to compose poetry in Greek and Latin. He urged instead that it turn away from composition toward ancient history and literature. Why study the ancients? Not for the reason today's conservatives offer, that there lie the fundamental principles of "Western Civilization." On the contrary, Mill thought the ancients worth studying precisely for how alien they are. The classical curriculum was Mill's version of multicultural education: its point is to get students out of the habit of parochial thinking, to recognize that their own customs, thoughts, and culture are neither universal nor necessary. (Modern cultures, he thought, were best studied directly, through travel to foreign lands rather than university courses.)

Nor did Mill endorse the conservative view that the ancients are to be valued for teaching that there is an immutable hierarchy of human beings, and for exemplifying the highest spiritual levels of this hierarchy. On the contrary, although he praised the ancients for holding up an example of excellence that could inspire moderns, he judged them to be spiritually simple and superficial compared to complex, brooding, self-conscious, psychologically insightful moderns. In his comparisons of ancients and moderns, Mill rejected the view that the pursuit of excellence requires the anti-democratic belief in a rank order of human beings. Instead, the ancients and moderns exemplify diverse dimensions of excellence and deficiency. The ancients are better at literary form and dialectical reasoning, the moderns at natural science and literary substance – that is, at expressing nuanced, complex, and deep feelings. We can learn even from those who are inferior to us in some respects, for they may be superior to us in others. Furthermore, as multiculturalism teaches us, we can learn from sheer cultural difference, too. In these passages we can hear Mill again undermining the simplistic dichotomy between elitism and democracy, conservative and utilitarian education.

More daringly, Mill challenged both reformers and traditionalists in upholding the importance of the fine arts, a subject absent from the favored curricula of both sides. He rejected Bentham's democracy of tastes in favor of cultivating "those high feelings, on which we mainly rely for lifting men above low and sordid objects, and giving them a higher conception of what constitutes success in life."[2] Mill saw the fine arts as inspiring the higher feelings and sentiments that motivate people to pursue noble aims.

Here, perhaps, the elitist strains in Mill are most clear. But are they as anti-democratic as they seem? A closer reading suggests not. For the nobler feelings include most prominently the "feeling of the miserable smallness of mere self in the face of . . . the collective mass of our fellow creatures – the poorness and insignificance of human life if it is to be all spent in making things comfortable for ourselves and our kin, and raising ourselves and them a step or two on the social ladder."[3] This passage appears to rebuke both elites and masses. As a check against elitist attitudes of individual superiority to the masses, he recommends humility before "the collective mass of our fellow creatures." Yet such humility cannot be based on the thought that the masses have worthier aims than elites: Mill instead castigates the masses for their small-minded egoistic materialism, and counsels them to aspire to higher aims. In other works, Mill made it clear that one function of an elite, educated class is to defend a vision of life's ends that transcends the petty selfishness, acquisitiveness, and social climbing of the middle-class.[4]

Mill's "Inaugural Address" thus navigates a difficult course through the conflict between elitism and democracy. Mill sought a democratic culture without a democracy of tastes: a democracy that could affirm the higher worth of some conceptions of life over others. And he identified a need for an educated elite to sustain democracy. Government must draw upon the expertise of an educated elite to frame and administer effective laws. An educated elite was needed to prevent democracy from degenerating into demagoguery. It was needed, also, to sustain a vision of higher ends against the homogenizing forces of democracy that pressure individuals into mass conformity, and against the narrowing forces of middle-class, crass commercialism that focus people's minds on the material interests of themselves and their small circle. Mill called upon higher education to cultivate such an elite. But once so formed and placed in an exalted role, what could prevent such an elite from looking down their noses at the masses? Wouldn't class-based contempt threaten to undermine democracy from above? And wouldn't this only reinforce the ingrained servility of the lower classes to elites that was pervasive in nineteenth-century Britain?

Arrogance from high stations, deference from below; here was a mass of sentiments inimical to democracy, of which Mill was well aware. And Mill deprived himself of a central utilitarian device for cutting away at these sentiments: the democracy of tastes, the relativist doctrine that one person's tastes are no better than anyone else's. Mill saw that democracy required not just scientific education, but an education of the sentiments. Sentimental education was an idea alien to orthodox utilitarianism. We need to examine more closely how Mill modified utilitarianism to accommodate this notion. Let us turn, then, to Mill's conception of moral sentiments, and the role he saw them playing in democratic culture.

UTILITARIAN AND DEMOCRATIC MORAL SENTIMENTS

We have seen that the orthodox utilitarians supported democracy in part by appealing to the equality of tastes. Utilitarians insist that every unit of happiness counts the same, regardless of who enjoys it or what the source of the enjoyment is. This principle tells us not to value the happiness of the aristocrat or aesthete more than the happiness of the worker or peasant. But this principle needn't support democratic equality. Democracy requires the equality of citizens, not just the equality of pleasures. Democratic equality is a substantive type of human relationship, opposed to hierarchy, domination, and servility, not just a principle for aggregating happiness.

At least three potential obstacles stand in the way of using utilitarianism to support democratic relations. One is *paternalism*: one party to a relationship may claim to know best what is in the joint interests of both, and thus claim entitlement to act without consulting the other party's wishes. Thus Mill's utilitarian father, James Mill, argued that because women's interests were included in the interests of their fathers and husbands, women could be happily excluded from political participation. Another is the possibility of an *aristocracy of hedonists*: some people may have vastly greater capacities for happiness and suffering than others. The utilitarian economist Francis Edgeworth claimed that the highest strata of culture were more susceptible to pleasure and pain than the lower. Happiness was therefore maximized by making the laboring classes, who suffer little from hard work, serve the aristocracy, who can enjoy far greater pleasure than the doltish masses but would suffer far more than they from having to work for their pleasures.[5] Finally, utilitarianism implies *indifference to distributive considerations*: it tells us to maximize total happiness, not to distribute happiness equally. It thus puts no principled obstacles in front of the grossest subjection of some for the sake of advancing the greater happiness of others. Even if everyone has equal capacities for happiness, the sheer numbers of people who enjoy the subordination or oppression of a minority may be sufficient to outweigh the suffering thereby inflicted on minorities.

These possibilities raise a question for utilitarians: why support democracy? This question has particular relevance for Mill, who, while a democrat at home, was an imperialist abroad. John Stuart Mill, like his father James Mill, was for decades a bureaucrat for the British East India Company. His views on imperial educational policy were considerably more elitist than his father's. James Mill argued that the Company should spend its educational funds on liberating the Indian masses from subjection to the selfish Brahman elite. It could do so by teaching useful knowledge – primarily English, which would give Indians access to the vast technical knowledge available in English language texts. Traditional Hindu teachings merely kept the subjugated masses in thrall to a selfish Brahman elite by promulgating superstition and intellectual despotism. John Stuart Mill opposed his father's educational views in a dispatch he drafted for the Company in 1836. There he argued that the Company should spend its educational funds on subsidizing schools of traditional Indian learning, which were attended by a tiny Indian cultural elite. He argued that such an elite was needed to keep Indian intellectual culture alive. Thus Mill wanted to enlist the forces of imperialism to maintain the cultural hierarchy of Indian society, against the more democratizing policies of his father.

Was Mill simply a hypocrite in advocating democracy at home and imperialism and aristocracy abroad? Or worse, was he a racist? A closer reading of the record suggests more complex answers. Ironically, Mill's support for traditional Indian learning reflected some qualms about cultural imperialism: he thought it arrogant and insensitive for Britain to undermine cultural traditions which Indians widely revered. Yet these qualms did not undermine his commitment to the imperialist project as such, which he justified on paternalist grounds, as bringing progress to backward civilizations. To attack cherished Indian cultural institutions would only alienate the people from the progressive projects promoted by the British East India Company. In supporting them, the Company would enlist the support of Indian cultural elites in interpreting and adapting useful British knowledge to Indian circumstances.[6]

Mill's views on imperialism and democracy reflect his historicism. He admitted that nothing in the logic of utilitarianism entailed support for egalitarian social relations or distributions of goods. For some historical circumstances, inequality, even slavery, is necessary. In the rudest ages of humanity, subjection to authoritarian rule was necessary to teach people in a state of savage independence how to live at peace with one another. Although the general historical tendencies of humanity are progressive, at any one time different civilizations are at different stages of development. The standard of utility must be applied with a view to the progressive character of human beings. Inequality is justified only as a means to develop human capacities to a more advanced stage. This provides a utilitarian rationale for imperialism, on condition that foreign rule actually advances the capacities of the colonized. Once inequality is no longer necessary for progress, equality in social relations is the rule of justice.

On Mill's view, then, there is something in the character of human progress that leads to equality as the preferred form of human relationship from a utilitarian point of view. What could this be? To orthodox utilitarians, progress consisted of scientific, technological and economic advancement, by which society enjoyed ever greater means to satisfy given wants or conceptions of happiness. Mill meant by progress something different: that people were progressing in their *capacity* for happiness. This notion is hard to square with the democracy of tastes, which measures pleasures by quantity, not quality. It is hard to see how people have the capacity to feel a greater quantity of pleasure now than in earlier ages. But Mill had a qualitative conception of pleasure, according to which some pleasures were higher in worth than others. The higher pleasures arise from the gratification of the higher faculties and sentiments. People were progressing in their capacities for happiness because their higher faculties and sentiments were becoming more developed.

So far, Mill's story of higher and progressing pleasures plays into Edgeworth's idea that there is an aristocracy of hedonists, a cultural elite with greater capacities for happiness and suffering than the common lot. And indeed, Mill thought this was so. This supports the temptation to read Mill's distinction between higher and lower pleasures as an expression of elitist snobbery, where the higher pleasures are taken in things the masses would never appreciate: refined poetry, esoteric philosophy, atonal music, and the like. It is as if Mill were retorting to Bentham by insisting that poetry is better than pushpin, after all.

Mill's belief in a cultural elite does not make him an elitist snob, however. He never took the sophisticated tastes of aesthetes and snobs as his exemplars of higher pleasures. The higher pleasures were rather the pleasures people take in the exercise of their capacities for autonomy and sympathy. The pleasures of autonomy or self-government consist in the pleasures we take in exercising imagination, judgment, choice, and initiative in leading our lives. The pleasures of sympathy and moral sentiments consist in the pleasures we take in caring about other people, the pleasures we take in other people's happiness, and in doing the right thing by them. Mill believed that in his society there were vast inequalities in the degree to which different people had actually developed these capacities. He did believe in a cultural elite, in this sense. But he was confident that society was progressing to the point where everyone would be able to develop their capacities for autonomy and sympathy to a high degree. Moreover, Mill saw the cultural elite as an essential caretaker and promoter of sympathy and autonomy, which are central values constitutive of democratic culture and institutions. The dominant middle classes threatened autonomy by homogenizing people's circumstances and pressuring people into conformity; they narrowed the scope of sympathy, singlemindedly focusing on the material advancement of their families. A cultural elite was needed to keep these homogenizing, conformist, egoistic tendencies at bay and promote the appeal of the higher pleasures.

Why call the pleasures of autonomy and sympathy *higher* pleasures? Mill offered one answer in his test for higher pleasures: one pleasure is higher than another if people experienced with both would, apart from any feeling of obligation to prefer one to the other, never prefer to give up the one entirely for any amount of the other. Mill's test has some notorious difficulties. One is that it doesn't distinguish a hierarchy of pleasures from a mere qualitative difference in pleasures. Two qualitatively distinct pleasures could pass the test, each in respect of the other, just so long as one had a preference for variety.

Mill suggested a better answer in his retort to those who charged utilitarians with a conception of goodness worthy only of animals. Humans could never be satisfied with wallowing in merely beastly pleasures, since such a life would be felt to be degrading. For a pleasure to contribute to human happiness, it must fit into a human's conception of happiness, the construction of which is governed by one's sense of dignity. The dignified person takes pride in her love of personal independence – the pleasures of autonomy – and in her interest in the happiness of others – the pleasures of sympathy. She feels ashamed of the pleasures of dependency and selfishness. The higher pleasures are higher, then, because they govern what other pleasures will fit into one's conception of happiness. Does the pleasure comport with one's autonomy and sense of unity with others? If not, eliminate it from one's conception of happiness, and count it not at all in the utilitarian calculus.

Mill's idea that we are progressing in our capacities to feel the higher pleasures of autonomy, sympathy, and dignity helps overcome the potential obstacles to utilitarian support for democratic social relations. If autonomy is a higher pleasure, then as people become more autonomous, paternalism (and hence imperialism) becomes a steadily less effective way to promote the happiness of others. If everyone is progressing in their capacities for happiness, then the aristocracy of hedonists is doomed. And if sympathy is a higher pleasure, then as people become more sympathetic, they will desire more and more equality. Or so Mill wanted to argue. But in arguing this, Mill subtly transformed the idea of sympathy from a utilitarian sentiment to one with distinctively Kantian overtones.

Utilitarian sympathy is a disturbingly ruthless sentiment. In prescribing the maximization of total human happiness, it sheds no tears over the sacrifice of some individuals to that end. So long as the individuals asked to bear the sacrifices are better off than average, its recommendations tend toward equality. But there is no theoretical limit to the sacrifices utilitarianism could ask some people to make for the sake of others. Mill's distinction between higher and lower pleasures starts to set some such limits. Recall that the higher pleasures may not be wholly sacrificed for any quantity of the lower. This principle works as well for interpersonal as for intrapersonal choices. Thus no one's autonomy may be utterly sacrificed for the sake of any amount of the lower pleasures enjoyed by any number of others. The slavery or subjection of even a tiny minority of people cannot be justified by any degree of mere amusement or luxury this would provide any number of other people. Still, it is consistent with utilitarianism supplemented by a hierarchy of pleasures to utterly sacrifice some people's happiness for the sake of increasing the sum total of *higher* pleasures enjoyed by others.

Whatever sentiment could license such treatment of others, it would not seem to be *sympathy*, as common sense understands this feeling. The sentiment underwriting the utilitarian policy is an attitude toward an aggregate – a mass of happiness. But sympathy is an attitude toward particular individuals. It is a concern we feel for *each* person for whom we are sympathetic, not just for some aggregate of all persons we sympathize with. It is also a concern that reserves its deepest feelings for the most downtrodden. It is the sort of feeling that makes us flinch from inflicting greater unhappiness on them, even when this brings about a greater mass of happiness to others. Sympathy thus has a *doubly distributive character*: it makes us care about the happiness of each person, not just of all together, and it makes us care especially about promoting the happiness of the worst off.

Mill thought that to have the genuine feeling of sympathy for others, one's identification of one's own happiness with that of others must not merely be conceived in the abstract, in allegiance to a principle, but in allegiance to actual people. And this allegiance cannot be just to people conceived as isolated atoms, but to people conceived in their social relations to oneself. Sympathy, or the feeling of unity with others, is expressed in a person's never conceiving of himself "otherwise than as a member of a body" whose governing. principle is that of a "society between equals," which "can only exist on the understanding that the interests of all are to be regarded equally" and "consulted." When perfected, the feeling of unity makes a person "never think of, or desire, any beneficial condition for himself in the benefits of which they are not included."[7] In other words, sympathy underwrites an egalitarian goal, not just an aggregative goal. But we shouldn't think of equality just as a principle for distributing divisible goods, making sure that each person gets a decent share. It involves also a disposition to adopt, as a central part of one's own happiness, common aims with others in cooperative relations. Most fundamentally, sympathy underwrites social relations of equality themselves. These are relations based on reciprocity, mutual consultation, and common aims, in which people take turns leading and being led, on terms mutually acceptable to everyone.

Mill's understanding of the demands of sympathy thus converges almost exactly with a Kantian understanding of the demands of respect: act only on principles that every reasonable person can accept. Such principles almost always require egalitarian social relations among people capable of self-government. But how did Mill, with his hedonistic psychology, arrive at the same point as Kant? The counterpart to the respect others owe oneself is one's own sense of dignity. And recall that the sense of dignity was what supported Mill's distinction between higher and lower pleasures, and thereby governed what pleasures get to count in one's conception of happiness. Sympathy directs us to care about the happiness of each person. But if others can't be happy when their dignity is compromised, then we can't express sympathy for others except by respecting their sense of dignity. Sympathy, then, makes us abhor not just the physical suffering and misery of others; it makes us recoil from making humiliating demands of them, and from treating others as mere servants or slaves. It makes us feel pain at their pain, and hence to feel pain at the undignified subjection of some to the wills of others.

So Mill was confident that human history manifested a progress of moral sentiments toward social equality. The original principles of social order were grounded in mutual fear and the rule of force. Christianity then taught the strong to show forbearance and generosity toward the weak, thus giving rise to paternalistic conceptions of justice. In the modern age, as individuals increased their knowledge and independence, justice was increasingly grounded in a cultivated sympathy among equals. This crude sketch of the history of moral sentiments raises the question: how did Mill imagine the cultivation of human sympathy to come about?

ORTHODOX UTILITARIAN MORAL EDUCATION

Mill framed the distinctive elements of his educational philosophy in reaction to the defects he saw in his father's philosophy and teaching methods. James Mill followed the orthodox utilitarian theory of education, which was based upon the psychological principles of hedonism, environmentalism, and associationism. Hedonism says that everything a person does is driven by the desire to avoid pain and enjoy pleasure. Environmentalism says that all of a person's thoughts and behavior can be explained by environmental influences. Associationism says that people will come to think of one thought upon exposure to another once they have been often enough exposed to the one in conjunction with the other. These three psychological doctrines lead to a simple and straightforward theory of moral education. The object of utilitarian moral education is to get people to behave in ways that benefit everyone to the greatest degree possible. This can be achieved, so long as people come to constantly associate thoughts of their own pleasure and pain with thoughts of the pleasure and pain of other people. The business of education is therefore to enforce this association by punishing people for harmful conduct and rewarding them for beneficial conduct. The constant association of others' pleasure with one's own pleasure, and others' pain with one's own pain, produces people who habitually seek paths of self-gratification that will benefit or at least not harm others.

This theory of moral education supports three mechanisms of moral behavior. One generates moral behavior by cognitive constraint: when calculating how to achieve their ends, people habitually think of means that benefit and don't harm others. Another generates moral behavior by external incentive: people engage in beneficial conduct and avoid harmful conduct in order to get the rewards and avoid the punishments meted out by society. The third mechanism actually works on people's sentiments by affecting their ultimate motivations: blame and punishment for harmful conduct may make people feel guilty about harming others, and the pangs of moral conscience may deter people from behaving badly.

While this may be a theory of moral education, it is not yet a theory of sympathetic education. It is a theory adapted to making people behave decently, but not by inducing them to care about other people for their own sakes. Most utilitarians regarded human motivations to be fixed and rather narrowly directed to self-interest and perhaps the interests of their families and closest friends. Rather than try to expand the horizons of people's sympathies to include other people, orthodox utilitarians thought it more efficient to rig the payoffs of different behaviors so that people could best advance their self-interest by means that happened to benefit others. Avoiding the pain of guilt looks like just another self-interested motive in this account. In the standard picture of utilitarian progress, society advances total happiness by channeling self-interested motivations along broadly beneficial paths. But it leaves people as pinched, parochial, smug, unimaginative, conventional, and selfish as they were before. It makes people happier without morally improving them, by satisfying their given conceptions of happiness rather than enabling them to frame and pursue superior conceptions of happiness.

James Mill added some distinctive elements to this classical utilitarian theory of moral education. Some were salutary. In one respect, he did pay attention to the importance of enlarging the scope of sympathy for others. He was vividly aware of the ways contempt for others interfered with sympathy for them, and of how easily children pick up habits of contempt from their elders. He thus insisted that children were not exposed to the obsessive ranking of individuals by the supposed worth of their occupation, income, religion, nationality or physique; it was this ranking that formed the basis of social contempt.

Other distinctive elements of James Mill's educational theory were chilling. He saw children as nothing more than budding tyrants. So he drew no distinction between disconsolate and manipulative crying. To his mind, crying was only the child's way to nag adults into submission. Adults should therefore ignore their children's cries, lest they teach them by association that they can get their way by annoying others. Adults should also teach infants from birth the natural consequences of their actions. He counseled parents not to rescue children from the naturally painful consequences of their ignorant behavior, lest they never learn to avoid imprudent conduct as adults. One may well wonder how infants could be expected to survive under his philosophy.

In his *Autobiography*, Mill's second great work on education, John Stuart Mill vividly described how his father put this educational philosophy into practice. James Mill exclusively directed his son's education from the age of 3 through adolescence. His theoretical suspicion of parental sentimentality toward children was reflected in practice by a harsh, cold, unrelentingly critical attitude toward his son. Just as his theory of education stressed cognitive over emotional and social development, his educational practice focused on academic subjects to the exclusion of everything else. John Stuart received no instruction in athletics, and very little even in the most basic practical arts. He was reading Greek before he could dress himself and tie his shoes. He was not allowed to play with other boys, and was therefore socially awkward around others. James Mill held the display of warm feelings in utter contempt. So John Stuart was starved of affection. The result was a hypertrophy of the intellect: by mid-adolescence, John Stuart Mill had an astonishing knowledge of Greek, Latin, English literature, world history, philosophy, psychology, mathematics and political economy, which was worthy of an educated person twenty years older. But this was combined with a profound shyness and reserve born of fear of his father's irascible temperament.

The two most striking faults Mill cited against his education were that he never got the chance to develop autonomy and sympathy, the two higher pleasures, without which Mill thought life wretched. The ability to express sympathy was out of reach of a child trained to extreme reserve and shyness by a quick-tempered father. The ability to assert one's will and initiative was also out of reach of a child whose life was comprehensively scheduled by his domineering father. The habit of leaving the initiative to his father continued in adulthood: James Mill chose John Stuart's first two professions, as a lawyer and then as a bureaucrat for the British East India Company. John Stuart was to work for decades directly under his father's supervision.

JOHN STUART MILL'S THEORY OF SENTIMENTAL EDUCATION

Mill learned from his own experience the deficiencies of utilitarian educational orthodoxy. He held the psychology underwriting classical utilitarian educational theory at fault. This psychology gave little consideration to the development of the capacities for the two higher pleasures of autonomy and sympathy. Its radical environmentalism led proponents to neglect the development of the inner sources of motivation: the senses of initiative, independence and imaginative inspiration, which lie at the root of autonomous activity. Environmentalism taught teachers always to look outside the individual for the direction of motivation, and to conceive of people as completely malleable according to whatever ideal the teacher demands, provided the right external incentives are applied. It was an educational philosophy of domination.

But what about sympathy? Even if the classical utilitarians were skeptical that human beings could expand the horizons of their sympathies much beyond their narrow circle, surely they ought to have supported extending people's sympathies wherever possible? Here we must confront the unfortunate cultural history of English utilitarianism, which appealed to a particularly stiff and cold class of partisans by means of a rhetoric of anti-sentimentalism. The classical utilitarians had to advance their radical political agenda against a moral discourse that supported conservative ends by appeal to the moral sentiments of humanity. Thus conservatives argued that utilitarian recommendations in favor of a right to divorce must be wrong, for they shock the conscience and offend people's moral sentiments! Utilitarians responded by relentlessly attacking the conservative rhetoric of moral sentiments. Their best argument against moral sentimentalism relied on the principle of association. Society could, by means of blame and punishment, associate the moral feelings of conscience, shock, and offense to any behavior, however beneficial, and the feeling of obligation to any other behavior, however harmful. Since moral sentiments are only artificially attached to behaviors by association, they can't function as independent arbiters of the moral worth of these behaviors.

It is hard to separate rhetoric from attitude: contempt for arguments that appeal to sentiments easily leads to contempt for sentiments themselves. It is hard to cultivate sympathy for others, including a consideration for their feelings, when one suspects their feelings express nothing more than irrational prejudices. No wonder utilitarianism tended to attract irreverent, cocky young men to its ranks, who enjoyed nothing more than criticizing their elders by attacking their most cherished doctrines in the most offensive and sectarian way possible. This could only reinforce the tendency in English culture, much lamented by Mill, to repress feelings and to undervalue the things such as poetry and art that can cultivate tender feelings for others.

Mill readily agreed with orthodox utilitarians that the moral sentiments of guilt and offense were purely a product of association, and thus could not serve as independent signs of right and wrong. But he denied that all moral sentiments were the product of association. Sympathy for others was intrinsic and natural to human beings. Mill drew his evidence for this claim from his experience in overcoming his youthful depression. In his *Autobiography*, Mill described his depression as a collapse of feeling and motivation brought about by relentless intellectual analysis. He desperately sought some emotional connection to others that could not be unnerved by the thought that he had it only because he had been drilled into it. Reading Marmontel's melancholy memoirs, Mill found himself driven to tears. *Here* was a sentiment, a genuine feeling of sympathy for another human being, which he knew wasn't just the product of his father's training! For his cold-hearted father had always starved him of affection, and treated the open expression of sympathy with contempt. Since this feeling of sympathy for others was not the product of association, it could not be unnerved by analysis. It could therefore serve as a motivational source of the appeal of utilitarianism that is intrinsic to human beings.

That Mill saw sympathy as intrinsic and natural to human beings doesn't imply that he thought it didn't have to be cultivated. Mill thought that people had to be educated to extend their sympathy in two dimensions. They had to learn to extend their sympathy beyond their narrow circle of acquaintances to people of other classes, religions, and countries. And they had to learn to engage their sympathies in considering issues beyond the petty concerns of personally getting on in life, issues concerning broader aims and higher aspirations than those they already had. These two extensions go together. Recall that for Mill, one feels sympathy not for people conceived in isolation, but for people conceived in real social relations to oneself. To engage with others in such relations demands that one concern oneself with common projects of broader significance than one's mere personal advancement.

Mill's theory of moral education thus included two models of how to educate the sentiments. One was the classical associationist model, which directs the moral conscience, the senses of guilt and obligation, by means of praise and blame, reward and punishment. The chief danger of relying on association alone to inculcate motives to promote general happiness is instability. Contrary incentives and moral judgments can direct the moral conscience in pernicious directions, and contemplation of the arbitrary connection between conscience and its objects can dissolve this connection. Mill also objected that associationist moral education took people's parochial, cramped, conventional and selfish motives too much for granted, as fixed motives to be channeled rather than transcended. Mill thought that these motives posed obstacles to human progress by standing in the way of experiments in living and the construction of wider communities of sympathy.

Mill's second model of sentimental education may be called the cultivation model. It applies to sympathy, which inherently rather than by mere association directs us to seek the good of others. Sympathy is cultivated – that is, extended to wider social circles and broader, higher concerns – by means of imagination, exercise, and public expression. Imagination enables us to conceive of what others are feeling, and to formulate new aspirations, common projects, and ways of life in response to these conceptions. Exercise habituates us to acting on such sympathetic imagination, and public expression puts the product of imagination to the test. Economists tend to assume that sympathy is a scarce motive that must therefore be economized. Society should not rely on it too much, or else people will soon stop behaving altruistically out of "charity fatigue." Mill disagreed. He thought one of the chief consequences of action was reinforcement of the motives from which one acts. So sympathy is more like physical fitness than like a fixed stock of food: it is enhanced with use. A society that doesn't exercise people's sympathies is a society of people with weak and narrow sympathies. Their charity fatigue is like the fatigue of an out-of-shape runner. The solution in both cases is to get them to exercise their capacities more.

THE PRACTICAL SCHOOLS OF SYMPATHY

Every mode of education has its schools. So what are the schools of sentimental education? Not the schools of formal education, to be sure. Mill knew as well as anyone that one doesn't learn to be moral by taking a class in moral philosophy. He argued in the "Inaugural Address" that aesthetic education – the study of poetry, literature, and the fine arts – could advance moral education by stimulating the imagination and feelings. But that isn't where the main action is. We should take most seriously Mill's claim that "the only school of genuine moral sentiment is a society between equals."[8] To fill out Mill's theory of sentimental education, we must study Mill's account of society between equals. Mill supported the advancement of three types of egalitarian society: workers' cooperatives, companionate marriages, and democracy. These were the practical schools of sentimental education, where people's sympathies were cultivated through exercise. The key to these settings is substantive social equality: here participants interact as equals, none superior or inferior to the others in status. To see how these settings cultivate sympathy, we must understand how they realize equality.

Mill thought that worker-managed firms represented a natural solution to the class conflict between workers and capitalists. The traditional conservative solution to class conflict was to tell the lower classes to submit to social hierarchy in return for the protection of a chivalrous aristocracy. Mill acknowledged that this arrangement cultivated favorable sentiments between the classes, but of servile gratitude on the one side, and condescending charity on the other. The advance of the rule of law made the conservative solution obsolete by granting protection to the lower classes independent of aristocrats. Now the poor met the condescension of the rich with resentment rather than gratitude. Education enlivened their sense of personal dignity and independence.

It is easy enough to see why a workers' cooperative would advance its participants' sense of personal worth and dignity. Workers would no longer be ordered around by others according to rules they didn't accept, but would govern their work by rules and goals they gave themselves. But how could such settings cultivate people's *sympathy* for others? We shouldn't be deceived by the word "sympathy" into thinking that it involves only tender and intimate emotions. Sympathy, remember, involves engaging in common aims with others on terms that are agreeable to and that benefit everyone else. Workers' cooperatives exercise the sentiment of sympathy through their democratic mode of operation: no participant can propose a project or work rule that can't be justified to everyone else, as advancing their interests, too. In a cooperative system of production, people would cease to honor people on account of birth or social status and reserve their admiration for those of genuine merit, where merit or virtue amounts to those qualities that advance everyone's interests.

Mill's second school of sympathy was companionate marriage. Mill believed that the appeal of true companionship would eventually overcome men's selfish interest in dominating their wives. As men came to think of love as a sentiment properly expressed within marriage, rather than something found only in extramarital relationships, they would want their wives to care for them out of genuine affection rather than fear. In addition, modern conditions made men spend more of their leisure time in the close company of women. They would feel a life spent in intimacy with inferiors to be insufferable. Yearning for a candid sharing of feelings, they would find their status as masters over their totally dependent wives only getting in the way of open communication. How could a woman tell her husband how she really felt about him when she lived in constant fear of reprimand or abandonment for telling the truth? Men could find no solace in comforting words expressed only out of fear, and no stimulation in conversation with wives educated only for drudgery.

To enjoy the goods of intimate companionship, men would have to accept marriage as a relation between equals. Only in a relationship of true reciprocity, where husband and wife took turns leading and being led, claiming nothing for themselves that they would not grant to their partners, rejecting power on the one side and obedience on the other, and sharing common purposes, could either party achieve domestic happiness. Only on terms of equality could they enjoy perfect candor in expressing their thoughts, as well as stimulating company. This prospect could be achieved only by educating women and reforming the law of marriage to permit divorce and make women legally equal to their husbands. Once achieved, the marriage of equals would become a school of moral cultivation, teaching the marriage partners and their children the daily habits and sentiments of egalitarian virtue.

Mill's third school of sympathy was democracy itself, that is, the institutions of representative government under a universal franchise. Indeed, his chief defense of democracy was not that it produced superior policies but that it advanced the virtue of citizens. By enlisting citizens in determining the course of public affairs, it enlarged their otherwise narrow intellectual horizons and stimulated their interest in common aims on a large scale. Mill defended the public ballot on the grounds that this would force citizens to justify their votes on terms that others could accept, and thus educate citizens to think and act for the sake of common rather than selfish interests. He supported widespread participation in public offices such as juries and vestries for their educative functions, in training citizens to act for the common interest.

The extension of the franchise served similar educative functions. Only by extending the franchise to workers and women would occupants of public office be forced to listen to what they had to say, and thereby learn how to take their interests into account. Sympathy is opposed to paternalism: it requires attention to people's interests as they see them, not as how the powerful define them. Conservatives objected to extending the franchise to women on the grounds that they already had influence over their husbands' votes, and that this influence was corrupting, since women urged their husbands to tend to the petty and parochial concerns that occupied their minds. Mill replied that conservatives confused cause and effect: women focused mainly on parochial concerns precisely because they were deprived of the ballot and so had no use for knowledge of public affairs and no sense of responsibility for the public. In being deprived of a vote, they were taught that they have no business involving themselves in public affairs. The right to vote would give women an interest in learning about public affairs and exercising public responsibility.

Mill thought that egalitarian social relations were mutually reinforcing. Thus he defended the enfranchisement of women as a way to promote companionate marriage. Men could not enjoy intimacy with wives who were not their intellectual equals, whose minds did not range as broadly as their own. If they were not to be dragged down to the petty interests of Mrs Grundy, they would need wives as engaged in public affairs as they were themselves. And this would not occur unless women could vote. Thus even achieving the sympathy of intimacy requires cultivating sympathy on a larger scale, at least on the level of democratic politics. Companionate marriages, for their part, provided essential support to democratic government. For they were the first school of justice for children, in which they would learn to express sympathy as a daily habit and thereby be prepared to extend it to the wider world of representative government.

Mill believed that historical forces were inducing people to enlarge their sympathies, and thereby promote the moral progress of humanity. He proposed two mechanisms for sentimental change, one working from the bottom up, the other from the top down. The first provided a material basis for the self-assertion of people on the bottom of the social hierarchy: as prosperity advanced, the lower classes would achieve economic independence from their social superiors and therefore feel disinclined to bow and scrape before them. They would repudiate habits of deference on their own because they no longer depended on elites for protection and subsistence. Mass public education would reinforce this trend, by teaching people how to think for themselves and endowing them with a sense of entitlement to do so. Mass education would expand people's knowledge beyond parochial matters and prevent working people from being hoodwinked by elite claims to superiority. Mill recognized the material basis for women's assertion of dignity and equality as well. So he argued that women could not achieve equality unless they were educated as highly as men and had the right to own property, to divorce, and to pursue careers on terms of equal opportunity with men. These reforms were needed as much to enable women to express their own thoughts, feelings, and interests on their own account as to deprive men of despotic power over their wives.

The second mechanism of sentimental change provided incentives for social superiors to repudiate their contempt for those placed beneath them. The expansion of the franchise to the working classes and women would force elites to recognize that they could not retain political power without taking seriously what these groups had to say. They would have to listen to their arguments and respond without condescension to their claims. Participants in democratic institutions enforce their own egalitarian rules of civility: they fiercely cut down all expressions of superiority, whether in the form of arrogance or condescension, and require elites to hide their pride and stifle their disdain. Respectful behavior initially practiced out of interest soon becomes a matter of habit. Through habituation, even strategic expressions of respect can become genuine.

A different interest would prompt men to accord respect to women. Mill was confident that the enormous appeal of the ideal of companionate marriage would give men a special interest in taking seriously their wives' thoughts and interests. For only by doing so could men enjoy a genuinely loving companion rather than a servile drudge. Once women attained equal education and the right to vote, men would learn to take seriously their wives' opinions about public affairs.

MILL'S EDUCATIONAL PHILOSOPHY: BEYOND ELITIST VERSUS DEMOCRATIC EDUCATION

Recall the conflict over educational visions that opened this essay. On one side, orthodox utilitarians promoted scientific and technical education for its usefulness to all of humanity, and disparaged the humanities as expressions of snobbish elitism, hard to justify once one accepts the democracy of tastes. On the other side, conservatives championed humanities education as necessary for sustaining the highest cultural values, at least among a tiny cultural elite, and found little use for modern science. Mill sided with orthodox utilitarians on the importance of science to politics: the right political aims and means could only be judged by considering the evidence according to scientific method. Thus science had to occupy a central place in education. However, in affirming a distinction between higher and lower pleasures, Mill rejected the orthodox utilitarian democracy of tastes and accepted the traditional view of the humanities as uplifting and improving human desires.

Mill might thus be seen as trying to combine elements from both educational visions. I have argued that he is better viewed as attempting to transform the terms of debate. Unlike the conservative moralists, Mill's distinction between higher and lower pleasures was not anti-democratic, because he identified the higher pleasures with the exercise of sympathy and autonomy. These are best cultivated and exercised in the context of democratic, egalitarian relationships. Mill also insisted on the necessity of an educated elite, at least under the historical conditions of nineteenth-century Britain. Yet his educational elitism was not anti-democratic. He argued that a liberally educated elite was needed to play several indispensable roles in democracy: to supply the expertise needed to frame and administer sound laws, prevent the degeneration of democracy into demagoguery, and counter the conformist, narrow-minded, egoistic character of the dominant middle class. Study of the arts and humanities advanced the last project of countering the excessive influence of middle-class commercialism: freedom of inquiry into the proper ends of life promoted autonomy against conformism, study of the classics promoted cosmopolitanism over narrow parochialism, the arts helped cultivate imagination, broader sympathies, and nobler goals than petty egoism.

Mill thought that the most important schools of moral sentiment lay outside the classroom, in the egalitarian social relationships of workers' cooperatives, companionate marriages, and democracy itself. He saw that the success of democracy requires that we overcome the sentiments of arrogance and deference, contempt and humility that interfere with people's effective participation in discussion of public affairs. He argued that we cultivate sympathy for others by participating in egalitarian institutions whose functioning demands that we frame common aims cooperatively and justify them on grounds that others can accept. These institutions teach the privileged to overcome their contempt for those occupying lower stations, and the disadvantaged to cast aside their deference in favor of autonomy and dignity.

Despite these powerful egalitarian strands in Mill's thought, Mill's devotion to egalitarianism was conditional. Mill was an imperialist as well as a democrat. He reconciled these two ideas through his progressive vision of history. Mill accepted the logic of paternalism in cases where a more advanced civilization could promote progress in backward civilizations by imperialism. Educational policies must always be designed with the aim of inspiring progress. In some cases, this meant supporting a cultural elite even at the expense of democratization. But Mill was confident that the end of human progress was an egalitarian society.

NOTES

1 In John Robson and Bruce Kinzer (eds) *Collected Works of John Stuart Mill*, vol. 21 (Toronto and Buffalo, University of Toronto Press, 1984), pp. 217–57.
2 "Inaugural Address," in *Collected Works, Mill* 21, p. 254.
3 Ibid.
4 See, for example, "M. de Tocqueville on Democracy in America," in *Collected Works, Mill* 18, p. 199.
5 Francis Edgeworth, *Mathematical Psychics* [1881] (London, C. Kegan Paul and Co., 1932), pp. 57ff.
6 For a full account of Mill's educational proposals for India, see Lynn Zastoupil, *John Stuart Mill and India* (Stanford, Calif., Stanford University Press, 1994), ch. 2.
7 John Stuart Mill, *Utilitarianism* [1861] (Indianapolis, Ind., Hackett, 1979), pp. 31, 32.
8 John Stuart Mill, *The Subjection of Women* [1869] in *Three Essays* (Oxford, Oxford University Press, 1975), p. 477.

SUGGESTIONS FOR FURTHER READING

John Stuart Mill's corpus is vast; here I shall point to sources for the themes of this essay that are not cited in footnotes. Mill's account of moral progress may be found in *Utilitarianism*, ch. 5 and *The Subjection of Women*, ch. I; his theory of higher and lower pleasures is in *Utilitarianism*, ch. 2. James Mill outlined his theory of education in his *Article on Education*, published in F. H. Cavenaugh (ed.) *James and John Stuart Mill on Education* (London, Cambridge University Press, 1931). Mill's *Autobiography* [1873] (Boston, Mass., Houghton Mifflin, 1969) is the single most important source on his own education and his two models of sentimental education. See also *Utilitarianism*, ch. 3 on sympathy and moral education. Mill offered noteworthy defenses of egalitarian institutions in *Principles of Political Economy* (in *Collected Works*, vol. 2), ch. 7 (workers' cooperatives), *The Subjection of Women*, chs 2 and 4 (companionate marriage), and "Considerations on representative government" [1861], in *Three Essays* (democratic government). He made his best arguments for extending the franchise in his parliamentary speeches. See especially "Representation of the people [13 April 1866]" in *Collected Works*, vol. 28, pp. 58–68 (workers' franchise); and "Admission of women to the electoral franchise [20 May 1867]" in *Collected Works*, vol. 28, pp. 151–62 (linking the ideals of democracy and companionate marriage).

The secondary literature on John Stuart Mill is even more vast than Mill's own writings. The single best work that focuses on Mill's egalitarian philosophy is Maria Morales, *Perfect Equality* (Lanham, Md., Rowman and Littlefield, 1996). The best work on Mill's imperialism is Lynn Zastoupil, *John Stuart Mill and India* (Stanford, Calif., Stanford University Press, 1994).

25

THE PAST IN THE PRESENT: PLATO AS EDUCATOR OF NINETEENTH-CENTURY BRITAIN

M. F. Burnyeat

Mankind can hardly be too often reminded, that there was once a man named Socrates, between whom and the legal authorities and public opinion of his time, there took place a memorable collision.

J. S. Mill

I am afraid mankind must contrive to do without a first parent.

B. Jowett

In 1871 George Grote was buried in Westminster Abbey – a rare mark of distinction. Among the pallbearers were John Stuart Mill and Benjamin Jowett. These three lovers of Plato are the focus of the present essay.[1] Let me introduce them one by one:

John Stuart Mill (1806–73): the most influential British philosopher of the nineteenth century; political reformist; defender of liberty and of women's rights; author of a humane version of Utilitarianism.

George Grote (1794–1871): Mill's older contemporary and friend; banker; political reformist; author of a ground-breaking multi-volume *History of Greece* and of a huge 3-volume study of Plato which remains a live presence in Platonic scholarship.

Benjamin Jowett (1817–93): elected Fellow of Balliol College Oxford while still an undergraduate; liberal theologian and one of the first thinkers in Britain to recognize the importance of Hegel; remembered today both for his translation of the dialogues of Plato and for his far-reaching influence as an educator on the minds and hearts of the civil servants and governing elite of his times.

Here are three nineteenth-century figures who contributed significantly both to the intellectual and to the political life of Britain, and who all found Plato an important presence in their thinking. I am not talking about mere influence. Of the three, only Jowett regards Plato as unqualifiedly his ally. The others take a more critical view of Plato's ideas. But this criticism, like Jowett's selection of what to admire in Plato, is part of a process of working out where they stand on the issues of their day in relation to Plato's discussion of the moral and social issues he confronted in the fourth century BC. In other words, all three find Plato *good to think with*, even though he wrote in a totally different society over 2,000 years ago.

This may seem a paradox. It is often asserted that there are no eternal questions in philosophy, and especially no eternal moral and social questions. The moral and social thought of the past being the portion most embedded in its historical context, it cannot without travesty and gross anachronism be lifted out of its original context and put to use at different times and places. The truth of the matter is that the scientific and theoretical works of the past date much more than the moral and social ones.

Throughout antiquity and for centuries after, the Number One work for finding out about Plato's philosophy was not the *Republic*, as it is now, but the *Timaeus*, where Plato presents a highly mathematical, Pythagoreanizing account of the physical world. I do not mean that the *Republic* was not widely read in antiquity. As a provocation, it stimulated Diogenes the Cynic and Zeno the Stoic to write rival *Republics* of their own. As a source of inspiration, it helped Platonist and Christian thinkers to keep alive a sense of spiritual values in the dark days of the Roman Empire. But if you asked where one finds out about Plato's philosophy, you would be directed to the *Timaeus*, whereas today you would be sent off to buy the Penguin *Republic*.

Now in the English-speaking world at least,[2] the person most responsible for bringing the *Republic* into the Number One place it occupies today was Benjamin Jowett. We will see that a corresponding marginalization of the *Timaeus*, by Jowett, was integral to the process whereby Plato and his *Republic* came to occupy the position he holds today (especially since the demise of Marxism) as one of the most widely read philosophers in the contemporary world. And I mean the whole world, from Europe through North and South America to Japan, Korea, Mongolia, Russia, and Zimbabwe, to mention just the countries where I personally know that Plato is read with care. The sun never sets on the reading of Plato. Always, someone somewhere is reading the *Republic*.

Contrast the state of affairs that John Stuart Mill depicts in 1834:

Considering the almost boundless reputation of the writings of Plato, not only among scholars, but (upon their authority) among nearly all who have any tincture of letters, it is a remarkable fact, that of the great writers of antiquity, there is scarcely one who, in this country at least, is not merely so little understood, but so little read. Our two great 'seats of learning', of which no real lover of learning can ever speak but in terms of indignant disgust, bestow attention upon the various branches of classical acquirement in exactly the reverse order to that which would be observed by persons who valued the ancient authors for what is valuable in them: namely, upon the mere niceties of the language *first*; next, upon a few of the poets; next, (but at a great distance) some of the historians; next, (but at a still greater interval) the orators; last of all, and just above nothing, the philosophers. An English bookseller, by the aid of a German scholar, recently produced an excellent edition of Plato;[3] the want of sale for which, by the way, is said to have been one of the causes of his insolvency. But, with the exception of the two dialogues edited by Dr. Routh,[4] we are aware of nothing to facilitate the study of the most gifted of Greek writers, which has ever emanated from either of the impostor-universities of England; and of the young men who have obtained university honours during the last ten years, we are much misinformed if there be six who had even looked into his writings. If such be the neglect of the best parts of classical learning among those whose special vocation and whose positive duty it is to cultivate them, what can be expected from others? Among those who are engaged in the incessant struggle which, in this country, constitutes more and more of the business of active life – every man's time and thoughts being wholly absorbed in the endeavour to rise, or in the endeavour not to fall, in running after riches, or in running away from bankruptcy – the tranquil pursuit not only of classical, but of any literature deserving the name, is almost at an end. The consequence is, that there are, probably, in this kingdom, not so many as a hundred persons who ever have read Plato, and not so many as twenty who ever *do*.[5]

This is Mill introducing a set of abridged translations of Platonic dialogues which he published, with considerable success, in a popular monthly magazine.

The works he translated were *Protagoras*, *Phaedrus*, *Gorgias*, *Apology*, *Charmides*, *Euthyphro*, *Laches*, *Lysis*, and *Parmenides*.[6] They show Socrates in debate, while the *Apology* shows him defending his practice of debate with all and sundry on moral questions. Evidently, it is Plato's presentation of Socrates as the debater and critic of conventional views that Mill values, as he confirms in his *Autobiography* (1873):

There is no author whom my father thought himself more indebted for his mental culture, than Plato, or whom he more frequently recommended to young students. I can bear similar testimony in regard to myself. The Socratic method, of which the Platonic dialogues are the chief example, is unsurpassed as a discipline for correcting the errors, and clearing up the confusions incident to the *intellectus sibi permissus*,[7] the understanding which has made up all its bundles of associations under the guidance of popular phraseology. The close, searching *elenchus* by which the man of vague generalities is constrained either to express his meaning to himself in definite terms, or to confess that he does not know what he is talking about; the perpetual testing of all general statements by particular instances; the siege in form which is laid to the meaning of large abstract terms, by fixing upon some still larger class-name which includes that and more, and dividing down to the thing sought – marking out its limits and definition by a series of accurately drawn distinctions between it and each of the cognate objects which are successively parted off from it – all this, as an education for precise thinking, is inestimable, and all this, even at that age [around 12 years old], took such hold of me that it became part of my own mind.[8]

As we see, in this valuation of the Socratic spirit of questioning inquiry, Mill is guided by the formidable figure of his father, James Mill, who taught his son Greek from the tender age of 3.[9] Readers who are surprised at the son's high esteem for Plato's method of division in the second half of the passage should turn to the father's *Essay on Government* (1820); it does not look like Socrates' description of division in Plato's *Phaedrus* (265d–266b) or the Eleatic Stranger's practice of it in the *Sophist* and *Statesman*, but it is structured throughout by the principles displayed in those works.[10] Or compare John Stuart Mill on Bentham:

> It is the introduction into the philosophy of human conduct, of this method of detail – of this practice of never reasoning about wholes till they have been resolved into their parts, nor about abstractions till they have been translated into realities – that constitutes the originality of Bentham in philosophy, and makes him the great reformer of the moral and political branch of it.[11]

In effect, the highest praise Mill can find for Bentham in this rather critical essay is that he rediscovered the Socratic method. Admittedly, 'Bentham was probably not aware that Plato had anticipated him in the process to which he too declared that he owed everything'.[12] So much the worse for Bentham, however. His 'incapacity to appreciate such men' as Socrates and Plato was in Mill's view 'a fact perfectly in unison with the general habits of [his] mind'.[13]

Now there is a famous passage in John Stuart Mill's *Autobiography* in which he reports reading the first six dialogues of Plato 'in the common arrangement', from *Euthyphro* to *Theaetetus*, in the original Greek, at the age of 7.[14] At that date (1813) the only dictionaries were Greek to Latin, which little John Stuart did not begin to learn (and simultaneously to teach his younger sister) until the age of 8. So his only recourse, when he met a word he did not know, was to ask his irascible father busy with his own work on the History of British India at the other side of the desk.

But it is not just the reading of Plato at so young an age that is extraordinary. It is also which dialogues Dad set him to read. He did not meet the *Republic* until he was 12 or 13. At 7 it was the first six works in the common arrangement: *Euthyphro*, *Apology*, *Crito*, *Phaedo*, *Theages*, *Erastai*, and *Theaetetus*[15] – very much the dialectical side of Plato again, the side beloved of analytic philosophers today.

Of the *Theaetetus* Mill says that it 'would have been better omitted, as it was totally impossible I should understand it'. This implies, by contrast, that he did get something out of the preceding dialogues. But the more important contrast lies elsewhere.

Shortly after my first quotation from Mill, we read this:

> We have all heard of Platonists, and the Platonic philosophy; but though, out of detached passages of his writings, philosophic systems have been subsequently manufactured, it is to this day a problem whether Plato *had* a philosophy; if he had, it certainly was *not* the philosophy of those who have called themselves Platonists.[16]

Likewise in the *Autobiography*, after praising the Socratic method in my second quotation, Mill goes on:

> I have felt ever since that the title of Platonist belongs by far better right to those who have been nourished in, and have endeavoured to practise Plato's mode of investigation, than to those who are distinguished only by the adoption of certain dogmatical conclusions, drawn mostly from the least intelligible of his works, and which the

character of his mind and writings makes it uncertain whether he himself regarded as anything more than poetic fancies, or philosophic conjectures.[17]

Who is he attacking?

Among those who did read Plato in Britain at the time, most were attracted by the mystical, transcendental side of Plato, which Mill would dismiss as poetic fancies – the side that many analytic philosophers still prefer to overlook. Chief among the mystical readers was Thomas Taylor, self-styled 'the Platonist', and very likely the immediate target of Mill's scorn. In 1804 Taylor had finally concluded a project begun by his older, more scholarly friend, Floyer Sydenham. He brought out the first complete English translation of Plato, whom he read, as people had been doing since Ficino and the Renaissance, through the eyes of Plotinus and the neo-Platonists, with mystery religions, the Hymns of Orpheus, the Chaldean Oracles, and much else thrown in.[18] Such was Taylor's enthusiasm that he was prepared to reject all the findings of contemporary science in favour of the *Timaeus* view that the Earth is the centre of the universe.[19]

Reviewing the work, James Mill (whose singular passion for Plato began during his student days at Edinburgh University), excoriated both the incompetence of Taylor's translation and his interpretations:

> He has not translated Plato; he has travestied him, in the most cruel and abominable manner. He has not elucidated, but covered him over with impenetrable darkness.[20]

He begins with an attack on the neo-Platonic commentators used by Taylor ('the *charlatans* of antient philosophy'); they more than any other influence have put people off reading Plato. Then comes a novel suggestion about the *Timaeus*. This is the dialogue that allows neo-Platonists like Proclus to claim Plato 'for the founder of that wild plan of mystic conjecture which they pursued in the name of philosophy'. But note that Plato chooses Timaeus rather than Socrates for his spokesman. This suggests, according to Mill, that the work is not designed by Plato to expound his own opinions. Rather, he wants to show that he can outdo previous natural philosophers in the ingenuity of his explanations, in much the same way as Aspasia's funeral speech in the *Menexenus* is Plato outdoing the orators.[21]

But it is not just the *Timaeus* that divides Taylor from the Mills. Taylor's neo-Platonic Plato is the author of a dogmatic Idealist system emanating from a transcendent Unity with which we may aspire to mystic union:

> 1. I believe in one first cause of all things, whose nature is so immensely transcendent that it is even super-essential; and that in consequence of this it cannot properly be named, or spoken of, or conceived by opinion, or be known, or perceived by any being.

> 2. I believe, however, that if it be lawful to give a name to that which is truly ineffable, the appellations of *the one* and *the good* are of all others the most adapted to it; the former of these names indicating that it is the principle of all things, and the latter that it is the ultimate object of desire in all things.[22]

Hardly the Mills' cup of tea.

Yet this is the Plato of the Romantic poets, who were avid readers of Taylor. Keats's 'Beauty is truth, truth beauty' might be easier to find in Plotinus than in Plato himself, but Wordsworth's 'Intimations of Immortality' could well have been entitled 'Ode to the Platonic Theory of Recollection'. (Wordsworth owned Taylor's 1793 translation of the *Cratylus*, *Phaedo*, *Parmenides* and *Timaeus*.) I remember as an undergraduate hearing Dr F. R. Leavis complain in a lecture that Shelley's lines,

> The One remains, the many change and pass;
> Heaven's light forever shines, earth's shadows fly;
> Life, like a dome of many-coloured glass,
> Stains the white radiance of eternity,
> Until Death tramples it to fragments.
>
> (*Adonais* 460–4)

simply do not make sense. They do if you have read the *Timaeus*, or if, like Shelley, you have translated the *Symposium*.

It was not only in Britain that Romantic minds were enthused by Taylor's translations of Plato and a host of neo-Platonic works. So too were Emerson and the Transcendentalists. Indeed, in the USA Taylor achieved considerable popularity. From New England Platonism spread to the mid-West, where a journal called *The Platonist* was still reprinting Taylor in the 1880s.[23] By contrast, when Emerson visited the aged Wordsworth in 1848, their conversation included the following:

> I told him, as I usually did all English scholars, that it was not creditable that no one in all the country knew anything of Thomas Taylor, the Platonist, whilst in every American library his books are found. I said, if Plato's Republic were published in England as a new book today, do you think it would find any readers? He confessed, it would not; – 'And yet,' added after a pause, (with that conceit that never deserts a trueborn Englishman) 'And yet, we have embodied it all.'[24]

The Romantics loved liberty and began as rebels against the Establishment. But they were much less interested than Grote and the Mills in the hard practical slog of getting things changed. This was the century in which Britain started out on its long slow journey towards democracy. Grote and the Mills were deeply involved. They were three of the four big names in a group called the 'Philosophic Radicals'.[25] The missing fourth person, who originated many of the ideas that the Mills and Grote took up, is Jeremy Bentham, the founding father of Utilitarianism and of numerous projects for radical reform.

Bentham himself, as we have seen, had no time for Socrates and Plato. But while he sat at the raised desk in his study writing volume upon volume of convoluted prose (much of it still unedited), the other three went out into the world of practical affairs. They joined committees and wrote for the general public. After the Great Reform Act of 1832, Grote and (much later) John Stuart Mill got themselves elected into Parliament. They were the activists. Accordingly, they were the ones who most felt the weight of Establishment resistance:

This aggregate of beliefs and predispositions to believe, ethical, religious, aesthetical, social, respecting what is true or false, probable or improbable, just or unjust, holy or unholy, honourable or base, respectable or contemptible, pure or impure, beautiful or ugly, decent or indecent, obligatory to do or obligatory to avoid, respecting the status and relations of each individual in the society, respecting even the admissible fashions of amusement and recreation – this is an established fact and condition of things, the real origin of which is for the most part unknown, but which each new member of the society is born to and finds subsisting. It is transmitted by tradition from parents to children, and is imbibed by the latter almost unconsciously from what they see and hear around, without any special season of teaching, or special persons to teach. It becomes a part of each person's nature – a standing habit of mind, or fixed set of mental tendencies, according to which, particular experience is interpreted and particular persons appreciated. It is not set forth in systematic proclamation, nor impugned, nor defended: it is enforced by a sanction of its own, the same real sanction or force in all countries, by fear of displeasure from the Gods, and by certainty of evil from neighbours and fellow-citizens. The community hate, despise, or deride, any individual member who proclaims his dissent from their social creed, or even openly calls it into question. Their hatred manifests itself in different ways, at different times and occasions, sometimes by burning or excommunication, sometimes by banishment or interdiction from fire and water;[26] at the very least, by exclusion from that amount of forbearance, goodwill, and estimation, without which the life of an individual becomes insupportable: for society, though its power to make an individual happy is but limited, has complete power, easily exercised, to make him miserable. The orthodox public do not recognise in any individual citizen a right to scrutinise their creed, and to reject it if not approved by his own rational judgement. They expect that he will embrace it in the natural course of things, by the mere force of authority and contagion – as they have adopted it themselves: as they have adopted also the current language, weights, measures, divisions of time, &c.[27]

Ostensibly, this powerful indictment˙ has nothing to do with the nineteenth century. It is Grote's description of what Socrates was up against. The passage continues directly:

If he dissents, he is guilty of an offence described in the terms of the indictment preferred against Sokrates – 'Sokrates commits crime, inasmuch as he does not believe in the Gods, in whom the city believes, but introduces new religious beliefs,' &c.

But this is a specimen of what Grote and the Mills call 'philosophical history'.[28] Socrates stands as a shining *exemplum* for a large generalization about 'the' community and 'the' individual.

The aggregate of prescriptive prejudice described here at such length Grote termed King Nomos, taking *nomos* in Pindar's much-quoted phrase *nomos basileus* to cover not only law, but 'positive morality and social aesthetical precepts, as well as civil or political, and even personal habits, such as that of abstinence from spitting or wiping the nose'.[29] One of the most forceful ancient descriptions of King Nomos he finds in the Great Speech of Protagoras in Plato's *Protagoras* (320c–328d), where Protagoras supports the Athenians' belief that, despite Socrates' doubts about whether virtue can be taught, it can. Virtue – or virtue as the Athenians conceive it – is taught in the same way as language and custom are taught: by everyone to everyone through a constant, often scarcely noticed, process of correction and bringing into line. Grote puts this into English, with direct reference to the speech Plato puts into the mouth of Protagoras, as 'the working of that spontaneous ever-present police by whom the authority of King Nomos is enforced in detail – a police not the less omnipotent because they wear no uniform, and carry no recognized title'.[30]

Later, in his chapter on the *Protagoras*, Grote commends the Great Speech for its accurate portrayal of 'the omnipresent agency of King Nomos and his numerous volunteers', and notes that it 'coincides completely' with James Mill's account of the transmission of established morality in his *A Fragment on Mackintosh* (1835).[31]

I have to say I find this a stunning interpretation of the Great Speech that Protagoras gives in the dialogue named after him. Modern scholars often admire the Speech because they find it a congenial, commonsensical alternative to the intellectualism of Socrates' doctrine that virtue is knowledge, to be gained only by philosophical inquiry. But Grote is right that Protagoras allows no space for reflective criticism and reassessment of inherited values.[32] His story is all about correcting, pressurizing, and punishing those who do not conform, with exile or death as the ultimate penalty for anyone who, like Socrates perhaps, persists in not toeing the line.

At the other end of the *Protagoras* (351bff.), in striking contrast to Protagoras' evocation of King Nomos, we find Socrates giving the first formulation of the idea of the hedonic calculus which was to be the foundation of Bentham's Utilitarianism. John Stuart Mill began his *Utilitarianism* (1861) by claiming outright that Socrates here asserts 'the theory of Utilitarianism against the popular morality of the so-called sophist'.[33] Grote is more exact and scholarly: Mill has omitted to mention that Socrates speaks of calculating, by quantities of pleasure and pain, which course of action will yield the greatest happiness *of the individual*, whereas Utilitarianism is about calculating, by quantities of pleasure and pain, which course of action will yield the greatest happiness *of the greatest number*.[34] Either way, the Philosophic Radicals, engaged as they were in the struggle for democracy and the promotion of more rational social arrangements generally, could fairly claim to find within the pages of a single dialogue a mirror of their own life and problems. The drama of the *Protagoras* is the clash between the unreasoning force of established morality and the attempt of autonomous reason to find better answers to practical problems by calculation and critical questioning.

This reading of the *Protagoras* casts a useful light on the wider Victorian debate over Athenian democracy. It was a real debate in the sense that the parties were simultaneously wondering whether democracy was a thing they should or must have, and if so, on what terms. Ancient Athens, even though it was a direct rather than a representative democracy, became the great precedent. Was it a dismal tale of rule by the rabble, egged on by demagogues and made worse by the corrupting influence of the Sophists? Or was it a splendid example of civic cooperation? Historical judgement on the Athenian constitution was a guide to immediate political action.[35]

Grote contributed to this debate by campaigning in and out of Parliament for secrecy of the ballot (not achieved until 1872, the year after his death) and through his scholarship. His *History of Greece* (1846–56) contains two immortal chapters written with contemporary issues in mind. Part II, chapter 67 demonstrates that the Sophists did not subvert morality and did not corrupt Athenian democracy; on the whole, they were rather conservative.[36] Chapter 68 manages the miracle of putting in the best possible light the two objects of Grote's most fervent admiration, Socrates and Athenian democracy, despite the fact that the one put the other to death for impiety.

By the time of his *Plato* (1865) and the reading of the *Protagoras* I have just adumbrated, Grote was an old man of 71. Experience had tempered his optimism about the prospects for successful reform. Even when achieved, democracy can easily suppress the liberty of individual judgement on which it is founded. Socrates flourished in Athens, but was finally silenced. A likely influence here is John Stuart Mill, whose essay *On Liberty*, published in 1859 (between Grote's *History* and his *Plato*), is an eloquent defence of the need to protect the liberty of individuals to form their own judgements and live out their chosen ways of life.[37] The enemy is not only the tyranny of the majority who scorn and do not want to know. There is also the tyranny of society itself, a 'despotism of custom' which is Grote's King Nomos in other words.[38]

This being the outlook of the Philosophic Radicals, what is to be done with the *Republic*? In the *Republic*, the Socratic method beloved by the Mills gives way to positive exposition. But unlike Thomas Taylor, James Mill did not take this for dogmatic systematizing:

> in the books concerning Polity and Laws, the business is to give specimens of investigation, to let in rays of light, to analyze particular points, and, by throwing out queries or hypotheses, to encourage speculation, rather than lay down and establish any system of opinions.[39]

Besides, he wholeheartedly agreed with Plato that the only security for good government is an identity of interests between the governors and the governed. True, Plato proposed to reorganize society, abolishing the family and private property for the governing class, so as to drive private interests out of existence. But the only reason for these 'extraordinary methods' was that Plato was 'ignorant, as all the ancients were, of the divine principle of representation'.[40]

John Stuart Mill was also quite positive. He endorsed Plato's view that the secret of good government is to have reluctant rulers, who want nothing from their office but to avoid being governed by people worse than themselves.[41] He approved the idea that government is a 'Skilled Employment', for which only superior minds are fit.[42] And he was inspired by Plato's argument in *Republic* IX (581e–583a) that only a philosopher is qualified to compare the pleasures of learning with other delights, so as to appreciate how much sweeter the intellectual pleasures really are. The result was a famous declaration in *Utilitarianism*:

> It is better to be a human being dissatisfied than a pig satisfied; better to be Socrates dissatisfied than a fool satisfied. And if the fool, or the pig, is of a different opinion, it is because they only know their own side of the question. The other party to the comparison knows both sides.[43]

But a scholarly study of Plato must do more than take up the ideas that please. Grote opens with a compliment to the *Republic*'s 'lofty pretensions as the great constructive work of Plato'.[44] The compliment turns out to be double-edged. Once the Socrates of the *Republic* has ceased to be the leader of opposition and has 'passed over to the ministerial benches',

> No new leader of opposition is allowed to replace him. The splendid constructive effort of the Republic would have been spoiled, if exposed to such an analytical cross-examination as that which we read in Menon, Lachēs, or Charmidēs.[45]

That cross-examination Grote supplies on his own initiative, in two long chapters of philosophical critique.[46] The critique, which takes in all the main moral and political theses of the *Republic*, is patient, fair, scholarly, and telling, supported when appropriate by reference to more recent philosophers. I recommend it as a model of how to write about ancient philosophy.

Right at the end, after pages of soberly restrained criticism, Grote comes to Plato's proposal (*Republic* VII 537c–539e) that in the ideal city dialectic and debate about moral values should be forbidden to the young and to anyone who has not been through military training (involving indoctrination about what is to be feared and what not) and a strenuous education in advanced mathematics, lasting until they are 30 years of age. Here is Grote on the great betrayal:

> In the Platonic Apology, we find Sokrates confessing his own ignorance, and proclaiming himself to be isolated among an uncongenial public falsely persuaded of their own knowledge. In several other dialogues, he is the same: he cannot teach anything, but can only cross-examine, test, and apply the spur to respondents. But the Republic presents him in a new character. He is no longer a dissenter amidst a community of fixed, inherited, convictions. He is himself in the throne of King Nomos: the infallible authority, temporal as well as spiritual, from whom all public sentiment emanates, and by whom orthodoxy is determined. Hence we find him passing to the opposite pole; taking up the orthodox, conservative, point of view, the same as Melētus and Anytus maintained in their accusation against Sokrates at Athens. He now expects every individual to fall into the place, and contract the opinions, prescribed by authority; including among those opinions deliberate ethical and political fictions, such as that about the gold and silver earthborn men. Free-thinking minds, who take views of their own, become inconvenient and dangerous. Neither the Sokrates of the Platonic Apology, nor his negative Dialectic, could be allowed to exist in the Platonic Republic.[47]

Further comment would be superfluous. I will simply quote Grote's response to John Stuart Mill's *An Examination of Sir William Hamilton's Philosophy* (1865): 'A dignified, judicial equanimity of tone is preserved from first to last.'[48]

Yet the *Republic* could and did help some Victorians who wanted to think for themselves and question received opinion.

In 1855 the Revd Benjamin Jowett, newly elected Regius Professor of Greek, was summoned to the vice-chancellor's office at the University of Oxford and made to sign again his allegiance to the Church of England's Thirty-Nine Articles of Religion.[49] Teachers at the universities of Oxford and Cambridge were required to subscribe to the established creed. Up until 1854 'subscription' was demanded from junior members as well; Bentham, entering Oxford in 1760 at the age of 12, had perforce to swallow his scruples about signing.[50] There were no religious tests in Scotland, but the only English university that did not require 'subscription' was the University of London (now University College London), known as the 'Godless College of Gower Street' and the 'Cockney College', which had been set up by the Philosophic Radicals and their allies as recently as 1826. An institution open, as the contemptuous nicknames complain, to members of any creed or class, including Roman Catholics, Jews and atheists, London was founded on the principle that there should be no religious or theological instruction at all.

Ten years before the summons was issued to Jowett, his colleague W. G. Ward (mathematics tutor at Balliol) had been publicly stripped of his degrees for supporting a High Church interpretation of the Thirty-Nine Articles by John Henry (later Cardinal) Newman. Eight years after his summons, Jowett would be charged with heresy before the Vice-Chancellor's Court at Oxford. Unlike Socrates, his life was not at risk from these attacks. But his career as a teacher most certainly was.

The cause of the summons in 1855 was that his edition of the Epistles of St Paul made use of the methods of historical criticism which had been developed by German scholars for the study of Homer. This gave rise to the (correct) suspicion that he entertained independent thoughts on the dogmas of religion.[51] The heresy indictment in 1863 was for his contribution, 'On the interpretation of scripture', to a collection of theological essays which aroused horror and scandal throughout the land.[52] Not only was this the century in which Britain began its long slow journey towards democracy. It was also the century in which Britain began the long slow journey towards secularism.

People agonized about religion with an earnestness we must take seriously if we are to understand the century which led up to our own. Faith was shaken both by the application to the Bible of 'the subtle shafts of German criticism',[53] and by the increasing plausibility to all rational standards of thought of the modern scientific world picture. Some of the assaults came from outside the established Church. But some also came from within.

The Philosophic Radicals were outsiders. When Grote was in his twenties, he was asked to write up Bentham's notes on the usefulness of religious belief. The result, published in 1822, was *An Analysis of the Influence of Natural Religion on the Temporal Happiness of Mankind* by 'Philip Beauchamp' (the publisher, Richard Carlile, did not need a pseudonym because he was already in Dorchester gaol for printing the theological and political works of Thomas Paine). James Mill showed the manuscript to his 16-year old son, on whom it had a formative effect.[54]

Jowett, by contrast, an ordained clergyman, was very much the insider. He supported the movement to abolish religious tests and in 1871 argued against 'subscription' before a Select Committee of the House of Lords; in the transcript their Lordships treat him with high respect.[55] What is more, as an educator – first, the charismatic but suspiciously unorthodox

363

tutor, from 1870 Master of Balliol, and finally (1882–6) Vice-Chancellor of Oxford University – Jowett did not agonize for himself alone. He was concerned with the morale, the morality in the broadest sense, of public life and public leaders. In short, with the character of King Nomos himself. If religion goes, or agreement about religion falls apart, what is to take its place?

Let us not be cynical. There is a rhetoric in public life which surely does not determine the behaviour of our leaders, but does set limits, however loose, to the kinds of policy they can get away with and the kinds of thing they can do without having to resign. It is a matter of enormous importance what values are acknowledged – sincerely or insincerely – in public discussion. King Nomos changes gradually over time. The Philosophic Radicals confronted him head-on, but when John Stuart Mill asked himself how a sense of principle could be maintained in public life now that 'the old opinions in religion, morals and politics, are so much discredited in the more intellectual minds', he had no answer.[56] A well-placed university teacher (then as now) can try to influence the way King Nomos will develop:

> My *Plato* is only a translation, but I have a satisfaction in feeling that it may influence the English and American world in the right direction long after I have gone.[57]

Such was the problem for which Jowett sought help from Plato. If the young were encouraged to read Plato for their 'Greats' tutorials, they would be ennobled by an 'Idealism' that would keep alive their devotion to duty and the public good when they went out into government or the Civil Service, at home or in the Empire.

Idealism for Jowett contrasted with Utilitarianism:

> If Mr. Grote should do me the honour to read any portion of this work he will probably remark that I have endeavoured to approach Plato from a point of view which is opposed to his own. The aim of the Introductions in these volumes has been to represent Plato as the father of Idealism, who is not to be measured by the standard of utilitarianism or any other modern philosophical system. He is the poet or maker of ideas, satisfying the wants of his own age, providing the instruments of thought for future generations. He is no dreamer, but a great philosophical genius struggling with the unequal conditions of light and knowledge under which he is living. He may be illustrated by the writings of moderns, but he must be interpreted by his own, and by his place in the history of philosophy. We are not concerned to determine what is the residuum of truth which remains for ourselves. His truth may not be our truth, and nevertheless may have an extraordinary value and interest for us.[58]

This is Jowett introducing the translation which 'succeeded in making Plato an English classic'.[59] He did the whole corpus singlehandedly, a task no other English speaker has undertaken.[60] Classical scholars delight to scoff at his inaccuracies,[61] but his prose is still a pleasure to read. And it was the prose that won him so many more readers than Taylor, whose knowledge of Greek really was defective.

Jowett's opposition to Utilitarianism is in fact quite mild. The greatest happiness principle, he says, is not the first principle of ethics, but it is the second: 'First duty, then happiness'.[62] And what he means by 'Idealism' comes out when he says that the Stoic or the Christian ideal, even if it is not realized in anyone's actual life, 'may serve as a basis for education, and may exercise an ennobling influence'.[63] More fully,

> Human life and conduct are affected by ideals in the same way that they are affected by the examples of eminent men. Neither the one nor the other are immediately applicable in practice, but there is a virtue flowing from them which tends to raise individuals above the common routine of society or trade, and to elevate States above the mere interest of commerce or the necessities of self-defence.[64]

That, for Jowett, is the point of studying Plato's account in the *Republic* of the ideally just individual and the ideally just city.

For this educative purpose it was important that Idealism, in the moral sense just sketched, should take first place among Plato's 'instruments of thought for future generations'. Metaphysical Idealism in Hegel's sense is explained in the Introduction to the *Sophist*, but this is in the hope of arousing interest in Hegel, not to equate ancient and modern Idealism.[65] Jowett makes clear that he has ceased to believe in Hegel's system, of which he is much more critical than he is of Utilitarianism. The former is conservative, the latter an inspiration to reform – and Jowett was as committed to practical reform as the Philosophic Radicals.[66] At the heart of his commitment was education of the young, to inspire them with moral Idealism. For this purpose, any too definite theological or metaphysical views would get in the way. They can be put down to 'the unequal conditions of light and knowledge' under which Plato was living, his 'place in the history of philosophy'. Hence Jowett, like James Mill, needs to marginalize the *Timaeus*:

> Of all the writings of Plato the Timaeus is the most obscure and repulsive to the modern reader, and has nevertheless had the greatest influence over the ancient and mediaeval world. The obscurity arises in the infancy of science, out of the confusion of theological, mathematical, and physiological notions, out of the desire to conceive the whole of nature without any adequate knowledge of the parts. . . . The influence which the Timaeus has exercised upon posterity is partly due to a misunderstanding. In the supposed depths of this dialogue the Neo-Platonists found hidden meanings and connections with the Jewish and Christian Scriptures, and out of them they elicited doctrines quite at variance with the spirit of Plato.[67] . . . A greater danger with modern interpreters of Plato is the tendency to regard the Timaeus as the centre of his system . . . But . . . we observe . . . that the dialogue is put into the mouth of a Pythagorean philosopher, not of Socrates . . . Nor does Plato himself attribute any importance to his guesses at science. He is not at all absorbed by them, as he is by the *idea* of good. . . . Thus we are led by Plato himself to regard the Timaeus, not as the centre or inmost shrine of the edifice, but as a detached building in a different style, framed, not after the Socratic, but after some Pythagorean model.[68]

Jowett is a bit more polite than James Mill, but the effect is the same. And Jowett was in a position of influence.

We are now ready to read the *Republic* as without rival the greatest of Plato's works:

no other Dialogue of Plato has the same largeness of view and the same perfection of style; <no other shows an equal knowledge of the world, or contains more of those thoughts which are new as well as old, and not of one age only but of all . . . He is the father of idealism in philosophy, in politics, in literature.> And many of the latest conceptions of modern thinkers and statesmen, such as the unity of knowledge, the reign of law, and the equality of the sexes, have been anticipated in a dream by him.[69]

The year after the translation appeared (1871), the *Republic* became a prescribed text for the 'Greats' examination at Oxford.[70] It has held this place of honour ever since.

What 'thoughts which are new as well as old' would Jowett have his readers find in the *Republic*? Here, from his Introduction to the dialogue, is a page that shows the *Republic* eliciting in the mind of a liberal Victorian clergyman some surprising thoughts on the proposal in Book V that women should be given the same education as man, to equip them for the same tasks (military and governmental) as the men will undertake:

[In no former age of the world would Plato's ideas on this subject have received so much assent as in our own. . . . He is as much in advance of modern nations as they are in advance of the customs of Greek society.] . . . The Athenian woman was in no way the equal of her husband; she was not the entertainer of his guests or the mistress of his house, but only his housekeeper and the mother of his children. She took no part in military or political matters. . . . A very different ideal of womanhood is held up by Plato to the world; she is to be the companion of man, and to share with him in the toils of war and in the cares of the government. She is to be similarly trained both in bodily and in mental exercises. She is to lose as far as possible the incidents of maternity and the characteristics of the female sex.

The modern antagonist of the equality of the sexes would argue that the differences between men and women are not confined to the single point urged by Plato; that sensibility, gentleness, grace, are the qualities of women, while energy, strength, higher intelligence, are to be looked for in men. And the criticism is true: the differences affect the whole nature, and are not, as Plato supposes, confined to a single point. But neither can we say how far these differences are due to education and the opinions of mankind, or physically inherited from the habits and opinions of former generations. Women have always been taught, not exactly that they are slaves,[71] but that they are in an inferior position, which is also supposed to have compensating advantages; and to this position they have conformed. Add to this that the physical form may easily change in the course of generations through the mode of life; and the weakness or delicacy, which was once a matter of opinion, may pass into a physical fact. The difference between the two sexes varies greatly in different countries and ranks of society, and at different ages in the same individuals. And Plato may have been right in denying that there was any ultimate difference in the sexes other than that which exists in animals, because all other differences may be conceived to disappear in other states of society, or under different circumstances of life and training.[72]

In other words – today's words – gender differences are socially constructed.

But so too are notions of property. Jowett will not condemn the communism of the *Republic*:

> The early Christians are believed to have held their property in common, and the principle is sanctioned by the words of Christ himself, and has been maintained as a counsel of perfection in almost all ages of the Church.[73]

Of course this sounds visionary in the world as we know it – Idealism at its most impractical. But perhaps 'our present individualism is . . . the artificial result of the industrial state of modern Europe'.[74] If so, it could one day be changed.

Eleven years earlier, in 1860, Jowett had been asked to read a three-volume work by Florence Nightingale which expressed radical views about religion and the position of women.[75] She wanted advice on preparing it for publication. John Stuart Mill had been encouraging, but advised condensing and a rearrangement of the ideas.[76] Jowett said the same, with rather more enthusiasm for Nightingale's theological speculations. He also urged her to soften the angry tone, so as to be more effective with readers.[77] Thus began a long friendship between Nightingale and Jowett.

They exchanged books, views, and practical advice. Each valued the other as a critic of their current writing project. In particular, Nightingale was the spur to many of the changes Jowett made for the second edition (1875) of his *Plato*.[78] It is a tempting speculation that over the years their friendship had made him more receptive than he might otherwise have been to Plato's suggestion that we should rethink the whole basis on which human society is organized.[79] At any rate, Jowett's final word on how readers might be ennobled by the *Republic* is a list of the ideals it continues to offer:

> The ideal of the State and of the life of the philosopher; the ideal of an education continuing through life *and extending equally to both sexes*; the ideal of the unity and correlation of knowledge; the faith in good and immortality.[80]

Would that the twentieth century could have matched that generous response to Plato.

ADDENDUM

After this essay had been submitted for publication, Alasdair MacIntyre pointed out to me that, in calling Jowett 'the person most responsible for bringing the *Republic* into the Number One place it occupies today' (p. 354 above), I overlook the considerable contribution of *The Republic of Plato*, translated into English, with an Introduction, Analysis, and Notes, by John Llewelyn Davies and David James Vaughan (Cambridge, Macmillan, 1852; 2nd edn, 1858). In 1852 Davies and Vaughan were young Fellows of Trinity College Cambridge, aged 26 and 27 respectively. Not only does their translation antedate Jowett's by nearly 20 years, but the third edition of 1866 was put into the popular Golden Treasury series, where it enjoyed no less than twenty-two reprints between 1868 and 1908. The Preface to the first edition speaks of the *Republic* as Plato's masterpiece, the Introductory Note to the third edition calls it his 'acknowledged masterpiece'. Clearly, the currents favouring the *Republic* within Oxford were matched by others in Cambridge and the wider world. That is hardly surprising. The relatively sudden rise in public appreciation of a philosophical work written nearly two and a half thousand years ago is not likely to have a simple, single-factor explanation.

NOTES

1 Which makes no claim to originality and offers no contribution to the subject called 'history of scholarship'. My aim is simply to share an enthusiasm with readers of this volume, making such use as I need of other scholars' work. Much the best and clearest treatment of the subject is to be found in two essays by John Glucker: 'Plato in England: the nineteenth century and after', in H. Funke (ed.) *Utopie und Tradition: Platons Lehre vom Staat in der Moderne* (Würzburg, Königshausen and Neumann, 1987), pp. 149–210, and 'The two Plato's of Victorian Britain', in K. A. Algra, P. W. van der Horst and D. T. Runia (eds) *Polyhistor: Studies in the History and Historiography of Ancient Philosophy* (Leiden, Brill, 1996), pp. 385–406. Besides the works mentioned in notes below, readers who want further information of a general kind can turn to the following: William Thomas, *The Philosophic Radicals: Nine Studies in Theory and Practice 1817–1841* (Oxford, Clarendon Press, 1979); Alexander Bain, *James Mill: a Biography* (London, Longmans, Green & Co., 1882); M. L. Clarke, *George Grote: a Biography* (London, Athlone Press, 1962); Geoffrey Faber, *Jowett: a Portrait with Background* (London, Faber, 1958).

2 Other countries' experience was very different, even if they arrived (eventually) at the same destination. For an instructive introduction to national differences, see Henri Wismann, '*Modus interpretandi*: Analyse comparée des études platoniciennes en France et en Allemagne au 19ième siècle', in M. Bollack, H. Wismann and T. Lindken (eds) *Philologie und Hermeneutik im 19. Jahrhundert* (Göttingen, 1983), vol. II, pp. 490–513.

3 *Platonis et quae vel Platonis esse feruntur vel Platonica solent comitari scripta Graece omnia*, with notes by Immanuel Bekker, 11 vols (London, 1826). On Mill's use of this edition, see n. 6 below. The bookseller (namely publisher) was A. J. Valpy, also responsible for the Delphine Classics and *The Classical Journal*.

4 *Platonis Euthydemus et Gorgias* (Greek and English), ed. Martin Joseph Routh (Oxford, 1784).

5 *The Collected Works of John Stuart Mill*, vol. XI: *Essays on Philosophy and the Classics*, ed. John M. Robson with Introduction by F. E. Sparshott (Toronto and London, University of Toronto Press, 1978), pp. 39–40. (The *Collected Works* are cited henceforth as Mill, *CW*.) Sparshott's Introduction, a splendidly knowledgeable assessment of Mill's dealings with classical topics, confirms the justice of Mill's complaint about the lack of scholarly editions from Oxford and Cambridge (see p. xxi with n. 65). But Mill's larger aspersions are mitigated by M. R. Stopper, 'Greek philosophy and the Victorians', *Phronesis* 26 (1981), pp. 267–85, who shows that there were lectures (and presumably tutorial teaching as well) on Plato in Oxford in the 1820s. I suspect that Mill had in front of him the very similar sentiments expressed by his father, much earlier and more truly, in the *Edinburgh Review* for 1809 (see n. 20 below), pp. 187–9, with reference to Scotland as well as England; if so, 'this kingdom' in the last sentence of the passage quoted means the United Kingdom, not just England.

6 Only the first four were published; for this and other details, see Sparshott, in Mill, *CW* XI, pp. xviii–xxi, who makes it virtually certain that Mill did his translations from Bekker's edition (n. 3 above). Bekker endorsed Schleiermacher's claim (in *Platons Werke*, Berlin, 1804–28) to have discovered 'the natural' (hence chronological) order in which to arrange the dialogues:

they were written in a sequence designed to prepare the reader stage by stage to embrace a philosophy premeditated by their author, beginning *Phaedrus*, *Lysis*, *Protagoras* and climaxing in the *Timaeus*. The dialogues translated by J. S. Mill are the first nine in Bekker's edition, forming the group which Schleiermacher considered 'elementary', plus the *Gorgias*. This explains the oddity of Mill's including the *Parmenides*; the oddity is Schleiermacher's considering it youthful and elementary. Schleiermacher may be consulted in William Dobson's English translation, *Schleiermacher's Introductions to the Dialogues of Plato* (Cambridge and London, 1863); Grote, *Plato*, vol. I, ch. 4, is a crushing critique of his views.

7 This phrase, which means 'the intellect left to go its own way', derives from Francis Bacon's *Novum Organon* (1620). Grote appeals to Bacon in the same terms for an identical appreciation of the Socratic method: see *A History of Greece*, Part II, ch. 68. Mill, reviewing the *History*, enthuses about the parallel between Socrates and Bacon: see Mill, *CW* XI, pp. 309–10 note.

8 Mill, *CW* I: *Autobiography and Literary Essays*, ed. John M. Robson and Jack Stillinger (1981), p. 25.

9 For comparison, Bentham's father was teaching him Latin, and at least the Greek alphabet, by the age of 5; Grote was taught Latin by his mother before he went to school at 5. James Mill's innovation was to start so early with Greek before Latin.

10 Readers should also bracket the now unassailable view that *Sophist* and *Statesman* are late works, Platonic rather than Socratic. This was first announced by Jowett's pupil, Lewis Campbell, in his famous 1867 edition of these dialogues, two years after the publication of Grote's *Plato*.

11 'Bentham' [1838] in Mill, *CW* X: *Essays on Ethics, Religion and Society*, ed. John M. Robson (1969), p. 86.

12 Ibid., p. 88.

13 Ibid., p. 90, referring to a passage of Bentham's *Deontology* which condemns Socrates and Plato for 'talking nonsense, on pretence of teaching morality and wisdom': see *The Collected Works of Jeremy Bentham: Deontology together with A Table of the Springs of Action and The Article on Utilitarianism*, ed. Amnon Goldworth (Oxford, Clarendon Press, 1983), p. 135.

14 Mill, *CW* I, p. 9.

15 Yes, that makes seven dialogues, not six; the *Autobiography* suffered a lapse of memory. I defend this claim, and give reasons for taking 'the common arrangement' to be the Stephanus order we still use for referencing the Platonic corpus, in 'What was "the common arrangement"? An inquiry into John Stuart Mill's boyhood reading of Plato', forthcoming. The relevant editorial annotations in *Collected Works*, Mill (vol. I, p. 9 note and vol. XI, p. xix, n. 54) assume that 'the common arrangement' is the order canonized in antiquity by Thrasyllus (Platonist philosopher and astrologer to the Emperor Tiberius) and familiar today from the Oxford Classical Text of Plato. That yields six dialogues with *Cratylus* in place of *Theages* and *Erastai*. The objection is that neither in 1813 nor in 1853 (when Mill wrote the first draft of his *Autobiography*) could Mill or his readers have thought of the Thrasyllan arrangement as, in any sense, 'the common' one.

16 Mill, *CW* XI, p. 40. Grote would agree. Part of the originality of his *Plato*, compared to previous scholarship, is its refusing to harmonize the dialogues into a system.

17 Mill, *CW* I, p. 25.

18 The full title is instructive: 'The Works of Plato, viz. His Fifty-five Dialogues [counting *Republic* as 10, *Laws* as 12], and Twelve Epistles, Translated from the Greek; Nine of the Dialogues by the Late Floyer Sydenham, and the Remainder by Thomas Taylor: with Occasional Annotations on the Nine Dialogues Translated by Sydenham, and Copious Notes, by the Latter Translator; in Which Is Given the Substance of Nearly All the Existing Greek MS. Commentaries on the Philosophy of Plato, and a Considerable Portion of Such as Are Already Published. 5 vols.' Those 'Copious Notes' are designed to feast the reader with neo-Platonizing interpretation.

19 *The Works of Plato*, vol. II, p. 425; cf. vol. I, pp. lxxix–lxxxiv, for Taylor's hostility towards Francis Bacon and the 'experimentalists'.

20 'Taylor's *Plato*', *Edinburgh Review* 14 (1809), p. 192. The review is anonymous, but an earlier onslaught against Taylor, in *The Literary Journal* 3 (1804), pp. 449–61 and 577–89, is signed 'M.'. Since Mill was the editor of this journal throughout its existence and a regular contributor, and since the two reviews are plainly from the same author, it is safe to ascribe both to his pen. For a discussion on this basis of James Mill's interest in Plato, see Kyriacos Demetriou, 'The development of Platonic studies in Britain and the role of the Utilitarians', *Utilitas* 8 (1996), pp. 15–37. J. S. Mill, at vol. XI, p. 42, repeats his father's judgement of Taylor's translation.

21 'Taylor's *Plato*' 200. The idea that the *Timaeus* does not express Plato's own convictions would be defended, on different grounds, a hundred years later in A. E. Taylor's controversial and deeply learned commentary on the work: *A Commentary on Plato's Timaeus* (Oxford, Clarendon, 1928).

22 These are the first two articles of Taylor's 'The Platonic philosopher's creed' [1805], available in Kathleen Raine and George Mills Harper (eds), *Thomas Taylor the Platonist: Selected Writings* (Princeton, NJ, Princeton University Press, 1969), 439.

23 A good account of Taylor's *fortuna* in the USA is George Mills Harper, 'Thomas Taylor in America' in Raine and Harper (eds) *Thomas Taylor*. In the same volume Kathleen Raine, 'Thomas Taylor in England', is an enthusiastic assessment of Taylor's intellectual career and of what he gave to the poets, especially William Blake.

24 Quoted from *The Journals and Miscellaneous Notebooks of Ralph Waldo Emerson*, ed. Merton M. Seaults, Jr., vol. V (Cambridge, Mass., Belkaap Press of Harvard University Press, 1973), p. 559.

25 The name was coined by John Stuart Mill for a parliamentary group of reformists, but was soon applied more widely. See his review of Fonblanque's *England under Seven Administrations* (1837) in *Collected Works, Mill*, vol. VI: *Essays on England, Ireland, and the Empire*, ed. John M. Robson (Toronto, 1982), p. 353; cf. also *Autobiography*, vol. I, pp. 107–11, pp. 203–5.

26 i.e. people refuse to light a fire for you, or to sit at meals and share the usual sacrifices with you. See Herodotus VII 231, Dinarchus, *Against Aristogiton*.

27 George Grote, *Plato and the Other Companions of Sokrates* [1865], 3rd edn (London, 1875) vol. I, pp. 250–1.

28 For more on this concept, see the illuminating essay by John Vaio, 'George Grote and James Mill: how to write history', in William M. Calder III and Stephen Trzaskoma (eds) *George Grote Reconsidered: a 200th Birthday Celebration* (Hildesheim, Weidmann, 1996), pp. 59–74.

29 Grote, *Plato*, vol. I, p. 252 note.

30 Ibid., 253.

31 Grote, *Plato*, vol. II, pp. 45–6 (cf. pp. 72–7).

32 So too Gregory Vlastos, Introduction to *Plato's* Protagoras, trans. B. Jowett and M. Ostwald (Indianapolis, Ind., and New York, Liberal Arts Press, 1956), pp. xx–xxi: 'Nothing in the process described in the Great Speech requires either learner or teacher to think for oneself, or even to think: to weigh evidence, analyze concepts, examine reasons.'

33 Mill, *CW*, X., p. 205; the phrase 'so-called sophist' reflects Mill's reading of the dramatic re-evaluation of the Sophists in Grote's *History*, of which more shortly.

34 Grote, *Plato*, vol. II, pp. 81–3.

35 The issues are well discussed in Frank M. Turner's outstanding book, *The Greek Heritage in Victorian Britain* (New Haven, Conn., and London, Yale University Press, 1981), ch. V.

36 Part II, ch. 67, on the Sophists does no more than mention Antiphon, who would now be the chief candidate for the role of subversive. The papyrus remains of his *Truth* were first published in 1914. If Grote were alive today, he would join Jonathan Barnes, *The Presocratic Philosophers* (London, Routledge and Kegan Paul, 1979), vol. II, pp. 206–14, in contesting the standard view that Antiphon's observations on the conflict between nature and convention imply an anarchic preference for nature. *Truth* tells us how things are, and the surviving fragments offer no advice for coping with the situation we find ourselves in.

37 On the change to a gloomier outlook, see Turner, *Greek Heritage*, pp. 294–5. For Grote's high opinion of *On Liberty*, see his review [1866] of Mill's *An Examination of Sir William Hamilton's Philosophy* in Alexander Bain (ed.) *The Minor Works of George Grote* (London, John Murray, 1873), pp. 288–90.

38 Mill, *CW*, XVIII: *Essays on Politics and Society*, ed. J. M. Robson (1977), pp. 219–20, 272–4. Yet another Millian variant on King Nomos is 'Commonplace'; see his review (1866) of Grote's *Plato* in *CW*, XI, p. 403.

39 *Edinburgh Review* 14 (1809), p. 199.

40 James Mill, *Political Writings*, ed. Terence Ball (Cambridge, Cambridge University Press, 1992), p. 311 (excerpt from *A Fragment on Mackintosh*).

41 *Considerations on Representative Government* in *Collected Works*, Mill, vol. XIX: *Essays on Politics and Society*, ed. J. M. Robson (Toronto, 1977), p. 498.

42 Review of Grote's *Plato*, in Mill, *CW* XI, p. 436.

43 *Collected Works*, vol. X, p. 212.

44 Grote, *Plato*, vol. III, p. 27; cf. p. 122.

45 Ibid., p. 165.

46 Ibid., chs 34–5. Grote in turn was subjected to cross-examination by Thrasymachus, Adeimantus, Glaucon and Socrates in an interesting little dialogue written by Henry Sidgwick and John Grote (Grote's younger brother, Professor of Moral Philosophy at Cambridge), in *Classical Review* 3 (1889), pp. 97–102.

47 Grote, *Plato*, vol. III, p. 240.

48 Bain (ed.) *Minor Works of Grote*, p. 290. Contrast the stridency with which Grote's criticism is repeated by Karl Popper, *The Open Society and its Enemies* [1945], 4th edn, vol. I: *The Spell of Plato* (London, Routledge and Kegan Paul, 1962), ch. 8, sect. vi with n. 55. I say 'criticism', not 'condemnation' (the word used by Turner, *Greek Heritage*, p. 395, n. 46), because Grote believed strongly that in philosophy reasoned untruth is to be valued more than unreasoned truth: *Plato*, vol. I, Preface, pp. v–vii.

49 In full, these are 'Articles agreed upon by the Archbishops and Bishops of both Provinces and the whole clergy in the Convocation holden at London in the year 1562 for the avoiding of diversities of opinions and for the establishing of consent touching true religion'. The Royal Declaration later prefixed to them by King Charles II expressly forbids 'any publick Reader in either of Our Universities, or any Head or Master of a College, or any other person respectively in either of them' to 'affix any new sense to any Article'.

50 The scruples are reported by J. S. Mill, 'Bentham', in Mill, *CW* X, p. 81, though he wrongly gives the age as 15.

51 *The Epistles of St Paul to the Thessalonians, Galatians, Romans: with critical notes and dissertations*, 2 vols (London, 1855). The essay 'The doctrine of the atonement', vol. II, pp. 468–82, caused particular offence.

52 *Essays and Reviews* [1860], 10th edn (London, 1862), pp. 399–527; Jowett's essay is reprinted in the 3rd edition of *The Epistles of St Paul*, brought out by Lewis Campbell in 1894.

53 Jowett, *Epistles of St Paul*, vol. I, p. 109. For an informative discussion of the issues, see Turner, *Greek Heritage*, ch. 4.

54 *Autobiography*, in Mill, *CW* I, p. 73.

55 Excerpts from the transcript are printed in *Letters of Benjamin Jowett*, ed. Evelyn Abbott and Lewis Campbell (London, 1899), pp. 19–39; the discussion is deeply impressive.

56 *Autobiography*, in Mill, *CW* I, pp. 245–7.

57 Abbott and Campbell (eds) *Letters of Jowett*, p. 182 (to R. B. D. Morier, 1870).

58 B. Jowett, *The Dialogues of Plato* [1871], 2nd edn, translated into English with analyses and introductions, 5 vols (Oxford, 1875), pp. viii–ix. Jowett ends with a warm tribute to Grote. They have their disagreements, large or small. 'But I "am not going to lay hands on my father Parmenides" [*Soph.* 241d], who will, I hope, forgive me for differing from him on these points.

I cannot close this Preface without expressing my deep respect for his noble and gentle character, and the great services which he has rendered to Greek Literature' (p. x).

59 Lewis Campbell in *Encyclopedia Britannica*, 11th edn, under 'Jowett'.

60 Pedantic correction: two very suspect dialogues, *Alcibiades* II and *Eryxias*, added to the 3rd edition (1892) of *The Dialogues of Plato*, were translated by Matthew Knight, the son of Jowett's servant (vol. II, p. 537). Jowett had been teaching him since boyhood; from the age of 14 he had been Jowett's amanuensis.

61 'Jowett's Plato: the best translation of a Greek philosopher which has ever been executed by a person who understood neither philosophy nor Greek' — so Housman, quoted in C. O. Brink, *English Classical Scholarship: Historical Reflections on Bentley, Porson and Houseman* (Cambridge, James Clarke; New York, Oxford University Press, 1985), p. 130. For an antidote, read Jowett's sensitive reflections on the difficulties of making Plato readable in English: *Dialogues of Plato*, vol. I, pp. xi–xviii (Preface to 2nd edn).

62 Jowett, *Dialogues of Plato*, vol. III, pp. 49–50.

63 Ibid., p. 24.

64 Ibid., p. 192.

65 Jowett, *Dialogues of Plato*, vol. IV, pp. 401–24 (added in 2nd edn).

66 A good way to get a sense of the range of Jowett's reforming interests is to read through the correspondence in *Letters of Jowett*.

67 'Neo-Platonists' here evidently includes Christians of the Roman Empire who shared a Platonic inheritance with the pagan philosophers.

68 Jowett, *Dialogues of Plato*, vol. III, pp. 523–5. Contrast Grote's calm at *Plato*, vol. III, pp. 243–7: while acknowledging that 'the Platonic Timaeus is positively anti-Sokratic', he still appreciates the epistemological modesty with which Plato presents his physical system (the earliest to be preserved intact) as at least as probable as any other.

69 Jowett, *Dialogues of Plato*, vol. III, pp. 1–2; angled brackets mark words added in 2nd edn.

70 For exact details, and corrections to the prevailing unjust assessment of Jowett's contribution to Oxford scholarship, see Stopper, 'Greek Philosophy and the Victorians'.

71 Possibly an allusion to J. S. Mill's recently published *The Subjection of Women* (1869). Mill makes much of the comparison with slavery, which had been abolished in the British empire only 36 years earlier; one of those who voted for the measure in 1833 was George Grote, newly elected to Parliament on an abolitionist platform.

72 Jowett, *Dialogues of Plato*, vol. III, pp. 159–60; square brackets mark words deleted in 2nd edn.

73 Ibid., p. 156.

74 Ibid., p. 158. On the historical contingency of notions of property, J. S. Mill agrees: see 'Chapters on Socialism' [1879], *Collected Works of Mill*, vol. V: *Essays on Economics and Society*, ed. J. M. Robson (Toronto, 1967), pp. 749–53. But he baulks at enlarging on alternatives for the future.

75 Vol. I *Suggestions for Thought to the Searchers after Truth among the Artizans of England*, vol. II–III *Suggestions for Thought to Searchers after Religious Truth* (privately printed, 1860).

76 *Collected Works*, Mill, vol. XV: *The Later Letters 1849–1873*, ed. Francis E. Mineka and Dwight N. Lindley (Toronto, 1972), pp. 706–12; cf. *The Subjection of Women*, vol. XXI: *Essays on Equality, Law, and Education*, ed. John M. Robson (Toronto, 1984), p. 319.

77 See the earliest letters in *Dear Miss Nightingale: a Selection of Benjamin Jowett's Letters to Florence Nightingale, 1860–1893*, ed. Vincent Quinn and John Prest (Oxford, Clarendon Press, 1987), with the editorial introduction, pp. xii–xiii. An interesting discussion of this episode (though slightly harsh on Jowett, in my view) is Elaine Showalter, 'Florence Nightingale's feminist complaint', *Signs* 6 (1981), pp. 395–412.

78 See *Dear Miss Nightingale*, pp. 218–21, 237, 245–6, 250, 256–8. My guess is that she would have exploded (affectionately) at the square-bracketed portion of the quotation on p. 366 above, leading Jowett to cut it out.

79 The Index to *Dear Miss Nightingale* has a sizeable entry under 'women'.
80 *Dialogues of Plato*, vol. III, p. 192; italics are mine.

This paper began as a lecture for an interdisciplinary course within the Faculty of Classics at Cambridge University, organized by my esteemed colleagues, Mary Beard and John Henderson. Thanks be to them for making me do it. Thanks also to Jonathan Barnes, Kyriacos Demetriou, Christopher Stray, and Robert Todd for advice and criticism.

26

MORAL EDUCATION IN
AND AFTER MARX

Richard W. Miller

When compassionate theorists think that their society is dominated by a rich elite whose interests conflict with the interests of the poor, they ask how the vast majority of the non-rich could acquire the motivations needed to change society. I will be investigating two answers to this question, one over a century old, the other in the process of creation. The old answer is Marx's account of how workers under capitalism acquire the motivation to carry out a socialist revolution. The new inquiry is an effort by those who have abandoned Marx's socialist hopes to see what role their residual Marxist beliefs could play in projects of reform.

Marx's writings as a whole constitute the great *Bildungsroman* of the nineteenth century, a story of the dawning insight and commitment of the Proletarian, with its subplot, the struggle to teach and to learn of the Communist. In this drama of enlightenment, capitalist oppression gives rise to new kinds of people, through "long struggles . . . transforming circumstances and men",[1] ultimately producing the goals and loyalties needed for a successful socialist revolution. My main effort will be to describe the mechanisms underlying this psychological transformation. What is most controversial in my interpretation can be summed up in the claim that the transformation of outlook on which Marx relies merits the label "moral education." This might seem perverse mislabeling. Marx scathingly dismisses appeals to impartial benevolence as an inadequate basis for socialist revolution, while emphasizing the deprivations that the capitalist labor market imposes on those who must sell their labor. This suggests that struggles against capitalism transform people by giving them new knowledge of resources for overcoming their own material deprivations – hardly a process of moral education.

In fact, when the nature and role of Marx's drama of enlightenment become clearer, it turns out to depend, crucially, on a different mechanism: changes in requirements for self-respect, brought about by resistance to domination, changes that produce a more extensive willingness to risk harm in the interests of others. New terms for self-respect convert mere material want into the revolutionary commitment that can transform society. Indeed, there is no other way that Marx could have reconciled his theory of the capitalist state with his expectation that capitalism would be overthrown as a result of rational revolutionary choices. So, despite his dismissals of mere preaching, Marx thinks that compassion will become politically effective through a process leading the vast majority to transcend self-interest. In addition, he may well have taken the new attitudes embodied in revolutionary proletarian class consciousness to be a basis for answering politically urgent questions of choice that impartial morality poses, but cannot answer. Thus, Marx's drama of enlightenment can be seen not just as the story of how people discover new facilities for relieving their individual burdens but as a story of how they develop a more determinate and effective conscience. It is, in short, a drama of moral education, one that challenges preconceptions of the relations between morality and impartiality, rationality and self-interest, self-assertion and self-sacrifice.

However, Marx wanted his drama of enlightenment to be a true story, not just an interesting yarn. In this he failed, or so I will assume. Capitalism will not be replaced by another system of social relations, radically enhancing the well-being of the vast majority of humanity. Still, despite the utopianism of Marx's hopes, many of Marx's large claims about capitalist domination remain extremely plausible. Having described the process of moral education that was implicit in Marx's whole theory of capitalism, I will end by exploring the question of what that remainder could contribute to a strategy of moral education in the interest of capitalism's victims that is believable over a century after Marx's death. In the tasks it assigns to intellectuals, this post-Marxist strategy will turn out to differ from Marx's both in content and in form, replacing his relatively unified vision of effective political engagement with a diverse array of roles, united only by a tense ethic of criticism and cooperation.

THE FETTERS OF IDEOLOGY

Like all great dramas of enlightenment, Marx's begins with an account of darkness, supplied by his theory of ideology. Although this is a familiar, exegetically uncontroversial part of his story, it is worth a bit of retelling, both because it helps to specify the tasks of enlightenment in Marx and because it contributes to the post-Marxist legacy whose current uses I will explore.

In Marx's view, people's ability to learn about their society is restricted by their location in the mode of material production, the technologies, work-relations and relations of control involved in the production of material goods. Above all, social stupidity is created by location in the class structure, the network of social relations of control over factors in material production. In a capitalist society, proletarians, who lack control over means of production, must work for capitalists, who control the surplus remaining when workers are paid and used-up physical means of production are replenished. Such dominance over the social surplus by a minority class is the single most important source of social stupidity: "The class that has the means of material production at its disposal has control, at the same time, over the means of mental production, so that thereby, generally speaking, the ideas of those who lack the means of mental production are subject to it" (*GI*, p. 65).

Of course (as Marx and Engels emphasize right after this passage), the propagation of beliefs and attitudes is, typically, the work of those outside the economic ruling class, for example, reporters or professors. But these idea-workers cannot use their ideas for food, clothing or other material equipment. Most of them are ultimately materially dependent on the support of the economic ruling class – directly in typical privately controlled institutions, or indirectly in public ones, owing to capitalist control of the state. Because of the costs of challenging class rule and the rewards of serving it, Marx thinks most idea-propagators will tend to put into circulation beliefs and sentiments more conservative than available evidence supports. And, Marx clearly thinks, they will often sincerely share these attitudes, even when they should know better. For attitudes, including beliefs, are molded by perceived interests. For example, although he takes the bourgeois underpinnings of their careers to have made respectable economists of his time "hired prizefighters" of the bourgeoisie (*C*, p. 25), Marx appreciates that the imperatives of self-respect make the apologists believe their apologias.

The outcome of this ruling class dominance of "mental production" is a milieu of institutionally sustained thoughts and sentiments representing the "interest [of the ruling class] as the common interest of all the members of society" (*GI*, pp. 65f.) and obscuring the common interest in social change of potentially revolutionary classes. A prime example of distortions of the second type are divisive views of a broadly racist kind. For example, Marx took the "antagonism" between English and Irish workers "artificially kept alive and intensified by the press, the pulpit, the comic papers, in short, by all the means at the disposal of the ruling classes" to be *the secret of the impotence of the English working class*, despite its organisation . . . the secret by which the capitalist class maintains its power."[2]

Apart from institutions which obscure social interests and social truths, Marx thinks social stupidity is inherent in certain class situations, above all, situations that give rise, simultaneously, to an aspiration toward change and a vision of how change will come about that guarantees defeat for that aspiration. For example, as a revolutionary in a largely peasant continent, Marx returns again and again to the analysis of peasant ideology. In discussing the small-holding peasants of France, he emphasizes both their legitimate fear that banking, agribusiness and industry will ruin the family farm, and their inability to unite as a nationwide movement, conscious of common interests, against these well-coordinated, politically powerful enemies. Marx traces this disunity to the relative self-sufficiency of the family farm, which produces "the great mass of the French nation . . . by simple addition of homologous magnitudes, much as potatoes in a sack form a sack of potatoes" (*EB* p. 172). The peasantry's combination of anxious hope for social salvation with paralyzing atomization produces the doomed wish for a Man on a Horse who restores peasant prosperity, which Louis Napoleon exploited. "They cannot represent themselves. They must be represented. Their representative must at the same time appear as their master . . . [A] man named Napoleon would bring all the glory back to them" (*EB*, p. 172).

"EVER-EXPANDING UNION"

No wonder that the *Communist Manifesto* proclaims that the "ruling ideas of each age have ever been the ideas of its [economic] ruling class" (p. 51). Add to this the thesis that the state serves to maintain class rule, so that "the executive of the modern state is but a committee for managing the common affairs of the whole bourgeoisie" (p. 37), and social revolution starts to seem as miraculous as the craziest messianic fantasy of the most stupefied peasantry. Of course, there has been enough oppression of enough working people to produce highly disruptive rebellions. But, despite the implicit trumpets in the background, the litany of class struggles with which the *Manifesto* begins ("freemen and slave, patrician and plebeian, lord and serf, master and journeyman, in a word, oppressor and oppressed," p. 36) is, in itself, reason for doubting the possibility of social change. In all these struggles, lack of sufficiently widespread unity, lack of coordination and illusions about the sources of social power prevented the oppressed from changing society.

In order to be a socialist revolutionary, Marx desperately needs a theory of moral education, i.e. a theory of the origins of the attitudes and insights required to improve the world as he thinks it can and should be improved. In particular, he needs an account of how vast numbers of working people acquire a commitment to make a revolution in their common interest which is sufficiently powerful to break the grip of the conservative vise he himself describes, in his theories of ideology and the state. The mode of production, the origin of this vise, is also the origin of that socialist transformation (as it was of previous social transformations, such as the triumph of capitalism, for which the label "moral education" is less apt). For it is "the advance of industry, whose involuntary promoter is the bourgeoisie, [which] replaces the isolation of the labourers, due to competition, by their revolutionary combination, due to association" (*CM*, p. 46).

In this process, the development of industrial capitalism creates new contexts and resources for workers' resistance, giving rise to new loyalties which are, in turn, a basis for further self-transforming struggles. (This is the process that deserves the label, "moral education", a process that sheds new light on the possible relations between morality, rationality and self-interest.) Thus the levelling of the special skills and prerogatives of crafts production when industrial techniques are introduced makes it harder for workers to advance their interests by the individual withdrawal of skilled labor, and creates a greater need for mutual aid, as in the collective resistance of the industrial strike or slow-down. The scale of such militant trade-unionism grows as the size of typical capitalist firms increases, improved transportation and mass literacy enhance communication and the interdependence of far-flung factories gives workers an appreciation of their common circumstances while making the national economy vulnerable to strikes in central industries. At the same time, the bureaucracy and the parliamentary democracy that helped the modern bourgeoisie to modernize the nation and mobilize it against international competitors became the focus of working-class political movements to set limits to capitalist oppression, for example, by shortening the working day.

Although Marx came to think that the immediate gains of non-revolutionary struggles had real value, saving workers from the fate of "broken wretches past salvation" (*WPP*, p. 228), his emphasis was always on a different outcome: "The real fruit of their battles lies, not in the immediate result, but in the ever-expanding union of the workers" (*CM* p. 43). The description of this process – whose main phases I have just presented – is the pivotal passage in the *Manifesto* (1848). In the climactic chapter of *Capital*, I (1867), Marx describes the working class as "disciplined, united, organised by the very mechanism of the process of capitalist production itself," and concludes, in an unusually flamboyant self-citation, by presenting a large chunk of the *Manifesto* passage (on p. 715). A great theme of *The Civil War in France* (1871), his last significant work but one, is the formation of international bonds and of ties between town and country by workers driven to resist the repressive and expansionist terrors of late-capitalist regimes.

Although this theme of ever-expanding loyalties keeps loudly recurring in Marx, it often alternates with another, psychologically simpler theme, which no one would identify with moral education: inevitable trends in capitalism make more and more workers, simultaneously, desperately deprived, give them access to transportation and communication necessary for their coordinated activity, and make production sufficiently concentrated and bureaucratic for the rapid achievement of collective workers' control. All of this is certainly necessary to the revolutionary process Marx describes. At times, this second theme, combining material deprivations and technical facilities for ending them, threatens to drown out the first theme, of moral education through ever-expanding commitment, as in the *Manifesto*'s final proclamation that proletarians will win the world because they have nothing to lose but their chains. Because industrial crises and capitalist wars, which inhibit or destroy production, are central to the process of "immiseration," the second theme is easier to harmonize with a technological-determinist reading of Marx, in which an alleged universal human drive to overcome social inhibitions to expanded production is the ultimate engine of social change. Partly for this reason, many of Marx's friends as well as many of his enemies have taken him to identify the typical participant's main motivation for taking part in a socialist revolution as a desire to end her own material deprivation together with dawning awareness that only capitalist social relations stand in her way. But in fact, Marx's account of the process of moral education plays an essential role in his theory of revolution. Without his distinctive account of novel, expansive loyalties, his theory would succumb to a charge of incoherence.[3]

SELF-INTEREST, CLASS-INTEREST AND MORALITY

The charge of incoherence is due to Mancur Olson. In his pioneering work on collective action, Olson noted that Marx's own view of the capitalist state and socialist revolution ruled out the identification of "the rational, selfish pursuit of individual interests" as proletarians' motivation for revolutionary activity.[4] After all, if Marx is right to suppose that the state, under capitalism, is "the national war-engine of capital against labor" (*CWF*, p. 290), then taking part in a socialist revolution is dangerous opposition to the best-established means of coercion, and requires the simultaneous activity of many people for its success. (I will call this consequence "the capitalist state thesis.") But Marx thinks that successful socialist revolution is a "public good" for proletarians, which would benefit all proletarian survivors, regardless of whether they took part. The gains are not a kind of war medal, for ex-combatants only. This public good thesis combines with the capitalist state thesis to make the following alternative the rational choice for a purely self-interested proletarian when there is an imminent prospect of revolution: seek a safe refuge, wishing the revolutionaries well. One fewer revolutionary will not make much difference to the prospects of success (which depends on large numbers), non-participation will reduce grave dangers, and, if the revolution succeeds, one can enjoy its triumph on emerging from one's cellar.

Olson thinks that this argument that the selfish, rational pursuit of individual interests will not motivate engagement in a socialist revolution establishes an incoherence in Marx. For he thinks that Marx is committed not just to the capitalist state thesis, the public good thesis, and the thesis that there will be a socialist revolution (all well-grounded attributions in which I have joined), but also to the view that the rational, selfish pursuit of individual interests is sufficient to motivate proletarians' revolutionary activity. This thesis of self-centered rationality would be entailed by the doctrine that individual proletarians' desires to overcome their respective material deprivations under the capitalist status quo are adequate and rational motivations for proletarian revolution. Fortunately for Marx, he does not explicitly subscribe to this doctrine, or otherwise proclaim the adequacy of "the rational, selfish pursuit of individual interests." But (to complete the case for Olson's charge), Marx does, clearly, regard the proletarians who make a socialist revolution as rational in their choices, and he scathingly denies that the impartial benevolence emphasized by prior socialists is an adequate basis for revolutionary change. ("The communists do not preach *morality* at all . . . They do not put to people the moral demand: love one another, do not be egoists, etc." (*GI*, p. 104).) These strategic assumptions might seem to leave too little room for the altruism Marx requires. Proletarians' informed awareness of their common interests is supposed to lead them to make a revolution. How can this be a rational choice if the capitalist state thesis is part of their information, a successful revolution is a public good, and impartial benevolence could not move them to take on revolutionary risks?

I have already proposed that the transformation of loyalties in the course of resistance to capitalism provides the answer, for Marx. But it might seem that his account of "the ever-expanding union of the workers" makes his neglect of impartial concern for humanity quite perverse, for just the reasons Olson exposes. When Marx describes specific class struggles in concrete detail, he acknowledges the need for risk-taking that would be irrational for a selfish person. For example, when he singles out the workers of the Paris Commune as paradigms of proletarian activism, he emphasizes their willingness to sacrifice themselves for a larger cause: they are "the self-sacrificing champions of a new and better society . . . The women joyfully give up their lives at the barricades"; he even salutes the destruction of buildings in door-to-door fighting as the "heroic self-holocaust" of working-class Paris (*CWF*, pp. 306f.). Evidently, the ever-expanding union involves the expansion of the group for whom a typical individual proletarian is willing to take unselfish risks. But if a proletarian can be motivated to take risks by unselfish concern for strangers, why is it important that the strangers be proletarians, as well?

A first response might be, "People simply are specially willing to take on unselfish risks when, if they should be lucky in their risk-taking, they can expect to benefit if the risky project succeeds." But this answer is doubly disappointing as a Marxist answer to Olson, even if it is true. First, while Marx takes successful proletarian revolution to be rational, it seems quite muddled to assess risks from an unselfish perspective while assessing pay-offs in a purely selfish way. So long as the relevant benefits of revolution (or the riskier sorts of trade union militancy) to the lucky activist are limited to her consumption of material goods, enjoyment of leisure and comfort, and similar pleasures, the crucial benefit-upon-success is sufficiently selfish to make an unselfish attitude toward risk a muddle. So we need to look for a rationale of a different kind. Second, even if the muddle could be overcome or tolerated, it will be quite unclear why the consequent motivation is powerful enough to motivate the grave risks that "revolutionary combination" requires. The thought, "I am taking part in a project aimed at my good among others'" might motivate risk-taking which the maximization of expected selfish benefit would not sustain, even when this unselfish risk-taking would not be motivated by the purely altruistic thought "I am taking part in a project to benefit others." But why should the added force be enough to motivate a serious risk of death, torture, exile, blacklisting, or similarly grave burdens? Not only must the rationale be very different from the neo-classical economist's goods-and-leisure package, it must be of some specially powerful kind, to motivate grave risks, unjustifiable in self-centered terms, among rational, informed people who are not prepared to take those risks just for the general benefit of humanity.

To meet these demands, Marx's theory of the moral education of the proletariat must base the ever-expanding union on expanding requirements for self-respect. In this conception of rational resistance, the rationality of an effort to reduce one's subordination to others and to oppressive institutions can depend, in crucial part, on the effort's expressing one's self-respect. Of course, likely consequences, including prospects of success, are relevant as well. Rational people always have a variety of interests other than self-assertion in the face of domination, including some which they could not neglect while respecting themselves. (Indeed, without interests in specific positive projects and attachments there would hardly be a self to assert.) Engagement in utterly hopeless rebellion is, at best, no more rational than the nobler sorts of suicide. Still, the need for self-respect (unlike any need independent of self-respect) can make active resistance rational even when the dominating power is so strong and pervasive that some path of acceptance would maximize expected gains in consumption, leisure and comfort.

If this is so, then, so long as societies are divided between oppressors and oppressed, people will rebel when pressed too far, rebelling even though they are rational, the oppressors are served by an efficient coercive apparatus and passivity would not mean death. Granted, resisting domination because one's self-respect demands it need not make a person disposed to take risks in the interests of another's struggles. However, other aspects of self-respect *are* potentially unifying, in Marx's view. If a strategy of mutual aid is a more feasible means of resisting common oppression than individual resistance, and all are aware of this, they will eventually try this strategy. (In crucial cases, the link between resistance and self-respect is needed to motivate the special risks sustained, which do not maximize expected selfish benefits.) Moreover, if the strategy of resistance succeeds to some extent, producing widespread benefits because of some participants' initial sacrifices, then accepting costs in order to reduce others' subordination becomes, itself, a dictate of self-respect, among those who have taken part in the project. (No doubt, this is true to some extent of all cooperation, but only a personal project as central as resisting domination would reliably motivate sacrifices to distant strangers and grave risk-taking, in the absence of a powerful enforcement agency.)

According to Marx's scenario, capitalist development gives rise to ever-expanding unity by making isolated resistance less feasible while enhancing the facilities for resistance based on far-flung mutuality. Initially, workers taking part in more collective resistance may be a few militants whose immediate hope is reciprocal aid by their co-workers, neighbors and a few militants elsewhere. But as the benefits of these endeavors spread, a commitment to bear burdens of cooperative resistance becomes a requirement of self-respect among more and more beneficiaries. So the magnitude of collective risk-taking grows, and more and more projects of resistance become feasible enterprises. Ultimately, the bonds that are forged become the basis for a great project of construction, the creation of a new mode of production that is founded on reciprocity, rather than the fear of unemployment.

Thus, guided by the development of industrial capitalism, the moral education of the proletariat takes place, most centrally, through activities that transform the prerequisites of self-respect, creating new needs to help in the liberation of others. This moral psychology is close to the surface of all of Marx's narratives of class struggle. It is also nearly explicit in the critique of Stirner's moral psychology which dominates *The German Ideology*. "The communists do not preach morality at all, such as Stirner preaches so extensively. They do not put to people the moral demand: love one another, do not be egoists, etc.; on the contrary, they are very well-aware that egoism, just as much as self-sacrifice, *is* in definite circumstances a necessary form of the self-assertion of individuals" (*GI*, p. 104f.). Hearing the opposition to moralistic preaching one can jump to Olson's conclusion that Marx does not mean to rely on interests transcending one's own comfort and leisure. But this is to be deaf to the rest of Marx's claim, his insistence that self-sacrifice can, in definite circumstances, be necessary for individual self-assertion. There is not much room for doubt that resistance to domination was at the core of self-assertion, in Marx's conception of workers' psychology. And it certainly pervaded his own self-conception, as recorded in the answers he used to give to the questionnaires that graced Victorian guestbooks: "Your idea of happiness: To fight. Your idea of misery: To submit. . . . The vice you detest most: Servility . . . Favorite hero: Spartacus, Kepler."[5]

Looking at the history of past social struggles, Marx could, plausibly, have concluded that the attempt to resist the powers dominating one's own life motivates grave risk-taking on the part of many people while mere concern for humanity at large does not. Perhaps some process of further-expanding union in which people of all walks of life and degrees of remoteness took up burdens to help others in central life projects would create sufficiently powerful impartial benevolence. But this has not happened yet. So Marx can avoid reliance on the "rational, selfish pursuit of self-interest", which Olson imputes to him, while still regarding appeals to class interest as the effective motivator of socialist revolution.

This emphasis on class interest leads to a final question about the "moral education of the proletariat": why call it "moral" at all? The response to Olson's challenge suggests one answer. If Marx's characterizations of capitalism and socialism are right, then the process in which "association" gives rise to "revolutionary combination" is the process by which people acquire a non-selfish motivation sufficient for activity that creates a better social system. Marx does not disdain to hail the Communards as "the self-sacrificing champions of a new and better society" (or to conclude *The Civil War in France* with the suggestion that history has

381

nailed the Commune's "exterminators . . . to that eternal pillory from which all the prayers of their priests will not avail to redeem them", pp. 306, 311). "Moral education" is hardly an inappropriate label for the way in which commitments transcending the self acquire the capacity to make a better society – in other words, the development of politically effective compassion.

A second connection between morality and the process of "revolutionary combination" is more intimate, but more speculative. Perhaps Marx thought that important indeterminacies left open by impartial morality had to be resolved by someone committed to social improvement, and regarded the perspective of the class-conscious proletarian revolutionary as the appropriate basis for resolving them. In all of his discussions of general moral topics, Marx emphasizes the superabundance of competing considerations that are relevant to every major kind of impartial moral judgment. When the demand for fairness is connected with specific rights, each right to fair treatment turns out to conflict with another, so that *"it is . . . a right of inequality in its content, like every right"* (CGP, p. 324). For example, the first stage of socialism neglects the right of the frail to reward according to effort in favor of reward according to total time spent working. By confiscating the factories of Horatio Algers and forbidding capitalist acts among consenting adults, this society violates rights to self-advancement through mutual agreement that capitalism respects, while instituting such non-capitalist rights as a right to non-degrading work. Similarly, in criticizing utilitarianism, Marx emphasizes the need to assess conflicts between the different kinds of enjoyment salient to people in different social situations (*GI*, pp. 114f.; *C*, p. 571). No mode of production is neutral between the zest of individual competition and the reassurance of solidarity, or neutral between the pleasure of consuming the products into which natural resources are made, on the one hand, the enjoyment of time off from production or the appreciation of unspoiled wilderness, on the other.

Probably no rational person assessing social alternatives from any impartial point of view could fail to prefer socialism to capitalism, if she were certain of the truth of all of Marx's characterizations of these alternatives. But even Marx may have appreciated the uncertainty of the characterizations. Indeed, such was his disdain for the task of "writing recipes for the kitchens of the future" that his institutional proposals for socialism consist of a few vague paragraphs, mostly in his last significant work, the *Critique of the Gotha Program*. How certain could anyone be about the consequences of so vague a project? In any case, Marx was well aware of uncertainties and harms that can make a choice of revolutionary *conduct* morally troubling, whatever the security of a preference for radically different institutions. The prospects of success for any particular socialist revolution are uncertain in the extreme, while it is certain that many innocent people are hurt in revolutions. Moreover, uncertainties to one side, acts that are crucial to successful revolution and to much successful non-revolutionary militance cause harm to innocents more directly than they produce their ultimate benefits. (A working-class neighborhood will be destroyed because troops are attacked; some of the strike-breakers who are beaten, to set an example, were driven by desperate poverty to take the job.) Unlike the detached observer who merely faces the daunting task of asking what choices are apt to make the world better, political agents face the problem of dirty hands.

Because of these difficulties, the conscientious choice of revolutionary or militant courses of action often involves an implicit evaluation of how important alleged advantages of change would be and an implicit judgment of whether the prospective benefits justify the costs and harms of pursuing them. Marx might plausibly have doubted that impartial morality can yield a decision in important, typical cases – a decision based, say, on an assessment of the value of socialist solidarity or of the moral urgency of certain revolutionary acts jeopardizing innocents. In these cases, the most defensible impartial moral perspectives are not determinate enough to tell the chooser if the socialist, revolutionary considerations are important enough to justify the activist choice. Yet indecision means the continual triumph of the bourgeois state. Perhaps, then, Marx thought that the questions which an improver of the world ought (morally) to confront ought to be resolved by taking up the perspective emerging from the ever-expanding union of proletarians. These experiences and inter-actions give rise to the distinctive character of the workers in Marx's narratives of the Chartists, the proletarian 1848'ers of Paris and Berlin and the Communards, a character that combines the hatred of oppression and angry contempt for oppressors, a concern for victims of oppression, including strangers, and the mutual well-wishing arising from cooperation against oppression. Perhaps Marx thought that unavoidable questions that impartial morality leaves open ought to be answered by taking up the perspective of these class-conscious proletarians, asking what their self-respect requires and what it permits.

But is this a perspective that one ought, *morally speaking*, to take up? Is Marx making morality more determinate, or should he be taken at his word when he says that his political movement "abolishes . . . all morality" (*CM*, p. 52), "shatter[s] the basis of all morality" (*GI*, p. 115), and thus sweeps away "ideological nonsense about rights and other trash so common among the democrats and French socialists" (*CGP*, p. 325)? If a moral basis for choice has to provide an impartial rationale, whose ultimate normative premises express impartial concern or respect for all, then Marx (as I have portrayed him) undermines morality. The needed degree of preference for solidarity over individualistic striving or for bold advance against oppression over submission that avoids direct harms is not an expression of impartial concern or respect for all. But if a moral perspective need only satisfy the constraints that valid impartial morality imposes while answering questions that impartial morality makes salient, then Marx need not be taken to undermine morality. If one adds that the more determinate perspective of the morally conscientious proletarian revolutionary is the self-transcending motivational structure whose prevalence improves the world, then this outlook might well be taken to clarify morality, rather than introducing an alien, nonmoral element.[6]

THE COMMUNIST INTELLECTUAL

I have been exploring Marx's account of the rise of the class-conscious proletarian. However, the focus of much current agony over how to change moral commitments in the interest of working people has been the role of the intellectual. I will conclude this synopsis of Marx's *Bildungsroman* with a brief glance at the analogous character in his story, the Communist, or, more precisely, the Communist Intellectual.

Marx thinks revolutions require leadership by organizations whose membership is smaller than the class they represent. Apart from tactical leadership, these groups work out and revise long-term goals and resist the ideology that intrudes on the process of ever-expanding union. Above all, "in the national struggles of the proletarians of the different countries, they point out and bring to the front the common interests of the proletariat, independent of all nationality" (*CM*, p. 46). In practice, and sometimes theoretically (for example, *CM*, p. 44), Marx gave intellectuals with non-proletarian origins a role as an important minority in this leadership. This role (his role) reflects the uses of book-learning, research, learned discussion and skilled advocacy in a movement in which political effectiveness depends on hard-won social insight and on countering truth-distorting social influences. But these teachers are also supposed to be educated by the working class they seek to educate, in the course of democratic participation in a largely working-class movement. Without this practice, most of them would be wholly enmeshed in universities and other such respectable institutions; their insight would be threatened by pressures toward conformity that make false belief a requirement of self-respect.

Whatever the failings of his large ego may have been, Marx did follow his prescriptions for educating the educator. He separated himself from respectable institutions, enmeshed himself in working-class activism, and learned from working-class activists. During the years in which he became a Marxist (1845–7), what Marx did that very few other intellectuals did was to make groups of working-class radicals the main focus of his political activities. After 1848 and the *Communist Manifesto*, all of the important changes in Marx's outlook are responses to working-class trade union and political activity which he knew at first or second hand. In the *Manifesto*, capitalism is portrayed as depressing wages to the minimum compatible with physical survival, while destroying traditional prejudices and illusions in its pursuit of "naked, shameless, direct, brutal exploitation" (p. 38). The first stage of socialism is portrayed as a use of the state apparatus inherited from capitalism to advance proletarian interests. Subsequently, during his London exile, British trade-unionism taught Marx that workers could resist that downward pressure on wages and that ethnic and national prejudices could be the main obstacle to the class unity he sought in the most advanced capitalist society.[7] Similarly, the political innovations of the Paris Commune led him to rethink his earlier tolerance of the hierarchical arrangements that are part of the most democratic capitalist political systems.

Marx has not been alone in this practice. From the time when he and Engels first frequented the working-class study groups of Brussels, working-class activists and working-class movements have played a central role in the lives of hundreds of thousands of intellectuals. One current task of an intellectual of the left is to reflect, unsentimentally but uncynically, on the costs of the loss of this connection in the course of the twentieth century.

POST-MARXISM

Marx's theory of the moral education of the proletariat surely describes some mechanisms driving the widening, deepening rebelliousness of workers that so impressed most well-informed people from the 1830s to the 1930s. It forces us to consider important options that much thinking about morality and rationality neglects: the vast terrain of rational motivations in between impartial morality and the pursuit of self-centered gains, moral points of view that are not ultimately impartial, and forms of rational self-assertion that are not self-centered. But such pay-offs fall far short of Marx's own goal. He intended to describe the origins of motivations sufficiently pervasive and powerful to produce successful socialist revolutions, profoundly improving the well-being of the vast majority of humanity. In this he failed. Capitalism has managed to prevent both the decline of real wages that Marx first envisaged and the inevitable increase of depressions and wars that was his later expectation. Increasingly elaborate hierarchies within capitalist firms have become a basis for promotion ladders sustaining hopes for advancement through conformity. A century after Marx's death, the worldwide circulation of goods and investments (whose importance he continually noted) insures that it will never be foolish to say that an increase in labor costs or tax-supported social services will make life worse for most workers in a capitalist economy, through the reduction of exports or the flight of investments abroad. Meanwhile, efforts to realize Marx's few prescriptions for a post-capitalist economy have given rise to enough disasters to convince the most class-conscious proletarian in an advanced industrial economy that the socialist remedy is apt to be worse than the capitalist disease.

Nevertheless, Marx's theory of capitalism has other parts, which could still be insightful. In particular, many of us who have abandoned Marx's radical hopes think that he was right in certain large claims about capitalist domination, economic, political and ideological. Emulating the pioneering ugliness of "post-structuralism" and "post-modernism", I will call this synthesis "post-Marxism." In the rest of this essay, I will describe this legacy, and explore its implications for a post-Marxist conception of education in the interest of social improvement.

Suppose that "capitalism" is understood, broadly and untendentiously, as an economy in which (a) the vast majority of households depend, for survival, on members working for firms that seek to sell their output for a profit and (b) the main mechanism of resource-allocation is the need of such firms to satisfy investors' desires to maximize returns on their investment. Like Marx, we post-Marxists think that in the labor market as a whole, in any such economy, there are enormous inequalities of bargaining power burdening those who must sell their labor and advantaging those whose income largely depends on investments, together with top managers. The local ties that make it irrational for most workers, worldwide, to chase high-paying jobs around the planet in the way in which firms chase cheap labor, the pressure to find a job quickly before one's life disintegrates, the difficulties of coordination among the sellers of labor, vastly more numerous than the buyers and living most of their waking lives under the workplace discipline of the buyers – these inequalities and others lead us to agree with Marx *and* Adam Smith that anyone who denies that "combinations of masters" are vastly more effective than "combinations of workers" "is as ignorant of the world as of the subject."[8] Because firms must (dare one use the word?) exploit these differences or go under, we see no way for most people under capitalism to have work that is sufficiently interesting, self-controlled and leisured to be a source of enjoyment rather than a burden. Because fear of unemployment is the basic incentive in a capitalist economy, we expect that insecurity will be common. We expect the capitalist need

385

for unemployment, together with demographic, technological and geographic shifts, to present some people with a horrid choice between irregular menial work and long-term unemployment. And we think that these differences in one generation will produce large differences in opportunity in the next.

For a great many people, this is not a good world, for reasons that have nothing to do with their individual failings. But it can be better or worse. Responding to the disheartening limits of what many are likely to achieve through reasonable individual effort, we post-Marxists seek the improvement of life-prospects, i.e. of prospects of a rewarding life given willingness to try to achieve one. In pursuing this improvement in opportunities, we agree with Marx that capitalist technological progress by itself does not substantially enhance opportunities for a rewarding life. Politics must intervene. And here, we accept certain claims about political dominance as hard truth. In a society with a capitalist economy, government will inevitably have a strong tendency to serve the interest in profits of the tiny minority whose income mainly depends on investments, regardless of whether those interests coincide with the vast majority's. As in Marx's own accounts of capitalist control of the state, no conspiracy is required, not even the quasi-conspiracy of purchasing influence with campaign contributions. When government decisions threaten profits, individual investors take their money out of firms engaged in production, switching to the most liquid assets or sending their money to another country. The mere prospect of the economic turmoil such non-conspiracy creates is a powerful disincentive. Moreover, the knowledge, experience and interpersonal connections required to elaborate and implement policy options at the highest level will typically be acquired in the course of rising through corporate hierarchies, dominated by imperatives of profit. In the United States, as part of the resulting circulation of personnel, two-thirds of the Secretaries of State, Defense and the Treasury since 1961 have come from the highest ranks of major industrial corporations, financial institutions and corporate law firms.[9]

No doubt, if it were clear when the interests of those who mainly depend on income from ownership clashed with the interests of the rest, the latter would prevail through sheer weight of numbers, in a parliamentary democracy. For financial wealth is highly concentrated: in the United States, the wealthiest 1 percent of households own 48 percent of it, the wealthiest 2 percent own 75 percent.[10] But the clash between bourgeois interests (we sometimes slip into these old usages) and the interests of the vast majority is rarely transparent. Increased labor costs do cause firms to go under and economies to stagnate. Expanded social services do increase the cost of doing business, raise inflation or increase trade deficits, in ways that can worsen most. We think that the interests of the best-off often, nonetheless, conflict with those of the vast majority of the not-so-well-off. But locating these trade-offs requires balanced judgment, and we see inevitable imbalance in the discourse of parliamentary politics.

We trace these limits of political discourse, in large part, to truth-distorting social forces, the ideological constraints that troubled Marx. Because of influence or control over "means of mental production" by those who ultimately control the means of material production, the mass media, educational institutions and electoral politics will, on the whole, foster illusions about equality of opportunity and the link between profits and the general good, while stigmatizing and isolating the worst-off. Moreover, people's inevitable fixations on the promotion-ladders that dominate their working lives will produce exaggerated assessments of the extent to which life can be made good by individual competitive effort. In short, the market in social ideas will be distorted by the forces that dominate the market in labor.

MORAL EDUCATION AFTER MARX

The currency of these views among many intellectuals has led to heated debate over a contemporary question about moral education in light of Marx: how should post-Marxists who have some independent capacity to influence others' outlook on social change use this access to make the world better? Part of the answer is obvious: because of their abandonment of Marx's radical hopes, post-Marxists will advocate piecemeal reforms, rather than the overthrow of capitalism. The further, hard question is whether the residual legacy of Marx ought to have any bearing on post-Marxists' effort to educate the electorate. Given the inevitability and the ideological powers of capitalism, using access to the public to argue that capitalism has limitations which cannot be changed seems perverse waste of a precious resource, in order to preach sermons that demoralize people whose morale is already sufficiently challenged. Perhaps, if her own theories are true, the post-Marxist should not theorize in public about the inevitable limits of capitalist reforms.

Completing the abandonment of all residual Marxism at the level of practice, post-Marxism might also seem to require the replacement of obsolete appeals to proletarian solidarity with appeals to patriotic solidarity, as a means of motivating support for government aid to the poor. Faced with the limited power of mere self-interest and impartial benevolence to motivate social improvement, Marx appealed to a group loyalty, defining terms of self-respect for members of the group, and claimed that such loyalties could provide the impetus that love of humanity and love of self could not. In the absence of the intense and widespread loyalty to the working class that Marx foresaw, a post-Marxist, respecting the Old Man's psychological acumen, should desire some analogous resource in a loyalty to a group embracing the poor, a loyalty that might make most of the non-poor ashamed to neglect them. Patriotism now seems the resource for solidarity most likely to play this role. So (to summarize these post-Marxist reasons for removing all practical residues of Marxism), perhaps a post-Marxist intellectual, attending to the political interests of the poor, should play the familiar, utterly non-Marxist role of a patriotic atheoretical reformist.[11]

In contrast, many post-Marxist intellectuals play the role of radical social critic, someone whose use of print and podium includes describing aspects of capitalism that make serious deprivation inevitable and deflating patriotic commitments that exceed a commitment to work with fellow-citizens to improve local justice in the place where one feels most at home and best knows how to take part in social improvement. Viewed through the lens of post-Marxism itself, is this a self-destructive exercise in nostalgia? Despite the case for a wholly patriotic, atheoretical practice, the radical social critic makes three kinds of special contributions to piecemeal reform.

(1) Radical social critics help to strengthen attitudes that respectable institutions tend, as a whole, to weaken, attitudes that can reduce suffering under capitalism.

One such contribution is the cosmopolitan project of making it vivid that people everywhere are equally deserving of concern and respect, so that policies should be opposed if they are not justifiable from the perspective of distant strangers. This cosmopolitanism is radical because it challenges the neglect of the interests of foreigners that is routine in the thought, speech and action of powerful people in a nation's respectable institutions. A patriotic atheoretical reformist, appealing to patriotic pride and rejoicing in his national identity, will consolidate this neglect. In disputes over immigration, foreign aid and aid to right-wing regimes and insurgencies, this contribution of the radical social critic benefits the poor in the world at large. Because of her willingness to oppose wars on account of what they do to kill non-citizens, she also often takes the lead in opposing carnage that victimizes the poor and the not-well-off of the homeland, such as the carnage of Vietnam, which Democratic politicians and labor union statesmen long sought to sustain with appeals to patriotic pride.[12]

What of the worry that this cosmopolitanism weakens a precious resource for the poor of the homeland: patriotic pride which can be converted to indignation at the lot of fellow citizens? In fact, patriotism is not a precious resource, so far as poor fellow-citizens are concerned. Granted, *if* patriotic pride combines strong, quasi-familial solidarity on a national scale with an accurate grasp of compatriots' needs and a tolerant view of personal differences within the national family, it is a powerful source of help to the nation's poor. But patriotism is at least as likely to encourage people to exaggerate the moral perfection that the nation has already achieved, to sacrifice social equality to military spending and to attribute economic failure to the choice of a life-style deviating from a presumed national norm.

A second motivational contribution of the radical social critic is a post-Marxist analogue of the proletarian class-consciousness that Marxists encouraged: a combination of sympathy with the poor (and not-well-off) with a refusal to organize hopes and sentiments around the wish that one's whole society will become a genuine community, in which all social roles dispose the role-players to make an adequate contribution to the well-being of others. This is valuable because the bad fit between this organizing wish and realities of interest and power creates its own utopianism, in which the inclusion of a labor representative on a corporate board seems an important step forward and noisy demonstrations seem merely a poor substitute for respectful dialogue with powerful people. (Shrewd radical critics are aware that sympathetic people of power are often glad of pressure from independent movements for change.)

(2) The radical social critic provides a general basis for questioning sources of opinion and attitude which are, in fact, biased against the poor.

In part, this skepticism is directed at the epistemic authority of the expert consensus on social issues as described by the major media and the epistemic authority of the presuppositions that major political figures share. Often, this limited spectrum of opinion is embodied in an agenda of questions worth discussing: how to break a cycle of dependency on welfare payments becomes the right focus for worries about the poor, how to keep inflation very low becomes the first question about the government's contribution to material well-being.

In addition to exposing the elite interests that ultimately distort these frameworks, the radical social critic reminds people of how contempt for the poor is encouraged by the individual struggles for self-advancement that can make a society resemble Marx's potatoes in a sack. It is very hard for most of us to reach the bottom rung of a good promotion-ladder and climb up it. These efforts have a greater impact on everyone's life than her individual political efforts to improve society. Self-definition as a victim of the system undermines the morale needed to pursue self-advancement and makes a person just plain depressed. So people are bound to concentrate on their chances of getting ahead by their own efforts. They will, then, overestimate the contribution of their efforts, as opposed to their backgrounds, to their chances of success – which makes it natural to underestimate the extent to which others' relative failures reflect their trying just as hard.

No doubt, the description of pressures toward falsehood in the daily life of the middle class has sometimes inspired self-isolating contempt on the part of intellectuals. The radical social critic has a remedy: similar self-scrutiny by intellectuals. The work lives of nearly all intellectuals are profoundly influenced by the pursuit of promotions, grants, and prestige, depending on fitting into an agenda that is supported by respectable institutions ultimately responsive to rich elites. An intellectual should regularly face the question of the extent to which her outlook and practice are determined by these facts of dependence rather than the facts she scrutinizes in her work. For example, a tendency to avoid questions of unequal social power might trouble the political philosopher who writes about equality, while a literary theorist might suspect his own inclination to practice the safest kind of subversion, namely, the subversion of meaning.

(3) Major social improvement in constitutional democracies has typically been caused, in part, by disruptive group actions, fixing attention on neglected harms and forcing large social changes to re-establish social peace. Concerned as she is with the inevitable limits of activism entirely confined to the rules of a capitalist democracy, the radical social critic directs attention to the productive ways in which the law and order of capitalist democracies have been defied.

Even in periods in which defiance is non-productive, there *will* be rebellion, since there will be plenty of police brutality, downsizing, give-backs and speed-ups. The radical social critic, with her special concern with the limits people face in improving their lives while obeying the rules, can play a special role in inspiring sympathy toward grievances under-lying these disorders and admiration of whatever is benevolent, disciplined and fraternal in them. Perhaps she will soon be able to play a more positive role, as well, helping to publicize, inform and support productive disorder within a large-scale movement for change, analogues of the sit-down strikes of the thirties or the anti-war sit-ins, mutinies, ghetto rebellions and wildcat strikes of the sixties. No one knows that widespread, productive defiance will break out in our time in the United States. But no one knows that it will not. Intellectuals know least of all. In their miserable record of failed predictions, confident predictions of the end of conflict, like Daniel Bell's announcement of "the end of ideology" in 1960, look quite as pathetic as Marx's giddy hope, after 1849, that each recession would be the start of the Great Crisis.

AN ETHIC FOR EDUCATORS

If post-Marxism is even approximately true, the radical social critic does not belong on a list of political types whose disappearance should not be mourned. But post-Marxism does not imitate the unity of Marx's *Bildungsroman*, by substituting the radical social critic for the communist intellectual. Rather, the outcome of post-Marxism is a division of labor in which many kinds of politically engaged intellectuals play a productive role, a division of labor implying a distinctive ethic of cooperation.

Some politically productive intellectuals provide politicians with advice, research or concrete policy proposals, and these projects are bound, to some degree or other, to foreshadow the patriotic atheoretical reformism involved in their ultimate enactment. Other intellectuals investigate concrete mechanisms of deprivation to which reformers had better attend, or write richly disturbing descriptions of social problems meant for a large audience. Whatever their sympathies with post-Marxism, they will often preserve access to the better sort of politician and the better sort of mass market book review by avoiding offense to patriotic atheoretical reformism. But they need not worship at its shrines to be effective, and (in a post-Marxist view) will hurt the poor if they do inspire patriotic exclusivity or false hopes of capitalist equity. Others investigate social problems with an eye to a narrower, more scholarly audience. They are freer to frame their inquiries in a radical way, though they, too, will want to avoid sectarianism. Others develop moral arguments for helping the poor based on minimal premises of the broadest possible appeal. They, too, will avoid unnecessary conflicts with patriotic atheoretical reformism, but, by the same token, they will avoid undermining the efforts of radical social critics seeking to persuade those who are not so far left. Finally, some intellectuals will productively openly engage in radical practices. They will investigate those mechanisms of deprivation that entail radical social criticism, explore the moral implications of the limits to capitalist improvement, or seek to win over as many people as possible to a radically critical stance. They will offend patriotic atheoretical reformism – though if they are serious people, they will be respectful and clear in appealing to patriotic atheoretical reformists.

Post-Marxism encourages a community of roles, bound by sympathy for the poor and wary respect for fellow-intellectuals who share it. As part of the ethic of this community, those who are mainly radical social critics will also uphold the importance of intellectual activity that respects limits imposed by major parties, mass media and national union leaderships, while warning of the complacency, elitism and careerism that such activity can promote. Those who are engaged in these important activities will respect the productive role of the criticism radical social critics provide and the disruption that they support, while warning of dangers of bitterness and naïveté. Each should take the others' warnings to heart.

In this ethic and in other ways, the perspective of post-Marxism is the perspective of maturity, recognizing inevitable and painful limits while seeking improvement within those limits, accepting the moral risks that are part of all efforts to make the world better while appreciating the need to resist reformers who succumb to temptation as they achieve political power. In projects guided by this ethic, post-Marxists will not be helped by Marx's vision of emerging revolutionary socialist unity. But they will be helped by his perception of how inequalities of power are constantly reproduced under capitalism. And as they seek to reform capitalism, they will constantly encounter the need for the ever-expanding union of workers which Marx studied and promoted. Never before has the threat, "If you don't like this work, workers somewhere else will do it," been more frightening. If workers' lives, worldwide, are not improved from the bottom up, pressure mounts to flatten them from the top down. Perhaps their need for unity will lead to effective reciprocity and a worldwide interdependence of bases for self-respect. Meanwhile, those who honor Marx's legacy can at least insist that this unity is the need of the non-rich of the world.

NOTES

1 *The Civil War in France*, p. 295. To simplify citation I will use the following abbreviations, with page references to *Selected Works*, except where indicated otherwise:

CWF   *The Civil War in France*, in Karl Marx and Frederick Engels, *Selected Works in One Volume* (New York, International Publishers, 1986)

CM   *Communist Manifesto* (written with Engels)

WLC   *Wage Labor and Capital*

EB   *The Eighteenth Brumaire of Louis Bonaparte*

WPP   *Wages, Price and Profit*

CGP   *Critique of the Gotha Program*

GI   *The German Ideology* (with Engels) (New York, International Publishers, 1970)

C   *Capital*, vol. 1 (Moscow, Progress Publishers, n.d.)

2 Marx notes that the anti-Irish attitude that makes English workers ineffective is "much the same as that of the 'poor whites' to the Negroes in the former slave states of the U.S.A.". Letter to Meyer and Vogt (ex-1848'ers living in St Louis), April 9, 1870, in Marx and Engels, *Selected Correspondence* (Moscow, Progress Publishers, n.d.), p. 222.

3 I do not mean to suggest that a technological-determinist Marx must regard desires for more goods or leisure as the only psychological mechanisms whose prevalence is required for successful social revolution. Partisans of this interpretation can admit that other mechanisms play an essential role, so long as they add that the prevalence of these mechanisms is explainable, in the final analysis, by appeal to the social inhibition of technological progress. Still, there is a real tension between this ecumenical view of essential psychological mechanisms and the technological determinist view of ultimate causes. Technological determinists ascribe to Marx the view that a social system is bound to change when its social relations of production inhibit technological progress. Why should this be so, if a desire for more goods and leisure would be an inadequate motivation for successful proletarian revolution, despite the material deprivations of proletarians and their material improvement if socialism is instituted? Gerald Cohen, *Karl Marx's Theory of History: a Defense* (Princeton, NJ, Princeton University Press, 1978) is the paradigmatic

modern defense of the technological determinist interpretation. I criticize this interpretation and offer a replacement for it in *Analyzing Marx: Morality, Power and History* (Princeton, NJ, Princeton University Press, 1984), chs 5 and 6.

4 Mancur Olson, *The Logic of Collective Action* (Cambridge, Mass., Harvard University Press, 1971), p. 108.

5 Saul Padover, *Karl Marx: an Intimate Biography* (New York, McGraw-Hill, 1978), pp. 627ff.

6 Most writing on Marx and morality has, understandably, concerned the shocking passages in which Marx seems to reject morality. In *Analyzing Marx*, chs 1 and 2, I argue that Marx's ultimate concern is to deny the availability of an evenhanded way of balancing the considerations that impartial morality puts in play. Allen Wood has defended a very different interpretation which also takes Marx's anti-moralism seriously, an interpretation in which Marx regards the major institutions of stable capitalist societies as just because his ascriptions of justice are ascriptions of a stabilizing social function. See *Karl Marx* (London, Routledge and Kegan Paul, 1981), especially chs 9 and 10. Our disagreements about Marx's metaethics depend, in large part, on disagreements about Marx's theory of the psychology and politics of revolution. George Brenkert, *Marx's Ethics of Freedom* (London, Routledge and Kegan Paul, 1983) is a revealing example of interpretations of Marx's apparent anti-moralism as the rejection of well-established moral perspectives of his time in favor of a different version of impartial morality.

7 Marx came to think that workers could maintain a roughly constant ratio of total labor devoted to producing goods workers consume to total labor devoted to producing goods that others consume or use to expand production. Technological progress would cause a long-term increase in real wages, but meanwhile workers' material needs would increase, partly because of their social and comparative dimension. ("Let a palace rise beside the little house, and it shrinks from a little house to a hut" (*WLC*, p. 84.)) Thus, as workers transform their loyalties, they also transform their needs.

8 See Adam Smith, *The Wealth of Nations* (Harmondsworth, Penguin Books, 1986), p. 169. In general, ch. 8, "The wages of labour", is a compelling and humane description of the inequalities of bargaining power dominating the labor market. Smith is much more appropriate as an emblem for post-Marxism than as a patron saint for *laissez-faire*.

9 I rely on Dennis Gilbert and Joseph Kahl, *The American Class Structure* (Belmont, Calf., Wadsworth, 1993), p. 215, for the 1961–1981 ratio. In his 1967 study, *Who Rules America?* (Englewood Cliffs, NJ, Prentice-Hall), G. William Domhoff noted that since 1932, eight of thirteen Secretaries of Defense or War and five of eight Secretaries of State had been listed in that manual of *haut-bourgeois* prestige, the *Social Register* (see pp. 97, 99).

10 These are 1983 estimates in Edward Wolff, "Estimates of household inequality in the U.S., 1962–1983", *Review of Income and Wealth* 33 (1987), p. 238. Financial wealth is net worth less the value of consumer durables, household inventories and net equity in owner-occupied housing. Wolff, *Top Heavy* (New York, New Press, 1996) contains similar figures for 1989. Drawing on a study by Kennickell and Woodbum, Gilbert and Kahl (*Class Structure*, p. 103) estimate that the top 10 percent of households owned 69 percent of the total net worth in the United States in 1990.

11 That intellectuals of the left should confine themselves to such advocacy is an important theme of Richard Rorty's writings. His insistence on the essential role of patriotism is shared by such prominent left-wing theorists as Eric Hobsbawm and David Miller, theorists who are well aware of the mythical ingredients in national identities and the frequent resort to patriotism by political scoundrels of the right. See, for example, Rorty, "Intellectuals in politics," *Dissent* 38 (1991), pp. 483–90: "The intellectuals at the end of socialism," *Yale Review* 80 (1992), pp. 1–16; "The unpatriotic academy," *New York Times*, February 13, 1994, Op-Ed page; Hobsbawm, "The cult of identity politics," *New Left Review* 217 (1996), esp. pp. 45–7; Miller, *On Nationality* (Oxford, Oxford University Press, 1995).

12 Some bias toward compatriots can be part of a political practice that is justifiable to distant strangers. Indeed, I have argued for such a bias in "Killing for the homeland," *Journal of Ethics* 1 (1997), pp. 165–85. But such a bias will fall far short of the neglect that is routine among leaders of respectable institutions, the insouciance displayed in General Powell's remark that the toll of Iraqis killed in the Gulf War is "really not a number I'm terribly interested in" (*New York Times*, March 22, 1991, an issue reporting expert estimates of 25,000 to 50,000 killed).

27

DEWEYAN PRAGMATISM AND AMERICAN EDUCATION

Alan Ryan

INTRODUCTION

This essay has three purposes: to show the connection between Dewey's pragmatism and his ideas about education; to link his conception of philosophy to his views about the character of modern society in general, and modern American society in particular; and to draw some lessons from these two discussions. I do not do this under these headings. I begin with the difficulty that many readers have in knowing quite what Dewey wanted to say about philosophy, education, and many other subjects, and then turn to an account of his educational ideas. I mostly concern myself with his early writings – that is, what he wrote in the ten years he was in Chicago and in the years immediately after that. The reason is that on education, these were the years of his greatest inventiveness, and thereafter he mostly defended himself against misunderstanding. On his politics, I focus, for what I think are good reasons, on his thoughts about American nationalism in the context of World War I. I end, very briefly, with an account of what I think we may learn from those First World War thoughts.

DEWEY AND DIFFICULTY

Dewey is said to be a 'difficult' writer. Such accusations are hard to refute: if readers find an author difficult, he is difficult, at any rate for them. Dewey's difficulty is not captured by that simple thought. Dewey is not so much difficult as *elusive*. In the ordinary sense his prose is not difficult; he uses no technical jargon, and no stylistic tricks. The problem he presents is that he was always groping for an appropriate vocabulary in which to express novel and unconventional ideas. The traditional vocabulary would not do: he strenuously tried to break out of every orthodoxy with which he was presented. He called himself an 'instrumentalist' until he thought the term misleading and preferred 'experimentalist'. He did not want certainty, did not suppose that anything he wrote captured the absolute truth, and later in life came to think that the purpose of philosophy was rather to enhance experience than to catalogue its features. For all his antipathy to philosophy as traditionally understood, however, he was sure that he was a philosopher; described as 'an educator', he would respond irritably.

394

Nowhere in Dewey is there an answer to traditional philosophical questions, such as 'Does the world exist independently of our perception of it?' and 'To what does the word "I" refer?' He thought the unanswerability of such questions showed not that they were deep but that we were muddled.[1] Philosophical problems are 'got over' rather than solved. That, however, tells us little about how we get over problems, or whether some ways are more effective than others. In the case of Dewey's writings on education, what is clearest is mostly negative. For instance, his reputation as an enemy to high standards and classical values – the complaint of conservative critics in Britain as well as in the United States – is clearly undeserved; but his positive views on classical values are less clear. A man who observed at his seventieth birthday celebrations that his favourite reading was Plato was not an enemy of high standards nor of a serious engagement with the classical tradition. Still no one reading Dewey can learn whether Dewey thought teenagers should or should not learn calculus, foreign languages, Latin and Greek, or European history; he barely even discusses the question of when elementary schools should insist on children learning the 'three Rs.'

One might expect Dewey's ten years in Chicago to cast light on his views on such practical matters. These were, after all, the years of the Laboratory School. In fact, his work with the school tells us little. In 1894, Dewey was a new boy in a new university; he was 35 years old, not well known, and only reluctantly appointed by President William Rainey Harper after a search for someone grander. As chairman of the Department of Philosophy, Psychology and Pedagogy, he was more preoccupied with raising the funds to keep the school going than with its curriculum. Before it opened, he wrote interestingly about what such a school could do, but in high-level philosophical terms, not in the terms that come naturally to a teacher planning a school week, let alone a lesson. Once the school was in operation, it had a principal and teachers of its own, and Dewey was not responsible for its day-to-day operations. As its name, 'the Laboratory School' suggests, the school was supposed to be a laboratory for students of social psychology. Funds had first been set aside for a more orthodox psychology laboratory; when there was no need for it, the funds were spent on the school. In the event, the school became a site for pedagogical demonstration, where visitors could see something of Dewey's ideas about elementary education in operation, as the familiar label of the 'Dewey school' suggests. For all that, it is not only later generations that have difficulty knowing what was 'Deweyan' about it; visitors often thought it was some sort of a Froebel kindergarten.[2]

Dewey was a great success as the theorist of, and the publicist for, a new approach to education, but he was a prophet without much honour in his own land. Reading and sending off endless querulous memoranda on the administration of his department occupied much of his working life. The Laboratory School was a constant source of anxiety because it had no endowment, and only a small subvention from the university. It was expensive. Personal care was lavished on the students, and required a generous ratio of teachers to pupils; creating a suitable environment for small children meant specially made chairs and tables and apparatus for the children to play on. The school in its original incarnation was always on the brink of extinction for purely economic reasons. In short, we cannot argue directly from what happened in the school to what Dewey's educational theory must have been, nor is there a simple deductive argument that links Dewey's philosophy to the school's practice. One has to turn to Dewey's writings about education to know what his philosophy of education was.

PRAGMATISM AND THE EDUCATIONAL VISIONARY

An important, if seemingly unlikely, feature of Dewey's pragmatism was that it resolved the tensions that had driven him to reject his mother's Congregationalist piety. Brought up in Vermont, Dewey experienced New England Protestantism as a creed that separated man from God, heart from mind, ethics from both science and poetry. His initial enthusiasm for the work of T. H. Green, the English Hegelian moral philosopher, waned when he came to think that Green's conception of the universal self in which all individual selves are to become members, itself replicated the 'apart thinking' of his mother's Protestant Christianity. He briefly turned to Hegel, but soon decided that Hegel's insights into the essentially cultural character of human thought and action should be divorced from a philosophy that aspired to the Absolute. Long after neo-Hegelianism had become a minority taste, Dewey assailed our hankering after the Absolute. *The Quest for Certainty, Experience and Nature*, and *A Common Faith* all argued that we could have the sense of belonging to the world – of being at home in it, and of somehow sharing in a cosmic purpose – that Hegel's devotees got from his work, without aspiring to see the world through the eyes of the Absolute. Whether pragmatism *really* resolved Dewey's problems is a question I here evade. But there is no doubting the continuity between Dewey's Hegelianism and his pragmatism, nor the usefulness of pragmatism for Dewey's somewhat dilute religiosity.

A characteristic display by Dewey the visionary is the little essay, 'My pedagogic creed'. It nicely displays the elusiveness I have in mind; it is written as a lay sermon rather than a proposal for curriculum review, and is clearer about the importance of education than about just how children are to be taught and just *what*. Dewey's aims as a teacher of teachers, or perhaps one might better say as a provider of moral and intellectual frameworks for teachers were pitched at a higher level than curriculum reform. 'My pedagogic creed' was Dewey's first famous statement of his educational convictions; he wrote it in 1896 for the *School Journal*,[3] and it is so replete with striking statements of the religious character of all true education, and with equally striking statements of the centrality of the school to social progress, and the centrality of the educational experience to all social understanding, that anyone writing about Dewey's views must be tempted to leave the job to Dewey.[4] After explaining the place of the school in rationally organized social change, elegantly rebutting the forced contrast between an individualism that lets the child run amok and a collectivism that stifles him, Dewey ends with the declaration: 'I believe that in this way the teacher always is the prophet of the true God and ushers in the true kingdom of God.'[5] As Lawrence Cremin observed, it was '[l]ittle wonder that American educators came to view this quiet little man with the dark mustache as a Moses who would eventually lead them toward the pedagogic promised land!'[6]

Dewey's comfort with the language of 'uplift' suggests the continuity of interests between his younger straightforwardly religious self and his later liberal and pragmatist self.

His philosophy of education was part of a worldview that smoothed away sharp oppositions and showed readers a strikingly optimistic vision of the future. Education was 'the art of giving shape to human powers and adapting them to social service'; so defined it was 'the supreme art', a claim calculated to jolt readers who remembered Aristotle's claim that politics was the highest art. Children came into the world neither as *tabula rasa* upon which teachers might write whatever they chose, nor as limbs of Satan, whose wills must be curbed to make them 'apt for society' as Hobbes once put it; they were bundles of intellectual, emotional, and moral potential, ready but not predestined to turn into useful and happy adults. As he did two decades later in *Democracy and Education*, Dewey took the chance to display his vision of the way individual and society might mesh. He asserted his belief that

> [T]he individual who is to be educated is a social individual, and society is an organic union of individuals. If we eliminate the social factor from the child we are left only with an abstraction; if we eliminate the individual factor from society, we are left only with an inert and lifeless mass. Education, therefore, must begin with a psychological insight into the child's capacities, interests, and habits. It must be controlled at every point by reference to these same considerations. These powers, interests, and habits must be continually interpreted – we must know what they mean. They must be translated into terms of their social equivalents – into terms of what they are capable of in the way of social service.[7]

This was the educational creed of a progressive, but not exactly the creed of a 'progressive educator'. 'Progressive education' later came to be a label for an educational theory that *over*emphasized the importance of teaching what interested the child, and *over*emphasized the child's responsibility for what went on at school. Dewey was utterly hostile to progressive education so described. He feared that his emphasis on the need to take the child's abilities and interests seriously had been taken as a licence to abandon teaching entirely. 'Child-centred' education had come to mean that it did not matter what the teacher did. For any such view he had complete contempt. His views were 'teacher centred'.

Politically, his position was decidedly progressive; his educational views presupposed that the school was an engine of social progress. Anyone less optimistic about social progress might have thought him naïve; Bertrand Russell observed that nobody ought to teach who did not have a profound feeling for the reality of original sin. Dewey had no such feeling. He knew there would be a need for a minimal amount of repressive discipline, but the need did not bulk large in his views. He thought that the integrated child would be a happy child, that virtue was both its own reward *and* the path to true happiness. A well-run school works with the grain of infant nature.

An aspect of Dewey's pragmatism that has lost none of its force in the intervening hundred years is its acceptance of the restlessness of modern society. In 1896 Dewey insisted that 'it is impossible to foretell definitely just what civilization will be twenty years from now. Hence it is impossible to prepare the child for any precise set of conditions.'[8] The only adequate form of preparation was that every pupil must be put 'in complete possession of all his powers'. Only by making children the masters both of what is already part of 'the funded capital' of society and giving them the ability to acquire what will be unpredictably added to it in the future do we prepare them for the world after school. In a general way, this is plainly *the* liberal view of education; if it seems banal, that is a sign of how far we have moved away from a belief in producing factory fodder, or in instilling political acquiescence in a lower class whose destiny is to take orders and do the world's work.

Nonetheless, the reader of Dewey's work is surprised by the minor place that the details of the curriculum occupy in Dewey's account even of the Lab School and its purpose. When Dewey writes about *The School and Society*, what he writes about is the place of the school in a democracy and the role of the school as an agent of social progress, not such down-to-earth issues as what mathematics to teach 8-year-olds. There is barely a dozen pages of curricular matter in the hundred-odd-page discussion of educational principle and description of the Lab School. Dewey opens *The School and Society* by observing that until recently education took place at home, because life was lived around the home. In the countryside the connection between getting a living and everyday life was visible and immediate. Children were socialized into becoming useful participants in the household and village economy. 'There was always something which really needed to be done, and a real necessity that each member of the household should do his own part faithfully and in cooperation with others.'[9]

The modern city broke that bond between the child, his upbringing and his finding a useful place in society. Dewey was fastidious about not giving a one-sided account:

> We must recognize our compensations – the increase in toleration, in breadth of social judgment, the larger acquaintance with human nature, the sharper alertness in reading signs of character and interpreting social situations, greater accuracy of adaptation to differing personalities, contact with greater commercial activities. These considerations mean much to the city-bred child of today.[10]

The change posed a question: 'How shall we retain these advantages and yet introduce into the school something representing the other side of life – occupations which exact personal responsibilities and which train the child in relation to the physical realities of life?'[11] There are several things to be said about this question. One is that Dewey saw elementary education – education up to the age of 13 – as a moral training and not a purely intellectual training. Indeed 'purely intellectual' would have been a term of abuse. There are two extremes from which Dewey has always been attacked, on the one side as someone who has an inadequate view of the need for discipline, order and instilled habit, and on the other as a theorist of the manipulation of children into docile membership of the corporate order.[12] Both are infinitely far from the truth. The sceptic must start, not from Dewey's desire that the powers of the child should find their natural fulfillment in life in a democratic society, but from his belief in such a natural harmony. What separates Dewey from more sceptical liberals is his assumption that something close to a complete harmony can be realized by intelligent action.

A second thing to notice is the light that Dewey's starting-point casts on his concern with 'manual training'. A familiar complaint against Dewey is that his emphasis on learning by doing was a recipe for preparing children to go on to vocational schools. American schools, like their British counterparts, put the brightest children into academic streams and the less bright into vocational streams; bright children would go on to be prosperous and well-rounded members of the managing classes while the less bright would be less prosperous members of the managed non-elite. So, all discussion of manual training tends to raise the unlovely spectre of an educational system that takes the existing division between managerial and manual work and reproduces it in the classroom. Dewey knew that. He thought that *if* there were an adequate system of trade schools, manual training in the elementary school would be an acceptable way of getting children to acquire the dexterity, discipline and work habits that trade schools could turn into the skills needed for wives and mothers on the one hand, and manual workers on the other. Characteristically, he went on to insist that to think of practical training in this way was 'unnecessarily narrow. We must conceive of work in wood and metal, of weaving, sewing and cooking, as methods of living and learning, not as distinct studies.'[13] *All* children were to acquire practical skills, as a moral imperative, even if only some of them would earn their living by using them.

Agricultural societies focused on farm and village showed the child the entire process by which life went on; nobody could turn a switch and have electric light. To get light, they had to kill animals, render tallow, and make their own candles. The school must show children the complexities of the modern world that has replaced that lost world. Dewey did not propose to do it by telling them about the way industry and commerce worked; swamping children with information in their early years was worse than useless; it bred superficial understanding, and sapped the ability to concentrate. The children must work their way through an activity from beginning to end; at the Lab School the children grew wheat in a corner of the schoolyard, ground it, and learned to make bread; when slightly older they learned about metal smelting and built their own furnace. To learn chemistry they cooked, and to cook they learned chemistry. This was how to acquire a hands-on understanding of the world. Dewey's pragmatism insisted on the practicality of knowledge; and here was the theory in practice. The vice of philosophers traditionally had been to think of all knowledge as spectatorial; Deweyan education started from the view that knowing was a form of engaging with the world.

A third feature of Dewey's discussion was his passionate belief that the educational process must make adequate ties with every aspect of the life around. In a chapter titled 'Waste in education' – an odd location for what he discussed – Dewey leaped in one bound from the concept of waste to that of organization, and then spread his wings on the topic of what organization meant for the school. He read his audience a sermon on the theme, 'All waste is due to isolation. Organization is nothing but getting things into connection with one another so that they work easily, flexibly and fully.'[14] The details of the picture do not matter. The frame of mind does. For 'organization' took on a decidedly super-managerial tone in the argument. The school was a spiritual entity. As a philosopher obsessed by the 'meaning' of events, Dewey emphasized that the school was a network of meanings rather than a collection of spaces in which children read, cooked, played, painted and whatever. The 'organization' Dewey had in mind was an emphasis on the school's ties to the whole social environment; cooking in the school kitchen linked the child to home, and to the countryside where food was grown, and thus to the school's own physical environment; sewing in the textile room tied the school both to the home, and then out to the world of business and industry.[15]

The School and Society was vastly popular; its popularity was a function of its combination of great clarity in general orientation and openness of argumentative texture. Dewey insisted over and over that schooling is part of life, not just a preparation for it, that children must use all their energies at school, not just intellectual ones and not just manual skills, that something of vast importance was happening in the school, since this was where the next generation was growing, and everyone knew that it was vastly easier to form children adequately than to have to reform them when they were teenage delinquents. All this was good news, and appreciated by his readers. One might complain that it did not yield very obvious conclusions about just what to teach and just how to teach it, but Dewey had headed off his critics in advance; the distinction between how to teach and what to teach was another of the separations that he deplored. Form and content, style and matter were to be adjusted to each other as we better understood what successful teaching was all about. We know that it is not about handing over slabs of undigested fact, we know it is a mistake to send the young out into the world primed with information but with no skills of processing and evaluating it; beyond that, *experientia docet*: people must experiment, report on their experiments, and hope to agree on good practice.

Dewey himself was ready to exploit even theories that he did not accept. He told the story of a visitor asking to see the kindergarten section of the Lab School and being told there was none. Then the visitor

> asked if there were not singing, drawing, manual training, plays and dramatizations, and attention to the children's social relations. When her questions were answered in the affirmative, she remarked, both triumphantly and indignantly, that that was what she understood by a kindergarten, and that she did not know what was meant by saying that the school had no kindergarten.[16]

Dewey agreed that what the school gave children between the ages of 4 and 13 did 'carry into effect certain principles which Froebel was perhaps the first consciously to set forth'.[17] But he was not a disciple of Froebel. Froebel could not give a sensible account of the role of play in early education because he lived in an authoritarian society to which such playful activities were anathema.[18] Dewey thought Froebel had had to give elaborate metaphysical justifications of the symbolic value of childish play-acting because he had to detach school activities from the outside world, in order to protect the child against the everyday world.[19] The American child as opposed to the Prussian child had an inalienable right to the pursuit of happiness, and his activities at school needed no metaphysical defence. His everyday desire for play could be part of the process of leading him gently towards adult life. Froebel's kindergarten methods were more useful when detached from Froebel's philosophy.

The same attitude marked Dewey's approach to Johann Herbart. Herbart was best known for the slogan that 'ontogeny recapitulates phylogeny', a misleading and distracting slogan in biology, and worse in its effect on the social sciences; what it means, literally, is that the growth of the individual takes place in stages that mirror the development of the species. What it meant in schools was that the curriculum was supposed to be governed by the individual child's gradual movement from an infancy in which he or she mimicked the mental and social relations of primitive peoples to an adult life in which he or she was a full member of a fully civilized community. Dewey wrote several papers disputing this as a picture of child development.[20] Yet the curriculum of the Lab School took something like it as a model; as a critic noticed, 'in the ordered progression of theme activities from preliterate man to modern society there were patent vestiges of the very recapitulation theory Dewey had attacked before the National Herbart Society'.[21]

But teaching children about the growth of human culture in an evolutionary fashion, and sophisticating the children's grasp of increasingly abstract material made good sense independently of Herbart. Dewey's thought was simply that children should be gradually weaned from their homes and the emotional and intellectual stimuli that home provided and on to a more abstract, more impersonal intellectual and social diet. It would have been possible to teach children history and social studies by starting with modern society and working backwards, but it takes little imagination to think of some reasons to prefer children to know a little about neolithic man and a lot about the contemporary world rather than a little about New York and a great deal about prehistory.

On the plausibility of Dewey's picture of child development, opinions have always varied. Practising infant teachers might think that Dewey had his eye too much on where children were going next, and not enough on the joys of the particular stage they had reached. Academically minded readers may flinch at how long it was before the children of the Lab School were supposed to settle down and learn some of the three Rs. What cannot be denied is that the gradual shift from what others would have denoted as play to what others would have denoted as 'real work' – neither of which Dewey would have so labeled – was always controlled by a clear idea of the child's destination. It was not nostalgia for a vanishing rural past that made Dewey start 6-year-olds on small-scale farming, harvesting, and cooking, but his belief that these were basic activities of human existence, and ones that children understood some part of by the time they reached school.

The homeliness of Dewey's manner, and the homeliness of his examples, are misleading as to the intellectual thrust of the syllabus he suggested. He did not think that all knowledge is applied knowledge, nor that all learning was to be assimilated to farming or washing the dishes; rather, he passionately believed that ideas made sense only as solutions to problems and that educationalists had neglected this fact. He saw his own contribution as suggesting ways of putting children into situations where they would grasp the problems to which increasingly sophisticated ideas and academic skills were solutions. Dewey steered a delicate path between simpler views that were not *wholly* wrong, but in his eyes missed the point. When he started writing about education, two opposed positions much in the public eye were the Herbartian emphasis on *interest* and the emphasis of his old mentor W. T. Harris on *effort*. Dewey thought the Herbartians' emphasis merely sugared the pill of a set curriculum, while Harris's emphasis on effort would create students who were either passive or rebellious. The point of Dewey's complicated argument about setting children *problems* and teaching them to *think* was that he believed that under those conditions they would be as interested as the Herbartians wished them to be and would make the effort that Harris and his colleagues so rightly stressed.[22]

401

All these arguments are so to speak 'pre-curricular', and Dewey's little pamphlet, *The Child and the Curriculum*, too, is not a discussion of the curriculum, but a plea for the abolition of sharp separations in methods of teaching where there should be none in the process of learning. The slogans of 'discipline' and 'interest' that opposed sides hurled at each other, one thinking to defend 'the subject' and the other to defend 'the child', reflected an analytical distinction inflated into a false vision of the world. Of course, children must learn something in particular, of course there was a particular direction in which they needed to be led, and so of course they needed to master the disciplines of learning; but to master anything in such a way as to have really been educated by it was a matter of absorbing it and turning it to one's own purposes, and this was a matter of our own interest. The only discipline worth having was self-discipline and the only interest worth gratifying was an interest capable of being sustained over a long enough run to enable us to learn a subject-matter thoroughly.

This lesson was spelled out for two hundred pages in *How We Think*. It was published in 1910, six years after Dewey left Chicago, but was essentially a 'Chicago' work. It offers exactly what Dewey intended, a guide to teachers who are puzzled to know what counts as intellectual progress on the part of their students and when they are in the presence of it. Practically oriented though it is, it still contains a good deal of philosophical provocation. The observation that 'Primarily, naturally, it is not we who think in any actively responsible sense; thinking is rather something that happens in us' is both true and shocking; the further suggestion that to say '*I* think' is to announce an achievement, is in the same vein.[23] Talking sense to teachers did not require Dewey to abandon his philosophical revolution.

Dewey was addressing himself to teachers who found themselves bombarded on all sides with panaceas; he refused to add to their number. He made good sense philosophically credible and morally uplifting, an achievement not to be sneered at. He refused to accept that teaching was to be left either to muddling through or to the flair of the individual teacher. There was a problem, or rather a set of problems – catching the child's attention, providing materials for thought, getting the child to think consecutively, coherently, organizedly, self-propelledly and relevantly, and watching always for how this contributed to what was to come next – and such problems were not soluble simply or by some trick; but they were not soluble at all by people who failed to identify them in the first place. As Dewey put it, the problem was to find 'the forms of activity (a) which are most congenial, best adapted, to the immature stage of development; (b) which have the most ulterior promise as preparation for the social responsibilities of adult life; and (c) which *at the same time*, have the maximum of influence in forming habits of acute observation and of consecutive inference.'[24]

Once we set up the issue like that, a heavily scientific education must look tremendously attractive, the more so to the extent that children themselves can devise their own experiments, build their own equipment, cooperate in designing and running their own projects, but still have to answer to someone else for the results. Yet even the reader who thinks Dewey has loaded the scales in favour of his view that good education is permeated with the scientific outlook must admit that the contrast between lugubrious modern discussions in which scientific education is assumed to have the one and only purpose of assisting the country in international trade, and Dewey's vision of a training that is simultaneously moral, social and intellectual is all in Dewey's favour.

One puzzle that this emphasis on problem-solving presents is whether Dewey's approach slights training in the humanities. Dewey's stress on problem-solving, on the social basis of knowledge, and on education as a form of social training, seems to make science central to education, and looks likely to turn history and geography into applied social science, as the study of how societies conceived as problem-solving organizations adapt to their environment by adjusting themselves to its opportunities and demands and adjusting it to their needs and techniques. Where in this is a love of poetry, art, or music for their own sakes, where is the cultivation of the eye and ear and a sense of rhythmic aptness? Where even is mere curiosity about the past? Dewey always believed that human beings had a natural urge to celebrate, commemorate, dance, play, sing, and paint, and had no difficulty in encouraging these as school activities. The difficulty lay in giving an account of their developed state, accommodating the not uncommon sentiment that Mozart operas are not 'good for' society but possess a special sort of value that gives a point to human existence. Throughout the 1930s, Dewey defended art education in elementary schools as an essential not a 'frill', and he knew what he was in favour of. The question of how it would fit into the schema he offered teachers was another matter.

A modern reader must see most of Dewey's ideas in *How We Think* as common sense; but it was Dewey who made them so. *How We Think* was addressed to working teachers; a large part of the teacher's trade at the turn of the century was conducting 'recitations', when, as the name suggests, children had to 'recite their lessons' and teachers 'heard' them. Dewey saw that unless they were conducted very well they were diseducative:

> To re-cite is to cite again, to tell over and over. If we were to call this period *reiteration*, the designation would hardly bring out more clearly than does the word *recitation* the complete domination of instruction by rehearsing of second-hand information, by memorizing for the sake of producing correct replies at the proper time.[25]

When foreign visitors to the United States encounter multiple choice tests they usually share Dewey's sentiments about reiteration.

When Dewey was writing, the better-trained teachers had got beyond recitations, and were accustomed to drawing up lesson plans along lines laid down by Johann Herbart. Herbart had claimed, as Dewey represents him at least, that

> there is a single 'general method' uniformly followed by the mind in an effective attack upon any subject. Whether it be a first-grade child mastering the rudiments of number, a grammar-school pupil studying history, or a college student dealing with philology, in each case the first step is preparation, the second presentation, followed in turn by comparison and generalization, ending in the application of the generalizations to new and specific instances.[26]

Suppose the lesson was to be a lesson on rivers – to take Dewey's example; as 'preparation', we would begin by getting the children to talk about streams and rivers they had seen, or about water flowing in gutters, and explain the purpose of the lesson; 'presentation' would then involve the formal presentation of films, photographs, models, perhaps a visit to look at rivers. Comparison and generalization are the stages by which the *in*essential features of the phenomenon are stripped way, so that a solid sense of what we are supposed to know about rivers is left. Finally, this knowledge would be anchored by being applied to new cases, so that children who knew about the Thames would go on to write about the Hudson. Dewey was in a dilemma *vis-à-vis* this Herbartian orthodoxy. He did not want to say that teachers should walk into class and play it by ear, but he did want to say that the five-stage schema was too pat, too neat, and in crucial ways misleading. He did not want to exaggerate the difference between his own view and the Herbartian, but he thought the Herbartian schema implied that imparting concepts and information *for their own sake* was the sum total of instruction. What was lacking was the purpose of instruction, the need to solve a problem.

Dewey offered his own five-stage schema, though he cheerfully admitted that it was never followed in all its steps, and that it was only a rough abridgment of how we think. Dewey's five stages of what he called 'the complete act of thought' were '(i) a felt difficulty; (ii) its location and definition; (iii) suggestion of a possible solution; (iv) development by reasoning of the bearings of the suggestion; (v) further observation and experiment leading to its acceptance or rejection; that is, the conclusion of belief or disbelief.'[27] Dewey's informal analysis is interesting because it suggests how difficult it is to map the process that Dewey so plausibly describes by a formal logical analysis. The fourth step in particular, where we convert a hypothesis into an explanation whose relevance to the phenomena is articulated and made obvious, is exceedingly hard to formalize, though logicians have laboured to create a 'relevance logic' for many years.

Dewey thought that his five-stage scheme overlapped Herbart's scheme, but brought out more clearly something central to the educational process. The crucial difference comes at the beginning. Dewey's children begin with a problem; the Herbartian schema begins with a teacher's lesson plan and the goals she was supposed to announce to the class before she started the lesson. Dewey's children acquire information on their way to solving a problem; information is assimilated in the process of thinking their way through to a solution. The Herbartian scheme does not exclude the idea that we think about what we learn but it does suggest that thought is incidental to information acquisition; Dewey insists always and throughout that acquiring information is incidental to problem-solving. Not emphasizing this made the Herbartian scheme misleading.

Guessing how much effect Dewey had on American education is difficult. His admirers often suggest he had rather little effect; one might parody their argument as the claim that since public education is still terrible, Dewey cannot have had much effect. His detractors sometimes seem to believe that he single-handedly debauched a fine system – which, seeing that he first wrote about education at a time when no more than 7 per cent of the population had a high school education and less than half of all children got even five years of schooling, is perhaps an exaggeration. Dewey himself was never sure which of his ideas were capable of large-scale implementation in the American public school system, and which would be hard to implement outside the Lab School. The Lab School taught classes of eight and ten, while most public schools had classes of forty or more.

Among the reasons why Dewey's influence was never likely to be as great as critics and defenders have claimed, three stand out. They are simple but conclusive. One is that Dewey schools are very expensive; they need small classes, a lot of equipment, and elaborate arrangements so that teachers can spend time and attention rethinking what they are doing. Dewey's vision of the school as a place of experiment was, it must be remembered, not a vision of an 'experimental school' in the sense of a place where eccentric, novel, or surprising things went on, but the vision of a place permeated by the experimental spirit. It could only be run by teachers who were able to get together to discuss their goals, their techniques, their successes and failures, and prospects for change.[28] The second is that Dewey schools are appallingly demanding of their teachers. Dewey may have assured teachers that they were doing God's work, but God's work is notoriously hard work. Since Dewey's educational philosophy was so determinedly teleological – at every stage, the child was seen as a creature about to embark on the *next* stage of growth – the teacher could not concentrate only on the child's current attainments and interests. Every encounter with a child was a chance to see how the moment might be turned to advantage in giving the child a grasp of arithmetic, languages, physics, chemistry, biology, geography, history, and whatever other skills we wish them to acquire. There never were many teachers' colleges capable of turning out teachers with that range of skills, and given the rates of pay for primary teachers, not many people with the ability to learn what this demanded were going to volunteer to become teachers. The third is that it is unclear just what a 'Deweyan' school is. Enormous numbers of people believe they attended one, but the schools they attended are exceedingly diverse. Since Dewey himself was not much interested in secondary education, and thought that by the time students attended college their mental habits were pretty well fixed, it is not surprising that there was little consensus over what a Deweyan allegiance meant at any level above the first few years of elementary school.

DEWEY'S AMERICANISM AND OURS

Having argued that Dewey's educational theory was in the ordinary sense of the term less a theory of education than a theory of the place of education in the politics of modern society, it remains to situate Dewey a little more firmly in the politics of his own time and ours. Dewey was a lifelong socialist, though a socialist of a liberal, Guild Socialist, stripe. He was an inveterate democrat, though 'democracy' as he understood it was a far cry from anything yet achieved in the United States or anywhere else. Without entirely ignoring those attachments, I here focus on his ideas about how we can build a modern, democratic nation from diverse, plural – in the modern terminology 'multicultural' – ingredients. Dewey came to maturity during the 1880s and 1890s, a time when the industrialization of the American economy was in full flood, and when enormous numbers of immigrants from Ireland, Germany, Scandinavia, and Eastern and Southern Europe were pouring into the country. The Chicago he encountered in 1894 was a city where barely a quarter of the inhabitants had two American-born parents.

Many Americans reacted to the arrival of these strangers with fear and distaste. Some denounced 'hyphenated' Americanism; they did not want a country full of 'German-Americans' or 'Jewish-Americans', but 100 per cent Americans. 'Racism' in those far-off days was more commonly an attitude towards new kinds of European migrant: Polish Jews, and southern Catholics in particular. Black Americans were below the horizon of consciousness in the northern states, to which, after all, the majority of immigrants went. Dewey was an American nationalist, but one of a peculiar stripe. He had no doubt that the United States was in some sense 'special', though he was even more sure that it was a *general* truth that human beings needed to acquire a sense of individual identity within a stable society with which they could identify. To the extent that American nationalism was an acceptable moral stance, it was because the United States was engaged in a moral undertaking that could properly engage the allegiances of a serious person. This distinguished it from European 'blood and soil' nationalisms. These issues came to a head during the First World War, when anti-German fury disfigured American politics and 'Americanism' became xenophobia. In an essay titled 'Nationalizing education', written in 1916, Dewey distinguished good and bad nationalism, in much the way that his contemporary Randolph Bourne had done a year before in his famous essay 'Transnational America': good nationalism creates an American culture and is consistent with internationalism, bad nationalism represses internal differences and is bellicose. A very Deweyan touch was the claim that American nationality is constituted by democracy; a second was his insistence that the 'hyphen' is good when it attaches, bad when it separates. Dewey was by this time the most famous educational theorist in the world, and it was an anxiety about the misuse of the educational system for political and propaganda purposes that led him to write this essay and several others in defense of pluralism.

The role of education, he argued in 'Nationalizing education', was not to inculcate one canonical image of American identity, but to foster mutual respect among the diversity of cultures and peoples that make up the American people. As to how to do it, he had nothing very surprising to suggest, but thought that one obvious way was to teach a view of American history that emphasized the positive contributions to American society of the successive waves of immigration. Eighty years later, this seems absolutely right, even though it raises some awkward questions about the tone to adopt in encouraging this mutual exchange of narratives. 'Immigration' is not exactly what happened to Africans who were brought to America as slaves, and even Dewey would have been hard put to it to find a wholly convincing way of telling the story of the African-American contribution to American history in such a way that it was neither a tale of passivity and victimization nor a Pollyanna-ish celebration of the successes of the downtrodden. Working out quite what we are to say to one another would surely be educative, however.

Dewey followed his student and colleague George Herbert Mead in thinking that the 'I' emerges only by distinction from the 'Me', so that we become self-conscious individuals only in a social setting. Individuality is thus a social achievement. Biological identity is a gift of nature, and biologically differentiated individuals are also differentiated experiential centres which can come to reflect on and to 'own' their particular streams of consciousness. But identity in any interesting sense is an accomplishment, and perhaps an intermittent one. It follows if not swiftly, then ineluctably, that the idea that Americans can be happily and for ever 'hyphenated' will not quite do for Dewey. The image of a melting pot is, if anything, worse. Both of these idioms stick too close to the surface of how things happen to be here and now; they do not link that surface to the deeper possibilities. Horace Kallen had defended pluralism against a 'melting pot' image of what America should do to its immigrants. He suggested that migrants might keep the cultural allegiances that stood, so to speak, to the left of the hyphen, while acquiring the political allegiances that stood to the right. 'German-Americans' would be cultural Germans and political Americans. The friends of the melting pot wanted cultural diversity to disappear as immigrants lost their former identities in a unitary American identity.

Dewey wanted something more than either party was looking for. In essence, he wished democracy to be a cultural and intellectual matter as well as a narrowly political one. As a good, if thoroughly lapsed, Hegelian, he wanted 'unity in difference' in a deeper sense than even the American national motto of 'e pluribus unum' had contemplated. A clue to what he hoped for lies in *Democracy and Education*, said by Dewey to be his most important book, and 'for many years the fullest expression of my philosophical position such as it is'. It made the argument (much resisted by philosophers, for whom the philosophy of education was a sort of 'service' subject reluctantly offered to student teachers) that *all* philosophy is the philosophy of education. This is a plausible implication of Dewey's pragmatism. Pragmatism approached epistemological issues in a genetic and naturalistic fashion, and aimed to understand how we acquire problem-solving competences in a great variety of contexts. This links philosophy and education; we must now tie both to a multicultural conception of democracy.

Connecting philosophy and democracy is no small task. *Democracy and Education* spelled out its case with Plato's defence of rule by Guardians and Rousseau's insistence that we must protect young Émile from a society that has been corrupted by the growth of the arts and sciences firmly in view. The entire book was a response to them. Dewey redefined democracy as a process of deep and organic communication on free and equal terms. The development of democracy was an expansion of sociality. The democratic community was in effect the community that best realized the very nature of sociability. Moral growth thus involved the acquisition of a capacity for communal life as well as personal fulfilment; we become more fully who we are as we become more able to offer ourselves to others. This is what one might expect from a thoroughly democratized Hegelian; one can see how Dewey could preach his brand of liberal democracy to Chinese audiences in the early 1920s who found Russell's more Millian liberalism very alien indeed.

The third crucial step is Dewey's emphasis on modernity; we live, like it or loathe it, in the *modern* world; just where the modern world is whether in space or time is never quite clear, since its *indicia* range from the achievements of the scientific revolution of the seventeenth century to the disorganization of the capitalist industrial world of the nineteenth. But its nature is easy enough to describe: social and geographical mobility, economic and moral individualism, moral subjectivity, and the beginnings of secularism.

How did Dewey integrate his account of modern identity and his account of the stresses of modernity, and get from that to an account of *American* identity? The answer is that his entire career was an attempt to do just this. His more arcane philosophical work and his more immediately accessible political journalism preach the same vision of how to make ourselves at home in the modern world by making the modern world more fit to be our home. 'Modern society' is the fundamental analytical category, and it is matched by a modern conception of identity: forward-looking, task-oriented, self-conscious and adaptable. Crises of identity Dewey almost uniformly analysed as a conflict between an old and backward-looking conception of identity and a modern social setting. 'Democracy' is the cultural – and then by inference the political – character of modern society; America is not modernity's only home, but it is where it is least obscured by everything else we have inherited. It is a *philosophical* as much as a sociological concept, because the investigation of modern thought is a philosophical activity – part of the social criticism of social criticisms that Dewey decided philosophy had now become. It thus follows that any account of American identity is one variation on the theme of modern identity, heightened perhaps but not unique nor morally special.

The implication for a pluralist conception of the social world now becomes clearer: against his Hegelian youth, Dewey repudiates the search for an Absolute, but in the spirit of that Hegelian youth he hangs on to the aspiration after a society in which fully transparent self-understanding and communication are possible; such a world does not obliterate differences of perspective and contribution, and is in that way friendly to pluralism, but it aspires after a kind of moral and intellectual unity that a naively empiricist and sociological pluralism might not care about. In that sense, Dewey was a theorist of Americanization inasmuch as he wanted to identify the American project with the project of achieving a novel form of emancipation that would not leave us deracinated but reracinated.

THE MORAL

Since the late 1970s, arguments over 'identity' and 'difference' have spread into every area of American political discussion. Their original home might have been in literary theory and the initial provocation questions of translation and interpretation, but questions of cultural attachment came during the 1980s to have considerable political resonance. In Canada the perennial issue of Québecois 'particularity', and the new demands of Inuit and other aboriginal peoples have caused great alarm; in the United States there has been a revival of old anxieties about immigration and a new depth of despair over the plight of the African-American poor, and at least some anxiety about recent assertions of the rights of women, sexual minorities and the disabled.

Unsurprisingly, demands to have our 'identities' respected and our 'differences' acknowledged have made their way into the classrooms of America at every level from kindergarten upwards. The debate represents a reversion to the ethical standards of Dewey's youth. From the perspective of the theorists of 'difference', the philosophical defence of human rights offered by the conventional liberalism of John Rawls and Robert Nozick is sociologically unsophisticated, and inattentive to the needs of groups and communities along with individuals. But it would have seemed so just after World War I, had it come to the notice of an audience which took it for granted that 'personality' and 'community' were the poles of debate. The one respect in which we differ from our predecessors is that we are

408

less confident that the circle can be squared and that plural identities can be made consistent with an overarching national identity.

It is at this point that Dewey's educational politics might decently be revived. For Dewey's conception of identity – as an achievement rather than a brute fact – usefully reminds us to take absolutely seriously the anti-essentialism that so many postmodernist critics preach but do not practice. Indeed, we might do well to let the notion of identity have a holiday and focus instead on the concept of a project. So conceived, American identity can again be what Dewey thought it ought to be, something defined in terms of the great experiment that Dewey had in mind: the attempt to build a society that would exploit all the resources of modernity, and allow all its members to feel both that they were contributing to a common project and that what they contributed was distinctively theirs.

Conversely, the various more localized identities to which people are properly attached can be emphasized without the sense that they trap their bearers – 'I am a black American, so how can I be an expert on Shakespeare?' has more than once been heard – or that they swallow up their bearers' lives. A gay racing driver may or may not pilot a Formula One car in a distinctively gay fashion, but if he is to stay alive on the track, it is the project of getting to the chequered flag quickly but safely that has to preoccupy him. The virtue of Deweyan experimentalism is that it teaches us to look for ways in which we can be all the things we are, and encourages us not to believe that there is characteristically only one and it must trump all the others all the time. There are surely many ways of providing an education that attends to that thought; but not all the kinds of education that we presently offer our children do so very well.

NOTES

1 The title of Cornel West's quick tour of the pragmatist tradition is nicely chosen: not only the title but the content, too, of *The American Evasion of Philosophy* leaves it squarely up to the reader to decide whether Americans – Dewey foremost among them – have simply ducked the hard issues of philosophy or have cleverly escaped the snares traditional philosophy sets for the unwary.

2 John Dewey, 'The School and Society', in *The Middle Works* (henceforth *MW*), p. 81. In this essay I cite *The Early Works* (*EW*) and *The Middle Works*, edited by Jo Ann Boydston (Carbondale, Ill., Southern Illinois University Press, 1972–80).

3 *EW* 5, pp. 84–95.

4 I am not the first commentator to have had that sensation: 'One is tempted to continue indefinitely quoting from this Creed,' wrote William H. Kilpatrick, in 'Dewey's influence on education', Paul Arthur Schilpp (ed.) *The Philosophy of John Dewey*, 2nd edn (New York, Open Court, 1971), p. 463.

5 'My pedagogic creed', *EW* 5, p. 95.

6 Lawrence A. Cremin, *The Transformation of the School* [1961] (New York, Vintage Books, 1964), p. 100.

7 'My pedagogic creed', *EW* 5, p. 86.

8 Ibid.

9 *MW* 1, p. 8.

10 *MW* 1, p. 9.

11 Ibid.

12 The latter was Christopher Lasch's criticism in *The New Radicalism in America* (New York, Knopf, 1965).

13 Ibid., p. 10.

14 Ibid., p. 39.

15 Ibid., pp. 41–3.

16 Ibid., p. 81.

17 Ibid.

18 In fact, the Prussian government banned the establishment of kindergartens in 1851; this seems to have been the result, not of an authoritarian government's suspicion of all forms of freedom, but of the Ministry of Education confusing the apolitical, mystical Friedrich Froebel with his nephew, Karl, a socialist (Harry G. Good and James D. Teller, *A History of Western Education* (New York, Macmillan Company, 1969), p. 287.

19 Bertrand Russell's two short books on education, *On Education*, and *Education and the Social Order*, do not go off on long metaphysical excursions, but there is something to be said for the thought that Russell's attachment to Froebel and Montessori teaching methods was part of a desire to protect children *from* society rather than a desire to integrate the child into society.

20 E.g. 'The interpretation of the savage mind', in *MW* 2, pp. 39–52.

21 Cremin, *Transformation of the School*, p. 141.

22 'Interest in relation to training of the will', in *EW* 5, pp. 111–50.

23 *How We Think*, in *MW* 6, p. 208.

24 Ibid., p. 215.

25 Ibid., p. 338.

26 Ibid., p. 339.

27 Ibid., p. 237.

28 I do not mean that this can *never* be done in the public school system. Debbie Mayers's success with the East Harlem school shows what can be done with an unusually talented principal and unusually devoted teachers; but nobody supposes that there is something here that can be set down as a recipe, whereas it is not too hard to see how a small school with a generous staff–student ratio would allow a Deweyan approach to flourish.

28

LEARNING FROM FREUD

Adam Phillips

In a talk given in 1950 to psychology and social-work students entitled, 'Yes, but how do we know it's true?', the British psychoanalyst D. W. Winnicott suggested that there were two stages people always go through when they are taught psychology. 'In the first stage', he writes,

> they learn what is being taught about psychology just as they learn other things. In the second stage they begin to wonder – yes, but is it true, is it real, how do we know? In the second stage the psychological teaching begins to separate out from the other as something that just can't be learnt. It has to be felt as real, or else it is irritating, or even maddening.[1]

The first stage of learning can be called, in Freud's language, identification; the student becomes like somebody who knows these things. In Winnicott's language it would be called compliance; the child fits in with the teacher's need to teach, and, by implication, with the culture's demand that these are the things one learns, and this is the way one learns them. In the first stage, that is to say, the student adapts to what is supposedly, the subject being taught.

In the second stage something akin to what Freud calls dream-work, and Winnicott calls object-usage goes on.[2] Each student, consciously and unconsciously, makes something of her own out of it all; finds the bits she can use, the bits that make personal sense. As in Winnicott's description of object-usage, the student attacks the subject with questions and criticisms, and finds out what's left after the assault; whatever survives this critique – this hatred – is felt to be of real substance (resilient, uncorruptible, worth banking on). In this way the student makes (or fails to make) psychology true for her. In the terms of Freud's account of dream-work, the subject-matter, the teaching, is like what Freud calls the dream-day – in which, quite unbeknownst to ourselves, we are selecting material for the night's dream. It's as if, while we go about our official business an artist inside us is all the time on the look-out for material to make a dream with. So from the point of view of the dream-work the student finds himself unwittingly drawn to specific bits of the subject being taught – whatever the emphasis of the teacher happens to be – which he will then, more or less secretly (even to himself) transform into something rather strange. If he did this while he was asleep we would call it a dream; if he does it while he is awake it will be called, a misunderstanding, a delusion, or an original contribution to the subject. In other words, in the second stage, the student makes the subject fit in with his unconscious project. He uses it for self-fashioning, or he dispenses with it. The first stage that Winnicott describes might be called the student's official education; the second stage, whether one redescribes it as object-usage or dream-work, may be rather more like the student's unofficial education.

In one sense, Winnicott's notion of object-usage is entirely compatible with the principles, if not the practice, of liberal education, liberal institutions favouring, as they claim to do, debate and critique, and the democratic (or agonistic) formulation of criteria of value. Freud's dream-work, however – to which Winnicott's useful concept is affiliated – has more radical implications for our stories about learning and teaching. One implication is that people can learn but they can't be taught; or at least, they can't be taught anything of real significance. And that is partly because people can never know beforehand, neither can their teachers, exactly what is of personal significance – that is, what each will find significant: to select our dream with, to remember or to forget. What is of interest to someone – what Freud called his 'preconditions for loving' – are both recondite, and profoundly idiosyncratic, a function of the strange weaving of personal history and unconscious desire, unpredictable and intelligible, if at all, only in retrospect. Because self-knowledge is always a reconstruction it is always out of date.

From a psychoanalytic point of view, I have my conscious preoccupations and ambitions, and these make me more or less educable. But I also have my unconscious desire and affinities – tropisms and drifts of attention – that can be quite at odds with my conscious ideals. I may go to a lecture on psychology and be fascinated; but I may dream that night about the ear-rings of the woman sitting next to me; which, if I were to associate to this detail in the dream might, like Proust's legendary madeleine, open up vistas of previously unacknowledged personal history. So, in Freud's view, virtue can be taught, but only to a part of the self (in Freud's metapsychology the super-ego is internalized initially from the parents, and then the ego has morality, as it were forced upon it by the super-ego, and through its own adaptation to its circumstances); other, more or equally powerful parts of the self – called variously by Freud, the id (basic instinct) or more inclusively, the unconscious (id plus dreaming self) – are either recalcitrant to influence or are living by their own rules (though where they learn these rules from Freud never considers). The ego, and to a far lesser extent the super-ego in this Freudian story are both, by definition, educable and keen to learn. Indeed from the ego's point of view acculturation is tantamount to survival (contemporary child psychotherapists always want to know whether the child is learning well in school). But it is what I am calling the dreaming self – with its dream-work and its idiosyncratic desire – that is the new Freudian contribution to the traditional questions about education. From the point of view of the dreaming self learning is a sublimation of desiring; there is no learning without desire, or none, in Winnicott's language, that is 'felt as real'. The dreaming self cannot be schooled in the traditional sense because it always chooses its teachers; any available cultural canon is simply like the dream day for the dreamer. From an unknowable (unconscious) set of criteria a person, unbeknown even to himself, picks out and transforms the bits he wants, the bits that can be used in the hidden projects of unconscious desire. In this process, which is like a kind of sleep-walking solitary self-education, the Freudian subject is, as it were, the Victorian autodidact romanticized.

So when Freud came to write about children's education he wrote more, and more interestingly, about children's self-education: about what they learned despite the adults not because of them. Indeed, Freud's implicit paradigm for teaching and learning – in which he was also alluding to the problematic teaching and learning of psychoanalysis itself – was the way children conducted what he called their 'sexual researches'. The ways in which children acquired their sexual theories, and the forms these theories took, were the daylight equivalent of night-times of dream-work. Children, Freud realized, couldn't really be taught about sex, they could only teach themselves: find out in their own ways, according to their own needs at the time. And because in Freud's view sex – in its fullest sense – was the only thing the child wanted to know about, learning about sex was the paradigm of learning. If children learn about sex in the same way that they dream, how could they be taught? (Imagine trying to teach someone how to dream.) 'The sexual behaviour of a human being', Freud writes in 'Civilized sexual morality and modern nervousness',[3] 'often lays down the pattern for all his other modes of reacting to life.' Integral, indeed constitutive of the sexual behaviour of children is their curiosity about sex. One could almost say, their curiosity IS their sexuality. And yet it is, in Freud's view, their very curiosity about sex that creates for them a fundamental conflict with what he calls the 'ideals of education'. Both what the children want to know, and how they go about learning it, puts them at odds with the adult world.

Children want to know about sexuality, but the grown-ups tell them they need to know about something else; and they need to know about something else – call it culture – to distract them from what they are really interested in. Education, Freud implies in this paper, teaches the child to lose interest in what matters most to her. Interest has to have something added to it, called education, to make it acceptable. Children dream, but adults want to teach them; children know what interests them, but adults want them educated.

This demonization of the adult world as exclusively repressive is, of course, an over-simplification. But by dramatizing in this way a war between curiosity and education Freud is describing his version of Romanticism, of what he will much later call civilization and its discontents. And by doing it in this way – by taking seriously the child's unofficial education of sexual research – Freud can get us to ask an interesting question: what would education look like if we took dreaming and children's sexual curiosity as the model for teaching and learning? What would our interest in things and people be like if we thought of our adult selves as more like dreamers and children, as Freud describes them?

One of the first words in psychoanalysis for what I am calling interest was curiosity. For Freud infantile sexuality was a kind of apotheosis of curiosity; it was both its origin for the individual, and the paradigm for all its later forms. In Freud's descriptions in the early works – pre-1910 – it is almost as though the child is lived by, or lives through, her sexual curiosity; it is what Strachey translates as the sexual researches of children. The index of the Standard Edition has more references under the heading 'sexual researches of children' than any of the other sexual subjects. What united, in Freud's view, the artist, the scientist, the lawyer, the teacher, was that they were all interested, in however disguised a form, in the sexual questions of childhood. Psychoanalysis was distinguished by being curious about curiosity, about its provenance and function in a person's life.

The child's profundity, in Freud's view, was in the quality of its curiosity. When he says that children, who have been told the facts of life but go on believing their own sexual theories, 'go on worshipping their own idols in secret', he is paying tribute to the child as someone unseduced by reality, unimpressed by other people's truths. The relentlessness of the child's questions, and the sense that the child's curiosity was his destiny, were what Freud took to heart. The child knew what he was interested in: where babies come from, the difference between the sexes, his parents' relationship. These were the child's inspiration; they weren't options – the child was not casting around for a hobby, or in some supermarket spoiled for choice – they were urgencies. And what the child's curiosity high-lighted was the child's need to know, and the impossibility of his being satisfied. As a kind of parody of theoretical or epistemological man, the Freudian child is driven by questions and doesn't believe any of the answers; he only finds his own satisfying. He is addicted to, driven by, what he doesn't know. But his well-being, if not his actual future depended on what Freud called his sexual researches, his making up of his theories. The child's sexual life was his theory-making; the child lived intensely his sensual life, out of which he made his necessary art. And the implications of this for psychoanalysis itself – and for education – are intriguing; Freud has identified with the curious child; the analyst and patient – or teacher and student – can now be pictured as two children exchanging their sexual theories. In 'On the sexual theories of children' Freud explicitly likens the child's fantastic sexual speculations to the theories of the adult. 'These false sexual theories', Freud writes,

> have one very curious characteristic. Although they go astray in a grotesque fashion, yet each one of them contains a fragment of real truth; and in this they are analogous to the attempts of adults, which are looked at as strokes of genius, at solving the problems of the universe which are too hard for human comprehension.[4] (IX, 215)

Freud gives us a theory of theorizing that puts all theory, including his own, into question. The origins of the child's theories, he writes, 'are the components of the sexual instinct which are already stirring in the childish organism'. The child is not exactly what we might call an empiricist; he simply uses so-called real things as food for thought, as what Henry James calls, in his notebooks, 'germs' for stories. What we might think of as the elaborate coherence of a theory Freud refers to as 'going astray in a grotesque fashion'. Knowledge for the child, as for the adult, is a sexually inspired project; just like the dream-work, out of a fragment of truth – of something real like a day residue – peculiar personal truths are woven out of unconscious desire. In Freud's scenario the 'fragment of truth' in the child's own theory comes from the biological facts of life (the facts of life are true in so far as one wants to have or avoid having a baby. If reproduction was not the project, or the purpose, what then would correspond to the fragment of truth? Once Freud positions himself as the one who can identify the fragment of truth in the child's theory he can differentiate himself from the child. He also has to find a position from which the child's position looks naïve, absurd or merely wrong. If no one's theory can be made to look ridiculous how are we going to tell our theories apart (the notion of truth in this context makes humiliation both possible and necessary)? There are fragments of truth and the going-astray in a grotesque fashion. This is the difference Freud both equivocates about and wants us to keep in mind.

All curiosity, in Freud's view, 're-awakens the traces, which have since become unconscious, of his first period of sexual interest'.[5] And these traces are traces of both knowledge and method: both what the child made (made up), and how he went about making it. Our own ways of being interested link us to the past. We have acquired official and unofficial habits of enquiry (and so have an official and unofficial personal development). Our preconditions for loving are bound up with, informed by, this first period of sexual interest.

What is clear in Freud's account of children's sexual curiosity is that it was akin to, or a form of appetite; it had to be satisfied, but by a fantasy, a story. It was as though the child's instinctual life partly took the form of a hunger for coherent narrative for satisfying fiction. Often stimulated, as Freud frequently points out, by the birth of a sibling – and other people, of course, were beginning to participate in Freud's psychoanalysis – these fantasies, whether they were sexual theories or the more disguised and sophisticated family romances, were the medium for the child's struggle for psychic survival: they were the child's attempts, however forlorn, to refind a place in the world. Theory, Freud intimates, is intrinsically rivalrous; it is about being better placed than someone else. The child's curiosity and theory-making were, in a real sense, about why he was there, and in what sense he was still there after the birth of the sibling. And this means, of course, that in a sense he was not still there; he had been displaced. He was elsewhere. Wishing is the sign of loss: wanting things to be otherwise because they are not as they are supposed to be. For the child to live his curiosity is itself an acknowledgement of loss.

And yet despite our hunger for elegeic knowledge – for knowledge as elegy – the child's discoveries in Freud's equivocal account are not quite or always as reassuringly painful as the by-now familiar post-Freudian talk of lack, disillusionment and mourning might suggest. Psychoanalytic theory has become obsessed by, indeed obsessional about, loss. But for Freud there is also an imaginative plenitude, a manifest exhilaration about the ways in which children go astray in a grotesque fashion. It is the child's always-paradoxical resilience – the inventions born of apparent insufficiency, the refusal of common sense, of the facts of life – that Freud is taken by. But it has been Freud's version of the child's formative helplessness that has been taken up in different ways by Lacan, Winnicott and Klein. For each of them the child is someone for whom something essential is missing, or is lost or about to be destroyed. The unified image in the mirror, the potential wealth and solace of the mother, the father's entitlement, the parents' sexual relationship – whichever way it is construed the child is essentially the maker of invidious comparisons. It is as though the child's strongest wishes or deepest desire is to grow up, to become more sexually or intellectually competent, to not be a child. The child seems to experience himself as exclusively inferior to the adult (whereas in certain forms of romanticism the adult is a diminished child). In other words, a potentially non-linear theory is underpinned by a simple linear progress myth. What children suffer from is not being what they think of as adults, or a growing acquaintance with the unappeasable nature of desire. You can become an adult who is supposed to know, or else a child with endless questions. Whether or not psychoanalysts try to escape from their question marks, they are committed to the idea of a life as somehow organized around, in relationship to, absence. We are the animals for whom something is missing, and for whom what is missing is always privileged. What is absent, ironically, is what is there for us to be interested in. Our curiosity depends upon a receding horizon. Good stories of profit and loss are indeed bewitching. And yet when we describe children, or adults, as insufficient we might wonder: insufficient compared to what? Why, for example, hasn't the death of God been the death of our preoccupation with ourselves as lacking? Our fantasies of plenitude make us look ridiculous, and it is in the child that these preoccupations get located. The theoretical vogue for lack and insufficiency has become a perverse boast: a way of disqualifying the child's very real imaginative achievements.

If there is a vividly frustrated child at the heart of psychoanalysis – a child who has stolen the show with his anguish, a child whose abject resourcelessness is somehow exemplary – there is another Freudian child who has been mislaid. This child is not merely the satisfied child. (However, he is alluded to, I think, in the fashionable accounts of the amazingly competent and accomplished infant of empirically based developmental theory; this child is a natural at the double act of infancy.)

The child I am referring to, whom psychoanalysis has mislaid – who is rarely the subject of psychoanalytic theory – is the child with an astonishing capacity for pleasure, and, indeed the pleasures of interest, with an unwilled relish or sensuous experience which often unsettles the adults who like to call it 'affection'. This child who can be deranged by hope and anticipation – by ice-cream – seems to have a passionate love of life – a curiosity about life – that for some reason isn't always easy to sustain. Of course the ordinary childhood experience of delight that I am describing has elements of omnipotence in it, but to call it merely omnipotence is to overload the dice. I would prefer to call it a kind of ecstasy of opportunity (Blake called it exuberance). But whatever it is, this childhood relish does not fit easily into the ordeal of psychoanalytic development. Because it is easy to sentimentalize and to idealize, the visionary qualities of the child, this part of the legacy of romanticism – that is in Blake and Wordsworth and Coleridge most explicitly – has been abrogated by psychoanalysis. Freud's child as sexual theorist, 'astray in a grotesque fashion', is a version of the visionary poet of romanticism who is, of course, neither innocent nor, in any sense, conflict-free. Or to put it more straightforwardly, children say some very strange things. They seem to care a lot about what is going on. And they are very interested in bodies. They really want to learn what goes in and out of them, and what goes on inside them.

Unfortunately, for the child of psychoanalysis there are usually only two genres available: romantic comedy or tragedy. In tragedy his curiosity ennobles the hero and kills him; in the comic romance his curiosity makes a mockery of him. It is the fate of what I am calling interest, in these genres, that it either invites agony and posthumous fame, or mild and enchanting humiliation. The child is Oedipus or the child is Don Quixote (both, in a sense, dreamers: both determined to find things out for themselves).

And yet in 'Civilised sexual morality and modern nervousness' and *The Interpretation of Dreams* Freud suggests, in his description of infantile sexuality and of dreaming, a quite different destiny for the child's curiosity. Or rather, he suggests that the fact that the child and the dreamer know exactly what interests her – that is, sexuality – makes desire, in the form of curiosity, a scandal for what Freud calls culture. The child inevitably sublimates;

there can be no sexuality without culture. She makes up theories in fantasy and language; but they are about nothing but sexuality: what goes in and out of bodies, and what goes on inside them and between them. But the child's forms of sublimation, just like the dreamer's, are also always refusing to play the game. He keeps, as it were, pointing at bodies and what they might do for pleasure and pain. In Freud's description of the child, the child represents what the dreamer reminds himself of each night in his dreams: the refusal of stoicism, the ambivalent aesthetics of an infinite curiosity. We are, Freud always intimates, terrified of quite how interested we are in people and things. Education can be used, just like symptoms, to temper curiosity: to anaesthetize, or muffle, desire.

If, improbably, we were to take the Freudian child and the Freudian dreamer as our paradigms for the not entirely connected processes of teaching and learning, then education would involve the student in re-finding his own ways of finding out. And it would take for granted that people know what they are interested in, even if they don't always know that they know (so laziness, for example, would be redescribed as fear of, or resistance to, one's own appetite). It would acknowledge the senses in which people bring their personal (and trans-generational) histories to bear on what they want to know about. But above all, it would have to take seriously the unpredictable ways each person makes something of their own out of what they are given. And if their education does not, one way or another, sustain their love of life – their appetite for it – then it's not worth having.

NOTES

1 D. W. Winnicott, *Thinking about Children* (London, Karnac, 1996), p. 13.
2 For Winnicott's concept of object-usage, see D. W. Winnicott, *Playing and Reality* (London, Tavistock Publications, 1971), pp. 101–11 and my 'On risk and solitude', in Adam Phillips, *On Kissing, Tickling and Being Bored* (Cambridge, Harvard University Press, 1993), pp. 22–39. For Freud's concept of dream-work see Freud, *The Interpretation of Dreams*, ch. 7, in *SE* IV, and Christopher Bollas, *Being a Character* (New York, Hill and Wang, 1992).
3 *Standard Edition of the Complete Psychological Works of Sigmund Freud (SE)*, trans. and ed. James Strachey (London, Hogarth Press and the Institute of Psycho-analysis, 1962), vol. IX, p. 198.
4 *SE* IX, p. 215.
5 *SE* IX, p. 225.

29

ENLIGHTENMENT AND THE VIENNA CIRCLE'S SCIENTIFIC WORLD-CONCEPTION

Thomas E. Uebel

At one of the heights of the Vienna Circle's complex debate about the question of the content, form and status of the observational evidence statements of science ('protocols') – a debate that ultimately turned on the question of what course the Circle's brave new philosophy was to take – Otto Neurath made a remarkable aside. In the course of his argument against Rudolf Carnap's 'methodologically solipsist' protocol language, he stated that Carnap's 'remarks might induce younger people to search for this protocol language. This easily leads to metaphysical deviations. Although metaphysics ultimately cannot be defeated by arguments, for the sake of waverers it is important to maintain physicalism in its most radical version.'[1]

What is startling about this passage is the clear implication of the educational intent of its author's position. Its expression is bound to provoke a certain sense of incredulity in the contemporary reader. What pastoral concerns were these? Moreover, we are likely to suspect some delusion of grandeur on their part: surely this is a case of overreaching philosophical ambition? Similar suspicions are raised by the closing sentence of the Vienna Circle's collectively written manifesto 'The Scientific World-conception: the Vienna Circle': "*The scientific world-conception serves life, and life receives it.*"[2] Is it not the case that logical positivism, even by its own admission, is singularly ill-equipped to handle the 'riddles of life'?[3] What relevance might the often difficult and sometimes abstruse argumentation of the protocol sentence debate therefore possess for 'life'?

Logical empiricism is rarely thought of nowadays as an educational project, let alone a viable one. Its anti-metaphysical teachings are associated with pedantry rather than pedagogics, if not with worse.[4] Surface appearances to the contrary, however, this reputation is ill-deserved. With the Vienna Circle, one of its points of origin, logical empiricism was steeped in the tradition of enlightenment thought and engaged in its continuation. Most important, it was engaged in its renewal; it was not a naïve progressivism. Moreover, in the hands of the Circle's most radical representative, Otto Neurath, philosophy – or what replaces or remains of it – became a self-reflexive experiment in learning. It was not by chance that in 1937 Neurath asked not only Nils Bohr and the Circle's old philosopher-cum-educationalist hero Bertrand Russell for 'outside' essays for the first volume of the *International Encyclopedia of Unified Science*, but also John Dewey, who subsequently contributed an entire monograph, his *Theory of Valuation*. In his first contribution Dewey explicitly touched on the issue of the 'human, cultural meaning of the unity of science', and in the second he stated: 'The practical problem that has to be faced is the establishment of cultural conditions that will support the kinds of behavior in which emotions and ideas, desires and appraisals, are integrated.'[5]

Initial scepticism is not easily assuaged by references to the associations kept by the later Neurath, however. Could it really be held that already the Circle's manifesto prepared the ground for the later collaboration? Thus it must be admitted that a sympathetic reading of it is required to discount occasional foundationalist-sounding appeals to 'reducibility to the given', but it can be added that such sympathy is justified. I take it to be one of the results of recent Vienna Circle scholarship that it is legitimate to discount such remarks as ultimately inessential accoutrements – the very point, incidentally, Neurath had to convince Dewey of before he agreed to take part in the *Encyclopedia*.[6] Even so disinfected, however, the Circle's vision seems a peculiarly one-sided, all-too austere affair of scientific reason.

> [W]hat is the *essence of the new scientific world-conception* in contrast with traditional philosophy[?] No special 'philosophic' assertions are established, assertions are merely clarified . . . *there is no such thing as philosophy as a basic or universal science alongside or above the various fields of the one empirical science*; there is no way to genuine knowledge other than the way of experience; there is no realm of ideas that stands over and beyond experience.[7]

Supposing that this short-hand can be anti-reductionistically defused, we may still ask, however, what educational gain may be expected of the recommended abstinence from metaphysics.

> The representatives of the scientific world-conception resolutely stand on the ground of simple human experience. They confidently approach the task of removing the metaphysical and theological debris of millennia. Or, as some have it: returning, after a metaphysical interlude, to a unified picture of this world which had, in a sense, been at the basis of magical beliefs, free from theology, in the earliest times.[8]

Are we not back to village positivism? What are we left with after such radical conceptual cleansing of traditional worldviews has taken place? Has scientific reason not been rendered absolute?

The answer I propose to investigate is that the scientific world-conception is properly understood as an enlightenment philosophy only if the current reassessment of the historical Vienna Circle (as opposed to the caricature still prevalent in the popular philosophical imagination) is once more extended to comprehend not only its thorough-going epistemological anti-foundationalism, but also the voluntarist point of its ethical 'non-cognitivism'.[9] That is to say, the scientific world-conception is properly understood as the opposite of village positivism only if it is recognized that it has an 'other' (as we may put it, staying with the anthropological idiom) and that the scientific world-conception was meant by its proponents to perform its enlightenment work only in conjunction with that other of scientific reason – ethical will and willing. The very austerity of the scientific world-conception represents an index of the place that is held for this other. Scientific reason cannot determine all there is to determine, it cannot determine the will. In this sense, there was, *pace* village positivism, more than scientific reason dreamt of. Scientific reason was not made absolute: rather, its (self-)clarification was required if a satisfactory view of its place in 'life' was to be attained. To confuse the work of reason and will was to cripple the prospect of sensible action. This was the reason why even the Circle's protocol sentence debate was ultimately of enlightenment relevance: our very 'image of knowledge' was one of the determinants of our conduct in life and it stood in need of repair.[10]

Investigation of this answer requires discussion of what the Circlists themselves discussed as such only rarely, if at all, in their publications: the embeddedness of the scientific world-conception in 'life'. In order to draw out their enlightenment legacy it is thus necessary to re-examine in its socio-historical and biographical context what the scientific world-conception was that the Vienna Circle wrote on the banners of early logical empiricism. My aim is to recover its educational meaning and, without claiming final vindication of their project, to display some of its virtues.

THE SOCIAL AND POLITICAL CONTEXT: RED VIENNA

A rough sketch may suffice to situate the Vienna Circle in the wider socio-political context of post-World War I Vienna. Building upon a fecund, if problematic past – its fin de siècle culture of avant-gardist artistic movements, its proliferation of middle-class-based social reform initiatives and its academic circles which moved in varying ways between the poles of artistic exploration and ethical engagement – post-WWI Vienna emerged from the ruins of the Habsburg empire first as the leader, then the last bastion of the experiment in democracy that was Austria's first republic. In 'Red' Vienna the surviving representatives of the pre-war modern movements, and those who grew up in reaction to them, showed an allegiance to the new republic that contrasted markedly with the alienation felt earlier towards the monarchy of 'Kakania'. This allegiance continued their pre-war concerns and found public expression in their support for, and their frequent participation in, the educational and cultural efforts undertaken either under the aegis of the City of Vienna or the sponsorship of the Austrian socialist party, even though many of them had not themselves converted to socialism. Thus for roughly fifteen years the modernists and modernizers in Vienna possessed critical political mass. In conjunction with the socialist party, they wielded the power to pursue a decidedly affirmative programme of reform in the areas of housing, health care, education and the arts and to create institutional frameworks for a project that could aptly be called the 'democratization of culture'.[11]

What is meant by this noble phrase? Obviously, the point of this project consisted in the 'empowerment' of the disadvantaged classes and minorities, but so as not to be misled by this use of an anachronistic term we must add that, inasmuch as we are concerned with the contribution of the Viennese intelligentsia, it was an intellectual, an educational, empowerment that it promoted. Besides others such as its famous housing programme, the City of Vienna under its socialist council funded projects that worked to provide the population with means to exercise its democratic rights in an informed and self-determined manner.

That meant first of all to provide access to the culture at large, which the lower classes typically were denied by circumstances of birth, 'culture' being understood widely as the field of cognitive, moral and aesthetic engagement of autonomous individuals. (The allusion to Kant is intentional: with Max Adler, one of its chief theoreticians, Austro-Marxism was explicitly neo-Kantian. That his particular philosophical interpretation of the common project was challenged, amongst others by Neurath, did not lessen its attraction for liberal intellectuals.) Typically the term used for this project, which ranged from remedial instruction to 'workers' universities', was not 'adult' education, but *Volksbildung*, literally 'people's' education (with 'education' being understood in the wide sense of *Bildung*, enabling participation as autonomous subjects).

I have painted a somewhat idealized picture, for it suffices for present purposes that this was the ideal of *Volksbildung* that informed the participation of members and associates of the Vienna Circle. This holds true not only of Otto Neurath and Edgar Zilsel, who belonged to its left wing, but also of Friedrich Waismann, who did not, to name but three. The emphasis of their educational work lay not on indoctrination, the provision of correct opinions on political issues, but rather on providing the tools whereby informed opinions could be formed. Thus Neurath's Social and Economic Museum, funded by the City of Vienna, developed methods of visually representing social and economic statistical data in easily accessible comparative form (the 'Vienna method of pictorial statistics') and produced permanent and travelling exhibitions for Vienna and abroad on themes of topical socio-political interest. Out of this work developed the outlines of a system for an international picture language ('ISOTYPE') for use in as varied educational efforts as health-care awareness campaigns and basic language instruction; early applications of the method were tested in Viennese schools in 1930–2.[12]

Of course, some engagements of some of the representatives of the scientific world-conception were party-political. But even when it came to socialist party agitation and propaganda Neurath stressed the need to provide information over indoctrination. In a lecture to youth group leaders he declared:

> Precisely because it is also educational, our agitation differs from that of the National Socialists and other class enemies . . . One could show over and over the worker with the flag in the wind, the column marching towards the sun, but the effect of such pictures is not stimulating and often even misleads. . . . How many debates get started when informational pictures contrast the taxes raised and their use by the City of Vienna with those raised and spent by the Federal Government. . . . Our principle: 'never forget to enlighten'.[13]

How well the work of his Social and Economic Museum fitted not only into the general Viennese programme of adult education, but also responded to its local political situation is evident from this remark. On a different front, Hans Hahn, serving as the leader of the Association of Socialist University Teachers, fought the influence of the Catholic Church on questions of federal educational reform.

It is well known that Schlick, to whom the manifesto was dedicated, found objectionable the way it linked the Circle's efforts to socialism, but this only shows that he refused to view the enlightenment project in party-political terms, not that he dissociated himself from the project itself. (He objected to the closure of the Ernst Mach Society by the Dollfuss regime in 1934 on just these apolitical grounds.)[14] Still, Schlick's displeasure underscores that the Vienna Circle was not a monolithic movement either in a philosophical or a political sense. A caveat to this effect was already entered obliquely by the manifesto's authors, just before its fiery ending quoted above:

> Of course, not every single adherent of the scientific world conception will be a fighter. Some, glad of solitude, will lead a withdrawn existence on the icy slopes of logic; some may even disdain mingling with the masses and regret the 'trivialized' form that these matters inevitably take on spreading. However, their achievements too will take a place among the historic developments. We witness the spirit of the scientific world-conception penetrating in growing measure the forms of personal and public life, in education, upbringing, architecture, and the shaping of economic and social life according to rational principles.[15]

Whether their engagement extended into party politics or not, it was the general project of the democratization of culture that the members and associates of the Vienna Circle sought to promote when they participated in the programmes of the municipal adult education institutes and the lecture series organized by the Ernst Mach Society. It was this project that provided the background against which the manifesto must be read, as was stressed, again, by its authors. After the dedicatory preface they begin:

> Many assert that metaphysical and theologising thought is again on the increase today, not only in life but also in science. . . . But likewise the opposite spirit of enlighten-ment and anti-metaphysical factual research is growing stronger today, in that it is becoming conscious of its existence and its task.[16]

The 'scientific world-conception' was the name given to the general philosophical outlook that was to characterize this renewed enlightenment spirit. That the Circle's differences about the precise form of the new philosophy found their reflection in how the scientific world-conception was understood is to be expected; I will follow the authors of the manifesto.

Yet how did 'life' receive them? Their contributions were valued in the *Volksbildung* movement and the lecture series of the Ernst Mach Society and related ones were recog-nized entries in the cultural calendar of Vienna. In official academia, however, the Circle remained a minority voice and already faced stiff opposition for appointments of its members and sympathizers in the 1920s.[17] At the same time the Circle could claim a certain following for its views among 'the more progressive portion of Viennese students', as one of its own student members recalled: 'up until the collapse in 1938, a relatively large part of the Vienna intelligentsia regarded the "Vienna Circle" as their representative philosophy'.[18] Until Austro-Fascism and Nazism put an end to the experiment in democracy, 'life' did receive, to some degree at least, the scientific world-conception.

THE SCIENTIFIC WORLD-CONCEPTION: ANTI-METAPHYSICS AND CONSTRUCTIVISM

The scientific world-conception was offered to serve as a conception of knowledge that was of use in the struggle for a democratic society. One may wonder, of course, whether the scientific world-conception was, or even could be, of such concrete use precisely because of its abstention from ethics, but several questions also arise about the propriety of the quasi-political alliance forged. How intimate was this alignment of philosophy and social practice? How was the practical engagement of the members of the Vienna Circle squared with the dispassionate analysis of scientific and philosophical reason? Was there an internal logic that led from their philosophy of science to their engagement in the enlightenment project of people's education?

Let us turn first of all to the scientific world-conception itself.

The scientific world conception is characterized not so much by theses of its own, but rather by its basic attitude, its points of view and direction of research. The goal ahead is unified science. . . . From this aim follows the emphasis on collective efforts, and also the emphasis on what can be grasped intersubjectively. . . . Neatness and clarity are striven for, and dark distances and unfathomable depths rejected. In science there are no 'depths'; there is surface everywhere: all experience forms a complex network, which cannot always be surveyed and can often be grasped only in parts. . . . Here is an affinity . . . with all those who stand for earthly being and the here and now. The scientific world conception knows no unsolvable riddle. Clarification of the traditional philosophical problems leads us partly to unmask them as pseudo-problems, and partly to transform them into empirical problems and thereby subject them to the judgment of experimental science.[19]

The scientific world-conception represented an epistemic attitude, not a system of philosophical propositions. It claimed the autonomy of scientific reason. For education the most relevant theses are the denial of the possibility of metaphysics and the rejection of traditional philosophy. These points are as obvious as they are problematic.

The sense of 'metaphysics' employed is crucial. Metaphysics was understood as 'the field of alleged knowledge of the essence of things which transcends the realm of the empirically founded, inductive science. Metaphysics in this sense includes systems like those of Fichte, Schelling, Hegel, Bergson, Heidegger. But it does not include endeavours towards a synthesis and generalization of the results of the various sciences.'[20] Talk of ontological commitment thus can be accommodated, when properly understood, in the metatheoretical departments of unified science. It is the metaphysics of essence and its epistemology of intuition that the Circle attacked in the first instance; only secondarily did it respond to the metaphysical deviations of leading scientists such as Planck.[21] Similarly, philosophies of value like Rickert's, which claimed to prove the existence of objective values to which different cultures approximated to different degrees, were rejected as metaphysical.[22]

The Circle's empirical criterion of meaningfulness, by whose measure metaphysics was to be banned, has, however, resisted precise formulation.[23] Its determination to stick to theses that can at least in principle be tested appears as simple-minded trust in a non-existent remedy. Yet we must note, first of all, that it was freely admitted that sufficient criteria for eliminating 'uncritical' theories from empiricist discourse could not be given in formal terms.[24] As a rough marker of the criterion of empirical meaningfulness, Ernst Mach's dictum – 'Where neither confirmation nor refutation is possible, science is not concerned' – was to be improved upon only by insisting also on the principled inconclusiveness of each instance of confirmation or falsification.

With a merely approximate criterion such as this it was of course impossible to escape some form of meaning holism (whole theories, not single concepts became the unit of analysis), so its edge against metaphysics seems blunted. Even if we allow shadings between the absolutes of atomism and holism, a conception of local holism may prevent metaphysical abuse only at the price of accepting the limits of formal explication. But perhaps this is only to be expected. The failure to provide necessary and sufficient conditions speaks against the project of defining empirical meaningfulness in the sense of saying what it 'really' consists in. There is no need to think that this is the project the Circle was engaged in. Its criterion of meaningfulness represented not a discovery but a proposal.[25] 'Explications' did less to retrace the previously undiscovered boundaries of given concepts than to consciously reshape them. That the formal explication of the concept of empirical meaningfulness remained incomplete only points to the openness of the concept involved.

Yet can an incomplete criterion do the anti-metaphysical job? That such incompleteness was by no means fatal to the project of explication has been argued for the case of the equally basic notion of formal science (what it is to be a 'formal' system).[26] This suggests that the inability to provide necessary and sufficient conditions for 'empirical' may also not be fatal, if we do not presume to start science from epistemic scratch. As a proposal for (meta-) language use the empiricist criterion of meaningfulness requires the exercise of a situational understanding that works by paradigmatic exemplar rather than formal definition, and presupposes a certain pre-understanding. Neurath, for one, would not have been surprised to learn this at all: it was in just this spirit that in the 1940s he opposed what he took to be the formalist scholasticization of orthodox logical empiricism. But Carnap too would have conceded that his logico-linguistic frameworks were but partial reconstructions that in no way pretended to replace our natural language in its entirety.

Note that already the manifesto allowed for this anti-foundationalist approach when it delineated what remained of philosophy:

> Nevertheless the work of 'philosophic' or 'foundational' investigations remains important in accord with the scientific world-conception. For the logical clarification of scientific concepts, statements and methods liberates one from inhibiting prejudices. Logical and epistemological analysis does not wish to set barriers to scientific enquiry; on the contrary, analysis provides science with as complete a range of formal possibilities as is possible, from which to select what best fits each empirical finding (example: non-Euclidean geometries and the theory of relativity).[27]

Foundational investigations became explorations of conceptual possibilities. This means not only that metatheory was included in science as a whole, that it was part of 'unified science'

– which in Neurath's hands assumed a non-reductive and non-hierarchic, patchwork form as regards the relation of the first-order sciences to each other[28] – but also that metatheory was understood more in engineering terms than in those of geographical discovery. This approach expressed a form of metaphilosophical anti-realism or conventionalism: I shall call it 'metatheoretical constructivism'.

If what has been said so far is roughly correct, then it is not the case that the scientific world-conception was powerless to isolate the metaphysics of essences (and objective values) and reject its epistemology of intuition. Naturally it had to start from somewhere, indeed the scientific world-conception rejected the very idea of presuppositionless knowledge. It took its stand from within science. As noted, there is nothing self-contradictory about this, unless we attribute to the Vienna Circle epistemologically foundationalist ambitions. On the left wing of the Circle Neurath proposed a new image of knowledge, poignantly articulated by his celebrated simile of the boat which we have to repair at sea.[29] Neurath's rejection of metaphysics involved the radical reorientation of philosophy itself, seeing its mission not in the provision of deeper philosophical knowledge of the world, but in the proper understanding of scientific knowledge.. Anti-foundationalist, anti-reductionist and naturalist in spirit, Neurath further constrained Carnap's meta-theoretical constructivism to focus on logico-linguistic frameworks that were not only 'realizable' in principle, but also sufficiently realistic to be of relevance for actual practice and our understanding of it.

Yet what was so educational about the anti-metaphysical, in effect, metaphilosophical message of the scientific world-conception that scientific reason is autonomous from metaphysical philosophy? The message comes in two parts, a negative and a positive one. Both are fused in the Vienna Circle's intention to *liberate* from metaphysics.

> The metaphysician and the theologian believe, thereby misunderstanding themselves, that their statements say something, or that they denote states of affairs. Analysis, however, shows that these statements say nothing but merely express a certain mood and spirit. To express such feelings for life can be a significant task. But the proper medium for doing so is art, for instance lyric poetry or music. It is dangerous to choose the linguistic garb of a theory instead: a theoretical content is simulated where none exists.[30]

Liberation recommended itself for two reasons. First, metaphysics failed to provide knowledge. Second, far from providing knowledge, metaphysics was also deemed 'inadequate' to fulfil the legitimate function which, as Carnap put it, 'arises from the need to give expression to a man's attitude in life, his emotional and volitional reaction to the environment, to society, to the tasks to which he devotes himself, to the misfortunes that befall him'.[31] Metaphysics was not just illusion, but a pernicious illusion. It simulated kinds of answers that could not in principle be given (it suggested closure where there could be none) and so undermined attempts to deal rationally with these types of questions ('rationally' precisely in the sense of being determined in awareness of insufficient evidence).

True rationality required insight into the limits of reason. The main points the Circle stressed were not only that the metaphysical realm of essences was unknowable, indeed that its very existence stood in doubt, and that human cognition was deeply fallible, but that one important limitation of reason was of an entirely different sort: what we now deem 'existential' questions called not for answers of which it could be held that they were true or false in any sense comparable to questions of fact — they called for a decision. Thus Carnap: 'The "riddles of life" are not questions, but are practical situations.'[32] Indeed all in the Circle would have agreed with Waismann's 1938 remark: 'Declaring oneself for a particular morality is a very deep process — I do not know another expression to designate our feeling that the core of our personality emerges or manifests itself in this choice.'[33]

Liberation from metaphysics was recommended, as we saw, not only for theoretical but also for practical reasons. There is, of course, very little practical advice that we get from the representatives of the scientific world-conception in their professional capacity, beyond the claim that rational life required that this form of mental hygiene be observed.[34] Still, given their voluntarist view of ethics, there could be but little argument with the ultimate value-judgments, which expressed themselves in the pursuit of personal religion or metaphysics, even though Carnap and Neurath did not share these valuations and considered them dangerously exploitable. These were emanations of 'character' or 'the will', not something to be derived from incontestable premises. Nothing could be said against such personal metaphysics — once, that is, the limits between faith and knowledge were drawn.[35]

Yet there was an argument to be made against social metaphysics, that is, against metaphysical systems that seek to underpin the forms of social life. A democratic society requires the consensus of the population to keep or change its institutions. Given the plurality of value-systems that characterizes modern societies, such a consensus cannot simply be assumed or be based upon metaphysical views. It must emerge from the intelligibility of the instrumental reasoning for or against such institutions and the persuasiveness of advocacy for certain basic aims. This was perhaps the deepest message of the Viennese experiment in democracy for which the representatives of the scientific world-conception engaged themselves. The relevance of their contribution is clear. The critique of social metaphysics was not only an exercise in conceptual hygiene, but formed an intrinsic part of the project of the democratization of culture.

In its historical place anti-metaphysical criticism turned positive and the reconceptualization of knowledge assumed a constructive role. Not, of course, that the critique issued in a normative theory for anything but epistemic conduct, it is rather that their metatheoretical constructivism turned out to have a deeply practical significance.

> The Vienna Circle believes that in collaborating with the Ernst Mach Society it fulfils a demand of the day: we have to fashion intellectual tools for everyday life, for the life of the scholar but also for the daily life of all those who in some way join in working at the conscious re-shaping of life.[36]

In promoting the scientific world-conception, its representatives did not seek to provide answers where decisions are needed, but instead to provide 'intellectual tools'. They recognized that images of knowledge possess a causal efficacy not only in the life of individuals but also of society and sought to provide a better image than the one they found dominant.

426

The manifesto was correct then to assert that 'endeavours toward a new organization of economic and social relations, toward the unification of mankind, toward a reform of school and education, all show an inner link with the scientific world-conception'.[37] No derivation of 'ought' from 'is' was here implied (as we earlier feared). The 'inner link' was the joint commitment of the Vienna Circle members to the enlightenment idea, not that the scientific world-conception derived or prescribed that enlightenment commitment. Beyond that, 'attitudes towards questions of life' were regarded as 'more closely related to the scientific world-conception than it might at first glance appear from a purely theoretical point of view'[38] only because of the presumed historical fact – one which Schlick, we noted, preferred to discount – that the scientific world-conception provided what the more empiricist theoretician of Austro-Marxism, Otto Bauer, had long noted was missing: 'Marxism requires a theory of knowledge which Mach and Avenarius, Poincaré and James cannot provide.'[39] (With both its constructivist empiricism and its overall abstention from moral discourse, we may note, the scientific world-conception provided a general philosophical outlook that competed with Adler's neo-Kantianism in Red Vienna.) Besides its intrinsic enlightenment concern with intellectual autonomy there obtains only a historically contingent connection between the scientific world-conception and party-political engagement. There is no reason, for instance, to suppose that 'the enemy' could not make use of its tools. (Relatedly Neurath once remarked: 'An institution related to those of the socialist future can be used against socialism and the proletariat, if it is ruled not by the proletariat but by the bourgeoisie . . . "Planning" within the context of German fascism means partly preparation for war, partly the subjugation of the working class.')[40]

Yet how then are we to understand, in terms of the scientific world-conception itself, the Circle's engagement, not only the socialist one, but also the general one with enlightenment? Here we touch on the other of scientific reason: ethical will. Any engagement was regarded as a moral decision on the part of the agent. Concerning its socialism the left wing of the Circle would argue that it simply thought through the sociological implications of pursuing the enlightenment project in its particular historical place and time. But it would equally admit what is important for us to note as a fundamental fact about the educational, indeed moral dimension of its scientific world-conception: *Sapere aude*, for them as for Kant the motto of enlightenment, required decision. But for them, enlightenment values themselves were not derived or proven a priori, they were adopted in the course of taking an existential stance in life. The Circle's enlightenment engagement reflected personal decision, it was not dictated by facts.

As with Wittgenstein's *Tractatus*, so with the Circle's scientific world-conception: its ethical dimension was little talked about and is revealed more by its self-conscious absence from the scientific discourse. The Circle's 'other', however, was not a hidden metaphysical system, as is often suggested, but an ethical engagement that was compatible with but not prescribed by its 'non-cognitivism'. The alignment of the scientific world-conception with the project of the 'conscious re-shaping of life' was predicated on the suitability of its new image of knowledge for the pursuit of that enlightenment project. It may even be conceded that for some of its proponents it was precisely the fact that it seemed to answer to 'the demands of the day', that motivated their work on the scientific world-conception and unified science. It remains the case that the enlightenment engagement of their 'philosophy' was not predicated on having committed a naturalistic fallacy. Their engagement for *Volksbildung* was a moral one, to be sure, but the conception of knowledge they sought to contribute did not in and of itself prescribe this moral stance.

EPISTEMIC AUTONOMY AND REFLEXIVITY

The scientific world-conception abjured claims to closure, its point being the expression of an epistemic attitude, not the provision of a complete picture. It was active and pragmatic, not contemplative. By liberating us from metaphysics it sought to liberate reason. Importantly this liberation not only implied the renunciation of hopeless pretensions, it also meant the reconfiguration of the relation between theory and practice. Scientific cognition presupposed a lived context of practical reason, which it could clarify, even transform, but whose limitations it could not fully escape. Scientific reason faced a twofold limit. On the one hand, it faced a horizon that arises from its embeddedness in history, the facticity of its material situatedness, on the other hand, it faced its other, the will. Scientific reason was foundationless, an epistemic practice that had to hold itself in place. Moreover, scientific reason could not ground ethical willing, provide unconditional imperatives – all the while it presupposed its own will to rationality.

It is of course just the conscious abstention from ethics that prompts our misgivings: even granted the Circlists' good intentions, surely this silence speaks volumes about the pedagogical potential of the scientific world-conception! Here it is important first of all to note that the Circle did not mean to disparage affairs of the ethical will. Rather, the Circle believed that a proper conduct of these affairs required the strict separation of facts and fundamental values. Once this basic distinction was observed, there was no need to deny that facts can inform value-judgements, nor that values can enter scientific problem-choice. (Its 'anti-philosophy' managed to engage with the enlightenment project of Red Vienna without contradiction only because the Circle observed this strict distinction.)

The educational intent of the scientific world-conception lies in recasting our expectations of scientific reason and in recognizing the role that our will and character must play. 'Life' required both reason and will. Even to engage with the life of reason required the will to be rational (the will that the Circle's analysis of reason presupposed); to engage in the moral life it required the will to be moral (which did not exclude the use of reason, of course). Consider again the constructivism of the scientific world-conception. Its representatives admitted that it too was not presuppositionless. Having renounced the apodicity of the synthetic a priori, they insisted that all a priori determinations of the object domains, investigative techniques and representational forms of the sciences were to be viewed as conventions. These conventions stood in need of intersubjectively intelligible justification; being conventions this could only consist in displays of their 'convenience' and so required an agreed-upon standard of measure according to which they were assessed. Such agreement could not be forced, of course, but it was nevertheless basic for the adoption of any convention. The point is rarely stressed, but it is clear that the scientific world-conception appealed to the autonomy of epistemic subjects, to their will to rationality.

It is no part of this analysis that all a priori presuppositions of a given scientific practice are consciously agreed by its participants; what is claimed is that an analysis can render these presuppositions rationally intelligible: they are not merely historically given. With the a priori historicized and conventionalized, the scientific world-conception declared our reflective conceptual universe to be reconstructible from within. Of course, this was a reconstruction in principle and in parts only and one hardly brought about by merely individual efforts. Nevertheless, with the recognition of the reconstructability of conceptual frameworks came the sense of 'responsibility' that Neurath had in mind when he remarked:

> It is already a nice result that scholars, who deal with the fundamental concepts of their science, do not seek the assistance of philosophers, but consider themselves competent and even personally obliged to engage in the clarification of the concepts of their science and *to take responsibility for these themselves.*[41]

(Again, this was no appeal to Cartesian individuals but to cooperating subjects in a social practice.)

Yet does the notion of epistemic responsibility not threaten the collapse of the entire edifice built on the separation of fact and value? Is the will to be rational not also a moral will? The Viennese answer is negative: there is no need to ascribe to them the view that science and technology, even scientific reason, was inherently good, nor that taking responsibility for one's concepts was a moral act any more than thinking clearly. (Of course, given most moral stances, disregard of reason would be a violation of their spirit.) It is rather that the exercise of epistemic responsibility is part of the autonomy of epistemic subjects. Not only must they decide between truth and falsity or confirmation and disconfirmation of assertions and the usefulness and disfunctionalities of postulates and methodological principles, they also had to decide the appropriateness of the concepts they employed.

To reject the charge of collapse, representatives of the scientific world-conception would thus have pointed to an important asymmetry between science and ethics. Epistemic norms were determinable within science. Once an epistemic goal was settled upon (truth or empirical adequacy) certain procedures recommended themselves as more instrumental than others for attaining it. The abstention, by contrast, from normative ethical theory followed from recognition of the sheer incompetence of scientific reason. Social utility maxima were not unambiguously determinable, different people's intuitions of moral ideals notoriously conflicted, and the categorical imperative was either empty or hid *völkisch* metaphysics. In comparison, disagreements about whether science should aim for truth or mere empirical adequacy constituted mere divergences in the metatheory and did not challenge the basic presumption that scientific knowledge always had to answer the call for intersubjectively available evidence. To determine ethical norms was to go beyond these bounds.

So far, so unexciting. Yet note that the Circle's intersubjective meaning criterion did not only play a negative but also a positive role (it was not merely an *ad hominem* device for segregating metaphysics). The notion of intersubjectivity also provided the framework within which it was possible for science to attain its autonomy from philosophy: it opened the possibility for replacing the 'metaphysical' idea of objectivity. The objectivity of science did not consist in the provision of distortionless reflections of reality – of 'views from nowhere' – but in the possibility for intersubjective control of perspectival views and assertions. This required not only the adoption of radical fallibilism, but also that the social character of scientific knowledge is recognized. 'Clear and distinct ideas' were created in social discourse. Carnap's formal explication of 'inductive support' represents such a proposal for future language use, as does Neurath's partly sociological explication of 'protocol'. Moreover, methodology had to consider the need to come to agreement in conditions of ignorance – if only to admit that no general and determinative rules of reason could be given for certain types of cases (even though strategies for reaching choices between equally weighted alternatives could be indicated).

Traditionally the autonomy of epistemic subjects showed itself in the critical use made of the tools of reason. The task now was to reconfigure the concept of autonomy in the absence of presuppositions of Cartesian self-sufficiency. Knowledge claims were to be publicly supportable and methodological postulates justifiable as instrumental conventions: the rationality and legitimacy of scientific concepts and procedures were to be made transparent to participants in a social practice.[42] This transparency was essential to the autonomy of the scientific world-conception from philosophy. But was it immune from the influence of basic values? A non-Cartesian theory of epistemic autonomy would have to deal also with the issue of the rationality of resistance to the consensus of a scientific community. Can we really be sure that such a rationality would not be grounded, if at all, in some moral stance? The refusal to provide a theory of substantive rather than instrumental rationality, in Weber's terms, of *Wert-* not only *Zweckrationalität*, does not on its own constitute an answer.

That a non-Cartesian conception of individual epistemic autonomy was recognized as being required is shown by Neurath's remark about epistemic responsibility. For him this meant something like an acute but not vertiginous awareness of the limitations of our data and tools as well as of the embeddedness of reason in 'life' – and so also of the embeddedness of instrumental in substantive rationality. The scientific world-conception did not deny the existence of the latter, nor need it be read as denying its relevance. Thus Neurath would add that about substantive rationality we can only discourse as morally engaged individuals, not as dispassionate objective inquirers – not, that is, as scientists or philosophers, but only as partisan cultural or social critics. With Neurath epistemic autonomy advised not only modesty for our claims, but also knowing when to be dispassionate and when to be partisan. Some may wonder whether now a dilemma threatens: for does it not follow that there exists a kind of reason and knowledge different from science? The scientific world-conception denies this. From the fact that the positing of ends is not decided by scientific reason it does not follow that normative advocacy employs another type of reason. Advocacy only goes beyond scientific reason in affirming as categorical certain values and arguing for oughts from this basis. This affirmation was an existential act, its performance an act of the will. The claim that the scientific world-conception was embedded in 'life' was indeed close to one we tend to associate with pragmatists like Dewey: reason is only part of what we must consider if we want to understand reason correctly.

Reason's awareness of its limits is, of course, a reflexive awareness; autonomy requires reflexivity. For Neurath the autonomy of epistemic subjects displayed itself, in the absence of epistemic foundations and objective values, in the awareness of the twofold limitation of reason. Not only did we have to cope with insufficient evidence, but it was also not enough to think things through; we also had to act upon what we thought. That thinking right does not yet make us act right is a simple thought, but not one without pedagogical consequences: implicit is yet another exhortation to the responsibility of the individual, albeit a very formal one. Scientific reason can, however, provide helpful data for the exercise of that responsibility. One of these helpful data, Neurath would argue, concerns precisely the relation of reason, value and will. Neurath's call to epistemic responsibility is a call for reflexive awareness also along this, as it were, vertical dimension.

Relatively little attention has so far been paid to the role of reflexivity in the philosophies of the Vienna Circle.[43] Already Neurath's famous simile shows that reflexivity was an issue of concern for at least some of them. It may be added that metatheoretically, reflexivity emerges in the seeming circularity that even Carnap's conventionalist reconstructionism shared with the radical naturalism of Neurath's theory of knowledge: metatheory was not exempt from the demands for validation it imposed upon first-order theories.[44] But recognition of the need for reflexivity emerges also in the fact that the scientific world-conception left room for, as I put it, the 'other' of scientific reason, indeed presupposed its contribution to perform its enlightenment work. Here the embedding of the scientific world-conception in 'life' is clearly, and reflexively, taken account of. Recognition of reflexivity, one is led to conclude, is essential to the scientific world-conception as enlightenment thought. The autonomy of scientific discourse and the epistemic autonomy of non-Cartesian subjects cannot be attained without it.

BEYOND VILLAGE POSITIVISM

We have come a long way from village positivism. This is not to say that all our doubts have been answered. Quite apart from what our hopes for a theory of substantive rationality may be, that philosophy as concern with *Wertrationalität* is but cultural criticism may sound a bit too 'postmodern' for some.

To show how the enlightenment was understood by the proponents of the scientific world-conception we may turn to Philipp Frank. (While Carnap, Hahn and Neurath were writing the manifesto with some help from Feigl and Waismann, Frank was organizing the Prague conference at which it was to be publicly presented: Frank may thus be considered a co-conspirator.) Frank's 1917 essay in memory of Ernst Mach provides insight into the views of a discussion group that has been dubbed the 'first' Vienna Circle and included Hahn and Neurath.[45] Its members' self-understanding is revealed in how they placed themselves *vis-à-vis* Mach as an enlightenment thinker. For Frank, an 'essential characteristic' of the enlightenment was its 'protest against the misuse of merely auxiliary concepts in general philosophical proofs'. A 'tragic feature' was even discerned in the enlightenment philosophy: 'It destroys the old system of concepts, but while it is constructing a new system, it is already laying the foundation for new misuse. For there is no theory without auxiliary concepts, and every such concept is necessarily misused in the course of time.'

'Hence,' Frank concluded, 'in every period a new Enlightenment is required in order to abolish this misuse.' Mach himself had seen his role to be not to fight 'against the Enlightenment of the 18th century but rather to continue its work'.[46] In this sense, it became the task of the first Vienna Circle in turn to study and criticize Mach and what his theories had become. How in detail the development of the Circle's philosophies is to be understood from this perspective is not our concern here, but it is clear that their appreciation of the need for reflexivity is rooted in their understanding of the enlightenment task (as their later constructivism is in their early conventionalist sympathies).

Frank's reflexive understanding of the enlightenment spirit – which anticipated aspects of Horkheimer and Adorno's *Dialectic of Enlightenment* by more than two decades[47] – was, on the face of it, a very theoretical one. That he only noted in passing that 'the ideas of the Age of Enlightenment were not pleasing to the ruling powers', does not mean, however, that the socio-political dimension of the enlightenment was neglected. When Frank remarked that 'theologic[al] concepts which were formed for dealing with certain psychic experiences of human beings, were made the foundation of all science throughout the Middle Ages and even at the beginning of the modern era', he was pointing amongst other things to the critique of social metaphysics.[48] Just that application lay closest to the heart of Neurath, the only trained social scientist in the Circle.

A reflexive understanding of the task of enlightenment also finds expression in Neurath's thought at an early date, indeed at the same time as the first employment of his famous simile in 1913. 'Rationalism sees its chief triumph in the clear recognition of the limits of actual insight.'[49] Appropriately to his social scientific interest, Neurath focused on the role of reason in public policy decisions. Here a proper understanding of what reason could and could not achieve was as essential as it was for the theory of science.

> With the progress of the Enlightenment men were more and more deprived of the traditional means which were suited to making unambiguous decisions possible. Therefore one turned to insight in order to squeeze an adequate substitute out of it with all possible force . . . The pseudo-rationalists always want to act from insight and are therefore grateful to anybody who is able to suggest to them that they had acted from insight . . . The question now is what will happen if psychological knowledge becomes so widespread that most citizens see through the apparatus of suggestion. Through this psychological enlightenment, suggestion may possibly be paralysed . . . If [people] do not return to superstition, to instinct or to absolute simplicity, nothing remains but seizing an auxiliary motive where insight does not reach far enough.[50]

An auxiliary motive postulated a pragmatic criterion for action in the face of inability to decide how best to realize a primary aim or to arrive at unanimity over what the ultimate aim should be. One of Neurath's early conclusions was that, owing to the principled inability to calculate unique and definite utility maxima, no normative prescriptions could follow from social science. Auxiliary motives represented alternative tools for reaching many of the agreements that had to be found for social policy decisions. 'The traditional uniformity of behaviour has to be replaced by conscious co-operation; the readiness of a human group to co-operate consciously, depends essentially on the character of individuals.'[51] The use to which the notion of auxiliary motives was put illustrates how the critique of metaphysics engaged in reflexive enlightenment: constructively. Admittedly, much of such work proceeded on a high level of abstraction: how was social enlightenment work to proceed *in concreto*?

Some examples from Neurath's educational writings may illustrate the trajectory of his thought. His earliest views are evident in his 1903 report on the 'Volksheim Ottakring'. Run as a community centre in one of the poor sections of Vienna, it was designed to pursue less the amelioration of material want than cultural ennoblement. '[I]f one wants to elevate and sensibilize their sentiments and their intellects,' Neurath noted, 'one should not shame them by material support, but must personally affect their wills and decisions directly and lift them intellectually and morally onto a higher level.'[52] It sounds very much as if direct normative instruction was what the 22-year old student envisaged: a certain paternalism cannot be denied. Several years later, in a series in which his wife Anna Schapire published on the history of and topical issues for the women's movement (as well as on Tolstoy), Neurath argued for the introduction into general education of courses on economics and civic studies. 'The democratization of the will of the state generally lacks the appropriate democratization of the knowledge from which to act. Nowadays the vote of the individual has its effect quite independently of whether a definite aim is consciously pursued or not.'[53] Neurath's emphasis had begun to shift to the provision of information, academically disinterested in the limits the authoritarian Prussian and Austro-Hungarian *Obrigkeitsstaat* put to the exercise of democratic rights.

Only after the 1918 November revolution Neurath made a convincing case for civic responsibility. *Ex officio* as an educationalist we can see him addressing the moral dimension of 'life', but still refraining from substantive prescription.

> [W]ith one blow the revolution has made every adult inhabitant of German territory into a member of a consistently implemented democracy. This means nothing less than that every man and every woman is co-responsible for what happens [there]. The social order has become, instead of our fate, our own deed, our sin. Everybody eligible to vote influences which forces and which principles will come into play. More than ever, it is incumbent on each individual to learn about the essential characteristics of our social order and other possible orders of life.[54]

Note that once we replace 'sin' by the less emotive 'failing', the contention that learning 'about the essential characteristics of our social order and other possible orders of life' is 'incumbent on each individual' turns out to be representing less the postulation of a basic value than an analysis of the dynamics of the social and historical situation. As described, the situation features morally autonomous subjects: the existential reality of moral conflict was by no means denied. Yet Neurath's appeal to moral duty was a purely formal one: beyond the demand to confront the situation in which they found themselves, nothing was prescribed for the autonomous subjects. (These subjects did well to help themselves to all the information unified scientific reason could give, but they should not expect reason to do their willing for them.)

433

Clearly, the conception of civic responsibility invoked here fitted the project of the democratization of culture, which Red Vienna was embarking upon at this time and which Neurath joined after his release from incarceration for his activities during the Bavarian revolution. But we may also note that the admonition to epistemic responsibility, which, we saw, Neurath delivered in the 1930s, represents but a transposition of the appeal to civic responsibility, transferred from the Munich *Räterepublik* to the 'republic of scholars'. In his *Anti-Spengler*, which, having written it partly in prison, he dedicated 'to the young and the future they shape', Neurath stated in the voice of a cultural critic of his age what he saw as, in so many words, the enlightenment task that lay ahead.

> [Spengler's] book satisfies a strong contemporary yearning for a complete world view. Is it mere accident that this wish is satisfied in such an inadequate, uncritical, pretentious and disruptive manner? In the long run blame will not help, only doing better will. . . . Ever more frequently the exaggerated specialization of recent decades takes vengeance in a conscious turning away from a total world view. . . . The special sciences require a world picture, otherwise they become victims of scepticism or recklessness, which Spengler's work links into a quaint communion.[55]

Here the task for the later scientific world-conception was clearly mapped out. Later the Circle used more confrontational terms to promote its incomplete 'world-conception' against the closed 'world views', not only of traditional metaphysics but also of the 'philosophies of life' (*Lebensphilosophie*) that were gaining great momentum in the wake of the lost World War. Against these adversaries' intimations of essences and mysteries, it sought to defend a clear-headed idea of what a conception of the totality of reality could possibly be. It was the proper understanding of the place of reason in life, the proper image of knowledge, that needed to be communicated to the youth of the first-ever republics in Austria and Germany.

Yet let us be sceptical once more. Does the scientific world-conception not remain toothless by failing to engage with the normative problem of character? Does it not hold that questions of will would settle themselves once one thought clearly and had the right idea of the relation of cognition and will? The official answer, of course, is 'No.' The scientific world-conception only said that scientific reason could inform but not determine the will; it did not say that no issues remained unresolved for the will. True, in keeping with its ethos the scientific world-conception stayed silent on the matter of guiding the will. But importantly, this did not stop the engagement of its proponents, as we saw, as cultural critics. What more could scientific reason do than register the existential reality of the moral realm? Of course, in light of the tremendous role that this other, whom the scientific world-conception presupposed, plays in the overall scheme of things, it is tempting to quip that the Circle's relative silence on the matter was an instance of 'being drunk with soberness', as Frank once described the enlightenment writings of Mach.[56]

Neurath and Frank, it seems, came to have second thoughts on whether enough had been said about the embeddedness of the scientific world-conception in 'life'. But they did not abandon the distinctions upon which it was built and which, in Neurath's case, were adopted in the disputes about the propriety of value-judgements of the Social Policy Association before World War I. Also since that time Neurath commented on the phenomenon of reflexive predictions in social science. That the constructivism later avowed by the scientific world-conception had the consequence that its pursuit did not remain contemplative but turned into a dialectic of action and reflection did not escape him. In his writings from the 1940s he repeatedly turned to this matter.

'What comes from an "experiment" with a modified scientific language will be analysed by a man who is modified by this "experiment", which is more than an experiment: it performs a kind of self-education.'[57] Neurath did not only recognize the reflexive nature of the process he envisaged by noting that the experimenter is 'modified' by the experiment. He also pointed to the necessary engagement for the idea of the enlightenment, for 'self-education', which works on the scientific world-conception required. In such a self-experiment, embedded as it is in 'life', recognition of the value-dimension is unavoidable.

> [A]ltering our scientific language is cohesive with altering our social and private life. There is no extraterritoriality for sociologists, or for other scientists, and this is not always sufficiently acknowledged. Sociologists are not only outside their scientific field in arguing, deciding, and acting like other human beings; they also argue, decide, and act like other human beings within their scientific field.[58]

In his very last paper Neurath stressed the point again:

> I do not think that one can distinguish between the problems of the scientists and the problems of the man in the street. In the end, they are more interlinked than people sometimes realize. Any synthesis of our intellectual life, any orchestration of various attempts to handle life and arguments should never forget these far reaching social implications.[59]

Neurath did not retract the claim that the determination of values lay beyond the brief of scientific reason, but he stressed the fact – the potential and the danger – of its situatedness in the whole of 'our social and personal life'. Paralleling earlier remarks in the manifesto, he pointed to work done in the Unity of Science movement during the war 'which serves everybody immediately by reducing the number of prejudices'.[60] This did not mean that science be 'ethicized', as it were, for such 'emancipatory' use of science was after all protected by the recognition of value-relevance in problem choice. But neither did it have to be decided once and for all just when resistance to scientific consensus was rational and when it was not. In place of these false universalisms Neurath urged that increased attention be given to historical, sociological and educational studies of science. Unless scientific reason investigated its own situatedness in 'life', it was indeed bound to remain, not toothless, but blind in its enlightenment pursuit.

The stress on historically and metatheoretically informed science education and research into external determinants of theory choice, which characterizes Frank's later writings, points in a similar direction.[61] Whether Neurath's and Frank's understanding of the scientific world-conception answers all sceptical doubts of its pedagogical potential need not be decided here. It should be clear, however, that the representatives of the scientific world-conception were not followers of a one-dimensional scientism, unwilling and unable to confront the presuppositions of its progressivist ethos – not in the least instance because they had long taken on board the idea that the enlightenment project must become a reflexive one. Pursuit of the scientific world-conception was an open-ended experiment in self-education.[62]

NOTES

1 O. Neurath, 'Protocol statements' [1932], trans. in O. Neurath, *Philosophical Papers 1913–1946*, ed. and trans. R. S. Cohen and M. Neurath (Dordrecht, Kluwer, 1983), p. 93: trans. altered.

2 R. Carnap, H. Hahn, O. Neurath, *The Scientific World Conception: the Vienna Circle* [1929]: hereafter 'CHN'; trans. in Otto Neurath, *Empiricism and Sociology*, ed. and trans. M. Neurath and R. S. Cohen (Dordrecht, Kluwer, 1973), p. 318.

3 R. Carnap, *The Logical Structure of the World* [1928], trans. R. A. George (Berkeley, Calif., University of California Press, 1963), §183.

4 Note M. Horkheimer's ill-considered insinuation that the Vienna Circle became an unwitting helpmate of fascism: 'The latest attack on metaphysics' [1937], trans. M. J. O'Connell in M. Horkheimer, *Critical Theory* (New York, Seabury Press, 1972).

5 John Dewey, 'Unity of science as social problem', in O. Neurath *et al. Encyclopedia and Unified Science* (Chicago, University of Chicago Press, 1938), p. 32, and *Theory of Valuation* (Chicago, University of Chicago Press, 1939), p. 65.

6 Ernest Nagel in C. Lamont (ed.) *Dialogue on John Dewey* (New York, Horizon, 1959), pp. 10–13. No monograph on the entire Vienna Circle from the emerging new perspective is available in English, but *Origins of Logical Empiricism*, ed. by R. N. Giere and Alan Richardson (Minneapolis, Minn., University of Minnesota Press, 1996) contains representative papers and a rich bibliography. An argument against the epistemologically foundationalist reading of the Circle is given in T. E. Uebel, 'Anti-foundationalism and the Vienna Circle's revolution in philosophy', *British Journal for the Philosophy of Science* 47 (1996).

7 CHN, p. 316.

8 Ibid., p. 317.

9 M. Schlick, *Problems of Ethics* [1930], trans. D. Rynin (New York, Prentice-Hall, 1939); O. Neurath, 'Sociology in the framework of physicalism' [1932], trans. in Neurath, *Philosophical Papers*; R. Carnap, 'Theoretische Fragen und praktische Entscheidungen' [1934], repr. in H. Schleichert (ed.) *Logischer Empirismus – der Wiener Kreis* (Munich, Fink, 1975).

10 A detailed reconstruction of the protocol sentence debate is given in T. E. Uebel, *Overcoming Logical Positivism from Within* (Amsterdam/Atlanta, Ga., Rodopi, 1992).

11 On Red Vienna see A. Rabinbach, *The Crisis of Austrian Socialism: from Red Vienna to the Civil War (1927–34)* (Chicago, University of Chicago Press, 1983); H. Gruber, *Red Vienna: Experiment in Working-Class Culture 1919–1934* (Oxford, Oxford University Press), 1991.

12 On Neurath's educational work see R. Haller, 'On Otto Neurath' [1977], J. Dvorak, 'Otto Neurath and adult education' [1982], and F. Stadler, 'Otto Neurath: encyclopedist, school reformer and people's educator' [1989], trans. in T. E. Uebel (ed.) *Rediscovering the Forgotten Vienna Circle* (Dordrecht, Kluwer, 1991), as well as L. Fleck [1979], Part I, in N. Cartwright, J. Cat, L. Fleck, T. E. Uebel, *Otto Neurath: Philosophy between Science and Politics* (Cambridge, Cambridge University Press, 1996).

13 O. Neurath, 'Jungfrontaktion und Bildungsarbeit (Aus einem Referat für Jungfrontfunktionäre)', *Bildungsarbeit* 19 (1932), pp. 165–6.

14 See F. Stadler, 'Aspects of the social background and position of the Vienna Circle at the University of Vienna' [1979], trans. in Uebel (ed.) *Forgotten Vienna Circle*.

15 CHN, pp. 317–18.

16 Ibid., p. 301.

17 See Stadler, 'Social background and position of the Vienna Circle'.

18 G. Bergmann, 'Memories of the Vienna Circle: letter to Otto Neurath (1938)', in F. Stadler (ed.) *Scientific Philosophy: Origins and Developments* (Dordrecht, Kluwer, 1993), pp. 198–9.

19 CHN, pp. 305–6.

20 R. Carnap, 'Remarks by the author (1957)' on 'The elimination of metaphysics through logical analysis of language' [1932], trans. A. Pap, in A. J. Ayer (ed.) *Logical Positivism* (New York, Free Press, 1959), p. 80.

21 M. Schlick, 'Positivism and realism' [1932], trans. D. Rynin, in Ayer (ed.) *Logical Positivism*.

22 O. Neurath, *Empirical Sociology* [1931], partly trans. as 'Empirical sociology', in Neurath, *Empiricism and Sociology*.

23 C. G. Hempel, 'Empiricist criteria of cognitive significance: problems and changes', in *Aspects of Scientific Explanation* (New York, Free Press, 1965).

24 O. Neurath, 'Sociology', p. 89.

25 T. Ricketts, 'Carnap's principle of tolerance, empiricism and conventionalism', in P. Clark and P. Hale (eds) *Reading Putnam* (Oxford, Blackwell Publishers, 1994).

26 A. Richardson, 'The limits of tolerance: Carnap's logico-philosophical project in logical syntax of language', in *Proceedings of the Aristotelian Society*, Supplementary Volume 1994.

27 CHN, p. 316.

28 See N. Cartwright and J. Cat, Part 3, in Cartwright *et al.*, *Otto Neurath*.

29 Neurath, 'Protocol statements', p. 92; for the history of Neurath's use of the simile, see T. E. Uebel, Part 2, in Cartwright *et al.*, *Otto Neurath*.

30 CHN, p. 307.

31 Carnap, 'Elimination', pp. 79–80.

32 Carnap, *Logical Structure*, §183.

33 F. Waismann, 'Ethik und Wissenschaft' [1938], quoted in H. Rutte, 'Ethics and the problem of value in the Vienna Circle' [1986], trans. in Uebel (ed.) *Forgotten Vienna Circle*, p. 156.

34 In their private voice Schlick and Neurath were not loath to write on issues of the conduct of life, Schlick's artistic-aristocratic attitude being apolitically individualistic ('On the meaning of life' [1927], trans. P. Heath, in M. Schlick, *Philosophical Papers*, vol. 2, ed. H. L. Mulder and B. v.d. Velde-Schlick (Dordrecht, Kluwer, 1979), while Neurath's more populist stance stressed collective action (*Personal Life and Class Struggle* [1928], excerpt trans. in Neurath, *Empiricism and Sociology*.

35 Carnap, 'Theoretische Fragen'; compare also the first quotation from Neurath in my opening paragraph.

36 CHN, p. 305.

37 Ibid., pp. 304–5.

38 Ibid., p. 304.

39 O. Bauer, 'Das Weltbild des Kapitalismus', in O. Jenssen (ed.) *Der lebendige Marxismus. Festgabe zum 70. Geburtstag von Karl Kautsky* (Jena, Thüringer Verlagsanstalt, 1924), p. 464.

40 O. Neurath, 'Sozialistischer Ausweg aus der Krise (Vortragsdisposition)', *Bildungsarbeit* 20 (1933), p. 196.

41 O. Neurath, *Le developpement du Cercle de Vienne et l'avenir de l'Empiricisme logique* [1936], trans. B. Treschmitzer and H. G. Zilian as 'Die Entwicklung des Wiener Kreises und die Zukunft des Logischen Empirismus', in O. Neurath, *Gesammelte philosophische und methodologische Schriften*, ed. R. Haller and H. Rutte (Vienna, Hölder-Pichler-Tempsky, 1981), p. 699.

42 On the theme of cognitive transparency compare P. Galison, 'Aufbau/Bauhaus: logical positivism and architectural modernism', *Critical Inquiry* 16 (1990), who develops it against the background of a more foundationalist interpretation of the Circle.

43 The notable exception is D. Zolo, *Reflexive Epistemology: the Philosophical Legacy of Otto Neurath* (Dordrecht, Kluwer, 1989). The present study confirms the thesis that the issue of reflexivity plays a central role in Neurath's thought, but unlike Zolo still seeks to locate Neurath this side of the postmodernist divide.

44 Cf. T. E. Uebel, 'Normativity and convention: on the constructivist element of Neurath's naturalism', in E. Nemeth and F. Stadler (eds) *Encyclopedia and Utopia* (Dordrecht, Kluwer, 1996).

45 R. Haller, 'The first Vienna Circle' [1985], trans. in Uebel (ed.) *Forgotten Vienna Circle*; P. Frank, 'Historical introduction', in *Modern Science and its Philosophy* (Cambridge, Mass., Harvard University Press, 1949).

46 P. Frank, 'The importance for our times of Ernst Mach's philosophy of science' [1917], trans. in *Modern Science*, pp. 73, 78, 73 and 75 respectively.

47 M. Horkheimer and T. W. Adorno, *Dialectic of Enlightenment* [1947], trans. J. Cumming (New York, Herder and Herder, 1972).

48 P. Frank, 'Importance for our times', p. 74.

49 O. Neurath, 'The lost wanderers and the auxiliary motive (On the psychology of decision)' [1913], trans. in Neurath, *Philosophical Papers*, p. 8.

50 Ibid., p. 8.

51 Ibid., p. 10.

52 O. Neurath, 'Eine soziale Niederlassung (Settlement) in Wien', *Der Arbeiterfreund* 41 (1903), p. 239.

53 O. Neurath, *Die allgemeine Einführung des volkswirtschaftlichen und staatsbürgerlichen Unterrichts* (Gautsch bei Leipzig, Dietrich, 1908), p. 3.

54 O. Neurath and W. Schumann, 'Zur Einführung', *Wirtschaft und Lebensordung* 1 (1919), p. 1.

55 O. Neurath, *Anti-Spengler* [1921], excerpts trans. in Neurath, *Empiricism and Sociology*, p. 162.

56 P. Frank, 'Importance for our times', p. 72.

57 O. Neurath, 'Universal jargon and terminology' [1941], repr. in Neurath, *Philosophical Papers*, p. 216.

58 O. Neurath, *Foundations of the Social Sciences* (Chicago, University of Chicago Press, 1944), pp. 46–7.

59 O. Neurath, 'After six years', *Synthese* 5 (1946), p. 79.

60 Ibid.

61 E.g. Frank, *Modern Science* and P. Frank (ed.) *The Validation of Scientific Theories* (Boston, Mass., Beacon Press, 1956).

62 I wish to thank the editor for helpful suggestions and Josef Simpson for stylistic advice.

30

EDUCATION AND SOCIAL EPISTEMOLOGY

Alvin I. Goldman

TRUTH, TEACHING, AND EXPERTISE

I believe in truth – "absolute" truth as it is sometimes called – and I believe that a great variety of human endeavors are dedicated, quite properly and understandably, to the discovery and dissemination of truths. Two motives drive truth-seeking: simple curiosity and practical advantage. The first is illustrated by the popular fascination with dinosaurs and their extinction. People want to know why the dinosaurs became extinct although this knowledge would serve no practical end in most cases. Moreover, they want to know the truth, i.e. what really happened, not simply what is generally believed (so truth must not be equated with consensual belief). The desire for truth also can have a prudential rationale. If a child has a nasty accident on a trip and needs immediate attention, the parents want a true answer to the question, "Where is the nearest emergency room?" Believing the truth is usually (though not invariably) a helpful means to achieving practical ends, such as prompt medical attention.

The interest in believing truths is amply demonstrated by the universal linguistic practice of asking questions. The standard aim of asking a question is to earn the true answer from the interlocutor. There are exceptions to this pattern. Teachers direct questions to students even when they (the teachers) already know the answers. Survey researchers ask questions of respondents simply to learn the latter's opinions, correct or incorrect. But the normal purpose of asking a question is to learn the true answer. This is why we direct questions, wherever possible, to people we regard as authoritative or knowledgeable, i.e. people in possession of the truth. I don't ask a random person on the street whether my department has a meeting scheduled for Friday; I call the department secretary, who knows about such matters.

Interest in true belief – or "knowledge," as I shall call it, using this term in a weak sense – is not confined to individuals. Many social institutions also have an interest in knowledge. Science aims to discover new knowledge; the law seeks the truth about who violated certain statutes, or who committed a tort, so that justice may be done. Finally, the fundamental aim of education, that is, of schooling systems at all levels, is to provide students with knowledge and to develop intellectual skills that improve their knowledge-acquiring abilities. This, at any rate, is the traditional image, and I know of no good reason to abandon it. I do not claim that factual knowledge and knowledge-acquiring skills are the *sole* ends of education; but they comprise, on my view, its most pervasive and characteristic aims.

Perhaps many people would agree with my emphasis on truth for a small sector of education, e.g. mathematics and science. Who would urge the teaching of false mathematics? But what about the rest of the curriculum? Well, even history should aim at teaching truths. *Which* historical truths should be taught is a difficult matter, but I do not think we should teach historical falsehoods, nor *misleading* historical theses, where a misleading thesis is one that is itself true but invites inferences to further conclusions that are false.

Several objections can readily be anticipated here. First, some people deny the existence of objective truth altogether; or they deny that there is truth in certain subject-matters, so my principles cannot apply there. Second, it may be observed that many truths are too complicated, or require too many qualifications, to inflict on young children. Surely it is permissible to simplify even at the cost of inaccuracy. Third, it may often be preferable to let students learn truths on their own rather than have teachers (or textbooks) present those truths. Fourth, who is to decide what is true and therefore what should be taught? How should schools and teachers proceed when there are divergent opinions in the local or professional community?

Starting with the first objection, I regret that I cannot fully here address a global skepticism or nihilism about truth.[1] But such global skepticism is highly counterintuitive. Consider the simple proposition that there are oil deposits beneath a certain parcel of land. Such a proposition is either true or false, independently of whether anybody has yet drilled for oil and discovered it there. The presence or absence of oil deposits does not depend on any social processes of negotiation, "construction," or even investigation of such deposits (although human *knowledge* of the presence or absence of oil does depend on human investigation). This kind of consideration leads me to reject global critiques of objective truth based on postmodernist, social constructivist, or relativist themes.

Let me turn, then, to restricted skepticism about truth. I grant that there may be domains lacking in truth-values, and my theses would have no direct application to those domains. But notice that in any domain we may distinguish *primary* judgments from *secondary* judgments. To illustrate, a primary judgment in the aesthetics of music might be: "Beethoven's *Eroica* is greater than Mozart's 41st Symphony." A secondary judgment in this area would be: "Some music lovers *think* (or *say*) that the *Eroica* is greater than Mozart's 41st for reasons A, B, and C." Even if primary judgments in this area lack truth-values, secondary judgments clearly have them, and it is plausible to expect teachers to aim at teaching some of these true secondary judgments. A similar point might be made in ethics. Even if it is conceded that primary statements of an ethical sort lack truth-values, there are truth-valuable secondary statements that may well be worth teaching; and the true ones are to be preferred to the false. In the ethical and social policy domain, moreover, there are plenty of pertinent factual truths about consequences (or probable consequences) of certain types of policies and courses of action. Many of these are certainly worth teaching.

Moving to the second objection – the need to simplify at the cost of inaccuracy – I completely concede the point. Often it is simplifications or approximations of the truth that should be given to young children; let my proposals be modified accordingly. Turning to the third objection, it is of course sometimes preferable to let students learn things on their own rather than instruct them didactically. That is why education aims to teach skills, not just facts. But the desired skills or methods of self-learning should be truth-conducive methods: techniques or skills that facilitate the identification of truth and the rejection of error. The most basic and universal skills that preoccupy education are the three Rs, and these can best be viewed as means to knowledge acquisition. Arithmetic competence enables a child to correctly determine (or know) whether she is receiving proper credit or change in financial transactions. Reading and writing skills enhance communicative competence, promote the receipt and transmission of relevant information, and thereby advance the knowledge prospects of the learner and the wider community. Another important skill is the ability to participate constructively in discussion and debate, which also, I believe, can be rationalized in terms of collective discovery and mutual persuasion of truth.[2]

The fourth objection concerns the integrity and viability of expertise. Expertise is an important topic in social epistemology, which is the context in which I approach it.[3] Let us define an expert as someone who has true answers to questions in the domain of expertise, or who has the capacity to readily acquire true answers when questions are raised. Thus, an opera expert is someone who can correctly answer questions about opera (without consulting a reference book), and an expert on automobile engines or kidneys is someone who can correctly determine why a particular token of the type is malfunctioning and what treatment would correct the malfunction. Expertise can be understood either in a *comparative* or an *absolute* sense. Someone is comparatively expert if her question-answering power ranks high compared with others; absolutely expert if her power ranks high in absolute terms. The definition of expertise, then, is relatively unproblematic.

The tougher question about expertise is whether it can be recognized or identified. Many people *claim* to be experts, but how should a community decide whether they are? When, if ever, should a community defer to the expertise or authority of educators (or the writers of textbooks) in deciding what is true? How can people decide who is an expert unless they know the relevant truths themselves, in which case there is no ground for deference? Finally, when does a teacher have an epistemic right to regard herself as sufficiently expert to present her opinions as truths? Mathematics instructors and texts often just present "truths," or teach certain techniques (e.g. long division, or square-root derivation) without typically proving their soundness; and this goes on in many other fields as well. What makes it epistemically appropriate, if and when it is? And can it be appropriate even when members of a local or professional community disagree?

I can only touch on this topic briefly, but the main point is this. It is sometimes possible for expertise to be demonstrated to novices, and when this happens deference to expertise is defensible and it is reasonable for an expert to deploy her expertise. Expertise can be demonstrated by what I call "truth-revealing situations." Weather forecasters predict the next day's weather, and novices can check on whether they get it right when the weather is "revealed" to all. Similarly for auto mechanics and medical diagnosticians. The diagnosis and treatment of a malfunctioning engine or kidney can often be checked by seeing whether the system or organ functions properly after treatment. Success or failure of the treatment can often be detected even by a novice, and can be used to calibrate the diagnostician's expertise.

In this fashion, non-experts can assess expertise. When expertise is thereby established, it seems reasonable to defer to experts (unless they have ulterior reasons to deceive or misrepresent their knowledge, as repair persons often do). Not all domains admit of "truth-revealing" situations, and there the possibility of consensus is dim. In such cases, claims to expertise cannot be honored in quite the same way. That is when teachers should move in the direction of teaching "secondary" statements rather than their own personally accepted "primary" statements in the subject-matter. For example, we would expect a high-school teacher to teach primary truths about the formal structure of government, where expertise can be established. But on issues of normative politics, e.g. which side is right in a territorial dispute, one would expect teachers not to press their own views on the rights and wrongs of the matter ("primary" statements), but to emphasize "secondary" truths, i.e. how each party to the dispute defends its territorial claim. In other words, a teacher can explain the position or conclusion that each side endorses and what their stated reasons or premises are for this conclusion. That specified positions are endorsed by indicated individuals or groups, and that they offer specified reasons for these positions are statements that have truth-values; and obviously it is better to teach the true ones than the false ones.

VERITISTIC EPISTEMOLOGY AND MULTICULTURALISM

The brand of epistemology I am advocating may be called *veritistic* epistemology because of its heavy emphasis on truth. This epistemology might initially seem committed to a certain position in the contemporary debate over the curriculum. It might seem to side necessarily with "essentialism" – espousal of a core curriculum – as opposed to "multiculturalism."[4] Aren't I, after all, just espousing the "tyranny of Truth" (with a capital "T") which is the heart of essentialism? Not at all. This association – between veritistic epistemology and essentialism – is by no means necessary, and the appearance of such a connection must be corrected.

The spirit of essentialism is succinctly expressed in the following argument from Robert Maynard Hutchins: "Education implies teaching. Teaching implies knowledge. Knowledge is truth. The truth is everywhere the same. Hence education should be everywhere the same."[5] Now the first several premises of this argument, a few quibbles aside, strike me as true. I accept that education implies teaching, that teaching (at least in large part) is the conveying of knowledge, and that knowledge is truth (more precisely, knowledge *entails* truth). What about the fourth premise, that truth is everywhere the same? This raises some technical issues about propositions, but let us restrict discussion to propositions devoid of any indexical or demonstrative elements like "I," "you," "here," "now," etc. Then I would agree that for any specified proposition P, its truth-value is the same at all times and places. (People's *beliefs* about a proposition's truth-value, of course, may vary over time, but that does not entail that the truth itself varies over time.) Since I accept all four premises, am I committed to the conclusion, i.e. that education should be everywhere the same? No, because the conclusion does not follow from the premises. The reason is simple. There are many truths; although each of these is *true* at all times and places, it does not follow that each should be *taught* at all times and places. Ignoring our earlier qualifications about simplification and approximation, we may say that being true is a *necessary* condition for being taught but not a *sufficient* condition. That leaves open the possibility of teaching different truths at different times and places.

Hutchins's conclusion might follow from the premises if the premises are taken to imply that there is a single truth, or a single totality of truths, that should be taught everywhere. Certainly one possible reading of the fourth premise, "*The truth* is everywhere the same," is that there is a single totality of truths. But even if we grant the premise, so understood, Hutchins would need a further premise to the effect that this totality should be taught everywhere, and that is dubious in the extreme. On a more plausible interpretation of the original premises, they do imply that *only* truths should be taught. But this is compatible with the idea that the particular subset of truths to be taught may be relativized to locale, culture, and context.

Some essentialists, no doubt, maintain that the truths of morality and human nature are found in certain classical works of the European tradition, and perhaps only in those works. If you hold that position, and you hold that the truths on those topics should be taught everywhere, then you get the doctrine that a certain canon should comprise the curriculum. But this doctrine does not follow from the objectivity of truth, or from objectivity conjoined with the view that education should teach truth. These views are compatible with the idea that truths are found in works from many different traditions, so that no particular tradition should monopolize the curriculum.

Furthermore, *even* if a particular tradition contains more truths than other traditions, it may be an important truth for students to learn that there are many traditions.[6] In a community as diverse as America, for example, it may be particularly important to teach about such diversity. But the existence of diverse races, genders, cultures, and ethnicities, and the range of distinctive values and perspectives that typically accompany these diverse identities, are themselves facts or truths. So educational multiculturalism need not stand in conflict with veritistic epistemology.

I just said that it may be particularly important to teach diversity. But what makes one truth more "important" to teach than another? Importance, I think, is a function of interests, but different types of interested parties and types of interests may be relevant. Let me start with the former. Two types of parties we can identify are individual believers (or learners), on the one hand, and the social systems or institutions of which they are a part, on the other. Although the interests of students are certainly relevant to the question of what should be taught, the interests of society as a whole should also be considered (certainly in the case of primary and secondary education). The situation is analogous to that of a criminal trial. Uninterested or unconscientious jurors may not care a whit whether they get the truth about the guilt of the defendant. But the judicial system as an institution certainly does have an interest in the rendering of a true verdict. Similarly, society may have an interest in its children learning certain truths, even if the children themselves are not terribly interested in those truths. Society's interest should not be ignored, just as the judicial system's interest should not be ignored.

Turning to the definition of "interest," let me focus on the learner's interests. There are three relevant senses or types of "interest". One measure of a question's interest is whether the learner finds it *interesting*, i.e. has an aroused curiosity or concern about the question's answer. Such concern can arise from intrinsic fascination or from recognition of the potential practical value of knowing a correct answer. A second measure of interest is dispositional rather than occurrent. Many questions *would* be interesting to a person if he or she only considered them. A third sense is more broadly dispositional: what would interest the learner *if* she knew certain things she does not currently know. Certain types of knowledge might be objectively in a student's interest, however unappreciative the student may be of this at the moment.

Returning to multiculturalism, an argument for it might be based on several of the foregoing factors. First, it may be in society's interest for students to have knowledge of the diversity of their world. Second, such knowledge may be in the students' interest (in the third sense of "interest"), whether they realize it now or not. Third, tailoring or adjusting curricula to the cultures of different student bodies may well be warranted by the obvious fact that material from one's own culture (or gender, or ethnicity, etc.) is more likely to be interesting (in the first sense of "interest"). Better learning takes place when there is active interest, and good learning of one subject often has beneficial consequences for other learning. Thus, even a veritistic approach to education offers many possible rationales for multiculturalism.

SOCIAL EPISTEMOLOGY, PEDAGOGY, AND ARGUMENTATION

I have characterized my form of epistemology as "veritistic" epistemology, but the title of my paper makes reference to *social* epistemology, and I have not fully explained what that is. I think of individual and social epistemology as two sectors of the subject. Individual epistemology studies intellectual activities of single cognitive agents in abstraction from others, to see how modes of belief formation promote or impede knowledge acquisition. Social epistemology studies the social or interactive practices of multiple agents, to see how their interactions encourage or obstruct knowledge acquisition. Two categories of social practices may be highlighted here. First, there are practices of speech, in which a speaker tries to inform or persuade an audience, often supporting his claims with reasons or argumentation. A second category of social practices are the inferential practices of hearers, who try to decide how much to trust what speakers say, assessing their credibility on the topic in question and their competence compared with other speakers and possible knowledge sources. Educational theory is obviously concerned with an appraisal of activities of both sorts. Which speech practices should be expected of teachers, and which inferential and learning practices of students ought to be expected or encouraged?

A number of recent writers on the philosophy of education have stressed the role of *reasons* in teaching, including Israel Scheffler, Harvey Siegel, and Kenneth Strike. Here is a representative passage by Scheffler, quoted approvingly by Siegel:

To teach . . . is at some points at least to submit oneself to the understanding and independent judgment of the pupil, to his demand for reasons, to his sense of what constitutes an adequate explanation. To teach someone that such and such is the case is not merely to try to get him to believe it: deception, for example, is not a method or mode of teaching. Teaching involves further that, if we try to get the student to believe that such and such is the case, we try also to get him to believe it for reasons that, within the limits of his capacity to grasp, are *our* reasons.[7]

Siegel endorses this idea and expands upon it in terms of an ideal of critical thinking.[8] He writes, for example:

> We want to get students to be able to think critically, and that means, in part, getting them to understand what the rules of assessment and criteria of evaluation of claims are. We want our students to learn, for example, the evidential criteria underlying our judgments that some piece of evidence supports claim X, but that another piece does not support claim Y.[9]

I am in broad sympathy with the position of Scheffler and Siegel, but I would like to base it on a deeper foundation, and also take some (limited) exception to their theses.

Reasons-giving, I suggest, should be viewed as argumentation. To give reasons for believing a certain proposition is to treat that proposition as a conclusion of an argument of which the reasons are premises. Now formal logic studies the deductive or inductive relations among propositions or sentences abstractly considered. But formal logic does not exhaust the subject of argumentation, where argumentation is construed as a complex speech act in which a speaker defends a thesis to an audience by appeal to reasons or premises.[10] In a previous paper, I have claimed that there are tacitly accepted rules governing the practice of argumentation, rules that go beyond those of formal logic or the theory of evidential relations.[11] For example, I suggest the following rules of good argumentation:

1 A speaker should assert a conclusion only if she believes it.
2 A speaker should assert a premise only if she believes it.
3 A speaker should assert a premise only if she is justified in believing it; and
4 A speaker should affirm a conclusion on the basis of stated premises only if (a) those premises strongly support the conclusion, (b) she believes that they strongly support it, and (c) she is justified in believing that they strongly support it.[12]

Now the theory of reasons and critical thinking advanced by Scheffler and Siegel makes little reference to the aims of true belief and error avoidance. But I suggest that the rationale for the rules of good argumentation is that they promote (or are thought to promote) these veritistic goals. For example, the first two rules instruct a speaker not to assert things that are false by her lights, because what is false by her lights may well *be* false; and assertion of such utterances is apt to induce false beliefs in the audience. The justification requirement in rules (3) and (4c) may be rationalized in similar terms. In particular, on a *reliabilist* approach to epistemic justification of the sort I have defended, justified beliefs are ones produced by belief-forming processes with high truth-ratios.[13] So justified beliefs are likely to be true; and confining oneself to premises and support relations that one is justified in believing will conduce to the assertion of true conclusions and hence to the production of true beliefs on the part of hearers who accept those conclusions. The aim of reasons-giving in the sense of proper argumentation, then, has its foundation in the aim of producing true belief and error avoidance. To the extent that teachers comply with the principles of good argumentation they can also be expected to serve the educational goal of advancing their students' knowledge. So reasons-giving, as thus far considered, is not a *distinct* goal from truth, but a means to that end. There is also a special reason for teachers to display the qualities of good argumentation, namely, that teachers are models and exemplars of speaking and thinking.[14] By displaying good argumentative practice under the rules I have sketched, teachers show what counts as good evidence and good argumentative speech, and through this exposure students may come to internalize the criteria of good evidence and the skills of good (internal) inference and good (public) argumentation. The latter are among the truth-promoting skills that an educational system should hope to instill in students.

Until now the rules of good argumentation we have considered pertain only to the speaker and her state of mind. Shouldn't there also be rules that bring the audience into the picture? Shouldn't the content of a good argument be sensitive to the intended audience, and isn't this particularly relevant to teachers as arguers or reasons givers? This point is at least partly appreciated by Kenneth Strike, who writes:

> Propositions that are objective evidence for some claim must be subjectively seen as evidence by the student. . . . [A] proposition or a phenomenon is only evidence for a claim in relation to a set of concepts that interpret it. . . . The suggestion that evidence is relative to the student's current concepts indicates a need on the part of the teacher to know what the student's current concepts are.[15]

I would say that a proposition is evidentially relevant for a hearer not only in relation to the hearer's *concepts* (as Strike says) but also in relation to the hearer's prior *beliefs* and *capacities for appreciating (deductive and inductive) support relations*. I would formulate this in terms of an additional rule of good argumentation:

5 A speaker addressing a particular audience should restrict her premises to statements that the audience is (or would be) justified in believing, and should restrict herself to a support relationship between premises and conclusion that the audience is capable of recognizing or appreciating.[16]

Although this rule applies to all speakers and audiences, we are interested in its application to teachers and students. The rule implies that a teacher must always take into account what students already believe or don't believe, since this determines whether the students would be justified in believing certain possible premises. In other words, the permissibility of using certain statements as premises depends on the students' prior informational states. As rule (5) implies, a good pedagogue should also take into account what inferential relations the students are capable of appreciating. It isn't enough that the support relation is in fact strong; the audience, in our case the students, should be capable of appreciating the strength of the relation.

AUTONOMY, TRUST, AND TESTIMONY-BASED BELIEF

An unrestricted form of the "reasons" thesis says that everything a teacher asserts must be backed up by reasons. But that is obviously too strong; a speaker's reasons must come to an end somewhere, namely, wherever her assertions are otherwise undefended premises. Rule (5), however, says that the premises of a good specimen of argumentation must be statements that the audience is, or would be, justified in believing. If this is right, justification for believing undefended premises must have a different source, not the current argument of the speaker. One possibility is that the hearer has prior independent information that justifies him in accepting the speaker's premises. But isn't there another possibility? Can't a hearer be justified in believing what a speaker asserts *simply because she asserts it?* Here we should refocus our discussion away from speech practices of speakers to belief practices of hearers, but the issue also bears on speech practices and educational practices generally, because it raises the issue of what students should be expected or encouraged to believe on the basis of teachers' assertions.

Many writers on education stress the need to respect the student's *autonomy*. Students, like all people, have a prima facie right and responsibility to be self-governing, and in the epistemic sphere this seems to mean that they have the right and responsibility to make belief decisions for themselves. Now in a sense this is trivial. There is clearly a sense in which everyone *necessarily* makes their own belief decisions. How can one person literally make a belief decision for another? What is presumably meant by a thesis of autonomy, then, has something to do with the rejection of trust. Strong autonomy would say that nobody should ever trust another in the sense of accepting what they say *simply because they say so*. If a hearer is justified in believing P because some speaker asserts P, it must be because the hearer has reasons to trust the speaker. Such trust has to be earned; it cannot come automatically. So teachers are not entitled to expect students to accept what they say simply because they say it.

This thesis has a nice liberal-sounding air to it; and it *may* be right. But recent discussions in the epistemology of testimony – a branch of social epistemology, as I would categorize it – create much room for doubt. Let us briefly review three historical positions on the epistemology of testimony, those of Locke, Hume, and Reid. Locke took the strictest position on intellectual self-reliance, claiming that we should not trust the faculties of others. He expressed doubts about granting even derivative authority to the opinions of others, that is, authority based on prior determination of the speaker's reliability.[17] Unlike Locke, Hume emphasized the usefulness of derivative authority. He appreciated the extent to which we rely on the opinions of others, but also insisted that we should rely on these opinions only to the degree that we have observational, non-testimonial reasons for thinking that they are reliable. Thomas Reid took a rather different position. He held that the testimony of others, or at least their sincere testimony, is prima facie credible, even if we do not have an independent check on the testifier's reliability. Reid thought that if our natural attitudes of trust, both in ourselves and in others, were not reasonable, the inevitable result would be skepticism. He therefore placed testimonial justification on an equal footing with perception and memory as a "first principle." This first principle, Reid held, is founded in certain innate dispositions: veracity, which disposes us to tell the truth, and credulity, which disposes us to believe what is said. For Reid, then, the child's default tendency to believe what he or she is told is epistemically in order, not something to be purged by an acid bath of autonomy.[18]

A Reidian position has been endorsed by a number of recent writers on testimony, especially Tyler Burge, Richard Foley, and Alvin Plantinga.[19] I find Foley's formulation of this position particularly congenial. Foley distinguishes *epistemic egoism* and *non-egoism*. The epistemic egoist grants no fundamental authority to others, just as the ethical egoist grants no fundamental value to the happiness of others. Epistemic egoists can grant derivative authority to others, but only on the basis of having personally established their reliability. Epistemic non-egoists, by analogy with ethical altruists, are prepared to grant others fundamental intellectual authority. In ethical theory, it has been debated whether egoism is a consistent position, the negative side holding that it is inconsistent to assign value to one's own happiness but not to other people's happiness, despite their similarity to oneself. In a similar spirit, Foley argues that if I grant fundamental intellectual authority to myself, I must in consistency grant it to others, because it is reasonable for me to think that their intellectual faculties and environment are broadly similar to my own. Foley goes on to say that when my own opinions conflict with those of a testifier, the prima facie authority of his testimony may be defeated or overridden by my opinions (especially when I take myself to have expertise on the subject in question). Thus, it isn't *always* appropriate to place final trust in other people's say-so. Nonetheless, as a default position, trust in others is warranted even when one has no independent grounds for certifying their reliability.

Several other recent writers have pressed the impossibility of verifying the reliability of testimony by non-testimonial means. C. A. J. Coady argues that it is practically impossible for an individual to personally check on more than a tiny percentage of testimonial reports, so the basis for an induction is too slim to provide much justification.[20] John Hardwig has pointed out that trust is an essential part of science, where collaboration is often required among multiple scientists and no specialist knows enough about the other specialities.[21] To take a recent example reported in *Science*, mathematical group theory has an Enormous Theorem (as it is affectionately called), describing the taxonomy of simple groups, the proof of which runs an estimated 15,000 pages spread over upwards of a thousand separate papers written by hundreds of researchers. The proof of the Enormous Theorem has so many pieces that even the experts who produced it rely on one another for assurance that the pieces fit together.[22] If even expert mathematicians rely on trust, why shouldn't students, especially young students, be epistemically permitted to exercise trust in their teachers?

Can the practice of trust be rationalized on veritistic grounds? It might be. If Reid is right that people have innate dispositions toward veracity and credulity, and if they are sufficiently competent, then trust may be a truth-conducive practice. For young children to decline to trust their elders would consign them to massive ignorance. The situation may be compared to language learning. Cognitive studies of language in the Chomskyan tradition indicate that young children have innate tendencies to lean toward certain hypotheses about the language corpora they encounter. This may be a bias, if you wish, but it is a bias that enables them to learn correctly the grammars of languages they actually encounter. Innate credulity might have similar properties.

Of course, as one grows older, one can do better than exercise unqualified credulity. (And indeed it seems plausible that if there is a credulity "module" at all, it ossifies as one leaves childhood, just as the language learning module becomes dysfunctional in adolescence.) So I do not mean to downplay the value of critical thinking. On the other hand, radical autonomism may well go too far, epistemically speaking, in disparaging the propriety of trust. We should not erect an epistemic standard for education that is excessively high. This is one of many issues in which educational theory and social epistemology have overlapping interests.[23]

NOTES

1 I present my views on this subject in ch. 2 of *Knowledge in a Social World* (forthcoming, Oxford University Press). A valuable treatment of truth from a realist perspective is William Alston, *A Realist Conception of Truth* (Ithaca, NY, Cornell University Press, 1996).

2 Again, my picture of intellectual discussion and debate diverges sharply from that of social constructivists, who view these processes as "negotiating", i.e. *creating*, the truth. I dispute the suggestion that truth, in general, is created by discussion or debate. No doubt, some discussions enact new social policies, and thereby create new policy facts. But intellectual (as opposed to practical) discussion is generally aimed at forming beliefs about antecedently existing truths or facts, not at creating new truths or facts.

3 I discuss it in similar terms in "Epistemic paternalism: communication control in law and society," *Journal of Philosophy* 88 (1991), pp. 113–31, sect. viii.

4 The label "essentialism" is used by Amy Gutmann in her editorial introduction to Charles Taylor, Amy Gutmann, Steven Rockefeller, Michael Walzer, and Susan Wolf, *Multiculturalism and the "Politics of Recognition"* (Princeton, NJ, Princeton University Press, 1992), p. 13.

5 Robert Maynard Hutchins, *The Higher Learning in America* (New Haven, Conn., Yale University Press, 1936), p. 66.

6 This point is emphasized, for example, by Susan Wolf in her comment on the essay by Charles Taylor, in *Multiculturalism and "The Politics of Recognition"*.

7 Israel Scheffler, *The Language of Education* (Springfield, Ill., Charles Thomas, 1960), p. 57.

8 Harvey Siegel, *Educating Reason: Rationality, Critical Thinking, and Education* (New York, Routledge, 1988).

9 Siegel, *Educating Reason*, pp. 44–5.

10 This approach traces back to Aristotle's *Rhetoric*.

11 Alvin I. Goldman, "Argumentation and social epistemology," *Journal of Philosophy* 91 (1994), pp. 27–49.

12 Goldman, "Argumentation and social epistemology," p. 34.

13 See my *Epistemology and Cognition* (Cambridge, Mass., Harvard University Press, 1986), chs 4–5, and *Liaisons: Philosophy Meets the Cognitive and Social Sciences* (Cambridge, Mass., MIT Press, 1992), esp. chs 6, 7, 9.

14 Compare Kenneth Strike, *Liberty and Learning* (New York, St Martins Press, 1982), partly reprinted in Peter Markie (ed.) *A Professor's Duties* (Lanham, Md., Rowman and Littlefield, 1994), p. 106.

15 Strike, *Liberty and Learning*, reprinted in Markie (ed.) *Professor's Duties*, p. 106.

16 This rule is suggested in my "Argumentation and interpersonal justification," in Frans H. van Eemeren, Rob Grootendorst, J. Anthony Blair, and Charles A. Willard (eds) *Perspectives and*

Approaches: Proceedings of the Third International ISSA Conference on Argumentation, vol. 1 (Amsterdam, 1995). It was partly inspired by Richard Feldman's person-relative analysis of good argumentation, in "Good arguments," in Frederick F. Schmitt (ed.) *Socializing Epistemology: The Social Dimensions of Knowledge* (Lanham, Md., Rowman and Littlefield, 1994).

17 "For, I think, we may as rationally hope to see with other Mens Eyes, as to know by other Mens Understandings. So much as we our selves consider and comprehend of Truth and Reason, so much we possess of real and true Knowledge. The floating of other Mens Opinions in our brains makes us not one jot the more knowing, though they happen to be true. What in them was science, is in us but Opiniatretry . . . . Such borrowed Wealth, like Fairy-money, though it were Gold in the hand from he received it, will be but Leaves and Dust when it comes to use" (*An Essay Concerning Human Understanding*, 2 vols, ed. A. C. Fraser (New York, Dover, 1959), Bk I, ch. iii, para. 23).

18 This is my formulation, not Reid's. Reid's discussion may be found in Thomas Reid, *Inquiry into the Human Mind*, ed. Timothy Duggan (Chicago, University of Chicago Press, 1970), ch. 6.

19 Tyler Burge, "Content preservation," *Philosophical Review* 102 (1993), pp. 457–88; Richard Foley, "Egoism in epistemology," in Schmitt (ed.) *Socializing Epistemology*; and Alvin Plantinga, *Warrant and Proper Function* (New York, Oxford University Press, 1993), ch. 4. For useful discussion, also see C. A. J. Coady, *Testimony: a Philosophical Study* (Oxford, Oxford University Press, 1992).

20 Coady, *Testimony*, ch. 4.

21 John Hardwig, "Epistemic dependence," *Journal of Philosophy* 82 (1985), pp. 335–49.

22 Barry Cipra, "At math meetings, Enormous Theorem eclipses Fermat," *Science* 275 (1995), pp. 794–5.

23 I wish to thank Harvey Siegel for the invitation to present this essay to the Philosophy of Education Society in March 1995, and for helpful bibliographical suggestions. Thanks also to my commentator, D. C. Phillips, for valuable comments, and to several people, especially Patrick Suppes and Sophie Haratounian, who raised particularly pertinent questions during the discussion period.

31

TRADITIONAL SHI'ITE EDUCATION IN QOM

Roy P. Mottahedeh

Before describing traditional education in Qom it is important to remember the likely path of education and socialization of the students who subsequently studied there. In traditional Iranian households the upbringing of a young Muslim boy rests firmly with his mother until about the age of six, when he starts to go to the public bath with his father instead of his mother. (Among the Shi'ites circumcision, often performed at birth, can be performed even as late as the sixth year.) At about the same age as a Muslim boy begins to accompany his father to the public bath he also begins to sit with his father and other male relations when male visitors are received at home. And, in Iranian society before the spread of universal primary education after the Second World War, many children also entered Qur'an schools in their sixth year. Although ties with mothers remained strong, the sudden introduction of Muslim boys into the world of men during their sixth year may have formed a model for the sense of sudden mastery of different levels of knowledge which characterizes much of the traditional Shi'ite system of education.

In the case of the older generation of students at Qom, such as Ayatollah Khomeini, this sense of abrupt change would be reinforced by their experience at Qur'an schools. (Such schools virtually ceased to exist in Iran after the Second World War, unlike other Islamic countries such as Morocco where they continue to exist in great numbers even today.) In a Qur'an school this sacred text was taught word by word in the original Arabic with little more than word-by-word glosses in Persian and not much grammatical explanation, even though Arabic grammar is far from easy and very different from Persian. Students who have gone through this system have described to me their initial sense of being completely at sea, and then their experience of a sudden leap in understanding. Incidentally, a fair number of the teachers at Qur'an schools for both boys and girls were women, and in village and tribal settings, boys and girls might be taught together.

Education at one of the seminaries or colleges (in Arabic and Persian *madrasas*) at Qom begins at about twelve to fourteen years of age, roughly the age of puberty, an association not without significance. There are a few separate seminaries for women, but there the students are taught by women, and female students can only listen to male teachers behind a curtain or similar barrier. Although the archetypal student in Qom will be represented as masculine throughout the rest of this essay, many of the statements about men also apply to women in their separate but parallel educational track. Qom is one of the two most prestigious centers of Twelver Shi'ite education, the other being Najaf in Iraq. Therefore students trained at less prestigious centers consider a period of study at Qom and/or Najaf essential to their accreditation in the higher stages of their education, and so new students of all ages arrive at Qom every year.

The first level of education is called "preliminaries" (*muqaddamāt*).[1] Grammar, rhetoric, and logic are the three subjects studied. These are, of course, identical with the trivium, the first stage of education in late antiquity and the European Middle Ages. Eton, in fact, was called a "trivial" school up into the eighteenth century. A connection between the seven "liberal arts" in the medieval Western tradition and the present system practiced at Qom is hard to establish but there is a basic similarity between the two systems. Both systems consider it appropriate that students be given fairly uniform training in the three basic "arts" or "sciences," because these subjects, which offer basic methods of textual analysis, necessarily precede exposure to more serious textbooks.

The texts for this first level of education are gathered in a single volume called *Jāmi' al-Muqaddamāt*, and the edition used is an offprint of a very old lithographic edition, and is therefore handwritten. Hence the very appearance of this volume suggests its continuity with the training of teachers for many generations past. The explanations of the basic texts that are printed between the handwritten lines and in the margins emphasize the fact that the transmission of the text has always required teachers.

In the pre-modern Middle Eastern educational system, a pupil usually needed the written permission of a teacher before he in turn could teach the book to others. While this system is no longer as prevalent as it once was, there still remains among students and teachers at Qom a conviction that a great deal of knowledge is passed "from chest to chest," that is, passed in the explanation and commentary offered by the teacher during the reading of the book.[2] Therefore, a book not studied with a master is not likely to have been properly assimilated by a student. For non-Arabic speaking students (the overwhelming majority in Qom), this need for a teacher is reinforced at the first level because all but two of the texts – the exceptions are a text in logic and a short Persian grammar of Arabic – are written in Arabic.

Already at the first level one encounters some of the pervasive features of the school texts used at all levels in traditional Shi'ite education. In Aristotelian logic (as modified by later thinkers) mutually exclusive statements are either contraries, such as "This man is blue-eyed" and "This man is brown-eyed," which are exclusive but do not exhaust all the possibilities of eye color; or contradictories, such as "Socrates existed" or "Socrates did not exist," which do exhaust all possibilities. Even the presentation of the morphology of the Arabic verb is given in schemata that show this basic understanding of the way an argument is conducted. The student therefore learns to construct solutions to problems into what we would call "decision trees." In cases where there are many contraries the students would necessarily have to memorize these contraries in order to master the subject. Consonant with this vision of knowledge as organized into decision trees is the view that items of knowledge are divided into "roots" (*uṣūl*) and "branches" (*furū'*). This distinction is already applied in the study of grammar; it is frequently repeated, especially in the later study of law and theology.

It is interesting to note that, in contrast with many Sunni systems of education, the Qur'an is not taught as such in the required curriculum (although there are classes in which the teacher offers a commentary on the Qur'an), nor is memorization of the Qur'an a formal prerequisite for entry into the Shi'ite system of education, as it once was in the most celebrated Sunni center of traditional education, the Azhar in Cairo. In fact, the Shi'ite system does not consciously regard itself as mnemonic, in contrast to most Sunni systems, although most serious Shi'ite students do memorize the Qur'an; and often, because of the slow and thorough way in which they proceed through their textbooks, students retain all or parts of some of these texts for life. Since misquotation of the Qur'an or any basic text is tantamount to losing an argument, memorization is very often a necessity, even if it is not overtly valued.

Talent in disputation or "dialectic" (*jadal*) is the most respected achievement of students, and is the key to understanding classroom techniques, and, indeed, an important aspect of the intellectual approach that traditional Shi'ite education fosters in its pupils. The study of rhetoric and logic are seen as contributing to dialectic, although their primary importance is to train students to reason properly about the derivation of substantive law, or "the branches" (*furū'*) of law from its "roots" (*uṣūl*). Students are encouraged to dispute points whether made in the textbook, or by other students, or even by the teacher himself. Here the student learns that by analyzing the text into contraries and contradictories he can demonstrate that certain positions can be refuted by showing that an opponent's argument leads to an infinite regress or a vicious circle. Of course, more mundane items of information also count in such disputations.

To prepare himself for class a student chooses a study partner called a "fellow discussant" (*ham-mobahese*) with whom he practices disputing the meaning of the text. The student also reads commentaries, some of which are written in a style reminiscent of disputation, that is, the commentary offers the original text with the words: "He says," and then adds after the quotation from the original: "But I say," followed by the remarks of the commentator. After classes the best student may hold a review session in which he reads his notes on the teacher's remarks; and, for more advanced textbooks or the highest stage of learning, which involves disputations outside the texts, these lecture notes or "reports" (*taqrīrāt*) are published with the teacher's permission, although with the name of this most favored student listed as the author on the title page.

The image of education as disputation is so powerful that in theory when a student wins a disputation with the teacher, the teacher should cede his place to another teacher. While this seldom happens, and while there are limits beyond which challenges to the teacher might amount to unacceptable behavior and/or an unacceptable denial of fundamental precepts of Islam, teachers are likely to teach only those texts over which they feel they have complete mastery. This self-selection more or less decides what level teachers achieve in the system. And, since students can shop around and find which teacher teaches the set textbooks in a way most congenial to him, there is a natural selection that "retires" unpopular teachers to provincial seminaries or other tasks in the Shi'ite religious establishment.

The middle level of education is called merely "texts" or, more literally, "surfaces" (*suṭūḥ*) of the texts, although the same analytical and dialectical approach employed in the first level is applied even more rigorously on this level, and the students are expected to go well below the surface. The textbooks for this level are on theology, law and – above all – jurisprudence, or as it is called in Arabic, "the roots of juridical understanding" (*uṣūl al-fiqh*). Whereas the colleges of Najaf claim superiority in understanding the Holy Law itself, the colleges of Qom claim superiority in understanding the more theoretical discipline of jurisprudence. At this stage the homogenization of the various branches of Islamic learning becomes yet clearer to the student because the techniques of the various disciplines are carried more fully across disciplinary lines.

A fairly homogeneous vocabulary is used in the different branches of learning, in part because a substantial number of the texts were written in the twelfth to the fifteenth centuries, a period in which Islamic learning was homogenized by great teachers such as Sa'd ad-Din Taftazani (d. 1389) in a newly established form of Islamic institution, the endowed school or *madrasa*. (The Shi'ite schools of Qom are, as we have said earlier, called *madrasas*.) For example, the word *hukm*, from an Arabic verb which means "to decide," is used for the grammatical governance of one word over another, for a general precept, for an actual law, for a sentence given in court, for jurisdiction, for legal provision, etc. The repeated discovery of a *hukm* or "ruling" in a variety of disciplines, as well as the repeated occurrence of such a word in the disciplines, suggests to the student that knowledge is governed by certain universal principles, an idea explicitly espoused by Shi'ite theology.

The third and highest level of education, called "outside the texts" (*khārij as-suṭūḥ*), is the level of pure disputation in which students exhibit all the information and dialectical skills acquired previously. A master teacher announces a subject of study and, usually without any books or notes, will cite key passages and contested areas in well-known works on this subject, which he introduces by declaring, "It has been said . . . " Then he will introduce his own reflections on the subject by adding, "But I say . . . " after which the student can respond, "But it can be said . . . " At this final level it becomes clear who has the capacity to become a *mujtahid*, a doctor of the law authorized by some previous doctor of the law to issue an authoritative opinion on Islamic law. Nowadays it is customary for a student who has shown skill at several classes at the third level to write a treatise on some area of the law before being accepted as *mujtahid*. To receive recognition from another *mujtahid* has always been sufficient to make someone a *mujtahid*, but such recognition is given exceedingly sparingly; there are only about two hundred *mujtahids* in the world.

Certain subjects considered slightly suspect according to the most orthodox scholars, yet highly esteemed by a great number of students and teachers, are taught in circles outside the *madrasa*. One such subject is philosophy, rejected as a subject by almost all Sunni *madrasas* but often (though not uniformly) accepted in Shi'ite circles, in part because Shi'ites, in contrast with many Sunnis, consider that *'aql*, "reason," is one of the sources of the law. Philosophical methods have influenced jurisprudence, the queen of the sciences in this system of education, and vice versa; so philosophy can be important to a student's understanding of advanced texts as well as to his ability to produce new texts himself. It should be noted, however, that all philosophy taught is of the school of Avicenna, as modified by major Shi'ite thinkers such as Mulla Sadra, who died in 1640.

The other highly important subject studied outside the *madrasas* is *'irfān*, or gnostic mysticism, which is often associated with philosophy insofar as it draws on a strong tradition of neo-Platonism in Islamic thought. This subject is taught privately with only teacher and pupil present, and involves the assignment and practice of mystical exercises meant to open the doors of perceptions and to purify the inner self. These private sessions establish a strong bond between teacher and pupil, and the world of the *mullahs* in Qom is honeycombed with ties created by mystical training. Such training reinforces the paradigm of learning as a long struggle with sudden leaps of understanding. It also creates a great self-confidence in those who feel that they have made this kind of "leap" in mystical development. As the ability to project self-confidence and to answer objections quickly and confidently, is a sign of mastery in the world of the *madrasa*, mysticism, like philosophy, can bring an added strength to its devotees in their careers as mullahs. Ayatollah Khomeini, incidentally, was perceived to be a master of gnostic mysticism, and was a good example of the kind of extraordinary self-confidence it can produce.

Economic resources, traditional status (as, for example, that enjoyed by sons of prominent *mujtahids* and/or descendants of the Prophet Muhammad), patronage, provincial loyalties, and the like, prevent this, like every other, educational system from being the pure meritocracy it imagines itself to be. Nevertheless, one of the significant aspects of the system is that it offers a clever boy as good a chance of advancement as the secular systems of education do.

This meritocracy is very much at work in the efforts of the *mullahs* in Qom to reach out for new pupils through networks in their province of origin. At the provincial levels the *mullahs* of the "small" community, the neighborhood and the village *mullah*, will actively recruit local young men with a serious interest in religion. Once these young recruits have arrived in Qom, the teacher from that province will often assume the responsibility for seeing to it that they receive some kind of very minimal stipend. If they remain in the system for a while most of them will return to their province to become *mullahs* and will maintain a connection with successful teachers in Qom from their province. They will also direct contributions to these teachers, who will be able to distribute further basic stipends. Such provincial ties based both on economic redistribution and differences in provincial culture still strongly felt in Iran, are shown in, for example, the continuing loyalty of the Isfahan area to Ayatollah Montazeri (from Najafabad, a town in that area) in spite of the coolness of the central government toward him.

Another characteristic of traditional education at Qom, as in so many systems of education, notably the English public school, is that it functions as a puberty rite, in an entirely male environment in which there is a sense of ordeal and a great sense of accomplishment for those who survive the ordeal. *Madrasa* students feel that ordinary people, lacking the dedication to pass sleepless nights in study, would not have achieved what these *madrasa* students have achieved. A contemporary *mullah*, Yusuf Ghulami, has given us a portrait of his student years which conforms closely to the accounts of other former students. On first seeing the rooms or *hujras* which line the upper storeys of the residential colleges – and the great majority of the students are boarders – he says: "My head began to hurt from looking at the rooms of this prison . . . Rooms two, three or four square meters in which two, three, and four people lived! [Nothing was to be seen in the students' rooms except] a mat, damp and colorless walls, a handful of books on one side, a few bowls and grains and an oil lamp on another, in the corner a bed and blanket." Their food is similarly modest, a typical dinner being bread, yoghurt, cucumber, salt, onion, and, occasionally, meatless meat soup. While some students were more privileged, most, even from well-to-do families, were made to live in such conditions as an essential part of their training. Such an ordeal must have made fellow-sufferers close to each other, and given them a heightened sense of their "heroism" and their "distinctiveness."[3]

A third characteristic of this education is that it is highly speculative about the formal relations of agreed sources of knowledge, but not necessarily about uncertain knowledge. In part, this is so because traditional Shi'ite education is textually centripetal, and, of course (as is the case for virtually all Islamic systems of education), ultimately centripetal to the text of revelation itself. The logic studied is deductive; induction, needed for dealing with necessarily uncertain matters, is not formally studied, although it is used to some extent in legal reasoning. Probabilistic thinking, and the sort of statistical orientation it supposes, is only involved when commonweal questions are raised, and commonweal is in the last resort a source of law when conclusions from the usual sources of jurisprudence must be suspended.

A fourth characteristic of this system is that, while encouraging disputation in class, outside the classroom students are very much bound to their teachers by feelings of deference and loyalty. Students believe they have a life-long debt to their teachers, and are cautious about issuing controversial opinions as long as there are senior scholars who are widely accepted as being learned. The genealogical view of knowledge – tracing one's teachers' teachers back to the early centuries of Islam – goes along with an ahistorical view of knowledge. Although intellectually very rigorous, this training develops little in the way of historical consciousness and little impulse to understand the thinking of past scholars of the tradition in the context of their time.

In this age in which many things are indiscriminately labeled "fundamentalist," it is important to notice that most aspects of the Shi'ite *madrasa* education described here would best be characterized as "traditional." There may be other aspects that would lead observers to characterize the system differently. But most teachers and students in pre-revolutionary Qom represented a very real continuity of intellectual approach in their teaching with teachers of a century ago. It remains to be seen which of the traditional features of this system of education will survive the political changes that Ayatollah Khomeini has wrought.

NOTES

It is my pleasure to thank Sayyid Muhammd Husain Jalali, Sayyid Reza Borqe'i, Shaikh Reza Ostadi, Ayatollah Majd ad-Din Mahallati, Dr Abbas Zaryab, and – above all – professor Hossein Modarressi for their unstinting generosity in discussing their education at Qom with me.

1 Mahdi Zavabiti, *Pazhuheshi dar Nezam-e Talabegi* (Teheran, 1359 [1940]), gives an overview of the methods and curriculum, although my informants have corrected several points of detail in this work.

2 While many works have been written on pre-modern Islamic education, the most comprehensive work on the transmission of texts remains Franz Rosenthal, *The Technique and Approach of Muslim Scholarship* (Rome, 1947).

3 Yusuf Ghulami, *Aya kasi sargozasht-e ma (talabeh-ha) ra bavar mikonad?* (Qom, 1403 [1982]), pp. 9–10.

32

THE YESHIVA

Moshe Halbertal and Tova Hartman Halbertal

Yeshiva life is a life of an ongoing conversation, a conversation that takes place in the Beit Midrash – a large, simple study hall – where students sit and study.[1] In the famous and big Yeshivas the Beit Midrash holds a few hundred students whose ages range from 16 to 40 years old or even older. The conversational mode of study is created through the institution of the *havruta* (in which students are divided into pairs). The pairs or partners spend twelve hours a day or more reading together the Talmud and its commentaries, exploring its meanings and debating its complexities. Thus the choice of one's partner is one of the most crucial decisions in the intellectual life of a Yeshiva student. The discursive mode of study is not restricted to the individual partner; questions and answers circulate across the Beit Midrash. It is very common for students to move around in order to discuss a problem with another *havruta* who has earned a reputation in the study hall. Since the whole Yeshiva studies the same tractate from the Talmud, the Beit Midrash becomes a microcosm of a cross-generational give and take. Young and old often discuss the same problem, which circulates around the hall as the issue of the day.

The Beit Midrash can be compared with another arena of study: the library. Libraries are areas where silent reading and isolated reflections on a text take place. Movement and noise are minimized as much as possible as they are considered a desecration of the silence of the sacred space. The Beit Midrash is noisy and full of body language, where study is experienced as a communal activity. The accumulation of the dozens and sometimes hundreds of small *havruta* discussions creates a steady and loud background noise – for the observer an impediment for learning – for the participant, almost a necessity for concentration. The movement of hands, the shaking of the bodies, the different ways of leaning on the "stender" (stand) the variety of facial expression ranging from a concentrated face troubled by a difficulty with the text to a triumphant and joyous smile of discovering a novel insight, all constitute the choreography of the Beit Midrash. This rich body language adds a dimension of physicality to the act of learning never experienced in lecture halls or libraries.

The conversational mode of the Beit Midrash affects the nature of frontal teaching at the Yeshiva. Students spend most of their time studying with their partner the same page of the Talmud that will be taught by their teacher in the classroom. The average ratio between hours of frontal lectures and time spent in *havruta* study at the Beit Midrash is approximately 1 to 20. Many students invest more time preparing for class than their teacher, developing their own ideas, and coming to their lesson ready not only to listen and learn but to argue and be heard. A usual class in the Yeshiva will quickly turn from a well-ordered presentation of the teacher into a lively and sometimes chaotic exchange between a few bright students and their teacher. The classroom does not function as the presentation of the truth by the all-knowing scholar imparting knowledge to ignorant or less knowledgeable receptacles, who write down all he says uncritically.

Yeshiva learning is conversational in yet another sense. Students do not write exams or papers at the end of a term. The evaluation of the students and the ranking of their achievements occurs through the students' participation in the ongoing exchange in the Beit Midrash. The close and intimate knowledge among students of each others' capabilities and achievements is remarkable given the lack of any systematized form of evaluation. The steady oral exchange, however, creates a reputation, and forms a clear picture – who is sharp, who is hard working, who is lazy and who is out of place – well known to the participants in the enclosed space of the study hall. In addition, writing is rare in the Yeshiva even when it comes to summarizing the teachers' classes or the students' own ideas. Teachers reading their lectures from a prepared text is a rare event.

The lack of writing highlights another feature of the Yeshiva. In the Beit Midrash ideas come and go, questions and answers are raised and forgotten. When the same tractate is to be studied again in the next cycle of learning,[2] teachers are expected not to repeat their old readings but to innovate. A good teacher and a bright student are not known for a particular thesis or theory which they have advanced, but rather for their unique style of teaching and approach towards a talmudic discussion. It is no wonder that teachers are selected and promoted not on the basis of written publications, but on their oral reputation in the Yeshiva world as sharp and knowledgeable Talmudists. In the Yeshiva both students and teachers own their talents and knowledge, not their ideas or theories.

Since being a Yeshiva student is being a contributor to an ongoing discussion at the Beit Midrash, older students and partners are far more crucial to the initiation of a student than teachers. Socialization at the Yeshiva occurs through successful integration into the stream of conversation at the Beit Midrash, in mastering its rules and in internalizing its discourse. There are no introductory classes to the Talmud at the Beit Midrash and there is no methodological orientation,[3] any entrance point in the conversation is as good as another.

The unique conversational structure of education in the Yeshiva and its attempt at maximizing cross-generational exchange aims at shaping the study of the Torah as a communal experience. Moreover, study is institutionalized in the Beit Midrash as a performative act carried out by the students' participation. In such a discursive mode students are not passive spectators in a reality shaped by teachers. A Beit Midrash is a learning space shaped by the intensity and quality of the ongoing exchange of its students. The conversational nature of the Yeshiva as an institution of study is captured in a very common term used to describe the practice of learning in Yiddish: "reden in learnen." This term, which has no parallel in English, translates literally as "talking in learning." Yeshiva life is the life of talking in learning. It is in this environment that the intellectual types of the "shmuzer" and "kibitzer" flourish.

Such a radically different method of study has far-reaching implications for the education development of its students. The conversational give and take leads to a unique approach in analyzing texts, in the questions raised and in the whole creative thought process. The conversational mode of study interestingly reflects the structure and content of the Talmud. A full account of the relationship between the central text studied and the methods of study employed in the analysis of these texts is a complex undertaking, since methodologies of learning in the history of Yeshivas have gone through many transformations. However, there is a central and relatively constant feature at the root of the conversational mode of study, which is deeply related to the nature of the Talmud as a particular type of text. In order to understand this process we will clarify what a page of the Talmud is.

The Babylonian Talmud is a compendium of statements and discussions conducted by the Amoraim (talmudic sages) from the first half of the third century until the end of the fifth century. The Talmud follows the order of the Mishnah, the interpretation of which is its primary concern. But the subject-matter of the Mishnah does not dominate the discussion. By way of associations, loose connections and indirect allusions, the talmudic *sugiya* (a unit of a discussion in the Talmud) drifts away from the Mishnah to a variety of subjects, ranging from profound theological observations to folk tales and from intricate legal discourse to magic, science and demonology. Edited as intergenerational arguments, layer upon layer, most talmudic discussions do not reach a definite legal opinion about the previous controversies. Rather, they preserve and clarify the wealth and multiplicity of approaches to the problem at hand. In many talmudic discussions, the *sugiya* does not proceed by way of selection aimed at approaching or approximating the right answer. Astonishingly, many *sugiyot* manifest the opposite tendency, since they progress dialectically. Instead of refuting and thereby favoring one of two or more opposing interpretations, they attempt to maintain the validity of opposing interpretations against potential challenges, challenges which are raised and refuted in turn. Through refutation of challenges the talmudic discussion advances multiple understandings of the Mishnah rather than narrowing those interpretative options as far as possible. Within this dialectical process, initial opinions are inevitably reinterpreted, sometimes rephrased or articulated within a new context and therefore perceived in a novel light.

What we know of the creation of the Talmud is that its editor (who is called the stama, "the anonymous") had before him the Mishnah accompanied by a mass of statements about it from the Amoraim, who had made statements without providing reasoning for them, statements that often contradicted each other. The editor wove a discussion from these traditions. He (or they) confronted one statement with another, creating a complex argument between them. What did *x* say when he was presented with this difficulty, how did he answer the challenges of *y* and what did *y* answer to the question of *x* relying on this or that distinction? The Talmud itself is thus an open-ended intergenerational discussion mostly imagined by the genius of its editor, the stama. The structure of learning in the Yeshiva is in its basic conversational mode a re-enactment of the imagined talmudic discussion. There is a deep affinity between the peculiar construction of the talmudic page and the way its learning is organized at the Beit Midrash. The students become attached to the tradition through their active participation in the ongoing argument. The text is the initial conversation which expands and develops by dialogue with it. Re-enactment is not a repetition: the student introduces a new interpretation, a novella or a *chidush* (a new way of approaching a problem).

The conversation is carried in an atemporal non-historical fashion. A Yeshiva student imagines himself as carrying on a direct argument with Rabbi Akiva of the second century, Nachmanides of the thirteenth century and Rabbi Chaim of Brisk of the nineteenth century. Historicity after all is a form of secularization; periodization creates a sense of distance and alienation. It is no wonder that very few Yeshiva students are capable of dating the material they spend hours analyzing. The historical philological methodology that was embraced in the nineteenth century by German Jewish *Wissenschaft des Judentumes* and subsequently by Jewish studies in the universities, was completely rejected by the world of the Yeshiva. The overall project of the nineteenth-century Jewish enlightenment was to locate the tradition within a historical context and thus to undermine its claim as an atemporal revelation. It also aimed at abstracting from the wealth of the material the essence of what Judaism is about, thus allowing for change in observance while maintaining the core. By contrast, the Yeshiva world abstracts the text from its historical formation. It also imbues every detail with equal importance. The Talmud is studied in the Yeshiva as it was received by tradition without any attempt to examine its version critically through careful philological comparative analysis of the different manuscripts. It is told of one of the founders of the contemporary Yeshiva approach, R. Chaim of Brisk, that after he provided an answer for a contradiction in Maimonides' code – the *Mishneh Torah*, one of his students pointed out to him that this same problem was raised before Maimonides by other scholars and that Maimonides provided a different and more local answer to it. R. Chaim, who paused to examine Maimonides' own answer uttered, after a while, "And this is *an* answer!".

The Beit Midrash mode of organizing and performing study is thus a serious re-enactment of a talmudic page. It is as if the Talmud is a text to investigate and a script to perform simultaneously. As a script, it has a dynamic function; it is more like a score for a jazz performance than a script for theater. The talmudic page provides a skeleton which is continuously enlarged through the incorporation of subsequent commentaries to the discussion, and through the improvisation of the students themselves. One can imagine what other types of texts would be suitable for the *havruta* technique of study. Among philosophical texts Wittgenstein's *Philosophical Investigations* is a good candidate. Wittgenstein conducts his argument through a subtle ongoing argument with an interlocutor. Unlike discursive texts, the *Investigations* has no clear entry or exit point; the text is cryptic enough to invite a close scrutiny and commentary.

The phenomenology of the talmudic page and its connection to the conversational technique also raises other pertinent general questions about theories of knowledge, questions about the relationship between modes of reasoning and the discursive process. Does the conversational structure of study penetrate the very nature of thinking and of approaching a problem? Do students trained at the Yeshiva not only experience learning differently but as a result think differently from the students in the libraries or the lecture halls? In short, does the conversational mode reflect not only a different performance of study but a different way of thinking? We have described the way talmudic reasoning

461

attempts to preserve the viability of counter-arguments. In this respect, a talmudic page proceeds counter to Popper's "scientific method of reasoning." As such, the aim of the argument is not to minimize the possible hypothesis stated at the starting-point of the discussion. A talmudic page would not achieve its purpose if at the end of the discussion one of the possible explanations of the Mishnah were refuted. The first stage of talmudic reasoning is rather to clarify what the argument is about ("So, what are they arguing about?" is a very common opener for a class). The second stage is the challenge of providing the best possible case both textually and conceptually for each of the opposing sides. This form of reasoning is achieved by the structure of study at the Beit Midrash. Taking sides and presenting arguments and counter-arguments gives vitality to a discussion. What is usually hard to achieve alone – giving weight to the other possibility, is secured through the institution of a constant interlocutor. In a *havruta* set-up, the processes of understanding and explaining become almost identical. While analyzing a text an isolated reader in the library might overlook inner contradictions or complexities which would be raised in the presence of a *havruta*. The Beit Midrash set-up is thus conducive to the purpose of preserving and enlarging the talmudic discourse. It is a training in acknowledging the existence of another point of view, presenting it, facing and struggling with it.

Given the environment that they are socialized into, Yeshiva students are encouraged to question, to see the other side of the problem and not to let go when they do not understand. However, this unique mode of training creates its own inner problems regarding the development of styles of reasoning. What is the fine line between a question that has weight and an empty one; between a distinction that clarifies an issue and a distinction that obscures or misfires? Overdoing is often more of a problem in a Yeshiva than "underdoing." The challenge of Yeshiva training is how to turn a student who is a clever arguer into a fine scholar. It is not about how to avoid mistakes but how to enter the frame of discussion where mistakes can begin to occur.

The training in seeing the other side of the argument and in preserving as many hypotheses as possible – which is so fundamental to the talmudic way of reasoning and lies at the core of organizing study in the Beit Midrash – led to the contemporary division of labor between the head of the Yeshiva (Rosh Yeshiva) and the rabbi (Posek) of the community. The rabbi has to rule. He has to address issues presented to him by laymen who adhere to Jewish law and seek direction over their actions. A rabbi has to issue norms that are related to the actual life of the *halakhah* (Jewish Law). A Yeshiva education is not a training in ruling since it does not relate to the Talmud as a source of clear-cut norms. A Yeshiva is not a place where rabbis are trained but where scholars are created. One famous anecdote reflects the deep difference of intellectual temperament between the head of the Yeshiva and the rabbi. It tells of a great head of a Yeshiva who would turn to the local rabbi for a ruling on a *halakhic* question. To this gesture – which appears surprising from a scholar who was no less knowledgeable than the rabbi about matters of Jewish law – the great scholar added another surprising request for the rabbi: "Please when you rule don't tell me your reasoning. As soon as you present it, I will have so many counter-arguments that I am not sure the problem will be resolved." A Yeshiva is therefore not a place were rabbis are trained; in a sense it is not a place where training occurs altogether. It is not a professional school. It serves no other goal but the continuous preoccupation and expansion of the discourse itself. (For instance, Yeshivas do not certify their students. If a student wants to be ordained as a rabbi, he will typically have to go somewhere else.)

What is the overall religious and intellectual context that provides meaning to the continuous preoccupation and expansion of the discourse for its own sake? The Yeshiva embodies the value of study of the Torah as the primary and most exalted value in Jewish life and it aims at shaping its ideal type: "the scholar."

The religious outlook which forms the basis of the value of Torah study for its own sake needs some clarification. The rise of the study of the Torah as a major religious ideal is one of the distinct innovations of the rabbinic period, in the early centuries of the common era. The study of the Torah as commanded in the Bible serves primarily a didactic role – to guarantee the continuity of memory and tradition. Scholars are not presented as ideal biblical figures, and the study of the Torah is not central to religious life as a spiritual mode of achieving intimacy with God. In the rabbinic period, in contrast, the Torah becomes an object of ongoing reflection and the ideal of learning comes to be considered a major religious obligation, equal if not superior to other religious obligations such as the practice of the *mitzvoth* and prayer. In the Talmud it is said, "The study of the Torah is greater then the daily sacrifices of the Temple."[4] Elsewhere Raba maintains that, "Anyone who studies the Torah needs neither the burnt offering nor the atonement sacrifice nor the guilt offering."[5] Along with the shift of authority from priest and prophet to scholar, the Torah came to be portrayed as the locus of God's presence. "Even one who studies the Torah alone, the Shechinah [God] is with him."[6] Study of the Torah is thus conceived as an intimate form of communication with God. Schematically, we could describe three approaches to the sacred; these of the priest, the prophet, and the scholar. In the priestly conception, God is manifest in a sacred geography; he has a territorial presence in the Temple. For the prophet, history serves as the stage for the divine drama, and God is revealed in sacred events. The scholar conceives the text as the medium for the sacred; it is in the Torah itself that God is found. Bereft of sacred territory after the destruction of the temple and alienated from divine history in their exile, Jews found comfort in the Torah, their portable temple.[7] The brilliance of this religious ideal is owed, in part, to the infinite possibilities it opens. New layers discovered in the text and the multiplicity of its interpretations are potentially identical with the infinity of divine presence. No wonder then that Jewish scholars entered every possible fissure in the text, followed every subtle allusion within it, and probed its depth with so many imaginative interpretative strategies.

The Yeshiva is an institutional embodiment of the trend in Jewish life that made the study of the Torah central and gave the ideal of the scholar its most extreme expression. The primacy of the ideal of study of the Torah is expressed in the structuring of the Yeshiva as a world substitute. The discursive and cross-generational way that it works enables it to serve an almost all-encompassing social and religious function. The learning of all particulars of a commandment is more important than the performance of that commandment itself. From the point of view of its staunch supporters the Yeshiva does not exist to serve the community, to produce teachers or rabbis; it is rather the fulfillment of the community's *telos*. It is through the practice of ongoing study in the Yeshiva that the community finds its goal. Yet in focusing upon the Talmud and its commentaries as the exclusive object of reflection, the Yeshiva world has made a crucial and interesting spiritual choice. The Talmud is mostly an anti-metaphysical, atheological text. The tractates which are usually studied at the Yeshiva relate to torts, contracts, evidence and family law. Tractates that discuss subjects not related to criminal or civil law (such as the tractate Shabbat in the Talmud) primarily define the legal category of work prohibited on the Sabbath, rather than the theological meaning of creation and rest. Systematic discussions of great theological and metaphysical issues that do exist in the Talmud are bracketed. In its anti-metaphysical thrust, the Yeshiva curriculum was deeply opposed by other Jewish traditions, which were concerned with metaphysical contemplation and mystical experience.[8] Medieval Jewish philosophers and mystics found the Talmud an inadequate object for exclusive reflection. It is told that the Baal Shem Tov, one of the famous Jewish mystics, confessed that when he studied the Talmud he meditated upon the white between the printed black letters on the page. The mystic who aims at abolishing individuation of thought finds that the intricate talmudic discussions distance him from the infinite. It is the white portions of the page which are most meaningful for such an ideal of mystical union with the divine. Joseph ibn-Caspi, the medieval Jewish philosopher who internalized the Aristotelian–Maimonidean definition of human perfection as attaining true knowledge, uttered the following complaint against talmudic education: "Is not the faculty of expounding the existence and unity of God as important as familiarity with the rule concerning small milk spoon?"[9] "God is in the details" would be the Yeshiva scholar's answer to such a complaint. For a medieval Aristotelian who poses the contemplation of nature and God as the fulfilment of the life of the intellect, the Talmud becomes an obstacle.[10] Yet in it anti-foundational mode, and in its overt ironic attitude to essences and rules, the Talmud has a great appeal to a modern and postmodern intellectual temperament. The talmudic skepticism towards systematic theological and metaphysical modes of thought is reflected in the following advice given by a reflective ex-Yeshiva student: "Rather than inquire how the fact of the revelation of the Torah at Sinai can be established – an issue which is anyhow out of reason's reach, it is better to discuss from which material the tablets of the ten commandments were made. When someone sincerely argues whether the tablets that Moses received at Sinai were made of marble or of wood, the problem of revelation as such is rendered superfluous." The justification of Yeshiva spirituality seems to be completely internal to the praxis itself.

Yeshiva education is self-sustaining in an even deeper way. The conversational mode attempts to structure a creative re-enactment of the Talmud. A good question assures a student's reputation in the study hall much more than a decent answer. And yet there are questions that are not asked. On the one hand, the ultimate goal in the training of the Yeshiva student is to educate an inquisitive mind, on the other hand, however, there are questions that may not be voiced. Questions aimed at the meaning of the practice as a whole, inquiries concerning theological and religious beliefs, historical contextualization and moral critique which might undermine claims for authority, are not part of the legitimate ongoing conversation. If these issues are raised they might be followed by a long discussion with one of the teachers or the head of the Yeshiva in an attempt to "deal" with the problem, sometimes in a sincere attempt to address it, though most often as a way of distancing it and dissolving it. If the questions do not get resolved quickly then the student will ultimately find himself outside of the Yeshiva. For this reason many books are not included in the Yeshiva library. Hence the mythic stories of Yeshiva students — who lost faith while in Yeshiva — reading heretical texts underneath their big printed Talmud.

Limitations are not peculiar to the Yeshiva. Most other educational institutions set clear boundaries of investigation. But a Yeshiva education creates a particular inner tension, which lies in the attempt to develop an inquisitive searching Talmudist while framing and channeling this search into well-defined boundaries. The Yeshivas with their conversational method of study can become a breeding ground for heretics who have asked one question too many. After all, who can control the direction in which a conversation within a *havruta* drifts in the long hours of study? The challenge of the Yeshiva is to direct the intense cultivated intellectual libido towards the internal goals of the system, in particular at times when powerful competing ideologies tend to capture the minds of the young. The questions that are prohibited are not announced as such, and the boundaries not to be crossed are not clearly marked. After all, declaring a boundary is a way of tempting one to cross it. The conversation itself in which the student is invited to participate, with all its intensity and in its all-encompassing nature, is meant to do the work of channeling curiosity.

Making the intellectual life of Torah study, and the ideal type of the scholar, the highest embodiment of religious values in the institution of the Yeshiva engenders a complex and fascinating concern of moral education at the Yeshiva. The ideal type of the scholar is in tension with other religious figures: the saint, the charismatic miracle maker, and the humble self-sacrificing pious person. A life of prayer is very different from a life of learning; an altruistic life dedicated to the poor and suffering is not the same as a life secluded in the study hall. Scholars tend to be competitive and arrogant, and the cultivation of intellectual self-perfection often becomes deeply narcissistic. A Yeshiva that continually rewards talent and intellectual achievement can be a cruel place to those less rigorous intellectually. The spectrum of talents that can be expressed is very narrow. Theories of "multiple intelligences" are completely foreign to a Yeshiva education.

Since its inception, the rabbinic tradition that postulated the scholar as its ideal type struggled with these concerns. It attempted to make the study of the Torah a form of worship while at the same time being painfully aware that it can become a tool for competitive intellectual pride. It sought to integrate within the life of scholarship the precious traits and virtues of the saintly and pious. Yet it produced a distinct religious ideal type. In the nineteenth century this intrinsic dilemma of the Yeshiva erupted in a conflict over the way to educate a student, which resulted in a major change to the institution. The struggle was initiated by the Musar movement,[11] it wished to address the neglect of character-building and moral education at the Yeshiva, and criticized the heightened intellectualism of its ideology. After growing pressure most Yeshivas established a position whose status was similar to the head of the Yeshiva: the "Mashgiach" (supervisor). The Mashgiach is responsible for the moral education of the students. He is not a particularly outstanding scholar but rather a figure of legendary moral character, who serves as a model for the Yeshiva students. At their best, some of the mashgichim produced perceptive and insightful tracts of moral psychology. Issues such as weakness of the will, cognition and emotion, humility and its inner contradictions, the disposition of faith and trust are examples of problems addressed by the Mashgiach.

With the introduction of this new role at the Yeshiva a curricular change was formed. In addition to the study of Talmud a small portion of the day was allocated to the study of literature that deals with virtues and moral character. For example, Rabbi Moshe Chaim Luzato's *Mesilat Yesharim* became a moral manual very popular at the Yeshivas. The Musar movement provided a variety of strategies and ideals of moral education, and the integration of the Musar sensibilities with the heightened intellectual ideal produced a spectrum of Yeshiva types: from a scholar-saint whose intellectual virtues are embodied in extreme piety and self-effacement to a scholar impatient with religious excess and false authenticity and distant from uninformed piety; from an unassuming modest scholar to a proud insider. The location of the student in this spectrum corresponds usually to the degree of his closeness to the ethos presented by the Mashgiach as a counter-voice in the Yeshiva. In addition, different Yeshivas stressed one or another of the character types. It is not uncommon to identify one of the types with a specific Yeshiva.

As a secluded institution, the Yeshiva functions as a space of exclusion as well. It is an institution of males and for males; women are excluded. Monasticism was never practiced in the intellectual elites among Jews since Jewish law obligates marriage for scholars. However the relations between scholars and students to their family and their wives is extremely complicated given the all-encompassing nature of the ideal of study and given the gender hierarchy attached to this form of life. The Mishnah states: "Students may go away to study the Torah, without the permission of their wives, for a period of thirty days" (*Ketuboth* 61b). A limit is set to the presence of a married student in a distant school away from home. The family seems to be a legitimate barrier to the function of the Yeshiva as a space of seclusion. Yet this is not the end of the story. The Talmud attempts to overcome the attachment to family obligation as a legitimate barrier and re-establish the absolute primacy of study: "R. Abba b. Ahabah, however, stated in the name of Rab: This is the view of R. Eliezer only, but the sages ruled: Students may go away to study Torah without the permission [of their wives even for] two or three years" (*Ketuboth* 62b). The Talmud allows a student to be a married monk, postulating the absolute claim of the Eros for wisdom.[12] Typical to the way a talmudic page progresses, this extension is undermined by a story which follows it:

> Rabba stated: The Rabbis relied on R. Abba b. Ahabah and acted accordingly at the risk of losing their lives. Thus R. Nehumi who was frequenting the school of Raba at Mhuza used to return home on the Eve of every Day of Atonement. On one occasion he was so attracted by his subject [that he forgot to return home]. His wife was expecting him every moment saying "He is coming soon, he is coming soon." As he did not arrive she became so depressed that tears began to flow from her eyes. He was [at that moment] sitting on a roof. The roof collapsed under him and he was killed.

The narcissistic involvement of the scholar with his study cost him his life, although the previous normative ruling legitimated such behavior. The Talmud in these rulings and counter-rulings, which are undermined in return by a story that recounts the punishment of the scholar by death for his cruel self-indulgence, reflects a deep ambivalence towards the secluded nature of study.

No ambivalence however, is manifested over the exclusion of women from the traditional Yeshiva at large, and from the intellectual endeavour of Talmud study in particular. The scholar's wife is there to wait for him to come home. The question that the Talmud deals with is how attuned he should be to her longing. In the Talmud Rabbi Akiva's wife, rather then waiting anxiously for her husband to return after his twelve years of studying, expresses a wish that he should stay away yet another twelve years, to study more. This story has become the paradigm in the education of young religious girls. Rabbi Akiva's wife is the ultimate wife fulfilling the woman's *telos*. The good woman is one who identifies with the community's highest value, of study. The "good enough wife" is one who, like Rabbi Akiva's wife, enables her husband to reach this goal by denying her own personal needs. The story of Rabbi Akiva and his wife is, however, just one of many stories in the talmudic passages about the relationship between scholar and spouse. Many of them have entirely different messages about the tragic consequences of absence from the family, leading sometimes to death or to alienation from one's children. However, this is a story of a woman's self-abasement, the story of her personal needs becoming completely subsumed under the higher values. Her role is thus to enable her husband to achieve the most significant goal of their tradition. She is, however, excluded from achieving this goal herself. This restriction thus prevents women from being partners in and contributors to the culture, a culture shaped by participation in the conversation at the Beit Midrash. It prevents women from achieving the positions of authority and power that are granted by excelling in this praxis. Women are assigned to be silent supporters of an intense conversation created and conducted by men for men, through bread-earning and raising children.

On the face of it, there seems nothing constitutive of the structuring of the Yeshiva that would exclude women. Although the Talmud itself, and many traditional Rabbis, do not allow them to study the Talmud, there are in fact interesting contemporary attempts to establish women's Yeshivas, or co-ed ones. The traditional justification of the Yeshivas as institutions of men for men is based on the doubt that women are intellectually competent, or emotionally mature enough, to engage in the highest levels of intellectual activity. This discussion must also pay attention to the fundamental relationship between the study of Talmud and the development of boys into men. It concerns gender identification and development. The Yeshivas were and still are institutions that define and constitute manliness. The Beit Midrash is not only a place to engage in an intellectual pursuit: membership and study define the ultimate man in the religious community. The most scholarly man is the most manly of men, the hero. It is not surprising then that women are excluded. To allow women to study would force an entirely new understanding of manliness. Similarly to other cultures that excluded women from either their most significant activity, or activities that defined manliness, traditional Judaism, through segregated institutions of learning, maintained the superiority of men and perhaps even more significantly the definition of the masculine gender.

Particular spaces of exclusion define the terms in which manliness is constituted in different societies. As institutions that define manliness, Yeshivas manifest a very peculiar form of gender differentiation. In Hellenistic cities, for example, genders were differentiated mainly through excluding women from civic and political life. This form of exclusion constituted men as citizens. Men alone were defined in the polis as political animals. As in the Greek community it was citizenship that marked gender, so in the Jewish community, it was scholarship; elsewhere the hierarchy is set by economic entrepreneurship. Defining the Beit Midrash as the space where manliness is formed has far-reaching implications towards the ideal of masculinity in the tradition. The Yeshiva student is pale, studious and disembodied; he lacks many features that are usually attached to masculinity.

One virtue central in Yeshiva education, in Yiddish termed *eidelkeit* (gentleness), is in stark opposition to alternative ideals of manliness. For the soldier-citizen-entrepreneur, *eidelkeit* is associated mostly with femininity. The Yeshiva example of gender differentiation is yet another example of how the division of labor and hierarchical structure is not premised on essential and natural differences between men and women. It rather depends upon what society defines as excellence and achievement and on the places from which women were excluded. The Yeshiva form of gender differentiation has its effect in many important ways on the division of labor within families. In Yeshiva families the economic responsibility is undertaken by the women. They support their husbands and children. Inevitably the woman also becomes more worldly and resourceful; and while she admires her husband as a scholar, she often also looks down at him as an incompetent *schlemiel*.

The Yeshiva is a fascinating institution because in it a deep link can be seen between the text at its center, the particular discursive form of its creative re-enactment and the mode of reasoning which fits both the text and its re-enactment. What links the different facets together is — conversation. A phenomenology of the Yeshiva contributes to the understanding of the Jewish tradition in particular, and besides this the organization of this institution challenges theories of education in general. What would other fields of knowledge look like if they were investigated in such a context? How would modes of reasoning, experiences of learning be affected if higher institutions of learning were established in a Yeshiva-like form? How would channels of intellectual exchange and forms of teacher–student relationships be shaped, if our universities had a Beit Midrash at their center? These questions suggest a rather wild thought-experiment, though it must be admitted an interesting one.

NOTES

1 Our essay focuses on contemporary Yeshivas. We take as our paradigm cases the important present Yeshivas such as Poneviz and Mir. These Yeshivas, which are modeled on the structure and ethos of the great Lithuanian Yeshivas that were destroyed in the holocaust, were founded by scholars who survived the holocaust, who studied there, and passed on their traditions. For a historical perspective of the development of the Lithuanian Yeshivas since the second half of the nineteenth century see S. Stampfer, *ha-Yeshiva ha-Litait be-Hithvuta*, Jerusalem, Magnes Press, 1995. An important account of the Medieval Yeshivas and their structure is given by M. Brueir, 'ha-Yeshiva ha-Ashkenazit be-shelei Yemei ha-Benaim, Ph.D. dissertation, Hebrew University, Jerusalem, 1967. For an interesting sociological approach to the Yeshiva, see W. B. Helmreich, *The World of the Yeshiva* (New Haven, Conn., Yale University Press, 1982).

2 Yeshivas have a cycle of learning which is completed in a few years, and during them a relatively fixed set of tractates from the Talmud are studied.

3 Students enter the Yeshiva already equipped for it by their years in various forms of elementary education of studying the Talmud.

4 Babylonian Talmud *Megilah* 3b.

5 Babylonian Talmud *Menachot* 110a and also *Sifrei Devarim* 41.

6 Babylonian Talmud *Berakhot* 6a.

7 See for example the detailed analogy between the temple and the Torah in Issac Duran (Efodi) *Ma'aseh Efod*, Vienna, 1865, p. 11–12.

8 The Talmud has long sections dealing with non-legal matters which include deep theological insights. It is very common in the Yeshiva to skip these sections!

9 Jewish dietary laws include instructions about dairy and non-dairy utensils.

10 On the construction of Jewish curriculum and its complexities see J. Katz, "Halakhah ve-Kabbalah ke-Nosei Limud Mitcharim," in *Halakhah ve-Kabbalah* (Jerusalem: Magnes, 1984), pp. 70–101; I. Twersky, "Talmudists, philosophers, kabbalists: the quest for spirituality in the sixteenth century," in B. Cooperman (ed.) *Jewish Thought in the Sixteenth Century* (Cambridge, Mass., Harvard University Press, 1983), pp. 431–59.

11 Musar literally means morals or ethics. For the origins of the Musar Movement and its founding figure see E. Etkes, *R. Israel Salanter ve-Reshita shel Tnuat ha-Musar* (Jerusalem, Magnes Press, 1982) and D. Katz, *Tnuat ha-Musar. Toldoteiah Isheiah ve-Shitoteiha* (Tel Aviv, Bitan Press, 1950–63).

12 For a deep analysis of this section in the Talmud and its relations to gender differentiation see D. Boyarin, *Carnal Israel* (Berkeley, Calif., University of California Press, l993), ch. 5.

We wish to thank Dr Menachem Lorberbaun for his helpful comments.

33

CIVIC EDUCATION IN THE LIBERAL STATE

William Galston

In most times and places the necessity and appropriateness of civic education has been accepted without question. It has been taken for granted that young human beings must be shaped into citizens and that public institutions have both the right and the responsibility to take the lead. In the United States today, however, civic education has become intensely controversial. Some skeptics believe that our political and social arrangements can function perfectly well without publicly defined (or directed) civic education. Others doubt that any one specification of civic education can be devised for a liberal polity in which individuals, families, and communities embrace fundamentally differing conceptions of choiceworthy lives. Still others argue that any unitary civic education violates the autonomy and conscience of many individuals and groups in a diverse society.

These objections are mistaken. It is both necessary and possible to carry out civic education in the liberal state. To do so properly, however, the partial truth of the critics' contentions must be recognized in the content and the conduct of that education.

PHILOSOPHIC EDUCATION VERSUS CIVIC EDUCATION

Let me begin with a distinction between two very different kinds of education. Philosophic education has as its basic objectives, first, the disposition to seek truth, and, second, the capacity to conduct rational inquiry. Training scientists, for example, requires the inculcation both of an ethic of inquiry – do not fabricate or distort results, take care to prevent your hypotheses (or desires) from affecting your observations – and the techniques of inquiry appropriate to the discipline.

There are of course many different forms of philosophic education, corresponding to the numerous ways in which truth may be pursued. Nevertheless, these forms of education share two key features. First, they are not decisively shaped by the specific social or political circumstances in which they are conducted, or, to put it the other way around, they are perverted when such circumstances come to have a substantive effect. There is no valid distinction between "Jewish" and "Aryan" physics, or between "bourgeois" and "socialist" biology; truth is one and universal. Second, and relatedly, philosophic education can have corrosive consequences for political communities in which it is allowed to take place. The pursuit of truth – scientific, historical, moral, or whatever – can undermine structures of unexamined but socially central belief.

Civic education differs from philosophic education in all these respects. Its purpose is not the pursuit and acquisition of truth, but rather the formation of individuals who can effectively conduct their lives within, and support, their political community. It is unlikely, to say the least, that the truth will be fully consistent with this purpose. Nor is civic education homogeneous and universal. It is by definition education within, and on behalf of, a particular political order. The conduct and content of civic education within a liberal democracy will therefore differ significantly from civic education within other kinds of polities. Nor, finally, does civic education stand in opposition to its political community. On the contrary, it fails – fundamentally – if it does not support and strengthen that community.

It might be argued that this alleged opposition between civic and philosophic education is far too sweeping. While some societies are dependent on myths and lies, others are far more open to truth. Liberal democracies, in particular, are founded on principles that can survive rational inspection, and their functioning is facilitated (or at least not crucially impaired) by unimpeded inquiry in every domain.

This argument does contain an important element of truth. The understanding of liberal society as an "open" society has important historical roots in early modern struggles against repressive tradition and superstition. It found classic formulation in John Stuart Mill's invocation of Socrates as liberal hero. In principle and in practice, liberal democracy does exhibit a degree of openness to philosophic education, and to its social consequences, that is probably without precedent in human history. This fact constitutes one of the most important arguments in favor of liberal democracy.

But it would be rash to conclude that the clash between rational inquiry and civic education in liberal societies has ceased to exist. On the level of theory, liberalism takes sides in a series of disputes about the meaning of equality, freedom, and the human good – disputes that cannot be regarded as definitively settled from a philosophic point of view. On the practical level, very few individuals will come to embrace the core commitments of liberal society through a process of rational inquiry. If children are to be brought to accept these commitments as valid and binding, it can only be through a pedagogy that is far more rhetorical than rational. For example, rigorous historical research will almost certainly vindicate complex "revisionist" accounts of key figures in American history. Civic education, however, requires a more noble, moralizing history: a pantheon of heroes who confer legitimacy on central institutions and constitute worthy objects of emulation.[1] It is unrealistic to believe that more than a few adult citizens of liberal societies will ever move beyond the kind of civic commitment engendered by such a pedagogy.

THE NEED FOR LIBERAL DEMOCRATIC CIVIC EDUCATION

There is a tradition of Mandevillean argument that liberal polities do not need – indeed, are distinctive in not needing – civic education directed to the formation of liberal citizens because social processes and political institutions can be arranged so as to render desired collective outcomes independent of individual character and belief. Albert Hirschman has traced the emergence in seventeenth- and eighteenth-century social thought of the thesis that republican government could best be secured not through civic virtue but through the liberation of the commercial-acquisitive "interests" of the middle class in opposition to the politically destructive "passions" of the aristocracy.[2] The most famous of the *Federalist Papers* (10 and 51) contain memorable formulations of the need to counteract interest with interest and passion with passion. Immanuel Kant, who was at once the most profound moral philosopher and the most devoted liberal theorist of his age, argued vigorously for the disjunction between individual virtue and republican government. A liberal government that fully protects individual rights "is only a question of a good organization of the state, whereby the powers of each selfish inclination are so arranged in opposition that one moderates or destroys the ruinous effect of the other. The consequence . . . is the same as if none of them existed, and man is forced to be a good citizen even if not a morally good person."[3]

The proposition that liberal societies are uniquely able to do without the fruits of civic education has been sharply challenged, however. Recent interpretations of the liberal theoretical tradition have emphasized the copresence of institutional and character-based arguments, as have rereadings of the *Federalist*.[4] Recent explorations of public policy problems – crime, drugs, dependency – have focused on the formation of character and belief as well as on the manipulation of incentives.[5] Historical inquiries into American public education have documented the driving role played by the perceived need for a civic pedagogy that could turn immigrants into citizens.[6] Groups across the political spectrum have re-emphasized their belief that a refurbished civic education is an urgent necessity:

> Democracy's survival depends upon our transmitting to each new generation the political vision of liberty and equality that unites us as Americans . . . Such values are neither revealed truths nor natural habits. There is no evidence that we are born with them. Devotion to human dignity and freedom, to equal rights, to social and economic justice, to the rule of law, to civility and truth, to tolerance of diversity, to mutual assistance, to personal and civic responsibility, to self-restraint and self-respect – all these must be taught and learned.[7]

Common experience buttresses what history and argument suggest: that the operation of liberal institutions and the functioning of liberal society are affected in important ways by the character and belief of individuals (and leaders) within the liberal polity. At some point the attenuation of civic spirit and competence will create pathologies with which liberal institutions, however perfect their technical design, simply cannot cope. To an extent difficult to measure but impossible to ignore, the viability of liberal society depends on its ability effectively to conduct civic education.

472

THE POSSIBILITY OF LIBERAL DEMOCRATIC CIVIC EDUCATION

Liberal democratic civic education may be necessary, but is it possible? In the same way that the religious diversity of liberal society makes it impossible to reach a religious consensus suitable for public endorsement, so too the moral and political diversity of the liberal polity might seem to undermine the possibility of a unitary civic pedagogy acceptable to, and binding on, all groups. Indeed, the movement from the religious neutrality of the liberal state to a wider moral and political neutrality is one of the defining characteristics of liberal theory in our time, a development with roots in the opinions of urban-based social elites.

This generalization of liberal neutrality is neither necessary nor wise. To the extent that we accept a shared citizenship, we have something important in common – a set of political institutions and of principles that underlie them. What we share, beyond all our differences, provides the basis for a civic education valid across the boundaries of our differences.

Some of the virtues needed to sustain the liberal state are requisites of every political community: the willingness to fight on behalf of one's country; the settled disposition to obey the law; and loyalty – the developed capacity to understand, to accept, and to act on the core principles of one's society. Some of the individual traits are specific to liberal society – independence, tolerance, and respect for individual excellences and accomplishments, for example. Still others are entailed by the key features of liberal democratic politics. For citizens, the disposition to respect the rights of others, the capacity to evaluate the talents, character, and performance of public officials, and the ability to moderate public desires in the face of public limits are essential. For leaders, the patience to work within social diversity and the ability to narrow the gap between wise policy and popular consent are fundamental. And the developed capacity to engage in public discourse and to test public policies against our deeper convictions is highly desirable for all members of the liberal community, whatever political station they may occupy.[8]

A leading contemporary theorist of civic education, Amy Gutmann, has reached conclusions parallel to but divergent from the theses just sketched. Her point of departure is democracy, and her argument is that our civic pedagogy should be oriented toward democratic virtue: "the ability to deliberate, and hence to participate in conscious social reproduction."[9] In my view, this is a piece – but only a piece – of the civic education appropriate to our situation, and it becomes a distortion when it is mistaken for the whole.

Let me begin with a methodological point. The adequacy of a conception of civic education cannot be determined in the abstract, but only through its congruence with the basic features of the society it is intended to sustain. To depart significantly from those features is to recommend a conception of civic education suitable for some society other than the one at hand. Differently put, it is to endorse a politics of transformation based on a general conception of the political good external to the concrete polity in question. I do not wish to deny the possibility or appropriateness of such theoretical practices. But I do not want to distinguish between them and the task of fitting pedagogical practices to existing communities.

It is at best a partial truth to characterize the United States as a democracy in Gutmann's sense. To begin with the obvious: in a liberal democracy the concern for individual rights and for what is sometimes called the private sphere entails limits on the legitimate power of majorities, and it suggests that cultivating the disposition to respect rights and privacies is one of the essential goals of liberal democratic civic education. In Gutmann's account, the power of the majority is limited by the requirement of "non-repression" and "nondiscrimination," but these limits are themselves derived from the conception of a democratic society all of whose members are equipped and authorized to share in ruling.[10] These considerations are not robust enough to generate anything like a liberal account of protections for individuals and groups against the possibility of majority usurpation.

A second liberal reservation against Gutmann's democracy is the distinction between momentary public whim and the settled will – that is, the considered judgment – of the community. This distinction is what underlies the liberal effort to construct a framework of relatively stable institutions partially insulated from shifting majorities. It is, in short, one of the motives for constitutions as distinct from acts of legislation as well as for processes that complicate the task of forging legislative majorities, at least for certain purposes. A form of pedagogy more fully appropriate than Gutmann's to a liberal democratic constitutional order would incorporate an understanding of these limitations on "conscious social reproduction."

Third, in liberal democracies representative institutions replace direct self-government for many purposes. A civic education congruent with such institutions will emphasize, as I have suggested, the virtues and competences needed to select representatives wisely, to relate to them appropriately, and to evaluate their performance in office soberly. These characteristics are related to, but in some respects quite distinct from, the traits needed for direct participation in political affairs. Perhaps it would be fair to say that the balance between participation and representation is not a settled question, in either theory or practice. A civic pedagogy for us may rightly incorporate participatory virtues. It may even accommodate a politics more hospitable to participation than are our current practices. But it is not free to give participatory virtues pride of place or to remain silent about the virtues that correspond to representative institutions.

Finally, in liberal democracies certain kinds of excellences are acknowledged, at least for certain purposes, to constitute legitimate claims to public authority. That is, in filling offices and settling policy, equalities of will and interest are counterbalanced by inequalities of training and accomplishment. Examples include the technical expertise of the public health official, the interpretive skill of the judge, and even the governance capabilities of political leaders. As paradoxical as it may appear, a tradition of political theory extending back to Aristotle has understood the selection of public officials through popular elections as significantly aristocratic in its effect. In American thought, some of our greatest democrats have embraced this view. Thomas Jefferson once wrote John Adams: "there is a natural aristocracy among men. The grounds of this are virtue and talents . . . May we not even say, that that form of government is best, which provides the most effectively for a pure selection of these natural *aristoi* into the offices of government? . . . I think the best [*way of doing this*] is exactly that provided by all our constitutions, to leave to the citizens the free election and separation of the *aristoi* from the *pseudo-aristoi*.[11]

To put this point more broadly: the problem that liberal democracy sets itself is to achieve the greatest possible conjunction between good judgment and virtue, on the one hand, and participation and consent on the other. Democratic processes, suitably refined, may hold out the best prospects for accomplishing this goal. But they are not ends in themselves; they are to be judged by their fruits. Liberal democratic civic education must therefore aim to engender, not only the full range of public excellences, but also the widest possible acceptance of the need for such excellences in the conduct of our public life. Populist rancor against the claims of liberal democratic excellence is understandable, and even at times a useful counterweight to arrogance and usurpation. But it cannot be allowed to obliterate the legitimacy of such claims.

CIVIC EDUCATION VERSUS LIBERAL PRIVACY

Civic education poses a special difficulty for liberal democracy. Most forms of government, classical and contemporary, have tacitly embraced the Aristotelian understanding of politics as the architectonic human association to which all others – family, tribe, economic groupings, even religion – are rightly subordinated. For all such political communities the government's authority to conduct civic education is unquestioned, because conflicts between political and subpolitical commitments are resolved by the belief that the political enjoys a principled primacy. In liberal societies, by contrast, the resolution of such conflicts is far less clear-cut. Reservations against public authority in the name of individual autonomy, parental rights, and religious conscience are both frequent and respectable. The liberal tradition is animated by the effort to carve out spheres that are substantially impervious to government – an effort set in motion by the historical lesson that the attempt to impose religious uniformity through public fiat undermines civil order as well as individual conscience. Thus, even if liberal theories, or public authorities moved by such theories, succeed in specifying a core of habits and beliefs supportive of the liberal polity, individuals and groups may nonetheless object to civic education that tries to foster these habits and beliefs universally.

Yet while the liberal tradition is sensitive to the claims of individual conscience, early liberal theorists were equally mindful of the dangers and limits of those claims. John Locke, for example, refused to expand his doctrine of religious toleration into an inviolable private sphere of conscience. On the contrary, he insisted that in cases of conflict, civil authority takes precedence over conscience or faith, however deeply held. The key criterion is the maintenance of civil order. Opinions that threaten the peace of society may be legitimately opposed or even suppressed: "No opinion contrary to human society, or to those moral Rules which are necessary to the preservation of Civil Society, are to be tolerated by the Magistrate." Nor did toleration preclude affirmative public discourse on behalf of those necessary rules. Locke distinguished between coercion and persuasion. The fact that the sovereign cannot legitimately command adherence to a specific belief does not mean that civil authority cannot offer systematic arguments for, or instruction in, that belief.[12] Thus, although Locke thought that in practice civic education would occur in families rather than through state mechanisms, his theory leads directly to the legitimation of the conduct of such education through public means, individual conscience to the contrary notwithstanding.

Two other lines of argument bolster this conclusion. In practice, the private sphere within which conscience is exercised can only be defended within civil society. In the classic American formulation, government is instituted "to secure these rights." It follows that individuals must be willing to surrender whatever portion of these rights must be sacrificed to the requirements of public order and institutional perpetuation. Individuals who seek to exercise, without compromise, the totality of their presocial rights will quickly find that conflict with other rights-bearers impedes the attainment of their ends and the security of their liberty. Even if we begin with a robust conception of individual rights defined theoretically rather than historically or politically, we are forced to conclude that public authority may legitimately restrict those rights in the name of maximizing their effective exercise. In particular, government may properly teach those beliefs and habits needed to bolster the institutions that secure liberal rights, and citizens of liberal polities who resist this civic education would be irrationally contradicting their own self-interest, rightly understood.

The second argument follows hard on the heels of the first. If citizenship means anything, it means a package of benefits and burdens shared, and accepted, by all. To be a citizen of a liberal polity is to be required to surrender so much of your own private conscience as is necessary for the secure enjoyment of what remains. To refuse this surrender is in effect to breach the agreement under which you are entitled to full membership in your community.

Now, it is perfectly possible to petition your community for special relief from the burdens accepted by your fellow citizens: "My conscience makes it impossible for me to fight in battle / pledge allegiance to the flag / or whatever." Public authority may then make a prudential determination as to whether granting your request will or won't impose unacceptable costs on public aims and institutions. If you are part of a small minority, and if the grounds on which you seek exemption from shared burdens are so narrow and idiosyncratic as to suggest that others are unlikely to follow suit, then it may be possible to grant the exemption. But if the facts suggest that acceding to you will open the floodgate for many others, then it would be rational for public authorities to reject your plea. The issue, to repeat, is one of concrete practice rather than general principle.

A variant of this problem arises when individuals or groups are willing to take the next step, abjuring the benefits of citizenship in order to gain release from its burdens. This is in effect to request a kind of resident alien status within one's community: you remain subject to basic laws of civil order, but you are no longer expected to attain the character, beliefs, and competences needed for effective political membership. Your real desire is simply to withdraw, to be left alone. Here again, as before, the issue is practical. If there is reason to believe that granting this request will generate significant ripple effects, there is a rational basis for public authority to resist it. Alternatively, it might be argued that withdrawal is an untenable halfway house between citizenship and actual physical exit. As long as your group remains located within the domain of wider community, it necessarily interacts with, and affects, that community in many ways. While some free-rider problems could be addressed through taxation, other difficulties would prove far less tractable. It is not clear that the political community could afford to remain indifferent to the example you might set for other potential withdrawers. (This is not intended as an argument against the right of physical exit, which rests on quite different foundations and raises different issues. The Soviets improperly used arguments parallel to those in this paragraph to thwart the emigration of disaffected groups.)

Perhaps the most poignant problem raised by liberal civic education is the clash between the content of that education and the desire of parents to pass their way of life on to their children. Few parents, I suspect, are unaware of or immune to the force of this desire. What could be more natural? If you believe that you are fit to be a parent, you must also believe that at least some of the choices you have made are worthy of emulation by your children, and the freedom to pass on the fruits of those choices must be highly valued. Conversely, who can contemplate without horror totalitarian societies in which families are compelled to yield all moral authority to the state?

Still, your child is at once a future adult and a future citizen. Your authority as a parent is limited by both these facts. For example, you are not free to treat your child in a manner that impedes normal development. You may not legitimately starve or beat your child or thwart the acquisition of basic linguistic and social skills. The systematic violation of these and related norms suffices to warrant state intervention. Similarly, you are not free to impede the child's acquisition of a basic civic education: the beliefs and habits that support the polity and enable individuals to function competently in public affairs. In particular, you are not free to act in ways that will lead your child to impose significant and avoidable burdens on the community. For example, the liberal state has a right to teach all children respect for the law, and you have no opposing right as a parent to undermine that respect. Similarly, the liberal state has a right to inculcate the expectation that all normal children will become adults capable of caring for themselves and their families.

Thus far the argument is reasonably strong and uncontroversial. But how much further may the liberal state go? Amy Gutmann argues that children must be taught both "mutual respect among persons" and "rational deliberation among ways of life," and that parents are unlikely to do this on their own. It is precisely because communities such as the Old Order Amish are morally committed to shielding their children from influences that might weaken their faith that the state is compelled to step in:

> The same principle that requires a state to grant adults personal political freedom also commits it to assuring children an education that makes those freedoms both possible and meaningful in the future. A state makes choice possible by teaching its future citizens respect for opposing points of view and ways of life. It makes choice meaningful by equipping children with the intellectual skills necessary to evaluate ways of life different from that of their parents.[13]

I do not believe that this argument can be sustained. In a liberal democratic polity, to be sure, the fact of social diversity means that the willingness to coexist peacefully with ways of life very different from one's own is essential. Further, the need for public evaluation of leaders and policies means that the state has an interest in developing citizens with at least the minimal conditions of reasonable public judgment. But neither of these civic requirements entails a need for public authority to take an interest in how children think about different ways of life. Civic tolerance of deep differences is perfectly compatible with unswerving belief in the correctness of one's own way of life. It rests on the conviction that the pursuit of the better course should be (and in many cases can only be) the result of persuasion rather than coercion – a classic Lockean premise that the liberal state does have an interest in articulating. Civic deliberation is also compatible with unshakable personal commitments. It requires only that each citizen accept the minimal civic commitments, already outlined, without which the liberal polity cannot long endure. In short, the civic standpoint does not warrant the conclusion that the state must (or may) structure public education to foster in children skeptical reflection on ways of life inherited from parents or local communities.

It is hardly accidental that Gutmann takes the argument in this direction. At the heart of much modern liberal democratic thought is a (sometimes tacit) commitment to the Socratic proposition that the unexamined life is an unworthy life, that individual freedom is incompatible with ways of life guided by unquestioned authority or unswerving faith. As philosophic conclusions these commitments have much to recommend them. The question, though, is whether the liberal state is justified in building them into its system of public education. The answer is that it cannot do so without throwing its weight behind a conception of the human good unrelated to the functional needs of its sociopolitical institutions and at odds with the deep beliefs of many of its loyal citizens. As a political matter liberal freedom entails the right to live unexamined as well as examined lives, a right whose effective exercise may require parental bulwarks against the corrosive influence of modernist skepticism. I might add that, in practice, there is today a widespread perception that our system of public education already embodies a bias against authority and faith. This perception, in large measure, is what underlies the controversy over "secular humanism" that is so incomprehensible to liberal elites.

It is not difficult to anticipate the objections that will be raised against the argument I have just advanced. There are, after all, three parties to the educational transaction: children, their parents, and the state. Perhaps the state has no direct right to shape public education in accordance with the norms of Socratic self-examination. But doesn't liberal freedom mean that children have the right to be exposed to a range of possible ways of life? If parents thwart this right by attempting, as we would say, to "brainwash" their children, doesn't the state have a right – indeed, a duty – to step in?

The answer is no on both counts. Children do have a wide range of rights that parents are bound to respect and that government is bound to enforce against parental violation. As I argued earlier, parents may not rightly impede the normal physical, intellectual, and emotional development of their children. Nor may they impede the acquisition of civic competence and loyalty. The state may act *in loco parentis* to overcome family-based obstacles to normal development. And it may use public instrumentalities, including the system of education, to promote the attainment by all children of the basic requisites of citizenship. These are legitimate intrusive state powers. But they are limited by their own inner logic. In a liberal state interventions that cannot be justified on this basis cannot be justified at all. That is how liberal democracies must draw the line between parental and public authority over the education of children, or, to put it less confrontationally, that is the principle on the basis of which such authority must be shared.[14]

But doesn't this position evade the emotional force of the objection? Does it legitimate parental brainwashing of children, which is a terrible thing? Again, the answer is no, for two reasons. First, the simple fact that authority is divided means that, from an early age, every child will see that he or she is answerable to institutions other than the family – institutions whose substantive requirements may well cut across the grain of parental wishes and beliefs. Some measure of reflection – or at least critical distance – is the likely result. Second, the basic features of liberal society make it virtually impossible for parents to seal their children off from knowledge of other ways of life. And, as every parent knows, possibilities that are known but forbidden take on an allure out of all proportion to their intrinsic merits.

To these points I would add a basic fact of liberal sociology: the greatest threat to children in modern liberal societies is not that they will believe in something too deeply, but that they will believe in nothing very deeply at all. Even to achieve the kind of free self-reflection that many liberals prize, it is better to begin by believing something. Rational deliberation among ways of life is far more meaningful (I am tempted to say that it can *only* be meaningful) if the stakes are meaningful – that is, if the deliberator has strong convictions against which competing claims can be weighed. The role of parents in fostering such convictions should be welcomed, not feared.

Despite the pluralism of liberal societies, it is perfectly possible to identify a core of civic commitments and competences whose broad acceptance undergirds a well-ordered liberal polity. The state has a right to ensure that this core is generally and effectively disseminated, either directly, through public civic education, or indirectly, through the regulation of private education. In cases of conflict this civic core takes priority over individual or group commitments (even the demands of conscience), and the state may legitimately use coercive mechanisms to enforce it.

But the liberal state must not venture beyond this point. It must not throw its weight behind ideals of personal excellence outside the shared understanding of civic excellence, and it must not give pride of place to understandings of personal freedom outside the shared understanding of civic freedom. For if it does so, the liberal state prescribes, as valid for and binding on all, a single debatable conception of how human beings should lead their lives. In the name of liberalism, it becomes totalitarian. It betrays its own deepest – and most defensible – principles.

NOTES

1 See Robert K. Fullinwider, "Civic education and traditional American values," *QQ* 6 (Summer 1986), pp. 5–8.

2 Albert Hirschman, *The Passions and the Interests* (Princeton, NJ, Princeton University Press, 1977).

3 Immanuel Kant, "Perpetual Peace," in Lewis White Beck (ed.) *Kant on History* (Indianapolis, Ind., Bobbs-Merrill, 1963), pp. 111–12.

4 See especially Rogers Smith, *Liberalism and American Constitutional Law* (Cambridge, Mass., Harvard University Press, 1985); Nathan Tarcov, *Locke's Education for Liberty* (Chicago, University of Chicago Press, 1984); Harvey Mansfield, Jr., "Constitutional government: the soul of modern democracy," *The Public Interest* 86 (Winter 1987), pp. 53–64.

5 James Q. Wilson, "The rediscovery of character: private virtue and public policy," *The Public Interest* 81 (Fall 1985), pp. 3–16.

6 Charles Glenn, Jr., *The Myth of the Common School* (Amherst, Mass., University of Massachusetts Press, 1988).

7 "Education for democracy: a statement of principles," (Washington, DC, American Federation of Teachers, 1987), p. 8.

8 This paragraph summarizes the central argument of my "Liberal virtues," *American Political Science Review* 82 (December 1988), pp. 1277–90.

9 Amy Gutmann, *Democratic Education* (Princeton, NJ, Princeton University Press, 1987), p. 39.

10 Ibid., pp. 44–6.

11 Alphaeus Mason, (ed.) *Free Government in the Making*, 3rd edn (New York, Oxford University Press, 1965), p. 385.

12 See William Galston, "Public morality and religion in the liberal state," *PS* 19 (Fall 1986), pp. 807–24.

13 Gutmann, *Democratic Education*, pp. 30–1.

14 For a very different way of drawing this line, see Bruce Ackerman, *Social Justice in the Liberal State* (New Haven, Conn., Yale University Press, 1980), ch. 5.